PUBLIC AND PRIVATE FAMILIES

PUBLIC AND PRIVATE FAMILIES: A READER

SECOND EDITION

Andrew J. Cherlin

Johns Hopkins University

Boston   Burr Ridge, IL   Dubuque, IA   Madison, WI   New York   San Francisco   St. Louis
Bangkok   Bogotá   Caracas   Lisbon   London   Madrid
Mexico City   Milan   New Delhi   Seoul   Singapore   Sydney   Taipei   Toronto

McGraw-Hill Higher Education

A Division of The McGraw-Hill Companies

PUBLIC AND PRIVATE FAMILIES: A READER

Published by McGraw-Hill, an imprint of The McGraw-Hill Companies, Inc. 1221 Avenue of the Americas, New York, NY 10020. Copyright © 2001, 1998 by The McGraw-Hill Companies, Inc. All rights reserved. No part of this publication may be reproduced or distributed in any form or by any means, or stored in a data base or retrieval system, without the prior written permission of The McGraw-Hill Companies, Inc.,including, but not limited to, in any network or other electronic storage or transmission, or broadcast for distance learning.

 This book is printed on acid-free paper.

2 3 4 5 6 7 8 9 0 FGR/FGR 0 9 8 7 6 5 4 3 2 1 0

ISBN 0–072–31992–5

Editorial director: *Phillip A. Butcher*
Sponsoring editor: *Sally Constable*
Marketing manager II: *Leslie A. Kraham*
Project manager: *Laura Ward Majersky*
Production supervisor: *Rose Hepburn*
Freelance design coordinator: *Laurie J. Entringer*
Media technology producer: *Kimberly Stark*
Cover photograph: *© Photodisc*
Compositor: *Shepherd Incorporated*
Typeface: *10.5/12 Times Roman*
Printer: *Quebecor Printing Book Group/Fairfield*

Library of Congress Cataloging-in Publication Data

Public and private families : a reader / Andrew J. Cherlin.— 2nd ed.
    p. cm.
   ISBN 0-07-231992-5 (softcover : alk. paper)
    1. Family—United States. 2. Family policy—United States. I. Cherlin, Andrew J., 1948-

HQ536 .P83 2001
306.85′0973—dc21

                                       00-036138

www.mhhe.com

CONTENTS

v

PREFACE

This volume consists of 32 readings that are keyed to the 16 chapters in a textbook I wrote for courses in the sociology of the family, *Public and Private Families: An Introduction.* Nevertheless, it can be used with other textbooks or no textbook at all. The metaphor of public and private families in my textbook and in the title of this reader reflects my sense that families matter in two senses. First, they perform activities of great importance to the public interest—most notably raising the next generation and caring for the frail elderly. Second, as the main site of our personal lives, they provide the private satisfactions of love, intimacy, and companionship. Think of viewing families through either of two lenses. When you are interested in caregiving, childrearing, and material support, you would look through the lens of the public family. When you are interested in intimacy, sentiment, and emotional support, you would look through the lens of the private family. The two lenses provide different ways of looking at the same group of family members. For example, a married couple may be providing each other with love and intimacy but also raising children. The two perspectives, then, can be thought of as complementary and sometimes overlapping ways of looking at the same reality: the institution of the family.

Many textbooks and readers focus more on the private family; they mainly describe how people manage their personal relationships as they proceed through the life course. I include this perspective, too, but I attempt to balance it with a consideration of the important public issues raised by the great recent changes in family life. Indeed, hardly a week goes by without some family issue—no-fault divorce, gay marriage, teenage childbearing, welfare reform, child care, deadbeat dads, domestic violence, and so forth—appearing on the front page of the newspapers.

Consequently, it's crucial that students studying the sociology of the family encounter not just studies of the individual life course but also of the ways that family life affects our society. I have attempted to provide both the public and private perspectives on the family in this reader.

I tried to cast a broad net while trawling for the articles and book excerpts presented here. Many pieces describe the stories of real families: for instance, Susan Sheehan's eye-opening report on the struggles of a working-class family, "Ain't No Middle Class," from *The New Yorker;* and Alex Kotlowitz's riveting portrait of Pharoah Rivers from his best-selling book, *There are No Children Here: The Story of Two Boys Growing Up in the Other America.* Others, such as Janet Z. Giele's essay on conservative, liberal, and feminist views on family policy, reflect debate and controversy within sociology about the future of the family. Still others are drawn from the current classics of the gender-studies approach to the sociology of the family, such as Arlie Hochschild's already-famous portrayal of Nancy and Evan Holt from *The Second Shift: Working Parents and the Revolution at Home.*

From outside of sociology, I have included insightful pieces by psychologists (Jamie K. Keshet's analysis of remarried couples), legal scholars (Elizabeth Batholet's discussion of adoption), and, in one case, a psychologist *and* a legal scholar (an analysis of joint custody by Eleanor Maccoby and Robert Mnookin). I also have imported a few excerpts from the large literature on family history: Steven Mintz's overview of men's family roles, Elaine Tyler May's discussion of the 1950s, and Ellen K. Rothman's description of the great changes in courtship during the twentieth century in the U.S.

In 1996, Congress enacted the so-called welfare reform bill, which constitutes the greatest change in social policy toward poor families since the Great Depression. Even after several years, there are few analyses of its potential impact on families and children. I have therefore written a background article, revised and updated for this second edition, that I hope will help students understand the implications of the new law for low-income families.

The second edition contains 12 new readings and two articles that have been revised—my welfare reform essay and Douglas J. Besharov's article on child abuse. Excerpts from several recent books are included, such as Katherine Newman's *No Shame in My Game: The Working Poor in the Inner City;* Mary Patillo-McCoy's *Black Picket Fences: Privilege and Peril among the Black Middle Class,* Pepper Schwartz and Virginia Rutter's *The Gender of Sexuality,* and Alan Wolfe's *One Nation, After All.* I also have included recent articles, such as Paula England and Nancy Folbre's "Who Should Pay for the Kids?" a discussion of the social benefits of raising children, and Steven Nock's "The Problem with Marriage," a critique of traditional arrangements that provide greater benefits for men and an appeal for support of gender-neutral marriage. It is my hope that the mix of readings retained from the first edition and readings added for this edition will produce a useful overview of the sociology of the family.

ABOUT THE AUTHOR

Andrew J. Cherlin is Benjamin H. Griswold III Professor of Public Policy in the Department of Sociology at Johns Hopkins University. He received a B.S. from Yale University in 1970 and a Ph.D. in sociology from the University of California at Los Angeles in 1976. His other books include *Marriage, Divorce, Remarriage* (revised and enlarged edition, 1992); *Divided Families: What Happens to Children When Parents Part* (with Frank F. Furstenberg, Jr., 1991); *The Changing American Family and Public Policy* (1988); and *The New American Grandparent: A Place in the Family, A Life Apart* (with Frank F. Furstenberg, Jr., 1986). In 1989–1990 he was chair of the Family Section, and in 1995–1996 he was chair of the Population Section of the American Sociological Association. In 1999 he was the president of the Population Association of America.

Professor Cherlin is a recipient of a MERIT (Method to Extend Research in Time) Award from the National Institutes of Health for his research on the effects of family structure on children. He was a member of both the Panel on Child Care Policy and the Committee on Child Development Research and Public Policy of the National Academy of Sciences. His recent articles include "Stepfamilies in the United States: A Reconsideration," in the *Annual Review of Sociology;* "Nostalgia as Family Policy," in *The Public Interest;* "Longitudinal Studies of the Effects of Divorce on Children," in *Science;* "Effects of Parental Divorce on Mental Health throughout the Life Course," in the *American Sociological Review;* and "By the Numbers," and "I'm O.K., You're Selfish," both in *The New York Times Magazine.* He also has written many short articles for

The New York Times, The Washington Post, Newsweek, and other periodicals. He has been interviewed on *ABC News Nightline,* the *Today Show,* network evening news programs, National Public Radio's *All Things Considered,* and other news programs and documentaries.

PUBLIC AND PRIVATE FAMILIES

PART ONE

INTRODUCTION

CHAPTER 1

Public and Private Families

The state of the American family—indeed, the state of the family in all industrialized nations—is a controversial issue, much debated by social commentators, politicians, and academic experts. A half-century ago, few observers seemed concerned. But since the 1960s, family life has changed greatly. Many users of this reader will have experienced these changes in their own families. Divorce is much more common; at current rates, about one in two marriages would end in divorce. Young adults are postponing marriage and often living with a partner prior to marrying. A growing number of children—currently about 30 percent—are born to mothers who are not married. And many more married women are working outside the home.

These trends aren't necessarily negative. For instance, married women's jobs often give them an improved sense of self-worth and boost their families' standards of living. Young adults may use living with a partner as a way to search for a more compatible spouse. In fact, some commentators hail the decline of the 1950s middle-class family in which wives usually stayed home and specialized in housework and child care. These breadwinner-homemaker families, it is alleged, restricted the lives of women and supported the continuation of conflict-ridden marriages that may have been worse for children than a parental divorce would have been. But the overall tone of the public commentary on family change has been one of concern.

In order to develop your own views on the subject, you first need to know the basic facts about changes in American families over the past several decades. In the first selection, demographers Sara McLanahan and Lynne Casper present an overview of four important demographic trends: the weakening role of marriage in family life, the increase in divorce, the changes in births to married and unmarried women, and the movement of mothers into the work force. All of these aspects have changed dramatically over the past half-century. The numbers and charts they present are the starting point for interpreting the controversy and debate that will be found in subsequent chapters. McLanahan and Casper also make the point that the United States has not been alone in experiencing these trends; rather, most Western European nations have experienced similar trends. This information suggests that the causes of the changes in family life are probably not narrow events in the United States but rather broad changes in the economy and in culture in the industrialized nations of Europe and North America.

What do most Americans think about these changes in family life? The conventional wisdom is that they are sharply divided into the conservative and liberal camps of a "culture war," with the former urging a return to the single-earner nuclear family that predominated in the mid-20th-century and the latter defending the more diverse arrangements of our day. Sociologist Alan Wolfe set out to learn whether middle-class, suburban Americans share a common world view. For his "Middle Class Moral-

ity Project," he and his assistants traveled to eight suburbs around the nation and spoke to residents—including African-Americans and Hispanics who had moved out of the city. In his book, *One Nation, After All,* he reports that many of the people he talked to were deeply ambivalent about the changes, lamenting the passage of the "traditional" family but supporting the rights of individuals to choose other forms of family life. To be sure, Wolfe's study is not a random sample nor, despite a few numbers, a statistical one. Rather, it is a more informal, intuitive look at people in eight communities that represent some, but by no means, all of American middle-class society. Read it as a source of insight rather than as scientific proof.

READING 1-1

Growing Diversity and Inequality in the American Family

Sara McLanahan and Lynne Casper

Dramatic changes have occurred in the American family over the last four decades, as reflected in popular television shows. In the 1950s the typical family portrayed in most situation comedies consisted of a breadwinner-husband, a homemaker-wife, and two or more children. This "ideal" American family was depicted in such shows as "Father Knows Best," "Leave It to Beaver," and "Ozzie and Harriet." The Nelson family—Ozzie, Harriet, and their children David and Ricky—has recently received renewed fame in the press and has come to symbolize the typical American family of the 1950s. It now serves as a baseline against which to compare current family arrangements. Although the Nelson family was more of an ideal than a reality for many people, even in the 1950s, Americans did share a common image of what a family should look like and how parents and children should behave, which reinforced the importance of the family and strengthened the institution of marriage. No such common understanding exists today, for better or for worse.

Since the 1950s, families like the Nelsons have become increasingly rare, as young men and women have delayed marriage and child-bearing, as wives and mothers have entered the labor force in greater numbers, and as divorce rates have soared. This does not mean that families are becoming extinct, but rather that they are taking on different forms. Along with the decline of families like the Nelsons, new types of families and living arrangements have become more dominant, including childless couples with two careers, one-parent families, and cohabiting couples with children. Nonfamily households—defined as households containing a single individual or people unrelated by either blood or marriage—have also become more prominent. Today, successful television shows, such as "thirtysomething," "LA Law," and "Murphy Brown," feature divorced and never-married characters, employed mothers, and single mothers (defined as divorced, separated, never-married, or widowed mothers raising children alone), reflecting the diversity of families that is characteristic of the 1990s. These "new families" indicate that Americans have more choices today than they did in the past about how to organize their private lives and intimate relationships (Goldscheider & Waite, 1991).

At the same time, greater diversity has meant greater economic inequality across households. Some of the new, nontraditional families, such as dual-earner couples, are doing very well; others, such as single-mother families, are doing poorly. In 1991, the typical dual-earner couple with children had an annual income of $46,629.[1] In contrast, the typical mother-only family had an income of only $13,012. Families like that of Ozzie and Harriet (working-husband, homemaker-wife, children) had an annual income of $33,961. The increase in single-mother families and dual-earner families during the 1970s and 1980s has led to increased inequality across households and to a feminization of poverty, with more and more of the poor being concentrated in families headed by unmarried mothers (Pearce, 1978). In 1960, 24 percent of poor families were headed by unmarried mothers; in 1990, the number was 53 percent. The diversity of families has also exacerbated racial and ethnic differences in economic well-being. Whereas the fastest growing white families are dual-earner families, a relatively advantaged group, the fastest growing black families are mother-only families, a relatively disadvantaged group.

Many people are concerned about what these changes mean for children and what government can (and should) do to help families and children adjust to change. Since women are spending more of their time working outside the home, their children are spending less time with them; and mothers are confronted with conflicting demands from the workplace and family. Despite the problems encountered by working mothers, today very few people believe that mothers' employment per se is harmful to children, except perhaps during the first year of life. And yet we used to think so, 40 years ago. Today, the policy debate about mothers' employment is primarily a debate over what constitutes quality childcare, how to make quality care accessible and affordable to families, and how to design parental leave policies to suit the needs of parents as well as employers (Da Vanzo, Rahman, & Wadhwa, 1994).

The public is much less sanguine about the future implications of marital disruption and single motherhood. When mothers work outside the home, children may spend less time with their parents, but the family also gains income. In contrast, when parents live in separate households, children experience a loss of parental time (typically the father's time) as well as a loss of income. Because the total loss of resources is substantial for children who live with single mothers, many people fear that this type of arrangement may be harmful to children. And indeed the empirical evidence supports their fears. Children who grow up with only one of their parents are less successful in adulthood, on average, than children who grow up with both parents. They are more likely to drop out of high school, to become teenage and single mothers, and to have trouble finding and keeping a steady job in young adulthood, even after adjusting for differences in parents' socioeconomic background (McLanahan & Sandefur, 1994). About

half of the disadvantages associated with single parenthood are due to lower incomes. Most of the rest are due to too little parental involvement and supervision and too much residential mobility. Given the public concern about the growth as well as the consequences of single motherhood, the policy debate in this area is not just about how to help children adapt to family change, it is about how to reverse change. We use the word single in this chapter to refer to adults who are not currently married and living with a spouse. Many of these people were married in the past or will be in the future.

The idea that government should try to prevent single-mother families from forming is a hotly contested issue. It raises questions about the causes underlying the decline in marriage and the causes of single motherhood. Those who want government to limit the growth of single-mother families often claim that government is responsible for the growth of such families. They argue that the rise in welfare benefits during the sixties and early seventies sent the message to young men and women that if they had children and did not marry, the government would take care of the mothers and children. Thus, fewer couples married and more young women became single mothers. Charles Murray, a leading proponent of this view, argues that the only way to save families is to eliminate welfare entirely, forcing poor young women either to stop having children or to place their newborns with adoption agencies (Murray, 1984, 1993).

At the other end of the political spectrum are those who believe that the decline in marriage is due to the decline in job opportunities for poor young men—jobs that would enable them to support a family (Wilson & Neckerman, 1986). They argue that young men with the least education and the fewest skills were the hardest hit during the 1970s and 1980s by the loss of jobs from central cities and the restructuring of the workplaces that occurred. With no visible means of support and with bleak prospects for the future, these young men are not seen as potential marriage partners by the young women they are dating, even when the women become pregnant. Nor are the parents of the girl likely to try to arrange a "shotgun marriage" as they might have done in the 1950s, when the likelihood of finding steady work was much greater for low-skilled men. In short, marriage has declined because the pool of marriageable men has declined.

These two theories tell us something about why marriage might have declined among women from disadvantaged backgrounds during the past few decades, but they do not explain why the trend also occurred among young women from more advantaged backgrounds. To fully understand what has happened to American families, we must look farther than welfare benefits and the loss of jobs for low-skilled men.

Another theory with considerable merit is that marriage declined because women became more economically independent; increased education, job opportunities, and hourly wages during the past three decades reduced the gains from marriage and gave women an alternative source of income outside marriage (Becker, 1981). This allowed them to be more selective in choosing mates and it encouraged them to leave bad marriages. The women's independence theory incorporates the two previous arguments. Welfare benefits, like earnings, provide less-educated women with an alternative source of income outside marriage. Similarly, the decline in good jobs for low-skilled men makes marriage less attractive for these women, especially if the level of welfare benefits remains constant.

Finally, some people blame the decline in marriage and increase in single motherhood on changes in American culture (Bellah et al., 1985; Lesthaeghe and Surkyn, 1988). The cultural argument has many different facets. Some people see the sexual revolution in the 1960s as the principal engine of change. Changes in attitudes about premarital sex made it easier for young men and women to live together without being married and destigmatized single motherhood. And improved and accessible birth control methods and more widely available abortions facilitated intimate relationships without the responsibilities and commitments they once entailed.

Other analysts focus on the shift in values that has taken place throughout the twentieth century, especially after 1960. The shift in values from those favoring family commitment and self-sacrifice to those favoring individual growth and personal freedom has given rise to the so-called "me generation." Many of the characters in recent television shows, such as "Northern Exposure," "Seinfeld," and "thirtysomething," show young people struggling with the tension arising from making permanent commitments to others while remaining true to their own ideals and personal growth.

The debate over the causes of family change has important policy implications. If welfare benefits are the major reason for the decline in marriage and the increase in single motherhood, reducing benefits or redesigning welfare incentives to be more marriage-neutral may have merit. If the decline in men's opportunities, the increase in women's employment opportunities, or value changes are the problem, eliminating welfare is not likely to have much effect on marriage, and it will definitely make poor children worse off economically. Ironically, if the increase in women's economic independence is a major cause of single motherhood, then encouraging welfare mothers to enter the labor force, which is a principal thrust of recent efforts to reform welfare, may actually exacerbate the trend in single motherhood, since it will increase the economic independence of women in the long run.

In this chapter we examine the changes that have made the prototypical Ozzie and Harriet family increasingly rare in the latter half of the 20th century. We begin by focusing on four major demographic trends: the decline in marriage, the rise in marital disruption, the changes in marital and nonmarital childbearing, and the increase in mothers' labor force participation. Certain of these trends, such as the rising divorce rate, are extensions of long-term patterns that have been reshaping family life since the turn of the century. Others, such as the employment of mothers with young children, are more recent and represent a break with the past.

We also examine demographic changes in other Western industrialized countries in order to place the U.S. experience in the broadest possible context. The cross-national comparisons help us think about the causes underlying the changes in the American family, and how we might minimize the cost of change for children. Too often, commentators and political pundits in the United States speak as though the changes affecting the American family were unique to this country. As noted above, the growth of single-mother families is often attributed to the increase in welfare benefits during the 1960s and early 1970s. As we shall see, however, the United States is not unique with respect to divorce, nonmarital childbearing, and women's employment. Nor is there a simple 1:1 relationship between the prevalence of single parenthood and the level of welfare benefits across different countries. Many European countries, such as France, Great Britain, and Sweden, are much more generous toward single mothers, and yet they have less single motherhood than we do.

In the second part of the chapter, we examine family diversity and its implications for the economic well-being of American women. Census data allow us to compare the characteristics of several different types of "new families," including single-mother families, single-father families, and cohabiting couples. They also allow us to examine the prevalence of different work and family roles among American women and the standard of living commensurate with these statuses. As in the previous section, we compare the U.S. case with other industrialized countries. We find that married-couple families in which the wife is employed have the lowest poverty rates in nearly all the countries examined, whereas families headed by nonemployed single mothers have the highest poverty rates. We also find that single mothers are much worse off in the United States, relative to other families with children, than in most other countries.

The final part of the chapter directly addresses the question of why marriage has declined during the past two decades. Here we present new evidence based on our own empirical analysis of marriage market characteristics in different metropolitan areas of the United States. We find that marriage is more common in areas where women's employment opportunities and earnings are low, where welfare benefits are low, and where men's employment opportunities and earnings are high. We also find that increases in women's employment opportunities can account for a good deal of the decline in marriage between 1970 and 1990 among white women but not among blacks. Our results do not support the argument that increases in welfare benefits or declines in men's employment opportunities have led to large declines in marriage.

FOUR DEMOGRAPHIC TRENDS

Four demographic changes have profoundly affected the American family in the past 40 years: the decline in marriage, the increase in marital instability, the change in marital and nonmarital fertility, and the increase in mothers' labor force participation. To understand what has happened to the family, we must understand what has happened in each of these domains (Da Vanzo & Rahman, 1994).

The Delay in Marriage

Throughout the 1950s, the typical young woman married when she was about 20 years old and the typical young man when he was about 23. This situation prevailed throughout the 1950s. By 1990, however, the median age at first marriage—the age at which half of the population has married for the first time—was 24 for women and 26 for men. In just three decades, the median age at first marriage increased by four years among women and by three years among men (see Figure 1).

The postponement of marriage that took place after 1960 led to a substantial increase in the percentage of never-married young adults. In 1970, about 6 percent of women and 9 percent of men aged 30–34 had never married. By 1990, the figures were 16 percent and 27 percent, respectively.[2] In one sense, the rise in the age at first marriage was not as unusual as it might at first appear. Marital patterns in the 1950s and early 1960s were unique (Cherlin, 1992). Never before in this century had so many people married, and never before had they married so young. Thus, using 1950 or 1960 as a benchmark against which to evaluate recent behavior makes the current situation appear much more unusual than it actually is. Had we used 1900 as our baseline, for example, we would have found a much smaller increase in the median age at first marriage—no change among men and only a two-year increase among women.

Yet, certain aspects of the relatively high age at first marriage today differ from those at the turn of the century. In 1900 most young adults lived with their parents or other relatives until they married: today they are more likely to leave home and establish independent households. Thus, the increase in the age at first marriage after the 1960s led to a substantial increase in nonfamily households—households containing a single person or several unrelated adults. This further undermined the institution of marriage, since it provided young people

FIGURE 1   **Median Age at First Marriage, by Sex and Year.**
(*Source:* U.S. Bureau of the Census. 1991. *Current Population Reports.* "Marital Status and Living Arrangements: March 1990." Series P–20, No. 450.)
Note: Data points after 1947 are plotted for single years.

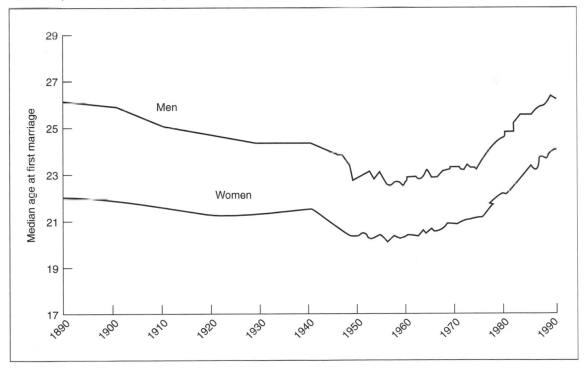

with an alternative way of establishing their independence from their families of origin.

Living away from home prior to marriage was especially pronounced throughout the 1960s and 1970s as the baby boom generation came of age, as contraception techniques improved, and as young men and women became active in the civil rights and women's liberation movements. During the 1980s, the trend reversed as economic conditions worsened for young people, who found it harder to find jobs and become self-supporting. Even so, the proportion of unmarried adults living on their own or with unrelated adults was substantially higher in 1990 than it was in 1970.

The increasing median age at first marriage and the rising percentage of never-married adults has coincided with an increase in cohabitation—two persons of the opposite sex living together in a marriagelike relationship. In 1960 and 1970, the earliest years for which cohabitation data are available, about 2 percent of unmarried adults were cohabiting.[3] After 1970, the percentage increased rapidly. Between 1980 and 1990, it grew from 5.3 percent to 7.9 percent among unmarried men and from 4.3 to 6.6 percent among unmarried women. The increase in cohabitation occurred among all age groups (except people over 65), but it was greatest among men and women in their late 20s and early 30s.

Although some analysts argue that cohabitation reinforces the institution of marriage by allowing people to "try out" potential marriage partners, thereby choosing their mates more carefully, there are several reasons for believing otherwise.[4] First, cohabiting unions are less stable than legal marriages and of much shorter duration (Bumpass, Sweet, & Cherlin, 1991). Second, a sizable proportion of cohabitors (10 percent) intend to continue living together, but do not intend to marry their current partner (Casper, 1992). For these couples, cohabitation is clearly an alternative rather than a precursor to marriage. There is another subset of cohabitors (7 percent) who plan to marry eventually

but who do not plan to marry the person they are currently living with (Sweet & Bumpass, 1992). And finally, regardless of how people view their relationship, the rights and obligations that go with legal marriage are much more difficult to enforce among cohabiting couples than among married couples. To take just one example: an unmarried woman who becomes a mother has a much weaker claim on the resources of the child's father than a woman who is married to the father. Only about 30 percent of children born outside marriage have a legally designated father (Garfinkel, 1992). Although the courts have been moving in the direction of extending "marital rights and obligations" to cohabiting couples, there continues to be a large disparity between these two types of partnerships.

The Increase in Marital Instability

A second major factor affecting families is the increase in divorce. Whereas in 1950, most people married once and remained married until they (or their spouses) died, as Ozzie and Harriet did, today over half of all couples end their marriages voluntarily. The divorce rate—the number of divorces each year per 1,000 married women—rose steadily during the first half of the 20th century and increased dramatically after 1960. Over half of all marriages contracted in the mid-1980s were projected to end in divorce (Castro-Martin & Bumpass, 1989). The divorce rate leveled off during the 1980s but this was not necessarily a sign of greater marital stability. We would have expected such a leveling off, given the increase in cohabitation (which means that the couples who do marry are likely to be the most committed), given the increase in the average age at first marriage, and given the fact that the large baby boom cohorts have reached middle age and passed through the period of their lives when they were most likely to divorce (Bumpass & Sweet 1989a).

The increase in divorce and the delay/decline in marriage led to a rise in the ratio of divorced to married people (Figure 2). In 1960, there

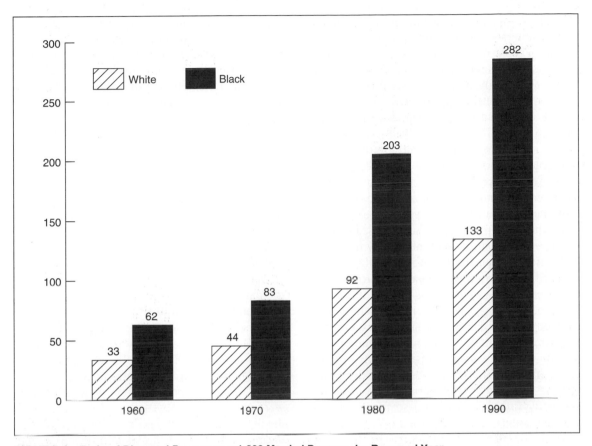

FIGURE 2 **Ratio of Divorced Persons per 1,000 Married Persons, by Race and Year.**
(*Source:* U.S. Bureau of the Census. 1991. *Current Population Reports.* "Marital Status and Living Arrangements: March 1990." Series P–20, No. 450.)

were 35 divorced men and women for every 1,000 married adults; by 1990, there were 140. The ratio of divorced to married people is nearly twice as large for blacks as for whites, and this was true throughout the period from 1960 to 1990. In just three decades, the ratio of divorced to married adults grew over fourfold! Although the ratio was higher for blacks than for whites, the percentage increase over time was the same for both races. The increase in the divorce ratio is likely to have a feedback effect on marriage. By increasing the chance that married and single people will interact with people who have ended their marriages through divorce, a high

divorce ratio makes divorce more acceptable and marriage more uncertain. In addition, legal changes since the 1950s have made divorce easier and more accessible. For example, until the 1960s, divorce was permissible in New York State only if one partner proved the other had committed adultery.

The Shift in Marital and Nonmarital Fertility

A third change affecting the American family is the shift in marital and nonmarital fertility rates. Between 1960 and 1990, marital fertility rates—births to married women between the ages of

15 and 44—declined sharply, while nonmarital fertility rates—births to unmarried women of similar ages—increased gradually. Together, these two trends represented a reduction in overall fertility while increasing the proportion of children born outside of marriage.

The rapid rise in the illegitimacy ratio—the proportion of all births each year occurring to unmarried women—has recently attracted considerable attention, as the public has become increasingly concerned about the economic and social costs of nonmarital childbearing for children, mothers, and the country at large.[5] What is often missing from such discussions, however, is the recognition that marital fertility has a significant effect on the trend in the illegitimacy ratio. Since married women account for a much larger proportion of all births than do unmarried women, a change in the fertility behavior of married women can have a large impact on this measure. In addition, an increase in the proportion of women who are single can also have a large effect on the proportion of children born outside marriage.[6] To understand why the illegitimacy ratio has gone up so fast in recent years, we must understand what is happening to both the marital and nonmarital birthrates as well as to the changing marital status composition of women, that is, the proportions of women who are married and unmarried.

The 1950s were an unusual decade. Not only did men and women marry at relatively young ages, they also became parents when they were quite young, and they gave birth to more children than in the previous decade. This increase in marital fertility caused what demographers called a baby boom from the mid-1940s to the early 1960s.

However, married women began to change their behavior in the early 1960s. Marital fertility rates declined by more than 40 percent between 1960 and 1975, from 157 births per 1,000 married women to 92 births per 1,000 married women. During this same period, nonmarital fertility hovered around 22–24 births per 1,000 unmarried women. The increase in the illegitimacy ratio between 1960 and 1975 was due to two factors: the decline in the fertility of married women and the delaying of marriage. But not to an increasing birthrate of unmarried women.

Beginning in the mid-1970s, marital fertility rates stopped declining, nonmarital fertility rates begin to rise, and the age at first marriage continued to rise. After 1975, the rise in the illegitimacy ratio was due to increases in nonmarital fertility as well as to increases in the number of women at risk of having a nonmarital birth (see Figure 3).

The distinctions between the different forces underlying the rises in the illegitimacy ratio are crucial for understanding the recent debate over the causes of out-of-wedlock childbearing. In this debate, policymakers and political pundits often point to the rise in the illegitimacy ratio as evidence that increases in welfare benefits were responsible for the increases in nonmarital childbearing. But their explanations do not fit the data. During the period when welfare benefits were going up—from 1960 to 1975—the rise in the illegitimacy ratio was driven primarily by the *decline* in marital birthrates and *delays* in marriage. Birthrates of unmarried women rose only 13 percent during this period. Not until the late 1970s and 1980s was the rise in the illegitimacy ratio driven by an actual increase in nonmarital fertility, and by that time, welfare benefits had started to decline in value. This does not mean that welfare has no impact on unmarried childbearing, but it does suggest that the relationship is much weaker and more complex than many people think. Clearly, the rise in the percentage of births occurring to unmarried women is not the simple consequence of more welfare benefits. And curtailing welfare benefits now will probably not reduce the illegitimacy ratio.

Changes in marital and nonmarital fertility altered family life in two major ways: they reduced the prevalence of parenthood overall, and

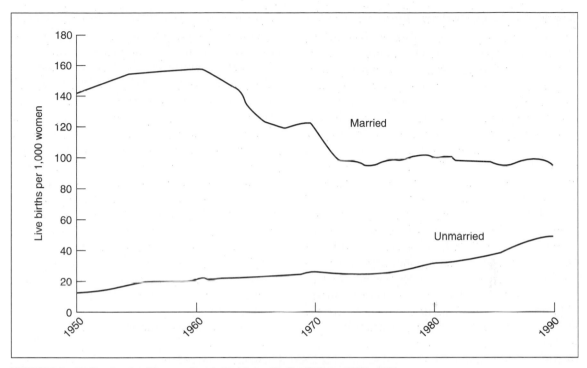

FIGURE 3 **Birthrates for Women Aged 15–44, by Marital Status: 1950–1991.**
(*Sources:* National Center for Health Statistics, *Vital Statistics of the U.S. 1988,* Vol. 1, Natality; National Center for Health Statistics, *Advance Report of Natality Statistics, 1993,* Vol. 41, No. 9.)

they increased the proportion of families headed by single mothers. In 1960, 44 percent of American households contained a married couple with a minor child. Recall that a household includes all the persons who share a dwelling unit, while a family includes two or more persons who share a dwelling unit *and* are related to each other by blood, marriage, or adoption. A person living alone is counted as a household but not a family. An additional 4 percent of households contained a child and either a single parent or neither parent (Wetzel, 1990). Thus, nearly half of all households included children, and nearly 90 percent of the households with children contained two parents. But by 1990, only about 35 percent of all households contained children, and an increasing proportion of households with children did not contain two parents. Between 1960 and 1990, the proportion of children living in single-parent families grew from 9 percent to 25 percent.[7] And this number understates the proportion of children that will ever experience single parenthood. Demographers estimate that over half of all children born in the late 1970s will live in a single-parent family at some point before reaching age 18 (Bumpass & Sweet, 1989a).

The growth of single-parent families is covered in more detail in the next section. For now, we simply note that single-parent families are very different from two-parent families in terms of their economic status, and this difference has important implications for the future well-being of children.

The Increase in Mothers' Employment

The final, and perhaps most fundamental, change affecting the American family is the increase in mothers' employment. Women's labor force participation—the percentage of women who are working or looking for work—has been going up since the beginning of the 20th century. In the early part of the century the increase occurred primarily among young unmarried women. After 1940, married women began entering the labor force in greater numbers, and after 1960, married mothers with children at home followed suit.

In the early 1950s, only about 30 percent of married mothers with school-aged children were working outside the home. By 1990, this number had risen to over 73 percent. In just four short decades, a behavior that once described only a minority of mothers now fit a large majority of mothers, and this was true of mothers of all marital statuses. The figures for mothers with preschool children (under age six) are even more dramatic. In 1960, only 19 percent of married mothers with preschool children were in the labor force, whereas by 1990, 59 percent were employed (Figure 4). By 1990, currently married mothers were nearly as likely to be in the labor force as formerly married single mothers (64 percent), and they were more likely to be employed than never-married mothers (49 percent).[8]

Race Differences

Racial and ethnic groups differed considerably in 1990 with respect to the prevalence of marriage, parenthood, and employment among mothers. The trends, however, were consistent for all of the groups we examined. White women were the most likely to be married in 1990; black women the least likely; and His-

FIGURE 4 Labor Force Participation Rates for Mothers with Children under Six.
(*Source:* Statistical Abstract of the United States, 1993.)
Notes: *Not available for 1960 and 1970.
"Other" includes widowed, divorced, and separated mothers.

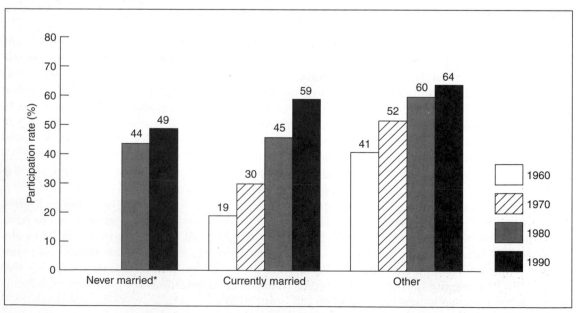

panic women fell in between. All three groups experienced a decline in the prevalence of marriage between 1980 and 1990.

The pattern for single parenthood was just the opposite. Black women were four times as likely as white women to be single mothers—28 percent versus 7 percent—and Hispanic women, again, were in the middle. Single includes women who reported they had never married or were divorced, separated, or widowed at the time of the census. The prevalence of single motherhood, as a percentage of all women, did not increase among white women during the 1980s, and increased by only 2 and 1 percentage points among blacks and Hispanics, respectively. (Single motherhood grew much more rapidly in the 1960s and 1970s than in the 1980s.) With respect to mothers' employment, all three racial and ethnic groups experienced an increase in mothers' labor force participation (mothers working at least 20 hours per week) between 1980 and 1990. White mothers were the most likely to be working outside the home in 1990, and Hispanic mothers were the least likely.

Cross-National Comparisons

The United States is not the only country to have experienced significant demographic changes during the past three decades. Declines in marriage, increases in divorce, growth in the proportion of children born outside marriage, and increases in the labor force participation of women have affected family life in most European countries as well as in Canada and the United States. The average age at marriage has risen since the beginning of the 1970s in most Western countries as it has in the United States. Europeans who were born in the 1950s and who came of age during the "free-love generation" of the 1960s initiated the retreat from marriage characterized by both later and less frequent marriage (Sorrentino, 1990). Indeed, the age at first marriage is actually lower in the United States than in most of the European countries.

Divorce rates have also increased throughout the Western world. While the United States had by far the highest rate of divorce in 1990, the increase over the past several decades was dramatic in nearly all of the Western countries (see Table 1). In Canada and the United Kingdom, the divorce rate grew from about 2 divorces per 1,000 married women in 1960 to 12 per 1,000 in 1990; in France it grew from 3 to 8 per 1,000 married women; and in the Netherlands from 2 to 8 per 1,000. Italy was the only European country that did not experience a sharp rise in divorce between 1960 and the mid-1980s.

The illegitimacy ratio also rose dramatically in nearly all of the Western countries. Sweden and Denmark experienced the largest percentage point increases (from 11 to 47 percent and from 8 to 46 percent for these two countries, respectively). While some countries had much higher illegitimacy ratios than the United States, they did not have a higher percentage of single-mother families. Nearly 23 percent of all families with children in the United States were headed by a single mother in the late 1980s, whereas the percentages were 20 and 13 percent in Denmark and Sweden, respectively. The higher prevalence of single motherhood in the United States is due in part to the fact that divorce is more common in the United States than in other countries and in part because children born outside of marriage are less likely to live with both parents in the United States than in other countries. In the United States about 25 percent of nonmarital births during the 1970s and 1980s were to cohabiting couples, whereas in Denmark and Sweden nearly all nonmarital births were to cohabiting couples (Bumpass & Sweet, 1989; Sorrentino, 1990).

Finally, women's labor force participation rates have been going up in nearly all the countries. In the late 1980s, Denmark and Sweden had the highest percentage of employed women, followed by Canada, France, and the United

TABLE 1

INTERNATIONAL COMPARISONS: DIVORCE RATES, ILLEGITIMACY RATIOS, SINGLE PARENTS AND EMPLOYED WOMEN

	Divorce rate[a]		Illegitimacy ratio[b]		Single parents[c]		Employed women[d]	
	1960[e]	1990[f]	1960	1990	1960	1988	1970[g]	1988
United States	9	21	5	28	9	23	45	73
Canada	2	12	4	24	9	15	41	75
Denmark	6	13	8	46	17	20	NA	90
France	3	8	6	30	9	12	52	75
Germany[h]	4	8	6	11	8	14	48	62
Italy	1	2	2	6	NA	NA	44	61
Netherlands	2	8	1	11	9	15	24	55
Sweden	5	12	11	47	9	13	61	89
United Kingdom	2	12	5	28	6	13	43	66

NA = Not Available.
[a]Divorce rate per 1,000 married women.
[b]Percentage of all births born to unmarried women.
[c]Percentage of all family households that are single-parent. 1971 and 1986 for Canada. 1976 and 1988 for Denmark. 1968 and 1988 for France. 1972 and 1988 for Germany. 1961 and 1985 for Netherlands. 1960 and 1985 for Sweden. 1961 and 1987 for United Kingdom. Age restrictions for children differ by country.
[d]Percentage of women aged 25–34 (25–39 in Italy) in the labor force.
[e]1970 for Italy.
[f]1989 for France: 1988 for United Kingdom.
[g]1977 for Italy.
[h]For former West Germany.
Sources: U.S. Bureau of the Census, Statistical Abstract of the United States, 1993: Sorrentino, 1990.

States. The increase in employment was greatest among women in the Netherlands. The labor force participation rates of Dutch women more than doubled, increasing from 24 percent to 55 percent! Canadian women also experienced relatively large increases in employment, from 41 percent in 1970 to 75 percent in 1988.

The labor force participation rate of mothers was lower than the rate of all women in the late 1980s, but a majority of mothers were working outside the home in most countries. Germany and Italy were the only countries in which less than half of mothers were in the labor force in the mid-1980s. Comparable numbers for the Netherlands are not available, but our own estimates indicate that Holland has one of the lowest labor force participation rates for mothers of all the Western European countries (McLanahan, Casper, & Sørensen, forthcoming).

ENDNOTES

1. U.S. Bureau of the Census (1992). "Money Income of Households, Families, and Persons in the United States: 1991."
2. U.S. Bureau of the Census (1991). "Marital Status and Living Arrangements: March 1990."
3. Percentages calculated from U.S. Bureau of the Census (1960). "Marital Status and Family Status: March 1970" (1981); "Marital Status and Living Arrangements: March 1980" (1991); and "Marital Status and Living Arrangements: Unpublished Tabulations."
4. Lynne Casper (1992). Also see Rindfuss, R. R., Vandenheuvel, A. (1990). Cohabitation: precursor to marriage or alternative to being single? *Population and Development Review,* 16, 103–126.
5. The term illegitimacy is a technical term used by demographers and is not intended to be judgmental.
6. For more information on the decomposition of the illegitimacy ratio see Smith, H. L., and

Cutright, C. (1988). Thinking about change in illegitimacy ratios: United States: 1963–1983. *Demography,* 25, 235–247.

7. U.S. Bureau of the Census (1991). "Household and Family Characteristics: March 1990 and 1989" (1991); and "Marital Status and Living Arrangements: March 1990."

8. U.S. Bureau of the Census (1991). Statistical Abstract of the United States, 1993.

REFERENCES

Becker, G. S. (1981). *A Treatise on the Family.* Cambridge, MA: Harvard University Press.

Bellah, R., Madsen, R., Swidler, A., Sullivan, W., & Tipton, S. (1985). *Habits of the Heart: Individualism and Commitment in American Life.* Berkeley, CA: University of California Press.

Bumpass, L. L., & Sweet, J. A. (1989). Children's experience in single-parent families: implications of cohabitation and marital transitions. *Family Planning Perspectives,* 21, 256–260.

Bumpass, L. L., Sweet, J. A., & Cherlin, A. J. (1991). The role of cohabitation in declining rates of marriage. *Journal of Marriage and the Family,* 53, 913–927.

Casper, L. M. (1992). Community norms and cohabitation: effects of level and degree of consensus. Paper presented at the annual meeting of the Population Association of America, Denver, CO.

Castro-Martin, T., & Bumpass, L. L. (1989). Recent trends and differentials in marital disruption. *Demography,* 26, 37–51.

Cherlin, A. J. (1992). *Marriage, Divorce, Remarriage.* Cambridge, MA: Harvard University Press.

Da Vanzo, J., & Rahman, O. (1994). American families: trends and correlates. *Population Index,* 59, 350–386.

Da Vanzo, J., Rahman, O., & Wadhwa, K. T. (1994). American families: policy issues. *Population Index,* 59, 547–566.

Garfinkel, I. (1992). *Assuring Child Support.* New York: Russell Sage Foundation.

Goldscheider, F. K. & Waite, L. J. (1991). *New Families, No Families?* Berkeley, CA: University of California Press.

Lesthaeghe, R., & Surkyn, J. (1988). Cultural dynamics and economic theories of fertility change. *Population and Development Review,* 14, 1–45.

McLanahan, S. & Sandefur, G. D. (1994). *Growing Up with a Single Parent.* Cambridge, MA: Harvard University Press.

Murray, C. (1984). *Losing Ground: American Social Policy, 1950–1980.* New York: Basic Books.

Murray, C. (1993). The coming white underclass. *The Wall Street Journal,* October 12, p. A13.

Pearce, Diana. (1978). The feminization of poverty: women, work, and welfare. *Urban and Social Change Review:* 28–36.

Sorrentino, C. (1990). The changing family in international perspective. *Monthly Labor Review,* 113, 41–58.

Sweet, J. A., & Bumpass, L. L. (1992). Young adults' views of marriage, cohabitation, and family. In S. South & S. Tolnay (Eds.), *The Changing American Family: Sociological and Demographic Perspectives* (pp. 143–170). Boulder, CO: Westview Press.

U.S. Bureau of the Census. *Statistical Abstract of the United States,* 1993. Washington, DC: U.S. Government Printing Office.

U.S. Bureau of the Census. (1991). *Current Population Reports,* Series P–20, no. 450, marital status and living arrangements. Washington, DC: U.S. Government Printing Office.

U.S. National Center for Health Statistics. (1988). *Vital Statistics of the U.S., 1988.* Vol. 1: Natality. Washington, DC: U.S. Government Printing Office.

U.S. National Center for Health Statistics. (1993). *Advance Report of Natality Statistics,* vol. 41, no. 9. Washington, DC: U.S. Government Printing Office.

Wetzel, J. R. (1990). American families: 25 years of change. *Monthly Labor Review,* 113, 4–13.

Wilson, W. J., & Neckerman, K. (1986). Poverty and family structure: the widening gap between evidence and public policy issues. In S. H. Danziger & D. H. Weinberg (Eds.), *Fighting Poverty: What Works and What Doesn't* (pp. 232–259). Cambridge, MA: Harvard University Press.

READING 1·2

The Culture War Within

Alan Wolfe

Katherine Mullins lives in a fairly expensive subdivision of Broken Arrow, a suburb of Tulsa, Oklahoma. Besides space, proximity to an airport is an important factor in where she chooses to live; she works for a company in Atlanta, having negotiated a deal in which, since she was going to be traveling most of the week, she could work out of her home. (Her husband, who is in the air-conditioning business, also travels frequently in his work.) Although she never went to college, and has no particular desire to send her sixteen- and eighteen-year-old sons to college either, Mrs. Mullins has had great success in the business world. Her income is considerable, her responsibilities great. Talking with her, one senses exactly why she has done so well. She is articulate, determined, opinionated, feisty, and, most of all, likable.

"You know, it's tough," she explains about her decision to pursue a career. "I know in Tulsa—I can't think of any friends or acquaintances that I know that both members of the family don't work full-time jobs." In recent years, according to her, downsizing has made it even tougher: "You did one job a year ago, now you do the job for three people." It's not nine-to-five anymore, especially for someone at her vice presidential level. Asked whether it was a hard decision for her to spend so much time at her job, she responds primarily in economic terms: "No, it was not. I had to do what I had to do to continue to make the money I needed to help support this family." As she shows off her comfortable and well-furnished home, she takes pride in herself as well as her family; look, she seems to be saying, if it were not for *my* income, we would not be living nearly as well as we do.

Still, it would be incorrect to view economics as the only reason Mrs. Mullins chooses to work. After all, she was once a child and, like most children, thought a great deal about the moral choices made by her own parents:

> My mother never worked, the whole time. . . . And quite frankly, until I was a teenager, [I led] pretty much a sheltered life, because Mother was always there and she was involved in everything. I don't necessarily think that's a good idea. I think it's better that the parents do work, and the kids have an opportunity to experience other people in life and situations, so when they grow up, it's not so tough. I've seen that, I've been there, I've done that. . . . So I disagree totally with the staying at home. I really do personally.

Clearly, Mrs. Mullins has been influenced by the social changes of the past thirty years, especially those that go under the heading of "feminism." Unlike her mother, she had a choice about what to do with her life; given her personality and ambition, it was not a hard one to make. She was born to be a career woman and knows full well that if, by force of tradition, she were not allowed that option, she would never have been comfortable in her own skin.

If Mrs. Mullins can be viewed as part of the world that feminism helped define, however, she is also anything but a feminist. Not a shred of bleeding-heart liberalism exists in Katherine Mullins's outlook on the world; whether the subject is crime in the inner city or welfare, she responds in a world-weary, it's-a-tough-world-out-there kind of tone. On economic matters in particular, it is not the women's movement that defines her outlook, but the conservative firebrands within the Republican Party. Mrs. Mullins worked for a Houston energy company in the late 1970s and had to lay off forty people before the company went bankrupt and she found herself out of a job. "Got a U-Haul truck, drove back to Tulsa," she continues. "Had no place to live, had about five bucks in our pocket." As Mrs. Mullins tells it, she and her husband did yard work and scraped by—no welfare for them—before things finally improved. In her view, it's all a question of attitude: you have it or you don't, and, luckily, she has it. Were Mrs. Mullins a man, everything she says about success, hard work, and rewards would sound like classic American entrepreneurialism; the only thing that makes her language even a bit unusual is her gender, not her words. Here is an American who believes that if government would just get out of the way, America would come to respect merit and individual initiative far more than it currently does. Katherine Mullins speaks in the language of classic American libertarianism.

And how does a libertarian raise her children? Conservatives, who would presumably like what Katherine Mullins has to say about the economy and personal responsibility, would not be pleased to hear what she has to say about family values or religion. For Mrs. Mullins, work comes first and family after: "When there's a job to be done, you don't get just to quit at five because you think you've got to come home to help the kids or bathe," she asserts with some finality. "The kids would have to understand that's what it's all about, and that working just a little harder gets you something just a little more."

"Did you ever think of quitting because you were not paying them enough time?" I ask her.

"No, absolutely not. No," she responds.

"Well, what about coming home a bit early from time to time to make dinner?"

"Absolutely not."

"And your husband? Does he support you in your decisions?"

"Like he has a choice," she laughs.

Since she believes that communication is very important, Mrs. Mullins stays in touch with her kids through a pager. But it has not been easy. Her youngest son is hyperactive and has had difficulties in school, where they have had to make spe-

cial arrangements for him. But not even this comment is made in a way that indicates any doubt or insecurity about her priorities as she understands them. When you come home from work, no matter how exhausted you might be, you just have to do the best you can. That's the way the world is, and, although Mrs. Mullins does not reflect directly on this, it is clear that from her point of view this is the way it ought to be.

Mrs. Mullins's views on religion also might make conservatives uncomfortable. Mrs. Mullins is one of those who, while not condoning homosexuality, also believes that it is no one's business what anyone does in private. When we asked her about matters of faith, she proved herself quite skeptical, if not downright distrustful, of any kind of organized religion: "I don't like structured, organized religion. I think that it's an incredible waste of money that we build these churches and pay for . . . preachers and . . . priests who drive better cars than I ever thought of driving, live better than I ever thought of living, you know, belong to country clubs and golf clubs," she said. Religion, in her view, is a personal thing and any public display of its features bothers her:

I'm very saddened that . . . people think that you have to leave your home and go to another place that you're helping to pay for the electricity, the gas, and that guy's salary to have a spiritual experience that should start in the heart and not because you all come together in a group. And some of the biggest bigots I know are just so incredibly into religion; . . . all of that just kind of just sickens me, too.

"I think you really have to believe in yourself strongly," concluded Mrs. Mullins, reflecting her deeply libertarian outlook on the world. People who believe in God instead strike her as "emotionally weak."

Mrs. Mullins's choices and beliefs illustrate a great deal of what is happening in America in the area of family matters. Of all the human groups to which modern people belong, none is more important than the family. To the degree that people give of themselves for others, the others to whom they make their offering are either loved ones chosen by themselves or those to whom they are tied by near mystical forces of blood and belonging. Families, which connect us to the past and the future, are societies in miniature. As alienated as Americans may be from politics, they tend to have high hopes for the family, or at least for their own; well over 60 percent of Americans routinely say that they are "very happy" with their marriages and over 70 percent think that being married is better than being single.[1] Roughly similar percentages find their roles as husbands and wives satisfying,[2] and the proportion of those who believe that married people are happier than unmarried people is in the same range.[3] Yet, with the possible exception of the church, no other institution has faced such intense criticism and nonetheless emerged in still-recognizable form as the modern family.

When those who write about family matters turn to this institution, which has engaged the best philosophers of the Western moral tradition since Aristotle, they seem to have no better language with which to express their disagreements than that of television.[4] Two popular situation comedies, one from yesterday and one from today, define the American debate over family values. On the one hand, there is *Ozzie and Harriet,* praised by defenders of the traditional family as the way things ought to be, condemned by others as unreal, hypocritical, and unrecognizable as a model for how adults and children should and do relate to each other under conditions of uncertainty and ambiguity.[5] On the other hand, there is *Murphy Brown,* lambasted, with counterproductive results, by a vice president of the United States and upheld by his critics as a refreshing look at how families actually are in this "postmodern" age.[6] Even when social scientists mobilize data and arguments around the question of whether the modern family is in decline, images of these two television programs lie behind the numbers and the theories.[7]

The questions in the debate about the family are clear enough.[8] Should women seek careers as well as men? How many children represent the ideal number? Are two parents necessary for the happiness and success of the children? Indeed, which is more important: happiness or success? Should parents who are unhappy with each other stay together for the sake of the children? How much does divorce constitute a social problem or is it the price we must pay for women's autonomy and freedom? Are the best interests of the children still the appropriate question in determining custody? Who is hurt more by divorce: men, women, or children? Should we make divorce harder to obtain? Has marriage lost its symbolic and ritualistic meaning? How important is religion in the upbringing of children? What faith should children be taught if their parents are of different religions? Does geographic and occupational mobility encourage freedom or destroy the bonds necessary for extended families? As passionate as the debates over such questions still are, surrounding them is a sense that the horse has already been stolen; economic and political transformations already had produced new family forms in post–World War II America before intellectuals and policy analysts were able to assess their consequences.

Nevertheless, contentious debate about the family is part and parcel of American political life these days. On one side, if we listen to the left, stand religious conservatives, defenders of male privilege, upholders of discipline, and homophobes, while on the other, if we listen to the right, can be found radical feminists, secularists, misguided idealists, and cultural relativists. So familiar have these images become that they turn into caricatures: rural Mississippi versus urban Manhattan, the angry husband confronting the working wife, the hardworking family struggling to protect its children versus kids lost to the lure of drugs and sex. Where, one wonders, does Katherine Mullins fit into such images? Equally contemptuous of bleeding-heart liberals and conservative Christian preachers, Mrs. Mullins, who is never going to be an actor in a morality play written by someone else, wants to lead her life according to principles chosen by herself. If we are ever to break new ground in the moral debate taking place over family values in the United States, it will be by hearing from those—not only Mrs. Mullins, but others who made very different choices from hers—who are trying to find their own ways to be faithful both to themselves and to others.

FAMILY OPTIONS

Katherine Mullins spends less time with her kids so that she can spend more time on her career. The Middle Class Morality Project also found a number of men who are spending less time on their careers so that they could spend more time with their kids—a potentially significant development if, as has recently been asserted, fatherhood is central to the raising of children.[9] Pedro Govea, a forty-nine-year-old second-generation Cuban, has an M.D. degree and a doctorate in biochemistry. Living in Brookline in close proximity to the largest concentration of scientific and medical institutions anywhere in the world, Dr. Govea, who at the time of our interview held a fellowship in hematology at one of the prestigious medical schools in the Boston area, would seem to be the kind of person for whom success and recognition would be driving forces in his moral accounting. Although ostensibly a member of the cognitive elite, Dr. Govea is close enough to his upbringing in a more traditional environment—his Cuban-born mother lives part of the year with him, his wife, and their three young children—to worry about the effects of modernity on the family. Just before we interviewed him, Dr. Govea had read an article in the *Atlantic Monthly* entitled "Dan Quayle Was Right," and its themes resonated with him. For Dr. Govea wants to do the right thing, and, for him, the right thing means sacrificing in work to spend more time at home.

"You have to make choices in this world," says Dr. Govea, sounding very much like Katherine Mullins. "You have to decide what is the ultimate goal." His goal, however, is the opposite of hers. "Whereas some of my single colleagues are still working at the hospital or working in the laboratory on research, I come home instead of doing the extra experiment. And I think it does have some detrimental effect on what academia and the 'type A personality' . . . looks at. . . . Well, that's life, I guess. You know, I've made that choice." Dr. Govea's values extend in two directions, for he laments not only the lack of time most parents spend with their children, but also the time they do not spend with their own parents, which seems to him so different from what he hears about the old country. "I get the impression from a lot of my senior patients that they get the feeling that their offspring don't appreciate them and their value," he tells us, which strikes him as not only inhumane, but also as bad from a medical point of view. Fortunately for Dr. Govea, his choice of career enables him to find that balance, even if the price is an income far lower than the ones commanded by his "type A" colleagues. If he has any regrets about this, they do not show. Pedro Govea simply knows what is important to him and organizes his life accordingly.

Not everyone has Dr. Govea's choices, of course; some men to whom we talked stayed home with the kids because they had lost their jobs, in many cases while their wives continued to work. The economic insecurity captured in the word "downsizing" has caused tremendous amounts of worry for many Americans, yet few have written about the other side of the coin, especially the way in which unemployment forces so many men to get to know their children. J. W. Cotton had worked for a defense contractor in the Tulsa area for twelve years before being laid off in response to cuts in the defense budget. Mr. Cotton, thirty-nine, has experienced what sociologist Judith Stacey calls "recombinant families."[10] His mother divorced at an early age, and Mr. Cotton found his stepfather, a truck driver, a phantom presence in his life: "He'd come in, deposit the money, say, 'Gotta go; see ya,' and off he'd go." In his own life, Mr. Cotton has a grown child from an earlier liaison and currently lives with his wife and ten-month-old baby. "That's one thing about [defense contractor] closing," he emphasizes. "I've been able to spend a whole year with my son of his life . . . I love it, I love it. I love it. He's my one, he's the most, best asset I've got." As uncomfortable with feminist language as Katherine Mullins, Mr. Cotton is not completely thrilled that his wife works outside of the house; he wishes she could work from home. But there's little doubt in his mind that it would be wrong for both parents to work full-time at the expense of the children. One of the parents ought to stay home, and, if it has to be him, then he is going to make the most of it.

In raising the examples of Pedro Govea and J. W. Cotton, and in contrasting them with Katherine Mullins, I am not making the point that there is a major reversal of gender roles taking place in the United States. It is certainly true that in the United States, the public, both men and women, have accepted the fact that women are now full-time in the labor force. Of those surveyed by the GSS in 1988, 49.5 percent agreed with the statement that "having a job is the best way for a woman to be an independent person," compared with the 31.5 percent who disagreed.[11] In addition, the Post-Modernity Project's survey on American values indicated that 90 percent of Americans believed that "the changes in the role of women in society" are good or mostly good compared with 9 percent, who thought they were bad or mostly bad. Such attitudes have produced changes worldwide that have profoundly altered the ways in which people live.[12] Still, for every woman who was as committed to her career as Mrs. Mullins, there were others in our sample who resolved pressures between work and family more in favor of

their families, just as far more men held views about the need to provide for the family that were more traditional than Dr. Govea's and Mr. Cotton's. The views of these three individuals are important for another reason: they underscore the degree to which decisions about how to raise families are the result of strategic picking between various available options.[13]

In order to discuss those options, it is important to distinguish between the kinds of families in which people actually live and the kinds in which they ought to live. Because the Middle Class Morality Project interviewed in suburbs, which are generally viewed as family-friendly places, it should come as no surprise that a little more than two-thirds of our respondents were married at the time we interviewed them (see Table 1). Three-quarters of them, moreover, had children; slightly more than 10 percent of them had four or more children. Although we did not ask our respondents questions about their own sexual preferences, two of them—one explicitly, the other implicitly—told us they were gay. In their actual family choices, in other words, the respondents to the Middle Class Morality Project were relatively conventional.

Whatever kinds of families people live in themselves, America's debate over the family involves public rather than private questions. Both those who defend conventional families and those who seek alternatives to them are concerned with the moral question of how people *should* live, not just the empirical question of

TABLE 1

FAMILY CHARACTERISTICS MIDDLE CLASS MORALITY PROJECT

Marital status		Children	
Married	153	No children	43
Single	19	1 child	38
Divorced (not remarried)	19	2 children	65
Separated	2	3 children	32
Widowed	7	4 or more children	22
Total	200	Total	200

how they actually *do* live. It does not follow that because people might live in conventional families themselves, they would conclude that everyone else should as well. I wanted to know what our respondents thought about the larger public debate taking place over family values in the United States. When I coded their responses, one position became clear very quickly: those who can be described as *traditionalists,* convinced of the goodness of nuclear family they associate with simpler times, wary of the changes that have taken place since, and persuaded that as many people as possible ought to be encouraged to return to it.

Forty-three of the two hundred people with whom we spoke could be classified as traditionalists (see Table 2). The history of what happened to the traditional family was succinctly narrated by an insurance accounts representative in Sand Springs, Oklahoma: "Women got liberated, and the men quit respecting them. Boom, 'bye went the family." With more seriousness, Adam Grant, also of Sand Springs, a graduate of the U.S. Naval Academy working as a quality control consultant, believes that our society is far too materialistic, so when women work to gain extra income, too often the money is used to buy a boat or a bigger house—unnecessary luxuries, when he thinks about it, that add little to the quality of family life. Nor, in his view, does America, for all its talk, really respect the family:

> Quayle spoke up for family values; look what happened to him. So I think we talk a good story, but we don't live it. Now, naturally, I'm gonna have a little stronger moral fiber, being a Christian, and [believing in] right and wrong. And this "Do what you want to do, don't bother anybody else and it's okay," I mean, that doesn't cut it.

Divorce, single parents these are what follow when Americans put their selfish needs first, in Mr. Grant's opinion. The result is a kind of relativism he finds chilling: "So the family unit, mother, father, children; no, I don't think that unit is valued any more today than the single parent."

Adam Grant's themes echoed throughout a number of the interviews we conducted. Jen Morgan, the conservative Christian who had strong views on questions of separation of church and state, was especially upset by efforts of homosexuals to claim family values:

> Now society wants us to think that two women are just as qualified to raise children, or two men are just as qualified to raise children. All of the . . . wrong morals that go along with that sort of a lifestyle and all . . . because of that, the whole definition of the family is changing. . . . It all is breaking the family down, because God wanted it to be man and woman raising a family. He must have had a reason for that.

TABLE 2					

ATTITUDES TOWARD THE FAMILY

	Traditional	Postmodern	Realist	Ambivalent	Insufficient information
Brookline	4	2	6	11	2
Medford	6	1	2	15	1
Broken Arrow	5	0	3	12	5
Sand Springs	7	1	2	14	1
DeKalb	5	0	7	9	4
Cobb	5	0	8	6	6
Eastlake	4	0	5	14	2
Rancho Bernardo	7	0	4	9	5
Total	43	4	37	90	26

Henry Pearson, who once taught history at a major midwestern university but now works as a risk management specialist in San Diego, told us: "It's so much a matter of . . . to use the current coin of the realm phrase, shifting the paradigm. Well, we've shifted the paradigm all right." He continued:

> And we've shifted society right into the trash can along with it. The simple truth of the matter is this: commitment today is transitory. . . . When it is convenient for us to be committed we are to another person. When it becomes inconvenient . . . the other person gets dumped along the way. I'm gonna get in trouble for this, but families work when there's a way to make sure that children, particularly until they're ten or eleven or twelve years old, are well cared for, are well directed, and are the prime focus of the family as a social unit. That doesn't happen when both parents work sixty-five hours a week.

Others felt the same way. "I think we're catering a lot to . . . nontraditional families," added Julie Skinner, the Mormon mother of six living in Medford, Massachusetts. "I'd like to see people saying that it's important that men and women marry before they have children, and raise their children, and treat them well and do the best that you can for them. Just the basics . . . you know? . . . I think it's important that the mother be at home when the children are young."

By the very nature of their views, people like these would not see their attachments to traditional values as a choice: for them, God created a preferred family form and those who live by its rules no more choose to do so than they choose to believe that God exists. Still, what was once the common pattern is increasingly becoming the exception; even though the Middle Class Morality Project interviewed only in the suburbs, where we presume that there are more women who want to stay home with their children, less than one-quarter of those with whom we spoke were traditional in their family outlook. On few other issues in America has public opinion experienced so

profound a shift over so short at a time as over the acceptance of new family forms.[14]

Diametrically opposed to traditionalists are *postmodernists,* a kind of family form whose emergence has been announced, sometimes with enthusiasm and sometimes with an air of inevitability, by feminist writers. As a result of a simultaneous collapse of the economy and the culture, the postmodern family form is ruled by an absence of rules: both spouses go in and out of the labor market; children are not necessarily the biological offspring of the adults with whom they live; sexual preference is polymorphous; and extended kin are not necessarily related by blood. According to their advocates, postmodern relationships in the family, especially contrasted with traditional ones, bring positive benefits to individuals: women are freer because they work, gays are treated with respect because their sexual preferences are acknowledged, and children are not punished because their unhappy parents mistakenly stay together for their sake.

The Middle Class Morality Project uncovered only four individuals who would advocate something like the postmodern vision of the family—and three of them lived around Boston. Alexandra Onafri, a Brookline resident who is a physical plant director at one of the universities in the Boston area, believes that families are the best venue for raising children, but, she continues, "I don't know that we've defined what family structure really means. You know, what is a family? Family is, you know, more than one person living together and what it entails." A committed feminist, Ms. Onafri believes that too much talk of strong families is an excuse for getting women back into the home. And would society be better off for that? Not at all, in her opinion. After all, active women not only work for a wage, but they also donate their services to the community: "Volunteer organizations were responsible for achieving an awful lot in the 1950s and 1960s and even the 1970s," Ms. Onafri points out. "And, you know, a tremendous amount of work was accomplished by

TABLE 3

"PEOPLE OF THE SAME SEX SHOULD BE ALLOWED TO MARRY"

	Strongly agree	Agree	No opinion	Disagree	Strongly disagree
Brookline	5	10	4	4	2
Medford	3	11	4	4	3
Broken Arrow	2	5	1	5	12
Sand Springs	2	4	4	6	9
DeKalb	0	5	5	6	9
Cobb	0	9	4	7	5
Eastlake	0	10	3	7	5
Rancho Bernardo	0	7	4	3	11
Total	12	61	29	42	56

spouses and women who were at home and who had a lot to offer, and were offering it in the nonpaying, nonprofit sector."

Robert Smithson, a minister in one of Brookline's more liberal churches, voices similar views. "I think the social order no longer has the ability to dictate what shall and shall not happen. . . . And parents are in some way caught in between," he says. "They are both expected to pick up the slack and also are the ones screaming that somebody has got to pick it up. Presumably other than themselves. So I see everybody under stress at this point on this one. And almost nobody is taking the larger responsibility for the public order." Finally, Susan Medina, a Medford interior designer, thought very much along the same lines: "I think if women can stop hanging on to the guilt of leaving their children to child care, I think that children can develop—I think for the most part, they may get brought up more professionally than they would at home—because, again, professionally, those people have been trained."

Not only is the postmodern family form an extreme minority taste, its affinity with a city like Boston suggests that it may be one of those phenomena more popular on the coasts than in the heartland. Our survey questions dealing with single-parent families and gay marriage confirm the notion that those who have the strongest

sympathy for nontraditional marriages are concentrated in particular places in America: no one strongly supported the rights of gays to marry in Georgia and California, for example, and only four did in Oklahoma (see Table 3). Similar results were found on the question of single-parent families, modified by the support for such families given by a number of African-Americans in DeKalb County (see Table 4).

The relative unpopularity of an "anything goes" approach to family life discovered by the Middle Class Morality Project is in accord with national survey data. Most polls show that a taste for individual choices in family life is by and large confined to questions of working women and acceptance of divorce, but does not include the view that any family form is as good as any other. Here is an area in which Americans like to make distinctions: over 80 percent of the American population, according to the Roper Organization, recognizes an unwed or divorced mother living with children as a family, but only between 20 percent and 30 percent recognize gay couples with children or unrelated adults as a family.[15] And even if single-parent families are considered families, they are not considered particularly good ones: 49.5 percent of GSS respondents disagreed that single parents can raise kids as well as two parents together compared with 36.1 percent who

---

TABLE 4

"FAMILIES WITHOUT FATHERS ARE JUST AS GOOD AS ANY OTHER KIND OF FAMILY"

	Strongly agree	Agree	No opinion	Disagree	Strongly disagree
Brookline	4	10	3	7	1
Medford	3	5	2	10	5
Broken Arrow	2	10	1	5	7
Sand Springs	1	11	1	10	2
DeKalb	4	8	2	11	0
Cobb	0	9	1	9	6
Eastlake	2	8	2	11	2
Rancho Bernardo	2	6	1	10	6
Total	18	67	13	73	29

---

agreed.[16] As they do on so many other issues, Americans split the difference on the question of the family: women should work, but not anything goes.

Perhaps the most important conclusion to be reached with respect to the question of the ideal family is that when we add the number of traditionalists and the number of postmodernists together, we shall have not reached 25 percent of our sample. Clearly, some other category is necessary to capture the essence of their views. I therefore added a third coding category, which can be called *realist*. These are individuals who may not be cheerleaders for a new, and decentered, form of family life, but who nonetheless feel that women ought to work and that access to divorce should be available when a marriage becomes unbearable, since both developments promote greater equality between the genders. The realist temperament is practical rather than ideological; instead of glorifying gay marriages or stepfamilies as a move away from the oppression of the nuclear family, people of this temperament acknowledge that changes have taken place in the family, and one simply has to adjust to them.

There are, as one might expect, people who conform to this definition in middle-class America, but once again their number is surprisingly small; only thirty-seven of our two hundred

respondents were coded as realists. Interestingly enough, I found the largest number of them in the South. Among whites, Cobb County contained a number of men and women whose economically libertarian outlook, which supports the idea that women should work, overcame their conservative and Christian ideal that they should not. "If a mother can work full-time and have everything under control at home, more power to her," said Frances Warren, who herself did not work and thinks she would become "a basket case" if she did. "Women working—that doesn't always hurt the family," added George Slade. "Naturally, it's rough on the children," as Jeremy Toole put it. "But . . . I don't think that today's children notice any difference because their parents have always worked. . . . As society grows, women grow, life grows. . . . My wife wants to work. She's bored if she's just at home doing gardening."

In nearby DeKalb County, where most of our respondents were black, we heard very similar themes. "I don't think you should have to sacrifice," Jamie Willis said. "If you want a career, I think you should go after a career, but you've got to learn to juggle the two," she added with reference to bringing up a family. African-American middle-class families, often dominated by strong women or by the absence of a man, were generally organized with the sense that a-person-has-to-do-what-a-person-has-to-do to get by in the modern world.[17] Indicative of this spirit was Vivian Teller, a forty-five-year-old woman living in DeKalb County, Georgia, who was in the process of obtaining a divorce when we talked with her. A mother of two, Ms. Teller had a strong opinion when asked whether, in the best of all possible worlds, women should stay home to raise their children:

> No, I would not like to see mothers . . . necessarily stay home more, because I find my work very fulfilling. I've been home. I stayed home for about five years, and it was great the first three. Those last two years were quite . . . they were awful. [Laughter.] I feel a lot better about myself now than I did then. I don't know. I think if somehow we can continue . . . in our careers and how somehow manage more quality time with our children . . . it would be a big help. That comes down to good time management. I found that, like myself, a lot of people are not good time managers.

Ms. Teller works as a nurse manager and has earned enough to send her teenage boy to a private school in the hopes of giving him a good start in life. Like many of the African-Americans to whom we spoke, she was a strong religious believer (Seventh-Day Adventist), but her faith in God, however important to her personally, could not in the final analysis determine her choices about marriage and work; economic realities did that, and Ms. Teller was determined to make the best of it.

Realists can be found in all sectors of American society and among men as well as women. "I think it's great that women are working and having a career. Personally, I would let my wife decide what she wanted to do. . . . I mean, I think it would be very hard to be at home all day. You just have to get out there," we were told by Robert Hertzo, a border patrol agent living in Eastlake, California. "If you have a woman who chooses to be in the workforce and really doesn't

want to be at home with the kids ever, and participate any way in their lives, well, of course that's gonna hurt, but you can have a woman staying at home who approaches that in the exact same way. The issue of love and involvement . . . is, to me, the crucial family issue, not where the time is spent," added Bea Cohen, a Jewish liberal in Cobb County. Timmy Sands, a landscaping business owner in Sand Springs, Oklahoma, was equally as practical: "I don't think having the mother and father working is a real problem as long as they work it out to where they're able to spend time with their kids and take care of everything that needs to be taken care of at home. Like I said, my mother and father worked and I think I turned out okay. But they balanced it out. I was able to play sports, do what I wanted to, there was always somebody there."

For all their reliance on pragmatic themes, however, even when the number of realists are added to those of both a traditional and postmodern orientation, they still constituted only eighty-five out of the two hundred individuals with whom we talked. That is one way of expressing the point that the single largest category into which our respondents can be divided when it comes to family values is not really a category at all; nearly half of those with whom we spoke—ninety out of two hundred—were so divided between traditional and modern conceptions of the family that they can only be described as *ambivalents*. The most striking aspect of the way ambivalents responded to the questions we asked about family values was to express their simultaneous faith in positions that, at least in the way the public debate over the family frames the issue, are impossible to reconcile.

"I love to work," says Louise Duffey, a twenty-nine-year-old credit marketing vice president in Rancho Bernardo. "I do like to work," she repeats herself. Then she pauses: "I don't know if that's really true. I mean, yes, the quality of time is a lot more important than the quantity, but when a child knows that when they come home after school that their mom is gonna be there and it's a lot different than . . . when the mom comes home she's so frazzled, the dad's so frazzled that they scramble up for dinner and they sit down in front of the TV for an hour and it's bedtime," Mrs. Duffey is the mother of one, with another on the way. When the conversation turns to how she personally would resolve the dilemma, she is equally ambivalent. She thinks of herself as "career-oriented," would prefer to work part-time, feels that a lack of maternal supervision has affected society in a negative way, but has yet to quit her job or reduce her hours. As she wrestles with all the thoughts she has on the subject, it becomes clear that Louise Duffey's views simply do not fit the categories we generally use when we think about how families ought to be organized—or, to put the matter slightly more accurately, her views fit many of them.

Men felt this ambivalence as strongly as women. "Is this a problem?" asks Ronald Klaus, a downsized executive working as a self-employed stockbroker, to the question of women working. "Maybe it is. Is it wrong? No, it isn't." Karl Johnson, a retired construction foreman in Sand Springs, admitted to being old-fashioned on the question: "It's kind of nice to have Mom home and supper on the table." But his personal experience contradicts his preferences: "Of course, both my first wife and this wife, they both work all the time and all five of those boys turned out well." Todd Smith feels that life would be more secure and the economy more healthy if women did not work, but the idea that women should stay home smacks of discrimination against them that, as an African-American, strikes him as unfair. Ambivalence—call it confusion if you want to—can be described as the default position for the American middle class; everything else being equal, people simply cannot make up their minds.

One possible response to this ambivalence is to suggest that middle-class Americans want incompatible things; their views about the family,

by this account, are very much like their desire to see taxes reduced while their favorite governmental programs are expanded. If people were more attuned to tough choices, conservatives in particular suggest, they would understand that if they want women to work, they must accept family decline; whereas if they want to stop family decline, they will have to accept less of a role for working women.[18] While Americans are quite adept in asserting seemingly contradictory beliefs with equal fervor, if one looks at the moral reasoning that undergirds ambivalent responses, the picture begins to look more consistent. Middle-class Americans, for all their uncertainty about the family, are nonetheless fairly certain about what moral principle should guide it: families should be organized to fit the needs of the individuals who compose them, rather than fitting the needs of individuals to some preestablished family structure. Given that there are many kinds of people and many kinds of families, the best way to fit the one to the other is to let people make those decisions that best fit themselves.

This notion that people ought to decide for themselves what kind of family form is appropriate for them emerged so persistently in our interviews that it can be illustrated through the respondents of one suburb. Asked what she thought about women who sacrificed their children for their careers, Mrs. Tartt of Broken Arrow, who sacrificed her career for her children, said this: "That's great. That's great for them." When it comes to herself, however, she made a different choice: "I did what was right for me and my family, my children." "It depends on the person," added her neighbor Stacey Williams. "I think everybody should evaluate what they think their capacities are." "You have to do cost-benefit," reflected Stephanie Proctor, an accountant. "I think it's all how you take care of your family," added Mr. Curry a nearby neighbor. His thoughts were seconded by Mrs. Behzadi born and raised in Iran: "I don't think it's necessarily just being home that qualifies you for being the best mom or having the best family values or standards. . . . I chose to stay home because I really do worry about my kids." Find out what kind of person you are and organize your family values accordingly: that is the advice these middle-class Americans would give to others.

The idea of putting the individual first and the family form second seemingly confirms the viewpoint of those critics who believe that Americans have become too focused on themselves to understand the need for commitment and loyalty essential to stable families. But before reaching that conclusion, a few caveats should be introduced.

For one thing, while Americans have embraced the idea that individuals must choose the kinds of families in which they will live, they have not done so enthusiastically. Arguing that two-career families are "happier, healthier, and better-off," Rosalind Barnett and Caryl Rivers describe situations in which both parents work in gushing terms.[19] There are, of course, some middle-class Americans, such as Katherine Mullins, who made a decisive and unblinking choice in favor of her career, understanding that, as a result, her children would pretty much have to fend for themselves. But the very unambivalent nature of her reflections makes her position a minority one among our sample. For most others, ambivalence is an indication that Americans are reluctant choosers when it comes to the modern family. As much as they expect to make individual decisions about how to balance career and family, they did not necessarily want to have that choice; changing circumstances, matters over which they have little control, such as the need for two incomes, imposed freedom on them. As a result, they feel not so much liberated by opportunity as weighted down by obligation. Both parents have obligations to themselves as individuals and to the economic well-being of the family to which they belong. And they have obligations to their children, whose demands on their time are inexhaustible,

when not irresistible. "If I knew the answer to that, I would run for God," responded Jesse O'Donnell of Eastlake, to our question about how people should divide their time between career and family.

Middle-class Americans seek not to do the right thing, but to do the workable thing; as Lisa Andrews, a paralegal in Eastlake, responded to a question about working women: "I don't think there's a hard and fast line on that." Some try to fit their work schedules to their life cycles: many women stay out of the labor force when their kids are very young, move up to part-time as they start school, and work full-time as the kids get older. Others obtain flextime, either from corporations sensitive to the needs of working parents or simply by taking it. Sometimes, men help out (and sometimes they don't). The point is to find the right balance. "I think that there has to be some kind of balance and some kind of compromise from both the standpoint of the father and the mother to try to make sure that things get done for the children and that there's some kind of supervision," Pedro Govea said in representative fashion.

What is most noticeable about the way middle-class Americans discuss family matters is that guilt is rarely an issue. Most people are reluctant to pass judgment on the choices other people make, religious injunctions play little role, and questions of how things ought to be take second place to how they actually are. The language of family life in middle-class America is profane rather than sacred, surely a disappointment to those who invest significant meaning in the family, as well as to those who believe we should pass judgment on the choices made by others.

Having heard from so many middle-class Americans about their feelings on the family, we are in a position to answer a question at the heart of the debate over the family: Is there a split in America between traditionalists who lament all the changes that have taken place in this country since *Ozzie and Harriet* and modernists who welcome the world of *Murphy*

Brown as a refreshing advance for personal freedom? Based on the interviews we conducted, my answer to that question is yes. Two very different models of family life exist in America: one that longs nostalgically for a world in which families stayed together, three generations lived in proximity to each other, children obeyed their parents, women remained at home, and everyone believed in God; and another in which both parents are free to pursue careers, children are anxious to escape the home and give themselves over to the attractions of a consumer and entertainment culture, grandparents try to avoid either being burdened by or dependent on their grown children, and the language of rights and self-fulfillment comes to play as much a role as the language of obligation and duty. There is little question, in other words, that America is furiously divided over the family.

Still, there is one thing very much out of focus in this picture: *These divisions over the family do not take place between camps of people; instead, they take place within most individuals.* The fact that the largest cluster of attitudes we found on the question of the proper family form was the ambivalent category suggests that the culture war lies within: middle-class Americans believe in both the traditional and the modern version of the family simultaneously. Longing for a world that no longer exists but having no intention of giving up the one that does, they are torn between nostalgia and necessity. As much as they lament the passing of the family meal, and they lament its passing mightily, they are too American not to appreciate the benefits that flow from both the material benefits of an additional salary and the political and social advantages of greater equality and personal liberty. Deep ambivalence, not ideological or religious certainty, characterizes the views of most Americans on family matters. What the sociologists Peter and Brigitte Berger called "the war over the family" may not be a war at all, but an inevitable, and perhaps even healthy, conflict between two different sets of needs, both of which

have compelling reasons to exist.[20] In theory, people cannot satisfy both needs at the same time; in practice, they are trying their hardest to do exactly that.

ENDNOTES

1. Bruce A. Chadwick and Tim B. Heaton, *Statistical Handbook on the American Family* (Phoenix, AZ: The Oryx Press, 1992), 21, 54; GSS, Trends, SATFAM. However, as Norval Glenn argues, the percentage of people in satisfactory marriages after ten years has probably declined in the United States. Norval D. Glenn, "The Recent Trend in Marital Success in the United States," *Journal of Marriage and the Family* 53 (May 1991): 261–70.
2. Roper Organization for Virginia Slims, *American Enterprise* 4 (September/October 1993): 91.
3. GSS, Trends, MARHAPPY.
4. For recent treatments of these issues, see Diana Tietjens, Kenneth Kipnist, and Cornelius F. Murphy, Jr., *Kindred Matters: Rethinking the Philosophy of the Family* (Ithaca: Cornell University Press, 1993).
5. Critics of the "Ozzie and Harriet" model include Stephanie Coontz, *The Way We Never Were: American Families and the Nostalgia Trap* (New York: Basic Books, 1992), Judith Stacey, *In the Name of the Family: Rethinking Family Values in the Postmodern Age* (Boston: Beacon Press, 1996), and Rosalind L. Barnett and Caryl Rivers, *She Works/He Works: How Two Income Families Are Happier, Healthier, and Better Off* (San Francisco: HarperCollins, 1996), the first chapter of which (pp. 1–8) is called "Ozzie and Harriet Are Dead." For the opposite point of view, but one that uses the same metaphor, see Daniel D. Polsby, "Ozzie and Harriet Had It Right," *Harvard Journal of Law and Public Policy* 18 (Spring 1995), 531–36.
6. Barbara DaFoe Whitehead, "Dan Quayle Was Right," *Atlantic* 271 (April 1993): 47–84, and Dan Quayle and Diane Medved, *The American Family: Discovering the Values That Make Us Strong* (New York: HarperColllns, 1996). For treatments along similar lines, see James Q. Wilson, "The Family Values Debate," *Commentary* 95 (April 1993): 24–31; Maggie Galagher, *The*

Abolition of Marriage: The Way We Destroy Lasting Love (Washington, D.C.: Regnery, 1996), and Barbara DaFoe Whitehead, *The Divorce Culture* (New York: Knopf, 1997).

7. On that debate, see David Popenoe, "American Family Decline, 1960–1990," *Journal of Marriage and the Family* 55 (August 1993): 527–42, and Judith Stacey, "Good Riddance to 'The Family,'" *Journal of Marriage and the Family* 55 (August 1993): 545–47.

8. For a treatment of many of these themes from a perspective that argues that many of the changes facing the family, especially divorce, are harmful, see David Popenoe, Jean Bethke Elshtain, and David Blankenhorn, eds., *Promises to Keep: Decline and Renewal of Marriage in America* (Lanham, MD: Rowman and Littlefield, 1996).

9. David Popenoe, *Life Without Father: Compelling New Evidence That Fatherhood and Marriage Are Indispensable for the Good of Children and Society* (New York: Martin Kessler Books of the Free Press, 1996); David Blankenhorn, *Fatherless America: Confronting Our Most Urgent Social Problem* (New York: Basic Books, 1995).

10. Judith Stacey, *Brave New Families: Stories of Domestic Upheaval in Late Twentieth Century America* (New York: Basic Books, 1990), 16–19. See also Stephanie Coontz, *The Way We Really Are: Coming to Terms with America's Changing Families* (New York: Basic Books, 1997).

11. GSS, Statistics, FEJOBIND; Post-Modernity Project, table 6.A. A similar survey found only 19 percent of the American population agrees with the statement: "Society made a mistake in encouraging so many women with families to work," while 76 percent agreed with the statement: "Society has been improved because women are now represented in the workplace." Pew Research Center for the People and the Press, "The Diminishing Divide: American Churches, American Politics," June 25, 1996, 67.

12. For Europe, see Duane F. Alwin, Michael Braun, and Jacqueline Scott, "The Separation of Work and the Family: Attitudes Towards Women's Labor Force Participation in Germany, Great Britain, and the United States," *European Journal of Sociology* 8 (May 1992): 13–37. The consequences of these transformations for America are discussed in Daphne Spain and Suzanne M. Bianchi, *Balancing Act: Motherhood, Marriage, and Employment Among American Women* (New York: Russell Sage Foundation, 1996).

13. Kathleen Gerson, *Hard Choices: How Women Decide About Work, Career, and Motherhood* (Berkeley and Los Angeles: University of California Press, 1985).

14. Arland Thorton, "Changing Attitudes Toward Family Issues in the United States," *Journal of Marriage and the Family* 51 (November 1989): 873–93.

15. *American Enterprise* 3 (July/August 1992): 101.

16. GSS, Statistics, SINGLPAR.

17. On gender relations among African-Americans, see Orlando Patterson, "The Crisis of Gender Relations Among African-Americans," in Anita Fay Hill and Emma Coleman Jordon, eds., *Race, Power, and Gender in America: The Legacy of the Hill-Thomas Hearings* (New York: Oxford University Press, 1995), 56–104.

18. David Galernter, "Why Mothers Should Stay Home," *Commentary* 101 (February 1996): 25–28.

19. Barnett and Rivers, *She Works/He Works,* passim.

20. Peter and Brigitte Berger, *The War Over the Family: Capturing the Middle Ground* (Garden City: Anchor Books, 1983).

CHAPTER 2

The History of the Family

Looking back on the 20th century, we can see that the most unusual and distinctive decade for family life was the 1950s. In the period from the end of World War II to the early 1960s, many of the century-long trends turned around. Birth rates rose sharply, creating the "baby boom." The age at which the typical person married dropped to a century-long low. Although the divorce rate continued to rise, it did so at a slower rate than in most other decades. Compared with any other decade, a larger proportion of children—slightly more than half—were being raised in a "breadwinner-homemaker family," consisting of a father who was employed outside the home and a mother who remained at home to care for the children and do the housework.

Observers at that time, and scholars now, speak of a more family-oriented value system in the 1950s. Perhaps it would be more accurate to call it marriage-centered because attitudes toward marriage were more positive in the 1950s than in subsequent decades. Some intriguing testimony is reported in *Homeward Bound: American Families in the Cold War Era* by his-

torian Elaine Tyler May, who studied a set of 300 interviews that had been conducted with white middle-class couples in 1955. The interviews show the high value women and men placed on home, children, and marriage. Nearly everyone cited the benefits of children, home, and marriage in their personal lives. Few had seriously considered divorce. By and large, they told the interviewers that the sacrifices they had to make for the sake of their home lives were worthwhile.

Nevertheless, as you will see, the sacrifices were not evenly distributed between husbands and wives. It was wives who were asked to make the greater sacrifice by forgoing employment outside the home. Bowing to the ideology, the vast majority of wives refrained from working outside the home at least until their youngest children were in school. Some did not wish to work for pay and therefore sacrificed little; others gave up their dreams. You will read about Ida Butler, who said she would have liked to have been a doctor but that now marriage was her career.

The 1950s nuclear family was the high-water mark of the *family wage*—the idea that fathers should earn enough money so that their wives could stay home and raise the children. It was an idea that emerged in the late 19th century when industrialization began to make working for wages the main source of jobs for American men. But after the 1950s, married women began to enter the paid work force in large numbers, undermining the family wage system. As factory work faded, the kinds of jobs fathers held changed. And as the role of breadwinner declined, no clear alternative role for fathers emerged. Rather, some fathers have become more involved parents while others who don't live with their children have faded from their lives. The cultural image of fathers has two faces—good dads and bad dads.[1]

Historian Steven Mintz notes, however, that there's nothing new about debates over fathers' proper roles in family life. At least since the 1870s, he argues in the second article in this chapter, there have been criticisms of fathers and controversies about what they should be doing with their children. Moreover, he maintains, during the 20th century cultural beliefs about what mothers should be doing also changed in important ways.

---

[1]Frank F. Furstenberg, Jr., 1988. "Good Dads—Bad Dads: Two Faces of Fatherhood," in *The Changing American Family and Public Policy,* Andrew J. Cherlin, ed. (Washington D.C: The Urban Institute Press), pp. 193–218.

Cold War, Warm Hearth

Elaine Tyler May

In summer of 1959, a young couple married and spent their honeymoon in a bomb shelter. *Life* magazine featured the "sheltered honeymoon" with a photograph of the duo smiling on their lawn, surrounded by dozens of canned goods and supplies. Another photograph showed them descending 12 feet underground into the 22-ton steel and concrete 8-by-11-foot shelter where they would spend the next two weeks. The article quipped that "fallout can be fun," and described the newlyweds' adventure—with obvious erotic undertones—as fourteen days of "unbroken togetherness."[1] As the couple embarked on family life, all they had to enhance their honeymoon were some consumer goods, their sexuality, and privacy. This is a powerful image of the nuclear family in the nuclear age: isolated, sexually charged, cushioned by abundance, and protected against impending doom by the wonders of modern technology.

The stunt was little more than a publicity device; yet, in retrospect it takes on symbolic significance. For in the early years of the cold war, amid a world of uncertainties brought about by World War II and its aftermath, the home seemed to offer a secure private nest removed from the dangers of the outside world. The message was ambivalent, however, for the family also seemed particularly vulnerable. It needed heavy protection against the intrusions of forces outside itself. The self-contained home held out

the promise of security in an insecure world. It also offered a vision of abundance and fulfillment. As the cold war began, young postwar Americans were homeward bound.

Demographic indicators show that in this period, Americans were more eager than ever to establish families. The bomb-shelter honeymooners were part of a cohort of Americans who lowered the age at marriage for both men and women, and quickly brought the birthrate to a twentieth-century high after more than a hundred years of steady decline, producing the "baby boom." These young adults established a trend of early marriage and relatively large families that lasted for more than two decades. From the 1940s through the early 1960s, Americans married at a higher rate and at a younger age than did their European counterparts . . .

To gain insight into this unique historical era, I have drawn on a wide range of sources, including evidence from the popular culture, especially movies, mass-circulation periodicals, and newspapers; the writings of professionals in numerous fields; and the papers and statements of those who influenced and formulated public policies. In addition, I have utilized a remarkable data collection—the Kelly Longitudinal Study (KLS)—which consists of several surveys of 600 white middle-class men and women who formed families during these years.[2] E. Lowell Kelly, a psychologist at the University of Michigan, was interested in long-term personality development among married persons. The 300 couples who participated in the study were contacted through announcements of engagements in the late 1930s in New England local newspapers. Kelly sent questionnaires to them every few years and took his most detailed and extensive surveys in 1955. By that time, most of the respondents had been married for at least a decade and were rearing their baby-boom children in suburban homes.

The KLS questionnaires are a valuable source for finding out why middle-class Americans adhered so strongly to a normative and quite specifically defined notion of family life at the time. Many respondents filled pages with their detailed testimonies, often attaching extra sheets to explain their answers more fully. They wrote about their lives, the decisions they made concerning their careers and children, the quality of their marriages, their family values, their sexual relationships, their physical and emotional health, and their major hopes and worries. They also reflected on their marriages, what they felt they had sacrificed, and what they had gained. In these open-ended responses, freed from Kelly's categories and concerns, they poured out their stories.[3]

The respondents to the KLS were among the cohort of Americans who began their families during the early 1940s, establishing the patterns and setting the trends that were to take hold of the nation for the next two decades. Their hopes for happy and stable marriages took shape during the depression, when many of their parents' generation struggled with disruption and hardship. They entered marriage when World War II thrust the nation into another major crisis, wreaking further havoc on families. They raised children as the cold war took shape, with its cloud of international tension and impending doom.

Yet, these women and men were hopeful that family life in the postwar era would be secure and liberated from the hardships of the past. They believed that affluence, consumer goods, satisfying sex, and children would strengthen their families, enabling them to steer clear of potential disruptions. In pursuing their quest for the "good life," they adhered to traditional gender roles and prized marital stability; few of them divorced. They represent a segment of the predominantly Protestant white population who were relatively well educated and who generally lived comfortable middle-class lives. In other words, they were among those Americans who would be most likely to live out the postwar American dream. Their poignant testimonies, however, reveal a strong undercurrent of discon-

tent; their hopes for domestic happiness often remained unfulfilled.

Since the KLS sample was all white and predominantly Protestant, it is important to keep in mind who was *not* included. Black Americans, as a result of institutionalized racism and widespread poverty, existed on the fringes of the middle-class family ideal. Suburbia was not part of the black experience, since blacks were systematically excluded from postwar suburbs. In segregated neighborhoods, black people created rich and thriving subcultures, rooted in unique historical traditions. Nevertheless, blacks as well as whites participated in the same postwar demographic trends. The fertility rates of blacks peaked in the late 1950s, as did those of whites, and the divorce rate among blacks and whites followed similar patterns.[4]

Although all groups contributed to the baby boom, it was the values of the white middle class that shaped the dominant political and economic institutions that affected all Americans. Those who did not conform to them were likely to be marginalized, stigmatized, and disadvantaged as a result. So although the KLS sample included only a few individuals from other ethnic or socioeconomic backgrounds, it was made up of men and women who wholeheartedly and self-consciously attempted to enact cultural norms. These norms represented the ideal toward which upwardly mobile Americans strove, and reflected the standard against which nonconforming individuals were judged. It is all the more important, then, to understand the standards of appropriate behavior established by the middle class. During the postwar years, there were no groups in the United States for whom these norms were irrelevant.

These white middle-class Americans were among the first to establish families according to the new domestic ideology. Relatively affluent, more highly educated than the average, they were among those Americans who were best able to take advantage of the postwar prosperity. They looked toward the home, rather than the public world, for personal fulfillment. No wonder that when they were asked what they thought they had sacrificed by marrying and raising a family, an overwhelming majority of them replied, "Nothing."

One of the striking characteristics of the KLS respondents was their apparent willingness to give up autonomy and independence for the sake of marriage and a family. Although the 1950s marked the beginning of the glamorization of bachelorhood, most of the men expressed a remarkable lack of nostalgia for the unencumbered freedom of a single life. Typical responses to the question, "What did you have to sacrifice or give up because of your marriage?" were "nothing but bad habits" and "the empty, aimless, lonely life of a bachelor." One who gave up only "a few fishing and hunting trips" claimed that "the time was better . . . spent at home." Many of these men had been married for over a decade and had their share of troubles. The comment for one man was especially poignant. Although he described his wife as addicted to alcohol and "sexually frigid," he claimed that "aside from the natural adjustment, I have given up only some of my personal independence. But I have gained so much more: children, home, etc. that I ought to answer . . . 'nothing at all.' "[5]

Women were equally quick to dismiss any sacrifices they may have made when they married. Few expressed regrets for devoting themselves to the homemaker role—a choice that effectively ruled out other life-long occupational avenues. Although 13 percent mentioned a "career" as something sacrificed, most claimed that they gained rather than lost in the bargain. One wife indicated how her early marriage affected the development of her adult identity: "Marriage has opened up far more avenues of interest than I ever would have had without it . . . I was at a very young and formative age when we were married and I think I have changed greatly over the years . . . I cannot conceive of life without him."[6]

Many wives who said they abandoned a career were quick to minimize its importance and to state that they "preferred marriage," which suggests that the pursuit of both was not viable. Many defined their domestic role as a career in itself. One woman defended her decision to give up her career: "I think I have probably contributed more to the world in the life I have lived." Another mentioned her sacrifices of "financial independence [and] freedom to choose a career. However, these have been replaced by the experience of being a mother and a help to other parents and children. Therefore the new career is equally as good or better than the old." Both men and women mentioned the responsibilities of married life as sources of personal fulfillment rather than sacrifice.[7]

Further evidence of the enormous commitment to family life appears in responses to the question, "What has marriage brought you that you could not have gained without your marriage?" Although the most common answers of men and women included family, children, love, and companionship, other typical answers were a sense of purpose, success, and security. It is interesting to note that respondents claimed that these elements of life would not have been possible without marriage. Women indicated that marriage gave them "a sense of responsibility I wouldn't have had had I remained single" or a feeling of "usefulness . . . for others dear to me." One said marriage gave her a "happy, full, complete life; children; a feeling of serving some purpose in life other than making money." Another remarked, "I'm not the 'career girl' type. I like being home and having a family . . . Working with my husband for our home and family brings a satisfaction that working alone could not."[8]

Men were equally emphatic about the satisfactions brought about by family responsibility. Nearly one-fourth claimed that marriage gave them a sense of purpose in life and a reason for striving. Aside from love and children, no other single reward of marriage was mentioned by so many of the husbands. Included in the gains they listed were "the incentive to succeed and save for the future of my family," "a purpose in the scheme of life," and "a motivation for intensive effort that would otherwise have been lacking." One man confessed, "Being somewhat lazy to begin with, the family and my wife's ambition have made me more eager to succeed business-wise and financially." A contented husband wrote of the "million treasures" contained in his family; another said that marriage offered "freedom from the boredom and futility of bachelorhood."

Others linked family life to civic virtues by claiming that marriage strengthened their patri-otism and morals, instilling them with "respon-sibility, community spirit, respect for children and family life, reverence for a Supreme Being, humility, love of country." Summing up the feel-ings of many in his generation, one husband said that marriage

> increased my horizons, defined my goals and pur-poses in life, strengthened my convictions, raised my intellectual standards and stimulated my in-centive to provide moral, spiritual, and material support; it has rewarded me with a realistic sense of family and security I never experienced during the first 24 years of my life.[9]

The respondents expressed a strong commit-ment to a new and expanded vision of family life, focused inwardly on parents and children and bolstered by affluence and sex. They claimed to have found their personal identities and achieved their individual goals largely through their families. Yet, the superlatives ring hollow, as if these women and men were trying to convince themselves that the families they had created fulfilled all their deepest wishes. For as their extensive responses to other ques-tions in the survey will show, they experienced disappointments, dashed hopes, and lowered ex-pectations. Many who gave their marriages high ratings had actually resigned themselves to a great deal of misery. As postwar Americans en-deavored to live in tune with the prevailing do-

mestic ideology, they found that the dividends required a heavy investment of self. For some, the costs were well worth the benefits; for oth-ers, the costs were too high.

Ida and George Butler were among those who felt the costs of marriage were worth the benefits. After more than a decade together, they both claimed that they were satisfied with the life they had built. When they first embarked on married life, they brought high hopes to their union. Ida wrote that George "very nearly measures up to my ideal Prince Charming." George, in turn, noted Ida's attractiveness, common sense, and similar ideas on home life and sex. He was glad she was not the "high stepping" type, but had "experience in cooking and housekeeping." For this down-to-earth couple, the home contained their sexuality, her career ambitions, his drive for success, and their desires for material and emotional comforts.

Yet, like all things worth a struggle, it did not come easy. Ida's choices reflect the constraints that faced postwar women. She sacrificed her plans for "a professional career—I would [have] liked to have been a doctor—but we both agreed that I should finish college, which I did." Fol-lowing her marriage, there were "obstacles" to her continuing to pursue a career in medicine. It was difficult to combine a professional life with a family. For one thing, the children were pri-marily her responsibility. She explained:

> My husband works very hard in his business and has many hobbies and friends. The care and prob-lems of children seem to overwhelm him and he admits being an "only" child ill prepared him for the pull and tug of family life. We work closely together on discipline and policies, but he is seri-ous minded and great joy and fun with the chil-dren [are] lacking.

If Prince Charming's shining armor tarnished a bit with the years, Ida was not one to complain. She had reasons for feeling contented with the family she helped build:

> I think a *stability* which runs through my life is important. I cannot recall any divorce or separa-

tion in my immediate family. We are a rural close-to-the-soil group and I was brought up to take the "bitter with the sweet"—"you made your own bed, now lie in it" philosophy, so it would not occur to me to "run home to mother."

Although marriage was not Ida's first career choice, it eventually became her central occupation: "Marriage is my career. I chose it and now it is up to me to see that I do the job successfully in spite of the stresses and strains of life." She felt that the sacrifices she made were outweighed by the gains—"children, a nice home, companionship, sex, many friends." George also claimed to be "completely satisfied" with the marriage. He wrote that it brought him an "understanding of other people's problems, 'give and take,' love and devotion." He felt that he sacrificed "nothing but so-called personal freedom." Her medical career and his so-called personal freedom seemed to be small prices to pay for the stable family life they created together.[10]

For couples like the Butlers, the gains were worth the sacrifices. But their claims of satisfaction carried a note of resignation. Combining a profession with a family seemed an unrealistic goal for Ida; combining personal freedom with the role of provider seemed equally out of reach for George. They both thought they faced an either/or situation, and they opted for their family roles. At first glance, this case appears unremarkable: two people who made a commitment to marriage and made the best of it. But the Butlers' choices and priorities take on a larger significance because they were typical of their generation, which was unique in its commitment to family life. The costs and benefits articulated by the Butlers—and their willingness to settle for less than they bargained for—were conditions they shared with their middle-class peers.

Unlike the Butlers, Joseph and Emily Burns emphasized the costs of family life. Haunted by the legacy of the Great Depression and World War II, Joseph expected marriage to yield the "model home" described by Nixon, where afflu-

ence, intimacy, and security would prevail. But the worrisome state of the world was inescapable for him, even in the family. Nevertheless, he articulated the way in which the world situation contributed to the intense familism of the postwar years.

At the time of his engagement, Joseph Burns had high expectations for his future marriage. He had chosen his fiancee because he could trust and respect her, her "past life has been admirable," she did not drink or smoke, and "she is pleasing to the eye." If anything made him uneasy about their prospects for future happiness, it was the fear of another depression: "If the stock market takes another drop . . . business will be all shot." The depression had already made him wary, but his disillusionment would be complete by the end of World War II.

Looking back over his life from the vantage point of the 1950s, Joseph Burns reflected:

> As I review the thoughts that were mine at the time of my marriage and as they are now, I would like to give an explanation that should be considered . . . A young couple, much in love, are looking forward to a happy life in a world that has been held up to them by elders as a beautiful world. Children are brought up by their parents to love God and other children, honesty is a must, obedience to the Ten Commandments and to the golden rule is necessary.
>
> With such training, I started out my life only to find out the whole thing is a farce. Blundering politicians lusting for power and self-glory have defiled what is clean and right, honesty is just a word in the dictionary, love of God—who really believes in God? Love of neighbor . . . get him before he gets you.
>
> I agree it does sound cynical, but let us face the facts. Mankind has been slowly degenerating, especially since 1914, and today, what do we have to look forward to? Civil defense tests, compulsory military training, cold wars, fear of the atomic bomb, the diseases that plague man, the mental case outlook? . . . I submit these things to show how a marriage can be vitally affected as

was ours and, therefore, many of my ideals, desires, and, most of all, my goal.

Joseph's cynicism toward the wider world made him place even higher hopes on the family to be a buffer. When world events intruded into that private world, he was devastated: "On December 7, 1941, the question burned in my mind, How can so-called Christian nations tear each other apart again?" Joseph resolved his personal anguish in a unique manner: he became a Jehovah's Witness. But he continued to cling to the family as security in a chaotic world. Although he claimed that the world situation had dashed his ideals, he still rated his marriage happier than average and said it gave him "the opportunity to think and reason." As far as what he sacrificed for his marriage, he wrote, "Whatever [I gave] up, which probably would have been material possessions, has been offset by the things [I] gained." Joseph's rage at the world was tempered by the benefits of having a family. He believed that the family provided him with security and satisfaction, and fulfilled at least some of the hopes he originally brought to it.

Emily Burns had a different view of their marriage, and found little comfort in her life with Joseph. Although his religious conversion was at the center of her dissatisfaction, her responses raise other issues as well. Emily complained about her husband's pessimism, coldness, aloofness, and lack of a love of beauty. She emphasized that her husband's change of religion had affected his whole life—"[his] attitude toward wife, children, home, friends, and world. Unless I become absorbed in [his religion], we [will come] to a parting of the ways, since I'm an outsider in my own home."

In addition to the major rift over her husband's conversion, Emily enumerated her sacrifices as follows:

1. A way of life (an easy one).
2. All friends of long duration; close relationships.

3. Independence and personal freedom.
4. What seemed to contribute to my personality.
5. Financial independence.
6. Goals in this life.
7. Idea as to size of family.
8. Personal achievements—type changed.
9. Close relationship with brother and mother and grandmother.

Her complaints add up to much more than religious incompatibility. They suggest some of the costs of adhering to the domestic ideology of the postwar era: an emphasis on the nuclear family at the expense of other relatives and friends, loss of personal freedom, financial independence, "goals" and "personal achievements." For Emily, like Ida Butler and others of their generation, marriage and family life led to a narrowing of options and activities. But it was a bargain she accepted because it appeared to be the best route toward achieving other goals in life. Although she would not have married the same person if she had to do it over again, she never considered divorce. The benefits she gained in marriage offset her discontent with her spouse. Her list of benefits reveals why she chose the domestic path:

1. The desire to give up all for the love of one.
2. The placing of self last.
3. A harmonious relationship until religion . . . changed this.
4. Two ideal children even though the boy is cold and indifferent like his father. (They have strong religious ties in common.)
5. A comfortable home independent of others.
6. Personal satisfaction if all turns out well.
7. Personal satisfaction in establishing a home.

In this list, Emily mentioned practically all the major subjective compensations that made marriage such an important commitment for so many women at the time. Yet, it was a qualified list. Her dissatisfaction was obvious even in her enumeration of her gains. So she struggled to improve her situation as best she could. While her husband used the last space in the questionnaire to brood over the world situation and explain his turn toward religion, Emily used it to reaffirm her faith in the potential for happiness in marriage. She wrote to Kelly and his research team: "Honestly wish this survey will help future generations to maintain happiness throughout marriage and that your book will become more than cold facts and figures. We have enough such now!"

Emily revealed a submerged feminist impulse that also surfaced in numerous testimonies of her peers. To help her formulate these ideas and influence her husband, she turned to experts:

> Have tried to arouse interest in the woman's point of view by reading parts of Dr. Marie Carmichael Stopes' works pertaining to marriage, to my husband. He says, "Oh, she is just a woman, what does she know about it?" and "How can such things (marriage relationship) be learned from a book?" I have ideas on marriage and when I see the same ideas expressed in print by a person of authority, at least I can see that I am not the only woman or person who thinks "such and such."

Recognizing that her husband was not sympathetic to her rebellion against female subordination, she predicted, "Because of a developing hard, slightly independent attitude on my part, I believe my husband's report on me will be anything but favorable."

Joseph and Emily Burns, in spite of their numerous complaints, stayed together. Through all their disillusionment and anger, they never wavered in their commitment to their imperfect relationship and insisted that their marriage was worth the struggle. Emily chafed against the limits to her freedom and turned to experts to bolster her status within the family. Joseph turned to the home to provide solace from the miseries that surrounded him in the public world. Both had invested a great deal of their personal identities in their domestic roles and were not willing to abandon them. Even if the

home did not fulfill their dreams of an emancipated, fulfilling life, it still provided more satisfaction and security than they were likely to find elsewhere. For all their struggles and strains, Joseph and Emily Burns had created something together that met their needs. In 1980, they were still married to each other.[11]

Like the Butlers, the Burnses demonstrate the powerful determination and the considerable sacrifice that went into the creation of the postwar family. Even if the result did not fully live up to their expectations, these husbands and wives never seriously considered bailing out. It is important to consider the limited options and alternatives that these men and women faced. It was not a perfect life, but it was secure and predictable. Forging an independent life outside marriage carried enormous risks of emotional and economic bankruptcy, along with social ostracism. As these couples sealed the psychological boundaries around the family, they also sealed their fates within it.

ENDNOTES

1. "Their Sheltered Honeymoon," *Life,* 10 August 1959, pp. 51–52.
2. This research used the *Kelly Longitudinal Study, 1935–1955* data set [made accessible in 1979, raw and machine-readable data files]. These data were collected by E. L. Kelly and donated to the archive of the Henry A. Murray Research Center of Radcliffe College, Cambridge, Massachusetts (Producer and Distributor). The data set is hereafter referred to as the KLS, in the text and notes. Two articles from the study were published: Charles F. Westoff, Elliot G. Meshler, and E. Lowell Kelly, "Preferences in Size of Family and Eventual Fertility Twenty Years After," *American Journal of Sociology* 62 (March 1957), pp. 491–97; and E. Lowell Kelly "Constancy of the Adult Personality," *American Psychologist* 10 (1955), pp. 659–81. An earlier article, based on a different data base, suggests the direction of Kelly's research in the early

years of the study: Kelly, "Marital Compatibility as Related to Personality Traits of Husbands and Wives as Rated by Self and Spouse, *Journal of Social Psychology* 13 (1941), pp. 193–98. Kelly spent years gathering, organizing, coding, and entering into machine-readable form an enormous amount of data. He then became involved in other projects without publishing a major work summarizing the findings of his study. Quotes from the KLS in the text have been edited slightly to correct spelling and punctuation, and occasionally grammar, since responses were often written in haste. Also, all names used are fictitious.

3. Kelly's data are a social historian's dream, but they are also something of a nightmare. Kelly devised his questionnaires for his purposes, not mine. As one among a growing number of social scientists who were interested in the scientific determinants of marital compatibility, he hoped to identify long-term patterns of marital adjustment that could be used as predictors of successful marriage in the future. His assumptions were implicitly ahistorical, since his study was based on the premise that personality characteristics are as likely to surface in one generation as another, regardless of historical circumstances. Accordingly, he believed that marriage is an institution grounded in personality adjustment, not social or cultural change. My assumptions are the opposite.

The questions Kelly asked locate his study in its era, in spite of the survey's presumed timeless objectivity. Kelly assumed, for example, that distinct domestic gender roles were universally endorsed. Thus, he asked women to rate their adequacy as "cooks" and "homemakers" and men to rate themselves as "handymen" and "providers." In addition to these value judgments, the questionnaires focused exclusively on personal life. There were literally hundreds of questions concerning the respondents' sex lives, but—remarkably—not one item about their political views, not even party affiliation. Kelly and his data, then, were raw material for this study, for they provide evidence of certain assumptions prevalent at the time. It is nevertheless frustrat-ing to draw on a collection of data so rich in some areas and so silent in others. The problem is unavoidable, since my intention is to break down the traditional disciplinary division between public and private lives—a division that provided the guiding assumptions for scholars such as Kelly.

4. Ronald R. Rindfuss and James A. Sweet, *Postwar Fertility Trends and Differentials in the United States* (New York: Academic Press, 1977), p. 191. On the similarities and differences of the demographic patterns of blacks and whites, see Cherlin, *Marriage, Divorce, Remarriage,* pp. 93–112. On the hardships blacks experienced during the Depression, see Jacqueline Jones, *Labor of Love, Labor of Sorrow: Black Women, Work and the Family from Slavery to the Present* (New York: Basic Books, 1985), chap. 6. For distinctive patterns of black family life, see, for example, Herbert Gutman, *The Black Family in Slavery and Freedom, 1750–1925* (New York: Pantheon, 1976); and Carol Stack, *All Our Kin* (New York: Harper & Row, 1974). On the exclusion of blacks from the suburbs, see Kenneth T. Jackson, *Crabgrass Frontier: The Suburbanization of the United States* (New York: Oxford University Press, 1985).

5. For a discussion of the rebellion against the breadwinner role, the glorification of bachelorhood, and the rise of the *Playboy* culture, see Barbara Ehrenreich, *The Hearts of Men* (Garden City, N.Y.: Doubleday & Co., 1983). Quotes are in responses to open-ended question #B.V.7, 1955 survey, KLS, "Looking back over your life, what did you have to sacrifice or give up because of your marriage?

6. Responses to #B.V.7, 1955 survey, KLS.

7. Ibid.

8. Responses to open-ended question #B.V.8, 1955 survey, KLS, "Looking back over your life, what has marriage brought you that you could not have gained without your marriage?"

9. Ibid.

10. Case 158, KLS. All names are fictitious; the KLS respondents were identified in the survey only by number.

11. Case 290, KLS.

READING 2-2

From Patriarchy to Androgyny and Other Myths: Placing Men's Family Roles in Historical Perspective

Steven Mintz
University of Houston

It is not a historical accident that Father's Day only became a national holiday in 1972, 58 years after Mother's Day received national recognition. Nor is it accidental that although Mother's Day is the busiest day of the year for telephone calls, Father's Day is just another Sunday (although it is the largest day for collect calls). Since the 1920s, Americans have held curiously ambivalent attitudes toward men's roles in families. Although sometimes admiring the family man as nurturer, protector, mentor, adviser, role model, authority figure, romantic partner, or big pal, popular culture has more often depicted such men in much more negative ways—as aloof and distant, inept and ineffectual, philandering or violent, neglectful and irresponsible, self-absorbed and emotionally insensitive, or simply superfluous. Lovable but pitiful bumblers, like Dagwood and Homer Simpson; henpecked louts like Ralph Kramden or Fred Flintstone; or fantasy-driven schemers like Al Bundy have been more common representations of fathers and husbands than the stammering but understanding Ozzie Nelson, the wacky but romantic Ricky Ricardo, or the authoritative and responsible Jim Anderson, Mike Brady, Ward Cleaver, and Cliff Huxtable.

Until very recently, it was quite properly said that the history of women was *terra incognita*.

Twenty-five years of intensive research by women's historians has begun to correct this omission, as women's historians have struggled to recover women's past cultural, domestic, economic, and political roles. What remains less charted, even today, is men's history . . .

MEN'S FAMILIAL ROLES SINCE THE 1870S

Since the 1870s, public anxiety over men's familial roles has generated controversies strikingly similar to those that rage today. Men's roles as fathers and husbands first became recognized social problems in the decade following the Civil War, when "family preservationists" and "child protectors" denounced the lazy, dissolute working-class father who violated every standard of manly decency by deserting or beating his wife and economically exploiting or abusing his children. In response, 11 states made desertion and nonsupport of destitute families a felony and three states instituted the whipping post where wife-beaters were punished with floggings (Gordon, 1988; Griswold, 1993; E. H. Pleck, 1987).

To combat the economic exploitation of children, reformers pressed for compulsory school attendance laws, child labor restrictions, orphanages, and "orphan trains" to place abused and neglected children (many of whom had one or two living parents) with farm families in the Midwest. Meanwhile, there were concerted campaigns to reduce the divorce rate (which an 1880 report had revealed to be the world's highest) by reducing the grounds for divorce, extending waiting periods, and establishing family courts, along with efforts to eliminate segregated male-only forms of recreation, campaigns that achieved ultimate success with the destruction of red-light districts throughout the country during the 1910s and of saloons following adoption of Prohibition in 1918 (Cohen, 1990; Peiss, 1986; Rosenzweig, 1983).

Around the turn of the century, the way that the problem of men in families was socially and culturally constructed underwent radical redefinition. Alongside heightened efforts to promote the male family wage, to allow a man to support his family without the contribution of wives and children, there was a growing concern about the immigrant father, who seemed to symbolize "Old World" values and obstruct efforts to Americanize his children. To promote assimilation, self-conscious efforts were made to use schools, settlement houses, and peer relationships to help first-generation wives and children break free from traditional cultural values, often symbolized by the bearded, unassimilated, foreign language-speaking adult man (Griswold, 1993).

During the 1920s, public concern shifted away from working class and immigrant men to the "new" middle class of salaried employees. Between 1880 and 1920, a fundamental shift occurred in the way that urban middle-class men earned a living, as individual proprietors, professionals, or artisans rapidly gave way to wage earners with far fewer opportunities for economic autonomy and independence. As older sources of male identity in independent work, sex-segregated politics, and community leadership disappeared, a host of educators, psychologists, sociologists, and advertisers argued that in a changing society men would find their greatest satisfaction in private life, especially relations with their wives and children (Griswold, 1993).

The new cultural ideal was the *companionate* family, in which husbands and wives would be "friends and lovers" and fathers and children would be "pals." Proponents of this new ideal argued that in a modern society it was imperative that a family based on male authority and hierarchy give way to new family relationships emphasizing sexual fulfillment, mutual respect, and emotional satisfaction. Fearful that wives were growing increasingly discontented and that men were becoming increasingly estranged from their families, advocates of the companionate ideal promoted courses in family education, a more active fatherly role in children's development, and, above all, participation in a host of leisure activities (such as car excursions, board games, hobbies, and attendance at sporting events) that would bring family members closer together (Griswold, 1993).

A source of particular concern was that boys, raised almost exclusively by women, were becoming overly feminized. In response, family professionals called on fathers to become buddies with their sons, share sports and hobbies with them, provide them with sex education, and serve as a model of masculine maturity. And yet, as Robert Griswold showed, this advice was not accompanied by sustained efforts to involve fathers in childrearing. Experts addressed their advice almost exclusively to mothers, and organizations, like the Parent-Teachers Association, which might have involved men in child development, limited their membership almost exclusively to women. The sole exceptions to this pattern of male exclusion were the Boy Scouts and the 4-H Clubs (and beginning in the late 1930s, the Little Leagues). Sports and outdoor activities became defined as the primary link between men and their children (Griswold, 1993).

The Great Depression and World War II elevated public concern about men's familial roles and reinforced an older ideal of man as protector, provider, and disciplinarian. Many observers were convinced that the depression drastically altered family roles. Many unemployed fathers saw their status lowered by the Great Depression. With no wages to punctuate their authority, they lost status as primary decision makers. In fact, large numbers of men who could not fulfill their role as breadwinners lost self-respect, became immobilized, and stopped looking for work, whereas others turned to alcohol and became self-destructive or abusive to their families. Still others walked out the door, never to return. A survey in 1940 revealed that more than 1.5 million married women had been deserted by their husbands. Convinced that preserving men's breadwinning role was a special national priority, government job programs focused largely on putting the male jobless to work. A major goal of New Deal policy was to restore the male breadwinner ideal (Griswold, 1993; Mintz & Kellogg, 1988).

World War II also thrust men's familial roles into the public spotlight. Intense fears flourished during the war years that father absence produced a host of social problems, including an upsurge in juvenile delinquency among boys and sexual promiscuity among teenage girls. A particular source of concern was that father absence resulted in maternal oversolicitousness toward children, producing boys who were spoiled sissies (Blankenhorn, 1995; Griswold, 1993).

As a result of the Great Depression and World War II, many postwar social analysts argued that fathers had a critically important role to play in children's personality development—not so much as playmate but as sex role model and disciplinarian. The lack of a proper male role model was blamed for a wide range of social problems. Rigid, distant, overbearing fathers, it was argued, produced authoritarian personalities in their children, whereas weak, ineffectual fathers produced schizophrenia or homosexuality. Absent or uninvolved fathers resulted in delinquency in boys or in an overcompensated hypermasculinity. Yet, although experts called on fathers to guide and befriend their children and play sports with them, they did not expect fathers to change diapers or take an active role in child care or housework, arguing that this would make it difficult for boys and girls to develop a clearly defined sex role identity (Griswold, 1993).

Since 1960, there has been heightened cultural and political focus on men's familial roles. The Moynihan Report (see United States Department of Labor, Office of Policy Planning and Research, 1965), "The Negro Family: The Case for National Action," raised the issue of absentee African American husbands and fathers—a specter that has haunted discussions of poverty until today. The rapid rise in the divorce rate during the late 1960s and 1970s touched off a mounting anxiety about the im-

pact of the loss of men's economic, psychological, and emotional contributions to the family, and also ignited a father's rights movement calling for increased legal rights to custody and visitation. To an unprecedented degree, men's roles as fathers and husbands became politicized (Griswold, 1993; Mintz & Kellogg, 1988).

NEW AGE MEN IN TROUBLED TIMES

Janus-like, recent media images of men in families reveal two very different faces. On one side is the "new" father and husband, far more involved, nurturing, and emotionally sensitive than the distant, disengaged dad of a generation ago. This image first reaching a broad audience in the 1979 film *Kramer vs. Kramer,* in which Dustin Hoffman was transformed from a workaholic absentee parent into a caring, nurturing, French-toast-making father. But it was *The Cosby Show,* which featured the comedian Bill Cosby as an obstetrician who refused to allow his professional responsibilities to stand in the way of his commitment to his family, that did the most effective job of popularizing the engaged, emotionally sensitive new man. Popular films like *Mr. Mom,* a gender-role-reversal film featuring a subtext highly critical of maternal employment, and *Mrs. Doubtfire,* the story of a divorced father who disguises himself as a maid and nanny in order to remain near his children, suggested that men could be even more nurturant than women (Furstenberg, 1988).

Yet, alongside of the Cosby image of the involved, sensitive new man, there were also disturbing images of deadbeat dads and abusive husbands, who fail to meet the most basic responsibilities of the masculine family role: to provide their children with emotional and financial support and to treat their wives and children in a civil, if not a loving, manner. One of the most profound social changes in recent years is the increasing absence of biological fathers from their children's home. Today, more than one third of the nation's children live apart from their biological father. White children have just a 50% chance of living with their father through age 18. A Black child has roughly 1 chance in 12. Yet, such figures only touch the surface of public concern. There is a widespread sense that even men who live in intact families are profoundly alienated from their children, that even "daddy trackers" are mere helpers and secondary caretakers who leave ultimate responsibility for housework and child care to their wives; and that men's primary connection with other family members is essentially economic, not emotional (Furstenberg, 1988).

In recent years, an older consensus about men's familial obligations has been thrown into question as the place of men in families has become highly politicized. The perception that American men are in a sea of confused identities, emasculated egos, and misplaced priorities has elicited a wide variety of responses. These include the "Promise Keepers" movement, the all-male Christian renewal movement that tells men to become the "spiritual leaders" of their homes; and the proliferation of mytho-poetic groups, whose members, inspired by the poet Robert Bly's 1990 book *Iron John,* explore their inner masculinity to the beating of drums. Other responses were evident in the 1995 "Million Man March," led by Louis Farrakhan, seeking to promote family responsibility among African American men; or in various grassroots movements to assert father's rights, which call for joint custody arrangements and expanded visitation rights after divorce (Griswold, 1993).

The "flight from fatherhood" and the "breakdown of the family" have elicited a variety of explanations that tend to break down along political lines, with liberals emphasizing economic forces and conservatives pointing to changes in cultural and moral standards. In his 1995 bestseller *Fatherless America: Confronting Our Most Urgent Social Problem,* Blankenhorn (1995), a prominent neo-traditionalist, attributed the retreat from fatherhood to changes in the dominant "cultural script" that tells men what

society expects of them. He linked the growing confusion about men's familial responsibilities to the ascendancy of a set of values destructive of commitment, obligation, responsibility, and sacrifice. In a sharply contrasting explanation, Griswold (1993), author of the first full-length history of fatherhood, stressed the reorganization of the household economy, which undermined the male breadwinning role that had undergirded male authority and defined male identity, and the reemergence of feminism, the first mass movement to directly challenge the gender division of labor in the family. Other authors emphasized the erosion of well-paying, low-skill entry level jobs, which made men without high school or college degrees less attractive as marriage partners, whereas the influx of women into the workforce gave them greater economic independence (Blankenhorn, 1995; Griswold, 1993; Wilson, 1987).

A lack of comparative perspective has exaggerated the novelty of current debates over men's familial roles. A fundamental paradox of our time is that the celebration of male involvement in families has been accompanied by a decline in actual amount of time that men spend in families. Men today are at once more and less involved in family life than a generation ago. On the one hand, many men are more prepared than in the past to play an active, nurturing role in the lives of their children and to participate more equally in child care and domestic chores. Although it is easy to exaggerate the extent of change, men are more likely than their predecessors to accompany their wives to prenatal examinations, attend their children's birth, change diapers, drop off children and pick them up at day-care centers, assume some day-to-day responsibilities for their children's well-being, and perform some housework. On the other hand, as a result of delayed marriage, unmarried cohabitation, and divorce, men also spend a declining proportion of their adult lives as fathers and husbands. Since the 1950s, the share of children living in mother-only families has quadrupled, from 6% to 24% of the nation's children. Which trend, one is eager to know, is stronger: The impulse toward engagement or toward disengagement? (Furstenberg, 1988).

History offers some clues. Although the nature of men's familial roles has changed profoundly across the past 300 years, one fact has remained constant: The authority and respect that men receive inside the home have been inextricably connected to their authority and status outside the home. I would like to suggest, by way of conclusion, that both the fragility of men's familial involvement and the indicators of greater engagement are connected to broader economic and cultural shifts.

In discussing the changes in men's familial roles, it is possible to point to many factors: The sexual revolution, which undermined the monogamy-for-sexual access bargain implicit in traditional marriage; the influx of women into the workforce, which diminished men's role as sole breadwinner; the legalization of abortion, which led many men to shed moral responsibility for a child's birth; the growth in divorce and nonmarital cohabitation, which have made families somewhat less stable than in the past. Here, however, I would draw attention to the impact of two long-term historical developments that have strongly shaped men's familial roles in recent years: The erosion of the family wage and its replacement by the individual wage; and the increasing emphasis attached to the mother–child dyad. The effect of both trends has been to weaken the necessity of male involvement in the family, making male involvement more voluntary and elective (Griswold, 1993; Taylor, 1992).

Throughout the 20th century, breadwinning has been a defining characteristic of men's familial roles, helping to define men's identity, providing their feelings of self-worth, and structuring the amount of time available for their family. The very language that men have used to describe their family roles since the 19th century—terms like *duty, responsibility, obliga-*tion, investment, and commitment—are words drawn from the economic sphere, a pattern that underscores the way that men's economic life has tended to interpenetrate their emotional and psychological life (Griswold, 1993; Weiss, 1990).

The nature of men's jobs, in turn, has had profound implications for their family orientations. Since the mid-20th century, middle-class men typically responded to the demands of work in certain characteristic ways. Some became careerists, focusing their energies almost exclusively on their jobs at the expense of their family ties. Others, who felt intense alienation from work, responded by becoming hobbyists, puttering in the basement, tinkering in the garage, tending the yard, coaching Little League, or leading a Scout troop. Still others coped with workplace tensions by rigidly compartmentalizing their family and work lives. Men's jobs often demanded socializing after work hours, either with their spouses or with other employees. Now that an earlier system in which men regarded themselves as the sole or primary breadwinner is eroding, it has become easier to assess the high psychic and emotional costs that each of these modes of adaptation exacted (Mintz & Kellogg, 1988).

Today we are in the midst of a profound and wrenching economic transformation, a shift from the family wage economy to an individual wage economy, echoing the earlier transition from family labor to the family wage economy. The individual wage economy differs in fundamental ways from the economy that preceded it: Based on the ideal of totally frictionless, mobile labor, the new economy has been characterized by the growth of temporary work, a declining assumption of lifetime employment by a single firm, and a movement away from benefit packages for entire families. Although often represented as a liberation from stifling, unproductive older forms of corporate organization, the shift to the individual wage economy has been accompanied by the stagnation or actual decline in real male wages and an increase in job instability. Despite limited growth in telecommuting and part-time work, which held out the promise of a more family-friendly work environment, for many employees, the tensions between the demands of work and family life have grown more intense in recent years, with an increase in evening and night work, longer work hours, and increasing demands for travel. Although many women increasingly define their identities around their job or career, the growing diversity of the workplace may have made the job less of a "club" or "community" for many White men (Schor, 1991).

Entry into the paid workforce has given women an unprecedented degree of economic independence, including the freedom to leave loveless and abusive marriages and the power to demand greater participation in housework from their husbands. Meanwhile, the stagnation or decline in average male real wages has apparently led some middle-class men to emphasize intense family ties as a class marker or as compensation for their inability to achieve greater success in the workplace. For some men, a conviction that traditional measures of success are inadequate has led to a greater investment in domestic life (Griswold, 1993).

One might suppose that the shift to the individual wage would have intensified spousal interdependence because two incomes are much higher than one. That this has not been the case is the result of many factors, including a growing unhappiness with what many women see as the unfairness of marriage, with its advantages flowing primarily to men while its burdens fall largely on their shoulders. Here, however, I stress a long-term historical trend that I believe has played a critical role in making male family commitment more optional and voluntary: The increasing cultural emphasis placed on the mother–child dyad.

During the 19th century, many middle-class women began to self-consciously define their identity in terms of motherhood. Yet compared to the 20th century, women's childrearing roles remained extensive rather than intensive. That is, intensive childrearing responsibilities were confined to a relatively limited number of years, a period that contemporaries referred to as infancy, which generally involved the period from birth to 3 to 6 years of age, and childrearing advice remained largely unsystematic. Furthermore, large families and other demands on women's energies sharply limited the amount of time mothers could devote to the care of individual children. Mothers typically shared day-to-day child care responsibilities with others, especially older daughters and, in the early part of the century, female neighbors who ran "dame schools," which provided care for very young children (often as young as 2 or 3 years old; Sklar, 1973; see also Hoffert, 1989; McMillen, 1990).

Even in the early 20th century, childrearing advice literature recommended a degree of maternal detachment that we find surprising today. Childrearing experts advised mothers to establish strict schedules for their children and avoid picking them up or caressing them. But during the 1930s, the mother–child axis began to stand at the very heart of family relationships, as children overwhelmingly identified the mother as the family's source of emotional sustenance. Since the Great Depression, the emphasis on the mother–child bond has intensified. The attachment theories of John Bowlby and the advice of such childrearing gurus as Benjamin Spock, Selma Fraiberg, T. Berry Brazelton, and Penelope Leach contributed to a belief that mothers were almost wholly responsible for their children's emotional, psychological, and social development and well-being. The rapid increase in the divorce rate further reinforced the impression that mothers are the only parents that children can count on in a pinch (Genevie & Margolies, 1987; Griswold, 1993; Parke, 1996).

Up until the 1960s, the increasing weight attached to the mother–child bond remained partially counterbalanced by the concept of gender complementarity: that husbands and wives each played distinctive roles in raising children. But during the 1960s and 1970s, feminism leveled two devastating criticisms against the idea of complementarity. The first was that complementary suggested a false equivalence between men and women's familial contributions. The concept obscured the fact that women were responsible for a wildly disproportionate share of child care and housework—and that the kinds of household labor that men performed, such as shopping or playing with children or mowing the lawn, were far less onerous than the demands placed on women. The other criticism was that insofar as men did convey certain gender-specific values to their children, these values had profoundly negative social consequences. The lessons that men transmitted to sons were overly masculine; they emphasized toughness, competitiveness, and emotional self-control, and encouraged sexism, aggression, and emotional repression (Miedzian, 1991).

The rapid entry of mothers into the workforce has not weakened the mother–child dyad. Although its form has changed somewhat, an ideal of intense mothering persists. Although mothers work in wholly unprecedented numbers, they also are now expected to breast feed their newborn, be familiar with the stages of child development, keep close tabs on their children during the day, and help them with their homework at night. The essential point is that over the course of the 20th century, mothers have become the primary parent, the key conduits and gatekeepers through which fathers relate to their children.

What possible messages can the history that we have examined offer contemporary social scientists? Looking to the past for present-day lessons is always a risky business, but if the discipline of history is to offer more than mere antiquarianism, it is essential that historians spell out with some specificity how their findings challenge current assumptions, which, I believe, tend to be profoundly ahistorical. By way of conclusion, I would suggest that the history we studied makes three essential points.

The first is that the history of men's roles in the family has not moved in a linear direction. Models of historical change that emphasize a long-term drift from patriarchy to androgyny and egalitarianism are wholly inadequate to capture the complexity of transformations that we have traced. Thus, I suggest that it would be a grave mistake for contemporary social scientists to assume that men's roles in the family are converging on a single destination or shifting in a uniform direction.

A second historical generalization is that at any particular point in time there has never been a single, unitary family role for men. Rather, we have seen profound variation along and across lines of race, ethnicity, class, and religion. Hence, we should not expect there to be a single characteristic or normative male role today. I suggest to you that the diversity that characterizes men's roles today—enshrined in such images as the wife beater, the "male mommy," the co-parent, the deadbeat dad, and countless others—is no greater than the range of behavior that we have witnessed in the past.

A third and perhaps a key lesson involves the historical roots of the contemporary crisis of men's authority in the family. Historically, men's family authority was rooted in certain concrete material conditions—ownership of property, control of craft skills, or men's role as the family's chief wage earner. If anything, the rise of the family wage that accompanied industrialization actually enhanced men's familial authority. A father's love could always be more conditional than a mother's precisely because other family members were in tangible respects dependent on him.

Across the past generation, however, the material bases of male familial authority have measurably declined. With the erosion of the family wage and its replacement by the individual wage, a central component of male identity, a critical factor in defining men's time commitments and roles in the family, has given way.

Men have adopted a host of adaptive strategies as they wrestle with the consequences of this historical shift. Very few men have responded by becoming co-parents and truly egalitarian husbands. Others have responded by attempting to assert a patriarchal authority grounded in religion. Still others have tried to function as noncustodial fathers. Most men have tried to muddle through—making greater, but still modest, contributions to housework and child care, but remaining secondary parents and continuing to define their spousal and parental identity largely as family breadwinner, despite the growing disjunction between this self-image and social realities. When the demands made on them become too great, many resolve this tension by disengaging or severing their family ties. Thus, 400 years of history of American men in families end not with a bang, but a whimper, an outcome particularly appropriate to a postmodernist age: fragmentation and splintering into diverse, indeed highly polarized adaptations.

REFERENCES

Alden, J. R. (1984). *George Washington: A biography.* Baton Rouge: Louisiana State University Press.

Amussen, S. D. (1988). *An ordered society: Gender and class in early modern England.* Oxford, England: Basil Blackwell.

Blankenhorn. D. (1995). *Fatherless America. Confronting our most urgent social problem.* New York: Basic Books.

Brodie, F. (1974). *Thomas Jefferson: An intimate history.* New York: Norton.

Carnes, M. C. (1989). *Secret ritual and manhood in Victorian America.* New Haven, CT: Yale University Press.

Carnes, M. C., & Griffen, C. (Eds.). (1990). *Meanings for manhood: Constructions of masculinity in Victorian America.* Chicago: University of Chicago Press.

Cohen, L. (1990). *Making a new deal: Industrial workers in Chicago, 1919–1939.* Cambridge, England: Cambridge University Press.

Cott, N. F. (1977). *The bonds of womanhood: "Woman's sphere" in New England, 1780–1835.* New Haven, CT: Yale University Press.

Danahay, M. A. (1993). *A community of one: Masculine autobiography and autonomy in nineteenth-century Britain.* Albany, NY: SUNY Press.

Davidoff, L., & Hall, C. (1987). *Family fortunes: Men and women of the English middle class.* Chicago: University of Chicago Press.

Degler, C. N. (1980). *At odds: Women and the family in America from the revolution to the present.* New York: Oxford University Press.

Demos, J. (1986). The changing faces of fatherhood. In J. Demos (Ed.), *Past, present, and personal: The family and the life course in American history.* New York: Oxford University Press.

Ditz. T. L. (1986). *Property and kinship: Inheritance in early Connecticut, 1750–1820.* Princeton, NJ: Princeton University Press.

Emery, N. (1982). *Alexander Hamilton: An intimate portrait.* New York: Putnam.

Ferling, J. E. (1988). *The first of men: A life of George Washington.* Knoxville: University of Tennessee Press.

Fischer, D. H. (1989). *Albion's seed: Four British folkways in America.* New York: Oxford University Press.

Fliegelman, J. (1982). *Prodigals and pilgrims: The American revolution against patriarchal authority, 1750–1800.* Cambridge, England: Cambridge University Press.

Frank, S. M. (1992). Rendering aid and comfort: Images of fatherhood in the letters of Civil War soldiers from Massachusetts and Michigan. *Journal of Social History, 26,* 5–31.

Furstenberg, F. F., Jr. (1988). "Good dads—bad dads: Two faces of fatherhood. In A. J. Cherlin (Ed.), *The changing American family and public policy* (pp. 193–218). Washington, DC: Urban Institute Press.

Genevie, L., &. Margolies, E. (1987). *The motherhood report.* New York: Macmillan.

Gerson, K. (1993). *No man's land: Men's changing commitments to family and work.* New York: Basic Books.

Gordon, L. (1988). *Heroes of their own lives: The politics and history of family violence, Boston, 1880–1960.* New York: Viking.

Greene, J. P. (1988). *Pursuits of happiness: The social development of early modern British colonies and the formation of American culture.* Chapel Hill: University of North Carolina Press.

Greven. P. J. (1970). *Four generations: Population, land, and family in colonial Andover, Massachusetts.* Ithaca, NY: Cornell University Press.

Greven. P. J. (1977). *The Protestant temperament: Patterns of child-rearing, religious experience, and the self in early America.* New York: Knopf.

Greven, P. J. (1991). *Spare the child: The religious roots of punishment and the psychological impact of physical abuse.* New York: Knopf.

Griswold, R. L. (1993). *Fatherhood in America: A history.* New York: Basic Books.

Hareven, T. K. (1982). *Family time and industrial time: The relationship between the family and work in a New England industrial community.* Cambridge, England: Cambridge University Press.

Hoffert, S. D. (1989). *Private matters: American attitudes toward childbearing and infant nurture in the urban North, 1800–1960.* Urbana: University of Illinois Press.

Kimmel, M. S. (Ed.). (1987). *Changing men: New directions in research on men and masculinity.* Newbury Park, CA: Sage.

Kimmel, M. S. (1996). *Manhood in America: A history.* New York: Free Press.

Koehler, L. (1980). *A search for power: The "weaker" sex in seventeenth-century New England.* Urbana, IL: University of Illinois Press.

Kulikoff, A. (1986). *Tobacco and slaves: The development of southern cultures in the Chesapeake, 1680–1800.* Chapel Hill: University of North Carolina Press.

Levy, B. (1988). *Quakers and the American family: British settlement in the Delaware Valley.* New York: Oxford University Press.

Lewis, J. (1983). *The pursuit of happiness: Family and values in Jefferson's Virginia.* Cambridge, England: Cambridge University Press.

Lopez, C.-A., & Herbert, E. W. (1975). *The private Franklin: The man and his family.* New York: Norton.

McDonald, F. (1979). *Alexander Hamilton: A biography.* New York: Norton.

McMillen, S. G. (1990). *Motherhood in the old south: Pregnancy, childbirth, and infant rearing.* Baton Rouge: Louisiana State University Press.

Miedzian, M. (1991). *Boys will be boys: Breaking the link between masculinity and violence.* New York: Doubleday.

Mintz, S. (1983). *A prison of expectations: The family in Victorian culture.* New York: University Press.

Mintz, S. (1992). Children, families, and the state: American family law in historical perspective. *Denver University Law Review, 69,* 639–640.

Mintz, S., & Kellogg, S. (1988). *Domestic revolutions: A social history of American family life.* New York: Free Press.

Moran, G. F. (1991). Adolescence in Colonial America. In R. Lerner, A. C. Petersen, & J. Brooks-Gunn, (Eds.), *Encyclopedia of adolescence* (pp. 164–167). New York: Garland.

Morgan, E. S. (1965). *The Puritan family* (rev. ed.). New York: Harper & Row.

Norton, M. B. (1996). *Founding mothers and fathers: Gendered power and the forming of American society.* New York: Knopf.

Ozment, S. E. (1983). *When fathers ruled: Family life in reformation Europe.* Cambridge, MA: Harvard University Press.

Parke, R. D. (1996). *Fatherhood.* Cambridge, MA: Harvard University Press.

Parke, R. D., & Stearns, P. N. (1993). Father and childrearing. In G. Elder, J. Modell, & R. D. Parke, (Eds.), *Children in time and place.* (pp. 147–150). New York: Cambridge University Press.

Peiss, K. L. (1986). *Cheap amusements: Working women and leisure in turn-of-the-century New York.* Philadelphia: Temple University Press.

Piore, M. J. (1979). *Birds of passage: Migrant labor, industrial societies.* Cambridge, England Cambridge University Press.

Pleck, E. H. (1987). *Domestic tyranny: The making of social policy against family violence from colonial times to the present.* New York: Oxford University Press.

Pleck, J. (1987). American fathering in historical perspective. In M. Kimmel (Ed.), *Changing men* (pp. 83–97). Newbury Park, CA: Sage.

Popenoe, D. (1996). *Life without father.* New York: Free Press.

Pugh, D. G. (1983). *Sons of liberty: The masculine mind in nineteenth-century America.* Westport, CT: Greenwood Press.

Reynolds, D. (1995). *Walt Whitman's America.* New York: Knopf.

Rorabaugh, W. J. (1979). *The alcoholic republic: An American tradition.* New York: Oxford University Press.

Rosenzweig, R. (1983). *Eight hours for what we will: Workers and leisure in an industrial city, 1870–1920.* Cambridge, England: Cambridge University Press.

Rotundo, A. (1985). American fatherhood: A historical perspective. *American Behavioral Scientist, XXIX,* 7–25.

Rotundo, A. (1993). *American manhood: Transformations in masculinity from the revolution to the modern era.* New York: Basic Books.

Rutman, D. B., & Rutman, A. H. (1984). *A place in time: Middlesex County, Virginia, 1650–1750.* New York: Norton.

Schochet, G. J. (1975). *Patriarchalism in political thought: The authoritarian family and political speculation and attitudes especially in seventeenth-century England.* New York: Basic Books.

Schor, J. (1991). *The overworked American: The unexpected decline of leisure.* New York: Basic Books.

Shammas, C., Samlon, M., & Dahlin, M. (Eds.). (1987). *Inheritance in America: From colonial times to the present.* New Brunswick, NJ: Rutgers University Press.

Sklar, K. K. (1973). *Catharine Beecher: A study in American domesticity.* New Haven, CT: Yale University Press.

Stearns, P. N. (1990). *Be a man!: Males in modern society* (2nd ed.). New York: Holmes & Meier.

Stearns, P. N. (1991). Fatherhood in historical perspective: The role of social change. In F. W. Bozett & S. M. H. Hanson (Eds.), *Fatherhood and families in cultural context* (pp. 28–52). New York: Springer.

Taylor, P. (1992, June 7). Life without father. *Washington Post,* p. C1.

Tentler, L. W. (1979). *Wage-earning women: Industrial work and family life in the United States, 1900–1930.* New York: Oxford University Press.

Thernstrom, S. (1984). *A history of the American people.* San Diego: Harcourt Brace Jovanovich.

Ulrich, L. T. (1982). *Good wives: Image and reality in the lives of women in northern New England, 1650–1750.* New York: Knopf.

U.S. Department of Labor, Office of Policy Planning and Research. (1965). *The Negro family: The case for national action.* Washington, DC: U.S. Government Printing Office.

Weiss, R. S. (1990). *Staying the course: The emotional and social lives of men who do well at work.* New York: Free Press.

Wilson, W. J. (1987). *The truly disadvantaged: The inner city, the underclass, and public policy.* Chicago: University of Chicago Press.

Wood, G. S. (1992). *The radicalism of the American Revolution.* New York: Knopf.

CHAPTER 3

Gender and Families

Over the past few decades, feminist scholarship on gender has greatly influenced how we view the family. In the middle of the 20th century, the predominant breadwinner-homemaker nuclear family was thought by many observers to be the natural way to organize a family—a timeless outgrowth of the deep-seated, and presumably biological, differences between women and men. Two generations of feminist scholarship on the division of labor in marriage, however, have produced evidence that the roles wives and husbands typically play in the breadwinner-homemaker family are not firmly rooted in biology but rather reflect the influence of culture and social structure. The first generation of scholarship emphasized the influence of large-scale forces: industrialization, which took males out of the household to earn wages in factories; the movement for a "family wage," which was discussed in Mintz's article in the previous chapter; the growth of the welfare state, which treated men differently from women; and so forth. These cultural and social structural forces, it was said, powerfully influenced the behavior of women and men in families. Jesse Bernard's 1981 article, "The Good-Provider Role—Its Rise and Fall," the first selection in this chapter, is probably the best-known example of this tradition in sociology.

The second generation of feminist scholars, while not disputing the influence of macro-level factors such as changes in the economy, nevertheless argued that gender differences also are reinforced day after day at the micro-level of individual personal interactions. Husbands and wives unthinkingly enact scripts that reproduce gender-typed behavior. In a frequently cited example, Sara Fenstermaker Berk[1] described a family in which the husband, a successful lawyer, smiled sheepishly as, try as he might, he was unable to sponge off a table without missing many of the crumbs. "He tries to be helpful. He tries," his wife said with resignation. Through continual interactions such as these, couples recreate gender differences or, in the language of feminist studies, "do gender."[2]

---

[1]Sara Fenstermaker Berk, *The Gender Factory: The Apportionment of Work in American Households* (New York: Plenum Press, 1985) p. 206.
[2]Candace West and Don H. Zimmerman, "Doing Gender." *Gender & Society* 2 (1987): 125–51.

In the second selection in this chapter, Marjorie L. DeVault presents an example of this second-generation scholarship. She examines the mundane and seemingly uncomplicated process by which most wives (and a few husbands) feed their families: planning meals, shopping, cooking, and cleaning. Why is most of this work done by women? She argues that women's food work is not "natural" but rather results from interactions that begin when little girls help their mothers, continue when pregnant women and new mothers concern themselves with feeding, and continue when husbands and wives reenact the scripts they learned as children.

READING 3-1

The Good-Provider Role—
Its Rise and Fall

Jessie Bernard

The Lord is my shepherd, I shall not want. He sets a table for me in the very sight of my enemies; my cup runs over (23rd Psalm). And when the Israelites were complaining about how hungry they were on their way from Egypt to Canaan, God told Moses to rest assured: There would be meat for dinner and bread for breakfast the next morning. And, indeed, there were quails that very night, enough to cover the camp, and in the morning the ground was covered with dew that proved to be bread (Exodus 16:12–13). In fact, in this role of good provider, God is sometimes almost synonymous with Providence. Many people, like Micawber, still wait for him, or Providence, to provide.

Granted, then, that the first great provider for the human species was God the Father, surely the second great provider for the human species was Mother, the gatherer, planter, and general factotum. Boulding (1976), citing Lee and deVore, tells us that in hunting and gathering societies, males contribute about one-fifth of the food of the clan, females the other four-fifths (p. 96). She also concludes that by 12,000 B.C. in the early agricultural villages, females provided four-fifths of human subsistence (p. 97). Not until large trading towns arose did the female contribution to human subsistence decline to equality with that of the male. And with the beginning of true cities, the provisioning work of women tended to become invisible. Still, in today's world it remains substantial.

Jessie Bernard, "The Good Provider Role: Its Rise and Fall" from *American Psychologist* 36 (1981). Copyright © 1981 by the American Psychological Association. Reprinted with the permission of Dorothy Jackson and the American Psychological Association.

Whatever the date of the virtuous woman described in the Old Testament (Proverbs 31: 10–27), she was the very model of a good provider. She was, in fact, a highly productive conglomerate. She woke up in the middle of the night to tend to her business; she oversaw a multiple-industry household; *her* candles did not go out at night; there was a ready market for the high-quality linen girdles she made and sold to the merchants in town; and she kept track of the real estate market and bought good land when it became available, cultivating vineyards quite profitably. All this time her husband sat at the gates talking with his cronies.

A recent counterpart to the virtuous woman was the busy and industrious shtetl woman:

> The earning of a livelihood is sexless, and the large majority of women . . . participate in some gainful occupation if they do not carry the chief burden of support. The wife of a "perennial student" is very apt to be the sole support of the family. The problem of managing both a business and a home is so common that no one recognizes it as special . . . To bustle about in search of a livelihood is merely another form of bustling about managing a home; both are aspects of . . . health and livelihood. (Zborowski & Herzog, 1952, p. 131)

In a subsistence economy in which husbands and wives ran farms, shops, or businesses together, a man might be a good, steady worker, but the idea that he was *the* provider would hardly ring true. Even the youth in the folk song who listed all the gifts he would bestow on his love if she would marry him—a golden comb, a paper of pins, and all the rest—was not necessarily promising to be a good provider.

I have not searched the literature to determine when the concept of the good provider entered our thinking. The term *provider* entered the English language in 1532, but was not yet male sex typed, as the older term *purveyor* already was in 1442. Webster's second edition defines the good provider as "one who provides, especially, colloq., one who provides food, clothing, etc. for his family; as, he is a good or an adequate provider." More simply, he could be defined as a man whose wife did not have to enter the labor force. The counterpart to the good provider was the housewife. However the term is defined, the role itself delineated relationships within a marriage and family in a way that added to the legal, religious, and other advantages men had over women.

Thus, under the common law, although the husband was legally head of the household and as such had the responsibility of providing for his wife and children, this provision was often made with help from the wife's personal property and earnings, to which he was entitled:

> He owned his wife's and children's services, and had the sole right to collect wages for their work outside the home. He owned his wife's personal property outright, and had the right to manage and control all of his wife's real property during marriage, which included the right to use or lease property, and to keep any rents and profits from it. (Babcock, Freedman, Norton, & Ross, 1975, p. 561)

So even when she was the actual provider, the legal recognition was granted the husband. Therefore, whatever the husband's legal responsibilities for support may have been, he was not necessarily a good provider in the way the term came to be understood. The wife may have been performing that role.

In our country in Colonial times women were still viewed as performing a providing role, and they pursued a variety of occupations. Abigail Adams managed the family estate, which provided the wherewithal for John to spend so much time in Philadelphia. In the 18th century "many women were active in business and professional pursuits. They ran inns and taverns; they managed a wide variety of stores and shops; and, at least occasionally, they worked in careers like publishing, journalism and medicine" (Demos, 1974, p. 430). Women sometimes even "joined the menfolk for work in the fields" (p. 430). Like the household of the proverbial virtuous woman, the Colonial household was a little factory that produced clothing, furniture, bedding, candles, and other accessories, and again, as in the case of the virtuous woman, the female role was central. It was taken for granted that women provided for the family along with men.

The good provider as a specialized male role seems to have arisen in the transition from subsistence to market—especially money—economies that accelerated with the industrial revolution. The good-provider role for males emerged in this country roughly, say, from the 1830s, when de Tocqueville was observing it, to the late 1970s, when the 1980 census declared that a male was not automatically to be assumed to be head of the household. This gives the role a life span of about a century and a half. Although relatively short-lived, while it lasted the role was a seemingly rocklike feature of the national landscape.

As a psychological and sociological phenomenon, the good-provider role had wide ramifications for all of our thinking about families. It marked a new kind of marriage. It did not have good effects on women: The role deprived them of many chips by placing them in a peculiarly vulnerable position. Because she was not reimbursed for her contribution to the family in either products or services, a wife was stripped to a considerable extent of her access to cash-mediated markets. By discouraging labor force participation, it deprived many women, especially affluent ones, of opportunities to achieve strength and competence. It deterred young women from acquiring productive skills. They dedicated themselves instead to winning a good provider who would "take care of" them. The wife of a more successful provider became for all intents and purposes a parasite, with little to do except indulge or pamper herself. The psychology of such dependence could become all but crippling. There were other concomitants of the good-provider role.

EXPRESSIVITY AND THE
GOOD-PROVIDER ROLE

The new industrial order that produced the good provider changed not so much the division of labor between the sexes as it did the site of the work they engaged in. Only two of the concomitants of this change in work site are selected for comment here, namely, (a) the identification of gender with work site as well as with work itself and (b) the reduction of time for personal interaction and intimacy within the family.

It is not so much the specific kinds of work men and women do—they have always varied from time to time and place to place—but the simple fact that the sexes do different kinds of work, whatever it is, which is in and of itself important. The division of labor by sex means that the work group becomes also a sex group. The very nature of maleness and femaleness becomes embedded in the sexual division of labor. One's sex and one's work are part of one another. One's work defines one's gender.

Any division of labor implies that people doing different kinds of work will occupy different work sites. When the division is based on sex, men and women will necessarily have different work sites. Even within the home itself, men and women had different work spaces. The woman's spinning wheel occupied a different area from the man's anvil. When the factory took over much of the work formerly done in the house, the separation of work space became especially marked. Not only did the separation of the sexes become spatially extended, but it came to relate work and gender in a special way. The work site as well as the work itself became associated with gender; each sex had its own turf. This sexual "territoriality" has had complicating effects on efforts to change any sexual division of labor. The good provider worked primarily in the outside male world of business and industry. The homemaker worked primarily in the home.

Spatial separation of the sexes not only identifies gender with work site and work but also reduces the amount of time available for spontaneous emotional give-and-take between husbands and wives. When men and women work in an economy based in the home, there are frequent occasions for interaction. (Consider, for example, the suggestive allusions made today to the rise in the birth rate nine months after a blackout.) When men and women are in close proximity, there is always the possibility of reassuring glances, the comfort of simple physical presence. But when the division of labor removes the man from the family dwelling for most of the day, intimate relationships become less feasible. De Tocqueville was one of the first to call our attention to this. In 1840 he noted that

> almost all men in democracies are engaged in public or professional life; and . . . the limited extent of common income obliges a wife to confine herself to the house, in order to watch in person and very closely over the details of domestic economy. All these distinct and compulsory occupations are so many natural barriers, which, by keeping the two sexes asunder, render the solicitations of the one less frequent and less ardent—the resistance of the other more easy. (de Tocqueville, 1840, p. 212)

Not directly related to the spatial constraints on emotional expression by men, but nevertheless a concomitant of the new industrial order with the same effect, was the enormous drive for achievement, for success, for "making it" that escalated the provider role into the good-provider role. De Tocqueville (1840) is again our source:

> The tumultuous and constantly harassed life which equality makes men lead [becoming good providers] not only distracts them from the passions of love, by denying them time to indulge in it, but it diverts them from it by another more secret but more certain road. All men who live in democratic ages more or less contract ways of thinking of the manufacturing and trading classes. (p. 221)

As a result of this male concentration on jobs and careers, much abnegation and "a constant sacrifice of her pleasures to her duties" (de Tocqueville, 1840, p. 212) were demanded of the American woman. The good-provider role, as it came to be shaped by this ambience, was thus restricted in what it was called upon to provide. Emotional expressivity was not included in the role. One of the things a parent might say about a man to persuade a daughter to marry him, or a daughter might say to explain to her parents why she wanted to, was not that he was a gentle, loving, or tender man but that he was a good provider. He might have many other qualities, good or bad, but if a man was a good provider, everything else was either gravy or the price one had to pay for a good provider.

Lack of expressivity did not imply neglect of the family. The good provider was a "family man." He set a good table, provided a decent home, paid the mortgage, bought the shoes, and kept his children warmly clothed. He might, with the help of the children's part-time jobs, have been able to finance their educations through high school and, sometimes, even college. There might even have been a little left over for an occasional celebration in most families. The good provider made a decent contribution to the church. His work might have been demanding, but he expected it to be. If in addition to being a good provider, a man was kind, gentle, generous, and not a heavy drinker or gambler, that was all frosting on the cake. Loving attention and emotional involvement in the family were not part of a woman's implicit bargain with the good provider.

By the time de Tocqueville published his observations in 1840, the general outlines of the good-provider role had taken shape. It called for a hardworking man who spent most of his time at his work. In the traditional conception of the role, a man's chief responsibility is his job, so that "by definition any family behaviors must be subordinate to it in terms of significance and [the job] has priority in the event of a clash" (Scanzoni, 1975, p. 38). This was the classic form of the good-provider role, which remained

a powerful component of our societal structure until well into the present century.

COSTS AND REWARDS OF THE GOOD-PROVIDER ROLE FOR MEN

There were both costs and rewards for those men attached to the good-provider role. The most serious cost was perhaps the identification of maleness not only with the work site but especially with success in the role. "The American male looks to his breadwinning role to confirm his manliness" (Brenton, 1966, p. 194).[1] To be a man one had to be not only a provider but a *good* provider. Success in the good-provider role came in time to define masculinity itself. The good provider had to achieve, to win, to succeed, to dominate. He was a bread*winner*. He had to show "strength, cunning, inventiveness, endurance—a whole range of traits henceforth defined as exclusively 'masculine'" (Demos, 1974, p. 436). Men were judged as men by the level of living they provided. They were judged by the myth "that endows a moneymaking man with sexiness and virility, and is based on man's dominance, strength, and ability to provide for and care for 'his' woman" (Gould, 1974, p. 97). The good provider became a player in the male competitive macho game. What one man provided for his family in the way of luxury and display had to be equaled or topped by what another could provide. Families became display cases for the success of the good provider.

The psychic costs could be high:

By depending so heavily on his breadwinning role to validate his sense of himself as a man, instead of also letting his roles as husband, father, and

---

[1]Rainwater and Yancey (1967), critiquing current welfare policies, note that they "have robbed men of their manhood, women of their husbands, and children of their fathers. To create a stable monogamous family we need to provide men with the opportunity to be men, and that involves enabling them to perform occupationally" (p. 235).

citizen of the community count as validating sources, the American male treads on psychically dangerous ground. It's always dangerous to put all of one's psychic eggs into one basket. (Brenton, 1966, p. 194)

The good-provider role not only put all of a man's gender-identifying eggs into one psychic basket, but it also put all the family-providing eggs into one basket. One individual became responsible for the support of the whole family. Countless stories portrayed the humiliation families underwent to keep wives and especially mothers out of the labor force, a circumstance that would admit to the world the male head's failure in the good-provider role. If a married woman had to enter the labor force at all, that was bad enough. If she made a good salary, however, she was "co-opting the man's passport to masculinity" (Gould, 1974, p. 98) and he was effectively castrated. A wife's earning capacity diminished a man's position as head of the household (Gould, 1974, p. 99).

Failure in the role of good provider, which employment of wives evidenced, could produce deep frustration. As Komarovsky (1940, p. 20) explains, this is "because in his own estimation he is failing to fulfill what is the central duty of his life, the very touchstone of his manhood—the role of family provider."

But just as there was punishment for failure in the good-provider role, so also were there rewards for successful performance. A man "derived strength from his role as provider" (Komarovsky, 1940, p. 205). He achieved a good deal of satisfaction from his ability to support his family. It won kudos. Being a good provider led to status in both the family and the community. Within the family it gave him the power of the purse and the right to decide about expenditures, standards of living, and what constituted good providing. "Every purchase of the family—the radio, his wife's new hat, the children's skates, the meals set before him—all were symbols of their dependence upon him" (Komarovsky, 1940, pp. 74–75). Such dependence gave him a

"profound sense of stability" (p. 74). It was a strong counterpoise vis-à-vis a wife with a stronger personality. "Whether he had considerable authority within the family and was recognized as its head, or whether the wife's stronger personality . . . dominated the family, he nevertheless derived strength from his role as a provider" (Komarovsky, 1940, p. 75). As recently as 1975, in a sample of 3,100 husbands and wives in 10 cities, Scanzoni found that despite increasing egalitarian norms, the good provider still had "considerable power in ultimate decision-making" and as "unique provider" had the right "to organize his life and the lives of other family members around his occupation" (p. 38).

A man who was successful in the good-provider role might be freed from other obligations to the family. But the flip side of this dispensation was that he could not make up for poor performance by excellence in other family roles. Since everything depended on his success as provider, everything was at stake. The good provider played an all-or-nothing game.

DIFFERENT WAYS OF PERFORMING THE GOOD-PROVIDER ROLE

Although the legal specifications for the role were laid out in the common law, in legislation, in legal precedents, in court decisions, and, most importantly, in custom and convention, in real-life situations the social and social-psychological specifications were set by the husband or, perhaps more accurately, by the community, alias the Joneses, and there were many ways to perform it.

Some men resented the burdens the role forced them to bear. A man could easily vent such resentment toward his family by keeping complete control over all expenditures, dispensing the money for household maintenance, and complaining about bills as though it were his wife's fault that shoes cost so much. He could, in effect, punish his family for his having to perform the role.

Since the money he earned belonged to him—was "his"—he could do with it what he pleased. Through extreme parsimony he could dole out his money in a mean, humiliating way, forcing his wife to come begging for pennies. By his reluctance and resentment he could make his family pay emotionally for the provisioning he supplied.

At the other extreme were the highly competitive men who were so involved in outdoing the Joneses that the fur coat became more important than the affectionate hug. They "bought off" their families. They sometimes succeeded so well in their extravagance that they sacrificed the family they were presumably providing for to the achievements that made it possible (Keniston, 1965).[2]

The Depression of the 1930s revealed in harsh detail what the loss of the role could mean both to the good provider and to his family, not only in the loss of income itself—which could be supplied by welfare agencies or even by other family members, including wives—but also and especially in the loss of face.

The Great Depression did not mark the demise of the good-provider role. But it did teach us what a slender thread the family hung on. It stimulated a whole array of programs designed to strengthen that thread, to ensure that it would never again be similarly threatened. Unemployment insurance was incorporated into the Social Security Act of 1935, for example, and a Full Employment Act was passed in 1946. But there proved to be many other ways in which the good-provider role could be subverted.

---

[2]Several years ago I presented a critique of what I called "extreme sex role specialization," including "work-intoxicated fathers." I noted that making success in the provider role the only test for real manliness was putting a lot of eggs into one basket. At both the blue-collar and the managerial levels, it was dysfunctional for families. I referred to the several attempts being made even then to correct the excesses of extreme sex role specialization: rural and urban communes, leaving jobs to take up small-scale enterprises that allowed more contact with families, and a rebellion against overtime in industry (Bernard, 1975, pp. 217–239).

ROLE REJECTORS AND ROLE OVERPERFORMERS

Recent research in psychology, anthropology, and sociology has familiarized us with the tremendous power of roles. But we also know that one of the fundamental principles of role behavior is that conformity to role norms is not universal. Not everyone lives up to the specifications of roles, either in the psychological or in the sociological definition of the concept. Two extremes have attracted research attention: (a) the men who could not live up to the norms of the good-provider role or did not want to, at one extreme, and (b) the men who overperformed the role, at the other. For the wide range in between, from blue-collar workers to professionals, there was fairly consistent acceptance of the role, however well or poorly, however grumblingly or willingly, performed.

First the nonconformists. Even in Colonial times, desertion and divorce occurred:

> Women may have deserted because, say, their husbands beat them; husbands, on the other hand, may have deserted because they were unable or unwilling to provide for their usually large families in the face of the wives' demands to do so. These demands were, of course, backed by community norms making the husband's financial support a sacred duty. (Scanzoni, 1979, pp. 24–25)

Fiedler (1962) has traced the theme of male escape from domestic responsibilities in the American novel from the time of Rip Van Winkle to the present:

> The figure of Rip Van Winkle presides over the birth of the American imagination; and it is fitting that our first successful home-grown legend should memorialize, however playfully, the flight of the dreamer from the shrew—into the mountains and out of time, away from the drab duties of home . . . anywhere to avoid . . . marriage and responsibility. One of the factors that determine theme and form in our great books is this strategy of evasion, this retreat to nature and childhood

which makes our literature (and life) so charmingly and infuriatingly "boyish." (pp. xx–xxi)

Among the men who pulled up stakes and departed for the West or went down to the sea in ships, there must have been a certain proportion who, like their mythic prototype, were simply fleeing the good-provider role.

The work of Demos (1974), a historian, offers considerable support for Fiedler's thesis. He tells us that the burdens thrust on men in the 19th century by the new patterns of work began to show their effects in the family. When "the [spatial] separation of the work lives of husbands and wives made communication so problematic," he asks, "what was the likelihood of meaningful communication?" (Demos, 1974, p. 438). The answer is, relatively little. Divorce and separation increased, either formally or by tacit consent—or simply by default, as in the case of a variety of defaulters—tramps, bums, hoboes—among them.

In this connection, "the development of the notorious 'tramp' phenomenon is worth noticing," Demos (1974, p. 438) tells us. The tramp was a man who just gave up, who dropped out of the role entirely. He preferred not to work, but he would do small chores or other small-scale work for a handout if he had to. He was not above begging the housewife for a meal, hoping she would not find work for him to do in repayment. Demos (1974) describes the type:

> Demoralized and destitute wanderers, their numbers mounting into the hundreds of thousands, tramps can be fairly characterized as men who had run away from their wives. . . . Their presence was mute testimony to the strains that tugged at the very core of American family life . . . Many observers noted that the tramps had created a virtual society of their own [a kind of counterculture] based on a principle of single-sex companionship. (p. 438)

A considerable number of them came to be described as "homeless men" and, as the country became more urbanized, landed ultimately on skid row. A large part of the task of social workers for almost a century was the care of the "evaded" women they left behind.[3] When the tramp became wholly demoralized, a chronic alcoholic, almost unreachable, he fell into a category of his own—he was a bum.

Quite a different kettle of fish was the hobo, the migratory worker who spent several months harvesting wheat and other large crops and the rest of the year in cities. Many were the so-called Wobblies, or Industrial Workers of the World, who repudiated the good-provider role on principle. They had contempt for the men who accepted it and could be called conscientious objectors to the role. "In some IWW circles, wives were regarded as the 'ball and chain.' In the West, IWW literature proclaimed that the migratory worker, usually a young, unmarried male, was 'the finest specimen of American manhood . . . the leaven of the revolutionary labor movement' " (Foner, 1979, p. 400). Exemplars of the Wobblies were the nomadic workers of the West. They were free men. The migratory worker, "unlike the factory slave of the Atlantic seaboard and the central

---

[3]In one department of a south Carolina cotton mill early in the century, "every worker was a grass widow" (Smuts, 1959, p. 54). Many women worked "because their husbands refused to provide for their families. There is no reason to think that husbands abandoned their duties more often than today, but the woman who was burdened by an irresponsible husband in 1890 usually had no recourse save taking on his responsibilities herself. If he deserted, the law-enforcement agencies of the time afforded little chance of finding and compelling him to provide support" (Smuts, 1959, p. 54). The situation is not greatly improved today. In divorce child support is allotted in only a small number of cases and enforced in even fewer. "Roughly half of all families with an absent parent don't have awards at all. . . Where awards do exist they are usually for small amounts, typically ranging from $7 to $18 per week per child" (Jones, 1976, abstract). A summary of all the studies available concludes that "approximately 20 percent of all divorced and separated mothers receive child support regularly, with an additional 7 percent receiving it 'sometimes'; 8 percent of all divorced and separated women receive alimony regularly or sometimes" (Jones, 1976, p. 23).

states, . . . was most emphatically 'not afraid of losing his job.' No wife and family cumbered him. The worker of the East, oppressed by the fear of want for wife and babies, dared not venture much" (Foner, 1979, p. 400). The reference to fear of loss of job was well taken; employers preferred married men, disciplined into the good-provider role, who had given hostages to fortune and were therefore more tractable.

Just on the verge between the area of conformity to the good-provider role—at whatever level—and the area of complete nonconformity to it was the non-good provider, the marginal group of workers usually made up of "the under-educated, the under-trained, the under-employed, or part-time employed, as well as the under-paid, and of course the unemployed" (Snyder, 1979, p. 597). These included men who wanted—sometimes desperately—to perform the good-provider role but who for one reason or another were unable to do so. Liebow (1966) has discussed the ramifications of failure among the black men of Tally's corner: The black man is

> under legal and social constraints to provide for them [their families], to be a husband to his wife and a father to his children. The chances are, however, that he is failing to provide for them, and failure in this primary function contaminates his performance as father in other respects as well. (p. 86)

In some cases, leaving the family entirely was the best substitute a man could supply. The community was left to take over.[4]

At the other extreme was the overperformer. De Tocqueville, quoted earlier, was already describing him as he manifested in the 1830s. And as late as 1955 Warner and Ablegglen were adding to the considerable literature on industrial leaders and tycoons, referring to their "driving concentration" on their careers and their "intense focusing" of interests, energies, and skills on these careers, "even limiting their sexual activity" (pp. 48–49). They came to be known as workaholics or work-intoxicated men. Their preoccupation with their work even at the expense of their families was, as I have already noted, quite acceptable in our society.

Poorly or well performed, the good-provider role lingered on. World War II initiated a challenge, this time in the form of attracting more and more married women into the labor force, but the challenge was papered over in the 1950s with an "age of togetherness" that all but apotheosized the good provider, his house in the suburbs, his homebody wife, and his third, fourth, even fifth, child. As late as the 1960s most housewives (87 percent) still saw breadwinning as their husband's primary role (Lopata, 1971, p. 91).[5]

INTRINSIC CONFLICT IN THE GOOD-PROVIDER ROLE

Since the good-provider role involved both family and work roles, most people believed that there was no incompatibility between them or at least that there should not be. But in the 1960s and 1970s evidence began to mount that maybe something was amiss.

De Tocqueville had documented the implicit conflict in the American businessman's devotion to his work at the expense of his family in the early years of the 19th century; the Industrial Workers of the World had proclaimed that the good-provider role which tied a man to his family was an impediment to the great revolution at the beginning of the 20th century; Fiedler (1962) had noted that

---

[4]Even though the annals of social work agencies are filled with cases of runaway husbands, in 1976 only 12.6 percent of all women were in the status of divorce and separation, and at least some of them were still being "provided for." Most men were at least trying to fulfill the good-provider role.

[5]Although all the women in Lopata's (1971) sample saw breadwinning as important, fewer employed women (54 percent) than either nonemployed urban (63 percent) or suburban (64 percent) women assigned it first place (p. 91).

throughout our history, in the male fantasy world, there was freedom from the responsibilities of this role; about 50 years ago Freud (1930/1958) had analyzed the intrinsic conflict between the demands of women and the family on one side and the demands of men's work on the other:

> Women represent the interests of the family and sexual life; the work of civilization has become more and more men's business; it confronts them with ever harder tasks, compels them to sublimations of instinct which women are not easily able to achieve. Since man has not an unlimited amount of mental energy at his disposal, he must accomplish his tasks by distributing his libido to the best advantage. What he employs for cultural [occupational] purposes he withdraws to a great extent from women, and his sexual life; his constant association with men and his dependence on his relations with them even estrange him from his duties as husband and father. Woman finds herself thus forced into the background by the claims of culture [work] and she adapts an inimical attitude towards it. (pp. 50–51)

In the last two decades, researchers have been raising questions relevant to Freud's statement of the problem. They have been asking people about the relative satisfactions they derive from these conflicting values—family and work. Among the earliest studies comparing family–work values was a Gallup poll in 1940 in which both men and women chose a happy home over an interesting job or wealth as a major life value. Since then there have been a number of such polls, and a considerable body of results has now accumulated. Pleck and Lang (1979) and Hesselbart (Note 1) have summarized the findings of these surveys. All agree that there is a clear bias in the direction of the family. Pleck and Lang conclude that "men's family role is far more psychologically significant to them than is their work role" (p. 29), and Hesselbart—however critical she is of the studies she summarizes—believes they should not be dismissed lightly and concludes that they certainly "chal-

lenge the idea that family is a 'secondary' valued role" (p. 14).[6] Douvan (Note 2) also found in a 1976 replication of a 1957 survey that family values retained priority over work: "Family roles almost uniformly rate higher in value production than the job role does" (p. 16).[7]

The very fact that researchers have asked such questions is itself interesting. Somehow or other both the researchers and the informants seem to be saying that all this complaining about the male neglect of the family, about the lack of family involvement by men, just is not warranted. Neither de Tocqueville nor Freud was right. Men do value family life more than they value their work. They do derive their major life satisfactions from their families rather than from their work.

It may well be true that men derive the greatest satisfaction from their family roles, but this does not necessarily mean they are willing to pay for this benefit. In any event, great attitudinal changes took place in the 1960s and 1970s.

---

[6]Pleck and Lang (1979) found only one serious study contradicting their own conclusions: "Using data from the 1973 NORC [National Opinion Research Center] General Social Survey, Harry analyzed the bivariate relationship of job and family satisfaction to life happiness in men classified by family life cycle stage. In three of the five groups of husbands . . . job satisfaction had a stronger association than family satisfaction to life happiness" (pp. 5–6).

[7]In 1978, a Yankelovich survey on "The New Work Psychology" suggested that leisure is now becoming a strict competitor for both family and work as a source of life satisfactions: "Family and work have grown less important than leisure; a majority of 60 percent say that although they enjoy their work, it is not their major source of satisfaction" (p. 46). A 1977 survey of Swedish men aged 18 to 35 found that the proportion saying the family was the main source of meaning in their lives declined from 45 percent in 1955 to 41 percent in 1977; the proportion indicating work as the main source of satisfaction dropped from 33 percent to 17 percent. The earlier tendency for men to identify themselves through their work is less marked these days. In the new value system, the individual says, in effect, "I am more than my role. I am myself" (Yankelovich, 1978). Is the increasing concern with leisure a way to escape the dissatisfaction with both the alienating relations found on the work site and the demands for increased involvement with the family?

Douvan (Note 2), on the basis of surveys in 1957 and 1976, found, for example, a considerable increase in the proportion of both men and women who found marriage and parenthood burdensome and restrictive. Almost three fifths (57 percent) of both married men and married women in 1976 saw marriage as "all burdens and restrictions," as compared with only 42 percent and 47 percent, respectively, in 1957. And almost half (45 percent) also viewed children as "all burdens and restrictions" in 1976, as compared with only 28 percent and 33 percent for married men and married woman, respectively, in 1957. The proportion of working men with a positive attitude toward marriage dropped drastically over this period, from 68 percent to 39 percent. Working women, who made up a fairly small number of all married women in 1957, hardly changed attitudes at all, dropping only from 43 percent to 42 percent. The proportion of working men who found marriage and children burdensome and restrictive more than doubled, from 25 percent to 56 percent and from 25 percent to 58 percent, respectively. Although some of these changes reflected greater willingness in 1976 than in 1957 to admit negative attitudes toward marriage and parenthood—itself significant—profound changes were clearly in process. More and more men and women were experiencing disaffection with family life.[8]

"ALL BURDENS AND RESTRICTIONS"

Apparently, the benefits of the good-provider role were greater than the costs for most men. Despite the legend of the flight of the American male (Fiedler, 1962), despite the defectors and dropouts, despite the tavern habitué's "ball and chain" cliché, men seemed to know that the good-provider role, if they could succeed in it, was good for them. But Douvan's (Note 2) findings suggest that recently their complaints have become serious, bone-deep. The family they have been providing for is not the same family it was in the past.

Smith (1979) calls the great trek of married women into the labor force a subtle revolution—revolutionary not in the sense of one class overthrowing a status quo and substituting its own regime, but revolutionary in its impact on both the family and the work roles of men and women. It diluted the prerogatives of the good-provider role. It increased the demands made on the good provider, especially in the form of more emotional investment in the family, more sharing of household responsibilities. The role became even more burdensome.

However men may now feel about the burdens and restrictions imposed on them by the good-provider role, most have, at least ostensibly, accepted them. The tramp and the bum had "voted with their feet" against the role; the hobo or Wobbly had rejected it on the basis of a revolutionary ideology that saw it as enslaving men to the corporation; tavern humor had glossed the resentment habitués felt against its demands. Now the "burdens-and-restrictions" motif has surfaced both in research reports and, more blatantly, in the male liberation movement. From time to time it has also appeared in the clinicians' notes.

Sometimes the resentment of the good provider takes the form of simply wanting more appreciation for the life-style he provides. All he does for his family seems to be taken for granted. Thus, for example, Goldberg (1976), a psychiatrist, recounts the case of a successful businessman:

> He's feeling a deepening sense of bitterness and frustration about his wife and family. He doesn't feel appreciated. It angers him the way they seem

---

[8]Men seem to be having problems with both work and family roles. Veroff (Note 3), for example, reports an increased "sense of dissatisfaction with the social relations in the work setting" and a "dissatisfaction with the affiliative nature of work" (p. 47). This dissatisfaction may be one of the factors that leads men to seek affiliative-need satisfaction in marriage, just as in the 19th century they looked to the home as shelter from the jungle of the outside world.

to take the things his earnings purchase for granted. They've come to expect it as their due. It particularly enrages him when his children put him down for his "materialistic middle-class trip." He'd like to tell them to get someone else to support them but he holds himself back. (p. 124)

Brenton (1966) quotes a social worker who describes an upper-middle-class woman: She has "gotten hold of a man who'll drive himself like mad to get money, and [is] denigrating him for being too interested in money, and not interested in music, or the arts, or in spending time with the children. But at the same time she's subtly driving him—and doesn't know it" (p. 226). What seems significant about such cases is not that men feel resentful about the lack of appreciation but that they are willing to justify their resentment. They are no longer willing to grin and bear it.

Sometimes there is even more than expressed resentment; there is an actual repudiation of the role. In the past, only a few men like the hobo or Wobbly were likely to give up. Today, Goldberg (1976) believes, more are ready to renounce the role, not on theoretical revolutionary grounds, however, but on purely selfish ones:

> Male growth will stem from openly avowed, unashamed, self-oriented motivations . . . Guilt-oriented "should" behavior will be rejected because it is always at the price of a hidden build-up of resentment and frustration and alienation from others and is, therefore, counterproductive. (p. 184)

The disaffection of the good provider is directed to both sides of his role. With respect to work, Lefkowitz (1979) has described men among whom the good-provider role is neither being completely rejected nor repudiated, but diluted. These men began their working lives in the conventional style, hopeful and ambitious. They found a job, married, raised a family, and "achieved a measure of economic security and earned the respect of . . . colleagues and neighbors" (Lefkowitz, 1979, p. 31). In brief, they successfully performed the good-provider role. But unlike their historical predecessors, they in time became disillusioned with their jobs—not jobs on assembly lines, not jobs usually characterized as alienating, but fairly prestigious jobs such as aeronautics engineer and government economist. They daydreamed about other interests. "The common theme which surfaced again and again in their histories, was the need to find a new social connection—to reassert control over their lives, to gain some sense of freedom" (Lefkowitz, 1979, p. 31). These men felt "entitled to freedom and independence." Middle-class, educated, self-assured, articulate, and for the most part white, they knew they could talk themselves into a job if they had to. Most of them did not want to desert their families. Indeed, most of them "wanted to rejoin the intimate circle they felt they had neglected in their years of work" (p. 31).

Though some of the men Lefkowitz studied sought closer ties with their families, in the case of those studied by Sarason (1977), a psychologist, career changes involved lower income and had a negative impact on families. Sarason's subjects were also men in high-level professions, the very men least likely to find marriage and parenthood burdensome and restrictive. Still, since career change often involved a reduction in pay, some wives were unwilling to accept it, with the result that the marriage deteriorated (p. 178). Sometimes it looked like a no-win game. The husband's earlier career brought him feelings of emptiness and alienation, but it also brought financial rewards for the family. Greater work satisfaction for him in lower paying work meant reduced satisfaction with life-style. These findings lead Sarason to raise a number of points with respect to the good-provider role. "How much," he asks, "does an individual or a family need in order to maintain a satisfactory existence? Is an individual being responsible to himself or his family if he provides them with little more than the bare essentials of living?" (p. 178). These are questions about the good-provider role that few men raised in the past.

Lefkowitz (1979) wonders how his downwardly mobile men lived when they left their jobs. "They put together a basic economic package which consisted of government assistance, contributions from family members who had not worked before and some bartering of goods and services" (p. 31). Especially interesting in this list of income sources are the "contributions from family members who had not worked before" (p. 31). Surely not mothers and sisters. Who, of course, but wives?

WOMEN AND THE PROVIDER ROLE

The present discussion began with the woman's part in the provider role. We saw how as more and more of the provisioning of the family came to be by way of monetary exchange, the woman's part shrank. A woman could still provide services, but could furnish little in the way of food, clothing, and shelter. But now that she is entering the labor force in large numbers, she can once more resume her ancient role, this time, like her male counterpart the provider, by way of a monetary contribution. More and more women are doing just this.

The assault on the good-provider role in the Depression was traumatic. But a modified version began to appear in the 1970s as a single income became inadequate for more and more families. Husbands have remained the major providers, but in an increasing number of cases the wife has begun to share this role. Thus, the proportion of married women aged 15 to 54 (living with their husbands) in the labor force more than doubled between 1950 and 1978, from 25.2 percent to 55.4 percent. The proportion for 1990 is estimated to reach 66.7 percent (Smith, 1979, p. 14). Fewer women are now fulltime housewives.

For some men the relief from the strain of sole responsibility for the provider role has been welcome. But for others the feeling of degradation resembles the feelings reported 40 years earlier in the Great Depression. It is not that they are no longer providing for the family but

that the role-sharing wife now feels justified in making demands on them. The good-provider role with all its prerogatives and perquisites has undergone profound changes. It will never be the same again.[9] Its death knell was sounded when, as noted above, the 1980 census no longer automatically assumed that the male member of the household was its head.

THE CURRENT SCENE

Among the new demands being made on the good-provider role, two deserve special consideration, namely, (*a*) more intimacy, expressivity, and nurturance—specifications never included in it as it originally took shape—and (*b*) more sharing of household responsibility and child care.

As the pampered wife in an affluent household came often to be an economic parasite, so also the good provider was often, in a way, a kind of emotional parasite. Implicit in the definition of the role was that he provided goods and material things. Tender loving care was not one of the requirements. Emotional ministrations from the family were his right; providing them was not a corresponding obligation. Therefore, as de Tocqueville had already noted by 1840, women suffered a kind of emotional deprivation labeled by Robert Weiss "relational deficit" (cited in Bernard, 1976). Only recently has this male rejection of emotional expression come to be challenged. Today, even blue-collar women are imposing "a host of new role expectations upon their husbands or lovers . . . A new role set asks the blue-collar male to strive for . . . deep-coursing intimacy" (Shostak,

---

[9]Among the indices of the waning of the good-provider role are the increasing number of married women in the labor force; the growth in the number of female-headed families; the growing trend toward egalitarian norms in marriage; the need for two earners in so many middle-class families; and the recognition of these trends in the abandonment of the identification of head of household as a male.

Note 4, p. 75). It was not only vis-à-vis his family that the good provider was lacking in expressivity. This lack was built into the whole male role script. Today not only women but also men are beginning to protest the repudiation of expressivity prescribed in male roles (David & Brannon, 1976; Farrell, 1974; Fasteau, 1974; Pleck & Sawyer, 1974).

Is there any relationship between the "imposing" on men of "deep-coursing intimacy" by women on one side and the increasing proportion of men who find marriage burdensome and restrictive on the other? Are men seeing the new emotional involvements being asked of them as "all burdens and restrictions"? Are they responding to the new involvements under duress? Are they feeling oppressed by them? Fearful of them?

From the standpoint of high-level pure-science research there may be something bizarre, if not even slightly absurd, in the growing corpus of serious research on how much or how little husbands of employed wives contribute to household chores and child care. Yet it is serious enough that all over the industrialized world such research is going on. Time studies in a dozen countries—communist as well as capitalist—trace the slow and bungling process by which marriage accommodates to changing conditions and by which women struggle to mold the changing conditions in their behalf. For everywhere the same picture shows up in the research: an image of women sharing the provider role and at the same time retaining responsibility for the household. Until recently such a topic would have been judged unworthy of serious attention. It was a subject that might be worth a good laugh, for instance, as when an all-thumbs man in a cartoon burns the potatoes or finds himself bumbling awkwardly over a diaper, demonstrating his—proud—male ineptness at such female work. But it is no longer funny.

The "politics of housework" (Mainardi, 1970) proves to be more profound than originally believed. It has to do not only with tasks but also with gender—and perhaps more with the site of the tasks than with their intrinsic nature. A man can cook magnificently if he does it on a hunting or fishing trip; he can wield a skillful needle if he does it mending a tent or a fishing net; he can even feed and clean a toddler on a camping trip. Few of the skills of the homemaker are beyond his reach so long as they are practiced in a suitably male environment. It is not only women's work in and of itself that is degrading but any work on female turf. It may be true, as Brenton (1966) says, that "the secure man can wash a dish, diaper a baby, and throw the dirty clothes into the washing machine—or do anything else women used to do exclusively—without thinking twice about it" (p. 211), but not all men are that secure. To a great many men such chores are demasculinizing. The apron is shameful on a man in the kitchen; it is all right at the carpenter's bench.

The male world may look upon the man who shares household responsibilities as, in effect, a scab. One informant tells the interviewer about a conversation on the job: "What, are you crazy?" his hard-hat fellow workers ask him when he speaks of helping his wife. "The guys want to kill me. 'You son of a bitch! You are getting us in trouble' . . . The men get really mad" (Lein, 1979, p. 492). Something more than persiflage is involved here. We are fairly familiar with the trauma associated with the invasion by women of the male work turf, the hazing women can be subjected to, and the male resentment of admitting them except into their own segregated areas. The corresponding entrance of men into the traditional turf of women—the kitchen or the nursery—has analogous but not identical concomitants.

Pleck and Lang (1979) tell us that men are now beginning to change in the direction of greater involvement in family life. "Men's family behavior is beginning to change, becoming increasingly congruent with the long-standing psychological significance of the family in their lives" (p. 1). They measure this greater involvement by way of the help they offer with homemaking chores. Scanzoni (1975), on the basis of a survey of over 3,000 husbands and wives, concludes that at least in households in which wives are in the labor force, there is the "possibility of a different pattern in which responsibility for households would unequivocally fall equally on husbands as well as wives" (p. 38). A brave new world indeed. Still, when we look at the reality around us, the pace seems intolerably slow. The responsibilities of the old good-provider role have attenuated far faster than have its prerogatives and privileges.

A considerable amount of thought has been devoted to studying the effects of the large influx of women into the work force. An equally interesting question is what the effect will be if a large number of men actually do increase their participation in the family and the household. Will men find the apron shameful? What if we were to ask fathers to alternate with mothers in being in the home when youngsters come home from school? Would fighting adolescent drug abuse be more successful if fathers and mothers were equally engaged in it? If the school could confer with fathers as often as with mothers? If the father accompanied children when they went shopping for clothes? If fathers spent as much time with children as do mothers?

Even as husbands, let alone as fathers, the new pattern is not without trauma. Hall and Hall (1979), in their study of two-career couples, report that the most serious fights among such couples occur not in the bedroom, but in the kitchen, between couples who profess a commitment to equality but who find actually implementing it difficult. A young professional reports that he is philosophically committed to egalitarianism in marriage and tries hard to practice it, but it does not work. He even feels guilty about this. The stresses involved in reworking roles may have an impact on health. A study of engineers and accountants finds poorer health among those with employed wives than among those with nonemployed wives (Burke & Wier, 1976). The processes involved in role change have been compared with those involved in deprogramming a cult member. Are they part of the increasing sense of marriage and parenthood as "all burdens and restrictions"?

The demise of the good-provider role also calls for consideration of other questions: What does the demotion of the good provider to the status of senior provider or even mere co-provider do to him? To marriage? To gender identity? What does expanding the role of housewife to that of junior provider or even co-provider do to her? To marriage? To gender identity? Much will of course depend on the social and psychological ambience in which changes take place.

A PARABLE

I began this essay with a proverbial woman. I close it with a modern parable by William H. Chafe (Note 5), a historian who also keeps his eye on the current scene. Jack and Jill, both planning professional careers, he as doctor, she as lawyer, marry at age 24. She works to put him through medical school in the expectation that he will then finance her through law school. A child is born during the husband's internship, as planned. But in order for him to support her through professional training as planned, he will have to take time out from his career. After two years, they decide that both will continue their training on a part-time basis, sharing household responsibilities and using day-care services. Both find part-time positions and work out flexible work schedules that leave both of them time for child care and companionship with one another. They live happily ever after.

That's the end? you ask incredulously. Well, not exactly. For, as Chafe (Note 5) points out, as usual the personal is also political:

Obviously such a scenario presumes a radical transformation of the personal values that today's young people bring to their relationships as well as a readiness on the part of social and economic institutions to encourage, or at least make possible, the development of equality between men and women. (p. 28)

The good-provider role may be on its way out, but its legitimate successor has not yet appeared on the scene.

REFERENCE NOTES

1. Hesselbart, S. *Some underemphasized issues about men, women, and work.* Unpublished manuscript, 1978.
2. Douvan, E. *Family roles in a twenty-year perspective.* Paper presented at the Radcliffe Pre-Centennial Conference, Cambridge, Massachusetts, April 2–4, 1978.
3. Veroff, J. *Psychological orientations to the work role: 1957–1976.* Unpublished manuscript, 1978.
4. Shostak, A. *Working class Americans at home: changing expectations of manhood.* Unpublished manuscript, 1973.
5. Chafe, W. *The challenge of sex equality: A new culture or old values revisited?* Paper presented at the Radcliffe Pre-Centennial Conference, Cambridge, Massachusetts, April 2–4, 1978.

REFERENCES

Babcock, B., Freedman, A. E., Norton, E. H., & Ross, S. C. *Sex discrimination and the law: Causes and remedies.* Boston: Little, Brown, 1975.

Bernard, J. *Women, wives, mothers.* Chicago: Aldine, 1975.

Bernard, J. Homosociality and female depression. *Journal of Social Issues,* 1976, *32,* 207–224.

Boulding, E. Familial constraints on women's work roles. *SIGNS: Journal of Women in Culture and Society,* 1976, *1,* 95–118.

Brenton, M. *The American male.* New York: Coward-McCann, 1966.

Burke, R., & Wier, T. Relationship of wives' employment status to husband, wife and pair satisfaction and performance. *Journal of Marriage and the Family,* 1976, *38,* 279–287.

David, D. S., & Brannon, R. (Eds.). *The forty-nine percent majority: The male sex role.* Reading, Mass.: Addison-Wesley, 1976.

Demos, J. The American family in past time. *American Scholar,* 1974, *43,* 422–446.

Farrell, W. *The liberated man.* New York: Random House, 1974.

Fasteau, M. F. *The male machine.* New York: McGraw-Hill, 1974.

Fiedler, L. *Love and death in the American novel.* New York: Meredith, 1962.

Foner, P. S. *Women and the American labor movement.* New York: Free Press, 1979.

Freud, S. *Civilization and its discontents.* New York: Doubleday-Anchor, 1958. (Originally published, 1930.)

Goldberg, H. *The hazards of being male.* New York: New American Library, 1976.

Gould, R. E. Measuring masculinity by the size of a paycheck. In J. E. Pleck & J. Sawyer (Eds.), *Men and masculinity.* Englewood Cliffs, N.J.: Prentice-Hall, 1974. (Also published in *Ms.,* June 1973, pp. 18ff.)

Hall, D., & Hall, F. *The two-career couple.* Reading, Mass.: Addison-Wesley, 1979.

Jones, C. A. *A review of child support payment performance.* Washington, D.C.: Urban Institute, 1976.

Keniston, K. *The uncommitted: Alienated youth in American society.* New York: Harcourt, Brace & World, 1965.

Komarovsky, M. *The unemployed man and his family.* New York: Dryden Press, 1940.

Lefkowitz, B. Life without work. *Newsweek,* May 14, 1979, p. 31.

Lein, L. Responsibility in the allocation of tasks. *Family Coordinator,* 1979, *28,* 489–496.

Liebow, E. *Tally's corner.* Boston: Little, Brown, 1966.

Lopata, H. *Occupation housewife.* New York: Oxford University Press, 1971.

Mainardi, P. The politics of housework. In R. Morgan (Ed.), *Sisterhood is powerful.* New York: Vintage Books, 1970.

Pleck, J. H., & Lang, L. Men's family work: Three perspectives and some new data. *Family Coordinator,* 1979, *28,* 481–488.

Pleck, J. H., & Sawyer, J. (Eds.). *Men and masculinity.* Englewood Cliffs, N.J.: Prentice-Hall, 1974.

Rainwater, L., & Yancey, W. L. *The Moynihan report and the politics of controversy.* Cambridge, Mass.: M.I.T. Press, 1967.

Sarason, S. B. *Work, aging, and social change.* New York: Free Press, 1977.

Scanzoni, J. H. *Sex roles, life styles, and childbearing: Changing patterns in marriage and the family.* New York: Free Press, 1975.

Scanzoni, J. H. An historical perspective on husband-wife bargaining power and marital dissolution. In G. Levinger & O. Moles (Eds.), *Divorce and separation in America.* New York: Basic Books, 1979.

Smith, R. E. (Ed.). *The subtle revolution.* Washington, D.C.: Urban Institute, 1979.

Smuts, R. W. *Women and work in America.* New York: Columbia University Press, 1959.

Snyder, L. The deserting, non-supporting father: Scapegoat of family non-policy. *Family Coordinator,* 1979, *38,* 594–598.

Tocqueville, A. de. *Democracy in America.* New York: J. & H. G. Langley, 1840.

Warner, W. L., & Ablegglen, J. O. *Big business leaders in America.* New York: Harper, 1955.

Yankelovich, D. The new psychological contracts at work. *Psychology Today,* May 1978, pp. 46–47; 49–50.

Zborowski, M., & Herzog, E. *Life is with people.* New York: Schocken Books, 1952.

READING 3-2

Feeding as "Women's Work"

Marjorie L. DeVault

The claim that housework is women's work hides a more complex reality. The home as an arena that requires women's domestic activity was actively constructed during the nineteenth century, partly in tandem with larger projects aimed at consolidating men's power (Hartmann 1981b; Smith 1985), and partly by women reformers who aimed to develop the home as a site of power and influence for women (Roth-

Marjorie L. DeVault, "Feeding as Women's Work" from *Feeding the Family: The Social Organization of Caring as Gendered Work.* Copyright © 1991 by Marjorie L. DeVault. Reprinted with the permission of the author and The University of Chicago Press.

man 1978). Actual practice, of course, has been far less uniform than the cultural ideals created during this period would suggest. In particular, the middle-class pattern of specialization in domesticity has rarely been an option for poor and minority women. Especially in working-class and minority families, the exigencies of survival have often required that all family members, regardless of gender, cooperate in maintaining households (Tilly and Scott 1978; Dill 1986). But the broad pattern of women taking responsibility for care at home has been pervasive and powerful. For feminists, women's responsibility for domestic life has been key to understanding women's subordination, and an important item on any agenda for change. Whether they have argued that women's domestic work must be acknowledged and compensated (e.g., Edmond and Fleming 1975), shared with men (e.g., Chodorow 1978; Hochschild 1989), or fundamentally reorganized (Hayden 1981), feminists have been concerned with understanding the processes of choice and enforcement through which women's responsibility for domestic life has been maintained.

In most households in this study, food work was done mostly by women. However, few of these households looked much like the "ideal home" of the nineteenth century—or even the "typical family" of the 1950s—and many of these women resisted the idea of domesticity as unquestioned fate. Although most of these women were doing most of the work of feeding their families, they did not necessarily do so automatically, without thought or negotiation. Some professed a desire to share the work of caring for children with their husbands, and had attempted to do so, with more or less success. Some actively resisted complete responsibility, and struggled to convince husbands to do more. But even couples who shared egalitarian ideals faced difficulties in developing equitable arrangements that in most cases pushed them toward more traditional patterns in actual practice. Further, both the material interests of women who might want to reduce their household work and the egalitarian ideals of sharing were undermined by the power of the socially organized practice and discourse of mothering. As these women grew up, they learned, both from their own mothers and from more general ideas about what mothers *should* be, to participate in the social relations that organize the family work of feeding. They also learned a skill or capacity—for attention to others—that allowed them as adults to see the responsibilities that arise out of the needs of others and of a group. I discuss one source for this kind of learning—participation in gendered activities, first as children observing mothers and female kin, and later as mothers themselves. There are, no doubt, other ways that women are recruited into the work of care. However, the influences of mothers and mothering were especially prominent in these accounts, and may be especially influential with respect to food work. . .

LEARNING FROM MOTHERS: RESPONSIBILITY

For most girls, learning about housework begins early. And one of the lessons that most women learn is that housework is "womanly" activity. More than a few of the informants in this study made some reference to fathers, as well as mothers, who cooked—especially in working-class families—and two reported that their fathers had done most of the cooking in their families when they were growing up. However, they also referred to these patterns as atypical, discounting the evidence of their own families in favor of assumptions about daily activities in other households. And while references to fathers' cooking were rather brief, many interviewees spoke at length about learning from mothers. As we talked, these women grew thoughtful and speculative; they knew they had learned from their mothers, but they were seldom very sure just what or how they had learned:

> She never sat down and said, "OK, this is how you do such and such." She may have done that

with something like baking cookies, but not everyday meals . . . So I think if I picked things up at all it would be through osmosis. And then kind of adapting, you know, things that I remember her cooking. That kind of thing.

The comment displays an effort to talk about learning this woman has rarely thought about: learning that is powerful, but informal and unsystematic.

Within households, or small networks of related households, much of the knowledge underlying the work of feeding is transmitted through activities that link women across generations. When families get together, for holiday meals, for instance, or in some everyday situations, the women of families work together at cooking tasks. For example, Susan's parents come to her house to eat every week, and she explains:

> Everyone gets involved, like washing the pots and stuff. It gives a chance for the women to get together.

Her comment is striking because it reveals the taken-for-granted character of the division of labor by gender. Though she begins by claiming that "everyone" is involved in the work, her next sentence reveals that she means "every woman"; the men of the family are exempt from consideration and disappear from her remark (as they do, literally, on these Sunday afternoons, one imagines). A Puerto Rican woman goes shopping on Saturdays with her mother; they go to several stores, and it takes a long time, but she says, "We also have fun on the way." Little girls often participate in these womanly projects. One woman told me, "I have these fond memories of shelling beans, on the front porch with my aunt." And Gloria explained:

> I used to watch my mother cook. And help her out. I was the one who cleaned the silver, I was the one who set the table . . . I don't know if she would ask me to help her, or if I would just hang around the kitchen and help her indirectly,

or just watch her and pick up a lot of things. I think a lot of it was just visual.

Women whose mothers live with them, or nearby, may continue to rely on their help with the work of feeding. In two Hispanic households I studied, grandmothers do much of the cooking. And Teresa, a Chicana woman whose mother lives next door, pools resources and effort with her mother. When she worked as a secretary, for example, her mother would help with her cooking:

If it was something that was going to take a lot of time, I'd leave it for my mother to do. I'd say, "Ma, why don't you do this, because it takes so long." So she'd start it off for me and then I'd come home and finish it up.

Women who visited their parents to eat talked about bringing home leftovers, and one even incorporated them into her planning. Susan reported:

And Monday and Tuesday—Monday we're going out at my mother's, and I'm begging for a leftover, [laughing] so we might skimp on Tuesday.

Even when informants did not see their relatives so often, their remarks occasionally suggested that women in their families were connected through feeding activities. For example, one working-class white woman, whose husband and children refuse to eat the kinds of food she likes best, explained:

It's mostly holidays, when his aunts come over, that we have the things that I really like, the sauerkraut and stuff. Because they make it—they know that I like it and they bring it over.

This kind of active network of women helping one another means that, consciously or not, many little girls learn that feeding is women's work. Robin, remembering her family's holiday dinners, commented on her "blissful ignorance" of the work involved in such events:

It was always the smell of all the food cooking, this is the kind of thing you think back on. You would play with all the cousins. And then they would call you when the food was ready. You just never gave a thought to anything else.

Now that she is grown, however, she feels responsible for such work: she is the one who works at preparing this kind of meal, even though her husband does almost all of the everyday cooking for their immediate family. She explained:

I love doing that, I love laying out a big meal. You know, roast beef, and ham, and potatoes, and you know, salad and dessert and the whole thing. I love doing that.

He likes to be in there too, because he thinks it's his kitchen. But he usually does more of the, being a good host. Making sure everybody's got drinks and stuff, while I'm in the kitchen.

Others, too, see learning about food as a way of continuing family traditions, and understand this guardianship as a particularly womanly responsibility. Susan, who had asked her mother for a "lesson" on gefilte fish, explained why:

Saturday I'm going over there for one of my ethnic cooking lessons. She's making food that I've had my whole life, that I don't know how to prepare. And I should . . . My mother's not really old. But there's the possibility that this might be our last holiday together—she might be retiring to Florida. So I said, someone has to make the fish. Someone has to learn how to do it.

Her comment reveals the powerful effect of observing throughout childhood that feeding is done mostly by women. The force of the idea that "someone has to do it"—a phrase that appeared in other women's talk as well—lies in the assumption (often not unfounded) that no one else will. And it is clear from the context for such remarks that "someone" actually means that "some woman" must do the work.

Often, the things that women have learned from mothers seem natural, because they are "just there":

I was lucky enough to grow up with lots of fresh vegetables. And no one ever preached about it.

Because it was just there, it was sort of an ingrained value.

In fact, the "naturalness" of this kind of learning seems more an element in the accounts people give than in the experience itself. Women cannot simply imitate their mothers, since the methods and standards for housework change from one generation to another, and the work varies from one household to another. But they often interpret their conduct of household work as making them, quite "naturally," like their mothers. For example, a young black woman whose mother was a domestic worker explained how she learned about cooking:

I've always been with her, on all of her jobs, when I was growing up—she took me with her, because I went to school where she worked at— so I just learned how to cook by nature; it was something I had to do. I had to learn how to clean, you know, because I worked with her, and she taught me what she knew. So it was from growing up, I grew up in an environment of cleaning and cooking . . . So I don't know, it came natural.

Though she describes her recruitment into cleaning and cooking as "natural," the example in fact highlights how varied and contingent the content and organization of housework can be while still producing a powerful sense that "womanliness" lies behind the variation. In this case, a black mother performed domestic work for pay, in someone else's household. Yet her daughter, who now works as a receptionist, still links her own quite differently organized family work to her mother's paid domestic labor.

Though learning about family life is not simply imitative, the privacy of the household does cause people to learn, initially at least, quite particular household routines. Households tend to be relatively closed groups, and people rarely know much about what others do inside them. From glimpses into other homes, and no doubt from the media as well, individuals compare, evaluate, and reflect on the practices they have observed in their family homes. For example, Jean talked nostalgically about the meals she had been served as a child, meals planned "with great care" by both of her parents together. Then she commented:

I didn't realize as a kid, but when I got older and went to other people's houses—you know, you go to someone's house and you'd be served a hot dog and you know, just potato chips, and a glass of milk. And I'd think, "But when is dinner coming?" Because, I mean, hot dogs were never served in my house when I was a kid.

Her own practices are different from her parents', but she retains a strong sense, from childhood, that meals and their conduct are very important. This kind of learning can be especially powerful. The pervasive day-to-day experience of household life can mean that particular practices come to be understood as "standards of excellence." One affluent white woman, for instance, wishes that her husband would recreate the "fatherly" conduct she remembers from childhood:

It was a matter of pride to my father, to be able to cut the meat just so. And it still is to me. It annoys me that my husband cuts it differently. I mean, he cuts it well, but he cuts it differently, you see. I get annoyed. I mean, there are certain standards of excellence, you know, they can't be expunged.

This kind of learning is implicit, and relatively unquestioned, part of a constructed sense of household "reality" (Berger and Luckmann 1967). More than specific techniques for cooking and serving food, it conveys strongly held beliefs about family, suffused with emotion. When they talked about learning from their mothers, many women spoke of global attitudes: of an "approach to cooking," or a "basic philosophy, of good food, at the expense of other things in some cases."

Perhaps most important, many women seem to learn from their mothers' practices what a meal should be and how it fits into a household routine. For example, when I asked about dinner, Laurel replied:

> Generally it's a full meal. I'm a product of my mother, I mean, I just see myself doing things—I remember as a child wanting so badly to have a soup and sandwich dinner, because other kids were having soup and sandwiches, which I really loved, but instead I had to eat pork chops, and potatoes, and vegetables, and salad. And I generally aim at that, at least.

Laurel runs a small mail-order business out of her home, and when she is busy with work she serves her family soup and sandwich suppers, but she refers to this as "just sliding," and says, "I feel like that's not really preparing a meal when it's not the full thing. Because my mother thought that."

Laurel does not simply imitate her mother, though she recognizes that this standard has come from childhood. She has reflected on the meaning of her mother's practice for her own life. She recognizes that her mother was "so rigid that she missed out on a lot because of it." But she sees reasons for her mother's behavior: her father was an invalid, and when Laurel reported that "Meals were always served," she added, "I guess that was my mother's effort—to at least keep up the appearance of normalcy." She has thought about her mother's approach to cooking, and has modified it to suit her own needs. She explained, "I got a lot of—which I have toned down for myself—but I got a lot of the right way to do things." What Laurel has learned from her mother, I would argue—though "toned down" for herself— is the importance of regular meals as part of the "right way" to do family life, and the idea that "normalcy" can be produced through this womanly work.

LEARNING FROM MOTHERING: ATTENTION

When women become mothers, their awareness of the importance of feeding, and sense of responsibility for it, are often heightened by the particularly female experiences of pregnancy and childbirth. This heightened awareness does not come automatically. Though pregnancy and childbirth are powerful experiences, uniquely female and biologically based, they are also as fully socially organized as any other activity. Women are taught to attend to their pregnancies, and a strong sense of responsibility for the next generation comes from a multitude of public sources as well as from women's own reflections on the individual physiological and psychological experiences of becoming a mother. I do not mean to suggest that mothering always produces a powerful commitment to feeding or caring work, or that it is the only kind of activity that recruits women into the work.[1] Certainly, women are motivated to take on such work for a variety of reasons, and women without children may be as committed to it as any mother. The discussion here is meant to show how in households such as these, where children are present, the organization of the work of mothering strongly reinforces women's involvement in feeding work.

Many of the women I talked with remembered their pregnancies as times when they became more conscious of food and nutrition and committed themselves to better feeding. Several learned more about food in formal pregnancy preparation courses, but they saw their new knowledge as generalizable beyond pregnancy. As one Puerto Rican woman explained:

> I thought if a pregnant woman has those nutritional needs then you would almost conclude that every human being would have them. The bread, the milk, the vegetables.

---

[1] My claim is that women who mother are likely to develop distinctive perspectives on group life (Ruddick 1980, 1989), but neither the activities nor the perspectives are associated in any simple way with women as a group, or even mothers as an undifferentiated group. Many women never do mothering work and still learn skills and associations like those discussed here from other sources; some men who care for children seem to develop similar perspectives (see e.g. Coltrane 1989, Hochschild 1989)

In addition to new knowledge, pregnancy provides a special reason for attending to food habits. Teresa, who was pregnant at the time of our interview, explained:

> Now that I'm pregnant I'm trying to have a pretty decent lunch. Before, if I felt like peanut butter and jelly I would have it, not worrying about getting enough vitamins and stuff. Now I'm more conscious about it.

Together, the special attention and new knowledge that come with pregnancy can lead to significant changes. Gloria's comment, below, shows how explicit teaching during pregnancy extends to her practices more generally:

> When I was pregnant, that was an important source of information about food. I learned a lot. And subsequently, although I backslide a little, I made some major changes. I think we're going through a period of backsliding now. But you know, each time I've been pregnant I've gone through a period of very systematically increasing intake of water, eating fresh foods—I've started parboiling the foods, or steaming them, trying to eat more fresh fruits and vegetables rather than canned. Just real basic kinds of changes, that come about primarily through the whole focusing on how you're going to start this newborn kid off.

The physiological experience of pregnancy—and all of the explicit teaching that surrounds it—enforces attention to feeding: a woman learns that she provides, very directly, the nourishment that carries the fetus to term.[2]

Attention to children's sustenance continues as they grow. Even when the physiological connection of pregnancy has ended, mothers are still usually more responsible than fathers for feeding their children. They watch them develop, and consider their responses to food. This relatively affluent white woman's comment shows her awareness that such monitoring and reflection take time:

> I think a full-time mother has got more time to be concerned about diet. You start thinking about it, because you know that that's when children form their basic food habits. You can just observe them and see how they'll eat anything at a certain age, and then their taste buds begin to develop and they start getting real fussy and so forth. It makes you conscious of food, and what you feed them.

Young mothers like this may talk together about what to do. Another reported:

> One of my friends likes to cook and is interested in cooking, and she had children at the same time I did, so we both would kind of compare notes about what was a good thing to do, and what would build strong bodies—how important early nutrition is for your life. You want them to eat good things, so they develop nice strong bodies. And you kind of feel responsible. It's one aspect of parenting.

While these comments come from "full-time mothers," others, too, reported a heightened attention to food after having children. They learn from public sources all around them about their responsibility for another life. Robin, for example, refers obliquely to television advertisements:

> Well, you know, Rick and I, yeah, it's not that important, but for Kate it's very important, because she's in her developing years, as they say, on the commercials for bread and everything.

Though her job does not allow her time for the study and reflection described above, she still feels the pressure of responsibility for the "developing years."

The textual sources from which many women learn about mothering emphasize the gravity of their responsibility for children. These instructions, and mothers' usually quite intense involvement with their children, push

---

[2]It is important to note, again, that while the processes I describe here are linked to the physiological experience of pregnancy, that experience is strongly conditioned by wider social relations. For example, the account I provide here describes the experience of women who have a network of support during pregnancy, and receive adequate prenatal care. For far too many women in the U.S., these conditions do not obtain.

women toward thinking about the work of feeding, and encourage them to practice "attention," an activity that supports the work. Attention is a central element in Sara Ruddick's analysis of "maternal thought." Drawing on the philosophies of Iris Murdoch and Simone Weil, Ruddick talks of attention as "an *intellectual* capacity connected even by definition with love, a special kind of 'knowledge of the individual'" (1980:358). She argues that "attentive love, the training to ask, 'What are you going through?' is central to maternal practices" (p. 359), and supports the kind of adaptation to growth and change that successful mothering requires. Her analysis is useful because she begins to identify actual practices and skills that give rise to features of mothering that have more often been seen as arising from emotional or psychological traits attributed to women. As I talked with women about feeding their families, I found that they often reported attending to individuals in their households, and that attention was an essential element in their conceptions of the work they did for others.

At the simplest level, attention involves simply noticing what someone needs. But children's needs for foods, and especially for foods of particular kinds, must be inferred by watching their responses. One woman explained, for example:

> I feel that there's a difference if I give Mark [the baby] something with a lot of sugar in it. I feel that he starts going off the wall. So I will try not to give him a lot of sugary type food.

This kind of knowledge requires monitoring the other's behavior over time and considering its sources. Margaret reported:

> Joey, he won't eat eggs. He just won't eat them at all. And you know, nutrition-wise, he gets that group in other things that he eats. And I don't like eggs either. I can't tolerate them, I'm allergic to them, so you know. And he eats french toast, so when he eats french toast he gets his egg in the toast.

"I'm allergic to them, so you know," she says, summarizing a train of unspoken thought: perhaps her son is allergic to eggs too, so that it may be best not to insist that he eat them.

This kind of attention must be a continuing project, and does not always have immediate results. Janice, for example, reported that she believes her teenaged daughter is much too thin, and that she has been concerned for some time that her daughter might be anorexic. I asked her what she does to keep track of the situation and she answered:

> Well, that's what mothers are for, isn't it? [MD: And what's involved in doing that?] I don't know if there's that much involved, except that I ask questions and hope to get the right answers. You know. Where have you been, where are you going, what's happening, are you going to do this, are you going to do that. [MD: So what does your daughter say?] She says, "Get off my back, Ma."

She knows that she cannot force her daughter to eat. Her job, then, is to pay attention, and to try to advise and help when she can.

Certainly all of these women are responding to some extent to public, textual sources of information about food and nutrition. They have received advice from physicians about children's needs, or have learned from media reports to watch for problems such as anorexia. But they put such knowledge to use in immediate, everyday ways by practicing attention. They learn, perhaps primarily by sharing experiences with mothers and peers, to monitor the health and well-being of family members, and to use whatever public knowledge they have to locate potential problems.

Paying attention in this way is a skill that these women recognize but often have trouble describing in words. As I talked with Jean, for example, she gave an example of the kind of strategizing she does about how to pay attention. But she spoke haltingly, and with some frustration, emphasizing how difficult it is to describe her thoughts about the process:

I guess I see that [keeping track] as one of my roles. But that is difficult at times. The tasks—you know they have to be done. But—this is very hard to verbalize—One of my daughters is a chronic complainer. And the other one never complains. So the older one, if she gets a nick, "Oh, I'm dying," you know, one of these kind of things. And the little one can be getting sicker and sicker by the moment, and I don't even notice it . . .

Some nights I sit and listen to [the older one] rant and rave about her various health problems, when there are none, and other nights I just simply brush her off.

I'm not doing this very well. I'm not saying what I really want to say. But I guess that is an area of concern. Because I really should pay more attention to the little one, and less to the big one. And yet it seems reversed. Because of just the way their personalities are.

Attention does not come naturally to mothers; it develops from both loving concern and the very strong societal prescription that mothers are responsible for their children's well-being. The concept refers to a set of activities that are not clearly articulated, that develop in practice through observation of others and in large part through trial and error, and through the kind of individual musing that Jean struggles to describe.

Over time, thoughtful attention results in knowledge that is tailored to specific situations. It develops through a woman's individual construction of belief and routine, and women's comments reveal the personal nature of these understandings. A woman with formal training in nursing, for example, explained that her education has influenced her household practice, but that she has really developed her own ideas about what is important. She reported:

I've actually done with food what I've done with religion, which is look around, listen a lot, and come up with my own version that I can live with.

This kind of gradual, continuous and personal learning is appropriate to the work of feeding. As Ruddick points out with respect to mothering, the continuous change associated with both mothering and feeding calls for "a kind of learning in which what one learns cannot be applied exactly, and often not even by analogy, to a new situation" (Ruddick 1980:353). The attention underlying such learning is often unrecognized, just because it is so continuous. According to Murdoch:

The task of attention goes on all the time and at apparently empty and everyday moments we are "looking," making those little peering efforts of imagination which have such important cumulative results. (cited in Ruddick 1980:358)

Her words were echoed by Bertie, trying to explain just how she had learned about feeding:

I believe that a lot of mothering, and homemaking, and child-rearing, is acquired—well, naturally acquired by experience—but the ability to pick up on that experience may be a process of maturation—you know what I mean? It's not that it's automatically there, but you know—survival. In order to survive you have to learn to do this. And for a person who cares about a family, it'll be perfectly natural for them to pick up on certain things. And maybe not even be aware that they're picking up on things, or learning to do certain things.

Because they find themselves responsible for families—because they have learned from watching the women around them that, as they say, "If I don't do it, then no one else will"—women pay attention. As they do so, they "pick up on" the knowledge that supports their work.

DOING GENDER

I began this chapter by describing several relatively distinct patterns of household responsibility in the families I studied. Some women do virtually all the work of feeding their families, while others share responsibility more equally with partners. Still, I have argued that feeding is "women's work." This claim, alongside considerable diversity, calls for some discussion of what it means to label feeding as "gendered activity."

At one level, the claim that feeding work is gendered refers to a continuing pattern in the allocation of the work: the fact that women typically do most of the work, and usually do its most important parts. Women continue to feel most responsible for feeding. The British study conducted by Murcott (1983) provides support for this claim. She found that even when men do some cooking, wives are the ones who prepare "cooked dinners," which are associated with home, health, and family. The asymmetry of men's and women's involvement shows up even more clearly in the patterns of solitary eating she describes. When either husbands or wives are home alone, they tend not to cook, but to "pick at" food or "snack" instead. Some— husbands much more often than wives—go to eat with relatives, where they are fed by the women of other families. This alternative is one the men feel entitled to; by contrast, when the women are served by someone else, they talk of "being spoiled."

This example also points to the more fundamental level at which we can refer to the gendered character of feeding activity. It is not just that women do more of the work of feeding, but also that feeding work has become one of the primary ways that women "do" gender. At this level, my approach to the concept of gendered activity draws on the understanding of gender as a product of "social doings" developed by Candace West and Don Zimmerman (1987). They propose that we analyze gender as "a routine, methodical, and recurring accomplishment" (p. 126), that is, as the outcome of people's joint activities in particular settings. In this view, activities like feeding a family are understood by those in families as "properly" women's work, and therefore become resources for the production of gender. By feeding the family, a woman conducts herself as recognizably womanly.

West and Zimmerman view gender as so fundamental to social interaction—at least in contemporary Western societies—that it is virtually always relevant to social conduct. Competent adult members of these societies have learned to view the differentiation between male and female as a fundamental and important one. Thus, much of their activity—virtually all the time, alongside other activities of different sorts—is activity that marks their sex category and identifies that of others. Doing gender, in this approach, is not just an individual performance, but an interactional process, a process of collective production and recognition of "adequate" women and men through concerted activity. West and Zimmerman propose that members of *this* society, at least, are virtually always "doing gender" in this sense—that is, they are conducting interactions, together and collaboratively, so as to mark themselves, and identify others, as acceptable men and women.

Through this ongoing process, activities such as feeding, which members of the society have learned to associate strongly with one gender, come to seem like "natural" expressions of gender. This observation does not imply that all women engage in such activity. Some choose not to do feeding. Others improvise and negotiate, developing idiosyncratic versions of this "womanly" work. And of course, some men do feeding work and remain recognizable men. But as long as feeding is understood, collectively, as somehow more "womanly" than "manly," the work stands as one kind of activity in which "womanliness" may be at issue. Thus, many couples apparently do organize their household activity around shared (or contested) assumptions about gendered activity, their versions of "properly" masculine or feminine behavior. Sarah Fenstermaker Berk (1985:204), using the concept of doing gender to interpret her study of household work, suggests that household tasks often become "occasions" for "reaffirmation of one's *gendered* relation to the work and to the world."

The material in this chapter begins to suggest how members of households learn to associate womanliness and feeding work, and how their later practices can sustain such an association.

At an early age, many children observe their mothers at work in the household, and girls are often recruited into womanly activities based on the principles of responsibility and attention; when they become mothers themselves these lessons are reinforced through the urgency and immediacy of infants' needs, as well as through textual instructions for mothers (Griffith and Smith 1987). New mothers are constantly reminded of these principles, and work at putting them into practice; they feel pleased when their efforts seem to succeed, and guilty when their children do not prosper. Fathers, of course, may take the same kinds of responsibility and learn similar skills. When they do so, however, they may be called to account for their "unnatural" conduct (Coltrane 1989). They, too, may have learned caring skills from their mothers (those I talked with suggested that this was so), but they typically have not developed the compelling sense, strongly felt by many women, that care for others is their duty. Women, by contrast, have been trained and encouraged to attend to others and care for them, and to resist these lessons is to risk their "womanly" character. Thus, for many, commitment to the work of caretaking has become an apparently "natural" part of the gendered self.

REFERENCES

Abel, Emily K. 1990. Family Care of the Frail Elderly. In Emily K. Abel and Margaret K. Nelson, eds., *Circles of Care,* 65–91. Albany: State University of New York Press.

Abel, Emily K., and Margaret K. Nelson, eds. 1990. *Circles of Care.* Albany: State University of New York Press.

Abramovitz, Mimi. 1988. *Regulating the Lives of Women: Social Welfare Policy from Colonial Times to the Present.* Boston: South End Press.

Acker, Joan. 1973. Women and Stratification: A Case of Intellectual Sexism. *American Journal of Sociology* 78:936–45.

———. 1988. Class, Gender and the Relations of Distribution. *Signs* 13:473–97.

Allan, Graham A. 1979. *A Sociology of Friendship and Kinship.* London: George Allen and Unwin.

Barrett, Michele, and Mary McIntosh. 1982. *The Anti-Social Family.* London: Verso.

Becker, Howard S. 1982. *Art Worlds.* Berkeley: University of California Press.

Belasco, Warren. 1990. *Appetite for Change: How the Counterculture Took on the Food Industry and What Happened When It Did, 1966–1986.* New York: Pantheon Books.

Benjamin, Esther R. 1988. Social Relations of Separated and Divorced Men and Women: A Class Comparison of the Effects of Marriage on the Middle- and Working-Class Divorce Experience. Ph.D. diss., Northwestern University, Evanston, IL.

Berger, Peter, and Thomas Luckmann. 1967. *The Social Construction of Reality.* New York: Doubleday.

Berheide, Catherine White, Sarah Fenstermaker Berk, and Richard A. Berk. 1976. Household Work in the Suburbs: The Job and its Participants. *Pacific Sociological Review* 19:491–517.

Berk, Richard A., and Sarah Fenstermaker Berk. 1979. *Labor and Leisure at Home: Content and Organization of the Household Day.* Beverly Hills, CA: Sage Publications.

Berk, Sarah Fenstermaker. 1985. *The Gender Factory: The Apportionment of Work in American Households.* New York: Plenum Press.

Bernardes, Jon. 1985. "Family Ideology": Identification and Exploration. *Sociological Review* 33:275–97.

———. 1987. "Doing Things with Words": Sociology and "Family Policy" Debates. *Sociological Review* 35:679–702.

Blaylock, James, Howard Elitzak, and Alden Manchester. 1989. Food Expenditures. *National Food Review* (U.S. Department of Agriculture) 12(2):16–24.

Blood, Robert O., and Donald M. Wolfe. 1960. *Husbands and Wives.* New York: Free Press.

Blumer, Herbert. 1969. *Symbolic Interactionism: Perspective and Method.* Englewood Cliffs, NJ: Prentice-Hall.

Blumstein, Philip, and Pepper Schwartz. 1983. *American Couples: Money, Work, Sex.* New York: William Morrow.

Bossard, James H. S., and Eleanor S. Boll. 1950. *Ritual in Family Living.* Philadelphia: University of Pennsylvania Press.

Bott, Elizabeth. 1957. *Family and Social Network: Roles, Norms, and External Relationships in Ordinary Urban Families.* New York: Free Press.

Braverman, Harry. 1974. *Labor and Monopoly Capital.* New York: Monthly Review Press.

Brown, Carol. 1981. Mothers, Fathers, and Children: From Private to Public Patriarchy. In Lydia Sargent, ed., *Women and Revolution,* 239–67. Boston: South End Press.

Brown, Judith K. 1975. Iroquois Women: An Ethnohistoric Note. In Rayna R. Reiter, ed., *Toward an Anthropology of Women,* 235–51. New York: Monthly Review Press.

Cancian, Francesca. 1987. *Love in America: Gender and Self Development.* New York: Cambridge University Press.

Caplovitz, David. 1967. *The Poor Pay More: Consumer Practices of Low-Income Families.* New York: Free Press.

Caulfield, Mina Davis. 1974. Imperialism, the Family, and Cultures of Resistance. *Socialist Review* 4(2):67–85.

Charles, Nickie, and Marion Kerr. 1988. *Women, Food and Families.* Manchester: Manchester University Press.

Chodorow, Nancy. 1978. *The Reproduction of Mothering.* Berkeley: University of California Press.

Collier, Jane, Michelle Z. Rosaldo, and Sylvia Yanagisako. 1982. Is There a Family? New Anthropological Views. In Barrie Thorne with Marilyn Yalom, eds., *Rethinking the Family,* 25–39. New York: Longman.

Collins, Patricia Hill. 1990. *Black Feminist Thought: Knowledge, Consciousness, and the Politics of Empowerment.* Boston: Unwin Hyman.

Coltrane, Scott. 1989. Household Labor and the Routine Production of Gender. *Social Problems* 5:473–90.

Comer, Lee. 1974. *Wedlocked Women.* Leeds: Feminist Books Ltd.

Connell, R. W. 1987. *Gender and Power: Society, the Person and Sexual Politics.* Stanford, CA: Stanford University Press.

Corrigan, Paul. 1977. The Welfare State as an Arena of Class Struggle. *Marxism Today,* March: 87–93.

Cott, Nancy F. 1977. *The Bonds of Womanhood: "Woman's Sphere" in New England, 1780–1835.* New Haven: Yale University Press.

Counihan, Carole M. 1988. Female Identity, Food and Power in Contemporary Florence. *Anthropological Quarterly* 61:51–62.

Coverman, Shelley. 1985. Explaining Husbands Participation in Domestic Labor. *Sociological Quarterly* 26:81–97.

Cowan, Ruth Schwartz. 1983. *More Work for Mother: The Ironies of Household Technology from the Open Hearth to the Microwave.* New York: Basic Books.

Daniels, Arlene Kaplan. 1987. Invisible Work. *Social Problems* 34:403–15.

———. 1988. *Invisible Careers: Women Civic Leaders from the Volunteer World.* Chicago: University of Chicago Press.

Davidoff, Leonore. 1973. *The Best Circles: Society, Etiquette and the Season.* London: Croom Helm.

———. 1976. The Rationalization of Housework. In Diana L. Barker and Sheila Allen, eds., *Dependence and Exploitation in Work and Marriage,* 121–51. London: Longman Group.

Davidoff, Leonore, and Catherine Hall. 1987. *Family Fortunes: Men and Women of the English Middle Class, 1780–1850.* Chicago: University of Chicago Press.

Davis, Angela Y. 1981. *Women, Race, and Class.* New York: Random House.

Delphy, Christine. 1976. Continuities and Discontinuities in Marriage and Divorce. In Diana L. Barker and Sheila Allen, eds., *Sexual Divisions and Society: Process and Change,* 76–89. London: Tavistock.

———. 1979. Sharing the Same Table: Consumption and the Family. In Chris Harris, ed., *The Sociology of the Family: New Directions for Britain,* 214–31. Keele: University of Keele.

DeVault, Ileen A. 1990. *Sons and Daughters of Labor: Class and Clerical Work in Turn-of-the-Century Pittsburgh.* Ithaca, NY: Cornell University Press.

DeVault, Marjorie L. 1990. Talking and Listening from Women's Standpoint: Feminist Strategies for Interviewing and Analysis. *Social Problems* 37:96–116.

DeVault, Marjorie L., and James P. Pitts. 1984. Surplus and Scarcity: Hunger and the Origins of the Food Stamp Program. *Social Problems* 31:545–57.

Diamond, Timothy. 1988. Social Policy and Everyday Life in Nursing Homes: A Critical Ethnography. In Anne Statham, Eleanor M. Miller, and

Hans O. Mauksch, eds., *The Worth of Women's Work: A Qualitative Synthesis,* 39–55. Albany: State University of New York Press.

———. N.d. *Making Gray Gold.* Chicago: University of Chicago Press. Forthcoming.

Dickinson, James. 1986. From Poor Law to Social Insurance: The Periodization of State Intervention in the Reproduction Process. In James Dickinson and Bob Russell, eds., *Family, Economy, and State,* 113–49. New York: St. Martin's Press.

Di Leonardo, Micaela. 1987. The Female World of Cards and Holidays: Women, Families, and the Work of Kinship. *Signs* 12:440–53.

Dill, Bonnie Thornton. 1986. Our Mothers' Grief: Racial Ethnic Women and the Maintenance of Families. Research Paper #4, Center for Research on Women. Memphis, TN: Memphis State University.

Dinnerstein, Dorothy. 1976. *The Mermaid and the Minotaur.* New York: Harper and Row.

Douglas, Mary. 1972. Deciphering a Meal. *Daedalus* 101:61–81.

———, ed. 1984. *Food in the Social Order: Studies of Food and Festivities in Three American Communities.* New York: Russell Sage.

Dudden, Faye E. 1983. *Serving Women: Household Service in Nineteenth-Century America.* Middletown, CT: Wesleyan University Press.

Edmond, Wendy, and Suzie Fleming, eds. 1975. *All Work and No Pay: Women, Housework and the Wages Due.* Montpelier, Bristol, U.K.: Falling Wall Press.

Ehrenreich, Barbara, and John Ehrenreich. 1979. The Professional-Managerial Class. In Pat Walker, ed., *Between Labor and Capital,* 5–45. Boston: South End Press.

Ehrenreich, Barbara, and Deirdre English. 1978. *For Her Own Good: 150 Years of the Experts' Advice to Women.* New York: Anchor.

Ellis, Rhian. 1983. The Way to a Man's Heart: Food in the Violent Home. In Anne Murcott, ed., *The Sociology of Food and Eating,* 164–71. Aldershot: Gower Publishing.

Evans, Sara. 1979. *Personal Politics: The Roots of Women's Liberation in the Civil Rights Movement and the New Left.* New York: Alfred A. Knopf.

Feldberg, Roslyn L. 1984. Comparable Worth: Toward Theory and Practice in the United States. *Signs* 10:311–28.

Finch, Janet, and Dulcie Groves, eds. 1983. *A Labour of Love: Women, Work and Caring.* London: Routledge and Kegan Paul.

Fisher, Berenice, and Joan Tronto. 1990. Toward a Feminist Theory of Caring. In Emily K. Abel and Margaret K. Nelson, eds., *Circles of Care,* 35–62. Albany: State University of New York Press.

Fishman, Pamela M. 1982. Interaction: The Work Women Do. In Rachel Kahn-Hut, Arlene K. Daniels and Richard Colvard, eds., *Women and Work: Problems and Perspectives,* 170–80. New York: Oxford University Press.

Freeman, Jo. 1975. *The Politics of Women's Liberation: A Case Study of an Emerging Social Movement and its Relation to the Policy Process.* New York: McKay.

Frye, Marilyn. 1983. *The Politics of Reality: Essays in Feminist Theory.* Trumansburg, NY: The Crossing Press.

Garfinkel, Harold. 1967. *Studies in Ethnomethodology.* Englewood Cliffs, NJ: Prentice-Hall.

Garmarnikow, Eva, David H. J. Morgan, Jane Purvis, and Daphne Taylorson, eds. 1983. *The Public and the Private.* London: Heinemann.

Gerstel, Naomi, and Harriet Engel Gross. 1987. *Families and Work.* Philadelphia: Temple University Press.

Gilligan, Carol. 1982. *In a Different Voice: Psychological Theory and Women's Development.* Cambridge: Harvard University Press.

Glazer, Nona Y. 1980. Overworking the Working Woman: The Double Day in a Mass Magazine. *Women's Studies International Quarterly* 3:79–83.

———. 1987. Servants to Capital: Unpaid Domestic Labor and Paid Work. In Naomi Gerstel and Harriet Engel Gross, eds., *Families and Work,* 236–55. Philadelphia: Temple University Press.

Glenn, Evelyn Nakano. 1985. Racial Ethnic Women's Labor: The Intersection of Race, Gender and Class Oppression. *Review of Radical Political Economics* 17:86–108.

———. 1990. White Women/Women of Color: The Racial Division of Social Reproduction. Paper presented at the Henry A. Murray Research Center, Radcliffe College, April, Cambridge.

Goode, William J. 1982. Why Men Resist. In Barrie Thorne with Marilyn Yalom, eds., *Rethinking the Family,* 131–50. New York: Longman.

Gough, Ian. 1980. *The Political Economy of the Welfare State.* London: Macmillan.

Graham, Hilary. 1983. Caring: A Labour of Love. In Janet Finch and Dulcie Groves, eds., *A Labour of Love: Women, Work and Caring,* 13–30. London: Routledge and Kegan Paul.

Griffith, Alison I. 1984. Ideology, Education and Single Parent Families: The Normative Ordering of Families Through Schooling. Ph.D. diss., University of Toronto.

Griffith, Alison I., and Dorothy E. Smith. 1987. Constructing Cultural Knowledge: Mothering as Discourse. In Jane Gaskell and Arlene McLaren, eds., *Women and Education: A Canadian Perspective,* 87–103. Calgary: Detselig Enterprises.

Gubrium, Jaber F., and James A. Holstein. 1990. *What Is Family?* Mountain View, CA: Mayfield.

Gussow, Joan. 1987. The Fragmentation of Need: Women, Food and Marketing. *Heresies,* no. 21:39–43.

Guyer, Jane I. 1981. The Raw, the Cooked, and the Half-Baked: A Note on the Division of Labor by Sex. African Studies Center, 125 Bay State Road, Boston, MA 02215.

Haavind, Hanne. 1984. Love and Power in Marriage. In Harriet Holter, ed., *Patriarchy in a Welfare Society,* 136–67. Oslo: Universitetsforlaget.

Hartmann, Heidi I. 1981a. The Family as the Locus of Gender, Class and Political Struggle: The Example of Housework. *Signs* 6:366–94.

———. 1981b. The Unhappy Marriage of Marxism and Feminism: Towards a More Progressive Union. In Lydia Sargent, ed., *Women and Revolution,* 1–41. Boston: South End Press.

Hawes, Jon M. 1982. *Retailing Strategies for Generic Brand Grocery Products.* Ann Arbor: UMI Research Press.

Hayden, Dolores. 1981. *The Grand Domestic Revolution: A History of Feminist Designs for American Homes, Neighborhoods, and Cities.* Cambridge: MIT Press.

Henley, Nancy M. 1977. *Body Politics: Power, Sex and Nonverbal Communication.* New York: Simon and Schuster.

Hertz, Rosanna. 1986. *More Equal Than Others: Women and Men in Dual-Career Marriages.* Berkeley: University of California Press.

Hertz, Rosanna, and Joy Charlton. 1989. Making Family Under a Shiftwork Schedule: Air Force Security Guards and Their Wives. *Social Problems* 36:491–507.

Hochschild, Arlie Russell. 1983. *The Managed Heart: Commercialization of Human Feeling.* Berkeley: University of California Press.

Hochschild, Arlie, with Anne Machung. 1989. *The Second Shift: Working Parents and the Revolution at Home.* New York: Viking.

Hood, Jane C. 1983. *Becoming a Two-Job Family.* New York: Praeger.

Hooks, Bell. 1984. *Feminist Theory from Margin to Center.* Boston: South End Press.

Hughes, Everett C. 1984. *The Sociological Eye.* New Brunswick, NJ: Transaction Books.

Humphries, Jane. 1977. The Working Class Family, Women's Liberation, and Class Struggle: The Case of Nineteenth-Century British History. *Review of Radical Political Economics* 9:25–41.

Illich, Ivan. 1981. *Shadow Work.* Boston: Marion Boyars.

International Association of Cooking Schools. 1982. Food Trends Panel. Discussion presented at Annual Meeting, Chicago, March 20.

Jones, Jacqueline. 1985. *Labor of Love, Labor of Sorrow: Black Women, Work, and the Family from Slavery to the Present.* New York: Basic.

Joseph, Gloria I. 1981. Black Mothers and Daughters: Their Roles and Functions in American Society. In Gloria I. Joseph and Jill Lewis, *Common Differences: Conflicts in Black and White Feminist Perspectives,* 75–126. Boston: South End Press.

Kahn, Alfred J., and Sheila B. Kamerman. 1987. *Child Care: Facing the Hard Choices.* Dover, MA: Auburn House.

Kahn-Hut, Rachel, Arlene Kaplan Daniels, and Richard Colvard. 1982. *Women and Work: Problems and Perspectives.* New York: Oxford University Press.

Kamerman, Sheila B. 1979. Work and Family in Industrialized Societies. *Signs* 4:632–50.

Kaplan, Jane Rachel, ed. 1980. *A Woman's Conflict: The Special Relationship Between Women and Food.* Englewood Cliffs, NJ: Prentice-Hall.

Komarovsky, Mirra. 1962. *Blue-Collar Marriage.* New York: Random House.

Ladd-Taylor, Molly. 1986. *Raising a Baby the Government Way: Mothers' Letters to the Children's*

Bureau 1915–1932. New Brunswick, NJ: Rutgers University Press.

Land, Hilary. 1978. Who Cares for the Family? *Journal of Social Policy* 7:257–84.

Lave, Jean, Michael Murtaugh, and Olivia de la Rocha. 1984. The Dialectic of Arithmetic in Grocery Shopping. In Barbara Rogoff and Jean Lave, eds., *Everyday Cognition: Its Development in Social Context,* 67–94. Cambridge: Harvard University Press.

Leibowitz, Lila. 1983. Origins of the Sexual Division of Labor. In Marian Lowe and Ruth Hubbard, eds., *Woman's Nature: Rationalizations of Inequality,* 123–47. New York: Pergamon.

Levenstein, Harvey A. 1988. *Revolution at the Table: The Transformation of the American Diet.* New York: Oxford University Press.

Lévi-Strauss, Claude. 1969. *The Raw and the Cooked.* Translated by John and Doreen Weightman. New York: Harper and Row.

Lopata, Helena Z. 1971. *Occupation: Housewife.* New York: Oxford University Press.

Luxton, Meg. 1980. *More Than a Labour of Love: Three Generations of Women's Work in the Home.* Toronto: The Women's Press.

MacKinnon, Catharine A. 1987. *Feminism Unmodified: Discourses on Life and Law.* Cambridge: Harvard University Press.

Matthews, Glenna. 1987. *"Just a Housewife": The Rise and Fall of Domesticity in America.* New York: Oxford University Press.

Mies, Maria. 1983. Towards a Methodology for Feminist Research. In Gloria Bowles and Renate Duelli Klein, eds., *Theories of Women's Studies,* 117–39. London: Routledge and Kegan Paul.

Mishler, Elliot G. 1986. *Research Interviewing: Context and Narrative.* Cambridge: Harvard University Press.

Murcott, Anne. 1983. "It's a Pleasure to Cook for Him": Food, Mealtimes and Gender in some South Wales Households. In Eva Garmarnikow, David H. J. Morgan, Jane Purvis, and Daphne Taylorson, eds., *The Public and the Private,* 78–90. London: Heinemann.

Noddings, Nel. 1984. *Caring: A Feminine Approach to Ethics and Moral Education.* Berkeley: University of California Press.

Novarra, Virginia. 1980. *Women's Work, Men's Work.* London: Marion Boyars.

Oakley, Ann. 1974. *The Sociology of Housework.* New York: Pantheon Books.

———. 1981. Interviewing Women: A Contradiction in Terms. In Helen Roberts, ed., *Doing Feminist Research,* 30–61. London: Routledge and Kegan Paul.

O'Kelly, Charlotte G. 1980. *Women and Men in Society.* New York: D. Van Nostrand.

O'Laughlin, Bridget. 1974. Mediation of Contradiction: Why Mbum Women Do Not Eat Chicken. In Michelle Zimbalist Rosaldo and Louise Lamphere, eds., *Woman, Culture and Society,* 301–18. Stanford, CA: Stanford University Press.

Oren, Laura. 1974. The Welfare of Women in Laboring Families: England, 1860–1950. In Mary S. Hartman and Lois Banner, eds., *Clio's Consciousness Raised,* 226–44. New York: Harper and Row.

Ortner, Sherry B. 1974. Is Female to Male as Nature is to Culture? In Michelle Zimbalist Rosaldo and Louise Lamphere, eds., *Woman, Culture and Society,* 67–87. Stanford, CA: Stanford University Press.

Paget, Marianne A. 1983. Experience and Knowledge. *Human Studies* 6:67–90.

Piven, Frances Fox, and Richard A. Cloward. 1979. *Poor People's Movements.* New York: Vintage.

Pleck, Joseph H. 1985. *Working Wives/Working Husbands.* Beverly Hills, CA: Sage Publications.

Rainwater, Lee, Richard P. Coleman, and Gerald Handel. 1959. *Workingman's Wife.* New York: Oceana Publications.

Rapp, Rayna. 1982. Family and Class in Contemporary America: Notes Toward an Understanding of Ideology. In Barrie Thorne with Marilyn Yalom, eds., *Rethinking the Family,* 168–87. New York: Longman.

Rich, Adrienne. 1976. *Of Woman Born: Motherhood as Experience and Institution.* New York: W. W. Norton.

Richardson, Laurel. 1988. The Collective Story: Postmodernism and the Writing of Sociology. *Sociological Focus* 21:199–208.

Riessman, Catherine Kohler. 1987. When Gender is Not Enough: Women Interviewing Women. *Gender and Society* 1:172–207.

Robertson, Claire. 1987. Never Underestimate the Power of Women: The Transforming Vision of African Women's History. Paper presented at the

Annual Meeting of the Organization of American Historians, April, Philadelphia.

Rollins, Judith. 1985. *Between Women: Domestics and Their Employers.* Philadelphia: Temple University Press.

Ross, Becki L. 1985. The Lodging of the Time Budget Method in Sexist Bedrock: A Feminist Excavation. Paper presented at The Motherwork Conference, October, Simone de Beauvoir Institute, Montreal.

Rothman, Sheila M. 1978. *Woman's Proper Place: A History of Changing Ideals and Practices, 1870 to the Present.* New York: Basic.

Rubin, Lillian Breslow. 1976. *Worlds of Pain.* New York: Basic.

Ruddick, Sara. 1980. Maternal Thinking. *Feminist Studies* 6:342–67.

———. 1989. *Maternal Thinking: Toward a Politics of Peace.* Boston: Beacon Press.

Sacks, Karen Brodkin. 1988. *Caring by the Hour: Women, Work, and Organizing at Duke Medical Center.* Urbana: University of Illinois Press.

Seifer, Nancy. 1973. *Absent from the Majority: Working Class Women in America.* New York: National Project on Ethnic America, American Jewish Committee.

Sered, Susan Starr. 1988. Food and Holiness: Cooking as a Sacred Act Among Middle-Eastern Jewish Women. *Anthropological Quarterly* 61:129–39.

Smith, Dorothy E. 1984. Textually-Mediated Social Organization. *The International Social Science Journal* 36:59–75.

———. 1985. Women, Class and Family. In Varda Burstyn and Dorothy E. Smith, *Women, Class, Family and the State,* 1–44. Toronto: Garamond Press.

———. 1987. *The Everyday World as Problematic: A Feminist Sociology.* Boston: Northeastern University Press.

———. 1990. Femininity as Discourse. In *Texts, Facts, and Femininity: Exploring the Relations of Ruling,* 159–208. New York: Routledge.

Sokoloff, Natalie J. 1980. *Between Money and Love: The Dialectics of Home and Market Work.* New York: Praeger.

Stack, Carol. 1974. *All Our Kin: Strategies for Survival in a Black Community.* New York: Harper and Row.

Strasser, Susan. 1982. *Never Done: A History of American Housework.* New York: Pantheon Books.

Thorne, Barrie. 1982. Feminist Rethinking of the Family: An Overview. In Barrie Thorne with Marilyn Yalom, eds., *Rethinking the Family,* 1–24. New York: Longman.

———. 1987. Re-visioning Women and Social Change: Where are the Children? *Gender and Society* 1:85–109.

Thorne, Barrie, with Marilyn Yalom, eds. 1982. *Rethinking the Family.* New York: Longman.

Tilly, Louise A., and Joan W. Scott. 1978. *Women, Work and Family.* New York: Holt, Rinehart and Winston.

Todd, Alexandra Dundas, and Sue Fisher, eds. 1988. *Gender and Discourse: The Power of Talk.* Norwood, NJ: Ablex.

Traustadottir, Rannveig. 1989. Constructing a Normal Family: Disability and Family Life. Unpublished paper. Center on Human Policy, Syracuse University, Syracuse, NY.

Tronto, Joan C. 1987. Beyond Gender Difference to a Theory of Care. *Signs* 12:644–63.

Ungerson, Clare. 1983a. Why Do Women Care? In Janet Finch and Dulcie Groves, eds., *A Labour of Love: Women, Work and Caring,* 31–49. London: Routledge and Kegan Paul.

———. 1983b. Women and Caring: Skills, Tasks and Taboos. In Eva Garmarnikow, David H. J. Morgan, Jane Purvis, and Daphne Taylorson, eds., *The Public and the Private,* 62–77. London: Heinemann.

U.S. Bureau of the Census. 1989. *Statistical Abstract of the United States,* 109th ed. Washington, D.C.: U.S. Government Printing Office.

U.S. Department of Agriculture, Economic Research Service. 1987a. Food Spending and Income. *National Food Review,* 1987 Yearbook, 24–33.

U.S. Department of Agriculture, Economic Research Service. 1987b. Food-service Trends. *National Food Review,* 1987 Yearbook, 10–15.

Vanek, Joann. 1974. Time Spent in Housework. *Scientific American* 231:116–20.

Wadel, Cato. 1979. The Hidden Work of Everyday Life. In Sandra Wallman, ed., *Social Anthropology of Work,* 365–84. London: Academic Press.

Waerness, Kari. 1984. The Rationality of Caring. *Economic and Industrial Democracy* 5:185–211.

Walker, Kathryn E., and Margaret E. Woods. 1976. *Time Use: A Measure of Household Production of Family Goods and Services.* Washington,

D.C.: Center for the Family, American Home Economics Association.

Waring, Marilyn. 1988. *If Women Counted: A New Feminist Economics.* New York: Harper and Row.

Weinbaum, Batya, and Amy Bridges. 1976. The Other Side of the Paycheck: Monopoly Capital and the Structure of Consumption. *Monthly Review* 28:88–103.

Welter, Barbara. 1966. The Cult of True Womanhood: 1820–1860. *American Quarterly* 18:151–74.

West, Candace, and Don H. Zimmerman. 1987. Doing Gender. *Gender and Society* 1:125–51.

West, Guida. 1981. *The National Welfare Rights Movement: The Social Protest of Poor Women.* New York: Praeger.

Willis, Ellen. 1972. "Consumerism" and Women. In Vivian Gornick and Barbara K. Moran, eds., *Woman in Sexist Society,* 658–65. New York: New American Library.

Wilson, William Julius. 1987. *The Truly Disadvantaged: The Inner City, the Underclass, and Public Policy.* Chicago: University of Chicago Press.

Woolf, Virginia. 1927. *To the Lighthouse.* New York: Harcourt, Brace.

Wright, Erik Olin. 1979. *Class, Crisis and the State.* London: Verso.

Wynn, Ruth L., and Jean Bowering. 1987. Homemaking Practices and Evening Meals in Married and Separated Families with Young Children. Paper presented at the Biannual Meeting of the Society for Research in Child Development, Baltimore, MD.

Yanagisako, Sylvia Junko. 1977. Women-Centered Kin Networks in Urban Bilateral Kinship. *American Ethnologist* 4:207–26.

Zaretsky, Eli. 1973. *Capitalism, the Family and Personal Life.* New York: Harper.

PART TWO

RACE, ETHNICITY, CLASS, AND THE STATE

CHAPTER 4

Social Class and Families

In the 1950s and 1960s, the American economy was strong and wages were rising. In fact, the average income of full-time workers, adjusted for inflation, doubled. Most workers without college educations could find jobs in the expanding factories of the nation. But the 1973 decision by oil-producing countries to sharply raise the price of oil sent the U.S. economy into a tailspin. Wages for workers without college degrees remained stagnant until the late 1990s. Even after the United States adjusted to the oil price shock, it became clear that our employment base in manufacturing was not growing the way it had in the past. Corporations moved production overseas in order to take advantage of the lower wages paid to workers in the developing world. Computers and other technologies allowed employers to replace some workers with machines, such as the robots on automobile assembly lines.

Consequently, adults without college educations have found it harder to obtain jobs with adequate wages, as I discuss in my textbook.[1]

These reduced prospects have hurt working-class families in two ways. First, young men who are unemployed, or who are employed but earn low wages, are often reluctant to marry because they don't think that they earn enough to help support a family. Young women realize the difficulty of finding a spouse who is a reliable earner, which may make them less likely to wait until marriage to have children. Thus, the stagnant wages may be related to the postponement of marriage and the growth of childbearing outside of marriage during the last two decades or so. Second, the marriages that do exist face more strain because of inadequate incomes. Most generations of Americans have expected to do better economically than their parents' generation. Now, a significant number of working-class families find that those expectations are not being met.

One such family, the Mertens of Des Moines, Iowa, was profiled in *The New Yorker* magazine in 1995 by Susan Sheehan, It is a story worth studying for what it says about working-class families in the United States today. Kenny Merten earned $7.00 an hour at his first job after marrying Bonita in 1972; his pay rose to $8.95

---

[1]Andrew J. Cherlin, *Public and Private Families: An Introduction,* 2nd ed. (New York: McGraw-Hill, 1999).

before he lost that job. Two decades later, working for a highway barricade company, he makes $7.30 an hour. During the two decades, the cost of consumer goods more than tripled because of inflation. Consequently, Kenny would have to be earning over $24 an hour to match the buying power he had in 1972. Instead, his buying power has declined by 70 percent. "There ain't no middle class no more," said Kenny, who had hoped to join it; "there's only rich and poor."

As you read the article, you might ask yourself what is responsible for the constant money troubles the Mertens have. Is it an inability to control spending? (Kenny impulsively bought the whole family mountain bikes.) An advertising industry that pushes consumption? (Bonita is unable to resist buying a pair of $89 Nike sneakers for Christopher.) An economy that doesn't pay adequate wages? ("I know I'll never be able to earn eleven-eighty an hour again," Kenny said. "The most I can hope for is a seven-dollar-an-hour job that doesn't involve swinging sandbags. Maybe if I come home less tired at the end of the day, I can handle an evening job.")

The 1950s and 1960s were also the era during which a substantial middle class began to emerge, for the first time, among African-Americans. Most large cities now contain black neighborhoods that are predominately composed of nonpoor families. Mary Patillo-McCoy did field research in one such neighborhood in Chicago, which she calls Groveland. Patillo-McCoy argues that the experience of being middle-class is different for blacks and whites. Most notably, she writes, black middle-class neighborhoods tend to be closer to poor black neighborhoods because of residential segregation and, in fact, usually contain some poor families. Morever, extended family ties typically link middle-class individuals with poorer relatives. As a result, she argues, it is harder for the black middle-class to shield their children from the lure of the of the street life, with its criminal behavior and drug usage. And middle-class residents must coexist with neighbors and relatives in the underground economy in ways most whites need not.

Ain't No Middle Class

Susan Sheehan

At 10 o'clock on a Tuesday night in September, Bonita Merten gets home from her job as a nursing-home aide on the evening shift at the Luther Park Health Center, in Des Moines, Iowa. Home is a two-story, three-bedroom house in the predominantly working-class East Side section of the city. The house, drab on the outside, was built in 1905 for factory and railroad workers. It has aluminum siding painted an off-shade of green, with white and dark-brown trim. Usually, Bonita's sons—Christopher, who is 16 and David, who is 20 and still in high school (a slow learner, he was found to be suffering from autism when he was eight)—are awake when she comes home, but tonight they are asleep. Bonita's husband, Kenny, who has picked her up at the nursing home—"Driving makes Mama nervous," Kenny often says—loses no time in going to bed himself. Bonita is wearing her nursing-home uniform, which consists of a short-sleeved navy-blue polyester top with "Luther Park" inscribed in white, matching navy slacks, and white shoes. She takes off her work shoes, which she describes as "any kind I can pick up for 10 or 12 dollars," puts on a pair of black boots and a pair of gloves, and goes out to the garage to get a pitchfork.

In the spring, Bonita planted a garden. She and David, who loves plants and flowers, have been picking strawberries, raspberries, tomatoes, and zucchini since June. Bonita's mother, who lives in Washington, Iowa, a small town

about a hundred miles from Des Moines, has always had a large garden—this summer, she gave the Mertens dozens of tomatoes from her 32 tomato plants—but her row of potato plants, which had been bountiful in the past, didn't yield a single potato. This is the first year that Bonita has put potato plants in her own garden. A frost has been predicted, and she is afraid her potatoes (if there are any) will die, so instead of plunking herself down in front of the television set, as she customarily does after work, she goes out to tend her small potato strip alongside the house.

The night is cool and moonless. The only light in the back yard, which is a block from the round-the-clock thrum of Interstate 235, is provided by a tall mercury arc lamp next to the garage. Traffic is steady on the freeway, but Bonita is used to the noise of the cars and trucks and doesn't hear a thing as she digs contentedly in the yellowy darkness. Bonita takes pleasure in the little things in life, and she excavates for potatoes with cheerful curiosity—"like I was digging for gold." Her pitchfork stabs and dents a large potato. Then, as she turns over the loosened dirt, she finds a second baking-size potato, says "Uh-huh!" to herself, and comes up with three smaller ones before calling it quits for the night.

"Twenty-two years ago, when Kenny and me got married, I agreed to marry him for richer or poorer," Bonita, who is 49, says. "I don't have no regrets, but I didn't have no idea for how much poorer. Nineteen-ninety-five has been a hard year in a pretty hard life. We had our water shut off in July *and* in August, and we ain't never had it turned off even once before, so I look on those five potatoes as a sign of hope. Maybe our luck will change."

When Bonita told Kenny she was going out to dig up her potatoes, he remembers thinking, Let her have fun. If she got the ambition, great. I'm kinda out of hope and I'm tired.

Kenny Merten is almost always tired when he gets home, after 5 P.M., from his job at Bonnie's

Barricades—a small company, started 10 years ago by a woman named Bonnie Ruggless, that puts up barriers, sandbags, and signs to protect construction crews at road sites. Some days, he drives a truck a hundred and fifty miles to rural counties across the state to set up roadblocks. Other days, he does a lot of heavy lifting. "The heaviest sandbags weigh between 35 and 40 pounds dry," he says. "Wet, they weigh 50 or 60 pounds, depending on how soaked they are. Sand holds a lot of water." Hauling the sandbags is not easy for Kenny, who contracted polio when he was 18 months old and wore a brace on his left leg until he was almost 20. He is now 51, walks with a pronounced limp, and twists his left ankle easily. "Bonnie's got a big heart and hires people who are down on their luck," he says.

Kenny went to work at Bonnie's Barricades two years ago, and after two raises he earns seven dollars and thirty cents an hour. "It's a small living—too small for me, on account of all the debts I got," he says. "I'd like to quit working when I'm 65, but Bonnie doesn't offer a retirement plan, so there's no way I can quit then, with 28 years left to pay on the house mortgage, plus a car loan and etceteras. So I'm looking around for something easier—maybe driving a forklift in a warehouse. Something with better raises and fringe benefits."

On a summer afternoon after work, Kenny sits down in a rose-colored La-Z-Boy recliner in the Merten's living room/dining room, turns on the TV—a 19-inch Sylvania color set he bought secondhand nine years ago for a hundred dollars—and watches local and national news until six-thirty, occasionally dozing off. After the newscasts, he gets out of his work uniform—navy-blue pants and a short-sleeved orange shirt with the word "Ken" over one shirt pocket and "Bonnie's Barricades" over the other—and takes a bath. The house has one bathroom, with a tub but no shower. Last Christmas, Bonita's mother and her three younger brothers gave the Mertens a shower for their basement, but it has yet to be hooked up—by Kenny, who, with the help of a friend, can do the work for much less than a licensed plumber.

Kenny's philosophy is: Never do today what can be put off until tomorrow—unless he really wants to do it. Not that he is physically lazy. If the Mertens' lawn needs mowing, he'll mow it, and the lawn of their elderly next-door neighbor, Eunice, as well. Sometimes he gets up at 4:30 A.M.—an hour earlier than necessary—if Larry, his half uncle, needs a ride to work. Larry, who lives in a rented apartment two miles from the Mertens and drives an old clunker that breaks down regularly, has been married and divorced several times and has paid a lot of money for child support over the years. He is a security guard at a tire company and makes five dollars an hour. "If he doesn't get to work, he'll lose his job," Kenny says. In addition, Kenny helps his half brother Bob, who is also divorced and paying child support, with lifts to work and with loans.

Around 7:30 P.M., Kenny, who has changed into a clean T-shirt and a pair of old jeans, fixes dinner for himself and his two sons. Dinner is often macaroni and cheese, or spaghetti with store-bought sauce or stewed tomatoes from Bonita's mother's garden. He doesn't prepare salad or a separate vegetable ("Sauce or stewed tomatoes *is* the vegetable," he says); dessert, which tends to be an Iowa brand of ice cream, Anderson Erickson, is a rare luxury. Kenny takes the boys out for Subway sandwiches whenever he gets "a hankering" for one. Once a week—most likely on Friday, when he gets paid—he takes them out for dinner, usually to McDonald's. "It's easier than cooking," Kenny says.

Because Bonita works the evening shift, Kenny spends more time with his sons than most fathers do; because she doesn't drive, he spends more time behind the wheel. Christopher, a short, trim, cute boy with hazel eyes and brown hair, is one badge away from becoming an Eagle Scout, and Kenny drives him to many Scouting activities. This summer, Kenny drove Eunice, who is 85, to the hospital to visit her

90-year-old husband, Tony, who had become seriously ill in August. After Tony's death, on September 12th, Kenny arranged for the funeral—choosing the casket and the flowers, buying a new shirt for Tony, and chauffeuring the boys to the private viewing at the funeral home. "Everyone was real appreciative," he says.

At around eight-thirty on evenings free from special transportation duties, Kenny unwinds by watching more television, playing solitaire, dozing again, and drinking his third Pepsi of the day. (He is a self-described "Pepsiholic.") Around nine-fifty, he drives two miles to the Luther Park nursing home for Bonita.

Bonita Merten leaves the house before 1 P.M., carrying a 16-ounce bottle of Pepsi (she, too, is a Pepsiholic), and catches the bus to work. She is dressed in her navy-blue uniform and white shoes. Since the uniforms cost 33 dollars, Bonita considers herself lucky to have been given a used one by a nurse's aide who quit, and she bought another, secondhand, for 10 dollars. Luther Park recently announced a mandatory change to forest-green uniforms, and Bonita does not look forward to having to shell out for new attire.

Bonita clocks in before one-forty-five, puts her Pepsi in the break-room refrigerator, and, with the other evening aides, makes rounds with the day aides. She and another aide are assigned to a wing with 20 long-term residents. "The residents have just been laid down on top of their beds before we get there," Bonita says. "First, I change water pitchers and give the residents ice—got to remember which ones don't want ice, just want plain water. We pass out snacks—shakes fortified with protein and vitamins, in strawberry, vanilla, or chocolate. They need the shakes, because they ordinarily don't want to eat their meals. While I'm doing that, the other aide has to pass out the gowns, washrags, and towels, and the Chux—great big absorbent pads—and Dri-Prides. They're adult snap pants with liners that fit inside them. We don't call them diapers because they're not actually diapers, and because residents got their pride to be considered."

At three-thirty, Bonita takes a 10-minute break and drinks some Pepsi. "We start getting the residents up and giving showers before our break and continue after," Bonita says. "Each resident gets two showers a week, and it works out so's I have to shower three patients a day."

One aide eats from four-thirty to five, the other from five to five-thirty. Until August 1st, Bonita bought a two-dollar meal ticket if she liked what was being offered in the employees' dining room. When the meal didn't appeal to her—she wouldn't spend the two dollars for, say, a turkey sandwich and a bowl of cream-of-mushroom soup ("I don't like it at all")—she either bought a bag of Cheetos from a vending machine or skipped eating altogether. On August 1st, the nursing home reduced meal tickets to a dollar. "Even a turkey sandwich is worth that much," she says.

The residents eat at five-thirty, in their dining room. "We pass trays and help feed people who can't feed themselves," Bonita says. "Sometimes we feed them like a baby or encourage them to do as much as they can." At six-thirty, Bonita charts their meals—"what percent they ate, how much they drank. They don't eat a whole lot, because they don't get a lot of exercise, either. We clear out the dining room and walk them or wheel them to their rooms. We lay them down, and we've got to wash them and position them. I always lay them on their side, because I like lying on my side. I put a pillow behind their back and a blanket between their legs. We take the false teeth out of those with false teeth, and put the dentures into a denture cup for those that will let us. A lot of them have mouthwash, and we're supposed to rinse their mouth. We're supposed to brush their teeth if they have them. After everyone is down, we chart. We check off that we positioned them and if we changed their liners. I'm supposed to get a 10-minute evening break, but I hardly ever take it. Charting, I'm off my feet, and there's just too much to do. Often we're short—I'll be alone on a hall for a few hours. The last thing we do is make rounds with the shift coming in. I clock out by nine-forty-five. Ninety-nine percent of the time, Kenny picks me up. When I had different hours and he'd be bowling, his half brother Bob picked me up, or I took a cab for five dollars. The bus is one dollar, but it stops running by seven o'clock."

Bonita has worked all three shifts at Luther Park. The evening shift currently pays 50 cents an hour more than the day shift and 50 cents less than the night shift, but days and nights involve more lifting. (In moving her patients, Bonita has injured her back more times than she can remember, and she now wears a wide black belt with straps which goes around her sacroiliac; she also uses a mechanical device to help carry heavy residents between their wheelchairs and their beds.) Bonita's 1994 earnings from Luther park were only 869 dollars higher than her 1993 earnings, reflecting an hourly increase in wages from six dollars and fifty cents to six-sixty-five and some overtime hours and holidays, for which she is paid time and a half. This July 1st, she received the grandest raise that she has ever had in her life—75 cents an hour—but she believes there is a hold-down on overtime, so she doesn't expect to earn substantially more in 1995. Luther Park gives her a ham for Easter, a turkey for Thanksgiving, 10 dollars for her birthday, and 20 dollars for Christmas.

Bonita rarely complains about working at the nursing home. "I don't mind emptying bedpans or cleaning up the residents' messes," she says. She regards her job, with its time clocks, uniforms, tedious chores, low wages, penny-ante raises, and Dickensian holiday rewards, as "a means to a life."

Bonita and Kenny Merten and their two sons live in a statistical land above the lowly welfare poor but far beneath the exalted rich. In 1994, they earned $31,216 between them. Kenny made $17,239 working for Bonnie's Barricades; Bonita made $13,977 at Luther Park. With an additional $1,212 income from other sources, including some money that Kenny withdrew from the retirement plan of a previous employer, the Mertens' gross income was $32,428. Last

year, as in most other years of their marriage, the Mertens spent more than they earned.

The Mertens' story is distinctive, but it is also representative of what has happened to the working poor of their generation. In 1974, Kenny Merten was making roughly the same hourly wage that he is today, and was able to buy a new Chevrolet Nova for less than 4,000 dollars; a similar vehicle today would cost 15,000 dollars—a sum that even Kenny, who is far more prone than Bonita to take on debt, might hesitate to finance. And though Kenny has brought on some of his own troubles by not always practicing thrift and by not always following principles of sound money management, his situation also reflects changing times.

In the 1960s, jobs for high-school graduates were plentiful. Young men could easily get work from one day to the next which paid a living wage, and that's what Kenny did at the time. By the mid-80s, many of these jobs were gone. In Des Moines, the Rock Island Motor Transit Company (part of the Chicago, Rock Island & Pacific Railroad) went belly up. Borden moved out of the city, and so did a division of the Ford Motor Company. Utility companies also began downsizing, and many factory jobs were replaced by service-industry jobs, which paid less. Although there is a chronic shortage of nurse's aides at Luther Park, those who stay are not rewarded. After 15 years of almost continuous employment, Bonita is paid 7 dollars and 40 cents an hour—55 cents an hour more than new aides coming onto the job.

Working for one employer, as men like Kenny's father-in-law used to do, is a novelty now. Des Moines has become one of the largest insurance cities in the United States, but the Mertens don't qualify for white-collar positions. Civil-service jobs, formerly held by high-school graduates, have become harder to obtain because of competition from college graduates, who face diminishing job opportunities themselves. Bonita's 37-year-old brother, Eugene, studied mechanical engineering at the University of Iowa, but after graduation he wasn't offered a position in his field. He went to work for a box company and later took the United States Postal Service exam. He passed. When Bonita and Kenny took the exam, they scored too low to be hired by the Post Office.

Although 31 percent of America's four-person families earned less in 1994 than the Mertens did, Kenny and Bonita do not feel like members of the middle class, as they did years ago. "There ain't no middle class no more," Kenny says. "There's only rich and poor."

This is where the $32,428 that the Mertens grossed last year went. They paid $2,481 in federal income taxes. Their Iowa income-tax bill was $1,142, and $2,388 was withheld from their paychecks for Social Security and Medicare. These items reduced their disposable income to $26,417. In 1994, Bonita had $9.64 withheld from her biweekly paycheck for medical insurance, and $14.21 for dental insurance—a $620.10 annual cost. The insurance brought their disposable income down to $25,797.

The highest expenditures in the Mertens' budget were for food and household supplies, for which they spent approximately $110 a week at various stores and farmers' markets, for a yearly total of $5,720. They tried to economize by buying hamburger and chicken and by limiting their treats. (All four Mertens like potato chips.) Kenny spent about eight dollars per working day on breakfast (two doughnuts and a Pepsi), lunch (a double cheeseburger or a chicken sandwich), and sodas on the road—an additional $2,000 annually. His weekly dinner out at McDonald's with his sons cost between 11 and 12 dollars—600 dollars a year more. Bonita's meals or snacks at work added up to about 300 dollars. Kenny sometimes went out to breakfast on Saturday—alone or with the boys—and the meals he and his sons ate at McDonald's or Subway and the dinners that all four Mertens ate at restaurants like Bonanza and Denny's probably came to another 600 dollars annually. David and Christopher's school

lunches cost a dollar-fifty a day; they received allowances of 10 dollars a week each, and that provided them with an extra 2 dollars and 50 cents to spend. The money the boys paid for food outside the house came to 500 dollars a year. The family spent a total of about $9,720 last year on dining in and out; on paper products and cleaning supplies; and on caring for their cats (they have two). This left them with $16,077.

The Mertens' next-highest expenditure in 1994 was $3,980 in property taxes and payments they made on a fixed-rate, 30-year, 32,000-dollar mortgage, on which they paid an interest rate of 8.75 percent. This left them with $12,097.

In April of 1994, Kenny's 1979 Oldsmobile, with 279,000 miles on it, was no longer worth repairing, so he bought a 1988 Grand Am from Bonita's brother Eugene for 3,000 dollars, on which he made four payments of 200 dollars a month. The Grand Am was damaged in an accident in September, whereupon he traded up to an 11,000 dollar 1991 Chevy Blazer, and his car-loan payments increased to $285 a month. Bonita has reproached Kenny for what she regards as a nonessential purchase. "A man's got his ego," he replies. "The Blazer is also safer—it has four-wheel drive." The insurance on Kenny's cars cost a total of $798, and he spent 500 dollars on replacement parts. Kenny figures that he spends about 20 dollars a week on gas, or about $1,040 for the year. After car expenses of $2,338 and after payments on the car loans of $1,655, the Mertens had $8,104 left to spend. A 10-day driving vacation in August of last year, highlighted by stops at the Indianapolis Motor Speedway, Mammoth Cave, in Kentucky, and the Hard Rock Cafe in Nashville, cost 1,500 dollars and left them with $6,604.

The Mertens' phone bill was approximately 25 dollars a month: the only long-distance calls Bonita made were to her mother and to her youngest brother, Todd, a 33-year-old aerospace engineer living in Seattle. She kept the calls short. "Most of our calls are incoming, and most of them are for Christopher," Bonita says. The Mertens' water-and-sewage bill was about 50 dollars a month; their gas-and-electric bill was about 150 dollars a month. "I have a hard time paying them bills now that the gas and electric companies have consolidated," Kenny says. "Before, if the gas was 75 dollars and the electric was 75 dollars, I could afford to pay one when I got paid. My take-home pay is too low to pay the two together." After paying approximately 2,700 dollars for utilities, including late charges, the Mertens had a disposable income of $3,904.

Much of that went toward making payments to a finance company on two of Kenny's loans. To help pay for the family's 1994 vacation, Kenny borrowed 1,100 dollars, incurring payments of about 75 dollars a month for two years and three months, at an interest rate of roughly 25 percent. Kenny was more reluctant to discuss the second loan, saying only that it consisted of previous loans he'd "consolidated" at a rate of about 25 percent, and that it cost him 175 dollars a month in payments. Also in 1994 he borrowed "a small sum" for "Christmas and odds and ends" from the credit union at Bonnie's Barricades; 25 dollars a week was deducted from his paycheck for that loan. Payments on the three loans—about 4,300 dollars last year— left the Merten family with a budget deficit even before their numerous other expenses were taken into account.

Except in a few small instances (according to their 1994 Iowa income-tax return, Bonita and Kenny paid H & R Block 102 dollars to prepare their 1993 return, and they gave 125 dollars to charity), it isn't possible to determine precisely what the rest of the Mertens' expenditures were in 1994. Several years ago, Kenny bounced a lot of checks, and he has not had a checking account since. Kenny exceeded the limits on both of their MasterCards a few years ago, and the cards were cancelled. Bonita has a J. C. Penney charge card but says, "I seldom dust it off." Now and then, Bonita went to a downtown outlet store, and if a dress caught her fancy she

might put it on layaway. On special occasions, she bought inexpensive outfits for herself and for Kenny. Before last year's summer holiday, she spent seven dollars on a top and a pair of shorts, and during the trip Kenny bought a 75 dollar denim jacket for himself and about 50 dollars' worth of T-shirts for the whole family at the Hard Rock Cafe. One consequence of Kenny's having had polio as a child is that his left foot is a size 5 1/2 and his right foot a size 7. If he wants a comfortable pair of shoes, he has to buy two pairs or order a pair consisting of a 5 1/2 and a 7. Often he compromises, buying sneakers in size 6 1/2. David wears T-shirts and jeans as long as they are black, the color worn by Garth Brooks, his favorite country singer. Christopher is partial to name brands, and Bonita couldn't say no to a pair of 89 dollar Nikes he coveted last year. The Mertens spent about 700 dollars last year on clothing, and tried to economize on dry cleaning. "I dry-clean our winter coats and one or two dresses, but I avoid buying anything with a 'Dry-clean only' label," Bonita says.

The Mertens' entertainment expenses usually come to a thousand dollars a year, but that amount was exceeded in 1994 when Kenny bought a mountain bike for every member of the family. The bikes (Bonita has yet to ride hers out of the driveway) cost 259 dollars apiece, and Kenny made the final payments on them earlier this year. This July, David rode Kenny's bike to a hardware store, and it was stolen while he was inside. Kenny yelled at David; Bonita told Kenny he was being too hard on him, and Kenny calmed down.

Bonita and Kenny don't buy books or magazines, and they don't subscribe to newspapers. (They routinely borrowed Eunice and Tony's Des Moines *Register* until Tony's death, when Eunice cancelled it.) They rarely go to the movies—"Too expensive," Kenny says—but regularly rent movies and video games, usually at Blockbuster. For amusement, they often go to malls, just to browse, but when they get a serious urge to buy they go to antique stores. Kenny believes in "collectibles." His most treasured possession is an assortment of Currier & Ives dishes and glasses.

The Mertens have never paid to send a fax, or to send a package via Federal Express, and they aren't on-line: they have no computer. They even avoid spending money on postage: Kenny pays his bills in person. Bonita used to send out a lot of Christmas cards, but, she says, "I didn't get a whole lot back, so I quit that, too." They spend little on gifts, except to members of Bonita's family.

Kenny knows how much Bonita loves red roses. Twenty-two years ago, he gave her one red rose after they had been married one month, two after they had been married two months, and continued until he reached 12 red roses on their first anniversary. He also gave her a dozen red roses when she had a miscarriage, in 1973, "to make her feel better." To celebrate the birth of David and of Christopher, he gave her a dozen red roses and one yellow one for each boy. And Kenny gives Bonita a glass rose every Christmas.

On a Sunday evening this summer, the four Mertens went to Dahl's, their supermarket of choice in Des Moines. They bought four rolls of toilet paper (69 cents); a toothbrush (99 cents); a box of Rice Krispies (on sale for $1.99); eight 16-ounce bottles of Pepsi ($1.67); a gallon of 2-percent milk ($2.07); a large package of the least expensive dishwasher detergent ($2.19), the Mertens having acquired their first dishwasher in 1993, for 125 dollars; two jars of Prego spaghetti sauce ($3); a box of Shake 'n Bake ($1.99); two rolls of film ($10.38), one for Kenny, who owns a Canon T50 he bought for 125 dollars at a pawnshop, and one for Christopher to take to Boy Scout camp in Colorado; a battery ($2.99) for Christopher's flashlight, also for camp; a pound of carrots (65 cents); a green pepper (79 cents); some Ziploc bags ($1.89); a Stain Stick ($1.89); a box of 2000 Flushes ($2.89); a package of shredded mozzarella ($1.39) to add to some pizza the Mertens already had in the freezer; and 12 cans of cat food ($3). Bonita bought one treat for herself—a box

of toaster pastries with raspberry filling ($2.05). Christopher asked for a Reese's peanut-butter cup (25 cents), a bottle of Crystal Light (75 cents), and a package of Pounce cat treats ($1.05). All three purchases were O.K.'d.

David, who is enchanted by electrical fixtures, was content to spend his time in the store browsing in the light-bulb section. He was born with a cataract in his left eye, and the Mertens were instructed to put drops in that eye and a patch over his "good" right eye for a few years, so that the left eye wouldn't become lazy. Sometimes when they put the drops in, they told David to look up at a light. Today, David's main obsession, which apparently dates back to the eyedrops, is light. "We'd go someplace with David, and if there was a light with a bulb out he'd say, 'Light out,'" Bonita recalls. "We'd tell him, 'Don't worry about that,' and pretty soon he was saying, 'Light out, don't worry about that.'"

At 20, David looks 15. A lanky young man with coppercolored hair, hearing aids in both ears, and eye-glasses with thick lenses, he attends Ruby Van Meter, a special public high school for the city's mentally challenged. He reads at a fifth-grade level, and he doesn't read much. For years, the Mertens have been applying—without success—for Supplemental Security Income for David. In June of this year, when his application for S.S.I. was once again turned down, the Mertens hired a lawyer to appeal the decision. David has held a series of jobs set aside for slow learners (working, for instance, as a busboy in the Iowa statehouse cafeteria and in the laundry room of the local Marriott hotel), but he says that his "mood was off" when he was interviewed for several possible jobs this summer, and he drifted quietly through his school vacation. He will not be permitted to remain in school past the age of 21. If David could receive monthly S.S.I. checks and Medicaid, the Mertens would worry less about what will happen to him after they are gone. They have never regarded David as a burden, and although he has always been in special-education classes, they have treated him as much as possible the way they treat Christopher. Say "special ed" to Bonita, and she will say, "Both my boys are very special."

The Dahl's bill came to $44.75. When Kenny failed to take money out of his pocket at the cash register, Bonita, looking upset, pulled out her checkbook. She had expected Kenny to pay for the groceries, and she had hoped that the bill would be 40 dollars or less. But Kenny was short of money. "Aargh," Bonita said, softly.

Bonita didn't want to write checks for groceries, because she has other ideas about where her biweekly paychecks—about 400 dollars take-home—should go. Most of her first check of the month goes toward the mortgage—$331.68 when she pays it before the 17th of the month, $344.26 when she doesn't. Bonita likes to put aside the second check for the two most important events in her year—the family's summer vacation and Christmas. In theory, Kenny is supposed to pay most of the other family expenses and to stick to a budget—a theory to which he sometimes has difficulty subscribing. "I don't like to work off a budget," he says. "I think it restricts you. My way is to see who we have to pay this week and go from there. I rob Peter to pay Paul and try to pay Peter back." In practice, Kenny rarely pays Peter back. With his take-home pay averaging about 235 dollars a week, he can't.

When a consumer counsellor, who does not know the Mertens, was questioned about the family's current financial predicament—specifically, their 1994 income and expenditures—she made numerous recommendations. Among her suggestions for major savings was that the Mertens cut their food bills dramatically, to 5,400 dollars a year. She proposed stretching the Mertens' food dollars by drastically curtailing their eating out and by buying in bulk from the supermarket. She said that Kenny should get rid of his high-interest loans, and use the money he was spending on usurious interest to convert his mortgage from 30 years to 15. The way Kenny and Bonita were

going, the counsellor pointed out, they would not finish paying off their current mortgage until they were 79 and 77 years old, respectively. The Mertens' principal asset is 8,000 dollars in equity they have in their house. If the Mertens wanted to retire at 65, they would need more than what they could expect to receive from Social Security.

The counsellor had many minor suggestions for economizing at the grocery store. The Mertens should buy powdered milk and mix it with one-percent milk instead of buying two-percent milk. They should cut down even further on buying meat; beans and lentils, the counsellor observed, are a nutritious and less costly form of protein. She recommended buying raisins rather than potato chips, which she characterized as "high-caloric, high-fat, and high-cost."

The counsellor had one word for the amount—between 1,500 and 2,500 dollars—that the Mertens spent on vacations: "outlandish." Their vacations, she said, should cost a maximum of 500 dollars a year. She recommended renting a cabin with another family at a nearby state park or a lake. She urged the Mertens to visit local museums and free festivals, and go on picnics, including "no-ant picnics"—on a blanket in their living room.

Kenny and Bonita were resistant to most of the suggestions that were passed on to them from the counsellor, who is funded mainly by creditors to dispense advice to those with bill-paying problems. According to Kenny, buying a dozen doughnuts at the supermarket and then taking breakfast to work would be "boring." Bonita says she tried powdered milk in the mid-80s, when Kenny was unemployed, and the kids wouldn't drink it. She does buy raisins, but the boys don't really like them. Bonita and Kenny both laugh at the prospect of a no-ant picnic. "Sitting on the living-room carpet don't seem like a picnic to me," Bonita says.

Bonita surmises that the counsellor hasn't experienced much of blue-collar life and therefore underestimates the necessity for vacations and other forms of having fun. "We couldn't afford vacations in the 80s, and if we don't take them now the kids will be grown," she says. Kenny reacted angrily to the idea of the boys' eating dried beans and other processed foods. "I lived on powdered milk, dried beans, surplus yellow cheese, and that kind of stuff for two years when I was a kid," he says. "I want better for my boys."

Kenny acknowledges that he tried to confine his responses to the consumer counsellor's minor suggestions, because he realizes that her major recommendations are sound. He also realizes that he isn't in a position to act on them. He dreams of being free of debt. He has tried a number of times to get a 15-year mortgage, and has been turned down each time. "We both work hard, we're not on welfare, and we just can't seem to do anything that will make a real difference in our lives," he says. "So I save 10 dollars a bowling season by not getting a locker at the alley to store my ball and shoes, and have to carry them back and forth. So I save 25 dollars by changing my own oil instead of going to Jiffy Lube. So what? Going out to dinner is as necessary to me as paying water bills."

Kenneth Deane Merten was born poor and illegitimate to Ruby Merten in her mother's home, outside Des Moines, on October 5, 1944; his maternal relatives declined to reveal his father's name, and he never met his father. Ruby Merten went on to marry a soldier and had another son, Robert. She divorced Bob's father, and later married Don Summers, a frequently unemployed laborer, with whom she had three more children. "Mr. Summers was so mean he made me stand up all night in the bed when I was eight years old," Kenny recalls. He has never hit his own sons, because "I know what it done to my life and I don't want it to get passed down." The family often moved in haste when the rent was due. Kenny attended eight or ten schools, some of them twice, before he completed sixth grade.

Kenny's mother died of cancer at 27, when he was 14. The three younger children stayed with Don Summers and a woman he married a month later. Kenny and Bob went to live with their maternal grandparents, and their lives became more stable. Even so, Kenny's school grades were low. "I had a hard time with math and science," he says. "Coulda been because of all the early moving around. I ain't stupid." He spent his high-school years at Des Moines Technical High School and graduated in 1964, when he was almost 20.

Two days later, he found a job as a shipping clerk for *Look* magazine. He kept the job until 1969, and left only when it became apparent that the magazine was cutting back its operations. He drove a cab from 1969 to 1972, drank too much, and did what he calls "some rowdy rambling." He had put much of that behind him when he got a job as a factory worker at EMCO Industries, a manufacturer of muffler parts and machinery bolts, in the fall of 1972, shortly before he met Bonita.

Bonita Anne Crooks was born on October 7, 1946, in Harper, Iowa. Her father, Cloyce Crooks, was employed all his working life by the Natural Gas Pipeline Company; his wife, Pauline, stayed home to take care of Bonita and her three younger brothers. Bonita was required to do chores, for which she was paid, and to deposit those earnings in a bank. She took tap-dancing lessons, wore braces on her teeth, and often went with her family on vacation to places like California and Texas. "Kenny's growing up was a lot worse than mine," she says. In 1965, Bonita graduated from a Catholic high school and became a nurse's aide, while living at home and continuing to bank her money. In 1971, she moved to Des Moines, and the following year she got a job as a keypunch operator for a large insurance company. Keypunching, however, proved too difficult for her (she couldn't combine accuracy with high speed), and she soon transferred within the company to a lower-paying position—that of a file clerk.

Bonita met Kenny in October 1972 on a blind date that had been arranged by a friend of hers. "I had been jilted by a younger man, and I knew Kenny was meant for me on our first date, when he told me he was born on October 5, 1944—

exactly two years and two days earlier than me," Bonita says. She and Kenny fell in love quickly and were married in a traditional ceremony at a Catholic church in Harper on June 30, 1973. The newlyweds set off for Colorado on their honeymoon, but Kenny's car, a secondhand 1966 Pontiac Bonneville convertible, broke down, and the couple ended up in the Black Hills of South Dakota. When they were courting, Kenny had asked Bonita what sort of engagement ring she wanted. She had declined a "chunky" diamond, and said that matching wedding bands would suffice. "I suspected Kenny had debts," Bonita says. "I just didn't know how many he had until we got home."

The couple moved into a modest two-bedroom house. Bonita kept her file-clerk job after David's birth, in April 1975, but when she became pregnant with Christopher, who was born in November 1979, her doctor ordered her to bed. From the window of her bedroom, Bonita could see the Luther Park nursing home being built "kinda like next to my back yard." She didn't return to the insurance company, because her pay couldn't cover the cost of daytime care for two children. Kenny was working days at EMCO, so in June 1980 Bonita took a job on the 3-to-11 P.M. shift at Luther Park. She earned more there than she had as a file clerk. On some nights, Kenny drove a cab. He needed two jobs, because he regularly spent more than he and Bonita earned, just as he had overspent his own pay when he was single. Every year or two, he bought a new car. "I shouldn't have bought those new cars, but life with Don Summers made me feel completely insecure," he says. "Driving new cars gave me a sense of self-worth."

Kenny lost his job at EMCO at the end of 1983. He says that he had asked his supervisor for permission to take some discarded aluminum parts, and that permission was granted. But as he was driving off EMCO's premises with the parts in the bed of his pickup he was accused of stealing them. His supervisor then denied having given Kenny permission to take the parts. A demoralized Kenny didn't seek a new job for a year. He had already stopped driving the cab—after being robbed twice—and had started mowing lawns part time in the spring and summer, and doing cleanup work and shovelling snow in the fall and winter. Kenny's business failed—"There were too many unemployed guys like me out there." Many of his prized belongings were repossessed, among them a Curtis-Mathes stereo console. For two weeks in the summer of 1984, the Mertens were without gas or electricity or telephone service. They went on food stamps. Bonita felt guilty about going to work in air-conditioned surroundings while her husband and children were at home in the heat. Kenny felt humiliated when Bonita's parents visited their dark, sweltering house over the Fourth of July weekend. While Kenny has done better financially than most of his side of the family, it pains him that he hasn't done as well as Bonita's brothers, and that they regard him as a spendthrift and an inadequate provider. "When they get down on Kenny, I feel like I'm caught between a rock and a crevice," Bonita says.

Kenny's starting salary at EMCO had been seven dollars an hour. By the time he was terminated, it was eight-ninety-five an hour. In 1985, he found several jobs he liked, but none paid more than seven dollars an hour. One such job was with Bob Allen Sportswear, and he kept it until 1987, when he was let go during the off-season. He occasionally filed unemployment claims, and the family qualified for food stamps and received some groceries from food banks. During the rocky period between 1984 and 1988, Kenny tried to continue making payments on bills that he owed, in order to avoid having to declare bankruptcy, but his debts grew to the point where they exceeded his assets by "I think 12 or 13 thousand dollars"; his creditors—mostly finance companies—got fed up with him, and then he had no choice. The Mertens were able to keep their house and their '79 Olds. Going on food stamps didn't embarrass them—the boys had to eat, and they went off food stamps whenever Kenny had a new job—but the bankruptcy filing was published in the newspaper and made Bonita feel ashamed.

In 1989, after seeing an ad on television, Kenny enrolled in electronics courses at a local vocational school and borrowed 7,200 dollars to pay for his studies. His deficiency in math came back to haunt him, and he eventually dropped out. While at school, he had heard of an opening as a janitor at Ryko Manufacturing, an Iowa manufacturer of car washes. He eventually moved up to a factory job, working full time at Ryko in the early 90s for three years. Those years were happy ones. He got regular raises, and during the April-to-December busy season he earned a lot of overtime. In the summer of 1991, the Mertens flew to Seattle to visit Bonita's brother Todd. They had just enough money to cover one plane fare, and asked Bonita's brother Eugene to lend them the money for the three other tickets. Bonita took three months off that year; by then, she had worked full time at Luther Park for 11 straight years and needed a break. Kenny was proud to be the family's main provider, and wanted Bonita to stay home and take it easy.

In February 1993 Ryko fired Kenny Merten. His supervisors said that the work he did on the assembly line was neither fast enough nor of a sufficiently high quality. He was earning 11 dollars and 80 cents an hour—almost 30,000 dollars a year including overtime—when he was terminated. "In today's job market, first-rate companies like Ryko can afford to be selective," he says. "They want to hire young men."

Around the same time, Luther Park announced that it intended to expand. The nursing home offered the Mertens 39,000 dollars for the house they had lived in for 18 years. Kenny and Bonita accepted the offer, and were allowed to stay on, free of charge, for six months while they went house hunting. After they sold their house, it became apparent that they had been using it to supplement their income. The house they had bought for 14,800 dollars had appreci-

ated handsomely in value, but they had kept remortgaging, and now they owed 29,000 dollars on it. As a result, they netted only 10,000 dollars from the sale. The purchase price of the Mertens' new home was 40,000 dollars. They spent 2,000 dollars from the sale of the old house on improvements to their new home, and this reduced the amount of the down payment they were able to afford to 8,000 dollars.

Kenny attempted to return to work at several of the companies where he had previously been employed, but they weren't hiring. It took him five months to find his current job with Bonnie's Barricades—far more arduous work, at lower wages than he had been paid at EMCO more than 20 years earlier. "I know I'll never be able to earn 11.80 an hour again," he says. "The most I can hope for is a seven-dollar-an-hour job that doesn't involve swinging sandbags. Maybe if I come home less tired at the end of the day, I can handle an evening job."

This year did not get off to a good start for Kenny. In January, he hocked two rings that Bonita had given him for a hundred dollars, in order to pay a utility bill. Then, three months later, true to form, Kenny spotted two rings at a local pawnshop that he wanted Bonita to have—a 199-dollar opal ring and a 399-dollar diamond-cluster ring. He asked the pawnshop owner to take the two rings out of the showcase and agreed to make periodic 20 dollar payments on them until they were paid off.

Kenny was not worried about how he would pay for the rings, or how he would pay for the family's annual summer vacation. In September of last year, a few days after the Mertens returned from that summer's driving trip, his Grand Am was rear-ended. After the collision, in which Kenny hurt his back, he hired a lawyer on a contingency basis. The young man who had caused the accident had adequate insurance, and Kenny expected to be reimbursed for medical bills and lost wages. (He hadn't been permitted to lift heavy objects for several weeks.) He also expected the insurance company to pay a sizable sum—10 or 15 thousand dollars—for pain and suffering. Kenny's lawyer told him that he could expect the insurance company to settle with him by March. When the insurance money failed to arrive that month, Kenny's lawyer told him to expect an offer in April, then in May, and then in June. In early July, the lawyer said that he could get Kenny 6,500 dollars by the end of the month—just in time to save the Mertens' summer vacation. The insurance payment and the annual vacation had been the focus of Bonita's attention for seven months. "If you don't go on vacation, a year has gone by with nothing to show for it," she says.

Bonita wanted the family to travel to Seattle to visit Todd because he had a new home and she was eager to see it. The Mertens made meticulous plans for a driving trip to the state of Washington. They decided they would get up at 4 A.M. on Saturday, August 5th, and drive to Rapid City, South Dakota. They would visit Mt. Rushmore, and Kenny, who has an eye for landscapes, would take photographs of the Devils Tower, in Wyoming, at sunrise and sunset. They would arrive at Todd's home on Wednesday, August 9th, spend a few days there, and return to Des Moines, by way of the Mall of America, in Bloomington, Minnesota, on August 19th. Both Bonita and Kenny had arranged with their employers to take one week off with pay and one without.

Six days before their departure, however, their lawyer called with crushing news; the insurance payment would not be arriving until September. The following evening, Bonita injured her shoulder lifting a patient at the nursing home, but she was still determined to have her vacation. Although Kenny was behind on almost all his bills—he had just borrowed 75 dollars from David to pay a water bill—he went to a bank and to his credit union on August 2nd to borrow 2,500 dollars to cover the cost of the vacation, figuring he would pay off this newest loan from the insurance money in September. On the evening of August 2nd, Bonita reinjured

her shoulder while helping another aide transfer a resident from her wheelchair to her bed.

Both the bank and the credit union turned Kenny down. Not only did he have too much outstanding debt of his own but he had also cosigned a loan on his half brother Bob's car. Without being able to borrow, the Mertens could not go on vacation. To make matters worse, Luther Park had sent Bonita to a doctor, and he informed her that she would require physical therapy three times a week for the next two weeks. The vacation would have to be cancelled. "When Kenny told me he'd been turned down for the loan, his jaw dropped about two inches," Bonita recalls. "Kenny was so shocked and disappointed for me that I couldn't be disappointed for myself."

The Mertens have had their share of disappointments, but they don't stay down long. On the morning they had set aside to pack for their trip, Bonita baked banana bread. That evening, after she finished work, Kenny took the whole family out to dinner. From there they drove to Blockbuster and bought two videos—"Sister Act 2" (David had loved the original) and a Beatles movie. They also rented two movies, and a video game that Christopher wanted. The boys spent the following week at their grandmother's. During the second vacation week, Bonita took David to the Iowa State Fair, in town. "Me and David really had fun together," she says.

Both Mertens spent a little money during the two weeks that they didn't go out West. Bonita made a payment to Fingerhut on a shelf that she had bought for David's room and on a game that she had bought him, and she finished paying Home Interiors for some mirrors, sconces, and a gold shelf that she had bought for her bedroom. "When I buy this stuff, I can see Kenny getting a little perturbed, but he doesn't say anything," she says. Later in August, the front brakes on Kenny's Blazer failed, and replacement parts cost about a hundred dollars. The labor would have cost him twice that much, but Eunice, the next-door neighbor, gave him some furniture that she no longer needed, and he bartered the furniture with a friend who is an auto mechanic. Kenny and Bonita agreed that driving with faulty brakes through the mountains on their way West would have been dangerous, so it was a blessing in disguise that they had been forced to remain at home.

On Friday, September 22nd, Kenny, feeling unusually fatigued, decided to take the day off from work. After lunch, he drove Bonita to their lawyer's office. The insurance company had agreed to pay Kenny 7,200 dollars. The lawyer would get a third—2,400 dollars—and Kenny owed 1,200 dollars in medical bills, so he would net 3,600 dollars. He had wanted more—to pay off more of his debts and bills—but this was three days after Bonita's lucky potato strike, and she was feeling optimistic. She persuaded Kenny to put the agony of waiting behind them and to accept the offer.

The next day, Kenny drove Bonita, David, and Christopher to the pawnshop. The proprietor, Doug Schlegel, was expecting them. At the cash register, Doug handed Kenny a small manila envelope with the opal ring inside. "Hey, Kiddo!" Kenny called out to Bonita as he removed the ring from the envelope. "Come here!"

Bonita tried to kiss Kenny, but he quickly moved away. "I love you," she said. After Bonita finished working the opal ring down the third finger of her left hand, checking to see whether it fitted properly, Doug told her, "You don't want to let it sit in the sun or put it in hot water."

"I know," Bonita said. "Opals are soft and touchy. They're my birthstone. I have one I bought for myself, but this is lots prettier."

Once the Mertens were back in the Blazer, Bonita asked Kenny, "Is the opal my birthday present?" Her 49th birthday was coming up in two weeks.

"It's a prebirthday present," Kenny replied. He didn't mention his plan to give her the more expensive ring—the one with the diamond cluster—for Christmas, provided he could make the payments in time.

"Thank you, Kenny. I love you," Bonita said.

"Sure," Kenny said. "You love to pick on me and drive me crazy."

Bonita touched Kenny's hand. "Leave me alone, I'm driving," he told her.

When Kenny stopped at a red light, Bonita said, "You're not driving now." But the light suddenly turned green.

Throughout the fall, Kenny Merten refused to fret over the very real possibility that he would have to file for bankruptcy again if he didn't get his financial house in order. He was thinking only as far ahead as Christmas—imagining himself putting the box that held the diamond-cluster ring for Bonita under the tree in their living room and marking it "Open this one last." Kenny predicts that when his brothers-in-law see the ring they will surely disapprove, but he doesn't care. "The rings shouldn't be in the budget, but they are," he says.

Kenny's mother's short life left him with a determination to marry once and to make that marriage succeed—something that few of his relatives have done. Bonita has often said that one reason she loves Kenny is that he surprises her every once in a while.

"Diamonds are a girl's best friend, next to her husband," Kenny says. "And Bonita's worth that ring, every bit of it. After all, she puts up with me."

READING 4-2

The Black Middle Class

Mary Patillo

On a tour of Chicago's neighborhoods, our jumbo coach bus drove through a predominantly African

---

Mary Patillo-McCoy, "The Black Middle Class" from *Black Picket Fences: Privilege and Peril Among the Black Middle Class.* Copyright © 1999. Reprinted with permission of the author and The University of Chicago Press.

American neighborhood not too far from Groveland, and just about as middle class. It was a cold autumn morning, and the tree-lined streets were completely empty. Yet there were conspicuous clues that somebody cared deeply about this neighborhood. Matching lampposts stood like sentries at the edge of each home's neat lot. Welcoming block-club placards on the corners—"Please Drive Slowly"—conveyed a concern for children who might be too engrossed in play to mind the traffic. The occasional candy wrapper or grocery bag on a few lawns did not ruin the overall tidiness. The homes with fresh paint, edged grasses, and decorative screen doors outnumbered the properties of loafers who had ceded victory to the weeds, or refused to sweep the sidewalk. As we took in the pleasant sights, our learned Chicago tour guide, who was white, reported to our group of sightseers, most of whom were also white, "From looking at it, some of you all might think this is a predominantly white neighborhood, but actually this neighborhood is all black." He spoke as if he had let us in on a little secret.

The guide's comment, dressed in its disclosing tone, initially struck me as narrow-minded, since I had, after all, grown up in a like neighborhood, and was not at all surprised by this find in Chicago. Yet with the near completeness of racial segregation in many large American cities, it would indeed be difficult for many whites to just happen upon a place like Groveland. For the most part—and especially in cities like Chicago, Milwaukee, St.Louis, Detroit, Newark, Buffalo, Philadelphia, and so on—African Americans live on the "black side of town," and whites on the "white side of town."[1] To a somewhat lesser extent and depending on the city, Hispanic and Asian American groups each have their "side of town," too. People's routine patterns ensure that they have little reason or opportunity to see Groveland and neighborhoods like it. The average nonblack citizen's ignorance of these enclaves is bolstered by the common belief in academia that the black middle class actually moved away from black

neighborhoods after the 1960s, leaving behind their poorer former neighbors. Recognizing all this, perhaps black middle-class neighborhoods *are* a secret. And the black middle class, while far from a secret, is shrouded in misperception.

Groveland's first generation of residents who entered adulthood in the immediate post–World War II era remember a time of largesse. With their stable jobs and in search of better housing, African American college-educated professionals move to Groveland. Along with them came customer service representatives, hairdressers, transit employees, and railroad workers. All earned enough to buy a home and perhaps send the children to Catholic school, or take a yearly trip back Down South. They replaced the white residents who were also benefiting from postwar prosperity, and were looking to move to the growing suburbs. Far from integration, the change in Groveland was complete racial turnover. As Groveland's African American residents established their stake in the neighborhood, the statues of Jesus in the old neighborhood churches were painted darker, the restaurants started serving soul food, and the drugstores stocked black haircare products. In their new, attractive neighborhood, Groveland's first generation began to reap the benefits of the civil rights movement.

The expansion of the black middle class in the 1950s, 1960s, and very early 1970s came to a halt in the last two-and-a-half decades of the twentieth century. The generations that followed Groveland's African American pioneer settlers have found it progressively more difficult to match what their parents amassed in those days of plenty. Executive profit-hoarding, corporate and government downsizing, and global labor markets have pillaged the wallets of the American middle class, both white and black. But with lower incomes and a flimsier financial cushion, African Americans are more susceptible than whites to slipping back down the class ladder. A contemporary profile of the black middle class reveals that higher-paid professionals and executives do not predominate as they do among the white middle class. Instead, office workers, salespeople, and technical consultants—all lower-middle-class jobs—make up the majority of black middle-class workers. Working-class African Americans, who have been even harder hit by production shifts, are also an integral part of neighborhoods like Groveland. Linda Brewer, a Groveland resident in her mid-thirties, listed the jobs that anchored her parent's generation. "A lot of these people around here, you know, post office workers, steel mills. They father had two jobs," she reflected. "But them jobs are no longer here. So now they kids are poor." The second generation, of which Linda is a member, struggles to buy homes, or maintain the houses their parents purchased. Along with the third generation of teenagers and young adults, they are somewhat bewildered by the fact that without a college degree, they often have to live with their parents in order to get full consumption and leisure mileage out of their lower-middle-class paychecks. The black middle class is particularly fragile. As Anna Morris summarized, "I get enough to get by. I don't get any more. I take care of my children. I think we're sort of well-to-do, but who could say. You could go any way any day."

In addition to being acutely affected by economic changes in production and the distribution of incomes, members of the black middle class are also unique in the kinds of neighborhoods in which they live. Racial segregation and disproportionate black poverty operate to cordon off black communities with higher poverty rates than equally segregated white communities. As the geographic span of high-poverty areas has expanded since the 1970s (Jargowsky 1997), they continue to push into nearby black middle-class neighborhoods. Groveland's unemployment and poverty rates have risen consistently since the 1970s. Black middle-class neighborhoods like Groveland subsequently have more crime, fewer services and resources, less political clout, and less adequate schools than most white neighborhoods. In the case of crime, the homicides that fill the evening news occur only a few blocks from the quiet streets of Groveland. Too often they happen in the neighborhood, challenging residents to devise strategies to keep their own children safe.

Parents, block-club leaders, church members, and all others who work toward keeping control of crime and disorder in Groveland make much use of the strong family and friendship ties that have developed since blacks first moved into the neighborhood. Instead of being despised aliens, the gang members and drug dealers in the neighborhood are recognized as someone's cousins, someone's grandchildren. This familiarity does not necessarily mean that residents are soft on the general problems of crime and violence. The landlord of a three-flat building in Groveland angrily addressed the police at a beat meeting. "I don't want no drug dealin' in or around my buildin'," the woman said out of frustration with the young men who had set up their illegal business in her rental property. "I got good tenants in that building and I want to keep them. If you need me, I'll go press charges. I want them in jail. I want 'em locked up." Yet despite these frequent and impassioned demands for beefed-up police protection, the simple fact that many residents have known each other for years often works to make Grovelandites feel more comfortable than would a squad car on every corner. At the same police beat meeting, Mr. McArthur, who was a youthful seventy years old, shared with his fellow residents how safe he felt on the streets of Groveland because the neighborhood youth involved in the drug trade are in fact the same kids he had watched as children.

> On my block I can walk up and down the street at any time of day or night. And my wife and daughter can too. I can walk down my street any time. And it's like a' inner fear they have. The kids that are out there doin' wrong, they know they doin' wrong and know they better not do nothin' in front of me. But I can walk down my street anytime

because I feel safe walkin' in my community, 'cause I've known these little kids since they was growin' up. And I tell you, I feel safe anytime out there because they're out there twenty-four hours a day. I feel bad callin' the police on these little kids 'cause every time I walk past, they are so nice [asking], "How you doin', Mr. McArthur? How you been?"

The dense networks across the lines of legitimacy, and fostered by residential stability, present a double-edged sword. Grovelandites, while not apathetic, make compromises on the destruction that gangs and drugs can bring because they also find certain comfort in their protective reach.

For Groveland youth, close-knit neighborhood life translates into a diverse group of role models. In their families, among their peer group, at school, and on their block, they have within their reach the ingredients for success, as well as the easy opportunity to join the wrong crowd. Again, it is the composition of black middle-class neighborhoods and the communities within which they are embedded that produces such a range of choices. While black middle-class families are indeed important "social buffers" (Wilson 1987) in the African American community,[2] their health is simultaneously under strain, because living with and near poverty exerts negative pressures on youth. Higher poverty rates mean that a sizable minority of the youth in black middle-class neighborhoods will be attracted to the financial perks of crime. With the opportunities in place, middle-class youth are also drawn to the fast money. White middle-class families and their children, who generally live in much more class-homogeneous neighborhoods, do not experience these same pressures.

Yet the *opportunity* to experiment in crime is not enough to account for the decision to sell drugs or join gangs by youth like Tyson Reed, whose mother sent him to the best schools and was herself a successful educator. Like other youth, black and white, Tyson and his peers revere popular-culture styles that valorize the ex-

citement of deviance. Tyson Reed was attracted to the flair of the underworld, despite his extensive middle-class exposures. He was quite cognizant of his mediating perch.

'Cause it's good to be educated and it's good to have the street sense. But sometimes it's bad just to be a hoodlum [who] don't know no better. Then sometimes it's real bad to be a damn nerd. You can have all the book smarts in the world, you ain't gon' make it in the real world. But then again, you could be the biggest hoodlum in the world and if you ain't got book sense, you know, law sense, you ain't gon' make it either. So, that's why I always felt it was best to have both of 'em.

Like Tyson, Spider also enjoyed straddling different worlds. Spider's father moved from Groveland into a predominantly white suburb. "It's quiet out there," he said about the suburbs. "Then, when it got too quiet, I come back out South for some good ol' South Side violence. Hear some guns shootin' off in the alley behind the crib [house]. Damn, I feel at home!" Liking the quiet of the suburbs, but simultaneously getting a thrill from the sound of gunshots, Spider melds "decent" and "street" orientations (Anderson 1991, 1994).

Despite their middle-class background, some youth are "seduced" by the criminal lifestyle (Katz 1988). They see Lance—the neighborhood's top-ranking Black Mobster—with a new Cadillac every few months, a mink coat, designer outfits, matching gym shoes, and the attentions of both women and men. The undecorated life of the teacher next door never inspires such awe. Groveland's teenage boys learn that money and power—no matter how they are earned—boost their status in the games of adolescent courtship. A young, overweight local kid named Kareem had no chance of winning a neighborhood beauty like Neisha Morris with either his looks or his sincere affections. But after Kareem moved up in the gang and began to profit from its drug business, Neisha grew fonder of him. For these reasons, some youth and young adults find the fast life more appealing than a safe middle-class existence.

Their attraction to the flashy lifestyle of the "gangsta" is nurtured by mass cultural productions. Black youth are an important target audience for marketers like Nike, whose shoes are ubiquitous in Groveland. Mass-culture industries employ black entertainers and athletes to endorse their products, and include black cultural themes in their advertising. More important, commercials, television shows, music, and the movies market more than just consumer goods. They market lifestyles. Gangster movies (black or otherwise), violent video games, fashion magazines, and rap music all supply the lifestyle images that young people in Groveland enjoy. Some of the behavior in Groveland clearly imitates this fantasy-world of the mass media.

White youth, of course, also contribute to Nike's multi-billion-dollar revenues. They also bomb each other playing Sega video games, line up to see the latest repackaging of *Scarface,* and try to walk with the bold swagger of gangsta rappers. Adolescence is color-blind in its demands for excitement and its propensity to test the boundaries. Groveland's young people are not alone in their attractions to the fast life. But the stakes are higher for Groveland youth. Gun violence is a more serious reality in black communities. When Ray Gibbs got involved with the gang in Groveland, he wound up getting shot as he walked through a nearby rival neighborhood. Ray survived the wound and his delinquent ventures into selling drugs, but fifteen-year-old Brandon Johnson—church youth-group member, YMCA participant, and young Black Mobster—did not. Even the youth who do not officially join the gang, and never commit a delinquent act, but who mimic media gangstas in their fashions, language, walk, and general disposition, are at risk of being misread by the more devoted badmen, or by the official agents of social control, like the police. Because of the mix of residents that poverty and segregation produce, the penalties for following the typ-ical adolescent urge for excitement can be severe in a neighborhood like Groveland, even for black middle-class youth. . .

RACE, CLASS, AND PLACE

African Americans have made impressive socioeconomic gains in this country, especially since World War II. Educational attainment has increased and performance has improved. The poverty rate for blacks, while still alarmingly high, is well below the 80 percent black poverty rate in 1950 (Jaynes and Williams 1989). Blacks have a visible presence in politics, business, and entertainment. And the black middle class has grown in terms of both absolute numbers and its proportion in the black community overall.

The status of the black middle class should be of paramount importance to those interested in the future of African Americans as a group. These are families and individuals who have invested in education and hard work in order to climb the occupational hierarchy into white-collar professional, sales, clerical, managerial, and entrepreneurial occupations. The older generation, born in the South, battled racist laws and practices and accepted the risks of northern migration to attain their present positions. Now they hold stable middle-class occupations as nurses, insurance brokers, phone operators, and managers. They have captured the American Dream of a single-family home with a backyard and a two-car garage. Some can afford elite private schools for their children, and many are able to retire with a solid pension, equity in their homes, and successful children to look after them. Yet despite these middle-class characteristics, African American families like the ones in Groveland still face unique economic, sociospatial, and cultural perils. The experience of middle-class status is not uniform across groups. Instead, it is colored by the crosscutting reality of race.

There are many manifestations of simultaneous racial and class stratification. As an example, the black middle class is disproportionately dependent on public-sector employment (Collins 1983, 1989; Freeman 1976; Grant et al. 1996; Steinberg 1995; Owens 1998). Government jobs have been the most positively affected by affirmative action policies (Leonard 1984, 1991), and the system of government-provided professional and social services that grew after the 1960s has been heavily staffed by black employees. Therefore, blacks are clustered in local, state, and federal jobs that interface with the black community. Even in the private sector, black workers and black businesses perform segregated functions that cater to a black clientele (Collins 1983, 1993). This stratified labor-market arrangement makes middle-class black occupations particularly vulnerable to waning public support for affirmative action and the fiscal support of welfare and social services.

Other examples of the intersection of race and class are the disparities in wealth (Jaynes and Williams 1989; Oliver and Shapiro 1995) and the daily experiences of racism (Cose 1993; Feagin and Sikes 1994). Regarding the latter, Harvard University professor Cornel West was reminded that neither money, nor education, nor prestige negated the fact that he was black. One empty cab after the next passed him as he attempted to get to a photo session to take pictures for the cover of his book. Middle-class blacks continue to face racial obstacles, and have yet to attain parity with whites.

The stories of Groveland families add the importance of *place* to this evidence of racial and class stratification. The lives of Grovelandites cannot, of course, speak for those of black middle-class Americans across the country. There are substantial regional differences; African Americans in some western and southern cities experience less racial segregation than those in the Rust Belt cities of the North and Northeast. Southern African Americans who stayed South while their relatives flocked to the North have yet another story to tell. Black immigrants from Africa or from the Caribbean islands bring an-

other history and lifestyle to what it means to be black and middle class. No research of the kind conducted in Groveland could characterize the diversity of black middle-class experiences. However, we do know that a slight majority of African Americans nationwide (53 percent) live in census tracts where over half of their neighbors are also African American, and the majority of these areas are not low-income neighborhoods (Urban Studies Group 1997). If only in terms of their residence in predominantly black, nonpoor neighborhoods, Groveland's residents share much in common with other black families across the country. The ecological context of black middle-class families is a basic feature of difference between the white and black middle class. The location of black middle-class neighborhoods dictates the experiences to which black middle-class youth will be exposed. Living near blighted, poor neighborhoods with substandard schools, crumbling institutions, and few businesses presents an extra challenge to managing the negative influences on black middle-class children.

Groveland parents try to curtail their children's negative involvements. They set limits on where their children can travel. They choose activities—church youth groups, magnet schools or accelerated programs in the local school, and the Boy Scouts and Girl Scouts—to increase the likelihood that their children will learn positive values and associate with youth from similar families. Still, many parents are working long hours to maintain their middle-class incomes. They cannot be with their children at all times. On their way to the grocery store or to school or to music lessons, Groveland's youth pass other young people whose parents are not as strict, who stay outside later, who have joined the local gang, or who earn enough money being a lookout at a drug house to buy new gym shoes. They also meet these peers in school and at the park, and in their music lessons as well. For some teenagers, the fast life looks much more exciting than what their parents have to offer them, and they are drawn to it. The simple fact of living in a neighborhood where not all families have sufficient resources to direct their children away from deviance makes it difficult for parents to ensure positive outcomes for their children and their neighborhood. For African Americans, then, there is a unique middle-class experience.

Middle class is a loaded term. As an economic term it is the most straightforward. It is relatively easy to look at the full distribution of incomes in the nation and slice out some "middle" proportion. Everyone captured in this range falls in the middle class by economic standards. But does that really jibe with what people think of when they say "middle class"? In casual or popular usage, the label "middle class" is often closer to the non-economic notion of "mainstream." When that comparison is explicitly recognized, the normative nature of the term becomes clear. "Mainstream" compared to whose "stream"? "Mainstream" in all realms, or only in key arenas like family and work, and who decides? "Mainstream" by today's standards or in a nostalgic sense? Can nonwhites even *be* "mainstream"?

The answers to these questions indicate that while "mainstream" and "middle class" may both be normative judgments in their lay use, the road to reaching middle-class status is structured by economic, political, and social forces that are larger than any one individual's efforts. If the spatial incarnation of "middle class" is actually "suburban," then African Americans are less able to be middle class by virtue of a history and present of racist lending, rental, and selling practices. If the cultural manifestation of "middle class" includes only those who almost always speak Standard English, then African Americans—along with immigrant groups and some rural whites—are disadvantaged because segregation affects the degree of exposure to those who decide what English vernacular is acceptable. If going to a good school is an educational component of being "mainstream," then

fewer blacks can be so labeled because of how their poorer neighborhoods undergird the discrepancies in school funding. And if "mainstream" means growing up with two biological parents, then a goodly proportion of both blacks and whites fall short of the bar. Black marriages may be especially at risk because of financial strains, but ever fewer Americans of all races can sustain the mainstream two-parent goal. The point in wading through this list of "mainstream-isms" is to illustrate that if African Americans are less likely to measure up to the normative notion of "middle class," it has much to do with the barriers that they face to reaching such a status.

Yet African American families make do with what they have, as the residents of Groveland illustrate. They mix strong cultural traditions with their economic resources to come up with their own "mainstream" practices. The role of the extended family is perhaps the best illustration of how black middle-class families adapt to an increasingly precarious economic context, following in the tradition of how poor African American families have coped with poverty. There were countless families in Groveland that flourished only because of the combined time and money resources and emotional help of many family members, sometimes all in one house and sometimes spread across the neighborhood and city. The family is the basis for upward mobility, as Terri Jones's family exemplified. Her mother's and aunts' strategy of having two sisters work outside the home and one work inside the home while watching the children allowed each to prosper. And Mr. Graham's four-generation family rests on his hard work and the constant help he gives, especially in the forms of babysitting and providing the home that his daughters can always come back to. The extended family is also the unit that is supportive in times of financial crisis. Mrs. French's daughter was solidly middle class until she split up with her husband, and then had to move with her son back to her parents' house. "Mainstream" might privilege the nuclear family model, but in reaction to their mostly lower-middle-class incomes, Groveland families keep alive a culturally based emphasis on the extended family in order to maintain an economically middle-class standard of living.

To manage the neighborhood context, Groveland families utilize the existing relationships between the do-gooders and the lawbreakers. A narrow definition of "middle class" might not include being friends with or a relative to a gang member or a drug dealer. But such a definition does not recognize the contingencies of being black and middle class. In order to achieve the "quiet neighborhood" that many Grovelandites agree that they have, the park supervisor allows the Black Mobsters to play dominoes in the field house, and the activists work with Lance despite his criminal position to vote the neighborhood dry. These are the mainstream behaviors that Grovelandites enact in light of their unique ecological situation.

Finally, Groveland youth adapt to the cultural context by balancing the mass-media imperatives of being a gangsta with "decent" aspirations, activities, and involvements. White middle-class youth are also attracted to the same "street" characters that are widespread in popular-culture productions. But young Grovelandites must be more vigilant in separating style from behavior, and particularly aware of who is reading their styles, and how those styles might be interpreted. In its conventional usage, "middle class" might exclude wearing baggy jeans or rapping along to an explicit song about rough sex and gunplay, but Groveland youth perform these styles simultaneously with participating in the church youth group, or going off to college.

The black middle class challenges the definition of middle class and mainstream, which follows a kind of majority-rule logic. Middle class and mainstream are both based on a white American model, which does not allow for the structurally and culturally determined adjustments that nonwhite groups must make to being middle class. Moreover, if there were a more developed literature on the lifestyles of the white middle class, the entire construct might buckle under the evidence that not even white families measure up. The findings might expose the pretense that the white middle class uniformly ascribes to and follows "mainstream" standards. Gangs, drugs, teenage sex, family dissolution, economic hardship, and generational cultural cleavages all exist among the white middle class. While there are fundamental axes upon which the black middle class differs, the white middle class may also exhibit behavioral adaptations that diverge from the sanitized notions of middle class and mainstream. Whatever the scenario among whites, the "mainstream" families in Groveland broaden the definition to include African Americans who speak both Black English and Standard English, who are single mothers, and who live next door to a drug dealer.

ENDNOTES

1. Massey (1996, 405) notes that the cities classified as "hypersegregated" in 1990 "contain 11 million African Americans, who together constitute 36% of the black population."

2. Wilson (1987, 7) writes that the presence of black working- and middle-class families "provided stability to inner-city neighborhoods and reinforced and perpetuated mainstream patterns of norms and behavior," and that "the black middle-class self-consciously imposed cultural constraints on lower-class culture" (1987, 55), and, finally, that in vertically integrated neighborhoods, there were a "sufficient number of working- and middle-class professional families to absorb the shock or cushion the effect of uneven economic growth and periodic recessions on inner-city neighborhoods" (1987, 144).

REFERENCES

Anderson, Elijah. 1991. "Neighborhood Effects on Teenage Pregnancy." pp. 375–98 in *The Urban Underclass*. Christopher Jencks and Paul E. Peterson, eds. Washington, D.C.: Brookings Institution.

———. 1994. "The Code of the Streets." *Atlantic Monthly* 273: 80–94.

Collins, Sharon M. 1983. "The Making of the Black Middle Class." *Social Problems* 30: 369–82.

———. 1989. "The Marginalization of Black Executives." *Social Problems* 36: 317–31.

———. 1993. "Blacks on the Bubble: The Vulnerability of Black Executives in White Corporations." *Sociological Quarterly* 34: 429–47.

Cose, Ellis. 1993. *The Rage of a Privileged Class*. New York: HarperCollins.

Feagin, Joe R., and Melvin P. Sikes. 1994. *Living with Racism: The Black Middle-Class Experience*. Boston: Beacon Press.

Fernandez, Roberto, and David Harris. 1992. "Social Isolation and the Underclass." pp. 257–93 in *Drugs, Crime, and Social Isolation: Barriers to Opportunity*. Adele Harrel and George Peterson, eds. Washington, D.C.: Urban Institute Press.

Freeman, Richard B. 1976. *Black Elite: The New Market for Highly Educated Black Americans*. New York: McGraw-Hill.

Grant, David, Melvin Oliver, and Angela James. 1996. "African Americans: Social and Economic Bifurcation." pp. 379–409 in *Ethnic Los Angeles*. Roger Waldinger and Mehdi Bozorgmehr, eds. New York: Russell Sage Foundation.

Jargowsky, Paul. 1997. *Poverty and Place: Ghettos, Barrios, and the American City*. New York: Russell Sage.

Jaynes, Gerald, and Robin Williams, eds. 1989. *A Common Destiny: Blacks and American Society*. Washington, D.C.: National Research Council.

Katz, Jack. 1988. *Seductions of Crime: Moral and Sensual Attractions of Doing Evil*. Stanford: Stanford University Press.

Leonard, Jonathan S. 1984. "Employment and Occupational Advance under Affirmative Action." *Review of Economics and Statistics* 66: 377–85.

———. 1991. "The Federal Anti-Bias Effort." *Essays on the Economics of Discrimination*. Emily Hoffman, ed. Kalamazoo, Mich.: Upjohn Institute for Employment Research.

Massey, Douglas. 1996. "The Age of Extremes: Concentrated Affluence and Poverty in the Twenty-First Century." *Demography* 33: 395–412.

Oliver, Melvin L., and Thomas M. Shapiro. 1995. *Black Wealth/White Wealth: A New Perspective on Racial Inequality*. New York: Routledge.

Owens, Michael Leo. 1998. "Government Jobs and Black Neighborhoods in New York City." Paper presented at the New York State Political Science Association meeting, Ithaca, New York.

Steinberg, Stephen. 1995. *Turning Back: The Retreat from Racial Justice in American Thought and Policy*. Boston: Beacon Press.

Wilson, William Julius. 1987. *The Truly Disadvantaged: The Inner City, the Underclass and Public Policy*. Chicago: University of Chicago Press.

CHAPTER 5

Race, Ethnicity, and Families

In 1903 the great African-American sociologist W. E. B. DuBois wrote in his book, *The Souls of Black Folk,* that "the problem of the twentieth century is the problem of the color line—the relation of the darker to the lighter races of men in Asia and Africa, in America, and the islands of the sea." Nearly a century later, the "problem" of color still looms large in discussions of American society, including family life. DuBois was referring to the difference between African-Americans and Americans of European descent. Although that black/white distinction is still a central part of American life, there are other "colors" now. The largest of the newer groups is comprised of people who speak Spanish and mostly trace their ancestry through Latin America. In the American political discourse they are increasingly lumped together as "Hispanics," even though there are sharp differences among the major Hispanic groups.

It's well known that the family patterns of African-Americans, non-Hispanic whites, and Hispanic groups such as Mexican Americans or Puerto Ricans differ in ways such as the prevalence of single-parent families and childbearing outside of marriage. But does this mean that family ties are weaker and assistance is less forthcoming? In the following excerpt from her book, *No Shame in My Game: The Working Poor and the Inner City,* anthropologist Katherine S. Newman describes the family lives of young African-Americans and Hispanics who worked for a fast-food restaurant chain in Harlem that she calls "Burger Barn." These young people and their families are part of the "working-poor," the millions of Americans whose low-wage jobs barely provide them with enough money to get by. Newman does not romanticize their family lives, but she tries to place both family strengths and family limitations in the context of life at the margins of poverty.

Newman's study suggests that part—although by no means all—of the differences in the family lives of racial and ethnic groups is really a reflection of the class differences among them. But because racial and ethnic group membership is easier to see than class membership, our public discussions often focus on race and ethnicity more than class. In fact, the public dialog about race has, if anything, become more intense in recent years. Lillian B. Rubin explored the reasons for the focus on race in the thinking of working-class families in her book, *Families on the Fault Line.* She argues, in part, that white working-class men and women, who often are struggling to get by in an unfriendly economy, find it easy to blame the groups below them—blacks and immigrants—for their economic troubles. Twenty years earlier, Rubin had interviewed families for her critique of working-class family life, *Worlds of Pain.* In the early 1990s, she reinterviewed many of these families and interviewed some new families. In this excerpt, she recounts her last visits to two of the families, one black and one Mexican American. Their comments provoked her to speculate on why race and ethnicity are still such major factors in the lives of working-class families.

READING 5-1

Family Values

Katherine Newman

Rosa Lee Cunningham, the subject of Leon Dash's Pulitzer Prize–winning series in the *Washington Post,* is an epitome of poverty for the end of the twentieth century.[1] Born the eldest girl in a Washington, D.C., family that had been liberated from the privations of southern sharecropping only in the 1930s, Rosa Lee quickly spiraled down into oblivion. Rosa Lee's first child was born when she was a mere fourteen years old. By the time she was twenty-four, Rosa Lee's children numbered eight and their six fathers were nowhere to be seen. She raised her kids on her own by waitressing in nightclubs, selling drugs, and shoplifting. In the wake of her own disillusionment and the overwhelming burden of taking care of her children, Rosa Lee was drawn to heroin. When stealing to support her family and her habit proved unreliable, she sold herself on the street and then turned her own daughter into a hooker to maintain the needed cash flow.

Responses to Dash's series, and the book that followed, have taken a predictable path: reviewers have been as worried as they have been disgusted by the cultural disintegration Rosa Lee and her ilk represent. Rosa Lee, who could not stay away from men of questionable character, and then did disastrously poorly by the children that resulted, takes center stage as the prototypical underclass mother, the prime mover in her own despair. And the crime and degradation that follow are depicted as the inevitable result of a culture of poverty so deep that it defies remedy. No jobs program, no drug program, no heavenly social worker, can res-

cue someone like Rosa Lee Cunningham. She is a lost soul, with children condemned to repeat her mistakes,[2] while the rest of society suffers the consequences of predatory criminals in its midst.

Powerful portraits of this kind have shaped public impressions of inner-city families. They present implicit explanations for how poor people fall to the bottom of society's heap: by failing to control their impulses. American culture is predisposed to find such an explanation appealing, since it rests upon the view that people are masters of their own destinies, that they can, by dint of individual effort, control the circumstances of their lives. Those that fail fall to the ground where they belong, not because they have been denied opportunity, or are victims of forces larger than anyone could control, but because they have succumbed to temptation or lack the brains to do any better—the story told by Herrnstein and Murray's book *The Bell Curve.* It is a story as old as the Puritans and as resonant today as it was in the seventeenth century.

The inner city does indeed have more than its share of families like the Cunninghams. Their problems reflect the crushing personal costs of living in parts of our country where good jobs have gone the way of the dinosaurs, where schools can be hard to distinguish from penitentiaries, and where holding families together has become women's work, while the means to do so have become the object of a fierce competition. More than a few in central Harlem have found themselves in Rosa Lee's situation.

But they are a minority, and a despised one at that. They are so far from the accepted, approved personification of motherhood and family life that they do not even belong in the same world with the families of Latoya or Carmen. Journalists and scholars who write about the Rosa Lees of this world have focused their energies on those inner-city residents who are the most troubled and who inflict the greatest damage on their neighbors. Their passions are understandable, for in keeping with the spirit that animated the original War on Poverty, they want to reawaken America's conscience and persuade us that we have a cancer growing in the midst of our prosperity. That message worked effectively in the 1960s, when the country was bursting with economic growth, the middle class was secure in its comforts, and faith in the capacity of government to eradicate social ills had not yet been eviscerated.

The same message delivered in the 1990s has had the opposite impact. Focusing on the deviant cases, on the whoring mothers, the criminal fathers, the wilding teenagers, and the abandoned toddlers, merely confirms a knowing hopelessness or worse: a Darwinian conviction that perhaps we should just "let it burn," sacrificing the present generation in the hope of rehabilitating future ghetto dwellers. Attitudes have hardened in part as the litany of broken lives dominates the only "news" in print from the inner city.

It would be absurd to suggest that the downbeat reports are untrue. The "underclass" story is a persistent, intractable, and most of all depressing reality for those who cannot escape it. But there is a war for the soul of the ghetto, and it has two sides. On the other side of deviance lie the families who embrace mainstream values, even if they don't look like Ozzie and Harriet, who push their children to do better, even when they have not progressed far in life themselves. Indeed, these families—the working poor and many a "welfare family" as well—are the first to condemn the Rosa Lees of their own neighborhood, to point to them as examples of what they don't want to be.

Who is winning this culture war? What are the *dominant* values of inner-city residents? The sociological emphasis on separated subcultures in the inner city has ignored the power of mainstream models and institutions like schools, the influence of the media, the convictions of poor parents, and the power of negative examples to shape the moral world of the ghetto poor. We must not confuse the irregular social structures of families—which do indeed depart from the canonical forms of middle-class society—with a separate set of values. Structure and culture can diverge in ghetto society as they do elsewhere in this country.

FAMILY VALUES

Latoya has a complicated family tree. Her mother, Ilene, who is on disability because of her diabetes, lives in the Bronx, far enough away to be in another world. Latoya's father, Alvin, has had many jobs in the course of his adult life—working mainly as a truck driver—and has only recently, in his later years, become once again a constant presence in Latoya's life. His problems with alcohol have made him a nuisance at times, but he has been welcomed back into the extended family fold because "he's blood" and has, for now at least, made a sincere effort to leave the booze behind.

Many years ago, Latoya's father began living with Elizabeth, then a recent migrant from rural Georgia, from a sleepy little town where there was nothing much to do and nowhere to go. First chance she got, Lizzie had boarded a bus for New York and begun her lifelong career cleaning houses for wealthy whites on New York's Upper East Side. She has been doing domestic work now for about twenty-five years, during which she gave birth to two daughters, Natasha and Stephanie, Latoya's half sisters through the father they share.

Though Alvin has been only sporadically in the picture, Latoya, Natasha, and Stephanie became a devoted band of sisters who look to Lizzie as the spiritual and practical head of the family. Together they form an extended family of long standing. They live within a few blocks of one another; they attend church together, especially on the important holidays.

Latoya was the first of the sisters to land a job at Burger Barn, but she was able to get Natasha on the crew not long thereafter. The two half sisters have worked together, covering for one another, blowing off the steam generated by confrontational customers, and supporting one another in the face of problem-seeking managers for nearly five years now. Little sister Stephanie, a junior in high school who has also had a summer stint at the Barn, makes it possible for Latoya to maintain a steady presence at work. It falls to Stephanie to retrieve Latoya's children from their city-funded day care center and after-school programs on those days when Latoya has to work late. Stephanie is often the one who stays with her nieces and nephews when Latoya has to work the night shift. Natasha used to do the same for Latoya.

Without the support that Natasha and Stephanie provide, Latoya would have a very hard time holding on to her job. But if we reduced the role these sisters play in Latoya's life to the instrumental need for emergency child care, we would miss the true depth of their interdependence. This is really one family, spread over several physical households in a pattern that will be familiar to readers of Carol Stack's classic book *All Our Kin*. Stack describes the complex exchange relations that characterize the families of the "Flats," a poor community in southern Illinois where goods and people circulate in a never-ending swap system. Reciprocal relations provide mothers with an insurance system against scarcity, unpredictable landlords, jobs that come and go, AFDC checks that get cut off without warning, and men who give what they can but much of the time find they have little to contribute.

FAMILY CIRCLES—SUPPORT STRUCTURES AMONG THE WORKING POOR

No one in Latoya's extended family network is on welfare; the adults are all working, even Alvin, drinking problem and all. The children are in school. Yet because they are poor as well, these folk live in clusters of households that are perpetually intertwined. Although Latoya and Lizzie are separate "heads of households" as the Census Bureau might define them, in a very real sense they are one social system with moving

parts that cannot stand alone. The older sisters, Natasha and Latoya, go out to clubs together when they can get Stephanie to baby-sit; together they hatch surprise birthday celebrations for Lizzie. Joining forces with their cousins, aunts, and uncles, they haul turkeys and cranberries up the stairs to whichever apartment can hold the largest number of people when it is time to host the Thanksgiving feast. And when Christmas comes, Latoya's children, sisters, and cousins and Lizzie and Alvin dress up in their Sunday best and lay claim to nearly a whole pew in the Baptist church several blocks away. Lizzie complains that her children don't attend church in the regular way she does, a habit born of her southern origins. But like many American families, Latoya and her sisters honor their mother's attachment to the church and participate in this family ritual.

Latoya, Natasha, Stephanie, and Lizzie have deliberately stayed close to one another not only because they need one another for practical support but because they value family above all else. "Family are your best friends," Natasha explains. Latoya is Natasha's closest friend, the person she socializes with, the person she confides in, her defender at work, the woman she goes shopping with when they want to look their best after hours. Danielle, cousin to them both, is part of the same inner circle, and together with her children they all form a tightly knit extended family.

Indeed, Latoya's three children look upon their aunts, Natasha and Stephanie, as permanent members of their household, people they can depend on to braid their hair for church, answer the occasional homework question, and bring them home an illicit burger or two. It was rare to find Latoya and her children at home without one of her half sisters as well.

Public perceptions of America center around middle-class nuclear families as the norm, the goal toward which others should be striving. Yet in those suburban households, it would be rare to find the intensity of relations that knits these sisters and cousins together, keeping them in daily contact with one another. Middle-class Americans value autonomy, including autonomous relations between generations and siblings once they reach adulthood. And, of course, if they have a stable hold on a decent income, there is little forcing them together into the sort of private safety net that Latoya and her relatives maintain.

The same could be said, and then some, for the immigrant families who make up a significant part of Harlem's low-wage workforce. Dominicans, Haitians, Jamaicans, West Africans, and South Americans from various countries have settled in Harlem's outer pockets. Immigrant workers in the low-wage economy depend upon extensive family networks—composed of seasoned migrants who have lived in New York for some time and those newly arrived—to organize their housing, child care, and a pool of income that they can tap when the need arises. Streaming into New York in an age-old pattern of chain migration, immigrants are often faced with the need to support family members back home while they attempt to meet the far higher costs of living they encounter in their adopted city. Families that are ineligible for government benefits routinely provided to the native-born must work long hours, pack a large number of people into small apartments, and recruit as many wage earners into the network as possible.

Immigrants cluster into apartment buildings in much the same fashion as the African-American poor do, both because relatives have been instrumental in helping their family members find housing and because proximity makes it that much easier to organize collective child-minding or communal meals. In Carmen's building there are five households linked together by kinship connections. Their members move freely between them, opening the refrigerator door in one to see whether there's anything good to eat, watching television in another because it has a cable hookup, using the one phone that hasn't been cut off for nonpayment.

Carmen's grandmother watches her grandchildren, a half-dozen in all now, so that their parents can go to work.

Yet to really understand the meaning of family in Carmen's life, one has to look back to the Dominican Republic, where her mother and one of her sisters still live. Carmen had to leave her mother behind to join her father and his kin, a transition necessitated both by her ambitions and by the declining purchasing power of her mother's paycheck. Carmen sends back money whenever she can, usually once a month, and that remittance spells the difference between a decent standard of living in *La Republica* and a slide into poverty.[3] For Carmen, though, this is a poor substitute for the intimacy she longs for, the daily love and affection of her mother. What she really wants, more than anything in this world, is to obtain a green card so that she can sponsor her mother and younger sister in New York. Now that she is a young parent herself, she wants her own mother close by so that she does not have to depend exclusively on her paternal relatives. That prospect is far off, though, and Carmen has to be content with the occasional trip back to her homeland, something she manages once every two or three years.

For immigrants, then, the meaning of family stretches over the seas and persists through long absences. It is organized into daisy chains of people who have followed each other, one by one, and then settled into pockets that turn into ethnic enclaves dense with interlocking ties. Families that lived next door to one another in Haiti land on adjacent blocks in Harlem. The same pattern organizes the native migrants from America's rural South, who also put down roots in Harlem neighborhoods. One can still find blocks dominated by people from particular towns in Georgia or the Carolinas and their descendants. In this respect, the native-born and the international migrant share common settlement patterns, which, in turn, provide the social structure that is so vital to the survival of the working poor.

Well-heeled families can buy the services they need to manage the demands of work and family. They can purchase child care, borrow from banks when they need to, pay their bills out of their salaries, and lean on health insurance when a doctor is needed. Affluence loosens the ties that remain tight, even oppressive at times, in poor communities. Yet there is an enduring uneasiness in our culture about the degree of independence generations and members of nuclear families maintain from one another, a sense that something has been lost. We look back with nostalgia at the close-knit family ties that were characteristic of the "immigrant generations" of the past and that still bind together newcomers to our shores, for the same reasons immigrants clung together at the turn of the century.[4]

What we fail to recognize is that many inner-city families, especially the majority who work to support themselves, maintain these close links with one another, preserving a form of social capital that has all but disappeared in many an American suburb.[5] These strong ties are the center of social life for the likes of Latoya and Natasha. It is true that these family values compete with other ambitions: the desire for a nice house and a picket fence in a suburb where graffiti doesn't mar the scenery and mothers needn't worry constantly about street violence. They dream about the prospect of owning a home and garden somewhere far away from Harlem. Yet if that miracle day arrived, they would be faced with a serious dilemma: unless they could afford to take everyone near and dear to them along on the adventure, they would find it very hard to live with the distance such a move would put between them and their relatives.

Why do we assume that family values of this kind are a thing of the past in the ghetto? While the answer lies in part on the emphasis that writers have given to people like Rosa Lee, it is just as much an artifact of the way we confuse kinship structures with the moral culture of family life in the inner city. Very few of the people who work for Burger Barn live in households that resemble the Bill Cosby model. Most are adult children in single-parent households, and some are single parents themselves. Latoya, for example, divorced her first husband when he turned to drugs, and has for a number of years now had a common-law relationship with Jason, the father of her son, the youngest child (at age two) in her household. Jason has lived with Latoya's family most of this time, taking on much of the financial responsibility for Latoya's children, since his earnings as a skilled craftsman are much higher than her Burger Barn wages. Still, their relationship has had its ups and downs; they have broken up and reconciled more than once.

Family patterns of this kind certainly do not sound like suburban America, or at least not the middle-class culture we would like to believe defines mainstream life.[6] The instability of family organization in America's ghettos has been the source of much hand-wringing. There can be little doubt that children born out of wedlock face an uphill battle, as they are more likely to be raised in poverty,[7] and that children of divorce, no matter what segment of society they come from, are similarly disadvantaged.[8]

However, we should not assume that "irregular" household structures suggest a diminished regard for the importance of family life, for the closeness of kin. Even though Latoya anguishes over Jason during their rough spots, she is no less attached to or attentive to her children. She draws the rest of her kin, especially her female kin, closer to her and builds a nest of loving relatives who sustain the familial bond and help her create a stable environment for her children. Latoya's values place family, particularly the well-being of her children, at the top of her priorities. Were we to look at the structure of her household and focus only on the ways it deviates from the nuclear family norm, we would miss what is most important about it: the quality of the relationships inside and the links between them and the web of kin who live in nearby apartments. Without them, it is true, Latoya would have a difficult time sustaining order or protecting her children in the dicey neighborhood where they live. But her story is a success in part because it is a story of a family that has pulled together against considerable adversity.

Patty began her career ten years ago at Burger Barn. She worked full-time for the entire nine months of her first pregnancy and didn't leave work until the baby was born. She continued working and finished high school even though her second child was on the way. Her attachment to the job, through the thick-and-thin of a failed marriage and a stint on welfare, reflects the values her mother instilled. Patty's mother has worked all her life as a home attendant, first with mothers recently home from the hospital with their new babies in tow and then with homebound elderly. Working as a home aide was something of an upward step in the family, for Patty's maternal grandmother spent her whole life as a housekeeper.

> My grandmother, who just passed [away], was my idol all during the time I was growing up. She bought a house in Queens off scrubbing floors. She bought that house and mortgaged it two or three times, so she had to start all over paying it off. But she did it.

Hence Patty and her sister, who also is in home health care, taking care of AIDS patients, have come from a long line of women who have shouldered the burdens of earning a living and raising their children. None of them would have been able to manage these responsibilities were it not for the fact that each in turn has made the extended family the core of her life. Patty's mother lives on the sixth floor of her building and still has her son, Patty's brother, under her wing. Patty's sister lives just a few blocks away. Their proximity has made a big difference in Patty's life, for with their collective help, she has been able to go to work knowing that there are other adults in her family who can help watch her children.

This web of kinship does not supersede the individual household or substitute collective child-rearing for that of the mother-in-charge. Patty remains the main figure around whom her kids' lives revolve. She is the one who feeds and clothes them, watches over their homework, and puts the Band-Aids on when they skin their knees. She keeps them safe from the pitfalls of the streets that surround her apartment in a Harlem public housing complex. She has gone without things she needs for herself so she could afford air-conditioning and a Nintendo machine, items that sound like luxuries but turn out to be the key—or at least one key—to keeping her kids indoors and safe through the hot summer months. They must have something to play with and somewhere to cool off if she is to leave the teenagers to their own devices while she is working. At least equally important, however, is Patty's reliance upon her siblings and her mother as substitute supervisors of her kids, her adjunct eyes and ears, when she is at work. Without them, she would be faced with some unhappy choices. . .

"ABSENT" MEN

Popular accounts of the ghetto world often lament the declining presence of men—especially fathers—in the life of the family. Men are in jail in record numbers; they have no interest in marrying the mothers of their children; they "hit" and run. That men cause grief to the women and children who need them is hardly news. As the divorce statistics remind us, this is a sad story repeated in every class. All over America there are children who need fathers but don't have them. We have developed a culture, both in the ghetto and outside it, that assigns to women the responsibility for raising children, leaving men peripheral to the task.

This is not to minimize the difference between a jailed father and a divorced father, a poor father who has never married the mother of his children and a more affluent father who fails to pay child support. There are differences, and they have consequences. Survey research tells us, for example, that single-parent children of never-married mothers are more likely than those of divorced parents to drop out of high school, and that daughters of never-married mothers are more likely than those of divorced parents to become teen mothers—though, it should be added, the differences are not as large as some pundits might claim.[9]

Yet it would be drawing too broad a brush stroke to suggest that men have absented themselves wholesale from the inner city. Uncles, fathers, brothers, sons, boyfriends—and husbands—are very much in evidence in the daily comings-and-goings of working poor families in Harlem. They help to support the households they live in and often provide regular infusions of cash, food, and time to the mothers of their children with whom they do not live.[10] The Bureau of the Census or a sociologist looking at a survey could easily miss the presence of men in Harlem households where they do not officially live, but to which they are nonetheless important as providers. Juan, father of Kyesha's son, is a case in point. He regularly gives part of his paycheck to his mother, who has several younger children and has been on AFDC for as long as he can remember. Juan also gives money to Kyesha to help take care of their son. Little of this check is left by the time he takes care of everyone who depends on him.

> It is a struggle to make ends meet. Like if I plan on buying something that week, then I got to hold back on that. 'Cause we got cable and you got to help out, you know. Or say the lights got to be paid. So I give a hundred dollars this week, fifty the next week. My mother has a bad habit sometimes. She doesn't think reasonably. So sometimes a lot of money has to come out of my pocket—I pay whole bills so I can get that off my back.

When the welfare authorities discovered that Juan was giving his mother money, they moved to take away some of her grant. He countered by finding a couch to sleep on in a friend's apart-ment so that his mother could report that he no longer lives in her home.

Reynaldo, whose mother is Puerto Rican and father from Ecuador, is a jack-of-all-trades who worked for a brief time at Burger Barn in between various hustles as a nonunion electrician, car repairman, carpenter, and cellular phone dealer for fellow Latinos in his Dominican neighborhood. A tall, stocky young man with a love of baggy pants and gold chains, Rey is a classic entrepreneur. He mixes and matches his job opportunities, picking up anything he can get on the side. For a time he had a job stocking shelves in a drugstore, but during his off-hours he made money fixing up broken-down cars for neighbors and rewiring a vacant apartment for his landlord. Rey works all the hours that are not consumed by school, his girlfriend, and hanging out with his younger brother.

No doubt he is influenced in his own brand of workaholism by the example of his father, Ernie, who taught him much of what he knows about electrical and machine repair. Ernie has never met a mechanical device he couldn't tear down to the foundation and rebuild just like new. Outside on the street curb sit the broken-down Fords, Dodges, and GM cars that await his attention. His auto repair shop is just the sidewalk in front of their apartment building, but everyone in the neighborhood knows that this is a business venue. Ernie is forever walking around with a cloth in his hands, wiping away the grease and oil from an old car he has torn apart and made whole again. The shelves of the family's back room are crammed with blow-torches, pliers, hammers, wrenches, reels of plastic-coated wiring—all the equipment needed to fix the long line of radios and TV sets that friends and friends of friends have left behind for repair.

As if he weren't busy enough, Ernie has a lively sideline as an off-the-books contractor, renovating apartments destined for immigrant families just like his own. Old apartment buildings in the Dominican neighborhoods have bad plumbing, plaster weeping off the walls, tiles missing, caulking cracked and flaking, windows shattered and taped. Landlords claim to have little money for keeping apartments up to code and in any case prefer to use local workers and avoid union labor. Their preferences keep Ernie in work as the apartments turn over. In turn, Ernie has kept Rey at his side and taught him everything he knows so he can turn over some of the work he has no time for, maintaining the opportunity "in the family."

Rey's mother is a student, working toward an Associate in Arts degree that will, she hopes, make it possible for her to work in computer administration someday. Most of her days are spent going to a community college that is a long subway ride from home. Until Mayor Giuliani canceled the policy, her education was subsidized by the city welfare system (in an effort to further the long-term career prospects of women on AFDC). After many years of working in a bra factory, she has come to understand the importance of credentials and is determined to accumulate them so that she can get a good job with decent pay.

Rey's younger brother, now sixteen, has staked his future on the prospect of going to college, for he seems to have the academic gifts. Where Rey coasts through school and sees little purpose in it, his brother would visit me at Columbia University and look eagerly at the college as heaven. He works during the summers and on the weekends for a print shop that is owned by a friend of the family.

In contrast to the households discussed earlier, whose earnings come mainly from the hard work of women, Rey's family relies largely on the income of the menfolk. While his mother has worked odd factory jobs now and again and hopes to find a real job when she finishes her studies, it is the entrepreneurial spirit of the men in the household that keeps the family going. Between them, father and sons earn enough in the (nontaxed) underground economy and the formal (wage-labor) system to keep the family

at a lower-working-class standard of living. They have nothing to spare, they cannot do without any of these sources of income, but they are not starving. They can even hope that the youngest child will be able to get through high school and make it into a public college, something that will require heavy doses of financial aid, but is not an unthinkable goal.

It is tempting to look at Rey's family as an inner-city exception, an icon of middle-class virtue. The two-parent family, the loving brothers, and the entrepreneurial energy all add up to an admirable portrait of a stable, supportive circle of kin pulling together. And there is much truth to the view. Yet, Rey's parents are actually divorced. They broke up years ago in order to qualify the household for welfare. Rey's father maintains an official address elsewhere.

If we were to look at an official government census of Rey's household, we would find that the adults within it are classified as out of the labor force. Indeed, it would be deemed a single-parent household supported by the welfare system. Harlem is populated by thousands of families whose official profiles look just like this. Yet there is a steady income stream coming into Rey's home, because most of the adults are indeed working, often in the mostly unregulated economy of small-scale services and self-employment, including home-based seamstresses, food vendors, gypsy cab drivers, and carpenters.[11] Most of this income never sees the tax man.

Much of what has been written about this underground system focuses on the drug world. But for thousands of poor people in New York who cannot afford a unionized plumber or electrician, unlicensed craftsmen and informal service workers (who provide child care or personal services) are more important exemplars of the shadow economy. Men like Rey and his father provide reasonably priced services and products, making it possible for people who would otherwise have to do without to get their cars fixed, their leaking roofs patched, or their children looked after. Immigrants who lack legal papers find employment in this shadow world, and those who are legal take second jobs in the underground economy.

It has proved extremely hard to estimate the size of this alternative system,[12] but it is so widespread in poor communities that it often rivals the formal economy. The multipurpose shop Rey's father runs from the living room and the street corner is the mainstay of the family's income, and in this they are hardly alone. The thoroughfares of Harlem have, for many years, had an active sidewalk market trade that is largely invisible to the Internal Revenue Service.[13]

Whether we look at employment or "family structure," Rey's household departs from the normative model of the nuclear family. The statistical observer or census-taker might lump this family together with others as dissolved, or as one whose adult members have been out of the labor force for many years. But anyone who is paying closer attention will see that this makes no sense. These people do make up an actively functioning family, and in fact kinship means everything to them. Their values place work and family at the center of their own culture in a form that would be embraced even by conservative forces in American society. And the men of the family are at least as committed to these norms as the women.

Jamal is the only income-earner in his tiny household. His common-law wife, Kathy, once received SSA, a government support provided to her because her father died when she was just a child. But once she ran away to live with Jamal, these funds were appropriated by her mother. Nowadays Jamal spends hours on the bus to reach his job sweeping floors and cleaning toilets in a Burger Barn in another borough. In Jamal's opinion, a real man earns a living and supports his family, and he puts his dictum into practice daily in a job that most Americans wouldn't waste their time on. In this, he follows a path, a cultural definition of manhood, that

continues to emphasize responsibility to family, responsibility that is sometimes expressed from a distance (as in Juan's case), while other times defined by coresidence (as is true for Ernie or Jamal).

Black men have been blanketed with negative publicity, excoriated as no good, irresponsible, swaggering in their masculinity, trapped in a swamp of "ghetto-related behavior."[14] Is this simply the force of stereotypes at work on a national psyche predisposed to believe the worst? Of course not. There are men in Harlem who have turned their backs on their mothers, wives, girlfriends, and children. Yet while we deplore the damage these males cause, we may overlook people like Jamal or Juan, or fifteen-year-old James, who brings his paycheck home to his parents to help with the rent, or Salvador, who works two jobs so that his wife, Carmen, and daughter will have a roof over their heads. We will not see the contributions that Latoya's common-law husband has made to the support of her children. And if we are to truly understand the role that men play in sustaining family values, we have to credit the existence of these honorable examples, while recognizing that many of their brethren have failed to follow through.

Some of those "failures" are young blacks who have irregular connections to family, who have no real place to live, whose seasonal labor is so poorly paid that there isn't much they can do to provide for their girlfriends even when they are so inclined.[15] Ron's mother died when he was a teenager. He now lives somewhat uneasily on the sufferance of his girlfriend while working at Burger Barn off and on. Since this relationship also is off and on, his living arrangements are precarious.

> You could say I work and pay my rent. I pay for where I stay at with my girl. My girl is my landlord, but nobody knows that. She does want money. I don't like to say this is my own bread, 'cause I don't like to be caught up in that "I'm gonna kick you out." So I always stay in contact

with my family. That way, if something happens between me and her, my sister lives in Brooklyn and she always has the door open for me until I make me another power move. My sister's household is secure, but me, I'm on the edge when it comes to financial things. 'Cause if Burger Barn falls off, then I'm off.

Ron is so close to the edge that he cannot do anything more than contribute some of his wages to whatever household he lands in for the time being. People in his situation have nothing left over for anyone else, which is one of the reasons they don't behave like people with commitments. This is no excuse for siring children they can't support, but it does point to the importance of steady, reasonably paid employment in encouraging responsibility, a point William Julius Wilson has brought to national attention in *When Work Disappears*. Men who lack the wherewithal to be good fathers, often aren't.

FAMILY FLAWS

In pointing to the continuous importance of family as a set of values expressed in practice, I do not mean to paint the households of the working poor as indistinguishable from the "mainstream model." Seen through middle-class eyes, there is much to worry about. Parents who work at the bottom of the income pyramid are stressed, tired, and stretched to the limit of their ability to cope. The irregularity of the income they receive, whether from low-wage jobs, undependable partners, or both, subjects families like Latoya's to unpredictable shortages, gnawing insecurities. Welfare reform is blowing like an ill wind through many of these kin networks, and because the working poor and the AFDC recipients are interleaved, policy directives aimed at the latter are derailing many of the former. Lacking vacations, having little left over to pamper themselves with after a long day flipping burgers, and seeing so little advancement ahead of them, Burger Barn workers are often short-tempered at home. Economic pressures

cannot descend upon families without showing their effects, especially on young kids.

Kyesha's two-year-old son, Anthony, spends much of his day in front of a television set tuned perpetually to soap operas and game shows. Sesame Street crosses the screen on occasion, but the purpose of the tube is not to educate little Anthony but to entertain his grandmother, stuck at home with him and several children of her own. Grandma Dana is not particularly attentive to Anthony's emotional needs, even though she keeps him fed and safe. He is never left alone, he does not run into the street, and his clothes are clean. But the focus stops there, and Anthony's behavior reflects the absence of sustained adult attention.

When Kyesha comes home, she wants to flop down on her bed and skim through movie star magazines. She lacks the energy to play with an active child.[16] She spends a lot of time figuring out how she is going to get to see her boyfriend and works on Dana in the hope that she will baby-sit Anthony for yet another evening so she can go out. The little boy is given to wandering into the tiny room they share and sounding off in an attempt to get Kyesha's attention. More often than not, she shoos him away so she can relax. If, like any normal two-year-old, he fails to obey, he is likely to be swatted.

Anthony will not start kindergarten knowing his colors and numbers, or the daily drill of communal "circle time" that is thoroughly familiar to any child who has spent time in a quality day care center. He will head down the road with a lack of basic experience that will weigh heavily when his teachers begin to assess his reading readiness or language fluency. There are consequences to growing up poor in a household of people who are pedaling hard just to stay afloat and have no time or reserve capacity left to provide the kind of enrichment that middle-class families can offer in abundance.

Shaquena has a rich array of people to turn to when she needs help. She has a web of kin and family friends living all around her, people who feed her and give her a place to hang out when all is not well at home. Yet her mother is a drug addict and her family broke up long ago under the strain. Had it not been for her grandmother, she would have found herself in foster care, her mother declared unfit. Hanging out with her girlfriends in the public housing project near her apartment in her younger years, she was known for getting into trouble. Fights, retaliation for insults, conflicts over boys—all have escalated to the point of serious violence. Shaquena's attachment to the work world is impressive because of this unlikely background, but the traces of her upbringing are visible enough in her temper, in the difficulty she has getting along with people at work from time to time. Her family cares about her, but to say that they are just as loving and stable in their irregular configuration as any Bill Cosby family in the suburbs would be pure romanticism.

Latoya and her common-law husband have had an on-again-off-again relationship that has caused her no end of grief. He messes up and she kicks him out. Left behind is his ten-year-old daughter by a previous relationship, not to mention the son they have in common. Latoya dreams of having a house in the suburbs, something she could afford if she could get her man to settle down, for he has a well-paid job as a carpenter, a unionized position that gives him benefits and upward of $15 an hour. Together they could make a break for it, but the instability of their relationship renders this fantasy almost unattainable. Latoya's heart bears the scars of his irresponsibility, and her children miss their dad when he is not around. Latoya's salary from Burger Barn barely stretches to meet the mounting expenses of a family of five, even with Jason's contributions. When they are together, though, their joint income puts them well above the poverty line, straight into the blue-collar working class. Hence family stability and standard of living go hand in hand in Latoya's household: when the family is together, everything looks rosy, and when things fall apart, the struggle is monumental.

Middle-class families have their ups and downs too, of course. Television is a babysitter in many families. Suburban marriages break up, leaving children in serious economic straits, with divorced mothers facing a job market that will not allow them to keep a secure hold on the lives their children are accustomed to.[17] The poor have no lock on the pitfalls of modern family life. Yet the consequences of family instability in poor neighborhoods are clearly more devastating because the whole institutional structure that surrounds folks at the bottom—the schools, the low-wage workplace, the overcrowded labor market, the potholed streets, the unsavory crack dealers on the front stoop—creates more vulnerability in families that have to deal with internal troubles. Support is more problematic, more likely to depend upon the resources of relatives and friends who are, in turn, also poor and troubled.

ENDNOTES

1. See Leon Dash, *Rosa Lee: A Mother and Her Family in Urban America* (Basic Books, 1996).
2. A couple of Rosa Lee's eight children, however, have taken very different paths. In *Rosa Lee: A Mother and Her Family in Urban America*, Dash writes about two of her sons who have never taken drugs or been to prison. Both have worked most of their adult lives, taking care of themselves and their families. One owns his home in a middle-class neighborhood.
3. In a 1980 survey of urban Santiago (DR) households that had relatives living abroad, about 20% of homes received sustained support from their absent members that averaged about $100 per month. Sherri Grasmuck and Patricia R. Pessar, *Between Two Islands: Dominican International Migration* (University of California Press, 1991).
4. Indeed, we often look right past the difficulties immigrants experienced in the urban villages of the nation's cities, especially the claustrophobia members of extended families felt when they could not get away from the prying eyes of

older generations. One of the major "push" factors that sent previous generations of inner-city dwellers to the suburbs was the desire to get away from the intrusive control of one's elders. See Herbert J. Gans, *The Urban Villagers: Group and Class in the Life of Italian Americans* (Free Press of Glencoe, 1962); and Herbert J. Gans, *Levittowners: Ways of Life and Politics in a New Suburban Community* (Pantheon Books, 1967).

5. Carol B. Stack, *All Our Kin: Strategies for Survival in a Black Community* (Harper & Row, 1974), even suggests that giving priority to maintaining close family bonds will dissuade ghetto dwellers from moving to better neighborhoods when they have the chance. Part of Stack's explanation lies in the difficulty of forecasting the permanence of good fortune among those poor people who discover that they have the opportunity to "get out." If they are confident that their money will last, then they may decide they can afford to cut the ties and go it alone. But few know for sure that the funds will continue to flow: jobs disappear, divorce may threaten . . . there are a thousand reasons for being skeptical of continuous good luck. And if one cannot be sure that resources will be stable, it may be more prudent to stay in the community where one's ties are strong and the private safety net continues to work. However, Stack also suggests that there is more to the desire to stay close to kin than just an instrumental need for their help. There is also a high cultural value placed on proximity, and a disdain for those who put mobility ahead of family ties.

6. However, see Judith Stacey, *Brave New Families: Stories of Domestic Upheaval in Late Twentieth Century America* (Basic Books, 1990), for an account of "postmodern" recombinant families, often constructed through remarriages and other agreements, that don't look too different. Our nation's domestic patterns have become increasingly diverse, and no single family model dominates. Only a minority of households in the United States still contain married couples with children. More children live with single mothers than in homes with paid-work fathers and full-time homemaker mothers. See Judith Stacey, *In the Name of the Family: Rethinking Family Values in the Postmodern Age* (Beacon Press, 1996).

7. Poverty has devastating effects, both direct and indirect, on children's well-being. A new set of studies, for example, clearly demonstrates that the negative outcomes for children associated with growing up in single-parent homes are related not only to home environment but to low income. While family disruptions such as divorce and remarriage often contribute to behavioral and psychological problems among children, the studies suggest that the net effects of poverty on cognitive ability and school achievement are at least as large as the effects of family disruptions. See Jeanne Brooks-Gunn, Greg J. Duncan, and Nancy Maritato, "Poor Families, Poor Outcomes: The Well-Being of Children and Youth," and Sara S. McLanahan, "Parent Absence or Poverty: Which Matters More?" both in Greg J. Duncan and Jeanne Brooks-Gunn, eds., *Consequences of Growing Up Poor* (Russell Sage Foundation, 1997), pp. 1–17, 35–48.

8. The experience of parental divorce is often traumatic for children. Research shows that children function better in a single-parent family than in a conflict-ridden two-parent home. James L. Peterson and Nicholas Zill, "Marital Disruption, Parent-Child Relationships, and Behavior Problems in Children," *Journal of Marriage and the Family* 48 (May 1986), pp. 295–307. But there is also ample evidence that children living with only one parent are worse off, on average, than children living with two parents (undoubtedly the quality of family interaction is more important than its form). Divorce has serious short-term effects on children, and, though less is known about adjustment to the separation many years later, many fewer children are thought to suffer long-term psychological harm. Analysis of statistical data from national surveys in Sara McLanahan and Gary Sandefur, *Growing Up with a Single Parent: What Hurts, What Helps* (Harvard University Press, 1994), shows that growing up in a single-parent home (including children born out of wedlock and those who as a result of divorce grow up in a one-parent household) is associated with diminished chances for a successful adult life. Low income—common among both unwed mothers and women divorcées, who almost always experience a sudden drop in income when a marriage breaks up—is by far the most important

factor in these children's lower achievement. In fact, low income accounts for about half of the disadvantage. See also Andrew J. Cherlin, *Marriage, Divorce, Remarriage,* (Harvard University Press, 1992); and Frank F. Furstenberg, Jr., and Andrew J. Cherlin, *Divided Families: What Happens to Children When Parents Part* (Harvard University Press, 1991).

9. The high school dropout risks for children with no family disruption, with single parent by divorce, with single parent by death of spouse, and with single parent by nonmarital birth are 13%, 31%, 15%, and 37% respectively. The teen birth risks for female children with no family disruption, with single parent by divorce, with single parent by death of spouse, and with single parent by nonmarital birth are 11%, 33%, 21%, and 37% respectively. Data come from the 1987 *National Survey of Families and Households,* Cohort 1, consisting of men and women between the ages of 20 and 34. The figures are adjusted for race, sex, mother's education, father's education, number of siblings, and place of residence. The children of widowed mothers probably do better as a group because parental conflict is not an issue and because widowed mothers as a group are more financially secure than other single mothers. McLanahan and Sandefur, *Growing Up with a Single Parent: What Hurts, What Helps,* pp. 65–68.

10. See Kathryn Edin and Laura Lein, *Making Ends Meet* (Russell Sage Foundation, 1997), for more on this point.

11. The severe local decline in the formal manufacturing sector has spurred opportunities for small-scale immigrant entrepreneurs, especially in low-wage apparel subcontracting. See Roger Waldinger, *Through the Eye of the Needle: Immigrants and Enterprises in New York's Garment Trades* (New York University Press, 1986). See also Grasmuck and Pessar, *Between Two Islands: Dominican International Migration,* pp. 162–98.

12. Studies have shown, however, that rapid "informalization" has occurred in several industries in New York City, including construction (in which an estimated 90% of internal work is done without a permit) and the furniture, footwear, and garment industries. In addition, subcontracting of back operations in consumer services (gourmet

food stores, custom-made clothes boutiques, caterers, etc.) is expanding into the informal economy. See Alejandro Portes and Saskia Sassen-Koob, "Making It Underground: Comparative Material on the Informal Sector in Western Market Economies," *American Journal of Sociology* 93, no. 1 (July 1987), pp. 30–61. According to Sassen-Koob, the ability of New York City to absorb such a large influx of immigrants from low-wage countries can be understood only by recognizing the profound restructuring of industrial sectors from formal to informal employment arrangements (including subcontracting, sweatshops, and homework). Saskia Sassen-Koob, 1989, "New York City's Informal Economy," in Alejandro Portes, Manuel Castells, and Lauren Benton, eds., *The Informal Economy: Studies in Advanced and Less Developed Countries* (Johns Hopkins University Press, 1989), pp. 60–77.

13. In 1994, over 1,000 unlicensed sidewalk vendors who crowded along Harlem's 125th Street shopping strip were evicted by the city in a series of police sweeps orchestrated by the Giuliani administration. They were offered an alternative open-air marketplace in an empty lot eight blocks south. While some local Harlem residents and political figures reviled the mayor for the removal, others, including business and development groups, praised the action, since the nontaxpaying vendors were thought to lure customers away from the stores, clogging the sidewalks and littering the street in front of their entrances. Many felt that there were legitimate complaints on both sides. About half the store owners along the strip are white; the street vendors, many of whom have moved to alternative Harlem locations, are overwhelmingly black (many are from West African countries). See Jonathan P. Hicks, "Vendors' Ouster and Boycott Divide Harlem," *New York Times,* October 23, 1994, p. A1.

14. "Ghetto-related behavior"—overt emphasis on sexuality, idleness, and public drinking; drug abuse, drug trafficking, crime, gang violence; and all the rest—is a term employed in William Julius Wilson, *When Work Disappears: The World of the New Urban Poor* (Knopf, 1996), pp. 51–86, to describe a set of practices—more prevalent in inner cities but also existent in mainstream society—that result from concentrated, persistent joblessness, poverty, and disconnection

from social resources and decent city services. Wilson's survey of Chicago's poor finds an abundance of residents with mainstream norms who vilify those engaging in such behavior but who can, nonetheless, cogently describe how a young male growing up in a barren, impoverished, and dangerous neighborhood can become attracted to this alternative. Wilson's point is clear: ghetto-related behaviors emerge from the structure of opportunity found in marginalized inner-city neighborhoods.

15. Elliot Liebow, *Tally's Corner* (Little, Brown, 1967), made this point long ago about poor black men in Washington, D.C. Men who have no money shy away from family obligations because this becomes yet another source of failure, another way they have fallen short of their own images of masculinity. Liebow argues that in this the street-corner men do not differ from the "mainstream" middle-class notions of appropriate behavior.

16. Working-poor parents rarely have the time, energy, or money to provide environments in which their children can thrive. A great deal of research shows that children from poor families exhibit lower levels of physical development, cognitive functioning, academic achievement, self-esteem, social development, and self-control than do children from more advantaged families. See Thomas L. Hanson, Sara McLanahan, and Elizabeth Thomson, "Economic Resources, Parental Practices, and Children's Well-Being," in Greg J. Duncan and Jeanne Brooks-Gunn, eds., *Consequences of Growing Up Poor* (Russell Sage Foundation, 1997), pp. 190–238. Indeed, the effects of poverty may be more pronounced for younger than for older children, since critical phases in brain cell development and in the capacity to form trusting emotional relationships occur in the first three years of life. Recent studies indicate that stimulation in the home environment can mediate the effects of family income on cognitive abilities, suggesting that less exposure to people and to learning interactions involving toys and books at home is a path toward lower achievement. This also suggests that childhood intervention programs that aim to enrich home environments are well founded. See Judith R. Smith, Jeanne Brooks-Gunn, and Pamela K. Klebanov, "Consequences of Living in Poverty for

Young Children's Cognitive and Verbal Ability and Early School Achievement," in Duncan and Brooks-Gunn, eds., *Consequences of Growing Up Poor*, pp. 132–89.

17. See Katherine Newman, *Falling from Grace: The Experience of Downward Mobility in the American Middle Class* (Free Press, 1988).

READING 5-2

Families on the Fault Line

Lillian B. Rubin

THE TOMALSONS

When I last met the Tomalsons, Gwen was working as a clerk in the office of a large Manhattan company and was also a student at a local college where she was studying nursing. George Tomalson, who had worked for three years in a furniture factory, where he laminated plastic to wooden frames, had been thrown out of a job when the company went bankrupt. He seemed a gentle man then, unhappy over the turn his life had taken but still wanting to believe that it would come out all right.

Now, as he sits before me in the still nearly bare apartment, George is angry. "If you're a black man in this country, you don't have a chance, that's all, not a chance. It's like no matter how hard you try, you're nothing but trash. I've been looking for work for over two years now, and there's nothing. White people are complaining all the time that black folks are getting a break. Yeah, well, I don't know who those people are, because it's not me or anybody else I

Lillian B. Rubin, "Families on the Fault Line" (editor's title) from *Families on the Fault Line: America's Working Class Speaks about the Family, the Economy, Race, and Ethnicity* (New York: HarperCollins Publishers, 1994) pp. 225–234 and 240–247. Copyright © 1994 by Lillian B. Rubin. Reprinted with the permission of the Rhoda Weyr Agency.

know. People see a black man coming, they run the other way, that's what I know."

"You haven't found any work at all for two years?" I ask.

"Some temporary jobs, a few weeks sometimes, a couple of months once, mostly doing shit work for peanuts. Nothing I could count on."

"If you could do any kind of work you want, what would you do?"

He smiles, "That's easy; I'd be a carpenter. I'm good with my hands, and I know a lot about it," he says, holding his hands out, palms up, and looking at them proudly. But his mood shifts quickly; the smile disappears; his voice turns harsh. "But that's not going to happen. I tried to get into the union, but there's no room there for a black guy. And in this city, without being in the union, you don't have a chance at a construction job. They've got it all locked up, and they're making sure they keep it for themselves."

When I talk with Gwen later, she worries about the intensity of her husband's resentment. "It's not like George; he's always been a real even guy. But he's moody now, and he's so angry, I sometimes wonder what he might do. This place is a hell hole," she says, referring to the housing project they live in. "It's getting worse all the time; kids with guns, all the drugs, grown men out of work all around. I'll bet there's hardly a man in this whole place who's got a job, leave alone a good one."

"Just what is it you worry about?"

She hesitates, clearly wondering whether to speak, how much to tell me about her fears, then says with a shrug, "I don't know, everything, I guess. There's so much crime and drugs and stuff out there. You can't help wondering whether he'll get tempted." She stops herself, looks at me intently, and says, "Look, don't get me wrong; I know it's crazy to think like that. He's not that kind of person. But when you live in times like these, you can't help worrying about everything.

"We both worry a lot about the kids at school. Every time I hear about another kid shot while they're at school, I get like a raving lu-

natic. What's going on in this world that kids are killing kids? Doesn't anybody care that so many black kids are dying like that? It's like a black child's life doesn't count for anything. How do they expect our kids to grow up to be good citizens when nobody cares about them?

"It's one of the things that drives George crazy, worrying about the kids. There's no way you can keep them safe around here. Sometimes I wonder why we send them to school. They're not getting much of an education there. Michelle just started, but Julia's in the fifth grade, and believe me, she's not learning much.

"We sit over her every night to make sure she does her homework and gets it right. But what good is it if the people at school aren't doing their job. Most of the teachers there don't give a damn. They just want the paycheck and the hell with the kids. Everybody knows it's not like that in the white schools; white people wouldn't stand for it.

"I keep thinking we've got to get out of here for the sake of the kids. I'd love to move someplace, anyplace out of the city where the schools aren't such a cesspool. But," she says dejectedly, "we'll never get out if George can't find a decent job. I'm just beginning my nursing career, and I know I've got a future now. But still, no matter what I do or how long I work at it, I can't make enough for that by myself."

George, too, has dreams of moving away, somewhere far from the city streets, away from the grime and the crime. "Look at this place," he says, his sweeping gesture taking in the whole landscape. "Is this any place to raise kids? Do you know what my little girls see every day they walk out the door? Filth, drugs, guys hanging on the corner waiting for trouble.

"If I could get any kind of a decent job, anything, we'd be out of here, far away, someplace outside the city where the kids could breathe clean and see a different life. It's so bad here, I take them over to my mother's a lot after school; it's a better neighborhood. Then we stay over there and eat sometimes. Mom likes it, she's lonely, and it helps us out. Not that she's got that much, but there's a little pension my father left.

"What about Gwen's family? Do they help out, too?"

"Her mother doesn't have anything to help with since her father died. He's long gone; he was killed by the cops when Gwen was a teenager," he says as calmly as if reporting the time of day.

"Killed by the cops!" The words leap out at me and jangle my brain. But why do they startle me so? Surely with all the discussion of police violence in the black community in recent years, I can't be surprised to hear that a black man was "killed by the cops."

It's the calmness with which the news is relayed that gets to me. And it's the realization once again of the distance between the lives and experiences of blacks and others, even poor others. Not one white person in this study reported a violent death in the family. Nor did any of the Latino and Asian families, although the Latinos spoke of a difficult and often antagonistic relationship with Anglo authorities, especially the police. But four black families (13 percent) told of relatives who had been murdered, one of the families with two victims—a teenage son and a 22-year-old daughter, both killed in violent street crimes.

But I'm also struck by the fact that Gwen never told me how her father died. True, I didn't ask. But I wonder now why she didn't offer the information. "Gwen didn't tell me," I say, as if trying to explain my surprise.

"She doesn't like to talk about it. Would you?" he replies somewhat curtly.

It's a moment or two before I can collect myself to speak again. Then I comment, "You talk about all this so calmly."

He leans forward, looks directly at me, and shakes his head. When he finally speaks, his voice is tight with the effort to control his rage. "What do you want? Should I rant and rave? You want me to say I want to go out and kill those mothers? Well, yeah, I do. They killed a good man just because he was black. He wasn't a criminal; he was a hard-working guy who just happened to be in the wrong place when the cops were looking for someone to shoot," he says, then sits back and stares stonily at the wall in front of him.

We both sit locked in silence until finally I break it. "How did it happen?"

He rouses himself at the sound of my voice. "They were after some dude who robbed a liquor store, and when they saw Gwen's dad, they didn't ask questions; they shot. The bastards. Then they said it was self-defense, that they saw a gun in his hand. That man never held a gun in his life, and nobody ever found one either. But nothing happens to them; it's no big deal, just another dead nigger," he concludes, his eyes blazing.

It's quiet again for a few moments, then, with a sardonic half smile, he says, "What would a nice, white middle-class lady like you know about any of that? You got all those degrees, writing books and all that. How are you going to write about people like us?"

"I was poor like you once, very poor," I say somewhat defensively.

He looks surprised, then retorts, "Poor and white; it's a big difference."

Thirty years before the beginning of the Civil War, Alexis de Tocqueville wrote: "If ever America undergoes great revolutions, they will be brought about by the presence of the black race on the soil of the United States; that is to say they will owe their origin, not to the equality, but to the "inequality of condition."[1] One hundred and sixty years later, relations between blacks and whites remain one of the great unresolved issues in American life, and "the inequality of condition" that de Tocqueville observed is still a primary part of the experience of black Americans.

I thought about de Tocqueville's words as I listened to George Tomalson and about how the years of unemployment had changed him from, as Gwen said, "a real even guy" to an angry and embittered one. And I was reminded, too, of de Tocqueville's observation that "the danger of conflict between the white and black inhabitants perpetually haunts the imagination of the [white] Americans, like a painful dream."[2] Fifteen generations later we're still paying the cost of those years when Americans held slaves—whites still living in fear, blacks in rage. "People see a black man coming, they run the other way," says George Tomalson.

Yet however deep the cancer our racial history has left on the body of the nation, most Americans, including many blacks, believe that things are better today than they were a few decades ago—a belief that's both true and not true.[3] There's no doubt that in ending the legal basis for discrimination and segregation, the nation took an important step toward fulfilling the promise of equality for all Americans. As more people meet as equals in the workplace, stereotypes begin to fall away and caricatures are transformed into real people. But it's also true that the economic problems of recent decades have raised the level of anxiety in American life to a new high. So although virtually all whites today give verbal assent to the need for racial justice and equality, they also find ways to resist the implementation of the belief when it seems to threaten their own status or economic well-being.

Our schizophrenia about race, our capacity to believe one thing and do another, is not new. Indeed, it is perhaps epitomized by Thomas Jefferson, the great liberator. For surely, as Gordon Wood writes in an essay in the *New York Review of Books,* "there is no greater irony in American history than the fact that America's supreme spokesman for liberty and equality was a lifelong aristocratic owner of slaves."[4]

Jefferson spoke compellingly about the evils of slavery, but he bought, sold, bred, and flogged slaves. He wrote eloquently about equality but he was convinced that blacks were an inferior race and endorsed the racial stereotypes that have characterized African Americans since their earliest days on this continent. He believed passionately in individual liberty, but he couldn't imagine free blacks living in America, maintaining instead that if the nation considered emancipating the slaves, it must also prepare for their expulsion.

No one talks seriously about expulsion anymore. Nor do many use the kind of language to describe African Americans that was so common in Jefferson's day. But the duality he embodied—his belief in justice, liberty, and equality alongside his conviction of black inferiority—still lives.

THE RIVERAS

Once again Ana Rivera and I sit at the table in her bright and cheerful kitchen. She's sipping coffee; I'm drinking some bubbly water while we make small talk and get reacquainted. After a while, we begin to talk about the years since we last met. "I'm a grandmother now," she says, her face wreathed in a smile. "My daughter Karen got married and had a baby, and he's the sweetest little boy, smart, too. He's only two and a half, but you should hear him. He sounds like five."

"When I talked to her the last time I was here, Karen was planning to go to college. What happened?" I ask.

She flushes uncomfortably. "She got pregnant, so she had to get married. I was heartbroken at first. She was only 19, and I wanted her to get an education so bad. It was awful; she had been working for a whole year to save money for college, then she got pregnant and couldn't go."

"You say she had to get married. Did she ever consider an abortion?"

"I don't know; we never talked about it. We're Catholic," she says by way of explanation. "I mean, I don't believe in abortion." She hesitates, seeming uncertain about what more she wants to say, then adds, "I have to admit, at a time like that, you have to ask yourself what you really believe. I don't think anybody's got the right to take a child's life. But when I thought about what having that baby would do to Karen's life, I couldn't help thinking, *What if . . . ?*" She stops, unable to bring herself to finish the sentence.

"Did you ever say that to Karen?"

"No, I would *never* do that. I didn't even tell my husband I thought such things. But, you know," she adds, her voice dropping to nearly a whisper, "if she had done it, I don't think I would have said a word."

"What about the rest of the kids?"

"Paul's going to be 19 soon; he's a problem," she sighs. "I mean, he's got a good head, but he won't use it. I don't know what's the matter with kids these days; it's like they want everything but they're not willing to work for anything. He hardly finished high school, so you can't talk to him about going to college. But what's he going to do? These days if you don't have a good education, you don't have a chance. No matter what we say, he doesn't listen, just goes on his smart-alecky way, hanging around the neighborhood with a bunch of no-good kids looking for trouble.

"Rick's so mad, he wants to throw him out of the house. But I say no, we can't do that because then what'll become of him? So we fight about that a lot, and I don't know what's going to happen."

"Does Paul work at all?"

"Sometimes, but mostly not. I'm afraid to think about where he gets money from. His father won't give him a dime. He borrows from me sometimes, but I don't have much to give him. And anyway, Rick would kill me if he knew."

I remember Paul as a gangly, shy 16-year-old, no macho posturing, none of the rage that shook his older brother, not a boy I would have thought would be heading for trouble. But then, Karen, too, had seemed so determined to grasp at a life that was different from the one her parents were living. What happens to these kids?

When I talk with Rick about these years, he, too, asks in bewilderment: What happened? "I don't know; we tried so hard to give the kids everything they needed. I mean, sure, we're not rich, and there's a lot of things we couldn't give them. But we were always here for them; we listened; we talked. What happened? First my daughter gets pregnant and has to get married; now my son is becoming a bum."

"Roberto—that's what we have to call him now," explains Rick, "he says it's what happens when people don't feel they've got respect. He says we'll keep losing our kids until they really believe they really have an equal chance. I don't know; I knew I had to *make* the Anglos respect me, and I had to make my chance. Why don't my kids see it like that?" he asks wearily, his shoulders seeming to sag lower with each sentence he speaks.

"I guess it's really different today, isn't it?" he sighs. "When I was coming up, you could still make your chance. I mean, I only went to high school, but I got a job and worked myself up. You can't do that anymore. Now you need to have some kind of special skills just to get a job that pays more than the minimum wage.

"And the schools, they don't teach kids anything anymore. I went to the same public schools my kids went to, but what a difference. It's like nobody cares anymore."

"How is Roberto doing?" I ask, remembering the hostile eighteen-year-old I interviewed several years earlier.

"He's still mad; he's always talking about injustice and things like that. But he's different than Paul. Roberto always had some goals. I used to worry about him because he's so angry all the time. But I see now that his anger helps him. He wants to fight for his people, to make things better for everybody. Paul, he's like the wind; nothing matters to him.

"Right now, Roberto has a job as an electrician's helper, learning the trade. He's been working there for a couple of years; he's pretty good at it. But I think—I hope—he's going to go to college. He heard that they're trying to get Chicano students to go to the university, so he applied. If he gets some aid, I think he'll go," Rick says, his face radiant at the thought that at least one of his children will fulfill his dream. "Ana and me, we tell him even if he doesn't get aid, he should go. We can't do a lot because we have to help Ana's parents and that takes a big hunk every month. But we'll help him, and he could work to make up the rest. I know it's hard to work and go to school, but people do it all the time, and he's smart; he could do it."

His gaze turns inward; then, as if talking to himself, he says, "I never thought I'd say this but I think Roberto's right. We've got something to learn from some of these kids. I told that to Roberto just the other day. He says Ana and me have been trying to pretend we're one of them all of our lives. I told him, 'I think you're right.' I kept thinking if I did everything right, I wouldn't be a 'greaser.' But after all these years, I'm still a 'greaser' in their eyes. It took my son to make me see it. Now I know. If I weren't I'd be head of the shipping department by now, not just one of the supervisors, and maybe Paul wouldn't be wasting his life on the corner."

We keep saying that family matters, that with a stable family and two caring parents children will grow to a satisfactory adulthood. But I've rarely met a family that's more constant or more concerned than the Riveras. Or one where both parents are so involved with their children. Ana was a full-time homemaker until Paul, their youngest, was 12. Rick has been with the same company for more than 25 years, having worked his way up from clerk to shift supervisor in its shipping department. Whatever the conflicts in their marriage, theirs is clearly a warm, respectful, and caring relationship. Yet their daughter got pregnant and gave up her plans for college, and a son is idling his youth away on a street corner.

Obviously, then, something more than family matters. Growing up in a world where opportunities are available makes a difference. As does being able to afford to take advantage of an opportunity when it comes by. Getting an education that broadens horizons and prepares a child for a productive adulthood makes a difference. As does being able to find work that nourishes self-respect and pays a living wage. Living in a world that doesn't judge you by the color of your skin makes a difference. As does feeling the respect of the people around you.

This is not to suggest that there aren't also real problems inside American families that deserve our serious and sustained attention. But the constant focus on the failure of family life as the locus of both our personal and social difficulties has become a mindless litany, a dangerous diversion from the economic and social realities that make family life so difficult today and that so often destroy it.

Two decades ago, when I began the research for *Worlds of Pain,* we were living in the immediate aftermath of the civil rights revolution that had convulsed the nation since the mid-1950s. Significant gains had been won. And despite the tenacity with which this headway had been resisted by some, most white Americans were feeling good about themselves. No one expected the nation's racial problems and conflicts to dissolve easily or quickly. But there was also a sense that we were moving in the right direction, that there was a national commitment to redressing at least some of the worst aspects of black–white inequality.

In the intervening years, however, the national economy buckled under the weight of three recessions, while the nation's industrial base was undergoing a massive restructuring. At the same time, government policies requiring preferential treatment were enabling African-Americans and other minorities to make small but visible inroads into what had been, until then, largely white terrain. The sense of scarcity, always a part of American life but intensified sharply by the history of these economic upheavals, made minority gains seem particularly threatening to white working-class families.

It isn't, of course, just working-class whites who feel threatened by minority progress. Wherever racial minorities make inroads into formerly all-white territory, tensions increase. But it's working-class families who feel the fluctuations in the economy most quickly and most keenly. For them, these last decades have been like a bumpy roller coaster ride. "Every time we think we might be able to get ahead, it seems like we get knocked down again," declares Tom Ahmundsen, a 42-year-old white construction worker. "Things look a little better; there's a little more work; then all of a sudden, boom, the economy falls apart and it's gone. You can't count on anything; it really gets you down."

This is the story I heard repeatedly: Each small climb was followed by a fall, each glimmer of hope replaced by despair. As the economic vise tightened, despair turned to anger. But partly because we have so little concept of class resentment and conflict in America, this anger isn't directed so much at those above as at those below. And when whites at or near the bottom of the ladder look down in this nation, they generally see blacks and other minorities.

True, during all of the 1980s and into the 1990s, white ire was fostered by national administrations that fanned racial discord as a way of fending off white discontent—of diverting anger about the state of the economy and the declining quality of urban life to the foreigners and racial others in our midst. But our history of racial animosity coupled with our lack of class consciousness made this easier to accomplish than it might otherwise have been.

The difficult realities of white working-class life not withstanding, however, their whiteness has accorded them significant advantages—both materially and psychologically—over people of color. Racial discrimination and segregation in the workplace have kept competition for the best jobs at a minimum. They do, obviously,

have to compete with each other for the resources available. But that's different. It's a competition among equals; they're all white. They don't think such things consciously, of course; they don't have to. It's understood, rooted in the culture and supported by the social contract that says they are the superior ones, the worthy ones. Indeed, this is precisely why, when the courts or the legislatures act in ways that seem to contravene that belief, whites experience themselves as victims.

From the earliest days of the republic, whiteness has been the ideal, and freedom and independence have been linked to being white. "Republicanism," writes labor historian David Roediger, "had long emphasized that the strength, virtue and resolve of a people guarded them from enslavement."[5] And it was whites who had these qualities in abundance, as was evident, in the peculiarly circuitous reasoning of the time, in the fact that they were not slaves.

By this logic, the enslavement of blacks could be seen as stemming from their "slavishness" rather than from the institution of slavery. Slavery is gone now, but the reasoning lingers on in white America, which still insists that the lowly estate of people of color is due to their deficits, whether personal or cultural, rather than to the prejudice, discrimination, and institutionalized racism that has barred them from full participation in the society.

This is not to say that culture is irrelevant, whether among black Americans or any other group in our society. The lifeways of a people develop out of their experiences—out of the daily events, large and small, that define their lives; out of the resources that are available to them to meet both individual and group needs; out of the place in the social, cultural, and political systems within which group life is embedded. In the case of a significant proportion of blacks in America's inner cities, centuries of racism and economic discrimination have produced a subculture that is both personally and socially destructive. But to fault culture or the failure of individual responsibility without understanding the larger context within which such behaviors occur is to miss a vital piece of the picture. Nor does acknowledging the existence of certain destructive subcultural forms among some African-Americans disavow or diminish the causal connections between the structural inequalities at the social, political, and economic levels and the serious social problems at the community level.

In his study of "working-class lads" in Birmingham, England, for example, Paul Willis observes that their very acts of resistance to middle-class norms—the defiance with which these young men express their anger at class inequalities—help to reinforce the class structure by further entrenching them in their working-class status.[6] The same can be said for some of the young men in the African-American community, whose active rejection of white norms and "in your face" behavior consigns them to the bottom of the American economic order.

To understand this doesn't make such behavior, whether in England or the United States, any more palatable. But it helps to explain the structural sources of cultural forms and to apprehend the social processes that undergird them. Like Willis's white "working-class lads," the hip-hoppers and rappers in the black community who are so determinedly "not white" are not just making a statement about black culture. They're also expressing their rage at white society for offering a promise of equality, then refusing to fulfill it. In the process, they're finding their own way to some accommodation and to a place in the world they can call their own, albeit one that ultimately reinforces their outsider status.

But, some might argue, white immigrants also suffered prejudice and discrimination in the years after they first arrived, but they found more socially acceptable ways to accommodate. It's true—and so do most of today's people of color, both immigrant and native born. Nevertheless, there's another truth as well. For wrenching as their early experiences were for

white ethnics, they had an out. Writing about the Irish, for example, Roediger shows how they were able to insist upon their whiteness and to prove it by adopting the racist attitudes and behaviors of other whites, in the process often becoming leaders in the assault against blacks. With time and their growing political power, they won the prize they sought—recognition as whites. "The imperative to define themselves as white," writes Roediger, "came from the particular 'public and psychological wages' whiteness offered to a desperate rural and often preindustrial Irish population coming to labor in industrializing American cities."[7]

Thus does whiteness bestow its psychological as well as material blessings on even the most demeaned. For no matter how far down the socioeconomic ladder whites may fall, the one thing they can't lose is their whiteness. No small matter because, as W. E. B. DuBois observed decades ago, the compensation of white workers includes a psychological wage, a bonus that enables them to believe in their inherent superiority over nonwhites.[8]

It's also true, however, that this same psychological bonus that white workers prize so highly has cost them dearly. For along with the importation of an immigrant population, the separation of black and white workers has given American capital a reserve labor force to call upon whenever white workers seemed to them to get too "uppity." Thus, while racist ideology enables white workers to maintain the belief in their superiority, they have paid for that conviction by becoming far more vulnerable in the struggle for decent wages and working conditions than they might otherwise have been.

Politically and economically, the ideology of white supremacy disables white workers from making the kind of interracial alliances that would benefit all of the working class. Psychologically, it leaves them exposed to the double-edged sword of which I spoke earlier. On one side, their belief in the superiority of whiteness helps to reassure them that they're not at the bottom of the social hierarchy. But their insistence that their achievements are based on their special capacities and virtues, that it's only incompetence that keeps others from grabbing a piece of the American dream, threatens their precarious sense of self-esteem. For if they're the superior ones, the deserving ones, the ones who earned their place solely through hard work and merit, there's nothing left but to blame themselves for their inadequacies when hard times strike.

In the opening sentences of *Worlds of Pain* I wrote that America was choking on its differences. If we were choking then, we're being asphyxiated now. As the economy continues to falter, and local, state, and federal governments keep cutting services, there are more and more acrimonious debates about who will share in the shrinking pie. Racial and ethnic groups, each in their own corners, square off as they ready themselves for what seems to be the fight of their lives. Meanwhile, the quality of life for all but the wealthiest Americans is spiraling downward—a plunge that's felt most deeply by those at the lower end of the class spectrum, regardless of color.[9]

As more and more mothers of young children work full-time outside the home, the question of who will raise the children comes center stage. Decent, affordable child care is scandalously scarce, with no government intervention in sight for this crucial need. In poor and working-class families, therefore, child care often is uncertain and inadequate, leaving parents apprehensive and children at risk. To deal with their fears, substantial numbers of couples now work different shifts, a solution to the child-care problem that puts its own particular strains on family life.

In families with two working parents, time has become their most precious commodity—time to attend to the necessary tasks of family life; time to nurture the relationships between wife and husband, between parents and children; time for oneself, time for others; time for solitude, time for a social life.[10] Today more than ever before, family life has become impoverished for want of time, adding another threat to the already fragile bonds that hold families together.

While women's presence in the labor force has given them a measure of independence unknown before, most also are stuck with doing two days' work in one—one on the job, the other when they get home at night. Unlike their counterparts in the earlier era, today's women are openly resentful about the burdens they carry, which makes for another dimension of conflict between wives and husbands.

Although the men generally say they've never heard of Robert Bly or any of the other modern-day gurus of manhood, the idea of men as victims has captured their imagination.[11] Given the enormous amount of publicity these men's advocates have garnered in the last few years, it's likely that some of their ideas have filtered into the awareness of the men in this study, even if they don't know how they got there. But their belief in their victimization is also a response to the politics of our time, when so many different groups—women, gays, racial minorities, the handicapped—have demanded special privileges and entitlements on the basis of past victimization. And once the language of victimization enters the political discourse, it becomes a useful tool for anyone wanting to resist the claims of others or to stake one of their own.

As the men see it, then, if their wives are victims because of the special burdens of women, the husbands, who bear their own particular hardships, can make the claim as well. If African-American men are victims because of past discrimination, then the effort to redress their grievances turns white men into victims of present discrimination.

To those who have been victimized by centuries of racism, sexism, homophobia, and the like, the idea that straight white men are victims, too, seems ludicrous. Yet it's not wholly unreal, at least not for the men in this study who have so little control over their fate and who so often feel unheard and invisible, like little more than shadows shouting into the wind.

Whether inside the family or in the larger world outside, white men keep hearing that they're the privileged ones, words that seem to them like a bad joke. How can they be advantaged when their inner experience is that they're perched precariously on the edge of a chasm that seems to have opened up in the earth around them? It's this sense of vulnerability, coupled with the conviction that their hardships go unseen and their pain unattended, that nourishes their claim to victimhood.

Some analysts of family and social life undoubtedly will argue that the picture I've presented here is too grim, that it gives insufficient weight to both the positive changes in family life and the gains in race relations over these past decades. It's true that the social and cultural changes we've witnessed have created families that, in some ways at least, are more responsive to the needs of their members, more democratic than any we have known before.[12] But it's also true that without the economic stability they need, even the most positive changes will not be enough to hold families together.

Certainly, too, alongside the racial and ethnic divisions that are so prominent a part of American life today is the reality that many more members of these warring groups than ever before are living peaceably together in our schools, our factories, our shops, our corporations, and our neighborhoods. And, except for black–white marriages, many more are marrying and raising children together than would have seemed possible a few decades ago.

At the same time, there's reason to fear. The rise of ethnicity and the growing racial separation also mean an escalating level of conflict that sometimes seems to threaten to fragment the nation. In this situation, ethnic entrepreneurs like Al Sharpton in New York and David Duke in Louisiana rise to power and prominence by fanning ethnic and racial discord. A tactic that works so well precisely because the economic

pressures are felt so keenly on all sides of the racial fissures, because both whites and people of color now feel so deeply that "it's not fair."

As I reflect on the differences in family and social life in the last two decades, it seems to me that we were living then in a more innocent age—a time, difficult though it was for the working-class families of our nation, when we could believe anything was possible. Whether about the economy, race relations, or life inside the family, most Americans believed that the future promised progress, that the solution to the social problems and inequities of the age were within our grasp, that sacrifice today would pay off tomorrow. This is perhaps the biggest change in the last 20 years: The innocence is gone.

But is this a cause for mourning? Perhaps only when innocence is gone and our eyes unveiled will we be able to grasp fully the depth of our conflicts and the sources from which they spring.

We live in difficult and dangerous times, in a country deeply divided by class, race, and social philosophy. The pain with which so many American families are living today, and the anger they feel, won't be alleviated by a retreat to false optimism and easy assurances. Only when we are willing to see and reckon with the magnitude of our nation's problems and our people's suffering, only when we take in the full measure of that reality, will we be able to find the path to change. Until then, all our attempts at solutions will fail. And this, ultimately, will be the real cause for mourning. For without substantial change in both our public and our private worlds, it is not just the future of the family that is imperiled but the very life of the nation itself.

ENDNOTES

1. Alexis de Tocqueville, *Democracy in America,* George Lawrence, trans., J. P. Mayer, ed. (New York: Anchor Books, 1969), p. 639.
2. Ibid.

3. For a longitudinal study of racial attitudes among both African Americans and whites, see Robert Blauner, *Black Lives, White Lives* (Berkeley: University of California Press, 1989).

4. *New York Review of Books,* May 13, 1993.

5. David R. Roediger, *Wages of Whiteness: Race & the Making of the American Working Class,* p. 35. (Pub by Verso UK 1991).

6. Paul Willis, *Learning to Labour* (New York: Columbia University Press, 1977).

7. David R. Roediger, *Wages of Whiteness: Race & the Making of the American Working Class,* p. 137. (Pub by Verso UK 1991). For a full discussion of this issue, see chapter 7, pp. 133–163, "Irish-American Workers and White Racial Formation in the Antebellum United States."

8. W. E. B. DuBois, *Black Reconstruction in the United States, 1860–1880* (New York: Harcourt Brace, 1935).

9. When adjusted for inflation, the average after-tax income of the one hundred million Americans who make up the bottom two-fifths of the income spectrum has fallen sharply since 1977. The average of the middle fifth of households has edged up 2–4 percent. But the average after-tax income of upper middle-income households has climbed more than 10 percent. And among the wealthiest 5 percent of taxpayers—those with incomes of $91,750 and more—after-tax income rose more than 60 percent during this period (Robert Greenstein, "The Kindest Cut," *The American Prospect* (Fall 1991): 49–57).

10. Juliet Schor, *The Overworked American: The Unexpected Decline of Leisure* (New York: Basic) shows that Americans now work 140 hours a year more than they did 20 years ago. Partly at least this is because most people need every dollar they can earn, so they're reluctant to give up any part of their income for leisure. In fact, large numbers of working-class people forgo taking their vacation time off and take the money instead while continuing to work, thereby earning double wages for the vacation period.

11. Robert Bly, *Iron John* (Reading, Mass.: Addison-Wesley, 1990). See also Sam Keen, *Fire in the Belly* (New York: Bantam Books, 1991).

12. See, for example, Judith Stacey, *Brave New Families* (New York: Basic Books, 1990); Stephanie Coontz, *The Way We Never Were;* and Arlene Skolnick, *Embattled Paradise.*

CHAPTER 6

The Family, the State, and Social Policy

In 1996, the U.S. Congress passed the most sweeping changes since the Great Depression in the program that provides cash assistance to poor families with children. President Bill Clinton, who had promised in his 1992 campaign to "end welfare as we know it," overcame misgivings about the bill and signed it. With the stroke of his pen, "welfare," as the program is commonly called, was transformed from an open-ended source of income to a program that required work and limited the amount of time that families could spend on the rolls. The debates over the new bill and its consequences reflect many of the main themes of the broader policy debates between liberals and conservatives over family issues.

Although several years have passed, there still are few good articles that provide the background to its passage, explain its main provisions, and discuss its consequences for children and families. I wrote an article, "How Will the 1996 Welfare Reform Laws Affect Poor Families?" for the first edition of this reader. I have revised it for the second edition to include the country's experience with welfare reform during the first three years since its passage. I hope

it will help the reader make sense of this momentous change in public policy toward poor families.

But the interrelationship between the family and the state extends well beyond government programs for the poor. In fact, many developed nations (although not the United States) provide general income support, in the form of "child allowances," to all parents who are raising children. The idea behind these programs is that parents are doing a valuable service to society when they raise children and they should be compensated for it—in part so that the next generation of young adults will continue to have enough children. Parents are doing a service, it is said, because each nation needs a sufficient number of productive, working-age adults; and without enough children, the next generation of workers will be too small. As Paula England and Nancy Folbre note in the second article in this chapter, workers in the United States and other countries pay the Social Security taxes that allow older people to collect their retirement checks. Those checks go to older people whether or not they raised children themselves. Thus, as

England and Folbre state in the language of economic theory, children are "public goods": Even the people who did not produce them (by remaining childless) cannot be stopped from enjoying the benefits derived from their existence (such as Social Security tax revenue). England and Folbre urge us to take a collective responsibility for children. They argue that the state should provide more compensation to parents to encourage even greater investments of time and effort into raising and educating the next generation.

READING 6-1

How Is the 1996 Welfare Reform Law Affecting Poor Families?

Andrew J. Cherlin

When Bill Clinton promised during the 1992 Presidential election campaign that he would "end welfare as we know it," he didn't realize how sweeping his promise would prove. In August 1996, he signed into law a striking bill that has thoroughly transformed the welfare system. When the legislation was passed, its supporters claimed that it would help poor families by restoring their motivation to work and making them self-sufficient. Its detractors argued that it would cause untold suffering and misery for poor families by cutting off their financial support. In truth, neither group knew for sure what the consequences of the new legislation would be for poor families. It was a great experiment with the lives of millions of parents and children. Since the passage of the law, the welfare rolls have gone down dramatically; and a booming economy has helped many former recipients find jobs. Yet little is still known about the effects on families.

POOR LAWS IN THE PAST

There's nothing particularly new about public assistance to the poor; it has been part of Western society for several hundred years. Before working for wages was common, most poor people were attached to the land, either farming their own plot or farming someone else's fields and keeping part of the harvest. Although there were plenty of poor families, they were not very visible. But as working for

wages became common and cities began to grow, many people migrated to urban areas in search of paid work. Those who could not find or keep steady jobs formed a dispossessed group that often was reduced to begging. Faced with this suddenly visible problem, societies began to formulate ways to reduce the worst of the misery they saw.

The early "poor laws" were based on principles that still characterize public assistance to the poor today. The principles were aimed, above all, at enforcing work among the poor. First, a distinction was made between the "deserving" and "undeserving" poor. Infants, the elderly, and chronically ill were held incapable of working and therefore "deserving" of public assistance. But older children and "able-bodied" adults were held to be capable of working and therefore "undeserving" of assistance. Second, the amount of assistance was kept lower than the prevailing wage in the area so that public aid would be less attractive than working. Third, assistance to the poor was administered by local, rather than national, authorities, on the theory that they knew best the local labor market conditions and need for workers. Thus, the early laws were designed to provide a bare minimum of assistance to persons deemed incapable of working and almost no assistance to persons deemed capable of working.

In the United States, these principles characterized assistance to the poor throughout the 1800s and the first few decades of the 1900s (Katz, 1986). Assistance to the poor was carried out by a mixture of local government agencies and private charities. There was no national program of assistance to the poor, although many states instituted pensions for widowed mothers in the early 1900s (Skocpol, 1992). But in the 1930s, the old system was overwhelmed by the demands of the huge number of people who were unable to find work during the Great Depression. After winning the 1932 election, Franklin D. Roosevelt expanded federal relief efforts and convinced Congress to pass landmark social legislation that greatly expanded the

Andrew J. Cherlin, "How Is the 1996 Welfare Reform Law Affecting Poor Families?" (original article, revised for 2e). Copyright © 1997 by Andrew J. Cherlin. Reprinted with the permission of the author.

federal government's role in assisting the poor, the unemployed, and the elderly.

FEDERAL WELFARE POLICY, 1935–1995

The major piece of legislation, the Social Security Act of 1935, began the modern era of government assistance to the poor. It established Social Security (the nation's system of retirement benefits), unemployment compensation for workers who lose their jobs, and Aid to Families with Dependent Children (AFDC), the program of cash assistance to low-income single parents and their children.[1] It was the AFDC program that came to be known informally as "welfare." All three programs were established as entitlements, meaning that if a person qualified for a benefit (by retiring or being laid off from work), the government had to provide it. But whereas Social Security was a national program in which the federal government merely issued checks, the AFDC program still followed many of old principles of assistance to the poor. AFDC was administered at the state rather than the national level, with each state free to set the amount of its benefits. In general, states with lower wages set their benefits rates lower. After the state established its benefit level, the federal government agreed to pay about half of the cost of the program. AFDC also excluded two-parent families because men were viewed as capable of working and supporting their families.

Most of the families that received AFDC in the 1930s were headed by widowed mothers; they were judged to be deserving of assistance so that they could stay home and raise their children. Because rates of divorce and childbearing outside of marriage were far lower than today, no one expected that large numbers of separated, divorced, and never-married mothers would be applying for assistance. But by the 1960s, changes in the American family had greatly altered the characteristics of the typical welfare-receiving parent. Due to increases in the divorce rate, declines in death rate, and increases in the proportion of births to unmarried mothers, the vast majority of adult recipients were not widowed but rather separated, divorced, or never married. Although it was just as hard for divorced single parents to raise children as for widowed single parents, some Americans viewed them as less deserving for having "chosen" to divorce or to have children outside of marriage.

Nor did anyone in 1935 foresee a time when most mothers, poor and nonpoor, would be working outside the home. But in the second half of the 20th century, millions of married and unmarried mothers poured into the paid labor force. By the 1990s, a majority of married mothers with children under 18—and even a majority of mothers with preschool-age children—were working outside the home (Cherlin, 1992). Because of this social change, it became more difficult to argue that poor mothers deserved assistance so that they could stay out of the work force and raise their children. Gradually, poor mothers shifted in public opinion from the "deserving" to the "undeserving" poor.

During the 1960s, the welfare rolls expanded sharply as states eased their eligibility requirements and advocates for the poor urged families to apply. Several factors underlay the increase. First, the Civil Rights movement had raised public consciousness of the plight of the poor. Second, the expanding American economy provided a larger pie from which to give the poor a slice. Third, African-Americans rioted in several cities, scaring and troubling politicians who subsequently raised benefits and loosened eligibility requirements for AFDC (Piven and Cloward, 1993). The expansion brought more minority families onto the rolls, many of whom were visibly concentrated in central city ghettos. (In 1996, about 37 percent of AFDC recipients were African-American; and 21 percent were

---

[1]The original program was named "Aid to Dependent Children," or ADC; the word "families" was added later.

Hispanics, who could be of any race [U.S. Administration for Children and Families, 1996b].)

As long as the economy was strong, few people seemed concerned about the expansion; but as the boom era ended in the 1970s, public sentiment against AFDC grew. Critics charged that the system discouraged work and instead encouraged people to become dependent on government support. The white majority's (mis)perception that the typical welfare family was black eroded their empathy for the families on the rolls (Quadagno, 1994). Another common complaint was that welfare was imposing too much of a tax burden on workers, even though AFDC cost far less than several other government social programs.[2]

Liberal defenders of AFDC argued that the number of recipients had increased because of a shortage of jobs for unskilled workers that paid enough to sustain a family. Therefore, according to this view, blaming poor families for receiving welfare amounted to "blaming the victims" of social inequality (Handler, 1995). Supporters of the program, however, were unable to prevent a series of changes to AFDC in the 1970s and 1980s that imposed ever-tougher work requirements for adult recipients.

By the late 1980s, even liberals seemed willing to concede that it was fair to ask poor mothers to work for pay if they were provided with adequate support. The new liberal sentiment was typified by David Ellwood, a poverty scholar who wrote a book proposing an overhaul of the welfare system (Ellwood, 1988). Although he acknowledged that it was often difficult for a welfare mother to find and keep a job, Ellwood recommended limiting the payment of cash assistance under AFDC to five years. During that period, recipients would be given extensive assistance in job training, job search, and education. The government would also make a greater efforts to collect unpaid child support payments from absent fathers of AFDC families. and would guarantee a minimum level of child support to poor single mothers. It would provide greater tax relief to the working poor, and it would provide health insurance to the millions of low-income families without it. If, at the end of the five years of cash assistance an AFDC parent still did not have a job, she would be provided with a public service job at the minimum wage.

TOWARD RADICAL WELFARE REFORM

Essentially, Ellwood proposed a carrot-and-stick reform with the carrot of greater support in obtaining work and the stick of just five years of cash payments. It was in this context that Clinton, influenced by welfare experts such as Ellwood, made his famous 1992 promise. But after his election, he chose to delay proposing changes to the welfare system while he attempted to convince Congress to enact legislation providing for universal health insurance coverage. Clinton failed, however, to convince Congress to pass his health insurance plan; and in the 1994 mid-term elections, the Republicans took control of Congress. After the election, the Republicans developed their own welfare reform plan. Their view harkened back to the pre-1935 tradition of public assistance. The sponsors of the bill and their conservative supporters argued that the main problem of families receiving AFDC was not a lack of jobs but a lack of work discipline.

The welfare system, conservatives argued, reduced poor people's initiative by providing them with unending cash benefits (Mead, 1986). Moreover, they argued that the combination of

---

[2]For example, in 1994, total federal and state expenditures for AFDC, job training for AFDC recipients, and child care for AFDC recipients and ex-recipients were $28.5 billion. In contrast, Social Security benefits for 1994 cost $316.8 billion. Medicaid, the program of health insurance benefits for the non-aged poor and for the elderly in nursing homes cost $143.6 billion. Food benefits, including food stamps and programs such as school breakfasts and lunches, cost $38.1 billion. (U.S. Bureau of the Census, 1996.)

AFDC payments, food stamps, medical coverage, and other benefits provided a higher standard of living than could be obtained from low-wage work. It was rational, they argued, for mothers to stay on welfare rather than look for paid work (Murray, 1984). Finally, some conservative thinkers argued that welfare programs worked better when private religious and charitable organizations played a major role, as had been the case prior to 1935. Therefore, they urged that government's role in helping the poor be minimized (Olasky, 1992).

The Republican majority introduced a bill that was much tougher than Clinton's version of welfare reform. First, it ended the entitlement to cash assistance. Instead of a commitment to provide welfare to all eligible families, the federal government would give a fixed amount of money to each state and allow the states to deny aid to eligible families if they exhausted their welfare funds. The federal contribution will not increase until 2003, at the earliest. Second, it limited cash assistance to a maximum of five years (states were free to set shorter time limits); but unlike the Ellwood plan, it provided no federal money for public service jobs for families that reached the time limit. Third, after two years, adults in most welfare families would be required to work at least part-time or their benefits would be cut off. The bill also provided far less in the way of job training, education, and tax benefits than did the liberal approach. In a sense, the Republican plan kept the stick of Clinton's program but threw away most of the carrots.

Twice the Republicans passed a welfare reform bill and twice Clinton, responding to pleas from liberal supporters, vetoed it. Then, in the summer of 1996, just before the start of the Presidential election campaign, the Republicans softened their bill a bit and passed it again. Clinton's welfare advisors urged another veto; but his political advisors, noting his 1992 promise and the unpopularity of welfare with the voters, urged him to sign it. In August, he signed it. After the election, several of his top welfare advisors resigned in protest from their posts in the Administration.[3]

The new law carries the somewhat grandiose title of "The Personal Responsibility and Work Opportunity Reconciliation Act of 1996" and has become known in policy circles by its acronym, PRWORA. It abolishes AFDC and replaces it with Temporary Assistance to Needy Families (TANF). States are now given a fixed amount of money—a so-called TANF block grant, and they are required to maintain their own spending at 75 percent (or more) of their previous levels. However, they have great flexibility in deciding how to spend their TANF funds. They may use the block grant to assist their poor residents in any reasonable way they choose. They may choose time limits shorter than five years (several have chosen time limits of two years or less). Overall, states have much greater control over their programs than before the new law.

THE CONSEQUENCES FOR MARRIAGE AND CHILDBEARING

The entire package—no entitlement, fixed federal payments, work requirement after two years, five-year lifetime limit, and other changes—is breathtaking in scope compared to previous rounds of welfare reform. As recently as the 1980s, no president—not even a conservative Republican such as Ronald Reagan—would have been able to push such a tough program through Congress. Its supporters claim that if recipients are forced to take responsibility for themselves by looking for work and taking any job they can get, they will be better off in the long run. They will have more self-esteem, it was said; their ability to be good parents will improve, and some will eventually move up the job ladder to better-paying work. The opponents

---

[3]One of those officials, Peter Edelman, subsequently described his objections in detail (Edelman, 1997).

of the 1996 legislation called it cruel and heartless. They argued that in today's economy there are not enough jobs for people with little in the way of skills or education. They warned of destitute families, of increases in homelessness, and of more children placed into the expensive and troubled foster care system.

It is commonly believed that the pre-1996 welfare system discouraged marriage, encouraged divorce, and encouraged childbearing outside of marriage among the poor. The reason is that, with few exceptions, two-parent families were not eligible for assistance. As a result, a couple who had a child could receive welfare payments only if they didn't marry or live together. And a married couple could receive welfare payments only if they separated or divorced. Despite the plausibility of these consequences of the welfare system, the social scientific evidence suggests that the effects on marriage are of moderate size, at most, although they may have been increasing in the 1980s (Moffitt, 1992). Under PRWORA, many states are allowing more poor two-parent families to apply for benefits; it remains to be seen whether this change will increase marital stability.

Before 1996, a recipient's benefits were increased if she had another child while on the rolls. During the deliberations on the welfare law, some members of Congress proposed a "family cap," under which a mother who is already receiving welfare benefits and who has another child would not receive an increase in benefits. Their reasoning was that the increase in benefits serves as an incentive for welfare recipients to have more children. Critics responded that the modest size of the increases makes them a minor factor in women's decisions about having children. The family cap provision was deleted from the federal bill before its passage, but the law did allow states to institute family caps if they wished; and by 1998, 23 states had done so (Center for Law and Social Policy, 1999). A study of the New Jersey family cap estimated that it had reduced

births to women receiving welfare by 14,000 but had also increased the number of abortions to women on welfare by 1,400 and denied benefits to 28,000 newborns (Center for Law and Social Policy, 1999). The evidence from other states on whether these family caps have diminished childbearing among welfare recipients is inconclusive.

One reason why the effects of welfare on marriage and childbearing may be smaller than commonly thought is that the value of the average AFDC benefit declined sharply between the 1970s and the 1990s. The decline occurred because most state legislatures refused to increase the benefit level even though inflation eroded its purchasing power. Adjusted for inflation and measured in 1994 dollars, the average state paid $792 per month in 1970 for a family of four and only $435 per month in 1994 for a similar family (Blank, 1997). If welfare benefits were a strong influence on marriage and fertility, one would expect that this drop in welfare benefits would have made marriage more attractive and childbearing outside of marriage less attractive. Yet divorce, cohabitation, and the percentage of births that occurred outside of marriage all increased during this period.

It is possible, nevertheless, that by 1970 welfare benefit levels had reached a high enough level that, even with some erosion, they supported family behaviors that weakened the place of marriage. But other influential changes also were occurring in American society. Since the early 1970s, the earning power of young men without college educations has lessened because of falling wages in the manufacturing sector of the economy. This trend might have made young men reluctant to marry, and it might have made young women skeptical of finding a partner with enough earning power to help sustain a family. A poor young woman who sees little prospect of finding a suitable husband is probably more likely to go ahead and have a child without marrying. In addition, a broad cultural shift away from marriage and toward individual fulfillment was occurring among all social classes.

THE CONSEQUENCES FOR CHILDREN

We know even less about how the new law is affecting poor children. Consider the possible consequences for children of limiting their mother's time on welfare and requiring them to work outside the home. Ronald Haskins, a developmental psychologist and Congressional staff member who was one of the architects of the 1996 law, speculated that the following consequences could occur (Haskins, 1995). On the negative side:

• Children's families could have lower incomes if mothers leave the welfare program for work at very low wages. In some states, the combination of cash welfare, food stamps, and other benefits can exceed the income from minimum-wage jobs. Moreover, low-wage jobs impose new costs (transportation, child care, clothes) and often do not include health insurance.
• Children could be placed in low-quality day care (e.g., too many children per caregiver) while their mothers work. This could hurt their cognitive and emotional development.
• Mothers may be less effective parents because of the increased responsibilities of combining paid work with childrearing. They will be available to their children for fewer hours. They may be more harried and pressed for time, and this may make them more irritable and impatient with their children.

On the positive side, Haskins listed:

• Mothers may be better parents because paid work will give them more self-esteem and satisfaction with their lives. It will improve the mood of those who were depressed because of their dependence on welfare. Consequently, mothers will be less harsh, angry, and punitive in their interactions with their children.
• Paid work imposes a daily routine—a set time to wake up, get to work, cook and eat dinner—that could increase order in the household.

Without a daily adult routine, it is harder for a parent to make sure that children get to school on time, keep doctors' appointments, and so forth.
• Employed parents may make better role models. Children will see parents who are attached to the world of work and may be more confident that they, too, will be able to find employment as adults. They may be more likely to stay in school and to postpone early, nonmarital childbearing.

We don't know which of these effects will dominate, or if other important effects will emerge. Haskins concluded, "Although claims of promoting child welfare will be tossed about by all sides during the debate, there is embarrassingly little good evidence about the impact of the welfare, intervention, and work strategies on children's long-term prospects" (1995, p. 267).

THE CONSEQUENCES FOR IMMIGRANT FAMILIES

The 1996 law also contained sharp restrictions on the receipt of other government benefits. These provisions had little to do with "welfare reform" itself; but they did provide much of the budgetary savings of the bill. A complex series of provisions drastically reduced the benefits that immigrants legally in the United States can receive (Primus, 1996), although many states have reinstated at least some benefits (Zimmermann and Tumlin, 1999). (Illegal immigrants already were ineligible for nearly all benefits and services except emergency medical care and public schools for their children.) Many new immigrants who enter the country legally are now ineligible for TANF, food stamps, or other federally funded benefits until they become citizens (which takes a minimum of five years). Even some legal immigrants who were already in the United States prior to the passage of the law have had food stamps and other benefits taken away.

Concern about public assistance to immigrants resulted from news reports about legal immigrants who brought their elderly parents to the United States and then had them apply for Supplemental Security Income (SSI), a program of cash assistance to the blind, the disabled, and the elderly poor. Studies confirmed that noncitizens were using SSI at a higher rate than citizens (Primus, 1996). Yet the same studies showed that noncitizens didn't have significantly higher rates of usage of other public assistance programs. Nevertheless, some supporters of these restrictions argued that generous U.S. public assistance programs attract excessive numbers of poor immigrants with negative consequences for the economy. Others argued that immigrants, like poor U.S.-born citizens, would be better served by low-wage work than by welfare.[4] (A small proportion of immigrants who are officially classified as political "refugees," such as many Southeast Asians from countries involved in the Vietnam War [Rumbaut, 1989], will remain eligible for all benefits.) Critics of the immigrant provisions predicted that hundreds of thousands of immigrant families would be pushed into poverty.

WHAT HAS HAPPENED SO FAR

Between 1996 and 1999, the welfare rolls continued the steep drop that began about a year before PRWORA was passed. Government statistics show that between January 1996 and December 1998, the number of families receiving welfare declined by 40 percent (U.S. Administration for Children and Families, 1999a). Part of this drop was caused by a tight labor market. The new welfare law had the good fortune of being launched during one of the greatest economic booms in the 20th century. By 1999, the unemployment rate had dropped to its lowest level in 30 years (U.S. Bureau of Labor

Statistics, 1999). Some employers had difficulty finding enough qualified workers and began to hire welfare recipients or other low-skilled workers who, in less prosperous times, would have had more difficulty finding jobs.

But in addition, it seems likely that the passage of the new law, and accompanying state legislation that is sometimes even tougher, has motivated some recipients to leave the rolls and discouraged other low-income families from even applying. Richard Nathan, a political scientist who has long observed the welfare system, argues that PRWORA has changed the culture of the welfare office far more than did previous changes in the law. Most welfare offices now emphasize job search and part-time employment. In some states, welfare intake-workers are allowed to give small cash grants to potential applicants to fix a car or eliminate some other problem that is preventing them from taking a job—on the condition that the applicant is not eligible for TANF for several months or a year. At the same time, mass media coverage of the changes and the drop in the rolls seems to have convinced most low-income family members that time limits and work requirements are here to stay. Nathan and Thomas L. Gais believe that the actions of national and state legislatures, welfare workers, and the mass media have had a "signaling effect" that has altered the behavior of current and potential welfare recipients (Nathan and Gais, 1999).

Even so, little is known about what has happened to recipients who have left the rolls. Several states have attempted to follow former adult recipients by examining employment records, and these studies indicate that half or more of former recipients were working in the months soon after they left welfare (Brauner and Loprest, 1999). A national telephone survey conducted in 1997 by the Urban Institute found that 61 percent of individuals who had left welfare in the previous two years were employed (Loprest, 1999). Their wages were comparable to the earnings of workers in low-income families that had not been on welfare at all in the

---

[4]See Espenshade et al. (1996) for a summary of these arguments.

previous two years. Supporters of PRWORA have taken early indicators such as these as evidence that the legislation has been successful in helping families make the transition from welfare to work. Still, 20 percent of those who left the rolls in the Urban Institute sample were neither working, in a family in which someone else was working, nor receiving government disability benefits. Almost two in five said that there had been a time during the previous year when they were not able to pay mortgage, rent, or utility bills. One-third said that sometime during the previous year they had had to cut the size of meals or skip meals because there wasn't enough food.

The opponents of PRWORA argue that we will not be able to judge its effectiveness until the next time the economy falters and the demand for workers declines. They also note that many former recipients still receive substantial assistance from their states. Because of the specifics of the law, states are receiving as much federal money as they did in 1995, even though their welfare rolls have dropped sharply. This surplus has led many states to provide more money for child-care assistance to former recipients and other working-poor families. Whether states will remain this generous during the next economic downturn is unclear.

In any case, we still know almost nothing about the consequences of PRWORA for the children of the adult former welfare recipients. Several studies are under way that will examine the ways that welfare reform has affected their lives. Key questions include the following: How have basic conditions of safety, diet, and housing changed? With parents in the work force, what kinds of child-care arrangements are being used? How many are receiving health insurance coverage? Are working parents providing more consistent emotional support and supervision to their children or has the quality of their parenting

skills deteriorated? It will be another few years until the answers to these questions are known.

CONCLUSION

The Personal Responsibility and Work Opportunity Reconciliation Act of 1996 may be the most important piece of poverty-policy legislation since the Great Depression. It repeals basic principles of assistance that were established in the Social Security Act of 1935: an entitlement to benefits among all families that qualify for them and a commitment to providing benefits for as long as a family still qualifies. It represents a return to an even older principle of assistance to the poor: that reliance on public assistance for more than a brief period saps people's initiative and self-reliance. According to this line of reasoning, the biggest problem poor people face is not low income but rather dependence on the support of others. Supporters hailed PRWORA for its support of "personal responsibility" and the creation (through time limits on benefits) of "work opportunities" that are in its title.

Critics argue that it may make the lives of many poor families even worse by limiting the assistance they can receive. According to the critics, the basic problem that poor families face is that there are not enough jobs for people without college educations at wages that can sustain a family (Wilson, 1996). They predict widespread hardship, more homelessness, and more domestic violence. They believe that poor children will suffer, rather than benefit, from the new lives their parents are forced to lead.

When PRWORA was passed, some veteran welfare-watchers (e.g., Blank, 1997) who had observed several unsuccessful attempts to enforce work through changes in the welfare laws argued that the legislation would produce less change than its supporters wished and than its critics dreaded. Welfare bureaucrats who sympathized with their clients, it was said, would find ways to work around the regulations; states would petition Congress for changes when they realized how difficult it would be to move large numbers of long-term welfare recipients into the work force. But it now appears that the 1996 law may prove to be the one that finally produces substantial changes in the lives of poor American families. Whether those changes will match the hopes of its defenders or the fears of its critics, we cannot yet say.

REFERENCES

Blank, Rebecca M. "The 1996 Welfare Reform." *Journal of Economic Perspectives* 11 (1997): 169–77.

Brauner, Sara, and Pamela Loprest. "Where Are They Now? What State's Studies of People Who Left Welfare Tell Us." *Assessing the New Federalism,* Series A, No. A-32. Washington, D.C.: The Urban Institute, 1999.

Cherlin, Andrew J. *Marriage, Divorce, Remarriage.* Revised and enlarged edition. Cambridge: Harvard University Press, 1992.

Edelman, Peter. "The Worst Thing Bill Clinton Has Done." *The Atlantic Monthly* (March 1997), pp. 43–56.

Ellwood, David T. *Poor Support: Poverty in the American Family.* New York: Basic Books, 1988.

Espenshade, Thomas J., Michael Fix, Wendy Zimmerman, and Thomas Corbett. "Immigration and Social Policy: New Interest in an Old Issue." *Focus* 18 (1996): 1–10.

Handler, Joel F. *The Poverty of Welfare Reform.* New Haven: Yale University Press, 1995.

Katz, Michael B. *In the Shadow of the Poorhouse: A Social History of Welfare in America.* New York: Basic Books, 1986.

Loprest, Pamela. "Families Who Left Welfare: Who Are They and How Are They Doing?" *Assessing the New Federalism,* Discussion Paper 99-102. Washington, D.C.: The Urban Institute, 1999.

Mead, Lawrence M. *Beyond Entitlement: The Social Obligations of Citizenship.* New York: Free Press, 1986.

Murray, Charles. *Losing Ground: American Social Policy,* 1950–1980. New York: Basic Books, 1984.

Nathan, Richard P., and Thomas L. Gais. "Implementing Welfare Reform." *Rockefeller Institute Bulletin, 1999* (1999): 5–22.

Olasky, Marvin. *The Tragedy of American Compassion.* Washington D.C.: Regnery, 1992.

Piven, Frances Fox, and Richard A. Cloward. *Regulating the Poor: The Functions of Public Welfare.* Updated edition. New York: Vintage Books, 1993.

Primus, Wendell. "Immigration Provisions in the New Welfare Law." *Focus* 18 (1996): 14–19.

Quadagno, Jill S. *The Color of Welfare: How Racism Undermined the War on Poverty.* New York: Oxford University Press, 1994.

Rumbaut, Rubén. G. "The Structure of Refuge: Southeast Asian Refugees in the United States, 1975–1985." *International Review of Comparative Public Policy* 1 (1989): 97–129.

Skocpol, Theda. *Protecting Mothers and Soldiers: The Political Origins of Social Policy in the United States.* Cambridge, MA: The Belknap Press of Harvard University Press, 1992.

U.S. Administration for Children and Families (1999a). "Change in Welfare Caseloads as of December 1998." Available online: www.acf.dhhs. gov/news/stats/cascload.htm (Accessed July 24, 1999).

U.S. Administration for Children and Families (1999b). "Characteristics and Financial Circumstances of AFDC Recipients, FY 96." Available online: www.acf.dhhs.gov/programs/ofa/cfc_fy96.htm (Accessed July 24, 1999).

U.S. Bureau of Labor Statistics. 1999. "Labor Force Statistics from the Current Population Survey." Available online: http://stats.bls.gov/cpsatabs.htm (Accessed July 24,1999).

U.S. Bureau of the Census. *Statistical Abstract of the United States: 1996.* Washington, D.C., U.S. Government Printing Office, 1996.

Wilson, William J. *When Work Disappears: the World of the New Urban Poor.* New York: Alfred A. Knopf, 1996.

Zimmermann, Wendy, and Karen C. Tumlin. "Patchwork Policies: State Assistance for Immigrants under Welfare Reform." *Assessing the New Federalism,* Occasional Paper no. 24. Washington, D.C.: The Urban Institute, 1999.

READING 6-2

Who Should Pay for the Kids?

Paula England and Nancy Folbre

Power never concedes anything without a struggle.
It never has and it never will.
—Frederick Douglass

The debate over family policy in the United States is dominated by rhetorical concern over children's welfare. However noble and sincere, this rhetoric tends to conceal some underlying distributional conflicts. Increased public support for child rearing—such as subsidized child care, universal health insurance, and more generous assistance to poor families with young children—would redistribute income from men to women, from adults and the elderly to the young, and, most likely, from the rich to the poor. In the short run, it would benefit the least powerful groups in our society at the expense of the more powerful. In the long run, however, a more equitable distribution of developing children's capabilities could help equalize opportunities and enhance economic efficiency.

These important issues are largely obscured by the lack of a coherent picture of the costs and benefits of children. In this article, we argue that the time, money, and care that parents devote to the development of children's capabilities create an important public good whose economic benefits are enjoyed by individuals and institutions who pay, at best, a small share of the costs. Economists define a public good as one that is difficult to put a price on because it is nonexcludable (someone can enjoy it without paying for it) and nonrival (one person can enjoy it

without diminishing someone else's enjoyment of it). Individuals who do not contribute to the production of a public good are likely to ride free on other people's efforts unless their responsibilities are enforced through explicit laws and rules, including taxes.

In the first section of this article, we explain why the conventional economic analysis of child-rearing decisions needs to be augmented by consideration of social institutions that affect the distribution of the costs of children between men and women, parents and nonparents, and old and young. An implicit social contract governing the relationship between parents, children, men, and women is now being renegotiated as the structure of family and work life is changing. Yet economists and policymakers have remarkably little to say about who should pay for the costs of rearing the next generation. Some seem to hold an implicit children-as-pets assumption—those who want them should pay for them. Our own view is just the opposite: We believe that all members of society have a moral responsibility to help develop children's capabilities. Even those who disagree with this claim, however, should agree that individuals and institutions enjoying the economic benefits of human capabilities should help pay the costs of developing them.

In the second section, we review the literature on the net costs of children (the difference between the economic costs and benefits). Most researchers have focused on the cost side; closer attention to the benefits leads toward more explicit consideration of what economists call positive externalities, or benefits that are not captured by the actual producers of children's capabilities, especially parents.[1] Both the taxation of the working-age population and less direct amenities enjoyed by friends, spouses, and employers mean that individuals who devote time and money to developing their children's capabilities generate important but unremunerated benefits for other people. As a concrete illustration, consider two individuals who have the same marriage and employment history—

they will receive exactly the same retirement benefits from Social Security, even if one of them raised three children who grew up to become productive members of society and to pay taxes on the income they earned, while the other raised none and simply enjoyed higher levels of personal consumption. Current policies in the United States socialize many of the economic benefits of children while requiring parents, mothers in particular, to pay most of the costs. Children themselves suffer from a high risk of poverty. . .

WHO SHOULD PAY THE COSTS OF CHILDREN?

There is something risky, perhaps even unpleasant, about applying the vocabulary of costs and benefits to children. Family life is one of the few areas of human endeavor that enjoy some protection from the cold logic of self-interest. But consideration of economic factors does not imply that these dominate family decisions. It simply calls attention to the economic consequences of the organization of family life, which has become increasingly costly for women in the United States over time. Women generally devote more time and money to children than men do. Over the last 25 years, they have substantially increased their overall hours of market work to help provide family income. Men, however, have only slightly increased their hours of child care and domestic labor. The percentage of families maintained by women alone is increasing, and enforcement of paternal child support responsibilities remains poor (Folbre 1994b, 1997; Bittman and Pixley 1997).

Over the same time period, the costs of raising children have increased. Education has a heightened impact on the probability of economic success, and the price of college and university services has gone up much faster than the general rate of inflation. As women's earnings have improved, the opportunity cost (or forgone earnings) of time devoted to family has increased. That many other traditional obstacles to gender inequality have been overturned means that parental responsibilities loom large as a current cause of lower earnings and restrictions on career advancement for women. Parents in general and mothers in particular remain highly susceptible to poverty in the United States (Wolff 1996; McLanahan and Kelly forthcoming). Furthermore, poverty rates among children in this country are among the highest in the industrialized world, largely as a result of public policies such as poor enforcement of paternal child support obligations and reluctance to extend public education to children under the age of 5 (Smeeding, Torrey, and Rein 1988; Garfinkel 1996; Bergmann 1996a).

How do economists interpret these trends? Mainstream neoclassical economists focus on adult decisions to maximize utility. By their account, individuals choose to have children and to continue caring for them, only if they get utility (or pleasure) from doing so. By definition, they must be better off as a result (Becker 1960). Applying this reasoning, Victor Fuchs (1988) suggests that single mothers are poor largely because they have stronger preferences for children than fathers do. The implication is that their utility gains must counterbalance their economic losses. Single mothers may have less money than fathers, but they also get more pleasure from their children.

This is consistent with what we call the children-as-pets approach. If people spend a lot of money on their golden retriever, it must be because it makes them happy to do so. In utility terms, they are no worse off than those who simply put an equivalent amount of money in the bank. From this point of view, people who acquire pets but cannot maintain them at a decent level of health and well-being are irresponsible and should be punished. The innocent pets may suffer in the meantime, but if all else fails they can be removed to the animal shelter (also known as the orphanage or foster care).

One can challenge this approach on moral and philosophical grounds. Amartya Sen (1993) argues persuasively that we should aim not to maximize utility but to promote the development of human capabilities. But one can also challenge the children-as-pets approach on its own terms by pointing out that children create far more significant positive externalities than pets do. This may sound obvious, but, as many feminist scholars have pointed out, the legacy of Western political theory from Thomas Hobbes to John Rawls dwells on relations between adult men, relegating mothers and children to the world of nature outside the social contract (Hartsock 1983; Pateman 1988; DiStefano 1991; Okin 1989). Neoclassical economic theory cannot take all the blame—the classical economic theories of Ricardo and Marx treat children as a nonproduced commodity.

Sociologists point out that children pay back their parents by raising children of their own, fulfilling an implicit contract that is obviously crucial to social reproduction (Davis 1937; Ryder 1973). But despite a widespread realization that fertility decline and modernization have transformed the nature of intergenerational relations, the terms of the payback have never been closely interrogated. We lack any systematic theory of what we collectively owe children and what they owe us. It is hardly surprising, therefore, that we lack a coherent vision of what we collectively owe those who take care of children.

HOW DO THE PUBLIC COSTS OF CHILDREN COMPARE TO THE PUBLIC BENEFITS?

Women who put time and energy into children are investing in what is essentially a "family public good." They pay most of the costs, but other family members, including children and fathers, claim an equal share of the benefits (Lommerud 1997). . . .

Individuals who devote time and energy to parenting often enjoy some economic as well as psychological benefits. Adult children seldom transfer much income to their parents, but they often provide care and assistance to those who are elderly. Partly as a result, elderly individuals with living children are less likely than others to require publicly subsidized nursing home care (Wolf in press). However, these private benefits are small compared to the transfers provided through taxation of the working-age population, as well as the less tangible benefits enjoyed by friends, spouses, and employers (Lee 1990; Folbre 1994a). Development economists have long emphasized that economic development is accompanied by a reversal in intergenerational income flows. In simple agrarian societies, children defray many of their economic costs by beginning work at an early age and continuing to contribute to family income as young adults. The more modern and technologically developed the society, however, the less likely parents are to capture the economic benefits of their child-rearing labor (Caldwell 1982). . . . However, the public payoff to investments in children's capabilities, or what neoclassical economists call child quality, tends to increase. . . .

The complete list of positive externalities created by parental and social investments in children's capabilities is quite large, and includes both returns to education and noncognitive skills such as "emotional intelligence" (Goleman 1994). These contribute directly to the stock of human capital and also to the network of relationships and climate of trust and reciprocity that is sometimes termed "social capital" (Gustafsson and Stafford 1997; Kennedy and Welling 1997).

Public expenditures on children are modest compared to those made by parents. Haveman and Wolfe estimate that the sum of public expenditures on children in the United States, composed mostly of education, housing, and income transfers, accounted for about 38 percent of the total cost, and their estimate of total cost is probably low (1995, 1829). Public expenditures on children in the United States are far lower per child than those in countries that, like France, provide subsidized child care for all children at age 3 and beyond (Bergmann 1996b). Over the last 30 years, the elderly in this country have received far greater transfers per capita than the young have (Preston 1984; Fuchs and Reklis 1992). . .

ENDNOTES

1. Parents are not the only producers of children's capabilities. We argue elsewhere that many individuals who engage in caring labor, such as teaching or child care, do so as well (England and Folbre 1999). Furthermore, children help produce their own capabilities. A full consideration of this issue is beyond the scope of this article.

REFERENCES

Becker, Gary. 1960. An Economic Analysis of Fertility. In *Demographic and Economic Change in Developed Countries.* Princeton, NJ: Princeton University Press.

Bergmann, Barbara. 1996a. Child Care: The Key to Ending Child Poverty. In *Social Policies for Children,* ed. Irwin Garfinkel, Jennifer L. Hochschild, and Sara McLanahan. Washington, DC: Brookings Institution.

————. 1996b. *Saving Our Children from Poverty: What the United States Can Learn from France.* New York: Russell Sage Foundation.

Bittman, Michael and Jocelyn Pixley. 1997. *The Double Life of the Family: Myth, Hope, and Experience.* Sydney: Allen & Unwin.

Burggraf, Shirley. 1993. How Should the Cost of Child Rearing Be Distributed? *Challenge* 37(5):48–55.

Caldwell, John. 1982. *The Theory of Fertility Decline.* New York: Academic Press.

Calhoun, Charles A. and Thomas J. Espenshade. 1988. Childbearing and Wives' Foregone Earnings. *Population Studies* 42:5–37.

Coleman, James S. 1988. Social Capital in the Creation of Human Capital. *American Journal of Sociology* 94(supp.):S95–120.

Davis, Kingsley. 1937. Reproductive Institutions and the Pressure for Population. *Sociological Review* 29:289–306.

Demeny, Paul. 1987. Re-Linking Fertility Behavior and Economic Security in Old Age: A Pronatalist Reform. *Population and Development Review* 13(1):128–32.

DiStefano, Christine. 1991. *Configurations of Masculinity: A Feminist Perspective on Modern Political Theory.* Ithaca, NY: Cornell University Press.

Duncan, Greg and Jeanne Brooks-Gunn, eds. 1997. *Consequences of Growing Up Poor.* New York: Russell Sage Foundation.

England, Paula and George Farkas. 1986. *Households, Employment, and Gender: A Social, Economic, and Demographic View.* Hawthorne, NY: Aldine de Gruyter.

England, Paula and Nancy Folbre. 1997. Reconceptualizing Human Capital. Paper presented at the annual meeting of the American Sociological Association.

————. 1999. The Cost of Caring. *The Annals* of the American Academy of Political and Social Science. 561 (Jan.):39–51.

Folbre, Nancy. 1994a. Children as Public Goods. *American Economic Review* 84(2):86–90.

————.1994b. *Who Pays for the Kids? Gender and the Structures of Constraint.* New York: Routledge.

————. 1997. The Future of the Elephant Bird. *Population and Development Review* 23(3):647–54.

Folbre, Nancy and Thomas Weisskopf. 1998. Did Father Know Best? Families, Markets and the Supply of Caring Labor. In *Economics, Values and Organization,* ed. Avner Ben-Ner and Louis Putterman. New York: Cambridge University Press.

Fuchs, Victor. 1988. *Women's Quest for Economic Equality.* Cambridge, MA: Harvard University Press.

Fuchs, Victor and Diane Reklis. 1992. America's Children: Economic Perspectives and Policy Options. *Science,* 3 Jan., 41–46.

Garfinkel, Irwin. 1996. Economic Security for Children: From Means Testing and Bifurcation to Universality. In *Social Policies for Children,* ed. Irwin Garfinkel, Jennifer L. Hochschild, and Sara McLanahan. Washington, DC: Brookings Institution.

Goleman, Daniel. 1994. *Emotional Intelligence.* New York: Bantam Books.

Gustafsson, Siv and Frank P. Stafford. 1997. Childcare, Human Capital, and Economic Efficiency. In *Economics of the Family and Family Policies,* ed. Inga Persson and Christina Jonung. New York: Routledge.

Hartsock, Nancy. 1983. *Money, Sex, and Power: Toward a Feminist Historical Materialism.* New York: Longman.

Haveman, Robert and Barbara Wolfe. 1995. The Determinants of Children's Attainments: A Review of Methods and Findings. *Journal of Economic Literature* 33(Dec.):1829–78.

Jorgenson, Dale W. and Barbara M. Fraumeni. 1990. Investment in Education and U.S. Economic Growth. In *The U.S. Savings Challenge,* ed. Charles E. Walker, Mark A. Bloomfield, and Margo Thorning. Boulder, CO: Westview Press.

Joshi, Heather. 1990. The Cash Opportunity Cost of Childbearing: An Approach to Estimation Using British Evidence. *Population Studies* 44:41–60.

———. 1991. Sex and Motherhood as Sources of Women's Economic Disadvantage. In *Women's Issues in Social Policy,* ed. D. Groves and M. McClean. New York: Routledge.

Juster, F. Thomas and Frank Stafford. 1991. The Allocation of Time: Empirical Findings, Behavioral Models, and Problems of Measurement. *Journal of Economic Literature* 24 (June):471–522.

Kamerman, Sheila B. and Alfred J. Kahn, eds. 1991. *Child Care, Parental Leave, and the Under 3s: Policy Innovation in Europe.* New York: Auburn House.

Kennedy, Peter W. and Linda Welling. 1997. Parental Externalities and the Private Provision of Childcare. *Canadian Journal of Economics* 30:822–34.

Kotlikoff, Laurence J. 1992. *Generational Accounting: Knowing Who Pays, and When, for What We Spend.* New York: Free Press.

Koven, Seth and Sonya Michel, eds. 1993. *Mothers of a New World: Maternalist Politics and the Origins of Welfare States.* New York: Routledge.

Lee, Ronald with the assistance of Tim Miller. 1990. Population Policy and Externalities to Childbearing. *The Annals* of the American Academy of Political and Social Science 510(July):17–32.

Leibowitz, Arleen. 1996. Child Care: Private Cost or Public Responsibility. In *Individual and Social Responsibility: Child Care, Education, Medical Care, and Long-Term Care in America,* ed. Victor R. Fuchs. Chicago: University of Chicago Press.

Lommerud, Kjell Erik. 1997. Battles of the Sexes: Non-Cooperative Games in the Theory of the Family. In *Economics of the Family and Family Policies,* ed. Inga Persson and Christina Jonung. New York: Routledge.

Mayer, Susan. 1997. *What Money Can't Buy: Family Income and Children's Life Chances.* Cambridge, MA: Harvard University Press.

McElroy, Marjorie. 1990. The Empirical Content of Nash-Bargained Household Behavior. *Journal of Human Resources* 25(4):559–83.

McLanahan, Sara and Erin L. Kelly. Forthcoming. The Feminization of Poverty: Past and Future. In *Handbook of Gender Sociology,* ed. Janet Chafetz. New York: Plenum.

Musgrave, Richard A. and Peggy B. Musgrave. 1989. *Public Finance in Theory and Practice.* New York: McGraw-Hill.

Nelson, Julie A. 1993. Household Equivalence Scales: Theory Versus Policy? *Journal of Labor Economics* 11(3):471–93.

Okin, Susan Moller. 1989. *Justice, Gender and the Family.* New York: Basic Books.

Pateman, Carol. 1988. *The Sexual Contract.* Stanford, CA: Stanford University Press.

Preston, Samuel. 1984. Children and the Elderly: Divergent Paths for America's Dependents. *Demography* 21:435–57.

Quadagno, Jill. 1994. *The Color of Welfare: How Racism Undermined the War on Poverty.* New York: Oxford University Press.

Ryder, Norman. 1973. A New Approach to the Economic Theory of Fertility Behavior: A Comment. *Journal of Political Economy* 81(2):S65–69.

Samuelson, Robert J. 1998. Investing in Our Children. *Newsweek,* 23 Feb., 45.

Sen, Amartya. 1993. Capability and Well-Being. In *The Quality of Life,* ed. Martha Nussbaum and Amartya Sen. Oxford: Clarendon Press.

Simon, Julian L. 1981. *The Ultimate Resource.* Princeton, NJ: Princeton University Press.

Skocpol, Theda. 1993. *Protecting Soldiers and Mothers: The Politics of Social Provision in the United States, 1870s–1920s.* Cambridge, MA: Harvard University Press.

Smeeding, Timothy M., Barbara Boyle Torrey, and Martin Rein. 1988. Patterns of Income and Poverty: The Economic Status of Children and the Elderly in Eight Countries. In *The Vulnerable,* ed. John L. Palmer, Timothy Smeeding, and Barbara Boyle Torrey. Washington, DC: Urban Institute.

U.S. Department of Agriculture. 1997. Expenditures on Children by Families, 1997 Annual Report. Washington, DC: Department of Agriculture. Available from http://www.huduscr. org/publications/publicassist/welreform.html.

Waldfogel, Jane. 1997. The Effects of Children on Women's Wages. *American Sociological Review* 62:209–17.

Willis, Robert. 1982. The Direction of Intergenerational Transfers and Demographic Transition: The Caldwell Hypothesis Reexamined. In *Income Distribution in the Family,* ed. Yoram Ben Porath, supp. to *Population and Development Review* 8:207–34.

Wolf, Douglas A. In press. Efficiency in the Allocation and Targeting of Community-Based Long-Term Care Resources. *Journal of Aging and Health.*

Wolff, Edward N. 1996. The Economic Status of Parents in Postwar America. Paper prepared for the meeting of the National Parenting Association, 20 Sept.

PART THREE

SEXUALITY, PARTNERSHIP, AND MARRIAGE

CHAPTER 7

Sexuality and Love

Sociology is here to tell you that sexual behavior, our most private activity, and romantic love, our most personal emotion, are heavily influenced by society. That might be obvious in a society where unmarried women's chastity is closely protected and parents choose their children's spouses. It might even be obvious were we to look back at the United States in the 1950s, when many young men and a majority of young women had first sexual intercourse with the person they chose to marry. But the claim is that although social influences are weaker now, sex and love are still structured in large part by society.

That is certainly the message of social scientists from the University of Chicago, who, in 1992, conducted the first comprehensive national survey of sexual behavior and attitudes. They published a long, scholarly work full of tables, *The Social Organization of Sexuality*.[1] A shorter, less technical version, *Sex in America:*

A Definitive Survey, from which the following excerpt is taken, was written in collaboration with science writer Gina Kolata. The authors argue that although sex may seem personal, it is also influenced by the social—by the attitudes of family members and friends, by laws, and by customs. They demonstrate this by analyzing the responses of people in the study to nine statements about sexuality (e.g., "premarital sex is always wrong"). They found that, based on responses to these statements, people can be classified into a few groups that differ sharply in their social characteristics. The authors attempt to draw lessons from these group differences about why debates over sexual issues are so heated.

But is sexuality totally constructed by society? Consider the differing ways women and men experience sexuality. Don't biological differences between women and men play a role? Indeed, best-selling books in the 1990s, such as *Men Are from Mars, Women Are from Venus,*[2]

---

[1]Edward O. Laumann, John H. Gagnon, Robert T. Michael, and Stuart Michaels, *The Social Organization of Sexuality: Sexual Practices in the United States* (Chicago: University of Chicago Press, 1994).

[2]John Gray, *Men Are From Mars, Women Are From Venus* (New York: HarperCollins, 1992).

argued that gender differences in sexuality are largely driven by biology. In contrast, most sociologists continue to insist that biological influences are minimal. In the following excerpt, sociologists Pepper Schwartz and Virginia Rutter search for a middle ground. Although partial to the position that social influences are greater than biological influences, Schwartz and Rutter maintain that *both* mechanisms must be included in a complete explanation of gender differences in sexual behavior and desire. In making their case, they present clear summaries of the opposing theoretical positions in this debate: sociobiology, which emphasizes evolutionary influences on human behavior, and social constructionism, which emphasizes social control.

Sex and Society

Robert T. Michael, John H. Gagnon, Edward O. Laumann, and Gina Kolata

In private and in public, within our families and among our friends, most of us are living the sexual lives that society has urged upon us. Social networks match up couples, sexual preferences are learned or mimicked within networks, social forces push Americans toward marriage and so richly reward wedded couples that marriage turns out to be the best way to have regular sex and the best way to have a happy sex life.

But there is more to social forces than social networks, social scripts, and a widespread conviction that marriage is the ultimate goal for nearly everyone. There also are social attitudes and beliefs, the very beliefs that show up in many of the contradictory messages that we all hear about the power and the pleasure—and the shame—of sexuality.

These attitudes and beliefs underlie some of the bitter social debates of our day. Should there be limits on a woman's right to an abortion? Should sex education be taught in schools? Should we treat homosexuality as just another lifestyle or should we consider it a sin or abnormality?

One way to look at the roots of these arguments is to ask whether there is any relationship between sexual behavior and deep-seated feelings about sexual morality. And if there is a relationship between behavior and beliefs, who is likely to hold which attitudes? Are highly educated people more likely to be libertarians? Do religious people have fewer sexual partners? Do

people who view sex as a form of recreation do different things in bed than people who say their sexual behavior is guided by their religious beliefs?

In a broader sense, looking for such a relationship tests our entire thesis that sexual behavior is a social behavior, determined, shaped, and molded by society like other more visible behaviors—religious practices or recreational habits, for example. If sexual behavior were a completely independent force, not subject to conscious thoughts but controlled instead by hormones, or whipped up by drives, then it should matter little what a person's attitudes are.

We asked our respondents about their attitudes and beliefs about sexual behavior, and, separately, we asked them what appealed to them sexually and what they did. This enabled us to put the pieces together. We found that there is a strong, robust link between attitudes and sexual behavior, and that it suggests why so many social issues related to sex are so contentious. Not only do people's underlying attitudes about questions of sexual morality predict what sort of sex they have in the privacy of their bedrooms, but they even predict how often people *think* about sex.

From the different attitudes and, correspondingly, different behavior of men and women, of older and younger people, and of people of different religions, we can suggest why it is that there is a war between the sexes, why it is that many women complain that men will not commit themselves to marriage, and why it is that many older people are dismayed by the sexual practices of the young.

To learn about attitudes and beliefs, we asked several questions about opinions regarding sexual behavior and other related topics, nine of which we discuss below. For example, we asked respondents to tell us how they felt about premarital sex. Was it always wrong, almost always wrong, sometimes wrong, or not wrong at all? We asked about sex between people of the same gender. Was it always, almost always, sometimes, or never wrong? We asked respondents if their religious beliefs guided their behavior. Then, with the replies to nine such questions in hand, we used a method called cluster analysis to divide the population into groups according to their opinions about those nine issues. Although people in each group varied, overall they had a general set of similar beliefs about key issues.

Cluster analysis is a frequently used tool of social scientists who often need to find patterns in masses of data and are not aided by strong theory in their quest. In our case, we did not know ahead of time how people would sort themselves out by their answers to these questions and we knew, at the outset, that there were a large number of possible combinations of answers to our nine questions. Since each person answered all nine questions about his or her attitudes and beliefs, and since we are focusing here on whether the respondents agreed or disagreed with each statement, there are a total of 2^9 or 512 ways to answer the set of nine questions. But, we reasoned, if there are logical or belief-driven patterns to the answers, there should be certain clusters of replies among all these possibilities. A man, for example, who says his religious convictions guide his views toward sexuality might also say that sex outside of marriage is always wrong, that teenage sex is always wrong, that extramarital sex is always wrong, and that abortions should be prohibited.

Cluster analysis underlies many studies in which people are categorized according to their replies to an array of questions rather than a single one. For example, a cluster analysis looking for voting patterns might group people according to their replies to such questions as: Should capital punishment be abolished? Should all companies be required to practice affirmative action? Should handguns be outlawed? Should women have the right to an abortion for any reason? Should states provide vouchers for parents who choose to send their children to private schools? People in each group would have similar answers to the questions. While no one question characterizes a person's political views, and while each person in a cluster will not give ex-

actly the same answers as every other person in the cluster, the pattern of their replies could be a good indication of their political leanings.

In this particular analysis, we divided the respondents into three broad categories on the basis of their attitudes. First is the *traditional* category, which includes about one-third of our sample. These people say that their religious beliefs always guide their sexual behavior. In addition, they say that homosexuality is always wrong, that there should be restrictions on legal abortions, that premarital sex, teenage sex, and extramarital sex are wrong.

Second is what we called the *relational* category, whose members believe that sex should be part of a loving relationship, but that it need not always be reserved for marriage. These people, who make up nearly half of our sample, disagree with the statement that premarital sex is always wrong, for example. Most, however, say that marital infidelity is always wrong and that they would not have sex with someone they did not love. The third group is the *recreational* category, who constitute a little more than a quarter of the sample. Their defining feature is their view that sex need not have anything to do with love. In addition, most of those in this third group oppose laws to prohibit the sale of pornography to adults.

Within each of these categories, however, people varied in their attitudes, and so we subdivided the categories to further characterize our respondents. A man would be part of the relational group, for example, if he thinks extramarital sex is always wrong and that he would not have sex with anyone unless he loved her. But he might also say that same-gender sex is always wrong. A woman who is in a different group in that category might agree with him about extra-marital sex and sex with a partner she loved, but disagree about same-gender sex being wrong.

Table 1 shows how the groups are categorized, according to people's replies to the nine questions on attitudes.

DESCRIPTION OF SEVEN NORMATIVE ORIENTATIONS TOWARD SEXUALITY

	Traditional			Relational		Recreational		Total sample
	Conservative	Pro-choice	Religious	Conventional	Contemporary religious	Pro-life	Libertarian	
1. Premarital sex is always wrong	100.0*	23.6	0.0	0.4	0.8	6.5	0.0	19.7
2. Premarital sex among teenagers is always wrong	99.5	90.3	78.6	29.1	33.6	65.7	19.7	60.8
3. Extramarital sex is always wrong	98.2	91.0	92.1	94.2	52.1	59.3	32.0	76.7
4. Same-gender sex is always wrong	96.4	94.4	81.9	65.4	6.4	85.9	9.0	64.8
5. There should be laws against the sale of pornography to adults	70.6	47.2	53.1	12.2	11.7	14.9	6.4	33.6
6. I would not have sex with someone unless I was in love with them	87.5	66.0	98.0	83.8	65.3	10.1	19.5	65.7
7. My religious beliefs have guided my sexual behavior	91.3	72.9	74.7	8.7	100.0	25.0	0.0	52.3
8. A woman should be able to obtain a legal abortion if she was raped	56.3	98.6	82.3	99.1	99.3	84.3	99.8	88.0
9. A woman should be able to obtain a legal abortion if she wants it for any reason	0.5	100.0	0.0	87.4	84.9	9.3	88.6	52.4
N = 2,843	15.4%	15.2%	19.1%	15.9%	9.3%	8.7%	16.4%	100.0%

Oversample was excluded from analysis, as were respondents who had missing values for one or more items. Clusters were derived by minimizing the squared Euclidean distance between members within each cluster. All items were dichotomized before clustering. Column percentages.
* Indicates the percentage of persons in the "Conservative Traditional" cluster who believe that premarital sex is always wrong.

161

TABLE 2

DISTRIBUTION OF NORMATIVE ORIENTATIONS WITHIN DEMOGRAPHIC GROUPS

Social characteristics	Normative orientation		
	Traditional	Relational	Recreational
Gender			
Men	26.9%	40.1%	33.0%
Women	33.7	47.6	18.7
Age			
Men			
18–24	17.4	46.9	35.7
25–29	21.0	46.2	32.9
30–39	26.2	38.6	35.2
40–49	31.2	38.2	30.5
50–59	40.1	31.3	28.6
Women			
18–24	23.0	51.8	25.3
25–29	27.5	54.6	17.9
30–39	34.6	46.6	18.8
40–49	34.5	44.9	20.6
50–59	47.0	43.4	9.6
Marital/Residential Status			
Men			
Noncohabiting	18.4	39.7	42.0
Cohabiting	8.6	48.4	43.0
Married	36.4	39.0	24.5
Women			
Noncohabiting	31.9	46.8	21.3
Cohabiting	23.9	50.4	25.6
Married	36.2	48.1	15.8

The columns show the percentages of our population who agree with the statements in the column on the left. We divided the traditional category into "conservative" and "pro-choice" groups essentially according to their opinions on abortion. Although people in this category nearly all believe that premarital sex among teenagers, same-gender sex, and extramarital sex are always wrong, they split on whether a women should be able to have an abortion.

The relational category breaks down into three groups, which we have labeled as religious, conventional, and contemporary religious. Those in the religious group said that religious beliefs shape their sexual behavior and tended to say that they oppose sex between people of the same gender and they oppose abortions. The conventional group is more tolerant than the religious group toward teenage sex, pornography, and abortion and are far less likely to say they are influenced by religious beliefs. But most think that same-gender sex and extramarital sex are always wrong. The contemporary religious group is much more tolerant of homosexuality but people in this group say that they are guided by their religious beliefs.

In the recreational category, there are two groups. One, which we call pro-life, consists of people who oppose both homosexuality and abortion for any reason but who are more accepting of teenage sex, extramarital sex, and pornography. The second group is the libertarian group. They have the most accepting position on all the items. None of this libertarian group considers religion as a guide to their sexual behavior.

TABLE 2 (continued)

DISTRIBUTION OF NORMATIVE ORIENTATIONS WITHIN DEMOGRAPHIC GROUPS

Social characteristics	Normative orientation		
	Traditional	Relational	Recreational
Education			
Men			
Less than high school	31.6	39.5	28.8
High school graduate or equivalent	28.3	40.9	30.8
Any college	25.0	39.8	35.2
Women			
Less than high school	36.6	47.6	15.9
High school graduate or equivalent	38.3	46.0	15.7
Any college	30.4	48.7	20.9
Religion			
Men			
None	11.7	39.1	49.2
Mainline Protestant	24.2	43.8	32.0
Conservative Protestant	44.5	30.1	25.3
Catholic	17.8	49.6	32.6
Women			
None	10.4	44.4	45.2
Mainline Protestant	30.9	51.4	17.7
Conservative Protestant	50.5	38.4	11.2
Catholic	22.2	58.0	19.8
Race/Ethnicity			
Men			
White	26.1	41.6	32.3
Black	32.4	25.4	42.3
Hispanic	25.3	45.1	29.7
Women			
White	30.5	48.3	21.2
Black	45.3	45.8	8.9
Hispanic	40.7	43.2	16.1

Note: Percentages in rows total 100 percent.

Just dividing the respondents into these groupings on the basis of their opinions, however, tells only part of the story. We also want to know how the groups differ by social characteristics. Men and women gravitate to different groups, as seen in Table 2. So do older and younger people and so do blacks and whites. The distribution of people into groups reveals why the formation of social policy regarding sexual issues is so contentious and so complex.

The top rows of Table 2 tell us that women are more likely to have the opinions we labeled "traditional" and are much less likely to have the views we called "recreational." By age, we see that the older men and women are disproportionately "traditional" and much less likely to hold the "recreational" views.

With distributions like this, it is no wonder that the battle between the sexes rages. Lance Morrow, a columnist for *Time* magazine, bemoaned men's fate. Women, he complained, have a particularly pejorative view of hapless men, thinking and saying something like "Men-are-animals-I-don't-care-if-they're-not-doing-anything-at-the-moment-they're-thinking-about-it-and-they-will-when-they-have-a-chance."

Some women, on the other hand, have sniped that men are not so blameless, pointing out that many men still leer at women when they walk down the street, and some men act like they have to be dragged kicking and screaming into marriage, behaving as if marriage is a ball and chain.

The distribution of men and women in the attitude clusters tells us, at least, that many more women than men are looking for love and consider marriage to be a prerequisite for sex. When women bitterly complain that the men they meet are not interested in long-term commitments, their laments have a ring of truth. Many more men than women are looking for sexual play and pleasure, with marriage or even love not necessarily a part of it. After all, men in the recreational category may be unlikely to feel that linking sex with marriage is high on their list of priorities. When men note that their girlfriends are always trying to lure them into making a commitment to exclusivity or that their relationships seem to end with an ultimatum—marry me or get out—there is a good reason for it.

The conflicting goals of men and women—and particularly young men and young women—are played out in the lines the men may use when they meet women. And at no time is this more true than in adolescence and young adulthood, the very time that men are most likely to be part of all-male groups who have recreational attitudes toward sex.

Elijah Anderson, a sociologist at the University of Pennsylvania, tells how black teenagers in an inner-city neighborhood take on these roles: "The lore of the streets says there is a contest going on between the boy and girl before they even meet. To the young man, the woman becomes, in the most profound sense, a sexual object. Her body and mind are the object of a sexual game, to be won for his personal aggrandizement." And to win a young woman, An-

derson says, the young man devises a rap, "whose object is to inspire sexual interest."*

The young women, on the other hand, want "a boyfriend, a fiancé, a husband, and the fairy-tale prospect of living happily ever after with one's children in a good house in a nice neighborhood," Anderson says. So the young man, trying to have sex with a woman, "shows her the side of himself that he knows she wants to see, that represents what she wants in a man." He may take the young woman to church, visit her family, help her with chores. But after the young man has sex with the young woman, he often leaves her for a new conquest.

The teenage woman "may know she is being played but given the effectiveness of his rap, his presentation of self, his looks, his age, his wit, his dancing ability, and his general popularity, infatuation often rules," Anderson notes.

Put differently, we see in this typical script the competitive marketplace for sexual partners. The young man is emphasizing those of his attributes that he thinks will attract the young woman. He engages in negotiations and interchanges designed, with all his strategic skills, to persuade her that a friendship that includes sex will be to her liking. She, similarly, emphasizes her attributes that she thinks might attract the most appealing guy. She carefully calibrates her encouragement and insists on behavior that wraps sex into the bundle of activities that she desires.

Whether the outcome is a single sex episode or a more steady dating relationship or even a longer-term sexual partnership, each of these young people offers and withholds, explores and considers, and reaches agreement about the sex. The strategic behavior by each, designed to at-

---

*Elijah Anderson, *Streetwise: Race, Class, and Change in an Urban Community* (Chicago: University of Chicago Press, 1990).

tract the partner and achieve the objective that each seeks, embeds the individual's endeavor in a social context that typically involves competition.

The table also shows us that the married men and women are least likely to hold the recreational view of sexuality, while the not-married men are far more likely to hold that set of views. The cohabiting men and women, on the other hand, are least likely to hold the traditional views of sexuality. Of course, these unmarried men and women are also likely to be younger than those who are married, so the pattern by marital status partly just mirrors the pattern we noted above that older (and married) people hold more traditional views while the younger (unmarried) people are more likely to be in the recreational category. This contributes to the battle of the generations. Older people, often the parents of teenagers or of people in their 20s, tend to have a very different view of the purpose of sex.

The age distribution also suggests the possibility that people change their attitudes over the years (though our data cannot confirm this), moving from times, in their youth, when they thought love need have nothing to do with sex to times, when they grow older, when loving relationships became more central to sexuality. People seem to move along the spectrum from libertarian toward conservative as they age. This could be one reason why 58 percent of our respondents who said premarital sex is always wrong also told us that they themselves had had sex before they were married. And it could explain why 26 percent of our respondents who told us that teenage sex is always wrong also said that they had had sex when they were teenagers. These differences by age might, on the other hand, reflect lifelong held differences of opinion of those born in the 1930s, the 1940s, and so on, but we speculate that these opinions change with age.

When we look at the relationship between race, religion, and education and attitudes about sex, we can see why people tend to feel more comfortable when they choose partners like themselves. The table shows, for example, that few who are not religious are part of the traditional category, but 48 percent of conservative Protestants are traditionalists. People with no religion are most likely to be part of the recreational category—nearly half are found here.

Our findings also show that the clichéd strife between black men and black women may, in fact, reflect fundamentally different attitudes about sex. Black women are more likely than white or Hispanic women to be traditionalists and are noticeably less likely than other women to be in the recreational category—fewer than 10 percent of black women have recreational views toward sex. But black men are noticeably more likely than other men to be in the recreational group—more than 40 percent have recreational views.

The pattern seen in Table 2 by education level is not dramatic, but it is quite systematic. Those with less than a high school level of education are more likely to hold traditional views about sexuality and less likely to hold recreational views; those with college education are just the opposite: they are more likely to hold the recreational views and least likely to hold the traditional views.

We did not have strong expectations or theories about how people's views of sexuality might be related to their social characteristics. But our findings seem to confirm the notion that people's beliefs about sexual morality are part of a much broader social and religious outlook that helps define who they are. Their orientations are reinforced by their friends and family and others in their social networks.

The next question is whether what people believe about sexual behavior is linked to what they actually do sexually. It is one thing to have a certain set of attitudes, but it is another thing to have those attitudes determine your most private acts, wishes, and thoughts. Yet that is what

TABLE 3

SELECTED SEXUAL BEHAVIORS WITHIN NORMATIVE GROUPS

	Panel A: Men		
	Normative orientation		
Sexual behaviors	Traditional	Relational	Recreational
Partners last year: Noncohabiting			
None	40.6%	22.4%	12.8%
One	30.2	41.0	27.9
Two or more	29.2	36.6	59.4
Partners last year: Married			
Zero or one	97.0	96.0	84.9
Two or more	3.0	4.0	15.1
Last year sex frequency			
None	12.5	8.8	8.4
Three times a month or less	31.4	34.2	35.9
Once a week or more	56.1	57.1	55.7
Think about sex			
Twice a month or less	13.4	14.1	7.1
Twice a week or less	40.8	35.3	27.0
Daily or more	45.8	50.6	65.9
Masturbate			
Never	50.2	35.5	25.6
Three times a month or less	32.1	38.5	39.4
Once a week or more	17.7	26.0	35.0
Had oral sex (active or passive) with primary partner in last year			
Yes	56.4	78.2	80.7
Had anal sex during lifetime			
Yes	18.7	23.1	32.3
Ever had same-gender partner since age 18			
Yes	2.6	4.5	7.8

we find, as seen in Table 3. Membership in a particular attitudinal group is closely associated with what their sexual practices are. It is even correlated with how often people think about sex and how often they have sex.

The top portion of both panels of Table 3 shows the number of sex partners in the past year for the men and women who are not living with a partner. We see there that those who have traditional views about sexuality mostly have zero or one partner and only a relatively small percentage had two or more sex partners in the past year: about 30 percent of the men and about 14 percent of the women have that many. But of those who held recreational views of sexuality, about 60 percent of the men and nearly 50 percent of the women had two or more sex partners in the past year. Their attitudes and opinions, as characterized by the three categories of traditional, relational, and recreational, do in fact distinguish these unmarried and non-cohabiting respondents quite effectively in terms of their number of sex partners in the past year.

To be sure, there are a few of those with a traditionalist view who have several sex partners, and a few of those with a recreationalist's view who have no sex partner or one partner, but in the main, the views they held are very

TABLE 3 (continued)

SELECTED SEXUAL BEHAVIORS WITHIN NORMATIVE GROUPS

	Panel B: Women		
	Normative orientation		
Sexual behaviors	Traditional	Relational	Recreational
Partners last year: Noncohabiting			
None	46.7	25.2	14.6
One	39.1	52.6	36.6
Two or more	14.1	22.2	48.8
Partners last year: Married			
Zero or one	98.0	98.5	92.5
Two or more	2.0	1.5	7.5
Last year sex frequency			
None	18.5	10.8	8.0
Three times a month or less	31.5	34.0	39.6
Once a week or more	50.0	55.1	52.4
Think about sex			
Twice a month or less	45.0	36.8	30.1
Twice a week or less	40.6	44.0	39.0
Daily or more	14.3	19.2	30.8
Masturbate			
Never	69.0	56.6	37.5
Three times a month or less	26.0	35.4	50.2
Once a week or more	5.0	8.1	12.3
Had oral sex (active or passive) with primary partner in last year			
Yes	55.9	73.9	83.6
Had anal sex during lifetime			
Yes	13.2	19.5	37.5
Ever had same-gender partner since age 18			
Yes	0.8	3.0	8.6

Note: Percentages in columns total 100 percent within the categories; the "no" percentages are omitted in the last three.

consistent with the number of partners they had in the past year.

The same is true of those who are married, as seen in the second set of rows in Table 3. For the men who were traditionalists or relationalists, only 3 or 4 percent had more than one sex partner in the past year, but as many as 15 percent of those who were recreationalists had more than one. The same pattern is seen for the married women where only 1 or 2 percent of the traditionalists and relationalists had more than one partner but more than 7 percent of the recreationalists had more than one. The tremendous influence of mar-

ital status on the number of sex partners is seen here, with a vast majority of the married men and women having zero or one sex partner in the past year, and the unmarried much more likely to have several, but within both marital statuses the influence of these opinions shines through.

In contrast, people's views about sex had little bearing on how often they had sex. Roughly half of those in each of the three categories report having sex once a week or more. Although somewhat fewer recreationalists said they did not have sex at all last year, the difference between them and those in other groups was not very great. We suspect it reflects the fact that people in the recreational group are more likely to be young and may not have yet found a sexual partner, however much they may want to.

Whether they are actually having sex or not, people who are recreationalists are much more likely than traditionalists to think about sex every day and are much more likely to masturbate. Those in the recreational group are twice as likely as those in the traditionalist group to report that they masturbated once a week or more.

Oral and anal sex and sex with someone of the same gender follow the same patterns, as is seen in the bottom three rows of Table 3. Recreationalists are more likely than traditionalists to have had oral sex in the last year with their partner. They also are more likely to have had anal sex. And they are more likely to have had same-gender sex. In fact, as we move along the scale from traditionalist to recreationalist, the frequency of oral sex, anal sex, and same-gender sex increases.

Overall, people's sexual opinions and their behavior mesh quite closely. We cannot tell whether the opinions prompted the behavior or whether the behavior prompted the opinions, or both, but the relationship is clear.

From these findings on attitudes, beliefs, and sexual behavior along with our findings on sexual networks and choices of sexual partners, we can start to see why America has such heated social policy debates about sexual issues such as abortion, public nudity, gay rights, and pornography.

As Table 2 showed, opinions and social characteristics seem to go hand in hand. The young have one set of opinions about sexuality while older adults have another; conservative Protestants have one set of views while those without religious affiliations have another; the less educated tend to have different views than the well educated. Table 3 showed that people's attitudes are reflected in their behavior, so different groups really do act differently.

We see that we have probably paired off with someone who has many of our own opinions

about sexuality. That is, in fact, probably a key reason why we choose partners from our own social group. Of course, opinions also may shift and become more similar as the partnership continues, but when that happens, it only makes the partnership stronger. It can be very difficult to maintain a sexual relationship with someone who strongly disagrees with you about such matters as whether abortion or extramarital sex is always wrong or whether religious beliefs always guide sexual behavior.

Our friends and families, the members of our social networks, also tend to be like us in social characteristics, and so they are likely to share many of our opinions about sexual behavior. Consequently, when we have discussions with our friends we tend to be speaking to people who are like us and who agree with us about sex. So we tend to get reinforcement for our views. That is probably one of the main reasons why our opinions are so internally consistent and so well reflected in our sexual behavior.

But all this reinforcement and consistency make it very threatening to change our views, to become convinced by an outside argument or to change an opinion about one aspect of sexual behavior, such as whether extramarital sex is always wrong, without changing any other opinions. Our opinions, behavior, and social networks all tend to encourage us to hold to those views that help tie all these opinions, beliefs, and behavior together. And when we see these sets of behaviors as woven together by our religious beliefs and our ethical principles, we are, quite understandably, reluctant to give ground. So the national debates on so many of these sexual issues become heated and all sides become entrenched. No wonder we are a nation that is deeply conflicted about sexual matters and that the disputes seem to go on forever, with no compromises in sight.

And with this we have traveled full circle, going from an investigation of what people do and who they are to who they are and what they do and what they believe about sex. We began our study by asking whether sexual behavior could be studied in the same way as other social behaviors and, if so, whether it followed any social rules. We asked whether the privateness of sexual behavior and the powerful myths put it in a class apart from other social behaviors or whether, when we drew back the curtain and looked at what really happens, sexual behavior would turn out to be not so mysterious after all.

In every instance, our data have shown that social forces are powerful and persistent in determining sexual behavior. We have found that our society constrains us, nudging us toward partners who are like ourselves. But, at the same time, it frees us, putting us together with people who have the same sorts of general understandings about sex that we do and so easing our way into sexual intimacies and revelations. We also found that although America may not be as sexy a place as it is often portrayed, most people are satisfied with the sexual lives they have chosen or that were imposed upon them.

America is not the golden land of eroticism where everybody who is young and beautiful has a hot sex life. Nor is it a land where vast hordes of miserable people, kicked out of the sexual banquet, lick their wounds in silence and resentment. Instead, it is a nation that uses social forces to encourage sexual norms and whose sexual behavior is, in large measure, socially determined. It is a nation of people who are for the most part content, or at least not highly dissatisfied, with the sexual lots they have drawn.

And, for those who feel the status quo is far from ideal, we have found that the costs of breaching the social pressures may be high, and the rewards of going along may be great. But by seeing where and how the pressures are brought to bear, we can break away from the myths and magical thinking that have captured us in the past. With unclouded eyes, we can ask whether we really want changes in sexual behavior and, if so, what the benefits and costs of these changes might be.

READING 7-2

Sexual Desire and Gender

Pepper Schwartz and Virginia Rutter

SOCIOBIOLOGY AND EVOLUTIONARY PSYCHOLOGY

The past few decades of research on sexuality have produced a new school of human behavior—sociobiology and a related discipline, evolutionary psychology—that explains most gender differences as strategies of sexual reproduction. According to evolutionary psychologist David Buss (1995), "Evolutionary psychologists predict that the sexes will differ in precisely those domains in which women and men have faced different sorts of adaptive problems" (p. 164). By "those domains," Buss refers to reproduction, which is the only human function that depends on a biological difference between men and women.

The key assumption of sociobiological/evolutionary theory is that humans have an innate, genetically triggered impulse to pass on their genetic material through successful reproduction: This impulse is called reproductive fitness. The human species, like other species that sociobiologists study, achieves immortality by having children who live to the age of reproductive maturity and produce children themselves. Sociobiologists and evolutionary psychologists seek to demonstrate that almost all male and female behavior, and especially sexuality, is influenced by this one simple but powerful proposition.

Sociobiologists start at the species level. Species are divided into *r* and *K* reproductive categories. Those with *r* strategies obtain immortality by mass production of eggs and

Pepper Schwartz and Virginia Rutter, "Sexual Desire and Gender" from *The Gender of Sexuality*. Copyright © 1998 by Pine Forge Press, Inc. Reprinted with the permission of the authors and Pine Forge Press, Inc.

sperm. The *r* species is best illustrated by fish. The female manufactures thousands of eggs, the male squirts millions of sperm over them, and that is the extent of parenting. According to this theory, the male and female fish need not pair up to nurture their offspring. Although thousands of fertilized fish eggs are consumed by predators, only a small proportion of the massive quantity of fertilized eggs must survive for the species to continue. In the *r* species, parents need not stay together for the sake of the kids.

In contrast, humans are a *K*-strategy species, which has a greater investment in each fertilized egg. Human females and most female mammals have very few eggs, especially compared to fish. Moreover, offspring take a long time to mature in the mother's womb and are quite helpless after they are born, with no independent survival ability. Human babies need years of supervision before they are independent. Thus, if a woman wants to pass on her genes (or at least the half her child will inherit from her), she must take good care of her dependent child. The baby is a scarce resource. Even if a woman is pregnant from sexual maturation until menopause, the number of children she can produce is quite limited. This limitation was particularly true thousands of years ago. Before medical advances of the nineteenth and twentieth centuries, women were highly unlikely to live to the age of menopause. Complications from childbirth commonly caused women to die in their 20s or 30s. Where the food supply was scarce, women were less likely to be successful at conceiving, further reducing the possibility of generating offspring.

Sociobiologists and evolutionary psychologists say that men inseminate, women incubate. The human female's reproductive constraints (usually one child at a time, only so many children over a life cycle, and a helpless infant for a long period of time) shape most of women's sexual and emotional approaches to men and mating. According to their theory, women have good reason to be more selective than men

about potential mates. They want to find a man who will stick around and continue to provide resources and protection to this child at least until the child has a good chance of survival. Furthermore, because a woman needs to create an incentive for a man to remain with her, females have developed more sophisticated sexual and emotional skills specifically geared toward creating male loyalty and commitment to their mutual offspring.

Sociobiologists and evolutionary psychologists say that differences in reproductive capacity and strategy also shape sexual desire. Buss asserts that reproductive strategies form most of the categories of desire: Older men generally pick younger women because they are more fertile; younger women seek older men who have more status, power, and resources (a cultural practice known as hypergamy) because such men can provide for their children. Furthermore, health and reproductive capacity make youth generally sexier, and even certain shapes of women's bodies (such as an "ideal" hip-to-waist ratio epitomized by an hourglass figure, which correlate with ability to readily reproduce), are widely preferred (Buss 1994)—despite varying standards of beauty across cultures. Likewise, men who have demonstrated their fertility by producing children are more sought after than men who have not (Buss 1994).

According to evolutionary psychologists, men's tastes for recreational sex, unambivalent lust, and a variety of partners are consistent with maximizing their production of children. Men's sexual interest is also more easily aroused because sex involves fewer costs to them than to women, and the ability for rapid ejaculation has a reproductive payoff. On the other hand, women's taste for relationship-based intimacy and greater investment in each sexual act is congruent with women's reproductive strategies.

In a field that tends to emphasize male's "natural" influence over reproductive strategies, evolutionary anthropologist Helen Fisher (1992) offers a feminist twist. Her study of hundreds of societies shows that divorce, or its informal equivalent, occurs most typically in the third or fourth year of a marriage and then peaks about every four years after that. Fisher hypothesizes that some of the breakups have to do with a woman's attempt to obtain the best genes and best survival chances for her offspring. In both agrarian and hunter-gatherer societies, Fisher explains, women breast-feed their child for three or four years—a practice that is economical and sometimes helps to prevent further pregnancy. At the end of this period, the woman is ready and able to have another child. She reenters the mating marketplace and assesses her options to see if she can improve on her previous mate. If she can get a better guy, she will leave the previous partner and team up with a new one. In Fisher's vision, unlike the traditional sociobiological view (see Table 1), different male and female reproductive strategies do not necessarily imply female sexual passivity and preference for lifelong monogamy.

Sociobiologists and evolutionary psychologists tell a fascinating story of how male and female reproductive differences might shape sexuality. To accept sociobiological arguments, one must accept the premise that most animal and human behavior is driven by the instinct to reproduce and improve the gene pool. Further-more, a flaw of sociobiology as a theory is that it does not provide a unique account of sexual behavior with the potential to be tested empirically. Furthermore, other social science explanations for the same phenomena are supported by more immediate, close-range evidence.

Consider hypergamy, the practice of women marrying men slightly older and "higher" on the social status ladder than they are. Sociobiologists would say women marry "up" to ensure the most fit provider for their offspring. But hypergamy makes little sense biologically. Younger men have more years of resources to provide, and they have somewhat more sexual resources. Empirically, however, hypergamy is fact. It is also a fact that men, overall and in nearly every subculture, have access to more rewards and status than women do. Furthermore, reams of imagery—in movies, advertising, novels—promote the appeal of older, more resourceful men. Why not, when older, more resourceful men are generating the images? Social practice, in this case, overrides what sociobiologists consider the biological imperative.

THE SOCIAL ORIGINS OF DESIRE

Your own experience should indicate that biology and genetics alone do not shape human sexuality. From the moment you entered the world, cues

---

TABLE 1

COMPARISON OF TRADITIONAL AND FEMINIST SOCIOBIOLOGICAL EXPLANATIONS OF GENDER DIFFERENCES IN SEXUALITY

Perspective	Gender difference	Explanation
Traditional	Men seek to maximize number of progeny by changing partners as often as possible. Women seek to maximize well-being of progeny by holding on to their partners as long as possible.	Men have biological capacity to inseminate many women in a short period of time; women's biological job is to incubate and nurture young.
Feminist	Men seek to maximize progeny; women seek to maximize well-being of progeny by exchanging partners when improved options are available.	Men and women both seek to maximize number of partners and quality of partners by exchanging when improved options are available.

from the environment were telling you which desires and behaviors were "normal" and which were not. The result is that people who grow up in different circumstances tend to have different sexualities. Who has not had their sexual behavior influenced by their parents' or guardians' explicit or implicit rules? You may break the rules or follow them, but you can't forget them. On a societal level, in Sweden, for example, premarital sex is accepted, and people are expected to be sexually knowledgeable and experienced. Swedes are likely to associate sex with pleasure in this "sex positive" society. In Ireland, however, Catholics are supposed to heed the Church's strict prohibitions against sex outside of marriage, birth control, and the expression of lust. In Ireland the experience of sexuality is different from the experience of sexuality in Sweden because the rules are different. Certainly, biology in Sweden is no different from biology in Ireland, nor is the physical capacity to experience pleasure different. But in Ireland, nonmarital sex is clandestine and shameful. Perhaps the taboo adds excitement to the experience. In Sweden, nonmarital sex is acceptable. In the absence of social constraint, it may even feel a bit mundane. These culturally specific sexual rules and experiences arise from different norms, the well-known, unwritten rules of society.

Another sign that social influences play a bigger role in shaping sexuality than does biology is the changing notions historically of male and female differences in desire. Throughout history, varied explanations of male and female desire have been popular. At times, woman was portrayed as the stormy temptress and man the reluctant participant, as in the Bible story of Adam and Eve. At other times, women were seen as pure in thought and deed while men were voracious sexual beasts, as the Victorians would have it.

These shifting ideas about gender are the social "clothing" for sexuality. The concept of gender typically relies on a dichotomy of male versus female sexual categories, just as the tradition of women wearing dresses and men wearing pants has in the past made the shape of men and women appear quite different. Consider high heels, an on-again-off-again Western fashion. Shoes have no innate sexual function, but high heels have often been understood to be "sexy" for women, even though (or perhaps because) they render women less physically agile. (Of course, women cope. As Ginger Rogers, the 1940s movie star and dancing partner to Fred Astaire, is said to have quipped, "I did everything Fred did, only backwards and in high heels.") Social norms of femininity have at times rendered high heels fashionable. So feminine are high heels understood to be that a man in high heels, in some sort of visual comedy gag, guarantees a laugh from the audience. Alternatively, high heels are a required emblem of femininity for cross-dressing men.

Such distinctions are an important tool of society; they provide guidance to human beings about how to be a "culturally correct" male or female. Theoretically, society could "clothe" its members with explicit norms of sexuality that de-emphasize difference and emphasize similarity or even multiplicity. Picture unisex hairstyles and men and women both free to wear skirts or pants, norms that prevail from time to time in some subcultures. What is remarkable about dichotomies is that even when distinctions, like male and female norms of fashion, are reduced, new ways to assert an ostensibly essential difference between men and women arise. Societies' rules, like clothes, are changeable. But societies' entrenched taste for constructing differences between men and women persists.

The Social Construction of Sexuality

Social constructionists believe that cues from the environment shape human beings from the moment they enter the world. The sexual customs, values, and expectations of a culture, passed on to the young through teaching and by example, exert a powerful influence over individuals. When Fletcher Christian sailed into Tahiti in Charles Nordhoff's 1932 account,

Mutiny on the Bounty, he and the rest of his nineteenth-century English crew were surprised at how sexually available, playful, guilt free, and amorous the Tahitian women were. Free from the Judeo-Christian precepts and straitlaced customs that inhibited English society, the women and girls of Tahiti regarded their sexuality joyfully and without shame. The English men were delighted and, small wonder, refused to leave the island. Such women did not exist in their own society. The women back in England had been socialized within their Victorian culture to be modest, scared of sex, protective of their reputation, and threatened by physical pleasure. As a result, they were unavailable before marriage and did not feel free to indulge in a whole lot of fun after it. The source of the difference was not physiological differences between Tahitian and English women; it was sexual socialization or the upbringing that they received within their differing families and cultures.

If we look back at the Victorian, nineteenth-century England that Nordhoff refers to, we can identify social structures that influenced the norms of women's and men's sexuality. A burgeoning, new, urban middle class created separate spheres in the division of family labor. Instead of sharing home and farm or small business, the tasks of adults in families became specialized: Men went out to earn money, women stayed home to raise children and take care of the home. Although this division of labor was not the norm in all classes and ethnicities in England at the time, the image of middle-class femininity and masculinity became pervasive. The new division of labor increased women's economic dependence on men, which further curbed women's sexual license but not men's. When gender organizes one aspect of life—such as men's and women's positions in the economy—it also organizes other aspects of life, including sex.

In a heterogeneous and individualistic culture like North America, sexual socialization is complex. A society creates an "ideal" sexuality, but different families and subcultures have their own values. For example, even though contemporary society at large may now accept premarital sexuality, a given family may lay down the law: Sex before marriage is against the family's religion and an offense against God's teaching. A teenager who grows up in such a household may suppress feelings of sexual arousal or channel them into outlets that are more acceptable to the family. Or the teenager may react against her or his background, reject parental and community opinion, and search for what she or he perceives to be a more "authentic" self. Variables like birth order or observations of a sibling's social and sexual expression can also influence a person's development.

As important as family and social background are, so are individual differences in response to that background. In the abstract, people raised to celebrate their sexuality must surely have a different approach to enjoying their bodies than those who are taught that their bodies will betray them and are a venal part of human nature. Yet whether or not a person is raised to be at ease with physicality does not always help predict adult sexual behavior. Sexual sybarites and libertines may have grown up in sexually repressive environments, as did pop culture icon and Catholic-raised Madonna. Sometimes individuals whose families promoted sex education and free personal expression are content with minimal sexual expression.

Even with the nearly infinite variety of sexuality that individual experience produces, social circumstances shape sexual patterns. For example, research shows that people who have had more premarital sexual intercourse are likely to have more extramarital intercourse, or sex with someone other than their spouse (Blumstein and Schwartz 1983). Perhaps early experience creates a desire for sexual variety and makes it harder for a person to be monogamous. On the other hand, higher levels of sexual desire may generate both the premarital and extramarital propensities. Or perhaps nonmonogamous, sexually active individuals are "rule breakers" in other areas also, and resist not only the traditional rules of sex but also other social norms they encounter. Sexual history is useful for predicting sexual future, but it does not provide a complete explanation.

To make explanations more useful, sociologists refer to societal-level explanations as the macro view and to individual-level explanations as the micro view. At the macrolevel, the questions pertain to the patterns among different groups. For example, we may note in our culture that some women wear skirts and all men do not. Why do women and men, generally speaking, differ in this way? Social conflict theory, which examines the way that groups gain and maintain power over resources and other groups, is often used to address macrolevel questions. One might ask: Whose interest does this custom serve and how did it evolve? What does it constrain or encourage? If the custom changes, what social forces have promoted the change? What social forces resist change? Who has power over customs at any given time, and why?

Symbolic interactionism supplements this macrolevel view by looking at the microlevel: How does a particular custom gain its meaning through social interaction? For example, what is really happening when a man opens a door for a woman? Symbolic interactionism proposes that social rules are learned and reinforced through everyday interaction in both small acts, such as a man's paying for a woman's dinner, and larger enactments of male and female roles, such as weddings, manners and advice books, movies, and television. Through such everyday social interaction, norms are confirmed or resisted. When an adult tells a little girl "good girls don't do this," or when boys make fun of her for wanting to be on the football team, or when she observes people scorning or stoning women who venture forth in inappropriate garb (as in countries where women are required to wear a veil), or when she sees women joining a military school getting hazed and harassed, she is learning her society's rules of behavior.

When it comes to sexuality, all these social and behavioral theories hold that biological impulses are subservient to the influence of social systems. Consider high heels again. As anyone who has done so knows, wearing high heels has physical consequences, such as flexed calves while wearing them and aching feet at the end of an evening. But nothing in the physiology of women makes wearing high-heeled shoes necessary, and the propensity to wear high heels is not programmed into women's DNA. A sociobiologist might note that any additional ways a society can invent for women to be sexy accelerate reproductive success. A symbolic interactionist would counter that most rules of sexuality go way beyond what's needed for reproductive success. Footwear has never been shown to be correlated with fertility. Instead, society orchestrates male and female sexuality so that its values are served. A social conflict theorist would go a step further and note that the enactment of gendered fashion norms, individual by individual, serves the political agenda of groups in power (in this case men) at the macrolevel.

An astounding example of gender-based social control of sexuality was the practice of binding the feet of upper-class women in China starting around the tenth century. Each foot was bound so tightly that the last two toes shriveled and fell off. What was left was so deformed that the woman could barely walk and had to be carried. The function was to allow upper-class men to control the mobility of their women. Bound feet, which were thus associated with status and wealth, became erotically charged. Unbound feet were seen as repugnant. By the eighteenth and nineteenth centuries, even poor women participated in this practice. This practice was so associated with sexual acceptability and marriageability that it was difficult to disrupt, even when nineteenth-century missionaries from the West labeled the practice barbaric and unsafe.

Only later, in the twentieth century, did foot binding become illegal (Greenhalgh 1977).

Social Control of Sexuality

So powerful are norms as they are transmitted through both social structures and everyday life that it is impossible to imagine the absence of norms that control sexuality. In fact, most images of "liberated" sexuality involve breaking a social norm—say, having sex in public rather than in private. The social norm is always the reference point. Because people are influenced from birth by the social and physical contexts of sexuality, their desires are shaped by those norms. There is no such thing as a truly free sexuality. For the past two centuries in North America, people have sought "true love" through personal choice in dating and mating (D'Emilio and Freedman 1988). Although this form of sexual liberation has generated a small increase in the number of mixed pairs—interracial, interethnic, interfaith pairs—the rule of homogamy, or marrying within one's class, religion, and ethnicity, still constitutes one of the robust social facts of romantic life. Freedom to choose the person one loves turns out not to be as free as one might suppose.

Despite the norm of true love currently accepted in our culture, personal choice and indiscriminate sexuality have often been construed across cultures and across history as socially disruptive. Disruptions to the social order include liaisons between poor and rich; between people of different races, ethnicities, or faiths; and between members of the same sex. Traditional norms of marriage and sexuality have maintained social order by keeping people in familiar and "appropriate" categories. Offenders have been punished by ostracism, curtailed civil rights, or in some societies, death. Conformists are rewarded with social approval and material advantages. Although it hardly seems possible today, mixed-race marriage was against the law in the United States until 1967. Committed same-sex couples continue to be denied legal marriage, income tax breaks, and health insurance, benefits, heterosexual couples take these social benefits for granted.

Some social theorists observe that societies control sexuality through construction of a dichotomized or gendered (male-female) sexuality (Foucault 1978). Society's rules about pleasure seeking and procreating are enforced by norms about appropriate male and female behavior. For example, saying that masculinity is enhanced by sexual experimentation while femininity is demeaned by it gives men sexual privilege (and pleasure) and denies it to women. Furthermore, according to Foucault, sexual desire is fueled by the experience of privilege and taboo regarding sexual pleasure. That is, the very rules that control sexual desire shape it and even enhance it. The social world could just as plausibly concentrate on how much alike are the ways that men and women experience sex and emphasize how broadly dispersed sexual conduct is across genders. However, social control turns pleasure into a scarce resource and endows leaders who regulate the pleasure of others with power. . . .

To summarize, social constructionists believe that a society influences sexual behavior through its norms. Some norms are explicit, such as laws against adult sexual activity with minors. Others are implicit, such as norms of fidelity and parental responsibility. In a stable, homogeneous society, it is relatively easy to understand such rules. But in a changing, complex society like the United States, the rules may be in flux or indistinct. Perhaps this ambiguity is what makes some issues of sexuality so controversial today.

AN INTEGRATIVE PERSPECTIVE ON GENDER AND SEXUALITY

Social constructionist explanations of contemporary sexual patterns are typically pitted against the biology of desire and the evolutionary understanding of biological adaptations. Some social constructionists believe there is no inflexible biological reality; everything we regard as either female or male sexuality is culturally imposed. In contrast, essentialists—those who take a biological, sociobiological, or evolutionary point of view—believe people's sexual desires and orientations are innate and hardwired and that social impact is minimal. Gender differences follow from reproductive differences. Men inseminate, women incubate. People are born with sexual drives, attractions, and natures that simply play themselves out at the appropriate developmental age. Even if social constraints conspire to make men and women more similar to each other (as in the 1990s, when the sensitive and nurturing new man is encouraged to get in touch with his so-called feminine, emotional side), people's essential nature is the same: Man is the hunter, warrior, and trailblazer, and woman is the gatherer, nurturer, and reproducer. To an essentialist, social differences, such as the different earning power of men and women, are the consequence of biological difference. In short, essentialists think the innate differences between women and men are the cause of gendered sexuality; social constructionists think the differences between men and women are the result of gendering sexuality through social processes.

Using either the social constructionist or essentialist approach to the exclusion of the other constrains understanding of sexuality. We believe the evidence shows that gender differences are more plausibly an outcome of social processes than the other way around. But a social constructionist view is most powerful when it takes the essentialist view into account. In Table 2, we describe this view of gender differences in sexual desire as integrative. Although people tend to think of sex as primarily a biological function—tab B goes into slot A—biology is only one part of the context of desire. Such sociological factors as family relationships and social structure also influence sex. A complex mix of anatomy, hormones, and the brain provides the basic outline for the range of acts and desires possible, but biology is neither where sexuality begins nor where it ends. Social and biological contexts link to define human sexual possibilities.

The integrative approach follows from a great deal that sexuality researchers have observed. Consider the following example: A research project, conducted over three decades ago, advertised for participants stating that its focus was how physical excitement influences a man's preference for one woman over another (Valins 1966). The researchers connected college men to a monitor that allowed them to hear their heartbeats as they looked at photographs of women models. The men were told that they would be able to hear their heartbeat when it surged in response to each photograph. A greater surge would suggest greater physical attraction. The participants were then shown a photograph of a dark-haired woman, then a blonde, then a redhead. Afterward, each man was asked to choose the picture that he would prefer to take home. In each case, the man chose the photograph of the woman who, as he believed from listening to his own speeding heartbeat, had most aroused him. Or at least the man thought he was choosing the woman who had aroused him most. In reality, the men had been listening to a faked heartbeat that was speeded up at random. The men thus actually chose the women whom they believed had aroused them most. In this case, the men's invented attraction was more powerful than their gut response. Their mind (a powerful sexual organ) told them their body was responding to a specific picture. The participants' physiological experience of arousal was eclipsed by the social context. When social circumstances influence sexual tastes, are those tastes real or sincere? Absolutely. The social world is as much a fact in people's lives as the biological world.

Now let us look at a case where the body's cues were misinterpreted by the mind. An attractive woman researcher stood at the end of a very stable bridge (Dutton and Aron 1974).

TABLE 2

EXPLANATIONS OF MALE AND FEMALE DIFFERENCES IN SEXUAL DESIRE

Explanations	Causes of desire	Consequences
Essentialist: Desire is biological and evolutionary	Genetically preprogrammed reproductive functions specific to males and females	Male independence in reproduction and female-centered child-rearing practices and passivity are the cause, rather than the result, of gendered social institutions
Social constructionist: Desire is sociological and contextual	Social institutions and social interaction signal and sanction "male" and "female," gendered norms of behavior	Support for or opposition to sex/gender-segregated reproductive and social practices depends on social definitions of men, women, and sexuality
Integrative: Desire is contextual and physical	Bodies, environments, relationships, families, governments shape sexualities	Policies address some biological differences (such as pregnancy and work); emphasize the impact of social forces, interaction, societal programs

She approached men after they had walked across the bridge, engaged them in conversation, and then gave the men her telephone number—in case they had further comments, she said. Then the researcher did the same thing with another group of participants, but at the end of an unstable, swinging bridge. People tend to feel a little nervous, excited, or even exhilarated when they make their way across such a bridge. The pulse rises. Adrenaline pumps. Indeed, the anxiety response of walking across the bridge is much like the arousal response caused by meeting a desirable new person. The question was, would that anxiety response confuse men into thinking that they were attracted to the woman at the end of the bridge, more so than the physiologically calm guys who met her on the stable bridge? Yes, a statistically significant, larger number of men from the swinging bridge called the woman. In this case, participants had interpreted an anxiety response as an attraction response, one compelling enough to warrant inviting a stranger on a date. The physical situation transformed the meaning of a casual meeting from anxiety to attraction, again showing the link between biological and social influences. . .

What do these examples from research illustrate? Sexual desire—in fact, all sexuality—is influenced by the cultural, personal, and situational. But these examples also tell us that people can't escape the biological context of sex and sexuality—nor can they rely on it. Such an integrative approach—the intimate relationship between social context and biological experience—is central to understanding sexuality.

What are the implications of using an integrative approach to sexuality? First, an integrationist will raise questions about biology when social context is emphasized as cause, and will raise questions about social context when biological causes are emphasized. The point is, everything sexual and physical occurs and achieves meaning in a social context.

REFERENCES

Buss, D. 1994. *The Evolution of Desire: Strategies of Human Mating.* New York: Basic Books.
———. 1995. "Psychological Sex Differences: Origins through Sexual Selection. *American Psychologist* 50:164–68.
Dutton, D. and A. Aron. 1974. "Some Evidence for Heightened Sexual Attraction under Conditions

of High Anxiety." *Journal of Personality and Social Psychology* 30:510–17.

Fisher, H. E. 1992. *Anatomy of Love: The Natural History of Monogamy, Adultery, and Divorce.* New York: Norton.

Foucault, M. 1978. *A History of Sexuality: Vol. 1. An Introduction.* New York: Pantheon.

Greenhalgh, S. 1977. "Hobbled Feet, Hobbled Lives: Women in Old China." *Frontiers* 2:7–21.

Malthus, T. R. [1798] 1929. *An Essay on the Principle of Population as It Affects the Future Improvement of Society.* New York and London: Macmillan.

Sexuality Information and Education Council of the United States. 1995. *A Report on Adolescent Sexuality.* New York: SIECUS.

Valins, S. 1966. "Cognitive Effects of False Heart-Rate Feedback." *Journal of Personality and Social Psychology* 4:400–8.

CHAPTER 8

Paths to Family Formation

The 20th century was a time of great change in the way in which most young people associated with age mates of the opposite sex, began romantic attachments, initiated sexual activity, lived with partners, and married. At the beginning of the century, this process was less private, more closely supervised by parents, and more directly tied to marriage. The now-quaint term "courtship" was used by experts who observed the process. In my textbook, I defined courtship as a publicly visible process with rules and restrictions through which young men and women find a partner to marry.[1] At the start of the 20th century, the process *was* public, it had many restrictions, and it was seen by all parties as leading to marriage. However, courtship, in this sense, hardly exists anymore. Historian Ellen K. Rothman tells the story of this transformation in the following excerpt from her book, *Hands and Hearts: A History of Courtship in America.* You will learn how and when dating and courtship evolved between 1920 and 1980.

---

[1] *Public and Private Families: An Introduction.*

At that point, Rothman's book ends. She notes the great rise in divorce in the 1960s and 1970s but concludes that the increase in divorce doesn't really threaten the institution of marriage. She cites social scientists (I was one of them) who reported that most divorced people remarried fairly quickly. But since 1980, rates of remarriage have declined, and cohabitation among previously married adults has increased greatly. Most demographers would no longer be so quick to conclude that the institution of marriage has been unharmed by frequent divorce.

With the rise in premarital sex and the post-1960 increases in age at marriage has come the "teenage pregnancy problem." There's nothing new about teenage pregnancy and childbearing, but until the 1960s most of it occurred to teenage women who were married. It is the decline in marriage, coupled with increasing sexual activity of the young and unmarried, that has caused public concern about unmarried teenagers having children. Yet among social scientists of late, there is disagreement over just how much of a "problem" teenage childbearing is. Some researchers have claimed recently that the problems of poor teenage mothers occur because they are poor, not because they are mothers. Even if these teenagers were to postpone childbearing, so this argument goes, their life prospects would not improve much. Other researchers claim that there are additional disadvantages to having a baby as a teenager—and that the baby is likely to be disadvantaged as well. In the following article, Kristin Luker attempts to untangle the strands of the teenage pregnancy problem in America.

READING 8-1

In Our Own Time, 1920–1980

Ellen K. Rothman

. . . Until the Second World War, Americans continued to marry at the age and rate characteristic of the 19th century. The median age at first marriage in 1900 was 21.9 for women and 25.9 for men; after "a slow and measured decline" in the first four decades of the 20th century, the figure in 1940 was 21.5 for women and 24.3 for men. The rate of marriage dipped in the early 1930s, but by 1939, it had returned to the 19th-century level. The 1940s brought a sudden interruption in this remarkable stability. The marriage rate rose and the median age at marriage fell, both dramatically. According to demographer Donald Bogue, during that one decade "the proportion of persons never married and the median age at first marriage declined by as much as they had during the entire preceding half-century." In the late 1940s, more than half of all women were married by the age of 21.[1]

The immediate dislocations of wartime may have accounted for the outbreak of what one commentator called "the war disease," but the epidemic did not subside after V–J Day. Young Americans continued to marry at an age that would, at any other time, have been considered dangerously young. In 1956, the median age at first marriage reached an all-time low (20.1 for women, 22.5 for men); and a year later, the birth rate reached its peak. Beginning about 1960, the median age at first marriage began a gradual rise. By the late 1970s, it had attained its prewar level. The children of the couples who had participated in the 1940s "marriage marathon" and produced the 1950s "baby boom" returned to patterns of family formation that their parents had broken.[2]

Thus the 20th century has been a time of demographic continuity. Except for the 1940s and 1950s, the transition to marriage appears as a steady line on the nation's statistical record. But when we turn from demographic trends to other forms of behavior, a different pattern emerges: a period of rapid change at the beginning (roughly 1910 to 1930); then more gradual, evolutionary change during the middle decades (1930 to about 1965); followed by another period of heightened change since the mid-1960s. The shifts of the last two decades can be gauged, at least indirectly, in the rise of cohabitation and teenage pregnancy; the discontinuity that marked the first quarter of the century is much harder to measure.

The subject of public consternation and celebration at the time, and of literary legend and historical debate ever since, "a first-class revolt against the accepted American order" took place among American youth in the 1920s. The "shock troops of the rebellion," as Frederick Lewis Allen called the fomenters of this "revolution in manners and morals," were not the first to breach the barricades. The assault on "the moral code of the country" had begun well before the battles along the Somme. What happened in the 1920s was that ideas and behavior which had once marked the outermost limits of acceptability moved to the center of middle-class youth culture. The sound of jazz, the smell of cigarette smoke, the discussions of Freud emanated not just from Greenwich Village but from Main Street and Fraternity Row. This was not a sudden eruption but rather a series of seismic tremors that occurred with increasing intensity and frequency through the 1910s and 1920s. The automobile, the moving picture, the close dance had all appeared before the First World War; but in the 1920s, they dominated and liberated American youth to an unprecedented extent. By 1930, the terrain through which young Americans passed en route to marriage would be almost unrecognizable to their parents.[3]

The men and women who courted circa 1900 and their children coming of age in the 1920s were separated by as wide a gulf as that between any two American generations. Standards for behavior had undergone change before, of course, but never so radically in such a short time. It was understandable that people who had ridden their wheels around town, danced the two-step at the bandstand, and kissed goodnight on the front porch would be alarmed to see their children go off on joy rides in closed cars, to "petting parties," or to "pictures with hot lovemaking in them."[4] In 1900, middle-class courtship was more carefully supervised and more formal than it had been at any time since the Revolution; by 1930, the supervision and formality had given way, like a poorly designed dam, and many of the familiar landmarks were swept aside. While the result may have looked like chaos and disarray, a new system, created and regulated by young people themselves, was in place almost as soon as the old one was abandoned. The youths of the 1920s, in the words of historian Paula Fass, "elaborated two basic rituals of social interaction—dating and petting."[5] Separately and together, these two rituals would define the experience of courtship for the next half-century.

The young women and men of the 1920s did not invent paired-off social behavior—couples had been "keeping company" for 200 years; nor were they the first to discover sexual pleasure.[6] What they did was to develop a systematic, peer-controlled approach to the social and sexual relationships of late adolescence and early adulthood. The date, one historian has recently observed, "had a compelling logic quite distinct from that of prior forms: it was a step in an ongoing negotiation with rules defined and deviations punished by age-peers." Dating provided a

way to manage the social demands of the peer society. It was an alternative to group activities, on the one hand, and to serious, marriage-oriented courtship, on the other. In a world where "press accounts of high school club dances [were] careful to emphasize the escort of each girl attending," the dating system ensured that a girl need not have a suitor in order to attend a dance.[7] Indeed, the fact that dating could operate independently of mate selection caused some observers to condemn it.

The sociologist Willard Waller, who studied campus life in the 1930s, concluded that dating "is not true courtship, since it is supposed not to eventuate in marriage; it is a sort of dalliance relationship." The decline of "formal modes of courtship" had, in Waller's view, been replaced by a "rating and dating complex" that rewarded "thrill-seeking" and "exploitative" behavior by young men and women. "Whether we approve or not" (and Waller made it clear that he did not), "courtship practices today allow for a great deal of pure thrill-seeking," he wrote in 1937. "Dancing, petting, necking, the automobile, amusement park, and a whole range of institutions and practices permit or facilitate thrill-seeking behavior." In this system, the goal was prestige rather than mate selection, plural rather than exclusive relationships. Men were rated according to the fraternity they belonged to, the clothes they wore, the amount of money they had to spend, and the skill they showed on the dance floor; what mattered was that they were "smooth" and had a "good line." For women, the important criteria were similar: "good clothes, a smooth line, ability to dance well, and popularity as a date."[8]

The pattern Waller described, based on a study conducted at Pennsylvania State University in the 1930s, was neither as novel nor as predominant as he thought.[9] A system oriented toward pluralistic, if not competitive, dating had evolved simultaneously among high school and college students well before the Crash.[10] The 1920s campus was above all a social scene, and that scene was designed around dating. Social activities rather than academic pursuits were what demanded time and conferred status. "Study in too enthusiastic a form" was widely considered "bad form . . . Too constant attendance at the Library is likely to lead to derogatory classification," the *Daily Princetonian* warned in 1926. Such misplaced enthusiasm was rare; at Ohio State that year, the average co-ed went on dates four nights a week. Because selection for fraternity and sorority membership "usually had more to do with superficial attractiveness and personality than rigid socio-economic class," "rating and dating" tended to flourish on campuses where the Greek societies were strong. Even there, however, it functioned alongside a more traditional social system. As one sociologist recently concluded, "rating and dating and less exploitive and pluralistic dating appear to have existed simultaneously."[11]

The social scientists saw good data and the journalists good copy in the collegian; but in 1930, less than 15 percent of the country's 18- to 21-year-olds were attending institutions of higher education. And off the campus, "going together" was the norm. The heroine of one 1920s novel described the "thing you called going together":

> You went with a boy. He was your fellow then and you were his girl. When you were old enough you got engaged and married . . . Going together was beautiful. You had fun then; all the fun there was. You were not an odd girl. You were not left out . . . You could belong to a crowd. You had somebody to walk home with you, pay for your ticket at shows, send you valentines, candy at Christmas.[12]

Whether they were dating many different people or "going together" with one special person (and most young people in and out of college probably experimented with both modes), middle-class youths organized their social lives around dating beginning well before 1930.

One of the chief characteristics—and attractions—of a date was that it took place away from home. In his survey of undergraduate life in the late 1920s, Robert Angell explained, "In seeking means of diversion together there seem to be two principal aims, to have as much privacy and at the same time as much excitement as possible." Angell realized that "the former has probably been present from time immemorial," but he thought that the latter had been "enormously developed in the past years by the automobile and other means of exciting recreation." The middle-class home was, by definition, neither private nor exciting. "Unless couples are engaged, they are rarely content to spend the afternoon or evening conversing in the parlor or even strolling together along shady walks." The same rule applied off the campus as well. In the Indiana town that the sociologists Robert and Helen Lynd called Middletown, in the 1920s, " a 'date' at home [was] 'slow' compared with motoring, a new film, or a dance in a near-by town." Half the boys and girls queried on the subject reported that they were home fewer than four evenings out of the week.[13]

The most popular pastime for both high school and college students was dancing. In the early 1920s, many high schools "instituted dances, in an effort of varying success to take the play away from commercial dance halls and road houses."[14] College students could attend dances sponsored by college organizations or patronize local cabarets. By the 1920s, dancing had become an activity for couples rather than groups; it encouraged sensuality rather than sociability. Angell commented on "the slight degree of mingling" at university dances. "Often a man and woman spend practically the whole evening together," he reported. Not only were they together, they were close together. The new dances "fostered an unheard of closeness between partners . . . Couples often held each other very close." There were rules governing proper behavior on the dance floor, but they were "usually treated in a cavalier fashion."[15] In spite of its sexual potential, however, dancing retained a certain innocent quality. Irene and Vernon Castle, who elevated cabaret dancing to respectability in the 1910s, "took the potentially seductive dance and made it 'fun.' " Irene Castle once explained, "If Vernon had ever looked into my eyes with smoldering passion during the tango, we should have both burst out laughing." Dancing, in the Castle style, offered young people "a means to experience physical closeness and erotic excitement, without the dangers of sexuality."[16]

Like the dance hall, the movie theater was another setting that offered young people privacy and excitement, within limits. As movies became an increasingly legitimate form of middle-class entertainment, they also became increasingly popular. Most collegians in the 1920s regularly attended the movies once a week, and high school students were no less devoted followers of Clara Bow and Rudolph Valentino. In Middletown in 1928, there were nine motion-picture theaters offering over 300 performances every week of the year. "Go to a motion picture and let yourself go," the readers of the *Saturday Evening Post* were told, and Americans heeded the call by the millions. In a typical week, one-third of Middletown's high school students attended the movies once; 20 percent went twice.[17]

Some of their teachers believed that movies were "a powerful factor in bringing about the 'early sophistication' of the young and the relaxing of social taboos," and the Lynds agreed that the "constant public watching of love-making on the screen" had a noticeable effect. The woman who happily sent her daughter "because a girl has to learn the ways of the world somehow and the movies are a good safe way" was not necessarily as naïve as she might have appeared to the Lynds. The movies presented both an opportunity and stimulation for sexual intimacy, but they left conventional boundaries in place. Robert Angell considered the excitement to be found at the movies "much milder" than at the dance hall. As historian Elaine Tyler May explains:

> The message of the plot reinforced the need for restraint. Love-struck viewers might hold hands or embrace in the darkened theater; but not much else could happen. They sat in a public place, fac-

ing the screen without talking to each other, watching attractive film idols instruct them in the art of gaining allure without losing virtue.[18]

Of all the new influences on the behavior of young women and men, none was more powerful than the automobile. Here, in the closed cars which were fast replacing open ones, anything *could* happen. Of the 30 girls charged with "sex crimes" in Middletown in 1924, 19 committed the offense in an automobile. In 1923, there were more than 6,000 cars in Middletown, two for every three families. Car ownership had reached the point of being an "accepted essential of normal living" for middle-class people.[19] It had become an "accepted essential of normal" courting for their children as well. The automobile was, however, no less revolutionary for being readily incorporated into normalcy. The Lynds concluded that the automobile had "revolutionized . . . leisure" in general and had specifically caused the "increasing relaxation of some of the traditional prohibitions upon the approaches of boys and girls to each other's persons." Robert Angell concurred. In 1928, he declared:

> To this invention must be assigned much responsibility . . . for the change, amounting to almost a revolution, which has come about during the last 15 years in the conduct of young men and women. The ease with which a couple can secure absolute privacy when in possession of a car and the spirit of reckless abandon which high speed and moonlight drives engender have combined to break down the traditional barriers between the sexes.[20]

Even at slower speeds and in broad daylight, the car allowed a level of intimacy and privacy reminiscent of the early republic. A Rhode Island woman explained in 1923, "You can be so nice and all alone in a machine, just a little one that you can go on crazy roads in and be miles away from anyone but each other." Fifteen years later, when Dorothy Bromley and Florence Britten published their study *Youth and Sex,* it was obvious that the car was "an incredible engine of escape." A boy called for his date, usually just by honking the horn, and the young couple was "off and away, out of reach of parental control. A youth now . . . has a refuge . . . complete privacy. He has taken full advantage of it, not only as a means of going places, but as a place to go where he can take his girl and hold hands, neck, pet, or if it's that kind of an affair, go the limit."[21]

The car provided far more privacy and excitement than either the dance hall or the movie theater, and the result was the spread of petting. In 1928, Robert Angell conceded that "what is vulgarly known as 'petting' is the rule rather than the exception in all classes of society"; and by 1930, Floyd Dell could refer to "the universal convention of petting" with little risk of overstatement.[22] The statistical pattern is clear. A 1924 study of "Certain Aspects of the Sex Life of the Adolescent Girl" found that 92 percent of the respondents (177 college girls) had indulged in "spooning" or "petting." (Spooning was a more old-fashioned term for kissing than petting, which included all forms of erotic behavior short of intercourse.[23]) This limited data was confirmed in the report on *Sexual Behavior in the Human Female* prepared by Alfred Kinsey and his associates in the early 1950s. About 80 percent of the women born just before 1900—in other words those who courted in the 1910s and 1920s—had engaged in some sort of petting, and the proportion increased with every decade. The story for men was similar. Among the older generation (born between 1895 and 1904), 65 percent had petting experience by age 18; while in the younger generation (born between 1917 and 1929), 85 percent had petted by that age.[24]

Much of this petting took place in the quasi-public setting of the "petting party." Petting parties were a regular feature of high school life in the 1920s. When asked if it was true that "nine out of every ten boys and girls of high school age have 'petting parties,' " 50 percent of the Middletown youths answered yes. Although

fewer students themselves admitted to petting, almost half of the boys and more than one-third of the girls indicated that they had taken part in a petting party. Such parties were not limited to the high school scene; college students indulged as well. In both cases, the petting party was, as Paula Fass points out, "a self-limiting form of experimentation . . . Here sexual activity was manifestly regulated by the group . . . a certain aura of intrigue and 'naughtiness' hovered around this semi-illicit behavior in the twenties."[25]

There was nothing *semi*-illicit about premarital coitus. "To maintain one's position with peers," Fass writes, "petting was permitted but intercourse was not." Only a minority violated the prohibition on premarital sexual intercourse, but their action was considered "an indiscretion and not a moral outrage." Virginity had ceased to be an absolute requirement in a bride, even if most men and women still considered it highly desirable. Although most of the young women in a 1936 study conducted by Phyllis Blanchard and Carlyn Manasses "assumed that it would make no difference to the men who wished to marry them if it was known that they had had previous sex experience," the authors concluded that "many girls draw a distinct line between the exploratory activities of the petting party and complete yielding of sexual favors to men." Blanchard and Manasses found a "decidedly tolerant attitude toward pre-marital sex experiences," and a 1936 effort to measure attitudinal change showed that "a consistent liberalizing of opinion" was taking place in the course of young people's college careers.[26]

While attitudes shifted toward greater tolerance for premarital sexual activities, the tie between love and sex remained strong. Indeed, it was, if anything, affirmed by the "rebels" of the 1920s. "I disapprove of promiscuous relations on moral grounds; not, however, between a man and woman in love," one co-ed told Blanchard and Manasses. In Fass's analysis, "it was emotional commitment above all that legitimized eroticism, for the young were true romantics who believed strongly in love." One college editor described the youth of his generation: "Where the ancient code had touched a vital principle he has hesitated to overstep its bounds." Even as they overthrew the "ancient code," young Americans preserved this principle. The bounds that marked off the sanctity of married love were readjusted, but they were not abandoned. "The revolution in sexual morality went on within the rules of the game," and the rules tied sex securely to love.[27]

Middle-class Americans had long considered love a "necessary condition" for sexual intimacy; what changed now was not the condition but the "point in the courtship process when it is applied." A growing minority of college students "altered the traditional notion of being a virgin when you marry to being a virgin when you reach engagement."[28] The commitment to this new standard is reflected in the fact that the increase in premarital coitus was largely confined to engaged couples. In the Kinsey Report, only a quarter of the women born before 1900 indicated they had had premarital intercourse, while for those born after 1900, the figure was close to 50 percent. However, at least one-half of the women in the 1920s who reported engaging in premarital coitus did so only with a future spouse. (Kinsey found a similar trend among his male respondents.)[29]

From data collected in the 1940s, Alfred Kinsey concluded that the greatest increase in premarital sexual activity occurred in the generation that reached adulthood in the late 1910s and early 1920s, and that "later generations appear to have accepted the new pattern and maintained or extended it." Observers in the 1930s agreed. The young no longer seemed to be diverting the mainstream into new directions, perhaps because the turbulence of the 1920s had already made the channel wide enough to accommodate a range of youthful experimentation. Some commentators even detected "a conservative reaction among the young to the 'Scott Fitzgerald wave'" of the early 1920s, but the retreat was more apparent than real. "The innovations of the 1920s," Fass writes, "had been solidified so that by the 30s the sexual mores begun by the college youth of the 20s were already a widespread and casual feature of behavior."[30]

When Helen and Robert Lynd returned to Middletown in 1935, they got "a sense of sharp, free behavior between the sexes (patterned on the movies) and of less disguise among the young." The liberalization of attitudes and behavior that had taken place in college in the 1920s now showed up among high school students. One young man, several years out of the Middletown high school, told the Lynds in 1935, "The fellows regard necking as a taken-for-granted part of a date. We fellows used occasionally to get slapped for doing things, but the girls don't do that much any more . . . Our high school students of both sexes . . . know everything and do everything—openly." The girls of Middletown might read in the local paper's advice columns, "A girl should never kiss a boy unless they are engaged," but few heeded such old-fashioned words.[31]

Petting was less notorious but no less popular than it had been in the 1920s. In their 1938 study of 1,300 undergraduates, Bromley and Britten found that, although at some colleges the terms *necking* and *petting* were no longer used, "the custom signified persists . . . on every campus and under many new names." As the novelty of petting wore off, it lost its more extreme, exhibitionistic qualities. Writing in 1937, the sociologist Theodore Newcomb argued that, while there had been "no quantitative decline in premarital sex relations since the alleged excesses" of the 1920s, there had been "changes in manners and morals associated with such behavior." Among the most important changes, Newcomb listed: "more widespread acceptance, particularly by females, of the 'naturalness' of sex intimacies, with or without coitus; less extreme 'petting' on first or early acquaintance; and more 'steady dating' with fewer inhibitions as to sex intimacy following long acquaintance." In June 1936, *Fortune* magazine reported, "As for sex, it is, of course, still with us. But the campus takes it more casually than it did ten years ago. Sex is no longer news."[32]

What was news was the worldwide economic crisis and the mounting threat of war in Europe. As the Depression tightened its grip on America, college enrollments fell, and the size and influence of campus fraternities declined. The Depression cast a long shadow and brought an altogether more somber mood to campus life. For many middle-class youths, college attendance represented a difficult sacrifice. The madcap social whirl of the 1920s was an extravagance few could afford. Academic pursuits and the students who excelled in them were rescued from the margins of college life and given new prestige. At the same time, college students expressed more eagerness for marriage and children than they had in the 1920s. In *Fortune*'s 1936 poll, 60 percent of the women and 50 percent of the men wanted to marry within a year or two of graduation; but when 50 percent to 85 percent of male college students were among the 13 million unemployed, these were dreams to be deferred.[33]

Deferred, but not abandoned. By the time war broke out in Europe, both the marriage rate and the age at marriage had returned to their pre-1930 levels.[34] With people rushing into marriage in response to the threat of separation and perhaps of death during wartime, symptoms of the "war disease" began to appear in ever younger people. From 1940 to 1948, the median age at first marriage fell by a full year, and three-quarters of women born between 1920 and 1924 were married by the age of 24.[35]

The "marriage marathon" was not the only sign of the war's impact on the social life of the middle-class young. At the University of Wisconsin in 1944, there were nine women for every man in the freshman class; and at Ohio State, the ratio was four to one. When a reporter from *Fortune* visited Cornell in 1942, he found Fraternity Row deserted, house parties suspended for the

duration, and only meager crowds at the football games. Male students left school early or attended classes year-round and prepared for active duty. Off the campus, most single men over 18 were in uniform and isolated from normal social life. "In comparison with the civilians, men in the armed forces had less spare time, fewer automobiles, and fewer contacts among the female population . . . Most servicemen were concentrated by the tens of thousands in one place or another . . . There were just not enough women to go around."[36] With men largely segregated in the armed forces and women in colleges or the war industries, the normal process and pace of social relationships were disrupted.

For younger groups, however, the social scene remained largely unaffected by the war. Petting was as common as ever. Of the women Kinsey interviewed in the late 1940s, 39 percent of those under 15 and 88 percent of those age 16 to 20 were having petting experience. For men in Kinsey's younger generation, 66 percent had petting experience by the age of 16; 93 percent by the time they were 20. Kinsey concluded that the incidence of petting had increased, and that men were starting to pet at an earlier age. Petting was no longer restricted to the back seat or the "petting party." "On doorsteps and on street corners, and on high school and college campuses . . . [it] may be observed in the daytime as well as in the evening hours," Kinsey wrote in 1948. Calling it "one of the most significant factors in the sexual lives of high school and college males and females," Kinsey hailed petting for the education it offered young people "in making socio-sexual contacts."[37]

Dating was the context within which most youthful petting took place, and it too functioned to educate young women and men about themselves and each other. While some observers still detected, and decried, a "rating and dating" complex at work in the "no strings attached" relationships many young people favored, other commentators recognized that it was precisely the association with freedom that gave dating its appeal. "Dating is a relationship expressing freedom, lack of commitment or public obligation for any sort of future action," wrote sociologist Samuel Lowrie in 1951.[38] At the same time, a contradictory pattern was emerging. Far from avoiding commitment, many young Americans were attaching strings with a vengeance. By the end of the Second World War, going steady had taken root, and the result was to impart "a different color to the social life of the youth. It makes it more serious, less frivolous." Writing in *Harper's* in 1957, Amherst College president George Cole expressed regret at what he saw happening to dating:

> In the twenties and early thirties, when the social pattern was one of multiple or polygamous dating— on the part of both boys and girls—young people did not think nearly so much about marriage as they do today . . . They dated each other for the fun of it, because they enjoyed each other's company, because they liked the same things, or merely because in the competitive social life of their time it was a good thing to have dates—the more, the better. Today young people often play with the idea of marriage as early as the second or third date, and they certainly think about it by the fifth or sixth. By the time they have been going steady for a while they are quite apt to be discussing the number and names of their future children.[39]

Indeed, with the marriage age dropping to an all-time low, large numbers of young people were moving through the dating system directly—and immediately—into marriage. Public policy and family values accounted for "the disappearance of the idea that a man should be able to support a wife before he gets married." New resources were available: The government subsidized mortgages and paid veterans a subsistence allowance—60 dollars if they were single, 75 if married—while they were in school. Working wives and parents supplemented that income. "Nowadays," Cole noted in 1957, "one or both sets of parents are expected to help."[40] Another less easily quantifiable factor was at work here, too. In 1958, *Parents Magazine* explained to its readers "Why They Can't Wait to Wed": "Youngsters want to grasp what little security they can in a world gone frighteningly insecure. The youngsters feel they will cultivate the one security that's possible—their own gardens, their own . . . home and families." That they had begun at an early age to "cultivate . . . security" in steady relationships gave "young people the feeling that they really know members of the opposite sex well enough to choose a marriage partner much earlier in life than people . . . would have dared to do . . . in an earlier day," sociologist David Riesman observed a year later.[41]

While public policy directly, and the political climate indirectly, encouraged early marriage, personal experience was the most important ingredient in the equation. By the 1950s, Americans began to acquire dating and petting experience as young teenagers. Winston Ehrmann found that, except for school, dating was the most time-consuming activity in his subjects' lives, beginning in junior high or even elementary school. Doubtless many parents disapproved of their children's early exposure to heterosexual socializing, but other parents clearly promoted it. In the April 1956 issue of *Good Housekeeping,* Phyllis McGinley bemoaned the fact that

> abetted, indeed pushed and prodded and egged on by their mothers or the PTA or scoutmasters, sixth-grade children are now making dates on the telephone and ineptly jitterbugging together every weekend evening . . . They are coaxed and bullied and enticed into "mingling." There are school dances and church dances and scout dances. There are Coke parties and local "assemblies" and what passes for dances at private homes.[42]

It was certainly true that by the time middle-class children entered junior high school, they were full participants in the first stages of dating ritual. Most began with "group dating": "Everything is done in gangs, although pairing off usually occurs sometimes during the evening," reported one student. Another described the process in greater detail:

> The boys and girls seldom attend the basketball games together, as couples, but prefer instead to drift in with a crowd of their own gender. When the lights are more discreetly lowered after the games, however, the boys tend to seek out their latest interests and pair off for dancing. At the end of such dances a few boys walk their "girls" home, but the majority of the crowd walks in groups of paired couples "en masse" down to the local hangout for a Coke.

For the clique that "set the pace for the others," there were two rituals of importance: the Saturday night date to the movies and "Coke parlor" afterward, and the more occasional private parties ("minus chaperons") at someone's house. The main attractions there were the games of "Spin the Bottle," "Postoffice," and "Spotlight."[43]

When these students went on to high school, they "began to date with real intent and purpose [and] played the field." Susan Allen Toth, who grew up in Ames, Iowa, in the 1950s, remembered that "high school courtship usually was meticulously slow, progressing through inquiry, phone calls, planned encounters in public places, double or triple dates, hand-holding, and finally a good-night kiss." Dates had a predictable form: "Movie, something to eat, and out to park. Movie, something to eat, come home, and perhaps neck there. Movie, home for something to eat, and then perhaps T.V.," a college student recalled. By senior year, the majority of the class was "going steady with someone." Many of those not going on to college married soon after graduation. College-bound students were less likely to marry their high school steadies than were classmates who went directly into the labor force.[44]

College enrollments rose at a slow rate during the years of Depression and war, but after the passage of the G.I. Bill in 1944, they surged ahead. More than twice as many Americans graduated from college in 1950 as had a decade earlier, and by 1960, 22 percent of the 18- to 24-year-old population was in school.[45] College students might not have talked about "going steady," a phrase with more currency in high school than collegiate circles, but "the institution was as strong in the latter as in the former." In a *Harper's* piece titled "American Youth Goes Monogamous," George Cole declared that "the present pre-marital monogamy of youth . . . is one of the most important phenomena of recent times." Nora Johnson, a 1954 graduate of Smith College, reported that when she was on campus in the early 1950s "everybody [was] doing it." In her view, "the phenomena of pinning, going steady, and being monogamous-minded [were] symptoms of our inclination to play it safe. . . . What a feeling of safety not to have to worry about a date for months ahead!" Johnson believed that the "male wish for dating security" was as strong as the woman's. "Their fraternity pins are burning holes in their lapels," she wryly observed. Getting "pinned" or "engaged to be engaged" was the ritual—and the symbol—for the college version of monogamy.[46]

Going steady or being pinned was not merely a source of social security. Sociologist Ira Reiss perceived that one of the great attractions of steady dating for teenagers was that "sex and affection can be quite easily combined"; and that especially for the girl, sexual behavior was "made respectable by going steady." In Nora Johnson's account, the "perpetual twosome" of the college scene was "often based on sex and convenience." Going steady allowed a woman to be respectable and available at the same time. It reconciled the two, often conflicting, principles by which middle-class girls operated: "One is that anything is all right if you're in love . . . and the other is that a girl must be respected, particularly by the man she wants to marry," as Johnson put it in "Sex and the College Girl." The "ideal girl," she suggested, "has done every possible kind of petting without actually having had intercourse. This gives her savoir-faire, while still maintaining her dignity."[47]

The "ideal girl" was also the typical girl: through the 1940s and 1950s, the increases in premarital sexual activity occurred in petting rather than coitus. By the mid-1950s, more than 90 percent of college-age men and women reported engaging in premarital petting. The incidence of premarital intercourse had remained fairly constant since the 1920s: between one-third and two-thirds of college men and about one-third of women reported that they had coitus before marriage. In one 1958 study, 10 percent of the co-eds had had sexual intercourse while in a dating relationship, 15 percent while going steady, and twice as many (31 percent) during engagement. The researchers concluded that "engagement was very often the prerequisite to a girl having premarital sexual intercourse." If a girl had coitus, it was likely to be with her fiancé, during the year or two before they were married.[48]

The frequency of this behavior reflects the acceptance among middle-class teenagers of what Ira Reiss has labeled "permissiveness with affection." High school couples "feel it is proper to engage in heavy petting if they are going steady, the justification being that they are in love or at least extremely fond of each other," he explained in 1961. Especially among a slightly older age group, similar reasoning supported the decision to have coitus during the late stages of the transition to marriage. One young man gave a typical rationale for why he and his girl friend "indulged in petting, and at times . . . heavy petting . . . [It] was the result of a drive that had something beside pure sex as a motivating factor. We didn't believe in petting because of the sex alone, but because we were very much in love and this was a means of expressing our love to each other." They refrained from sleeping together not because they thought it was wrong, but because they "didn't want to take any unnecessary chances."[49]

This young man and his girl friend agreed on where to draw the limits in their sexual relationship; but, in general, "permissiveness with af-

fection" figured more largely in the female than in the male code of sexual ethics. Boys may have been more sexually experienced (more than twice as many boys as girls had coitus in their teens), but they were also more conservative, in the sense that they were more likely to embrace the traditional double standard which sanctioned conduct in men that it condemned in women. However, during the 1950s, young men evinced "increased willingness . . . to accept some coitus on the part of females, especially if it occurs when the girl is in love and/or engaged." An even more egalitarian standard, which made premarital intercourse right for both sexes, gained ground among older teenagers, particularly those in college. By 1959, a majority of the men in Ehrmann's study of college students adhered to a single standard; and for most of them, it was a *liberal* single standard.[50]

Ehrmann concluded that, in spite of these attitudinal changes, women were still the arbiters and enforcers of sexual codes. A survey published in the *Ladies' Home Journal* in January 1962 summarized the sentiments of women 16- to 21-years old: "They feel a special responsibility for sex *because* they are women." In their comments, these young women revealed an understanding of the different roles played by men and women in the sexual game. "A woman has much more to lose than a man," one woman said. "Girls especially should have a great deal of self-control, seeing quite a few boys don't," was another's response. One young woman declared, "A man will go as far as a woman will let him," and another agreed, "A girl has to set the standard."[51]

The standard was based on emotion more than on eroticism. For the women in Ehrmann's study, sexual expression was "primarily and profoundly related to being in love and going steady"; while for the men, "sexuality is more indirectly and less exclusively associated with romanticism and intimate relationships." Ehrmann noticed an even more striking difference in the sexual standards of young men and women: "The degree of physical intimacy actually experienced or considered permissible is among males *inversely* related and among females *directly* related to the intensity of and familiarity and affection in the male-female relation." In other words, the more a young woman loved a man, the more permissive she was likely to be; the more a young man loved a woman, the less permissive he was likely to be. Furthermore, where women rarely went beyond the limits set by their codes, men were often prevented by their partners from going "as far sexually as their codes permit."[52]

By the end of the 1950s, the differences between male and female standards were fading. Men were moving away from the traditional double standard toward permissiveness with affection; while women's attitudes were shifting toward the "transitional double standard—coitus is all right for men under any condition, but it is acceptable for women only if they are in love." Investigators detected signs of a related change in the "steady decrease in the tendency to express different standards for members of one's own sex than for members of the opposite sex." By 1968, the double standard had not disappeared, but its decline was noticeable. It was being eroded by an overall liberalization of sexual attitudes. The new ground broken by the youths of the 1950s was not so much in the incidence of premarital coitus as in the wider acceptance of it.[53]

Reflecting on this convergence of sexual attitudes and behavior, Ira Reiss speculated in 1966, "We may well witness soon an increase in many forms of sexual behavior . . . The stage is set for another upward cycle of increasing sexual behavior and sexual acceptance." Reiss was soon proved right. After decades of relative stability, the rate of premarital coitus showed a dramatic increase. The most marked change for men occurred among those in college. Half of the college-bound men in a 1972 survey had had premarital intercourse by the age of 17, more

than twice the rate in the Kinsey Report. (Among males not in college, the increase was substantially lower.)[54] The change for women was even more dramatic. The percentage of women who had first intercourse by the age of 17 doubled between the 1940–49 and 1950–59 birth cohorts. A range of studies yielded higher premarital coital rates among college women in the late 1960s than in the 1950s and early 1960s. Only two studies showed a nonvirgin rate below 30 percent for college women, and most found between 40 percent and 55 percent.[55]

When Ira Reiss described the teenage girl in 1961 as "the guardian of sexual limits," he observed that "she appears increasingly to be a half-willing guardian who more and more seeks her self-satisfaction and strives to achieve sexual equality." By the late 1960s, she was drawing closer to this goal. It was not just the rate of premarital intercourse that increased dramatically in the 1960s; the context changed as well. In a 1968 replication of a 1958 study, Robert Bell and Jay Chaskes found that, in 10 years, the proportion of women having premarital coitus while in dating relationships had gone from 10 percent to 23 percent; for those going steady, the increase was from 15 percent to 28 percent. The rise in the rate of premarital intercourse during engagement was smaller, from 31 percent to 39 percent. The authors concluded that in 1968 women were more likely than a decade before to have their first sexual experience prior to becoming engaged. Furthermore, the young women in the 1968 sample were far more likely than those in the 1958 group to feel comfortable with that decision. The percentage of co-eds who felt they had gone "too far" was cut in half for all three dating levels. Other investigators uncovered a similar pattern: there was a general decline in the proportion of women who reported feeling guilt or remorse after their first coital experience. "What was done by a female in 1925 acting as a rebel and a deviant can be done by a female in 1965 as a conformist," Reiss declared.[56]

While her parents were likely to be more critical than her peers, by the early 1970s older as well as younger Americans were evincing more liberal attitudes toward premarital sex. In a 1969 Gallup Poll, 68 percent of a national sample believed premarital sex was wrong; four years later, only 48 percent agreed. Older respondents remained more conservative than younger ones, but a shift toward permissiveness had taken place among all age groups. "Marriage no longer seemed to occupy its place as the dividing line between socially approved and socially disapproved sexual intimacy," sociologist Robert Sorensen observed. More than half of the teenagers in his 1973 nationwide study thought it was "abnormal or unnatural for a boy not to have sex until he gets married." (That the double standard lingered on is reflected in the fact that only 42 percent of the boys and 27 percent of the girls answered yes when the same question was asked about girls.) The concept of "premarital sex" was fast disappearing. Teenagers assumed "there is nothing wrong with sex without marriage."[57]

Sex without love, on the other hand, was another matter. This generation preserved the rule that had guided their parents: "It's all right for young people to have sex before getting married if they are in love with each other." Behavior patterns suggest that "permissiveness with affection" was still the prevailing standard. In Morton Hunt's 1972 study, twice as many women reported having had premarital coitus as in Kinsey's sample, but the proportion of those whose premarital experience was confined to one partner remained the same. Of the women born between 1948 and 1955 (in other words, those who reached early adulthood in the late 1960s and early 1970s), 53 percent had premarital coitus only with their future husbands. "Today's 'nice' girl is still guiding herself according to romantic and historically rooted values," Hunt concluded in 1974.[58] For the next generation, the teenagers of the 1970s, those values appear to have lost some of their hold.

Magazines might remind their young female readers of "Your Right to Say No," but more and more teenage girls were saying yes. In 1979, 50 percent of the teenage girls living in metropolitan areas had had premarital sex, an increase of 20 percent since the start of the decade.[59]

Young people in the 1970s may have been sexually active at a younger age than earlier generations, but most acquired this sexual experience in settings that would have been familiar to their parents and grandparents.[60] There was, however, one important addition: a growing minority of young men and women lived together before marriage. Just as the "sexual revolution" of the first quarter of the 20th century involved the innoculation of mainstream youth with a germ incubated in bohemia, so too the dramatic rise in cohabitation reflects the diffusion of an alternative life style throughout middle-class culture. In the late 1960s, unmarried couples who lived together were described in the pages of the *New York Times* as a "tiny minority" within "the dissident youth subculture—the intellectual, politically liberal to radical, from middle- and upper-middle-class backgrounds, antimaterialistic and anti-Establishment." Between 1970 and 1982, the number of cohabiting couples tripled. While some of these couples were older people, a leading demographer concluded that the increase was "accounted for . . . primarily by *young couples without children.*" During the 1970s, the number of cohabiting couples under 25 with no children increased eightfold.[61]

In spite of the alarms sounded by parents and the press, cohabitation posed little threat to marriage. An unmarried couple told the *Times* in 1969 that the usual sequence was to "slide from dating into shacking up into marriage." As parents saw their children sliding into marriage rather than into a life in the counter culture, fears subsided. A report on the 1980 census remarked that "young Americans are becoming increasingly attracted to this lifestyle, and their parents are becoming less critical of this behavior." An occasional couple found themselves at odds with the law or a censorious landlord, and many young people continued to conceal their living arrangements from their parents; but by the early 1980s, cohabitation had lost its association with the "dissident youth subculture" that had spawned it. A 1981 research team described it as "part of the courtship process rather than a long-term alternative to marriage."[62]

When couples made the transition from living together to marriage, as so many eventually did, they observed the same rituals as their noncohabiting comtemporaries.[63] While a small minority devised "alternative" weddings, most Americans who married in the late 1960s and the 1970s followed a familiar pattern. Three out of four first-time brides received an engagement ring; 85 percent of them wore a formal bridal gown. "We Americans are getting married almost precisely as we did a hundred years ago," Marcia Seligson wrote in 1973:

> We are adorning ourselves in long white romantic gowns, going to church or to a hotel or country club, repeating established vows we have heard at other folks' weddings for years, sipping champagne, cutting cake, dancing, tossing the bouquet, posing for pictures, fleeing through a shower of rice as we head for our Caribbean honeymoon.

This list, which would have served as a guide to American wedding ritual any time between 1920 and 1980, explains the growth of the "wedding industry" in the past 50 years. Americans who married in 1979 and their families spent about $12.5 billion dollars on rings, wedding expenses, home furnishings, and honeymoons; and the wedding market seemed immune to hard times. In May of 1982, the *New York Times* reported on a "return to traditionalism," noting that for "bridal merchants, it's a state of bliss."[64]

Were the objects of all this commercial activity equally blissful? Presumably so, yet at a time when one in every two marriages was likely to

end in divorce, couples could not help but approach the altar with some sense that they were taking on a challenge at which many of them would fail. Lorenzo Dow's 1833 reflection on matrimony, "If a man have a farm and don't like it, he can pull it down and build another. But this is for life!" had ceased to describe the American experience. Although the annual divorce rate had been rising steadily for well over a century (with the exception of a drop during the Depression and an upsurge after both world wars), it has increased more sharply in the 1960s and 1970s than ever before. Between 1966 and 1976, the divorce rate doubled and then, in the late 1970s, showed signs of leveling off. The rate of remarriage declined (along with the rate of first marriage) during the 1970s, but Americans had not lost faith in marriage. Four out of every five divorced persons remarried, half of them within three years, and in 1983, two and a half million marriages were recorded.[65]

When a boyhood friend announced his engagement in the fall of 1905, Walter Price sent his congratulations: "The union of a man and a woman in these days where precedents are disregarded & 'Novelty holds sway' is the one old fashioned thing to which people cling. Without it life's a shipwreck."[66] In the perilous world of the 1980s, Americans are no more willing to let go than their grandparents were.

ENDNOTES

1. U.S. Census, Current Population Reports, "Marital Status and Living Arrangements," series P-20, no. 365, March 1980, pp. 1–2; Andrew J. Cherlin, *Marriage Divorce Remarriage* (Cambridge, MA, 1981), Figures 1.1, 1.2; Donald J. Bogue, *The Population of the United States* (Glencoe, IL, 1959), p. 215.

Related changes that occurred in the 1940s were the increasing independence of the transition to marriage from the transition to labor force participation and from parenthood; and the sharp reduction in the spread of ages at which Americans married. For a detailed examination of these phenomena, see John Modell, Frank Furstenberg, Jr., and Douglas Strong, "The Timing of Marriage in the Transition to Adulthood: Continuity and Change, 1860–1975," in John Demos and Sarane Spence Boocock, eds. *Turning Points,* supplement to *AJS* 84 (1978): S122–47. Here, and elsewhere in this chapter, the figures apply only to whites. Cherlin discusses the similarities and differences in the demographic patterns of the black and white populations (*Marriage,* chap. 4, passim).

2. Cherlin, *Marriage,* chap. 1, passim.

One important new pattern that appears to be developing in the early 1980s is the increase, among 25- to 29-year-olds, of those who are single. According to the 1980 census, one-fifth of the women in that age group had not yet married, a twofold increase since 1970. There was a 70 percent increase for men, from one-fifth in 1970 to one-third in 1980. One result of this trend was to raise the median age at first marriage; by 1983, Americans were marrying later than at any time since 1890.

3. Frederick Lewis Allen, *Only Yesterday: An Informal History of the 1920s* (New York, 1931; Perennial Library ed. 1964), p. 73. For the classic statement of the changes under way in American life before the First World War, see Henry F. May, *The End of American Innocence* (New York, 1959), pp. 138–39, 266–67.

4. Lynd and Lynd, *Middletown,* p. 139.

5. Paula Fass, *The Damned and the Beautiful: American Youth in the 1920s* (New York, 1977), p. 262. While Fass has a tendency to overgeneralize from the college youth who are the focus of her book, *The Damned and the Beautiful* is an indispensable resource to anyone interested in the experience of young Americans during the 1920s.

6. Alfred Kinsey recognized that older generations had engaged in "flirting, flirtage, courting, bundling, spooning, mugging, smooching, larking, sparking, and other activities which were simply petting under another name." Alfred C. Kinsey, et al., *Sexual Behavior in the Human Female* [hereafter cited as *SBHF*] (Philadelphia, 1953), p. 231.

7. John Modell, "Dating Becomes the Way of American Youth," in *Essays on the Family and Historical Change,* ed. by Leslie Page Moch and Gary D. Stark (College Station, TX, 1983),

p. 102; Lynd and Lynd, *Middletown,* p. 138. I am grateful to Professor Modell for sharing this essay with me before publication.

8. Willard Waller, "The Rating and Dating Complex," *ASR* 2 (1937): 729, 728, 730. Christopher Lasch discusses the challenge Waller presented to sociological orthodoxy in the 1920s and 1930s; see *Haven in a Heartless World* (New York, 1977), pp. 50–55.

9. Michael Gordon suggests that Penn State may have been especially well suited to support a "rating and dating complex": it was geographically isolated; it had six males for every female student (as opposed to ratios of three to one at Cornell and two to one at Michigan); and its student body represented the lower rather than the upper reaches of the middle class. Michael Gordon, "Was Waller Ever Right? The Rating and Dating Complex Reconsidered," *JMF,* 43 (February 1981): 69, n.3.

10. Modell argues persuasively that Fass's account of the development of dating needs to be revised to take into account the importance of peer-group activities, especially dating, on the high school level. He points out that "high schools had almost even sex ratios—a demography far more conducive to widespread dating than that in college" ("Dating," p. 104).

11. Fass, *The Damned,* pp. 175, 200, 153; Gordon, "Was Waller Ever Right?" [11]: 73.

12. Louise Dutton, *Going Together* (Indianapolis, IN, 1923), pp. 20–21.

13. Robert Angell, *The Campus: A Study of Contemporary Undergraduate Life in the American University* (New York, 1928), pp. 165–69; Lynd and Lynd, *Middletown,* p. 134.

This distaste for home dates held true when Susan Allen Toth was growing up in Ames, Iowa, in the 1950s. She recalled that young couples rarely spent time in each other's homes. "We might not have been bothered," Toth explained, "but we really wouldn't have been alone. Cars were our private space, a rolling parlor, the only place we could relax and be ourselves . . . Driving gave us a feeling of freedom." Susan Allen Toth, *Blooming: A Small Town Girlhood* (Boston, 1981), p. 52.

14. Modell, "Dating," p. 106.

15. Lewis Erenberg, *Steppin' Out: New York Nightlife and the Transformation of American*

Culture, 1890–1930 (Westport, CT, 1981), pp. 154–55; Angell, *Campus,* p. 169; Fass, *The Damned,* p. 196.

16. Elaine Tyler May, *Great Expectations: Marriage and Divorce in Post-Victorian America* (Chicago, 1980), p. 69. Erenberg examines the Castle phenomenon at length in *Steppin' Out,* pp. 146–76.

17. Fass, *The Damned,* p. 206; Lynd and Lynd, *Middletown,* pp. 263–64.

    Children unaccompanied by a parent accounted for the largest share of the movie audience in Middletown, prompting the Lynds to wonder about the "decentralizing tendency of the movies upon the family" (p. 265).

18. Lynd and Lynd, *Middletown,* pp. 267, 139, 268; Angell, *Campus,* p. 169; May, *Great Expectations,* p. 69.

    The Lynds suggested that the "sex adventure" magazines which were widely read in Middletown had some of the same effects as the movies (pp. 241–42). For a discussion of the evolution of movies as a reflection of and stimulus to middle-class values, see Lary May, *Screening Out the Past: The Birth of Mass Culture and the Motion Picture Industry, 1896–1929* (New York: 1980).

19. Lynd and Lynd, *Middletown,* pp. 258, 253. As the car became a measure of social status, it also became a source of parent-child conflict. In Middletown, "among the high school set, ownership of a car by one's family has become an important criterion of social fitness; a boy almost never takes a girl to a dance except in a car; there are persistent rumors of the buying of a car by local families to help their children's social standing in high school." Ibid., p. 137.

20. Ibid., p. 137; Angell, *Campus,* p. 169.

21. Katharine Merrill to William McCormick, 25 August, 1923, PC; Dorothy Dunbar Bromley and Florence Haxton Britten, *Youth and Sex: A Study of 1300 College Students* (New York, 1938), p. 11.

22. Angell, *Campus,* p. 169; Floyd Dell, *Love in the Machine Age* (New York, 1930), p. 166. According to Modell, petting in the 1920s "was almost universal, in the sense that all daters petted at some time, but not in the sense that all couples petted." ("Dating," p. 100).

23. According to Kinsey, "distinctions between necking and petting, mild and heavy petting, and still other classifications which are current among American youth, appear to differentiate nothing more than various techniques, or the parts of the body which are involved in the contacts, or the level of arousal which is effected." Alfred Kinsey, Wardell B. Pomeroy, and Clyde E. Martin, *Sexual Behavior in the Human Male* [hereafter cited as *SBHM*] (Philadelphia, 1948), p. 228.

24. Geraldine Frances Smith, "Certain Aspects of the Sex Life of the Adolescent Girl," *JAP* (September 1924) 348–49; *SBHF,* pp. 298–301; *SBHM,* p. 406.

25. Lynd and Lynd, *Middletown,* pp. 138–39; Fass, *The Damned,* pp. 266–69.

26. Fass, *The Damned,* pp. 266, 278, 268; Phyllis Blanchard and Carlyn Manasses, *New Girls for Old* (New York, 1930), pp. 69, 73, 75; Walter Buck, "A Measurement of Changes in Attitudes and Interests of University Students over a Ten-Year Period," *JASP* 31 (1936):14.

27. Blanchard and Manasses, *New Girls,* p. 71; Fass, *The Damned,* pp. 273, 274, 276.

28. Robert R. Bell and Jack V. Buerkle, "Mother and Daughter Attitudes to Premarital Sexual Behavior," *MFL* 23 (1961):391. This statement was written about the 1950s, but it is an accurate description of a process that began in the 1920s and 1930s.

29. *SBHF,* table 83, figure 50, p. 339; Fass, *The Damned,* p. 455, n. 28; *SBHM,* pp. 410–13.

30. *SBHF* [8], p. 299; Robert S. Lynd and Helen Merrell Lynd, *Middletown in Transition: A Study in Cultural Conflicts* (New York, 1937), p. 170; Fass, *The Damned,* p. 271.

31. Lynd and Lynd, *Middletown in Transition,* p. 170.

32. Bromley and Britten, *Youth and Sex,* pp. 15–16; Theodore Newcomb, "Recent Changes in Attitudes toward Sex and Marriage," *ASR* 2 (1937):667, 662; "Youth in College," *Fortune* 13, 3 June 1936, p. 101.

    Michael Gordon has tried to explain the apparent contradictions between the views of 1930s campus life offered by Waller and Newcomb; see "Was Waller Ever Right?" pp. 68–69.

33. Fass, *The Damned,* p. 180; "Youth in College," p. 101; Calvin B. Lee, *Campus USA 1900–1970: Changing Styles in Undergraduate Life* (New York, 1970), p. 48.

34. The marriage rate fell from 10.14 per 1,000 in 1929 to 7.9 in 1932 and then started up again, reaching its late 1920s level by 1934 and surpassing it by 1940. Paul Glick and Hugh Carter, *Marriage and Divorce: A Social and Economic Study* (Cambridge, Mass., 1970), p. 41.

35. U.S. Census, Current Population Reports, "Statistical Portrait of Women in the United States: 1978," series P-23, no. 100, p. 24; Cherlin, *Marriage* [3], p. 9.

36. Lee, *Campus USA,* p. 76; "Education for War," *Fortune,* December 1942, p. 146; Winston Ehrmann, *Premarital Dating Behavior* (New York, 1959), p. 76.

37. *SBHF,* p. 234; *SBHM,* pp. 406, 539, 541.

    While Kinsey recognized the educational value of petting, he had grave doubts about it on other grounds. He saw petting as the way college groups "attempt to avoid pre-marital intercourse." He was appalled by "the mixture of scientifically supported logic, and of utter illogic, which shapes the petting behavior of most of these youths. . . . They are particularly concerned with the avoidance of genital union. The fact that petting involved erotic contacts which are as effective as genital union . . . does not disturb the youth so much as actual intercourse would." He suggested that the lower incidence of petting among working-class men reflected their lack of respect for the distinction that was all important to the college group. *SBHM,* pp. 541, 543–44.

38. Lowrie, "Dating Theories," p. 337. Lowrie takes a prodating position. He attacks the negative view of dating offered by Waller and others by showing that students themselves emphasized the learning rather than the thrill-seeking aspects of dating behavior.

39. Ira Reiss, "Sexual Codes in Teen-Age Culture," *AAAPSS* (November 1961):54; Charles W. Cole, "American Youth Goes Monogamous," *Harper's Magazine,* March 1957, p. 32. What Cole missed in the 1950s approach to dating are precisely those elements that Willard Waller found so disturbing in the 1930s.

40. Cole, "American Youth," p. 32.

    Co-residence with parents was, however, not a popular strategy. After 1947, the "prevalence of family extension declined abruptly" (Modell, Furstenberg, and Strong, "Timing of Marriage," pp. S136–37).

41. Mildred Gilman, "Why They Can't Wait to Wed," *Parents Magazine,* November 1958, p. 46; David Riesman, "Permissiveness and Sex Roles," *MFL* (August 1959):21.

    Elaine Tyler May has recently suggested that one of the attractions of early marriage in the 1950s was the containment of sexuality which, like communism and atomic war, threatened American stability and order ("Explosive Issues: Sex, Women, and the Bomb in Post-War America," unpublished paper, American Historical Association, December 1982). The couples who married during this period were the "only cohorts in the last hundred years to show a substantial, sustained shortfall in their lifetime levels of divorce": that is, they had a lower rate of divorce than one would expect from the long-term trends (see Cherlin, *Marriage,* p. 25).

42. Ehrmann, *Premarital Dating,* p. 268; Phyllis McGinley, "The Fearful Aspect of Too-Early Dating," *Good Housekeeping,* April 1956, pp. 60–61, 287–88.

    Ira Reiss attributed this early socialization to the spread of junior high schools: "The anticipatory socialization of sex games like 'spin the bottle,' . . . begins prior to junior high levels and thus prepares students for dating in junior high" ("Sexual Codes," p. 54, n. 3).

43. Jesse Bernard, Helen E. Buchanan, and William M. Smith, Jr., *Dating, Mating and Marriage* (Cleveland, OH, 1958), pp. 34, 25–28. The Bernard book is unusual among marriage and family texts in that it takes a "documentary case approach." The "informants" are unidentified college students, presumably enrolled in the authors' courses.

44. Ibid., pp. 27–28; Toth, *Blooming,* p. 49.

45. Godfrey Hodgson, *America in Our Time* (New York, 1978), pp. 53–54; *Historical Statistics of the United States from Colonial Times to 1970,* Bicentennial Edition (Washington, D.C., 1975), part I, p. 383.

46. Cole, "American Youth," pp. 30, 33; Nora Johnson, "Sex and the College Girl," *Atlantic,* November 1959, pp. 57–58.

    Pinning was "made quite a bit of in the fraternity set" on at least one campus. The couple would announce, after the weekly chapter meeting, that they were about to become pinned; and "then the next weekend the 'fellow' and several of his friends came to the sorority house and there was singing and 'serenading.' After that the pinning was official. Depinning was also a ritual. Both announced after chapter meetings that they were no longer pinned. It was the custom for no one to ask any questions or even to discuss it." Bernard, Buchanan, and Smith, *Dating,* p. 43.

47. Reiss, "Sexual Codes," pp. 55, 59; Johnson, "College Girl," pp. 57, 59, 60.

48. Ehrmann, *Premarital Dating,* p. 36, tables 1.6, 1.7; Robert R. Bell and Jay B. Chaskes, "Premarital Sexual Experience among Coeds, 1958–1968," *JMF* 32 (February 1970):83.

Ehrmann pointed out the "curious fact [that] there exist more quantitative data about the incidence rates of coitus, the most taboo of premarital heterosexual activities, than about kissing and hugging, the most socially acceptable" (p. 32).

49. Reiss, "Sexual Codes," 55; Bernard, Buchanan, and Smith, *Dating,* p. 58. Reiss's *Premarital Sexual Standards in America* (Glencoe, IL, 1961) is a detailed inquiry into the values underlying sexual standards in America.

50. Reiss, "Sexual Codes," 59; Ehrmann, *Premarital Dating,* p. 270.

51. "Shaping the 60s . . . Foreshadowing the 70s," *Ladies' Home Journal,* January 1962, pp. 30, 73.

In spite of the fact that "so few they would hardly count supported greater sexual freedom for men and women than our society condones," George Gallup concluded from this poll that these girls were "unconventional in their attitudes toward sex." Ibid., p. 30.

52. Ehrmann, *Premarital Dating,* p. 269. All of these distinctions prompted Ehrmann to suggest that there were "distinct male and female subcultures" in the world of American youth; see pp. 270–77, for his discussion of this idea.

53. Edwin O. Smigel and Rita Seiden, "Decline and Fall of the Double Standard," *AAAPSS* 376 (March 1968): 12; Gilbert R. Kaats and Keith E. Davis, "The Dynamics of Sexual Behavior of College Students," *JMF* 32 (August 1970):391; Ira Reiss, "The Sexual Renaissance: A Summary and Analysis," *JSI* 22 (1966): 126.

54. Reiss, "Sexual Renaissance," p. 126; Morton Hunt, *Sex in the 70s* (Chicago, 1974), p. 149.

55. J. Richard Udry, Karl E. Bauman, and Naomi M. Morris, "Changes in Premarital Coital Experience of Recent Decade-of-Birth Cohorts of American Women," *JMF* 37 (November 1975): 784; Kenneth L. Cannon and Richard Long, "Premarital Sexual Behavior in the 60s," *JMF* 33 (February 1971): 40; Kaats and Davis, "Dynamics," 391.

56. Reiss, "Sexual Codes," pp. 58–59; Bell and Chaskes, "Premarital Sexual Experience," pp. 82–83; Cannon and Long, "Premarital Sexual Behavior," p. 41; Reiss, "Sexual Renaissance," p. 126.

57. Hunt, *Sex in the 70s,* p. 21; Smigel and Seiden, "Decline and Fall," p. 14; Robert C. Sorensen, *Adolescent Sexuality in Contemporary America* (New York, 1973), pp. 341, 242, 100.

Sorenson suggests that his subjects' lack of interest in marriage was a reflection of the developmental nature of adolescence. Adolescents do not "seek lifelong companionship and financial security in their immediate post-adolescent life. They are moving away from their own family ties, and few seek to replace them with new ones . . . Commitment to the future is not to their liking, and when most adolescents think of marriage, they think of commitment" (p. 345). While this argument is sensible, it fails to explain the phenomenon of teenage pregnancy— and parenthood.

58. Sorenson, *Adolescent Sexuality,* p. 100; Hunt, *Sex in the 70s,* pp. 151–53.

59. Sally Helgesen, "Your Right to Say No," *Seventeen,* August 1981, pp. 284–85; Melvin Zelnik and Jon F. Kantner, "Sexual Activity, Contraceptive Use and Pregnancy among Metropolitan-Area Teenagers," *FPP* 12 (September/October 1980):230–31.

Virtually all of the growth in coitus between 1976 and 1979 occurred among white teenagers. This increase in teenage sexual activity was accompanied by a steady increase in teenage pregnancy and abortion. In 1979, 16 percent of all teenage women had been premaritally pregnant; 37 percent of these pregnancies were terminated by induced abortion. In spite of "increased and more consistent" use of contraception by teenagers, pregnancy rates were rising, perhaps because many adolescents were substituting withdrawal for more effective methods, such as the pill and the IUD. See Zelnik and Kantner, "Sexual Activity," p. 237.

60. One entirely new setting has recently been introduced to the college social scene. In January 1983, the *New York Times* reported that computer centers were "to some extent replacing libraries as a focus of student life, both academic and social." *New York Times,* 2 January 1983, p. A:1.

61. Arno Karlen, "Unmarried Marrieds on Campus," *New York Times Magazine,* 26 January 1969, p. 77; U.S. Census, "Marital Status," p. 1; Paul Glick and Graham B. Spanier, "Married and Unmarried Cohabitation in the United States." *JMF* 42 (February 1980):20–21.

Some of this increase is the result of the absolute increase in the numbers of young adults in the population and of greater frankness in reporting; but all analysts agree that while it may be exaggerated by the statistics, the real magnitude of the change is very great.

62. Karlen, "Unmarrieds," p. 78; Glick and Spanier, "Married and Unmarried Cohabitation," 21; Barbara J. Risman et al., "Living Together in College: Implications for Courtship," *JMF* 43 (February 1981):82.

63. Risman et al., found some evidence that cohabiting couples were more likely to have smaller and, presumably, less formal weddings than their noncohabiting counterparts ("Living Together," p. 82).

64. "Big Weddings Are Back," *McCall's,* April 1981, pp. 124–34; Marcia Seligson, *The Eternal Bliss Machine: America's Way of Wedding* (New York, 1973), p. 4; *New York Times,* 26 October 1980, p. C:19; *New York Times,* 18 May 1982, p. B:2.

65. Lorenzo Dow, "Reflections on Matrimony," in Peggy Dow, *Vicissitudes in the Wilderness* (Norwich, CT, 1833), p. 156; Cherlin, *Marriage,* pp. 22–23; Arthur J. Norton and Paul C. Glick, "Marital Instability in America: Past, Present, and Future," in *Divorce and Separation,* ed. by George Levinger and Oliver C. Moles (New York, 1979), p. 13.

66. Walter W. Price to James Lee Laidlaw, 8 September 1905, Harriet Burton Laidlaw Papers, SL.

READING 8-2

Dubious Conceptions: The Controversy over Teen Pregnancy

Kristin Luker

The conventional wisdom has it that an epidemic of teen pregnancy is today ruining the lives of young women and their children and perpetuating poverty in America. In polite circles, people speak regretfully of "babies having babies." Other Americans are more blunt. "I don't mind paying to help people in need," one angry radio talk show host told Michael Katz, a historian of poverty, "but I don't want my tax dollars to pay for the sexual pleasure of adolescents who won't use birth control."

By framing the issue in these terms, Americans have imagined that the persistence of poverty and other social problems can be traced to youngsters who are too impulsive or too ignorant to postpone sexual activity, to use contraception, to seek an abortion, or failing all that, especially if they are white, to give their babies up for adoption to "better" parents. Defining the problem this way, many Americans, including those in a position to influence public policy, have come to believe that one attractive avenue to reducing poverty and other social ills is to reduce teen birth rates. Their remedy is to persuade teenagers to postpone childbearing, either by convincing them of the virtues of chastity (a strategy conservatives prefer) or by making abortion, sex education, and contraception more freely available (the strategy liberals prefer).

Reducing teen pregnancy would almost certainly be a good thing. After all, the rate of teen childbearing in the United States is more similar to the rates prevailing in the poor countries of the world than in the modern, industrial nations we think of as our peers. However, neither the problem of teen pregnancy nor the remedies for it are as simple as most people think.

In particular, the link between poverty and teen pregnancy is a complicated one. We do know that teen mothers are poorer than women who wait past their 20th birthday to have a child. But stereotypes to the contrary, it is not clear whether early motherhood causes poverty or the reverse. Worse yet, even if teen pregnancy does have some independent force in making teen parents poorer than they would otherwise be, it remains to be seen whether any policies in effect or under discussion can do much to reduce teen birth rates.

These uncertainties raise questions about our political culture as well as our public choices. How did Americans become convinced that teen pregnancy is a major cause of poverty and that reducing one would reduce the other? The answer is a tale of good intentions, rising cultural anxieties about teen sex and family breakdown, and the uses—and misuses—of social science.

HOW TEEN PREGNANCY BECAME AN ISSUE

Prior to the mid-1970s, few people talked about "teen pregnancy." Pregnancy was defined as a social problem primarily when a woman was unmarried; no one thought anything amiss when an 18- or 19-year-old got married and had children. And concern about pregnancies among unmarried women certainly did not stop when the woman turned 20.

But in 1975, when Congress held the first of many hearings on the issue of adolescent fertility, expert witnesses began to speak of an "epidemic" of a "million pregnant teenagers" a year. Most of these witnesses were drawing on statistics supplied by the Alan Guttmacher Institute,

which a year later published the data in an influential booklet, *Eleven Million Teenagers*. Data from that document were later cited—often down to the decimal point—in most discussions of the teenage pregnancy "epidemic."

Many people hearing these statistics must have assumed that the "million pregnant teenagers" a year were all unmarried. The Guttmacher Institute's figures, however, included married 19-year-olds along with younger, unmarried teenage girls. In fact, almost two-thirds of the "million pregnant teenagers" were 18- and 19-year olds; about 40 percent of them were married, and about two-thirds of the married women were married prior to the pregnancy.

Moreover, despite the language of epidemic, pregnancy rates among teenagers were not dramatically increasing. From the turn of the century until the end of World War II, birth rates among teenagers were reasonably stable at approximately 50 to 60 births per thousand women. Teen birth rates, like all American birth rates, increased dramatically in the period after World War II, doubling in the baby boom years to a peak of about 97 births per thousand teenage women in 1957. Subsequently, teen birth rates declined, and by 1975 they had gone back down to their traditional levels, where, for the most part, they have stayed (see Figure 1).

Were teen births declining in recent decades only because of higher rates of abortion? Here, too, trends are different from what many people suppose. The legalization of abortion in January of 1973 made it possible for the first time to get reliable statistics on abortions for women, teenagers and older. The rate among teenagers rose from about 27.0 to 42.9 abortions per 1,000 women between 1974 and 1980. Since 1980 teen abortion rates have stabilized, and may even have declined somewhat. Moreover, teenagers account for a declining proportion of all abortions: in the years just after *Roe v. Wade,* teenagers obtained almost a third of all abortions in the country; now they obtain about a quarter. A stable teen birth rate and a stabilizing

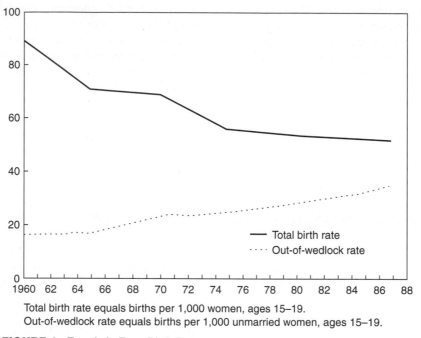

Total birth rate equals births per 1,000 women, ages 15–19.
Out-of-wedlock rate equals births per 1,000 unmarried women, ages 15–19.

FIGURE 1 Trends in Teen Birth Rates.
(Sources: National Center for Health Statistics, *Annual Vital Statistics,* and *Monthly Vital Statistics Reports;* U.S. DHEW, Vital and Health Statistics, "Trends in Illegitimacy, U.S. 1940–1965.")

teen abortion rate means that pregnancy rates, which rose modestly in the 1970s, have in recent years leveled off.

What has been increasing—and increasing dramatically—is the percentage of teen births that are out-of-wedlock (Figure 1). In 1970 babies born out of wedlock represented about a third of all babies born to teen mothers. By 1980 out-of-wedlock births were about half; and by 1986 almost two-thirds. Beneath these overall figures lie important racial variations. Between 1955 and 1988 the out-of-wedlock rate rose from 6 to 24.8 per thousand unmarried, teenage, white women, while for unmarried, nonwhite teenagers the rate rose from 77.6 to 98.3 per thousand. In other words, while the out-of-wedlock birth rate was rising 25 percent among nonwhite teens, it was actually quadrupling among white teens.

The immediate source for this rise in out-of-wedlock teen pregnancy might seem to be obvious. Since 1970 young women have increasingly postponed marriage without rediscovering the virtues of chastity. Only about 6 percent of teenagers were married in 1984, compared to 12 percent in 1970. And although estimates vary, sexual activity among single teenagers has increased sharply, probably doubling. By 1984 almost half of all American teenage women were both unmarried and sexually active, up from only one in four in 1970.

Yet the growth of out-of-wedlock births has not occurred only among teens; in fact, the increase has been more rapid among older women. In 1970 teens made up almost half of all out-of-wedlock births in America; at present they account for a little less than a third. On the other hand, out-of-wedlock births represent a much larger percentage of births to teens than of births to older women. Perhaps for that reason, teenagers have become the symbol of a problem that, to many Americans, is "out of control."

Whatever misunderstandings may have been encouraged by reports of a "million pregnant teenagers" a year, the new concept of "teen pregnancy" had a remarkable impact. By the mid-1980s, Congress had created a new federal office on adolescent pregnancy and parenting; 23 states had set up task forces; the media had published over 200 articles, including cover stories in both *Time* and *Newsweek;* American philanthropy had moved teen pregnancy into a high priority funding item; and a 1985 Harris poll showed that 80 percent of Americans thought teen pregnancy was a "serious problem" facing the nation, a concern shared across racial, geographic, and economic boundaries.

But while this public consensus has been taking shape, a debate has emerged about many of its premises. A growing number of social scientists have come to question whether teen pregnancy causes the social problems linked to it. Yet these criticisms have at times been interpreted as either an ivory-tower indifference to the fate of teen parents and their babies or a Panglossian optimism that teen childbearing is just one more alternate lifestyle. As a result, clarity on these issues has gotten lost in clouds of ideological mistrust. To straighten out these matters, we need to understand what is known, and not known, about the relation of teen pregnancy to poverty and other social problems.[1]

DISTINGUISHING CAUSES FROM CORRELATIONS

As the Guttmacher Institute's report made clear, numerous studies have documented an association between births to teenagers and a host of bad medical and social outcomes. Compared to women who have babies later in life, teen mothers are in poorer health, have more medically treacherous pregnancies, more stillbirths and

newborn deaths, and more low-birth-weight and medically compromised babies.

Later in life, women who have babies as teenagers are also worse off than other women. By their late 20s, women who gave birth as teenagers are less likely to have finished high school and thus not to have received any subsequent higher education. They are more likely to have routine, unsatisfying, and dead-end jobs, to be on welfare, and to be single parents either because they were never married or their marriage ended in divorce. In short, they often lead what the writer Mike Rose has called "lives on the boundary."

Yet an interesting thing has happened over the last 20 years. A description of the lives of teenage mothers and their children was transmuted into a causal sequence, and the often-blighted lives of young mothers were assumed to flow from their early childbearing. Indeed, this is what the data would show, if the women who gave birth as teenagers were the same in every way as women who give birth later. But they are not.

Although there is little published data on the social origins of teen parents, studies have documented the effects of social disadvantage at every step along the path to teenage motherhood. First, since poor and minority youth tend to become sexually active at an earlier age than more advantaged youngsters, they are "at risk" for a longer period of time, including years when they are less cognitively mature. Young teens are also less likely to use contraceptives than older teenagers. Second, the use of contraception is more common among teens who are white, come from more affluent homes, have higher educational aspirations, and who are doing well in school. And, finally, among youngsters who become pregnant, abortions are more common if they are affluent, white, urban, of higher socio-economic status, get good grades, come from two-parent families, and aspire to higher education. Thus, more advantaged youth get filtered out of the pool of young women at risk of teen parenthood.

Two kinds of background factors influence which teens are likely to become pregnant and give birth outside of marriage. First is inherited disadvantage. Young women from families that are poor, or rural, or from a disadvantaged minority, or headed by a single parent are more likely to be teen mothers than are their counterparts from more privileged backgrounds. Yet young mothers are not just disadvantaged; they are also discouraged. Studies suggest that a young woman who has other troubles—who is not doing well in school, has lower "measured ability," and lacks high aspirations for herself—is also at risk of becoming a teenage mother.

Race plays an independent part in the route to teen motherhood. Within each racial group, according to Linda Waite and her colleagues at the Rand Corporation, teen birth rates are highest for those who have the greatest economic disadvantage and lowest academic ability. The effects of disadvantage, however, vary depending on the group. The Rand study found that among young high-ability, affluent black women from homes with two parents, only about one in a hundred become single, teenage mothers. For comparable whites, the risk was one in a thousand. By contrast, a poor, black teenager from a female-headed household who scores low on standardized tests has an astonishing one in four chance of becoming an unwed mother in her teens. Her white counterpart has 1 chance in 12. Unwed motherhood thus reflects the intersecting influences of race, class, and gender; race and class each has a distinct impact on the life histories of young women.

Since many, if not most, teenage unwed mothers are already both disadvantaged and discouraged before they get pregnant, the poor outcomes of their pregnancies as well as their later difficulties in life are not surprising. Consider the health issues. As the demographer Jane Menken pointed out some time ago (and as many other studies have corroborated), the medical complications associated with teen pregnancy are largely due not to age but to the poverty of young mothers. As poor people, they suffer not from some biological risk due to youth, but from restricted access to medical care, particularly to prenatal care. (To be fair, some research suggests that there may be special biological risks for the very youngest mothers, those under age 15 when they give birth, who constitute about 2 percent of all teen mothers.)

Or, to take a more complicated example, consider whether bearing a child blocks teenagers from getting an education. In the aggregate, teen mothers do get less education than women who do not have babies at an early age. But teen mothers are different from their childless peers along exactly those dimensions we would expect independently to contribute to reduced schooling. More of them are poor, come from single-parent households, and have lower aspirations for themselves, lowered measured ability, and more problems with school absenteeism and discipline. Given the nature of the available data, it is difficult to sort out the effects of a teen birth apart from the personal and social factors that predispose young women to both teen motherhood and less education. Few would argue that having a baby as a teenager enhances educational opportunities, but the exact effect of teen birth is a matter of debate.

Educational differences between teen mothers and other women may also be declining, at least in terms of graduating from high school. Legislation that took effect in 1975 forbade schools to expel pregnant teens. Contrary to current skepticism about federal intervention, this regulation seems to have worked. According to a study by Dawn Upchurch and James McCarthy, only 18.6 percent of teenagers who had a baby in 1958 subsequently graduated from high school. Graduation rates among teen mothers reached 29.2 percent in 1975; by 1986 they climbed to 55 percent. Teen mothers were still not graduating at a rate equal to other women (as of 1985, about 87 percent of women ages 25 to 29 had a high school diploma or its equivalent). But over the decade prior to 1986, graduation rates had increased more quickly for teen mothers than for other women, suggesting that federal policies tailored to their special circumstances may have made a difference.

Since education is so closely tied to later status, teasing out the relationship between teen pregnancy and schooling is critical. The matter is complicated, however, because young people do many things simultaneously, and sorting out the order is no easy task. In 1984 Peter Morrison of the Rand team reported that between a half and a third of teen mothers in high school and beyond dropped out before they got pregnant. Upchurch and McCarthy, using a different and more recent sample, found that the majority of female dropouts in their study left school before they got pregnant and that teens who got pregnant while still in school were not particularly likely to drop out. On the other hand, those teens who first drop out and then get pregnant are significantly less likely to return to school than other dropouts who do not get pregnant. Thus the conventional causal view that teens get pregnant, drop out of school, and as a result end up educationally and occupationally disadvantaged simply does not match the order of events in many people's lives.

THE SEXUAL ROOTS OF PUBLIC ANXIETY

Teen pregnancy probably would not have "taken off" as a public issue quite so dramatically, were it not for the fact it intersects with other recent social changes in America, particularly the emergence of widespread, anxiety-producing shifts in teen sex. Academics debate whether there has been a genuine "sexual revolution" among adults, but there is no doubt in regard to teenagers. Today, by the time American teenagers reach age 20, an estimated 70 percent of the girls and 80 percent of the boys have had sexual experiences outside of marriage. Virtually all studies confirm that this is a dramatic historical change, particularly for young women. (As usual, much less is known about the historical experiences of young men.) For

example, Sandra Hofferth and her colleagues, using nationally representative data from the 1982 National Survey of Family Growth, found that women navigating adolescence in the late 1950s had a 38.9 percent chance of being sexually active before marriage during their teenage years. Women who reached their 20th birthday between 1979 and 1981, in contrast, had a 68.3 percent likelihood.

Yet even these statistics do not capture how profoundly different this teen sexuality is from that of earlier eras. As sources such as the Kinsey Report (1953) suggest, premarital sex for many American women before the 1960s was "engagement" sex. The woman's involvement, at least, was exclusive, and she generally went on to marry her partner in a relatively short period of time. Almost half of the women in the Kinsey data who had premarital sex had it only with their fiancés.

But as the age at first marriage has risen and the age at first intercourse has dropped, teen sexuality has changed. Not surprisingly, what scattered data we have about numbers of partners suggest that as the period of sexual activity before marriage has increased, so has the number of partners. In 1971, for example, almost two-thirds of sexually active teenaged women in metropolitan areas had had only one sexual partner; by 1979 fewer than half did. Data from the 1988 National Survey of Family Growth confirm this pattern for the nation as a whole, where about 60 percent of teens have had two or more partners. Similarly, for metropolitan teens, only a small fraction (about 10 percent) were engaged at the time of their first sexual experience, although about half described themselves as "going steady."

Profound changes in other aspects of American life have complicated the problem. Recent figures suggest that the average age at first marriage has increased to almost 24 years for women and over 25 years for men, the oldest since reliable data have been collected. Moreover, the age of sexual maturity over the last century has decreased by a little under six months each decade owing to nutritional and other changes. Today the average American girl has her first menstrual period at age 12 and a half, although there are wide individual variations. (There is less research on the sexual maturity of young men.) On average, consequently, American girls and their boyfriends face over a decade of their lives when they are sexually mature and single.

As teenagers pass through this reproductive minefield, the instructions they receive on how to conduct themselves sexually are at best mixed. At least according to public opinion polls, most Americans have come, however reluctantly, to accept premarital sex. Yet one suspects that what they approve is something closer to Kinsey-era sex: sexual relations en route to a marriage. Present-day teenage sex, however, starts for many young people not when they move out of the family and into the orbit of what will be a new family or couple, but while they are still defined primarily as children.

When young people, particularly young women, are still living at home (or even at school) under the control, however nominal, of parents, sexual activity raises profound questions for adults. Many Americans feel troubled about "casual" sex, that is, sex which is not intimately tied to the process by which people form couples and settle down. Yet many teenagers are almost by definition disqualified as too young to "get serious." Thus the kinds of sexuality for which they are socially eligible—sex based in pleasure, not procreation, and in short-term relationships rather than as a prelude to marriage— challenge fundamental values about sexuality held by many adults. These ambiguities and uncertainties have given rise to broad anxieties about teen sexuality that have found expression in the recent alarm about teen pregnancy.

RAISING CHILDREN WITHOUT FATHERS

While Americans have had to confront the meaning and purpose of sexuality in the lives of teenagers, a second revolution is forcing them to

think about the role—and boundaries—of marriage and family. Increasingly for Americans, childbearing and, more dramatically, childrearing have been severed from marriage. The demographer Larry Bumpass and his colleagues have estimated that under present trends, half or more of all American children will spend at least part of their childhood in a single-parent (mainly mother-only) family, due to the fact that an estimated 60 percent of recent marriages will end in divorce.

At the same time, as I indicated earlier, out-of-wedlock births are on the rise. At present, 26 percent of all births are to single women. If present trends continue, Bumpass and others estimate, almost one out of every six white women and seven out of ten black women will give birth to a child without being married. In short, single childbearing is becoming a common pattern of family formation for all American women, teenagers and older.

This reality intersects with still another fact of American life. The real value of inflation-adjusted wages, which grew 2.5 to 3.0 percent a year from the end of World War II to at least 1973, has now begun to stagnate and for certain groups decline; some recent studies point to greater polarization of economic well-being. Americans increasingly worry about their own standard of living and their taxes, and much of that worry has focused on the "underclass." Along with the elderly and the disabled, single women and their children have been the traditional recipients of public aid in America. In recent years, however, they have become especially visible among the dependent poor for at least two reasons. First, the incomes of the elderly have improved, leaving behind single mothers as a higher percentage of the poor; and second, the number of female-headed households has increased sharply. Between 1960 and 1984, households headed by women went from 9.0 percent to 12.0 percent of all white households, and from 22.0 percent to 43 percent of all black households. The incomes of about half of all families headed by women, as of 1984, fell below federal poverty levels.

Raising children as a single mother presents economic problems for women of all ages, but the problem is especially severe for teenagers with limited education and job experience. Partly for that reason, teenagers became a focus of public concern about the impact of illegitimacy and single parenthood on welfare costs. Data published in the 1970s and replicated in the 1980s suggested that about half of all families supported by Aid to Families with Dependent Children (AFDC) were started while the mother was still a teenager. One estimate calculated that in 1975 the costs for these families of public assistance alone (not including Medicaid or food stamps) amounted to $5 billion; by 1985, that figure increased to $8.3 billion.

Yet other findings—and caveats—have been ignored. For example, while about half of all AFDC cases may be families begun while the woman was still a teenager, teens represent only about 7 percent of the caseload at any one time. Moreover, the studies assessing the welfare costs of families started by teens counted any welfare family as being the result of a teen birth if the woman first had a child when under age 20. But, of course, that same woman—given her prior circumstances—might have been no less likely to draw welfare assistance if, let us say, she had a baby at age 20 instead of 19. Richard Wertheimer and Kristin Moore, the source of much of what we know about this area, have been careful to note that the relevant costs are the marginal costs—namely, how much less in welfare costs society would pay if teen mothers postponed their first births, rather than forgoing them entirely.

It turns out, not surprisingly, that calculated this way, the savings are more modest. Wertheimer and Moore have estimated that if by some miracle we could cut the teen birth rate in half, welfare costs would be reduced by 20 percent, rather than 50 percent, because many of these young women would still need welfare for children born to them when they were no longer teens.

Still other research suggests that most young women spend a transitional period on welfare, while finishing school and entering the job market. Other data also suggest that teen mothers may both enter and leave the welfare ranks earlier than poor women who postpone childbearing. Thus teen births by themselves may have more of an effect on the timing of welfare in the chain of life events than on the extent of welfare dependency. In a study of 300 teen mothers and their children originally interviewed in the mid-1960s, Frank Furstenberg and his colleagues found 17 years later that two-thirds of those followed up had received no welfare in the previous five years, although some 70 percent of them had received public assistance at some point after the birth of their child. A quarter had achieved middle-class incomes, despite their poverty at the time of the child's birth.

None of this is to deny that teen mothers have a higher probability of being on welfare in the first place than women who begin their families at a later age, or that teen mothers may be disproportionately represented among those who find themselves chronically dependent on welfare. Given the disproportionate number of teen mothers who come from socially disadvantaged origins (and who are less motivated and perhaps less able students), it would be surprising if they were not overrepresented among those needing public assistance, whenever they had their children. Only if we are prepared to argue that these kinds of women should never have children—which is the implicit alternative at the heart of much public debate—could we be confident that they would never enter the AFDC rolls.

RETHINKING TEEN PREGNANCY

The original formulation of the teen pregnancy crisis seductively glossed over some of these hard realities. Teen motherhood is largely the province of those youngsters who are already disadvantaged by their position in our society.

The major institutions of American life—families, schools, job markets, the medical system—are not working for them. But by framing the issue as teenage pregnancy, Americans could turn this reality around and ascribe the persistence of poverty and other social ills to the failure of individual teenagers to control their sexual impulses.

Framing the problem as teen pregnancy, curiously enough, also made it appear universal. Everyone is a teenager once. In fact, the rhetoric has sometimes claimed that the risk of teen pregnancy is universal, respecting no boundaries of class or race. But clearly, while teenage pregnancies do occur in virtually all walks of life, they do not occur with equal frequency. The concept of "teen pregnancy" has the advantage, therefore, of appearing neutral and universal while, in fact, being directed at people disadvantaged by class, race, and gender.

If focusing on teen pregnancy cast the problem as deceptively universal, it also cast the solution as deceptively simple. Teens just have to wait. In fact, the tacit subtext of at least some of the debate on teen pregnancy is not that young women should wait until they are past their teens, but until they are "ready." Yet in the terms that many Americans have in mind, large numbers of these youngsters will never be "ready." They have already dropped out of school and will face a marginal future in the labor market whether or not they have a baby. And as William J. Wilson has noted, many young black women in inner-city communities will not have the option of marrying because of the dearth of eligible men their age as a result of high rates of unemployment, underemployment, imprisonment, and early death.

Not long ago, Arline Geronimous, an assistant professor of public health at the University of Michigan, caused a stir when she argued that teens, especially black teens, had little to gain (and perhaps something to lose) in postponing pregnancy. The longer teenagers wait, she noted, the more they risk ill health and infertility, and the less likely their mothers are to be alive and able to help rear a child of theirs. Some observers quickly took Geronimous to mean that teen mothers are "rational," affirmatively choosing their pregnancies.

Yet, as Geronimous herself has emphasized, what sort of choices do these young women have? While teen mothers typically report knowing about contraception (which they often say they have used) and knowing about abortion, they tell researchers that their pregnancies were unplanned. In the 1988 National Survey of Family Growth, for example, a little over 70 percent of the pregnancies to teens were reported as unplanned; the teenagers described the bulk of these pregnancies as wanted, just arriving sooner than they had planned.

Researchers typically layer their own views on these data. Those who see teens as victims point to the data indicating most teen pregnancies are unplanned. Those who see teens as acting rationally look at their decisions not to use contraceptives or seek an abortion. According to Frank Furstenberg, however, the very indecisiveness of these young people is the critical finding. Youngsters often drift into pregnancy and then into parenthood, not because they affirmatively choose pregnancy as a first choice among many options, but rather because they see so few satisfying alternatives. As Laurie Zabin, a Johns Hopkins researcher on teen pregnancy, puts it, "As long as people don't have a vision of the future which having a baby at a very early age will jeopardize, they won't go to all the lengths necessary to prevent pregnancy."

Many people talk about teen pregnancy as if there were an implicit social contract in America. They seem to suggest that if poor women would just postpone having babies until they were past their teens they could have better lives for themselves and their children. But for teenagers already at the margins of American life, this is a contract that American society may be hard put to honor. What if, in fact, they are acting reasonably? What can public policy do about teen pregnancy if many teenagers drift into childbearing as the only vaguely promising option in a life whose options are already constrained by gender, poverty, race, and failure?

The trouble is that there is little reason to think any of the "quick fixes" currently being proposed will resolve the fundamental issues involved. Liberals, for example, argue that the answer is more access to contraception, more readily available abortion, and more sex education. Some combination of these strategies probably has had some effect on teen births, particularly in keeping the teen pregnancy rate from soaring as the number of sexually active teens increased. But the inner logic of this approach is that teens and adults have the same goal: keeping teens from pregnancies they do not want. Some teens, however, do want their pregnancies, while others drift into pregnancy and parenthood without ever actively deciding what they want. Consequently, increased access to contraceptives, sex education, and abortion services are unlikely to have a big impact in reducing their pregnancies.

Conservatives, on the other hand, often long for what they imagine was the traditional nuclear family, where people had children only in marriage, married only when they could prudently afford children, and then continued to provide support for their children if the marriage ended. Although no one fully understands the complex of social, economic, and cultural factors that brought us to the present situation, it is probably safe to predict that we shall not turn the clock back to that vision, which in any event is highly colored by nostalgia.

This is not to say that there is nothing public policy can do. Increased job opportunities for both young men and young women; meaningful job training programs (which do not slot young women into traditional low-paying women's jobs); and child support programs . . . would all serve either to make marriage more feasible for those who wish to marry or to support children whose parents are not married. But older ages at first marriage, high rates of sex outside of marriage, a significant portion of all births out of wedlock, and problems with absent fathers tend to be common patterns in Western, industrialized nations.

In their attempts to undo these patterns, many conservatives propose punitive policies to sanction unmarried parents, especially unmarried mothers, by changing the "incentive structure" young people face. The new welfare reform bill of 1988, for example, made it more difficult for teens to set up their own households, at least in part because legislators were worried about the effects of welfare on the willingness to have a child out of wedlock. Other, more draconian writers have called for the children of unwed teen parents to be forcibly removed and placed into foster care, or for the reduction of welfare benefits for women who have more than one child out of wedlock.

Leave aside, for the moment, that these policies would single out only the most vulnerable in this population. The more troublesome issue is such policies often fall most heavily on the children. Americans, as the legal historian Michael Grossberg has shown, have traditionally and justifiably been leery of policies that regulate adult behavior at children's expense.

The things that public policy could do for these young people are unfortunately neither easy to implement nor inexpensive. However, if teens become parents because they lack options, public policy toward teen pregnancy and teenage childbearing will have to focus on enlarging the array of perceived options these young people face. And these must be changes in their real alternatives. Programs that seek to teach teens "future planning," while doing nothing about the futures they can expect, are probably doomed to failure.

We live in a society that continues to idealize marriage and family as expected lifetime roles for women, even as it adds on the expectation that women will also work and be self-supporting. Planning for the trade-offs entailed in a lifetime of paid employment in the labor market and raising a family taxes the skills of our most advantaged young women. We should not be surprised that women who face discrimination by race and class in addition to that of gender are often even less adept at coping with these large and contradictory demands.

Those who worry about teenagers should probably worry about three different dangers as Americans debate policies on teen pregnancy. First, we should worry that things will continue as they have and that public policy will continue to see teens as unwitting victims, albeit victims who themselves cause a whole host of social ills. The working assumption here will be that teens genuinely do not want the children that they are having, and that the task of public policy is to meet the needs of both society and the women involved by helping them not to have babies. What is good for society, therefore, is good for the individual woman.

This vision, for all the reasons already considered, distorts current reality, and as such, is unlikely to lower the teen birth rate significantly, though it may be effective in keeping the teen birth rate from further increasing. To the extent that it is ineffective, it sets the stage for another risk.

This second risk is that the ineffectiveness of programs to lower teen pregnancy dramatically may inadvertently give legitimacy to those who want more punitive control over teenagers, particularly minority and poor teens. If incentives and persuasion do not lead teenagers to conduct their sexual and reproductive lives in ways that adults would prefer, more coercive remedies may be advocated. The youth of teen mothers may make intrusive social control seem more acceptable than it would for older women.

Finally, the most subtle danger is that the new work on teen pregnancy will be used to argue that because teen pregnancy is not the linchpin that holds together myriad other social ills, it is not a problem at all. Concern about teen pregnancy has at least directed attention and resources to young, poor, and minority women; it has awakened many Americans to their diminished life chances. If measures aimed at reducing teen pregnancy are not the quick fix for much of what ails American society, there is the powerful temptation to forget these young women altogether and allow them to slip back to their traditional invisible place in American public debate.

Teen pregnancy is less about young women and their sex lives than it is about restricted horizons and the boundaries of hope. It is about race and class and how those realities limit opportunities for young people. Most centrally, however, it is typically about being young, female, poor, and nonwhite and about how having a child seems to be one of the few avenues of satisfaction, fulfillment, and self-esteem. It would be a tragedy to stop worrying about these young women—and their partners—because their behavior is the measure rather than the cause of their blighted hopes.

ENDNOTE

1. Teen pregnancy affects both young men and young women, but few data are gathered on young men. The availability of data leads me to speak of "teen mothers" throughout this article, but it is important to realize that this reflects an underlying, gendered definition of the situation.

CHAPTER 9

Spouses and Partners

The expectations that wives and husbands have for their marriages changed greatly during the 20th century. Ernest Burgess described the evolution of marital relations during the first half of the century as a "transition from an institution to a companionship." The "institutional" marriage was governed by the formal authority of the husband, which was backed by community pressure. There was little emphasis on the emotional side of marriage. Marriage as a "companionship," a form that peaked at mid-century, emphasized romantic love, mutual affection, and friendship. Still, there was a sharp distinction between the ideal roles of wives and husbands—she was the homemaker; he was the breadwinner. Moreover, in the companionship marriage, wives held the main responsibility for maintaining the family's emotional life by expressing feeling and providing emotional support to husbands and children.

The companionship marriage was a partnership in which fulfilling one's roles—being a good homemaker, earning the family's income—provided the highest satisfactions. Much of a person's gratifications, then, occurred through activities external to the self. But after the 1950s, marriages, and the rising numbers of heterosexual and homosexual nonmarital partnerships, came to be defined more in terms of individual growth and development than in terms of fulfilling prescribed roles. Sociologist Francesca Cancian, in the following excerpt from her book, *Love in America: Gender and Self-Development,* calls this a transition "from role to self" in the focus of personal rewards in marriages and partnerships.

Cancian maintains that love itself was "feminized" under the older kinds of marriage because emotion was seen as the domain of women. Now, love is more "androgynous," meaning that both women and men are concerned about expressing love and emotional support. Correspondingly, autonomy and self-development were emphasized more for men, whereas now these goals are put forth for both genders. To provide evidence for her view of the evolution of marriage, she studied articles on marriage in popular magazines between 1900 and 1979. Their shifting content, she argues, demonstrates the shift from role to self.

Married couples often find that the birth of a first child alters their relationship. Most couples expect positive change: a greater closeness as a family, a sense of sharing and mutuality. Few are prepared for the unwanted changes that also frequently occur. Studies show that in the months after a first child is born, the relationship between the mother and father often becomes less satisfying, more conflictual, and more distant. Developmental psychologist Jay Belsky studied 250 couples before and after the birth of their first child. He found that 12 to 13 percent became so divided that the quality of their marriages declined severely. For both partners, feelings of love and communication dropped sharply and feelings of conflict and ambivalence rose. Another 38 percent experienced a more moderate decline in marital quality. Thus, half the couples found that the new child reduced their satisfaction with their marriages. These declines weren't inevitable: 30 percent of the couples experienced little or no change in marital quality and 19 percent reported that the birth brought them closer together.

In the excerpt reprinted here from his book with writer John Kelly, *The Transition to Parenthood: How a First Child Changes a Marriage*, Belsky describes the factors that tend to push spouses apart and the factors that tend to pull them together. He argues, as have others, that the transition to parenthood typically is experienced very differently by women and men.

READING 9-1

From Role to Self: The Emergence of Androgynous Love in the 20th Century

Francesca M. Cancian

In the long run, the social changes that began in the 19th century destroyed Victorian family patterns. The ideal of masculine independence spread to women and the private sphere, undermining people's willingness to be restricted by narrow family and gender roles. Wives became less subordinate and absorbed by mothering, as they had fewer children and increasingly joined the labor force, and many husbands became less consumed by their work as leisure time expanded and jobs became bureaucratized. Through most of the 20th century, there has been a trend towards more fluid, androgynous family roles and more involvement in self-development and personal life. Americans have become more concerned with individual happiness and pleasure, more tolerant of alternative life styles, more committed to equality for women and men, and more prone to divorce.

Francesca M. Cancian, "From Role to Self: The Emergence of Androgynous Love in the Twentieth Century" from *Love in America: Gender and Self-Development*, pp. 30–45. Copyright © 1987 by Cambridge University Press. Reprinted with the permission of the author and Cambridge University Press.

The trend to androgynous love has been discontinuous. In eras that emphasized personal liberation like the 20s and the late 60s, the trend accelerated, while in the 50s the long-range trend reversed as gender roles became more rigid and tolerance declined. These discontinuities can be used to identify different periods in the social organization of marriage, each dominated by a different family blueprint, or a different mix of blueprints.[1] Each blueprint combines a cultural image of the ideal marriage with expectations for daily life that guide behavior.

Figure 1 presents the major blueprints of marriage since the 19th century. First is the Victorian blueprint of family duty in which love is the woman's responsibility. Then come the three blueprints that dominate contemporary marriage: the more traditional companionship blueprint that first evolved in the 20s, and the newer blueprints of independence and interdependence in which the woman and the man share the obligation to work on their relationship, and the goal of self-development replaces conformity to roles. This chapter gives a general description of these changes in blueprints of marriage, and then presents quantitative data on the major trends.

THE DECLINE OF THE FAMILY DUTY BLUEPRINT

The family duty blueprint was the first solution to the problem of maintaining family bonds in an increasingly individualistic society. According to this image of family life, as we have seen,

	Who is responsible for love?	What is love?
Feminized love		
Family duty (19th century)	woman	fulfill duty to family
Companionship (1920–)	woman	intimacy in marriage
Androgynous love		
Independence (1970–)	woman and man	individual self-development and intimacy
Interdependence (1970–)	woman and man	mutual self-development, intimacy, and support

FIGURE 1 Blueprints of Love.

the ideal family was a nuclear household consisting of a father who left home every day to make the money to support the family, a loving mother who was the center of family life, and the children. Marriage was forever, and a man had considerable authority over his wife and children. The relation between husband and wife began with falling in love and might develop into companionship, although intimacy and sexual relations between spouses were not central and both spouses had important ties with relatives and friends of their own sex. The key relation was an intense, emotional tie between mothers and children, and raising moral, respectable, and healthy children was a woman's major task.

This ideal dominated in the United States from about 1840 to 1880 and then began to show signs of decline.[2] The divorce rate was increasing at the end of the century, and it doubled between 1900 and 1920. The proportion of women remaining single was rising, and so many affluent women were childless that some social critics raised the spectre of "race suicide" and "race sterility." Others criticized the family as an oppressive institution that deprived Americans of freedom and equality. Feminists attacked the tyranny of husbands over wives; plays like Ibsen's *A Doll's House* attacked the childlike position of women; advocates of free love protested against sexual repression; and sociologists viewed the difficulty of divorce as an unnecessary impediment to self-development.

By the turn of the century there was widespread debate in government, churches, and the mass media on the future of the family, the decline of sexual morality, and especially divorce. Opponents of divorce believed that it would destroy the family, which they saw as the basis of civilization. Divorce was attributed to "dangerous individualism," especially individualism in women, and women were charged with being spoiled, romantic, "jealous of men and usurpers of the male's time-honored functions." But by 1910, the opposition was overwhelmed and divorce was accepted.[3]

The 1920s witnessed the dissolution of Victorian family patterns. Social commentators believed that a "revolution in manners and morals" was sweeping the country, and, according to William Chafe, "almost all agreed that the age was one of unprecedented personal liberation."[4] The historian of the family, Arthur Calhoun, writing in 1917, believed he was witnessing the passing of patriarchy and devotion to the family, as people became more and more individualistic.

In the Roaring Twenties, college students and other young people cast aside Victorian clothes and pursued sexual liberation and exciting personal experiences.[5] The institution of dating developed—the pattern of young men and women seeing each other without chaperones, and without any intention of marriage, to "have a good time." High school students in Muncie, Indiana, in 1924 went to necking and petting parties and only with difficulty could be persuaded to be home for dinner three nights a week. On college campuses, dedication to social reform gave way to social activities organized by sororities and fraternities.[6] Women from respectable families smoked in public, wore short skirts and cosmetics, worked as secretaries before they married, and modeled the new image of a woman with an expensive wardrobe and sex appeal. The response of many older, more conservative Americans to all this was horror at the decline of morality and the sexual orgies (real and imagined) of the young.[7]

The causes of the decline of the family duty blueprint include changes in the sexual division of labor and an increasing value placed on self-fulfillment. Women's daily activities shifted away from motherhood and toward more participation in the public sphere. The ideal of the free, self-made man was spreading, and women were beginning to be seen as similar and equal to men, as persons who should develop themselves. The declining birth rate reduced the burdens of motherhood, although many housewives were busier than ever as standards for a clean and attractive home rose. Employment opportunities for women expanded through the growth of respectable jobs such as being a secretary or a saleswoman. "Nowadays," said suffragist Frances Willard in 1897, "a girl may be anything from a college president down to a seamstress or a cash girl. It depends only upon the girl what rank she shall take in her chosen calling."[8] In fact, most working women were segregated in a few low-paying jobs, and it remained shameful for married women to work, but being a single career woman was becoming a respected way of life.[9]

The Victorian ideal that woman's place was in the home was also challenged by women's participation in the temperance movement and in other social reform movements of the early 20th century. The movement for women's suffrage, which obtained the vote for women in 1920 and involved an estimated two million women, most directly undermined the family duty blueprint.[10] The suffragists used the rhetoric of separate spheres and argued that women needed the vote because they were more moral and altruistic than men, but women's suffrage removed a major barrier to women's participation in public life.[11]

Men's lives also changed as routine white-collar jobs expanded with the growth of large corporations, and the 40-hour work week became more common. Men's work became more sedentary and regimented, and less heroic. According to several social historians, as many men found less validation for their masculinity in work, their personal identification with their jobs diminished and they became more involved with their personal lives, their families, and leisure activities.[12] Work probably continued to be the center of life for men pursuing challenging and prestigious careers, but personal life became increasingly important for men as the 20th century advanced.[13]

The increasing focus on personal life and self-development and decreasing commitment to traditional roles was fueled by several changes. Security—experiencing the world as safe and abundant—seems to promote a concern with self-development, and the average person's sense of security probably rose in the early 20th century because of gradual improvements in the standard of living and the widespread economic boom during the early 20s.[14] The growth of consumerism and advertising also encouraged people to develop new personal needs and try to fulfill them. "The American citizen's first importance to his country," editorialized the Muncie newspaper in the 1920s, is "that of consumer."[15] Valuing self-development and independence over conformity to roles was also encouraged by public education, which expanded enormously for both sexes.[16] In 1924, high-school diplomas were awarded to 213,000 men and 281,000 women, an increase since 1900 of about 500 percent for both sexes, while the population had only increased by 50 percent.[17] Finally, the social reform movements of the Progressive Era challenged traditional roles and political institutions, and the unpopularity of World War I further undermined established authority, leading people to seek direction and meaning in their own personal lives.[18]

THE COMPANIONSHIP BLUEPRINT

As the Victorian blueprint of duty to family roles was disintegrating, a new ideal was being articulated in academia and the mass media: the companionship family. This blueprint identified the family with marriage, not parenthood, and emphasized emotional and sexual intimacy between husband and wife.

Sociologists proposed a new family ideal focused on affection and supporting each other's personalities, now that families had lost their traditional economic and social functions. The modern family was "a unity of interacting personalities" in the famous phrase of sociologist Ernest Burgess, and had evolved "from institution to companionship."[19] The first principles of family life, according to Burgess, are "that the highest personal happiness comes from marriage based on romantic love" and "that love and marriage are essentially personal and private and are, perhaps, even more than other aspects of life to be controlled by the individual himself."[20] Marriage, in this view, is a private arena of self-fulfillment, not duty. With the spread of the companionship blueprint, affective individualism and a more androgynous self became part of mainstream American culture.

For the first time, popular advice books suggested that having children might weaken a family, and in 1931, for the first time, there were more advertisements for cosmetics than for food in the *Ladies' Home Journal.* Being an attractive companion was becoming more important than being a competent homemaker. Dorothy Dix, in her syndicated newspaper column for women, advised: "The old idea used to be that the way for a woman to help her husband was by being thrifty and industrious . . . but a domestic drudge is not a help to her husband, she is a hindrance . . . The woman who cultivates a circle of worth-while people, who belongs to clubs, who makes herself interesting and agreeable . . . is a help to her husband."[21]

The companionship family blueprint emphasized the similarity of husband and wife much more than the family duty blueprint. Both partners were expected to need and to give affection and understanding, and increasingly, both were expected to enjoy sexual intimacy. But love was still feminized, and wives were still expected to be economically dependent and submissive to their husbands. Marriage was to be all of a woman's life but only part of a man's. There was no column by Dorothy Dix instructing a man on how to be a help to his wife, and the magazines of the period consistently told women that it was their responsibility to create successful marriages.[22] Despite some changes towards androgyny, gender roles remained fairly polarized in the companionship blueprint.

The reality of family life in the 20s, according to Robert and Helen Lynd's study of Muncie, is more similar to the family duty blueprint than to the world of companionship marriage and libertine flappers. In the business class (the top 30 percent of the families), wives did not work, and the social status of the family was a primary concern to both husband and wife. Most couples did not place a very high value on companionship in marriage, and frankness between spouses was not encouraged. Husbands described wives as purer, morally better, and more emotional and impractical than men, and their wives agreed. The motto of one of the women's clubs was "Men are God's trees; Women are his flowers."[23] Social life was organized primarily around couples, although men and women were also active in sex-segregated clubs and friendships were important to the women. Wives were very child-centered, while husbands had little contact with their children beyond meals and family auto trips. Husbands were, however, beginning to share in the housework. In the working class, a substantial minority of the wives worked, but marital relations were even farther from the companionship ideal. Husbands and wives rarely talked, and in the absence of other methods of birth control wives kept away from their husbands sexually. Only the beginnings of the companionship family were observable in Muncie; an intimate emotional and sexual bond between two developing personalities was seldom achieved or even strongly desired. Contrary to what many historians have suggested, marital intimacy was rare, as late as the 20s.

The Great Depression from 1929 to 1941 was probably the major force in reversing the trend towards individual freedom of the 20s. As the economy collapsed, people faced an insecure, hostile environment, and adopted a rigid version of the companionship ideal that emphasized traditional family and gender roles more than personal development. Although domestic politics became more radical in the 30s, with the growing power of labor unions and the social programs of the New Deal, family life became more conservative.

College students in the early 30s expressed less approval of divorce and extramarital sex than in the 20s and there was a rise in the proportion of students who intended to marry and have children.[24] Opposition to women's entering the labor force reappeared as more and more men lost their jobs, and employers increasingly denied married women the right to work. A survey of 1,500 school systems in 1930 reported that 77 percent refused to hire wives and 63 percent fired women teachers if they married. When the Gallup Poll asked Americans in 1936 whether wives should work if their husbands were employed, 82 percent said "no."[25] Women's magazines "urged their readers to return to femininity and constructed an elaborate ideology in support of the home and marriage to facilitate the process," according to historian William Chafe.[26] *The Ladies' Home Journal* told its readers that "the creation and fulfillment of a successful home is a bit of craftsmanship that compares favorably with building a beautiful cathedral," while *McCall's* observed that only as a wife and mother could the American woman "arrive at her true eminence."[27]

The effects of economic insecurity on commitment to traditional family roles is documented by Glen Elder's study of people who grew up during the Depression. Compared with people whose families had not suffered economically, men and women from families that had suffered substantial economic losses in the Depression placed a greater value on family life as opposed to work and leisure, and were more interested in raising children and less interested in husband–wife companionship. The deprived men actually had a larger number of children, on the average, than men from nondeprived backgrounds. Another finding that supports the link between economic deprivation and traditionalism is that working-class people have more traditional attitudes about family and gender than middle-class people.[28]

World War II ended the Depression and interrupted normal life for many families as men went off to war and women to work. Between 1940 and 1944, the proportion of married women in the labor force rose from 17 percent to 20 percent.[29] Although there was an effort to push women workers back into the home after the war, married women continued to enter the work force in growing numbers, radically changing the division of labor between husbands and wives that had persisted since the 19th century.

The postwar decades were a period of extreme commitment to the family and to split gender roles. People married earlier, had more children, and avoided childlessness, causing the famous baby boom. The divorce rate stayed unusually steady,[30] and new suburban tracts provided a setting for a family-centered way of life. There was a resurgence of antifeminism and a revival of the 19th-century theme of separate spheres. Thus the head of one women's college advocated that preparing women for "the task of creating a good home and raising good children" be made the primary purposes of women's colleges.[31] Women's magazines described the joys of femininity and togetherness, and public opinion, which had supported wives working during the war, once again opposed their working if their husbands could support them. Most people also supported a traditional division of labor in which men determined where a family lived and how it spent its money.[32] Yet all the while, more and more wives were working.

The blueprint for family life was a revised version of the companionship family of the 20s and 30s.[33] The companionship ideal of the 50s was based on intimate affection between husband and wife. Although the relation between mother and children was vitally important, a woman was warned not to let motherhood weaken her relation with her husband or to smother her children with too much attention. The couple was expected to lead an active social life but not to have close ties outside the nuclear family. The Victorian ideology of separate spheres was still partly intact; it was the husband's job to support the family, while the wife was the center of home life. But the authority of the husband had declined—he was to be more of a pal to his children and more of a companion to his wife. The concept of family togetherness—of mom, dad, and the kids barbecuing dinner together in the backyard—softened the separation of men's and women's spheres. Marriage began with falling in love and developed into companionship; but if love died, divorce might be the best solution.

This family ideal was endorsed by most intellectuals and social scientists in the postwar era. Talcott Parsons provided a theoretical justification with his argument that a well-functioning family required an instrumental father and an expressive mother. Other sociologists obscured the gender differentiation in the companionship model by emphasizing its equality and flexibility in comparison with the patriarchal Victorian family or the marriages of conservative Americans. Few observers noted that as long as marriage was defined as the wife's responsibility and love was feminized, emphasizing companionship increased her dependency on her husband.[34] The Victorian wife at least had her separate sphere of children and women friends. For the wife in a companionship marriage, her husband was her sphere, and her life was focused on getting the right emotional response from him. The price of companionship marriage was high, especially for the educated, middle-class women who valued their independence the most.[35]

The strong commitment to traditional family roles throughout the 50s and early 60s is somewhat puzzling since many social conditions encouraged androgyny and self-development. A growing number of wives had jobs and became less economically dependent on their husbands. By 1965, 45 percent of married women with school-age children worked, compared with 26 percent in 1948. There was an unprecedented economic prosperity in the postwar era, and a very large expansion of public higher education. One would expect these conditions to accelerate the trend from role to self, but this did not happen until the late 60s, when a wave of protest movements and the Vietnam War produced a counterculture that rejected traditional roles and beliefs, including the companionship family blueprint.[36]

THE DECLINE OF THE COMPANIONSHIP BLUEPRINT

Another period of personal liberation began in the sixties. This time many observers felt that a major boundary of social organization had been crossed—that we had passed from an era in which people's private lives were regulated by the obligations of family roles into a new era of the self.[37] There was a rapid reversal of the familism of the 50s. Divorces accelerated sharply and fertility declined to an all time low. The rate of couples living together without being married doubled between 1970 and 1979, and there was a large increase in the number of persons living alone. Premarital sexual experience, which had been increasing since the 20s, became much more frequent; for example, the percentage of single 17-year-old girls who had experienced sex rose from 27 to 41 percent between 1971 and 1976.[38]

The trend toward wives working for money was probably the underlying cause of the decline of the companionship family. But the immediate cause was the antiestablishment social movements of the 60s and 70s. The 60s began a period of "revolution in manners and morals" similar to the twenties, literally a "counterculture."[39] The civil rights movement, the antiwar movement, and the women's movement involved a large minority of Americans in demonstrations, drug trips, petition campaigns and consciousness-raising groups, all of which undermined the patriotism and devotion to family of the postwar era.

The women's movement, in particular, attacked the companionship family blueprint. Conservative feminists endorsed the "two-career family," in which both husband and wife were equally committed to glamorous careers and to childrearing and homemaking. Radical feminists rejected the family as the preferred living arrangement and developed images of homosexual households or socialist collectives. By the early 70s, ideas about gender equality diffused throughout the nation as the women's movement received a great deal of media coverage and achieved a rapid series of legislative victories supporting expanded opportunities for women in the labor force and in education.[40]

Once again, a strong women's movement had undermined traditional family roles. As long as family blueprints emphasized self-sacrifice and polarized gender roles, women's freedom conflicted with family bonds. Thus Carl Degler concludes his history of women and the family in America by observing that "the great values for which the family stands are at odds . . . with those of the women's movement."[41]

Companionship family roles were also attacked by the human potential movement. Popular psychology books like Gail Sheehy's *Passages* rejected the role of successful provider and cheerful housewife as hypocritical and deadening. They urged people to free themselves from restrictive obligations, get in touch with their feelings, and experience their full potential. New therapies and growth centers sprung up—encounter groups, Esalen, Primal Scream, EST—all of them encouraging adult men and women to develop themselves and reject traditional roles. In contrast to the orthodox therapies of previous decades that had urged patients to adjust to traditional family and gender roles, the new therapies preached androgyny, and urged men and women to reject the expectations of others and develop their own true selves.[42]

The decline of the companionship blueprint was welcomed by some groups and opposed by others. Not surprisingly, women supported the new flexibility in gender roles more than men, especially highly educated professional women.[43] These women valued independence the most and could benefit the most from improved career opportunities. Thus, in the political struggle over abortion, the "pro-choice" activists were mostly well-educated, career-oriented women who placed a high value on individual freedom and self-development. The "pro life" women

were primarily less educated housewives with a deep commitment to religion and to the traditional roles of the loving housewife and the strong husband who provides for her.[44] For these women and for many other Americans, the companionship family continued to be their ideal.

THE NEW BLUEPRINTS: INDEPENDENCE AND INTERDEPENDENCE

By the middle of the 70s, new androgynous images of close relationships were beginning to crystallize. A prolonged economic recession dampened people's aspirations for freedom, and academics and the mass media began to criticize the human potential movement as selfish and narcissistic.[45] The need for intimacy began to seem more pressing than the need to combat oppressive family and gender roles.

The new blueprints emphasize three sets of qualities that I label *self-fulfillment, flexible roles,* and *intimacy and open communication.* First, in the new images of love, both partners are expected to develop a fulfilled and independent self, instead of sacrificing themselves for the other person. Second, family and gender roles are flexible and are continually renegotiated. Third, the relationship centers on intimate communication of needs and feelings, and on openly confronting problems. Self-development and love are integrated in these blueprints, and love is the responsibility of the man as well as the woman. The independence and the interdependence blueprints both emphasize these qualities; they differ on the issue of self-sufficiency and independence versus mutual support and commitment.

The new blueprints of relationships began to emerge in the middle of the 60s, according to a study of women's magazines. Women were advised that they must develop an independent self in order to be loving, and they were told to build a vital, spontaneous relationship without fixed rules, by communicating openly about feelings and working through conflicts. In contrast, in the 50s, "putting aside of self was defined as loving behavior," and women were advised to sacrifice themselves for their families, follow traditional sex roles, and strive for harmony and togetherness.[46]

When Ann Swidler interviewed 60 residents of an affluent California suburb around 1980, she found that most of them emphasized self-fulfillment and accepted the "therepautic ideal" of love promoted by psychologists and the human potential movement. They believed that love is partly expressed by sharing oneself and one's feelings; therefore, a person must develop a somewhat independent self in order to be loving. For example, a young wife explained that she had had problems with her husband, Thomas, because "I was doing things just for him and ignoring things for myself." Now, since her therapy, she feels more independent and self-confident. "The better I feel about myself, I feel I have a whole lot that I can contribute to Thomas."[47]

Good communication is crucial in the new blueprints, both to express one's self, and to negotiate a unique, flexible relationship in the absence of definite family and gender roles. Verbal communication is also part of being intimate and working on the relationship. As a college man commented, "You have to work at your marriage, it's like a job." A poll conducted for *Playboy* magazine in 1976 indicates the importance of communication to contemporary American men. "Someone to be totally open and honest with" was the most frequently mentioned quality for an ideal lover.[48]

The new blueprints are radically androgynous and anti-institutional. The themes of self-fulfillment and intimate communication resemble the companionship blueprint, and its concern with personality development and marital interaction. But unlike the companionship ideal, the new blueprints do not legitimate predetermined roles or a sexual division of labor; they are blueprints for relationships, not marriages. Both partners are expected to work on the relationship, communicate openly and develop themselves. Wives are advised to cultivate independent interests and goals, while husbands are encouraged to express their feelings. Love is no longer part of women's special sphere.

The independence blueprint adds to these themes a strong emphasis on being self-sufficient and avoiding obligations. Developing an independent self and expressing one's needs and feelings is seen as a precondition to love. In contrast, couples who follow the interdependence blueprint believe that they owe each other mutual support and affection, and that love is a precondition to full self-development.

Sociologists disagree about the relative importance of these two blueprints. Robert Bellah and his associates conclude that independence is becoming the dominant image of love in America. People are increasingly avoiding commitments, they argue and support their interpretation by quoting from Swidler's interviews. For example a counselor commented: "I guess, if there is anyone who needs to owe anybody anything, it is honesty in letting each other know how they feel about each other, and that if feelings change, to be open and receptive, to accept those changes, knowing that people in a relationship are not cement."[49]

In contrast, my study of 133 adults in 1980 indicates that Interdependence, not Independence, is the dominant blueprint of love. The respondents, who came from diverse social backgrounds, were asked about the "qualities that are most important for a good marriage or love relationship" . . . Contrary to the argument of Bellah et al., the second most frequently mentioned quality was "support and caring." "Good, open communication" was most frequently mentioned, while "tolerance, flexibility and understanding" was third, "honesty" was fourth, and "commitment" was fifth. Individuals who emphasized "support and caring" usually talked about the obligation to be nurturant and attentive, and many of them connected support and caring with self-development. For example, when a 30-year-old minister in San Diego was asked what he most valued in his wife, he replied:

I trust her to react in a reaffirming way to me when I share with her . . . I know that she will respond to me in a positive way. She will share the pain or frustration or triumph of the day with me, and I feel like what I have to say about me is very important, because it's me in a sense.

Although there is disagreement about the importance of mutual support and commitment in contemporary relationships, researchers agree on the growing importance of self-fulfillment, flexible roles, and intimate, open communication. With the decline of the companionship blueprint, the trend from role to self accelerated, producing new, more androgynous images of love.

It is possible that another shift back to traditional roles has begun, partly as a result of the continued economic difficulties of the 70s and 80s. The slight drop in the divorce rate and the reversal of feminist gains in affirmative action and abortion rights may be signs of such a shift. But the evidence that would document this change is not yet available.

EVIDENCE FROM POPULAR MAGAZINES

The changes in family blueprints that I have just described are clearly reflected in magazine articles that give advice on how to have a happy marriage. I analyzed a sample of articles from 1900 to 1979 and measured the proportion of articles in each decade that endorsed the traditional family duty and companionship blueprints versus the modern themes of self-fulfillment, flexible roles, and intimacy. The results confirm the long-range trend from role to self during the 20th century, and also show that the 20s and 60s were unusually modern while the 50s were unusually traditional. Studies by other researchers show this same pattern of change.

I examined 128 articles on marriage from high circulation magazines like the *Ladies' Home Journal, McCalls,* and *The Reader's Digest.* The articles are addressed primarily to women, and advise them on how to produce a happy, loving marriage and how to overcome feelings of disap-

pointment and loneliness. For each five-year period, I randomly selected eight articles listed in the *Reader's Guide to Periodicals* under the topic "Marriage." The content of each article was coded according to the dominant message that the article seemed to communicate to readers.[50]

The categories used to analyze the articles focused on self-fulfillment, flexible roles, and intimacy and open communication. One category that measured self-fulfillment was "self-sacrifice versus self-fulfillment." An example of endorsing self-sacrifice is a 1909 editorial in *Harper's Bazaar* that advised: "Marriage means self-discipline. Marriage is *not* for the individual, but for the race . . . Marriage is the slow growth of two persons into one—one person with one pursuit, one mind, one heart, one interest . . . one ideal."[51] In contrast, a *Ladies' Home Journal* article in 1978, illustrating the self-fulfillment theme, warned that it was a myth to believe that marriage should "meet all the emotional needs of both spouses," that it "is an all-encompassing blend of two personalities fused into one. A marriage like this leaves no breathing space for two individuals to retain their own personalities."[52]

A category for measuring flexible roles was "rigid versus flexible female gender role." The traditional side of this category is illustrated by a 1940s article which comments that, compared to men, "women have much less time for action, being absorbed, consciously or unconsciously, by their preoccupation with love and maternity."[53] Intimate communication was measured by the category "avoid conflict, and keep up a front versus communicate openly and confront problems." Illustrating the modern view of communication, an article in the *Reader's Digest* in 1974 asserted that "if spouses are thoughtful toward each other on *all* occasions, they probably have a sick marriage."[54]

Table 1 shows the number of articles in each decade that support traditional versus modern themes in these three categories. The percent of modern themes—combining the three categories— gradually rises, as shown at the bottom of the

TABLE 1

TRENDS IN MAGAZINE ARTICLES ON MARRIAGE, 1900–1979: NUMBER OF ARTICLES SUPPORTING TRADITIONAL VERSUS MODERN THEMES

Traditional [T]		Modern [M]	1900–1909		1910–1919		1920–1929		1930–1939		1940–1949		1950–1959		1960–1969		1970–1979	
			T	M	T	M	T	M	T	M	T	M	T	M	T	M	T	M
1 self-sacrifice compromise	vs.	self-fulfillment individuality	7	1	4	3	5	1	7	2	10	0	11	0	7	7	5	2
2 rigid female role	vs.	flexible female role	10	7	14	4	8	10	11	7	8	9	13	5	8	10	6	13
3 avoid conflict, keep up a front	vs.	communicate openly, confront problems	1	2	2	0	3	2	5	3	4	0	4	6	4	8	3	10
Percent of modern themes			36%		26%		45%		34%		29%		28%		57%		64%	

table. There are also discontinuities; for instance, there are more articles endorsing flexible gender roles in the 1920s than in the next three decades. Thus a 1925 article in *The Ladies' Home Journal* proclaimed: "The woman of today acknowledges no master." Women now regard marriage as "a social partnership, an adventure, an experiment even, but it must always be on a fifty-fifty basis."[55] And in every decade, there is considerable variation in what the magazines are saying, and a substantial number of both traditional and modern themes.

The trend from role to self and the discontinuities in this trend are more clearly displayed in the graph in Figure 2. The graph shows the percent of themes in each decade that support self-fulfillment, flexible roles, and intimate communication, combining eight categories that include the three already discussed. For example, "flexible roles" is measured by the previously discussed category

about the female role, as well as categories about the male role and the acceptability of divorce . . .

The graph shows a trend to modern themes over the 20th century. In the first two decades of the century, about 30 percent of the themes are modern, compared to about 70 percent in the 1970s. There is also a clear up-and-down pattern of change, with modern themes predominating in the 20s and again in the 60s and 70s.

The causes of the trend from role to self, as I have discussed, probably include economic prosperity, increasing leisure and education, and the tendency of women as well as men to work for individual wages. The discontinuities can partly be explained by the same factors; in particular, economic hard times apparently reversed the trend in the 30s. Other researchers have emphasized demographic shifts in explaining discontinuities in American family life, and unpopular wars may also be important.[56]

FIGURE 2 Modern themes in magazine articles on marriage, 1900–1979: Percent of themes supporting self-fulfillment, flexible roles, and intimacy.

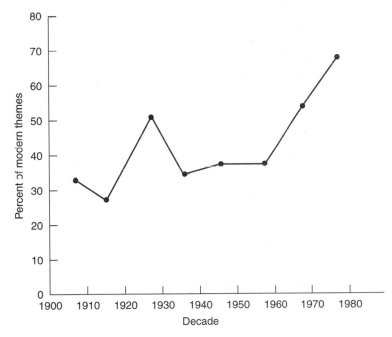

The intriguing association between the women's movement and images of marriage suggests other explanations of the discontinuities— explanations that point to the great importance of gender roles in understanding the American family. A strong women's movement accompanied or preceded the extreme emphasis on personal freedom and self-fulfillment in the 20s and again in the late 60s. The women's movement, as measured by the amount of coverage of women in the *New York Times* and popular magazines, was strongest between 1905 and 1920. It reached its low point between 1950 and the early 60s, and then rose again in the late sixties. . . The rise and fall of the women's movement thus parallels the rise and fall of modern images of marriage, as shown in Figure 2, except that the highpoint of the movement around 1910 preceded the change in marital images by about a decade.

This relationship between the women's movement and the trend from role to self is not surprising, and has been noted by social historians. The women's movement usually has urged women to avoid self-sacrifice and traditional gender roles, and participating in the movement probably made women more powerful and independent of their families as they acquired new skills and friends, and new ideas about women's proper place.

The conflict between traditional family roles and women's rights may also produce a self-generating cycle of change. When there is a strong commitment to a traditional family blueprint (i.e., the family duty or companionship blueprint), individual freedom and self-development are suppressed, especially for women. But freedom and self-development are highly valued in America, leading to a conflict that eventually undermines the blueprint and produces a period of personal liberation like the 1920s. Greater freedom to develop oneself, especially for women, then threatens people's needs for attachments, creating a readiness to accept a new family blueprint. This cyclic tendency, if it exists, will be weakened by the diffusion of the interdependence blueprint, which combines stable attachments and self-development.

Whatever the causes of the changing images of marriage, two patterns of change emerge clearly from my analysis of magazine articles. There has been a gradual trend towards self-fulfillment, flexible roles, and intimate communication, as well as some major discontinuities.

ENDNOTES

1. Fixing the date of these periods is only approximate, and is based on the sources quoted in this and the previous chapter.
2. The Civil War occurred in the middle of this period, but, surprisingly, most historians do not attribute great social consequences to it. Eleanor Flexner's history of women is an exception.
3. O'Neil, 1978, pp. 143–44.
4. Chafe, 1972, p. 49.
5. Fass, 1977.
6. Rothman, 1978.
7. Fass, 1977; Newcomb, 1937.
8. Quoted in Rothman, 1978, p. 43.
9. For a poignant description of how respectable but poor married women had to hide the fact that they were working see Rothman, 1978, Chapter 2. Single life was not unattractive, given the close bonds among women, especially for the privileged few with a college education. The women born between 1865 and 1874 "married later and less frequently than any group before or since," and by the turn of the century "nearly one in five married women was childless" (Ryan, 1979, p. 142).
10. Ryan, 1979, p. 140.
11. Many of its supporters and opponents believed that women's winning the vote would change their role in the family and drastically after electoral politics. The large amounts of money spent by the liquor industry and urban political machines to fight women's suffrage are an indication of the importance they attributed to it. On the high hopes of many suffragists about the changes that would occur after women got the vote, see Flexner, 1974; and O'Neil, 1978. O'Neil documents the conservative and occasionally racist rhetoric of the suffrage movement.

12. The eight-hour day became common during World War I and the 40-hour week was mandated by New Deal legislation in the thirties (Harris & Levey, 1975, p. 1, 511). On the declining masculinity of work, see Hantover, 1980, pp. 285–302, and also Filene, 1974.
13. For a supporting argument, see Zaretsky, 1976, and for supporting evidence see Pleck, 1985; and Veroff et al., 1981.
14. On the economic changes, see U.S. Bureau of the Census, 1976, pp. 164–5. On the relation of security and self-development, see Maslow's theory of the hierarchy of needs, 1970.
15. The quotation is from Lynd & Lynd, 1937, p. 80. For a description of this period, also see Chafe, 1972, and Rothman, 1978.
16. Educated people, according to many studies, are more likely to believe that they control their lives and to question authority and traditional rules. See Kohn, 1969.
17. U.S. Bureau of the Census, 1976, pp. 379 and 380. In 1924 B.A.s or first professional degrees were awarded to 55,000 men and 28,000 women, an increase since 1900 of about 200 percent for men and 500 percent for women.
18. I am indebted to Thomas Kemper for this observation.
19. Quoted in Lasch, 1977, p. 31.
20. These quotes are taken from Rothman, 1978, p. 180.
21. Quoted in Lynd & Lynd, 1937, p. 116.
22. See the thought-provoking analysis of magazines from 1921 to 1940 by Johns-Heine and Gerth, 1949.
23. Lynd & Lynd, 1937, p. 118.
24. Newcomb, 1937. In contrast, the Lynds report that high school students in Muncie became more accepting of premarital sex and women's working between 1924 and 1935. This may be an instance of a lag in changes among working class and provincial people compared to college students.
25. Chafe, 1972, Chapter 4. The proportion of college teachers who were women began to fall in the 30s and continued to decline until the late 50s.
26. Chafe, 1972, p. 105.
27. Quoted in Chafe, 1972, p. 105.
28. Elder, 1974, analyzes the effects of the depression. Virtually all researchers find that middle-class people tend to be more modern. They value companionship between husband and wife more and having children less, and place more emphasis on self-fulfillment, tolerance of diversity, and flexible gender roles. This pattern confirms the hypothesis that economic security, prosperity, and education promote the shift from role to self. The classic study of class and child-rearing values is Melvin Kohn's *Class and Conformity,* 1969. The preference of middle-class people for self-actualization and esteem, and working-class people for belonging and security, is shown in an interesting British study using Abraham Maslow's theory of the hierarchy of needs by Gratton, 1980. Duncan et al., 1973, document the greater importance of job security for working-class people. Also see Gurin et al., 1960; Mason et al., 1976; Gecas, 1979; and Rubin, 1976.
29. U.S. Bureau of the Census, 1976, p. 133.
30. Cherlin, 1981.
31. Chafe, 1972, p. 208.
32. Ibid., p. 178.
33. For a similar interpretation, see Rothman, 1978, p. 218.
34. For an example, see Hicks and Platt's widely quoted and basically sound review of the literature on marital adjustment, published in 1970. Even Komarovsky (1962), usually very sensitive to issues of gender, took for granted the superiority of companionship marriage. She criticized the blue-collar pattern of restricted communication and separate social activities for husbands and wives as a form of "social disorganization," failing to see that the husband's buddies and the wife's close ties with relatives and friends might provide a valuable counterbalance to the tendency of women to be overdependent on their husbands in companionship marriages. Evidence on the role of relatives and friends in limiting wives' dependency on husbands comes from a study of British working-class families by Michael Young and Peter Willmott. They found that wives became more dependent after they moved away from their old community into a suburb.
35. Evidence of the discontent of college educated wives with their marriage is presented in Campbell et al., 1976. Also Pahl & Pahl, 1971.
36. See Cherlin, 1981, for data on changes in women working and an analysis of how the fifties interrupted many long-term demographic and family

trends. For quantitative data on the postwar boom, see U.S. Bureau of the Census, 1976, and Lebergott 1976. Generation and politics may explain the unusual familism of the 1950s. Perhaps the generation that raised their families in the 50s had too many frightening memories of depression and war to feel secure, despite their new prosperity. And perhaps American politics of cold war and McCarthyism diminished people's sense of self-direction and the importance of their personal lives by enhancing the significance of government actions and patriotic values.

37. The phrase "from role to self" was suggested to me by Almond's essay (1977) on the transitions from character to role to self since the 19th century. Also see Turner's influential paper (1976).

38. For more detailed information on these trends see Cherlin, 1981, and U.S. Bureau of the Census, 1982. The survey on premarital sex is reported in Zelnik and Kantner, 1980.

39. Several studies document substantial shifts of public opinion towards personal liberation and away from the standards of the companionship family between the middle of the sixties and the middle of the seventies. See, for example, Yankelovich, 1974. Cherlin, 1982, also suggests that the acceptance of divorce accelerated in the late 60s and early 70s.

40. For a history of the women's movement, see Carden, 1974; and Hole and Levine, 1971. Freeman, 1975, gives an excellent account of its legislative victories. For an analysis of media coverage of the movement, see Cancian and Ross, 1981.

41. Degler, 1980, p. 471.

42. See Friedan, 1963, on the conservative message of Freudian and other therapists in the 1950s.

43. See, for example Osmond & Martin, 1975.

44. Luker, 1984.

45. Clecak, 1983, reviews this criticism. Christopher Lasch's book, *The Culture of Narcissism,* 1978, is the critical book that had the greatest impact. On the need for commitment, see Yankelovich, 1981.

46. Kidd, 1974 and 1975. Zube's study (1972) of changing concepts of morality in the *Ladies' Home Journal* from 1948 to 1969 comes up with an interpretation similar to Kidd's. Her quantitative analysis shows a clear shift from values oriented to the future and active "doing," to values oriented to "being" in the present.

47. Bellah *et al.,* 1985, pp. 93 and 100; and Swidler, 1982, pp. 7–8. Similar findings are reported by Quinn, 1982, who did intensive interviews with eleven couples in North Carolina.

48. Harris, 1979.

49. Bellah et al., 1985, p. 101.

50. Here is more detail in the methodology. The high circulation magazines that were included were taken from a list in Kidd, 1975. In the early decades, I also selected articles listed in the *Readers' Guide* from *Harper's* and *Atlantic.* Because of the ease of obtaining articles from *Reader's Digest,* I randomly selected four articles from *Reader's Digest* and four from other magazines, after *Reader's Digest* began publication in the early 1920s. The coding system was originally developed to study changes in magazines between 1950 and 1970; therefore the categories are progressively less applicable as we move towards the beginning of the century, and the earlier articles receive fewer codes in any of the categories. The categories about gender roles are an exception; every article was coded as traditional or modern on these categories. A few articles contained very contradictory messages and were "double-scored" or counted as both traditional and modern on some categories; however, double-scoring was avoided whenever possible. The category system was refined until I reached a criterion of two coders agreeing on 85 percent of the coding for a particular article. This method of measuring changes in popular images of marriage has several problems. The intended audience of the magazines seems to come from a higher social class in the earlier decades, and the content of the articles partly reflects the policies of editors and advertisers and the attitudes of the writers. Nonetheless, the magazines seem to provide a fairly valid measure, since my findings are consistent with the other sources of data described in this chapter.

51. *Harper's Bazaar,* September 1909.

52. Vahanian & Olds, 1978.

53. Maurois, 1940.

54. Lederer & Jackson, 1974.

55. Miller, 1925.

56. Easterlin, 1980, emphasizes the changing size of birth cohorts. He sees very little change in fam-

ily blueprints and gender roles since World War II. What has changed, in his view, is young people's income relative to the standard of living they grew up with. When their income was relatively high, they lived according to their family ideals, and wives stayed home and had many children as happened in the 50s. When the baby boom generation (or cohort) reached the labor market in the late 70s wages were relatively low because the cohort was so large that wages were depressed. As a result, they were unable to live according to their ideals and had fewer children. When their children reach the labor market, their income will be relatively high because their cohort is so small, and the cycle will repeat. The relative merits of his theory and mine will be clarified by changes in the family during the recession that began in the 70s. Easterlin predicts a decline in family attachments as relative income declines. I predict a rise because hard times lower people's aspirations for freedom. See Cherlin, 1981, for an excellent analysis and critique of Easterlin. Although I agree with Easterlin that the changes in gender roles are often exaggerated, he exaggerates the stability. For evidence of major changes in women's goals since the late 60s, see Parelius, 1975; Roper & Labeff, 1977; Duncan et al., 1973; Thornton et al., 1983. Cherlin argues that the pattern of family change is not cyclical; rather there have been gradual changes since 1900 interrupted by the peculiar 50s. Another explanation sociologists have developed is the marriage squeeze argument advanced by Oppenheimer, 1973, and others. They argue that, because women marry men about three years older than themselves, it will be difficult for women to find attractive husbands in historical periods following a rise in fertility, since there will be more younger women on the marriage market than older men. This situation occurred in the 70s, following the baby boom. According to Heer and Grossbard-Shectman's interpretation (1981), the unfavorable marriage market for women in the 70s helps explain why a growing proportion of women did not marry, why they turned to employment instead and became involved in a women's movement to improve their situation at work.

REFERENCES

Almond, Richard (1977). "Character, Role and Self: Evolution in Personality Styles." Unpublished manuscript. Palo Alto, California.

Bellah, Robert, Richard Madsen, William Sullivan, Ann Swidler and Steven Tipton (1985). *Habits of the Heart.* Berkeley: University of California Press.

Burgess, Ernest W. and Harvey J. Locke (1960). *The Family: From Institution to Companionship.* New York: American Book Co.

Calhoun, Arthur W. (1917). A Social History of the American Family. Cleveland: Arthur Clark.

Campbell, Angus, Philip Converse and Willard L. Rodgers (1976). *The Quality of American Life.* New York: Russell Sage.

Cancian, Francesca and Bonnie Ross (1981). "Mass Media and the Women's Movement." *Journal of Applied Behavioral Science* 17:9–26.

Carden, Maren L. (1974). *The New Feminist Movement.* New York: Russell Sage Foundation.

Chafe, William H. (1972). *The American Woman.* New York: Oxford University Press.

Cherlin, Andrew (1981). *Marriage, Divorce, Remarriage.* Cambridge, Massachusetts: Harvard University Press.

Clecak, Peter (1983). *America's Quest for the Ideal Self.* New York: Oxford University Press.

Degler, Carl N.(1980). *At Odds: Women and the Family in America from the Revolution to the Present.* New York: Oxford University Press.

Duncan, Otis Dudley, Howard Schuman and Beverly Duncan (1973). *Social Change in a Metropolitan Community.* New York: Russell Sage.

Easterlin, Richard A. (1980). *Birth and Fortune.* New York: Basic Books.

Elder, Glen (1974). *Children of the Great Depression.* Chicago: University of Chicago Press.

Fass, Paula S. (1977). *The Damned and the Beautiful.* New York: Oxford University Press.

Filene, Peter (1974). *Him/Her/Self: Sex Roles in Modern America.* New York: Harcourt Brace Jovanovich.

Flexner, Eleanor (1974). *Century of Struggle.* New York: Atheneum.

Freeman, Jo (1975). *The Politics of Women's Liberation.* New York: David McKay.

Friedan, Betty (1963). *The Feminine Mystique.* New York: Norton. (1981). *The Second Stage.* New York: Simon Schuster.

Gecas, V. (1979). "The Influence of Social Class on Socialization." In W. Burr *et al.* (eds.) *Contemporary Theories about the Family,* Vol. I. New York: Free Press.

Gratton, Lynda C. (1980). "Analysis of Maslow's Need Hierarchy with Three Social Class Groups." *Social Indicators Research* 7:463–76.

Gurin, Gerald, J. Veroff and S. Feld (1960). Americans View Their Mental Health. New York: Basic Books.

Hantover, Jeffrey P. (1980). "The Boy Scouts and the Validation of Masculinity." In Elizabeth Pleck and Joseph Pleck, *The American Man.* Englewood, New Jersey: Prentice Hall.

Harris, Louis and Associates (1979). *The Playboy Report on American Men.* Playboy Inc.

Harris, William H. and Judith Levy (eds.) (1975). *The New Columbia Encyclopedia.* New York: Columbia University Press.

Heer, David M. and Amyra Grossbard-Shechtman (1981). "The Impact of the Female Marriage Squeeze and the Contraceptive Revolution on Sex Roles and the Women's Liberation Movement in the U.S. 1960–1975." *Journal of Marriage and the Family* February, 43:49–65.

Hicks, Mary W. and Marilyn Platt (1970). "Marital Happiness and Stability: A Review of Research in the Sixties." *Journal of Marriage and the Family* 32:553–74.

Hole, J. and E. Levine (1971). *The Rebirth of Feminism.* New York: Quadrangle.

Johns-Heine, Patrick and Hans Gerth (1949). "Values in Mass Periodical Fiction, 1921–1940." *Public Opinion Quarterly* 13:105–113.

Kidd, Virginia (1974). "Happy Ever After and Other Relationship Styles." Ph.D Dissertation. Department of Speech, University of Minnesota.

Kohn, Melvin (1969). *Class and Conformity: A Study in Values.* Homewood, Illinois: Dorsey Press.

Komarovsky, Mirra (1962). *Blue-Collar Marriage.* New York: Random House. (1976). *Dilemmas of Masculinity.* New York: W.W. Norton.

Lasch, Christopher (1977). *Haven in a Heartless World.* New York: Basic Books.

Lebergott, Stanley (1976). *The American Economy.* Princeton, New Jersey: Princeton University Press.

Lederer, William and Don Jackson (1974). "Do People Really Marry for Love?" *Reader's Digest,* January.

Luker, Kristin (1984). *Abortion and the Politics of Motherhood.* Berkeley: University of California Press.

Lynd, Robert S. and Helen Lynd (1929). *Middletown.* New York: Harcourt, Brace and Co.

Maslow, Abraham (1970). *Motivation and Personality,* Second Edition. New York: Harper and Row.

Mason, Karen, John Czajka and Sara Arber (1976). "Change in U.S. Women's Sex-Role Attitudes, 1969–1974." *American Sociological Review* 41:573–96.

Maurois, Andre (1940). "The Art of Marriage." *Ladies' Home Journal,* April.

Miller, Ruth Scott (1925). "Masterless Wives and Divorce." *Ladies' Home Journal,* January.

Newcomb, Theodore (1937). "Recent Change in Attitudes Toward Sex and Marriage." *American Sociological Review* 1:659–67.

O'Neil, William (1978). "Divorce in the Progressive Era." In M. Gordon (ed.) *The American Family in Social-Historical Perspective.* New York: St. Martin's Press, pp. 140–51.

Oppenheimer, Valerie Kincade (1973). "Demographic Influence on Female Employment and the Status of Women." *American Journal of Sociology* 78:946–61.

Osmond, Marie W. and Patricia Y. Martin (1975). "Sex and Sexism." *Journal of Marriage and the Family* 37:744–59.

Pahl, J. M. and R. E. Pahl (1971). *Managers and their Wives.* London: Allen Love and Penguin Press.

Parelius, Ann P. (1975). "Emerging Sex-Role Attitudes, Expectations and Strains among College Women." *Journal of Marriage and the Family* 37:146–54.

Parsons, Talcott and Robert F Bales (1955). *Family, Socialization and Interaction Process.* Glencoe, Illinois: The Free Press.

Pleck, Joseph (1985). *Working Wives, Working Husbands.* New York: Sage Publications.

Quinn, Naomi (1982). " 'Commitment' in American Marriage: a Cultural Analysis." *American Ethnologist* 9:775–98.

Roper, Brent S. and Emily Labeff (1977). "Sex Roles and Feminism Revisited: An Intergenerational Attitude Comparison." *Journal of Marriage and the Family* 39:113–20.

Rothman, Sheila M. (1978). *Women's Proper Place: A History of Changing Ideals and Practices 1870 to the Present.* New York: Basic Books.

Ryan, Mary (1979). *Womanhood in America (From Colonial Times to the Present).* Second Edition. New York: New Viewpoints.

Sheehy, Gail (1976). *Passages.* New York: Dutton.

Swidler, Ann (1980). "Love and Adulthood in American Culture." In N. Smelser and E. Erikson (eds.) *Themes of Work and Love in Adulthood.* Cambridge, Massachusetts: Harvard University Press, pp. 120–47.

———. (1982). "Ideologies of Love in Middle Class America." Paper read at Annual Meeting of Pacific Sociological Association, San Diego.

Thornton, Arland, Duane Alwin, and Donald Camburn (1983). "Causes and Consequences of Sex-Role Attitudes and Attitude Change." American Sociological Review 48:211–27.

Turner, Ralph (1976). "The Real Self: From Institution to Impulse." *American Journal of Sociology* 81:789–1,016.

U.S. Bureau of the Census (1976). *The Statistical History of the United States.* New York: Basic Books.

Vahanian, Tilla and Sally Olds (1978). "How Good Is Your Marriage." *Ladies' Home Journal,* January.

Veroff, Joseph, Elizabeth Douran and Richard Kulka (1981). *The Inner American: A Self-Portrait from 1957 to 1976.* New York: Basic Books.

Yankelovich, Daniel (1974). *The New Morality.* New York: McGraw-Hill. (1981). *New Rules.* New York: Random House.

Young, Michael and Peter Willmott (1957). *Family and Kinship in East London.* London: Routledge and Kegan Paul.

Zaretsky, Eli (1976). *Capitalism, the Family and Personal Life.* New York: Harper Colophon.

Zelnik, Melvin and John Kantner (1980). "Sexual Activity, Contraceptive Use and Pregnancy." *Family Planning Perspectives,* 12:230–37.

Zube, Margaret (1972). "Changing Concepts of Morality: 1948–1969." *Social Forces* 50:385–96.

READING 9-2

The His and Hers Transition

Jay Belsky and John Kelly

WHAT DIVIDES US

New parents disagree about many things, but when they fight, they usually fight about one of five things: division of labor, money, work, their relationship (who is responsible for the hole that has opened up in it), and social life (are we getting out enough). These five issues are so big, important, and all-pervasive, they might be said to constitute the raw material of marital change during the transition. Quite simply, couples who manage to resolve these issues in a mutually satisfactory way generally become happier with their marriages, whereas those who do not become unhappier. In order to understand how these five issues operate in a couple's relationship, it will help to know more about the issues themselves and how biology, upbringing, and perhaps evolution have conspired to make men and women see them so differently.

Chores and Division of Labor

On the whole, husbands and wives agree that this is the major stress of the transition. They also agree that while they expected the baby to create a lot more work, that expectation did not prepare them for what they actually encountered. One of our project mothers compared the difference to "watching a tornado on TV and having one actually blow the roof off your house."

Some recent figures explain why the reality of a baby's impact is so much greater than the

Jay Belsky and John Kelly. "The His and Hers Transition" from *The Transition to Parenthood: How a First Child Changes a Marriage,* pp. 32–50. Copyright © 1994 by Jay Belsky, Ph.D. and John Kelly. Reprinted with the permission of Delacourt Press, a division of the Random House, Inc.

expectation. Typically nonbaby tasks, such as dishwashing, increase from once or twice a day to four times, laundry from one load a week to four or five, shopping from one expedition per week to three, meal preparation from twice a day to four times, and household cleaning from once a week to usually once a day. Nursing chores add further to the workload. On average a baby needs to be diapered six or seven times and bathed two or three times per day, soothed two or three times per night and often as many as five times per day. His helplessness also transforms once-simple tasks into complex, time-consuming ones. "These days," said one new father, not bothering to hide his exasperation, "going out for ice cream is like planning a moon shot. First I have to check Alex to see if he's wet. Then I have to wrestle him into his clothes, then into the stroller. Next I have to pack an extra diaper in case he wets himself and a bottle in case he starts acting up."

Compared with his 1960s counterpart, a man like this father is notably more involved in baby and household chores. Studies show that, on average, 30 years ago a man devoted 11 hours per week to home and baby, while today he devotes 15 or 16 hours. But this three- to four-hour increase has not significantly alleviated the new mother's burden. Even in a home where a woman works full-time, we found that her contributions to child care, such as diapering, feeding, and bathing, often exceed her husband's by nearly 300 percent. Or to put it another way, for every three diapers he changes, she changes eight. The new mother's contribution to household chores also increases during the transition, usually by about 20 percent.

One of the major changes that has occurred within her transition over the past 15 years is the way women themselves view this division of labor. What was acceptable for earlier generations of new mothers is not acceptable for new mothers of this generation. A combination of factors, including maternal employment, feminism, and egalitarianism, has made today's woman expect and feel entitled to a significant

amount of help from a man. By the same token, men have not been untouched by the winds of change either. Men today want to be more involved with home and child, and they also realize that their wives shoulder burdens their own mothers never dreamed of shouldering.

Yet despite these changes, when men and women sit down to discuss who does what, they usually end up sounding like a project couple I interviewed several years ago:

> Husband (with some self-congratulation): "My dad is always telling me and my brother he never changed a diaper in his life. I change them all the time, and I think I'm a better parent and a better husband for it."
>
> Wife (after husband left the room): "David knows his father never helped his mother, and since he gives me a little help, he thinks he's Mother Teresa. The truth is, I do about 80 percent of everything. You know what really burns me up though? The way David acts when his parents visit. Usually he does a little more then, and of course they think he's wonderful. 'Wow,' his dad keeps saying, 'I never did any of that stuff.' Ohhh, when I hear that, I'd like to take the pair of them . . ."

Why do so many new mothers feel that they don't get the help and support they need? Part of the answer lies in several aspects of his transition that make a man perceive his contribution to home and baby differently than his wife. One is that a man uses a different yardstick to measure his contribution to the division of labor. A wife measures what a husband does against what she does. And because what a man does looks small when measured by this yardstick, the woman often ends up as unhappy and disgruntled as the project wife above. The man, on the other hand, usually measures his contribution to chores against what his father did. And because by that yardstick his 15 to 16 hours per week represent a 30 to 40 percent increase over what his father did, he often ends up feeling as good about himself and his contribution to the division of labor as the project father above.

Frequently the man's perception of who does what is also influenced by the fact that, at least temporarily, he becomes the family's sole breadwinner. And because this is a role he has been taught to equate with parenting, fulfilling it not only makes a new father feel like he is already satisfying his parental obligation, it also makes the 20 percent he does at home seem like 200 percent to him. How can his wife not appreciate his contribution? The nature of transition chores can also shape a man's perception of the division-of-labor issue. Because his wife is usually more skilled at baby chores, the man sometimes concludes that his help is really not needed. The new father who hops on this train of thought usually gets off at the same station as the project husband who said to me, "I expected to do more, I really did. But then I started thinking. Since Brenda's breastfeeding Jenny, Brenda should get up with Jenny. Then, pretty soon, 'getting up with Jenny is Brenda's job' became 'Jenny is Brenda's job.'"

Sometimes aspects of her transition can also contribute to an unequal division of labor. For example the yardstick a new mother uses to measure a husband's contribution to chores can produce such maternal disgruntlement and withholding that the man does even less because he does not get the gratitude he feels he is entitled to for surpassing his father's. In addition a woman's significant biological investment in the child can make her so critical of her husband's parenting that, without intending to, she drives him away.

I witnessed a dramatic example of this phenomenon at a neighborhood picnic last year. I was talking to another father—a man I'll call Jake—when a scream erupted from a nearby meadow. While we were talking, Jake's two-year-old, Bobby, had wandered off, fallen, and cut his forehead. As Jake comforted him, wife Nora, who had been off getting hot dogs with their older son, appeared. Grabbing Bobby out of Jake's arms, she asked, "What happened?" in a voice full of upset and reproach. Jake told her, then added defensively, "It's only a scratch." Nora, however, was unmollified. "I'm taking

Bobby to the nurse," she announced, and proceeded to march off. "Wait," Jake said, running after her, "I'll come with you." "No," said Nora, spinning around. "You stay here. You've already done your work for the day."

As he watched his wife and sons disappear over a hill, I could see Jake struggling with himself. He knew Nora's sharpness was a product of her concern for Bobby, not a personal attack on him. She had simply "lost it" for a moment. Still, the sharpness hurt, and in the end that hurt won out. "Next time let her take the both of them to get a hot dog," Jake said. "I've had it."

Men who find themselves continually criticized for their inadequate diapering, bathing, and dressing skills often end up feeling similarly conflicted. On one level they know that their wives do not really mean to be hurtfully critical; on another level, like Jake, they feel humiliated and often conclude that the best (and safest) policy to adopt vis-à-vis child-care chores is a hands-off policy.

Money Worries

Income among project couples averaged $25,000 per annum (or about $30,000 in current dollars). This is about the national average for new parents, and it explains why finances are also a major transition issue. Twenty-five thousand dollars does not go very far, particularly when, in addition to covering ongoing expenses such as mortgage and car payments, it has to cover the new expenses created by the baby, who despite his small size can be a formidable consumer. For example, the packages of Pampers or Huggies he goes through every three or four days cost $9.50 to $12.50; the Osh-Kosh jeans and shoes he outgrows every few months cost $20 and $30 if he is one year old and $30 and $40 if he is two. On average his new winter coat costs up to $50; his new stroller anywhere from $80 to $250. Depending on where he lives, his visits to the pediatrician can cost between $25 and $75. If his mother continues to work, child-care costs can run as high as $20,000 per year in some cities.

Most of the disagreements new mothers and fathers have about these expenses arise from another difference between members of the his and hers transition: Parenting changes men's and women's self-perceptions in very different ways. When a couple joined the project, one of the first things we asked them to do was play what we called the penny game. We gave the husband and wife 15 pennies each and asked them to allot their money to three roles: spouse, worker, and parent, depending upon how closely they identified with these roles. At the start of the transition, women allotted almost as many pennies as men to the worker role—which is to say that mothers-to-be were almost as likely as fathers-to-be to identify themselves as workers. But after the baby's birth a divergence developed. Women (including working women) began allotting more and more of their pennies to the parenting role, men relatively more to the worker role.

The different forms of economic logic that new mothers and fathers develop arise from this divergence in self-perception. Many a man's thinking about money issues is dominated by his worker impulse to conserve and enhance financial resources. A new father frequently works longer hours to increase income and begins cutting back on his own consumption. Now he shuts off the lights when he leaves a room and brings a sandwich to work instead of eating lunch out. Many a woman's economic logic is often shaped by her close identification with the parenting role. New mothers also turn out lights and "brown-bag it" to save money. However, because a mother sees herself first and foremost as a nurturer, the woman's chief concern becomes the baby's well-being. And this often produces economic choices that put her in conflict with her conservation-minded husband.

Exhibit A of this phenomenon was project wife Betty van der Hovel's decision to have the living-room windows babyproofed with sliding metal guards two weeks after son Luke's birth. Because husband Ted felt the windows would not pose a hazard until Luke was two or three years old, Betty's decision baffled and annoyed him. "Now on top of everything else I have to find a hundred and fifty dollars to pay for those goddamn guards," he told me one day. "Why couldn't Betty have waited?" But Betty felt that Ted had missed the point entirely. The issue was not money, it was their son's safety. And how could he possibly put economic considerations ahead of that? "Sometimes, you can be such a jerk," I overheard her tell Ted one afternoon during a conversation about the window guards.

Exhibit B of this phenomenon is a disagreement I witnessed one evening at the home of project couple Tom and Maggie Davis. I was sitting in the kitchen with Tom when Maggie arrived home with a bagful of new baby clothes. "Look at these, Tom," she said, pulling a smock, hat, and booties out of the bag in rapid succession. "Won't Alexis look adorable in them?"

In a transition where conservation is an overriding priority, expensive baby clothes make as little economic sense as sliding metal guards, so Tom reacted to this fashion show the way Ted van der Hovel had to the guards. "Jesus, Maggie, how many times do we have to go through this?" he said. "We just bought a house, we're not making much money, we can't afford to keep buying baby clothes. How many dresses does Alexis need, anyway? She doesn't look in a mirror."

Maggie groaned as if to say, "You don't get it, do you?" And from the perspective of her transition, Tom had not gotten it. Often for women new baby clothes represent a sensible economic choice because they advance another of the new mother's priorities: social presentation. This is the name given to her desire to present her baby—her creation—to the larger world of family and friends for admiration and praise. And since a 30-dollar Osh-Kosh outfit and a 40-dollar pair of shoes will make her new creation look even more irresistible to that larger world, frequently the new mother believes them to be a sound investment.

One interesting sidelight of the employed-mother revolution is that it may have enhanced the incidence of clothes and toy buying for baby. When men were providing most of the family's income, a mother often had to curb her buying impulse if a husband said, "Enough," because it was money he earned that she was spending. But now that many new mothers have independent sources of income, they feel (within limits of course) that they have a right to spend their money as they choose.

Relationship Difficulties

It is harder to draw a statistical profile of marital estrangement and drift, but several numbers suggest why it is also an important transition issue. One comes from a recent *Parenting* magazine survey that found that new mothers and fathers are twice as likely to kiss the baby as they are each other. A recent University of Michigan study found that the incidence of sexual intercourse drops 30 to 40 percent in the first year after the baby's arrival.

Fatigue, of course, is partly responsible for these changes, and so is the baby, who attracts attention and affection his parents used to direct at each other. But the principal reason new parents touch less frequently is that they feel less connected, less in tune with each other. It is not accidental that one of the most enduring pieces of transition folklore—one that has been passed down from one generation of new parents to the next—is the story of the couple who, on their first night out alone, run out of things to say within five minutes. The sense of drift, estrangement, and loneliness that produces such tongue-tiedness is as much a feature of the transition in most marriages as are money worries and division-of-labor concerns. But once again, differences in upbringing and biology often make men and women blame these problems on very different things.

For men the chief culprit is maternal preoccupation with the baby. While most new fathers expect the baby to become the main priority in the family, many are stunned at how little wifely attention or affection is left over for them. Our project fathers complained that after the baby's arrival much less interest was shown in their work, hobbies, concerns, or sexual desires. One project husband described a recent sexual encounter with his wife this way: "Last Sunday, while Ellen and I were lying in bed, I reached over and touched her. She'd been half asleep, but as soon as I put my hand on her breast, she bolted upright, pulled a sheet over her and said, 'Don't. Not now. That's for Jonathan.' Believe me, if I ever had any doubts about her priorities, that incident cleared them up in a hurry."

Often adding to the man's sense of estrangement is the coterie of advisers that surrounds the new mother. While men know why this happens, these figures—who include mothers, sisters, aunts, and other female relatives and friends—possess nurturing skills a man often does not. Their sudden importance in a wife's life often makes a husband feel shunted aside and unimportant. A University of Minnesota study found that while in-laws were not among the top five transition complaints of new mothers, they were the number-one complaint of new fathers, many of whom singled out mothers-in-law and sisters-in-law as sources of alienation and estrangement. "Sometimes I wonder if anyone remembers I'm still here," a project father said to me one day.

When women talk about transition-time loneliness and estrangement, their chief culprit is what I call male self-focus. Because of upbringing and perhaps biology as well, a man's emotional energy and attention all too frequently tend to flow inward toward his own concerns and needs. Shared experiences which pull a man outside of himself and force him to concentrate on his partner's needs can sometimes disrupt this flow. But because none of the transition's major events absolutely require male participation—a man does not have to be in the delivery room if he does not want to be, for example—often the new father's focus remains relatively undisrupted. As before the baby's arrival, he continues to be preoccupied with his own wants and needs.

An example of how this self-focus can contribute to maternal estrangement and disaffection is a story a project wife told me about a visit to her husband's parents six weeks after her child's birth. "I'd had a cesarean," the woman said, "so Norman carried Natasha into the house. But he was so concerned about getting to the TV set and the football game that the minute he got through the door, he practically threw her on the floor. He didn't take her out of her baby seat or unwrap her blanket; he didn't ask me what I wanted. He didn't do anything except vanish. Sometimes I wonder whether he realizes the two of us even exist."

An encounter another project wife had with male self-focus left her feeling even more estranged and alienated. One night about three months after daughter Sarah's birth, mother Jill was standing in front of the bedroom mirror in her bra and panties when she happened to catch a glimpse of husband, Michael, examining her from the opposite side of the bedroom. The look on his face so horrified her that Jill rushed to the closet for a bathrobe. When she told one of our female observers about this incident, Jill said it confirmed what she had already begun to suspect about Michael: He was so wrapped up in what he wanted—"a perfect little beauty queen of a wife"—he had no understanding of or sympathy for what she was going through.

The association men make between work and parenting also contributes to maternal loneliness and estrangement. Just at the point when a new mother wants her husband home by her side, this association will often make the husband pull himself out of the family and immerse himself more deeply in his work. "I know Ralph means well," one of our wives told me, "but I don't understand why he only equates parenting with money. It's important, but right now having him here is a lot more important to me than the few extra dollars his overtime brings in."

Career and Work

At the project's start in 1982, 30 percent of our wives were employed in the baby's first year, and most held traditionally female jobs. They were beauticians, nurses, teachers, and clerks. Most also worked for a traditionally female reason: Their families could not get by without their paychecks. At the project's conclusion in 1988, maternal employment stood at 45 percent, and now our employed mothers included more professional women, such as accountants, lawyers, and office managers. An increasing number of our women also looked upon their work, whatever they did, as a career or as the stepping-stone to one. Our data closely mirror national trends, which show that between 1970 and 1990 the number of employed mothers with young children almost doubled, from 30 percent to 53 percent.

This change in maternal employment has fueled another equally momentous change. For reasons of both ideology and need, over the past decade more and more employed mothers have come to embrace the notion of egalitarian role sharing. While today's employed mother expects parity or near parity on division of labor, her adherence to this ideal often leads her to expect something much deeper—marital parity. She expects her partner to share emotional responsibility for their child and family and to share in career sacrifices if they have to be made. Not every woman who goes to work embraces egalitarianism, of course, but enough do to have created another potent source of divisiveness between members of the his and hers transitions.

Some men share their wives' egalitarianism. During the project, we encountered a number of committed male egalitarians, and interestingly the ones most steadfast in their commitment to this ideal tended to be alike . . . For the most part they were low-key, usually nonideological (i.e., they did not have any special intellectual commitment to either egalitarianism or feminism), extremely secure, and often domestically skilled. Also noteworthy, they were all deeply in love with their wives. However, these husbands represented the exception. The norm among project husbands—and I strongly suspect among husbands in general—is a man in transition. This individual also loves his wife and wants to support her, especially when she holds a paying job. But because he has a lingering allegiance to certain aspects of the traditional male role, he is often psychologically and emotionally unprepared to be the full partner his wife wants and expects.

Take chores. The woman's desire for parity or near parity on the division-of-labor issue frequently causes conflict because it bumps into the transitional man's belief that while a husband should contribute, a wife should remain first among equals in the nursery, kitchen, and laundry room. The working mother's belief that emotional responsibility for child and home should be shared also frequently causes conflict. Unlike his father or grandfather, a transitional man will bathe and diaper the baby. But like them he believes, or at least acts as if he believes, that chores that involve assuming emotional responsibility for home and child, such as scheduling pediatrician's visits, overseeing child-care arrangements, and making out shopping lists, are a woman's work—whether she has a job outside the home or not.

Career conflicts are also common between this man and his wife because his view of himself as the family's principal breadwinner (whatever the reality of the situation) produces an expectation that career sacrifices are also his wife's job. One area where this expectation caused a great many problems for project mothers was when they had to work late. Usually if a man's desk was clear at five, he would agree to pick up the baby at the sitter or child-care center. However, if it wasn't—even if there wasn't anything terribly pressing on it—he would generally say, "No, I can't. I have to work too. You'll just have to make other arrangements."

Social Isolation

The weeks immediately following the baby's birth are a whirlwind of social activity. But sometime around the end of the first month the congratulatory calls and visits begin to taper off, and that is when the stress of social isolation really starts to make itself felt. Among project participants, recreational activities in the form of visits to movies, restaurants, and friends' homes declined by 40 percent during the first year of the transition. And several findings from the *Parenting* magazine study suggest that their experience is the rule, not the exception. More than half the survey respondents reported that they did not go out at all during the first six months after the baby's birth unless a relative was able to sit. Even after the first year more than 81 percent had yet to spend a weekend alone, and 91 percent to take a vacation of five or more days alone.

On the whole, new mothers tend to suffer more from isolation than fathers, and new stay-at-home mothers suffer most of all. Said one such mother, "Sometimes it gets so bad, I find myself actually dreading Kate's naps. But when she's up, I spend most of my time wishing I had another adult here to talk to." Work protects men from this kind of desperate isolation. But the lack of date nights, parties, vacations, and extracurricular activities such as Saturday afternoon racquetball takes its toll on them too. In conversations we found men and women equally likely to complain about feeling isolated and cut off. But we also found that like the other major transition stresses, this one is perceived very differently by the two sexes.

Men generally take the position of Mike Evans, one of our project husbands, who felt that the principal reason for his and wife Phoebe's isolation was what he called Phoebe's obsession with the baby. "She won't leave him alone," Mike complained one day. "I know mothers are supposed to be devoted to their babies, but Phoebe's gone way overboard. Every time David hiccups, she makes a federal case out of it. She won't eat unless he's on her lap or leave him if she thinks the slightest thing is wrong. Last week, an hour before we were supposed to go to the movies, Phoebe marched into the living room and announced that she'd just canceled the sitter. She thought David was coming down with a cold and didn't want to leave him. I went ballistic. We've been out exactly three times in the last eight months."

When I talked to Phoebe Evans a few days later, she was still feeling vaguely guilty about this incident. "I know sometimes I overfocus on David," she admitted, "but it's taken me a while to recognize that and also to recognize that it won't change unless I make an effort to change it." But like most women Phoebe also felt that a major factor in the Evans's isolation was her husband's attitude. "Mike's always telling me, 'Come on. Let's go out, let's go out,' and I want to, but I say no because I'm too exhausted. And that's Mike's fault. He barely lifts a finger to help me."

WHAT UNITES US

"One day, when Michela was four months old, I had an incredible experience with her. She'd been crying and I was trying to soothe her, but nothing worked. So finally, out of desperation, I began singing 'Row, Row, Row Your Boat' very softly. All of a sudden the tears stopped, her eyes got shiny and as big as nickels, and her little mouth formed into a perfect 'O.' She was straining every ounce to focus on me. No one had ever looked at me that intently before—as if I were the sun, moon, and stars all wrapped up in one. It made me so happy, I took Michela's little hand in mine and began waltzing her round and round the kitchen."

This story from a project mother indicates what is wrong with the portrait of the transition I've painted over the last 15-odd pages—it leaves out all the good parts. If becoming a parent were an endless conflict about money, chores, work, the relationship, and social activ-

ity, babies would be a lot rarer than they are. But of course it is not an endless conflict. Along with the tumult, the exhaustion, the loneliness, and hurt feelings there are also moments of sublime happiness, moments when the new parent literally begins dancing with joy. And for the most part what sets new parents to dancing is the same. Among project husbands and wives there was as much agreement about the transition's gratifications as there was about its stresses. But just as men and women perceive the stresses differently, often they also perceive its gratifications differently.

Take what everyone agrees is the transition's most exquisite gratification: the baby himself. Often when new mothers talk about why he is so wonderful, they speak the language of love. They say the baby has introduced them to a new dimension of this feeling, one they did not know—had not dreamed—existed before. Project mothers tried to explain the uniqueness of this love in many different ways. Some attempted to delineate its parameters in words, and often the words they chose were ones people use when they are trying to describe a profound spiritual awakening. Women talked about being seized by an "all-embracing," "all-encompassing" love. Other mothers employed metaphors to describe the specialness of what they felt. Said one project woman, "Tilly's opened a door in me I didn't even know was there." Still others described the transforming effect of their new feelings. "The love that flows through Adam's eyes when I hold him makes me tingle," said one mother, while another compared her baby's smile to a "magic wand" that "chases my blues away." We also had a fair amount of new mothers who believed that human language had not yet invented words powerful enough to describe what they felt. "I love Cynthia more than words can say," declared one mother when I asked her to describe how she felt about her new baby.

While new fathers are also set to dancing by the baby, they usually dance more slowly and for different reasons. We had a few men who were as swept away by love as any new mother. Representative of this group was the man who said, "I can't fully express the feelings of love I have for Michael. He's a magnificent blessing. He's increased the love I receive and the love I give." But most new fathers are swept away by the baby for more traditional male reasons. Many look upon him as a terrific new playmate. A number of project fathers echoed the sentiment of the man who described his new son as being "more fun than TV." Even more men seem to see the baby as a wonderful new cement that strengthens their feelings toward wife and family. "I feel much more deeply committed to my marriage now," said one new father.

While men and women used different verbal styles to describe their feelings about baby, when they talked about him, I noticed that they both used the same facial expression: They smiled.

Changes in feeling about oneself ranks as the second major transition gratification. At one point or another almost all of our mothers and fathers reported that parenthood had made them feel more mature, more grown-up. But these words meant different things to men and to women. Usually when a man used them, he meant that he felt more responsible about his work. Sometimes this would lead him to devote more hours to it; other times, to begin looking at it in a new way. Instead of seeing it simply as a source of revenue, now the new father would begin to look at his job as part of a larger life plan. As the child grew, the family's income needs would increase; did his job offer an opportunity for advancement? And even more important, his family would need a secure source of income. Did his present job provide that security?

New mothers also equated maturity with responsibility. But when a woman talked about responsibility, usually she meant the responsibility of shaping and molding a new life. Many women reported that motherhood made them behave more sensibly. "I used to be a real speed demon," said one woman. "But not anymore. Since Amy's birth, I don't think I've gone more than 45 miles per hour. My husband can't believe it. But now that she's a part of my life, I don't feel I can afford to take risks anymore." Other women reported that their new sense of responsibility had awakened them to larger concerns. "I never paid much attention to environmental issues," one of our mothers told me one day. "I figured I don't live in Brazil, so why should I worry about the rain forest, and I'm not an Eskimo, so why should I worry about the whales? But Eddie's changed that. These things are a part of the world he's going to live in, and I want to make sure that when he's grown-up, they're still there for him to enjoy."

The new sense of family that the baby creates ranks as a third major transition gratification for most new parents. And interestingly it is one that mothers and fathers experience in the same way. When we asked project participants why the baby enhanced their sense of family, men were as likely as women to cite the same reasons. One was that the new child had given the husband and wife what they had not had before: a biological connection. One project father spoke for many of our study participants when he said, "Since the baby, I feel a lot closer to my wife emotionally and spiritually because she's not just my partner anymore. She's the mother of my child." The need to pull together to meet the demands of the transition can also enhance a couple's sense of being part of the same unit. "Suddenly you realize if you're going to survive this thing intact," said one woman, "the two of you are going to have to learn to work together in a new way, and that creates a tremendous sense of unity." The remark of another project participant hints at a third reason why the baby often enhances a couple's sense of family: "When I was a little girl," she said, "we used to spend every summer on the Jersey shore. Since Jane's birth Everett and I have spent a lot of time talking about the traditions we want to create for our new family."

In interviews project participants singled out one other aspect of the transition as being particularly gratifying: It brought them closer to their own parents. Sometimes this bond arose from empathy. Now that they were parents themselves, participants said they had a better appreciation of what their parents had given them and what they had gone through to give it. Said one man, "Being a dad myself, I realize what a good job my parents did with me and how much I owe them." A project mother added, "It took me 28 years, but I'm finally beginning to understand all the sacrifices my mom and dad made for me."

Other times the new bond with one's own parents was generational. Suddenly the mother and father felt linked in a great family chain that stretched back into some unknown past and now forward into the baby's future. Being part of this chain evoked powerful feelings in a new parent. A particularly dramatic case in point was the project father who ended a five-year dispute with his father after his daughter's birth. The two men had not spoken since having a falling-out over the family business. "I felt my father had behaved very pigheadedly," the man said,

"and I was angry at him. But after Natalie's birth I felt it was time to put our dispute aside. We're all part of the same family, and it would be silly to allow a business disagreement to continue disrupting the family. So I gulped hard and called him."

One of the things that became clear early in the project is that couples who are able to focus their attention on what unites them and produces mutual joy usually end up at the end of the transition with a better, happier marriage. I think the reasons for this are fairly self-evident. The transition gives a couple dozens of new and potentially much deeper points of connection. There is the baby and the new biological link he creates between husband and wife; there is the new sense of unity, of family they experience as they join together to nurture him; and there is also the enormous satisfaction of knowing that you and your partner are growing together and growing in the same direction. However, in order to take advantage of these new points of connection, a couple first must learn how to deal with the new differences and divisions the transition also creates.

PART FOUR

POWER, CONFLICT, AND DISRUPTION

CHAPTER 10

Work and Families

No family issue reflects the tensions caused by the movement of married women into the labor force more than the division of labor in the home. In the 1950s, when most married women with children did not work outside the home, housework and child care were seen as their job. Husbands may have helped out a bit, but wives did most of the work. Now, most married women with children are working for pay outside the home. Yet men still do not share equally in domestic work. A series of surveys carried out between 1965 and 1985 showed that women had cut back the number of hours they spent in domestic work and that men had increased their hours by a smaller amount. So, overall, less household work was getting done and men were doing a larger share of it. But women still did over 70 percent of the work.[1] I know of no recent survey that can be compared with the 1965–1985 figures. We do not know, therefore, how much men may have increased their share since the mid-1980s. Impressionistic evidence suggests that men do somewhat more but that the division is still unequal. Wives work for pay all day and then come home to what Arlie Hochschild called "the second shift."

The first reading for this chapter is an article I originally wrote for *The New York Times Magazine* about the transformation of motherhood since the middle of the 20th century. The great social changes in the lives of mothers since then have included more employment outside the home, more childbearing outside of marriage, fewer births, and more divorce and remarriage. In the article, I review developments such as these and discuss their implications for mothers, fathers, and society.

A major question for sociologists is why, despite massive social change, the unequal division of labor between mothers and fathers persists. One answer, favored by social exchange theorists, is that men still have better labor market opportunities than women, which makes married women economically dependent on their husbands. It is said that although wives earn more relative to their husbands than they used to, they still need a husband's earnings to pool with theirs. Thus, with an implied threat of

---

[1]John F. Robinson, "Who's Doing the Housework?" *American Demographics,* December 1988, 24ff.

divorce, the middle-class husband can make his wife do more than half of the housework in return for his greater financial contribution.

As valid as the social exchange perspective is, it seems incomplete. Even men whose wives have earnings close to (or more than) theirs often do not share fully in the housework. A number of sociologists, seeking to unravel this puzzle, have turned to the persistence of beliefs about culturally appropriate behavior for women and men. People have "gender ideologies," to use Hochschild's term, that stubbornly affect what they do around the house. It is important to the self-image of many men that their wives be seen as the main workers around the house because, they think, men aren't supposed to do much work around the house. Hochschild studied some working-class husbands who did a great deal of domestic work but insisted that they were just helping out their wives.

For women, the inner conflict can be greater. Those who were raised after the feminist revolution of the 1960s typically believe that women should be able to work outside the home and that their husbands should share the housework and child care. But they also may want to prove to their husbands that they are fulfilling the role of a good wife; and this desire may lead them to display how much housework they still do. Or they may want to do more of the housework to support the ego of a husband who is not earning much money and therefore is not fulfilling the culturally prescribed male role. Faced with these tensions, as well as with the grim economic situation of many divorced women, wives may accept an unequal division of labor despite their preferences for greater sharing.

In "Joey's Problem: Nancy and Evan Holt," a chapter from her book, *The Second Shift: Working Parents and the Revolution at Home,* Hochschild tells the story of a married couple who do not share the housework and child care equally even though the wife works full-time outside of the home. Nancy struggles to reconcile the reality of the division of labor in her marriage with her ideals. Hochschild provides an insightful account of the tensions in their marriage and how they were resolved.

The Transformation of Motherhood

Andrew J. Cherlin

To understand the transformation that has occurred in American attitudes toward the role of mothers, consider this question, which has been asked in national surveys over two decades: "Do you agree or disagree that it is much better for everyone involved if the man is the achiever outside the home and the woman takes care of the home and the family?" In 1977, 66 percent of adults agreed. By 1996, the figure had fallen to 38 percent.

In 1977, many employed women viewed their jobs as necessitated by the need for a second income. And many felt guilty about being away from their children: 42 percent of working mothers with preschool children agreed that "a preschool child is likely to suffer if his or her mother works." That guilt has lessened, although it has not disappeared: in 1996, 23 percent of comparable women agreed with the statement.

What has happened is a cultural redefinition of the meaning of motherhood. At midcentury, motherhood was a way of life, almost a calling. Today, it is a social role—still highly valued, but now competing with career and personal growth as a source of a woman's identity. Yet this great change is so recent that society hasn't fully adjusted to it. Even conservatives are coming to accept the inevitability of mothers working outside the home. But neither employers nor government nor many men recognize the inescapable consequence: working mothers need support if they are to balance their double burden. Think for a moment about the trends that demonstrate this new unstable equilibrium in mothers' lives.

More Employment   The percentage of married women who work outside the home has increased significantly. In 1996, 77 percent of all married women with school-age children were employed or looking for work. The figure was 63 percent for those with preschool-age children—five times what it was in 1950.

Less Marriage   Men and women marry about four years later than they did at midcentury. Moreover, the proportion who will never marry has risen to about 10 percent among whites and 25 to 30 percent among African-Americans. In addition, many more women are having children outside marriage—32 percent of all births in 1995, compared with just 5 percent in 1960.

Fewer Births   The typical mother who came of age in the 1950's had three or more children; today, she is likely to have two. And more women are pursuing careers, waiting until their 30's and 40's to start families, when it is harder to become pregnant.

More Divorce and Remarriage   The probability of divorce doubled between the early 1960's and 1980; since then it has dropped slightly. At current rates, about half of all marriages will end in divorce. In the majority of cases, children live with their mothers after a divorce. And because of remarriage, about one-third of all mothers will be part of a stepfamily before their children reach 18.

Overall, marriage plays a much smaller role in mother's lives than it used to. The decline of marriage as an institution is one of the most significant changes in family life since the 1950's. And its weakening has both economic and cultural roots. As for economics, the worsening prospects for poorly educated men have made it harder for poor and working-class women to find men they can count on for steady earnings. The sociologist

Frank F. Furstenberg Jr. has suggested that for many poor women and men marriage is a "luxury consumer item," the preferred form of coupling, but one that is ever more out of reach.

Yet economic problems can't explain the middle-class decline in marriage, and studies suggest that they can't even fully explain the drop-off among the poor. There has also been a cultural change since midcentury in Americans' attitudes toward marriage and family life. In 1957 and again in 1976, Americans were asked what they would think about a person if all they knew was that he or she did not want to get married. In 1957, half said that the person must be selfish, sick or immoral. But in 1976, only one-third responded with negative comments; most were neutral or positive.

This is not to imply that the two-parent breadwinner-homemaker family has disappeared. In 1995, about one-fifth of all children lived with an employed father and a stay-at-home mom—down from an all-time high of only 57 percent in 1960. But stay-at-home moms today are different from their 1950's counterparts. To begin with, some use child care. According to the 1990 National Child Care Survey, 1 in 7 stay-at-home wives with children under 3 used child care (provided by nonrelatives) regularly—conduct that would have been unthinkable a generation ago.

Why has this happened? In part because lower birth rates and longer adult lives have made child rearing, for most women, a temporary job. Rearing children occupies less of a mother's lifetime than it did in the past, so women are investing much more in developing careers. They are postponing marriage and using that time to get a foothold in the labor market. Many also have a strong incentive to keep working at least part time so that their skills and seniority don't deteriorate.

Of course, the time demands are greatest for mothers who combine paid work with child rearing. Much has been written about "the second shift," in sociologist Arlie Hochschild's phrase, that working mothers must take on when they come home. Part of the problem is simply fitting children's needs into parents' work schedules. But much of the problem is the behavior of husbands, who have not filled the gap left at home by their employed wives.

In 1965, 1975 and 1985, the sociologist John P. Robinson and others asked adults to keep a log of what they did all day, noting the starting and ending times of all activities. The results showed that between 1965 and 1985, married mothers cut their housework hours from 30 to 20, while their husbands' housework hours increased from 5 to 10.

But Robinson's logs showed no increase in the time men spent performing child-care duties. Whether there has been an increase since then, we do not know. While magazines and movies feature fathers trying to balance work with parenting, there's no hard evidence that fathers are spending more time caring for their children.

It is true that a small but growing number of children—about 4 percent in 1996—live in single-father families. Although these fathers would seem to be the real-life equivalents of the heroic single dads of the movies, few of them live alone with their children. Most are sharing their households with mothers, sisters or new girlfriends, who may be doing much of the child care. And certainly, in a far larger number of families, fathers are simply not around: 24 percent of all children were being reared by unmarried mothers in 1996, up from 11 percent in 1970.

How can society accommodate itself to the historic change in motherhood—to the poor and working-class mothers who must now work and the middle-class married mothers who want to combine careers and children? Although these behavioral changes have been going on for decades, the end of the cultural war over whether mothers should work outside the home has come into view only in the last few years. Oddly enough, welfare reform has been an accidental ally. The conventional wisdom is that welfare reform is tough on families. But the fact is, it has done what three decades of feminist activism could not accomplish: make most Americans accept the propriety of mothers working outside the home.

Throughout the 1970's and 80's, most conservatives championed the full-time mother as a bulwark of capitalism and democracy. In 1971, when President Richard M. Nixon vetoed legislation that would have created federally financed child-development centers, he did so in words that equated child care with communism. Federal support, he said, "would commit the vast moral authority of the national government to the side of communal approaches to child rearing over against the family centered approach."

During the last 10 years, however, starting with the Family Support Act of 1988, conservatives have argued that mothers on welfare must find jobs. This view was codified in the landmark welfare-reform legislation of 1996, which requires most welfare recipients to start working within two years of going on the rolls and puts a time limit on federal welfare benefits.

The contradiction for conservatives is that their support of welfare-to-work programs has impaired their ability to defend full-time homemakers. It is difficult to argue that poor mothers should find jobs but that middle-class mothers should stay home. Child-care policy shows this contradiction most clearly. The 1996 legislation provides a year of transitional child-care assistance for women who leave welfare for work. Some states are supplementing that assistance with child-care funds for low-income working families—including those that have not been on welfare. This broad assistance further undermines the argument that it's better for mothers to stay home.

Consequently, Republicans in Congress are now forced to accept child-care assistance for the working and middle classes while arguing for parallel assistance for mothers who don't work. When President Bill Clinton proposed a major child-care initiative in his 1998 State of the Union Message—a package of measures that would increase subsidies for low-income families, expand the tax credit for child-care expenses and provide financing for after-school care—the Senate majority leader, Trent Lott, in the Republican response, conceded its passage

in some form by saying only, "Give stay-at-home parents the same tax breaks and benefits available to parents who use day care."

In searching for solutions, many people look to western Europe and its more generous economic support for mothers—both stay-at-home and employed. The European approach would greatly ease the burden on American families. But it is not without its drawbacks. For example, the high taxes and high unemployment rates that currently bedevil Europe's social democracies are partly a result of the costly, comprehensive social programs that have given so much support to mothers.

Still, we cannot escape the fact that the United States, especially when compared with many other nations, is downright stingy in its family benefits. A recent United Nations study found that the U.S. is one of the few countries in the world without a national policy requiring paid maternity leave. In addition, nearly every western European country has a child allowance—a flat payment to families for each child they have, whether the mother is employed or not, and regardless of income. The U.S. came close to establishing such an allowance in 1997 when Congress passed a child tax credit for families with children under 17. But in a stunning display of middle-class selfishness, Congress excluded millions of low-income households. Only families with income-tax liabilities will receive the credit; if you don't make enough money to pay any income tax, you will simply not be eligible.

Since the 1980's, corporations have been addressing the difficulty of combining employment and parenting—largely out of self-interest. By one estimate, two-thirds of the new entrants to the labor force in the 1990's have been women, many of whom have families. Most large companies now have some personnel policies to help employees balance work and family responsibilities. But much of the assistance is limited and low cost, like flexible hours and information and referral offices to match parents with child-care openings.

Paid child-care benefits are rarer. For instance, of all employees in companies that had 100 or more workers in 1995, only 8 percent reported that their employers provided child-care-assistance benefits. And fewer small companies offer family-friendly benefits of any kind.

As a result, a two-tiered class system is developing. Larger businesses, which tend to have better-paying, steadier jobs and better-educated work forces, offer better policies to help workers achieve balance between the demands of work and family. Smaller businesses, which tend to have lower-paying, less-steady jobs and less-educated work forces, provide less help. The unskilled workers in low-paying jobs who most need assistance are the ones least likely to get it.

In October 1997, 26 years after Richard Nixon rejected child-care assistance as creeping socialism, President Clinton convened the first White House conference on child care. The conference, in turn, led to the proposals the President announced in his State of the Union Message. These efforts will help. But more needs to be done, and not just by Government and corporations. Unless fathers do a greater share of the work at home, mothers will remain disadvantaged in working outside the home.

READING 10-2

Joey's Problem: Nancy and Evan Holt

Arlie Hochschild

Nancy Holt arrives home from work, her son, Joey, in one hand and a bag of groceries in the other. As she puts down the groceries and opens

the front door, she sees a spill of mail on the hall floor, Joey's half-eaten piece of cinnamon toast on the hall table, and the phone machine's winking red light: a still-life reminder of the morning's frantic rush to distribute the family to the world outside. Nancy, for seven years a social worker, is a short, lithe blond woman of 30 who talks and moves rapidly. She scoops the mail onto the hall table and heads for the kitchen, unbuttoning her coat as she goes. Joey sticks close behind her, intently explaining to her how dump trucks dump things. Joey is a fat-cheeked, lively four-year-old who chuckles easily at things that please him.

Having parked their red station wagon, Evan, her husband, comes in and hangs up his coat. He has picked her up at work and they've arrived home together. Apparently unready to face the kitchen commotion but not quite entitled to relax with the newspaper in the living room, he slowly studies the mail. Also 30, Evan, a warehouse furniture salesman, has thinning pale blond hair, a stocky build, and a tendency to lean on one foot. In his manner there is something both affable and hesitant.

From the beginning, Nancy describes herself as an "ardent feminist," an egalitarian (she wants a similar balance of spheres and equal power). Nancy began her marriage hoping that she and Evan would base their identities in both their parenthood and their careers, but clearly tilted toward parenthood. Evan felt it was fine for Nancy to have a career, if she could handle the family too.

As I observe in their home on this evening, I notice a small ripple on the surface of family waters. From the commotion of the kitchen, Nancy calls, "Eva-an, will you *please* set the table?" The word *please* is thick with irritation. Scurrying between refrigerator, sink, and oven, with Joey at her feet, Nancy wants Evan to help; she has asked him, but reluctantly. She seems to resent having to ask. (Later she tells me, "I *hate* to ask; why should I ask? It's begging.") Evan looks up from the mail and flashes an irritated glance toward the kitchen, stung, perhaps, to be asked in a way so barren of appreciation and respect. He begins setting out knives and forks, asks if she will need spoons, then answers the doorbell. A neighbor's child. No, Joey can't play right now. The moment of irritation has passed.

Later as I interview Nancy and Evan separately, they describe their family life as unusually happy—except for Joey's "problem." Joey has great difficulty getting to sleep. They start trying to put him to bed at 8:00. Evan tries but Joey rebuffs him; Nancy has better luck. By 8:30 they have him *on* the bed but not *in* it; he crawls and bounds playfully. After 9:00 he still calls out for water or toys, and sneaks out of bed to switch on the light. This continues past 9:30, then 10:00 and 10:30. At about 11:00 Joey complains that his bed is "scary," that he can only go to sleep in his parents' bedroom. Worn down, Nancy accepts this proposition. And it is part of their current arrangement that putting Joey to bed is "Nancy's job." Nancy and Evan can't get into bed until midnight or later, when Evan is tired and Nancy exhausted. She used to enjoy their love-making, Nancy tells me, but now sex seems like "more work." The Holts consider their fatigue and impoverished sex life as results of Joey's problem.

The official history of Joey's problem—the interpretation Nancy and Evan give me—begins with Joey's fierce attachment to Nancy, and Nancy's strong attachment to him. On an afternoon walk through Golden Gate Park, Nancy devotes herself to Joey's every move. Now Joey sees a squirrel; Nancy tells me she must remember to bring nuts next time. Now Joey is going up the slide; she notices that his pants are too short—she must take them down tonight. The two enjoy each other. (Off the official record, neighbors and Joey's baby-sitter say that Nancy is a wonderful mother, but privately they add how much she is "also like a single mother.")

For his part, Evan sees little of Joey. He has his evening routine, working with his tools in the basement, and Joey always seems happy to be with Nancy. In fact, Joey shows little interest in Evan, and Evan hesitates to see that as a problem. "Little kids need their moms more than they need their dads," he explains philosophically; "All boys go through an oedipal phase."

Perfectly normal things happen. After a long day, mother, father, and son sit down to dinner. Evan and Nancy get the first chance all day to talk to each other, but both turn anxiously to Joey, expecting his mood to deteriorate. Nancy asks him if he wants celery with peanut butter on it. Joey says yes. "Are you sure that's how you want it?" "Yes." Then the fidgeting begins. "I don't like the strings on my celery." "Celery is made up of strings." "The celery is too big." Nancy grimly slices the celery. A certain tension mounts. Every time one parent begins a conversation with the other, Joey interrupts. "I don't have anything to drink." Nancy gets him juice. And finally, "Feed me." By the end of the meal, no one has obstructed Joey's victory. He has his mother's reluctant attention and his father is reaching for a beer. But talking about it later, they say, "This is normal when you have kids."

Sometimes when Evan knocks on the baby-sitter's door to pick up Joey, the boy looks past his father, searching for a face behind him: "Where's Mommy?" Sometimes he outright refuses to go home with his father. Eventually Joey even swats at his father, once quite hard, on the face for "no reason at all." This makes it hard to keep imagining Joey's relation to Evan as "perfectly normal." Evan and Nancy begin to talk seriously about a "swatting problem."

Evan decides to seek ways to compensate for his emotional distance from Joey. He brings Joey a surprise every week or so—a Tonka truck, a Tootsie Roll. He turns weekends into father-and-son times. One Saturday, Evan proposes the zoo, and hesitantly, Joey agrees. Father and son have their coats on and are nearing the front door. Suddenly Nancy decides she wants to join them, and as she walks down the steps with Joey in her arms, she explains to Evan, "I want to help things out."

Evan gets few signs of love from Joey and feels helpless to do much about it. "I just don't feel good about me and Joey," he tells me one evening; "that's all I can say." Evan loves Joey. He feels proud of him, this bright, good-looking, happy child. But Evan also seems to feel that being a father is vaguely hurtful and hard to talk about.

The official history of Joey's problem was that Joey felt the "normal" oedipal attachment of a male child to his mother. Joey was having the emotional problems of growing up that any parent can expect. But Evan and Nancy add the point that Joey's problems are exacerbated by Evan's difficulties being an active father, which stem, they feel, from the way Evan's own father, an emotionally remote self-made businessman, had treated him. Evan tells me, "When Joey gets older, we're going to play baseball together and go fishing."

As I recorded this official version of Joey's problem through interviews and observation, I began to feel doubts about it. For one thing, clues to another interpretation appeared in the simple pattern of footsteps on a typical evening. There was the steady pacing of Nancy, preparing dinner in the kitchen, moving in zigzags from counter to refrigerator to counter to stove. There were the lighter, faster steps of Joey, running in large figure eights through the house, dashing from his Tonka truck to his motorcycle man, reclaiming his sense of belonging in this house, among his things. After dinner, Nancy and Evan mingled footsteps in the kitchen, as they cleaned up. Then Nancy's steps began again: click, click, click, down to the basement for laundry, then thuck, thuck, thuck up the carpeted stairs to the first floor. Then to the bathroom where she runs Joey's bath, then into Joey's room, then back to the bath with Joey. Evan moved less—from the living room chair to Nancy in the kitchen, then back to the living room. He moved to the dining room to eat dinner and to the kitchen to help clean up. After dinner he went down to his hobby shop in the basement to sort out his tools; later he came up for a beer, then went back down. The footsteps

suggest what is going on: Nancy was at work on her second shift.

BEHIND THE FOOTSTEPS

Between 8:05 A.M. and 6:05 P.M., both Nancy and Evan are away from home, working a "first shift" at full-time jobs. The rest of the time they deal with the varied tasks of the second shift: shopping, cooking, paying bills; taking care of the car, the garden, and yard; keeping harmony with Evan's mother who drops over quite a bit, "concerned" about Joey, with neighbors, their voluble baby-sitter, and each other. And Nancy's talk reflects a series of second-shift thoughts: "We're out of barbecue sauce . . . Joey needs a Halloween costume . . . The car needs a wash . . ." and so on. She reflects a certain "second-shift sensibility," a continual attunement to the task of striking and restriking the right emotional balance between child, spouse, home, and outside job.

When I first met the Holts, Nancy was absorbing far more of the second shift than Evan. She said she was doing 80 percent of the housework and 90 percent of the childcare. Evan said she did 60 percent of the housework, 70 percent of the childcare. Joey said, "I vacuum the rug, and fold the dinner napkins," finally concluding, "Mom and I do it all." A neighbor agreed with Joey. Clearly, between Nancy and Evan, there was a "leisure gap": Evan had more than Nancy. I asked both of them, in separate interviews, to explain to me how they had dealt with housework and childcare since their marriage began.

One evening in the fifth year of their marriage, Nancy told me, when Joey was two months old and almost four years before I met the Holts, she first seriously raised the issue with Evan. "I told him: 'Look, Evan, it's not working. I do the housework, I take the major care of Joey, *and* I work a full-time job. I get pissed. This is *your* house too. Joey is *your* child too. It's not all *my* job to care for them.' When I cooled down I put to him, 'Look, how about this: I'll cook Mondays, Wednesdays, and Fridays. You cook Tuesdays, Thursdays, and Saturdays. And we'll share or go out Sundays.' "

According to Nancy, Evan said he didn't like "rigid schedules." He said he didn't necessarily agree with her standards of housekeeping, and didn't like that standard "imposed" on him, especially if she was "sluffing off" tasks on him, which from time to time he felt she was. But he went along with the idea in principle. Nancy said the first week of the new plan went as follows. On Monday, she cooked. For Tuesday, Evan planned a meal that required shopping for a few ingredients, but on his way home he forgot to shop for them. He came home, saw nothing he could use in the refrigerator or in the cupboard, and suggested to Nancy that they go out for Chinese food. On Wednesday, Nancy cooked. On Thursday morning, Nancy reminded Evan, "Tonight it's your turn." That night Evan fixed hamburgers and french fries and Nancy was quick to praise him. On Friday, Nancy cooked. On Saturday, Evan forgot again.

As this pattern continued, Nancy's reminders became sharper. The sharper they became, the more actively Evan forgot—perhaps anticipating even sharper reprimands if he resisted more directly. This cycle of passive refusal followed by disappointment and anger gradually tightened, and before long the struggle had spread to the task of doing the laundry. Nancy said it was only fair that Evan share the laundry. He agreed in principle, but anxious that Evan would not share, Nancy wanted a clear, explicit agreement. "You ought to wash and fold every other load," she had told him. Evan experienced this "plan" as a yoke around his neck. On many weekdays, at this point, a huge pile of laundry sat like a disheveled guest on the living-room couch.

In her frustration, Nancy began to make subtle emotional jabs at Evan. "I don't know *what's* for

dinner," she would say with a sigh. Or "I can't cook now; I've got to deal with this pile of laundry." She tensed at the slightest criticism about household disorder; if Evan wouldn't do the housework, he had absolutely *no* right to criticize how she did it. She would burst out angrily at Evan. She recalled telling him: "After work *my* feet are just as tired as *your* feet. I'm just as wound up as you are. I come home. I cook dinner. I wash and I clean. Here we are, planning a second child, and I can't cope with the one we have."

About two years after I first began visiting the Holts, I began to see their problem in a certain light: as a conflict between their two gender ideologies. Nancy wanted to be the sort of woman who was needed and appreciated both at home and at work—like Lacey, she told me, on the television show "Cagney and Lacey." She wanted Evan to appreciate her for being a caring social worker, a committed wife, and a wonderful mother. But she cared just as much that she be able to appreciate *Evan* for what *he* contributed at home, not just for how he supported the family. She would feel proud to explain to women friends that she was married to one of these rare "new men."

A gender ideology is often rooted in early experience, and fueled by motives formed early on and such motives can often be traced to some cautionary tale in early life. So it was for Nancy. Nancy described her mother:

> My mom was wonderful, a real aristocrat, but she was also terribly depressed being a housewife. My dad treated her like a doormat. She didn't have any self-confidence. And growing up, I can remember her being really depressed. I grew up bound and determined not to be like her and not to marry a man like my father. As long as Evan doesn't do the housework, I feel it means he's going to be like my father—coming home, putting his feet up, and hollering at my mom to serve him. That's my biggest fear. I've had *bad* dreams about that.

Nancy thought that women friends her age, also in traditional marriages, had come to similarly bad ends. She described a high school friend: "Martha barely made it through City College. She had no interest in learning anything. She spent nine years trailing around behind her husband [a salesman]. It's a miserable marriage. She hand washes all his shirts. The high point of her life was when she was 18 and the two of us were running around Miami Beach in a Mustang convertible. She's gained seventy pounds and she hates her life." To Nancy, Martha was a younger version of her mother, depressed, lacking in self-esteem, a cautionary tale whose moral was "if you want to be happy, develop a career and get your husband to share at home." Asking Evan to help again and again felt like "hard work" but it was essential to establishing her role as a career woman.

For his own reasons, Evan imagined things very differently. He loved Nancy and if Nancy loved being a social worker, he was happy and proud to support her in it. He knew that because she took her caseload so seriously, it was draining work. But at the same time, he did not see why, just because she chose this demanding career, *he* had to change *his own* life. Why should her personal decision to work outside the home require him to do more inside it? Nancy earned about two-thirds as much as Evan, and her salary was a big help, but as Nancy confided, "If push came to shove, we could do without it." Nancy was a social worker because she loved it. Doing daily chores at home was thankless work, and certainly not something Evan needed her to appreciate about him. Equality in the second shift meant a loss in his standard of living, and despite all the high-flown talk, he felt he hadn't *really* bargained for it. He was happy to help Nancy at home if she needed help; that was fine. That was only decent. But it was too sticky a matter "committing" himself to sharing.

Two other beliefs probably fueled his resistance as well. The first was his suspicion that if he shared the second shift with Nancy, she would "dominate him." Nancy would ask him to do this, ask him to do that. It felt to Evan as if

Nancy had won so many small victories that he had to draw the line somewhere. Nancy had a declarative personality; and as Nancy said, "Evan's mother sat me down and told me once that I was too forceful, that Evan needed to take more authority." Both Nancy and Evan agreed that Evan's sense of career and self was in fact shakier than Nancy's. He had been unemployed. She never had. He had had some bouts of drinking in the past. Drinking was foreign to her. Evan thought that sharing housework would upset a certain balance of power that felt culturally "right." He held the purse strings and made the major decisions about large purchases (like their house) because he "knew more about finances" and because he'd chipped in more inheritance than she when they married. His job difficulties had lowered his self-respect, and now as a couple they had achieved some ineffable "balance"—tilted in his favor, she thought—which, if corrected to equalize the burden of chores, would result in his giving in "too much." A certain driving anxiety behind Nancy's strategy of actively renegotiating roles had made Evan see agreement as "giving in." When he wasn't feeling good about work, he dreaded the idea of being under his wife's thumb at home.

Underneath these feelings, Evan perhaps also feared that Nancy was avoiding taking care of *him*. His own mother, a mild-mannered alcoholic, had by imperceptible steps phased herself out of a mother's role, leaving him very much on his own. Perhaps a personal motive to prevent that happening in his marriage—a guess on my part, and unarticulated on his—underlay his strategy of passive resistance. And he wasn't altogether wrong to fear this. Meanwhile, he felt he was "offering" Nancy the chance to stay home, or cut back her hours, and that she was refusing his "gift," while Nancy felt that, given her feelings about work, this offer was hardly a gift.

In the sixth year of her marriage, when Nancy again intensified her pressure on Evan to commit himself to equal sharing, Evan recalled saying, "Nancy, why don't you cut back to half time; that way you can fit everything in." At first Nancy was baffled: "We've been married all this time, and you *still* don't get it. Work is important to me. I worked *hard* to get my MSW. Why *should* I give it up?" Nancy also explained to Evan and later to me, "I think my degree and my job has been my way of reassuring myself that I won't end up like my mother." Yet she'd received little emotional support in getting her degree from either her parents or in-laws. (Her mother had avoided asking about her thesis, and her in-laws, though invited, did not attend her graduation, later claiming they'd never been invited.)

In addition, Nancy was more excited about seeing her elderly clients in tenderloin hotels than Evan was about selling couches to furniture salesmen with greased-back hair. Why shouldn't Evan make as many compromises with his career ambitions and his leisure as she'd made with hers? She couldn't see it Evan's way, and Evan couldn't see it hers.

In years of alternating struggle and compromise, Nancy had seen only fleeting mirages of cooperation, visions that appeared when she got sick or withdrew, and disappeared when she got better or came forward.

After seven years of loving marriage, Nancy and Evan had finally come to a terrible impasse. Their emotional standard of living had drastically declined: they began to snap at each other, to criticize, to carp. Each felt taken advantage of: Evan, because his offering of a good arrangement was deemed unacceptable, and Nancy, because Evan wouldn't do what she deeply felt was "fair."

This struggle made its way into their sexual life—first through Nancy directly, and then through Joey. Nancy had always disdained any form of feminine wiliness or manipulation. Her family saw her as "a flaming feminist" and that was how she saw herself. As such, she felt above the underhanded ways traditional women used to get around men. She mused, "When I was a teenager, I vowed I would *never* use sex to get my way with a man. It is not self-respecting; it's de-

meaning. But when Evan refused to carry his load at home, I did, I used sex. I said, 'Look, Evan, I would not be this exhausted and asexual every night if I didn't have so much to face every morning.' " She felt reduced to an old "strategy," and her modern ideas made her ashamed of it. At the same time, she'd run out of other, modern ways.

The idea of a separation arose, and they became frightened. Nancy looked at the deteriorating marriages and fresh divorces of couples with young children around them. One unhappy husband they knew had become so uninvolved in family life (they didn't know whether his unhappiness made him uninvolved, or whether his lack of involvement had caused his wife to be unhappy) that his wife left him. In another case, Nancy felt the wife had "nagged" her husband so much that he abandoned her for another woman. In both cases, the couple was less happy after the divorce than before, and both wives took the children and struggled desperately to survive financially. Nancy took stock. She asked herself, "Why wreck a marriage over a dirty frying pan?" Is it really worth it?

UPSTAIRS-DOWNSTAIRS: A FAMILY MYTH AS "SOLUTION"

Not long after this crisis in the Holts' marriage, there was a dramatic lessening of tension over the issue of the second shift. It was as if the issue was closed. Evan had won. Nancy would do the second shift. Evan expressed vague guilt but beyond that he had nothing to say. Nancy had wearied of continually raising the topic, wearied of the lack of resolution. Now in the exhaustion of defeat, she wanted the struggle to be over too. Evan was "so good" in *other* ways, why debilitate their marriage by continual quarreling. Besides, she told me, "Women always adjust more, don't they?"

One day, when I asked Nancy to tell me who did which tasks from a long list of household chores, she interrupted me with a broad wave of her hand and said, "I do the upstairs; Evan does the downstairs." What does that mean? I asked.

Matter-of-factly, she explained that the upstairs included the living room, the dining room, the kitchen, two bedrooms, and two baths. The downstairs meant the garage, a place for storage and hobbies—Evan's hobbies. She explained this as a "sharing" arrangement, without humor or irony—just as Evan did later. Both said they had agreed it was the best solution to their dispute. Evan would take care of the car, the garage, and Max, the family dog. As Nancy explained, "the dog is all Evan's problem. I don't have to deal with the dog." Nancy took care of the rest.

For purposes of accommodating the second shift, then, the Holts' garage was elevated to the full moral and practical equivalent of the rest of the house. For Nancy and Evan, "upstairs and downstairs," "inside and outside," was vaguely described like "half and half," a fair division of labor based on a natural division of their house.

The Holts presented their upstairs-downstairs agreement as a perfectly equitable solution to a problem they "once had." This belief is what we might call a "family myth," even a modest delusional system. Why did they believe it? I think they believed it because they needed to believe it, because it solved a terrible problem. It allowed Nancy to continue thinking of herself as the sort of woman whose husband didn't abuse her—a self-conception that mattered a great deal to her. And it avoided the hard truth that, in his stolid, passive way, Evan had refused to share. It avoided the truth, too, that in their showdown, Nancy was more afraid of divorce than Evan was. This outer cover to their family life, this family myth, was jointly devised. It was an attempt to agree that there was no conflict over the second shift, no tension between their versions of manhood and womanhood, and that the powerful crisis that had arisen was temporary and minor.

The wish to avoid such a conflict is natural enough. But their avoidance was tacitly supported by the surrounding culture, especially the image of the woman with the flying hair. After all, this admirable woman also proudly does the "upstairs" each day without a husband's help and without conflict.

After Nancy and Evan reached their upstairs-downstairs agreement, their confrontations ended. They were nearly forgotten. Yet, as she described their daily life months after the agreement, Nancy's resentment still seemed alive and well. For example, she said:

> Evan and I eventually divided the labor so that I do the upstairs and Evan does the downstairs and the dog. So the dog is my husband's problem. But when I was getting the dog outside and getting Joey ready for childcare, and cleaning up the mess of feeding the cat, and getting the lunches together, and having my son wipe his nose on my outfit so I would have to change—then I was pissed! I felt that I was doing *everything*. All Evan was doing was getting up, having coffee, reading the paper, and saying, "Well, I have to go now," and often forgetting the lunch I'd bothered to make.

She also mentioned that she had fallen into the habit of putting Joey to bed in a certain way: he asked to be swung around by the arms, dropped on the bed, nuzzled and hugged, whispered to in his ear. Joey waited for her attention. He didn't go to sleep without it. But, increasingly, when Nancy tried it at eight or nine, the ritual didn't put Joey to sleep. On the contrary, it woke him up. It was then that Joey began to say he could only go to sleep in his parents' bed, that he began to sleep in their bed and to encroach on their sexual life.

Near the end of my visits, it struck me that Nancy was putting Joey to bed in an "exciting" way, later and later at night, in order to tell Evan something important: "You win; I'll go on doing all the work at home, but I'm angry about it and I'll make you pay." Evan had won the battle but lost the war. According to the family myth, all was well: the struggle had been resolved by the upstairs-downstairs agreement. But suppressed in one area of their marriage, this struggle lived on in another—as Joey's problem, and as theirs.

NANCY'S "PROGRAM" TO SUSTAIN THE MYTH

There was a moment, I believe, when Nancy seemed to *decide* to give up on this one. She decided to try not to resent Evan. Whether or not other women face a moment just like this, at the very least they face the need to deal with all the feelings that naturally arise from a clash between a treasured ideal and an incompatible reality. In the age of a stalled revolution, it is a problem a great many women face.

Emotionally, Nancy's compromise from time to time slipped; she would forget and grow resentful again. Her new resolve needed maintenance. Only half aware that she was doing so, Nancy went to extraordinary lengths to maintain it. She could tell me now, a year or so after her "decision," in a matter-of-fact and noncritical way: "Evan likes to come home to a hot meal. He doesn't like to clear the table. He doesn't like to do the dishes. He likes to go watch TV. He likes to play with his son when he feels like it and not feel like he should be with him more." She seemed resigned.

Everything was "fine." But it had taken an extraordinary amount of complex "emotion work"—the work of *trying* to feel the "right" feeling, the feeling she wanted to feel—to make and keep everything "fine." Across the nation at this particular time in history, this emotion work is often all that stands between the stalled revolution on the one hand, and broken marriages on the other.

It would have been easier for Nancy Holt to do what some other women did: indignantly cling to her goal of sharing the second shift. Or she could have cynically renounced all forms of feminism as misguided, could have cleared away any ideological supports to her indignation, so as to smooth her troubled bond with Evan. Or, like her mother, she could have sunk into quiet depression, disguised perhaps by overbusyness, drinking, overeating. She did none of these things. Instead, she did something more complicated. She became *benignly* accommodating.

How did Nancy manage to accommodate graciously? How did she really live with it? In the most general terms, she had to bring herself to *believe* the myth that the upstairs-downstairs division of housework was fair, and that it had resolved her struggle with Evan. She had to decide to accept an arrangement which in her heart of hearts she had felt was unfair. At the same time, she did not relinquish her deep beliefs about fairness.

Instead, she did something more complicated. Intuitively, Nancy seemed to *avoid* all the mental associations that reminded her of this sore point: the connections between Evan's care of the dog and her care of their child and house, between her share of family work and equality in their marriage; and between equality and love. In short, Nancy refused to consciously recognize the entire chain of associations that made her feel that something was wrong. The maintenance program she designed to avoid thinking about these things and to avoid the connections between them, was, in one way, a matter of denial. But in another way, it was a matter of intuitive genius.

First, it involved dissociating the inequity in the second shift from the inequity in their marriage, and in marriages in general. Nancy continued to care about sharing the work at home, about having an "equal marriage" and about other people having them too. For reasons that went back to her depressed "doormat" mother, and to her consequent determination to forge an independent identity as an educated, middle-class woman for whom career opportunities had opened up in the early 1980s, Nancy cared about these things. Egalitarianism as an ideology made sense of her biography, her circumstances, and the way she had forged the two. How could she *not* care? But to ensure that her concern for equality did not make her resentful in her marriage to a man remarkably resistant to change, she "rezoned" this anger-inducing territory. She made that territory much smaller: only if Evan did not take care of the dog would she be indignant. Now she wouldn't need to be upset about the double day *in general*. She could still be a feminist, still believe in 50–50 with housework, and still believe that working toward equality was an expression of respect and respect the basis of love. But this chain of associations was now anchored more safely to a more minor matter: how lovingly Evan groomed, fed, and walked the dog.

For Evan, also, the dog came to symbolize the entire second shift: it became a fetish. Other men, I found, had second-shift fetishes too. When I asked one man what he did to share the work of the home, he answered, "I make all the pies we eat." He didn't have to share much responsibility for the home; "pies" did it for him. Another man grilled fish. Another baked bread. In their pies, their fish, and their bread, such men converted a single act into a substitute for a multitude of chores in the second shift, a token. Evan took care of the dog.

Another way in which Nancy encapsulated her anger was to think about her work in a different way. Feeling unable to cope at home, she had with some difficulty finally arranged a half-time schedule with her boss at work. This eased her load, but it did not resolve the more elusive moral problem: within their marriage, her work and her time "mattered less" than Evan's. What Evan did with his time corresponded to what he wanted her to depend on him for, to appreciate him for; what she did with her time did not. To deal with this, she devised the idea of dividing all of her own work in the new schedule into "shifts." As she explained: "I've been resentful, yes. I was feeling mistreated, and I became a bitch to live with. Now that I've gone part-time, I figure that when I'm at the office from eight to one, and when I come home and take care of Joey and make dinner at five—all that time from eight to six is my shift. So I don't mind making dinner every night *since it's on my shift*. Before, I had to make dinner on time I considered to be *after* my shift and I resented always having to do it."

Another plank in Nancy's maintenance program was to suppress any comparison between her hours of leisure and Evan's. In this effort she had Evan's cooperation, for they both clung hard to the notion that they enjoyed an equal marriage. What they did was to deny any connection between this equal marriage and equal access to leisure. They agreed it couldn't be meaningfully claimed that Evan had more leisure than Nancy or that his fatigue mattered more, or that he enjoyed more discretion over his time, or that he lived his life more as he preferred. Such comparisons could suggest that they were both treating Evan as if he were *worth more* than Nancy, and for Nancy, from that point on, it would be a quick fall down a slippery slope to the idea that Evan did not love and honor her as much as she honored and loved him.

For Nancy, the leisure gap between Evan and herself had never seemed to her a simple, practical matter of her greater fatigue. Had it been just that, she would have felt tired but not indignant. Had it been only that, working part time for a while would have been a wonderful solution, as many other women have said, "the best of both worlds." What troubled Nancy was the matter of her worth. As she told me one day: "It's not that I mind taking care of Joey. I love doing that. I don't even mind cooking or doing laundry. It's that I feel sometimes that Evan thinks his work, his time, is worth more than mine. He'll wait for me to get the phone. It's like his time is more sacred."

As Nancy explained: "Evan and I look for different signs of love. Evan feels loved when we make love. Sexual expression is very important to him. I feel loved when he makes dinner for me or cleans up. He knows I like that, and he does it sometimes." For Nancy, feeling loved was connected to feeling her husband was being considerate of her needs, and honoring her ideal of sharing and equity. To Evan, "fairness" and respect seemed impersonal moral concepts, abstractions rudely imposed on love. He thought he expressed his respect for Nancy by listening carefully to her opinions on the elderly, on welfare, on all sorts of topics, and by consulting her on major purchases. But who did the dishes had to do with a person's role in the family, not with fairness and certainly not with love. In my interviews, a surprising number of women spoke of their fathers helping their mothers "out of love" or consideration. As one woman said, "My dad helped around a lot. He really loved my mom." But in describing their fathers, not one man I interviewed made this link between help at home and love.

SUPPRESSING THE POLITICS OF COMPARISON

In the past, Nancy had compared her responsibilities at home, her identity, and her life to Evan's, and had compared Evan to other men they knew. Now, to avoid resentment, she seemed to compare herself more to *other working mothers*—how organized, energetic, and successful she was compared to them. By this standard, she was doing great: Jocy was blooming, her marriage was fine, her job was all she could expect.

Nancy also compared herself to single women who had moved further ahead in their careers, but they fit another mental category. There were two kinds of women, she thought—married and single. "A single woman could move ahead in her career but a married woman has to do a wife's work and mother's work as well." She did not make this distinction for men.

When Nancy decided to stop comparing Evan to men who helped more around the house, she had to suppress an important issue that she had often discussed with Evan: How *unusually* helpful was Evan? How unusually lucky was she? Did he do more or less than men in general? Than middle-class, educated men? What was the "going rate"?

Before she made her decision, Nancy had claimed that Bill Beaumont, who lived two

doors down the street, did half the housework without being reminded. Evan gave her Bill Beaumont, but said Bill was an exception. Compared to *most men,* Evan said, he did more. This was true if "most men" meant Evan's old friends. Nancy felt "upwardly mobile" compared to the wives of those men, and she believed that they looked upon Evan as a model for their own husbands, just as she used to look up to women whose husbands did more than Evan. She also noted how much the dangerous "unionizer" she had appeared to a male friend of theirs:

> One of our friends is a traditional Irish cop whose wife doesn't work. But the way they wrote that marriage, even when she had the kid and worked full time, she did everything. He couldn't understand our arrangement where my husband would help out and cook part time and do the dishes once in a while and help out with the laundry [an arrangement that didn't last]. We were *banned* from his house for a while because he told Evan, "Every time your wife comes over and talks to my wife, I get in trouble," I was considered a flaming liberal.

When the wife of Joe Collins, a neighbor on the other side, complained that Joe didn't take equal responsibility, Joe in turn would look down the invisible chain of sharing, half-sharing, and nonsharing males to someone low on his wife's list of helpful husbands and say, "At least I do a hell of a lot more than *he* does." In reply, Joe's wife would name a husband she knew who took fully half the responsibility of caring for the child and the home. Joe would answer that this man was either imaginary or independently wealthy, and then cite the example of another male friend who, though a great humorist and fisherman, did far less at home.

I began to imagine the same evening argument extending down the street of this middle-class Irish neighborhood, across the city to other cities, states, regions . . . wives pointing to husbands who did more, husbands pointing to men who did less. Comparisons like these—between Evan and other men, between Nancy and other women—

reflect a semiconscious sense of *the going rates for a desirable attitude or behavior in an available member of the same and opposite sex.* If most of the men in their middle-class circle of friends had been given to drinking heavily, beating their wives, and having affairs, Nancy would have considered herself "lucky" to have Evan, because he didn't do those things. But most of the men they knew weren't like that either, so Nancy didn't consider Evan "above the going rate" in this way. Most of those men only halfheartedly encouraged their wives to advance at work, so Nancy felt lucky to have Evan's enthusiastic encouragement.

This idea of a "going rate" indicated the market value, so to speak, of a man's behavior or attitudes. If a man was really "rare," his wife intuitively felt grateful, or at least both of them felt she ought to. How far the whole culture, and their particular corner of it had gotten through the feminist agenda—criminalizing wife battery, disapproving of a woman's need for her husband's "permission" to work, and so on—became the cultural foundation of the judgment about how rare and desirable a man was.

The "going rate" was a tool in the marital struggle, useful in this case mainly on the male side. If Evan could convince Nancy that he did as much or more than "most men," she couldn't as seriously expect him to do more. Like most other men who didn't share, Evan felt the male "norm" was evidence on his side: men "out there" did less. Nancy was lucky he did as much as he did.

Nancy thought men "out there" did more at home but were embarrassed to say so. Given her view of "men out there," Nancy felt less lucky than seemed right to Evan, given his picture of things. Besides that, Nancy felt that sheer rarity was not the only or best measure. She felt that Evan's share of the work at home should be assessed, not by comparing it to the real inequalities in other people's lives, but by comparing it to the ideal of sharing.

Comparisons between Evan and the going rate of male helpfulness was one basis on which

to appraise Evan's offerings to their marriage and the credit and gratitude due him for those offerings. The more rare, the more credit. Their ideals of manhood and womanhood formed another basis. The closer to the ideal, the more credit. And the harder it was to live up to the ideal, the more pride-swallowing it took, or the more effort shown, the more credit. Since Evan and Nancy didn't see this going rate the same way, since they differed in their ideals, and since Evan hadn't actually shown much effort in changing, Nancy had not been as grateful to Evan as he felt she should have been. Not only had she not been grateful, she'd resented him.

But now, under the new "maintenance program" to support the necessary myth of equality in her marriage, Nancy set aside the tangles in the give and take of credit. She thought now in a more "segregated" way. She compared women to women, and men to men, and based her sense of gratitude on that way of thinking. Since the going rate was unfavorable to women, Nancy felt she should feel more grateful for what Evan gave her (because it was so rare in the world) than Evan should feel for what she gave him (which was more common). Nancy did not have to feel grateful because Evan had compromised his own views on manhood; actually he had made few concessions. But she did feel she owed him gratitude for supporting her work so wholeheartedly; that was unusual.

For his part, Evan didn't talk much about feeling grateful to Nancy. He actually felt she wasn't doing enough around the house. But he said this in a curious way that avoided an Evan-Nancy comparison. He erased the distinction between Nancy and himself: his "I" disappeared into "we," leaving no "me" to compare to "you." For example, when I asked him if he felt that he did enough around the house, he laughed, surprised to be asked point-blank, and replied mildly: "No, I don't think so. No. I would have to admit that we probably could do more." Then using "we" in an apparently different way, he went on: "But I also have to say that I think we could do more in terms of the household chores than we really do. See, we let a lot more slide than we should."

Nancy made no more comparisons to Bill Beaumont, no more unfavorable comparisons to the "going rate." Without these frames of reference, the deal with Evan seemed "fair." This did not mean that Nancy ceased to care about equality between the sexes. On the contrary, she cut out magazine articles about how males rose faster in social welfare than females, and she complained about the condescending way male psychiatrists treat female social workers. She pushed her feminism "out" into the world of work, a safe distance away from the upstairs-downstairs arrangement at home.

Nancy now blamed her fatigue on "everything she had to do." When she occasionally spoke of conflict, it was conflict between her job and Joey, or between Joey and housework. Evan slid out of the equation. As Nancy spoke of him now, he had no part in the conflict.

Since Nancy and Evan no longer conceived of themselves as comparable, Nancy let it pass when Evan spoke of housework in a "male" way, as something he "would do" or "would not do," or something he did when he got around to it. Like most women, when Nancy spoke of housework, she spoke simply of what had to be done. The difference in the way she and Evan talked seemed to emphasize that their viewpoints were "naturally" different and again helped push the problem out of mind.

Many couples traded off tasks as the need arose; whoever came home first started dinner. In the past, Evan had used flexibility in the second shift to camouflage his retreat from it; he hadn't liked "rigid schedules." He had once explained to me: "We don't really keep count of who does what. Whoever gets home first is likely to start dinner. Whoever has the time deals with Joey or cleans up." He had disparaged a female neighbor who kept strict track of tasks as "uptight" and "compulsive." A couple,

he had felt, ought to be "open to the flow." Dinner, he had said, could be anytime. The very notion of a leisure gap disappeared into Evan's celebration of happy, spontaneous anarchy. But now that the struggle was over, Evan didn't talk of dinner at "anytime." Dinner was at six.

Nancy's program to keep up her gracious resignation included another tactic: she would focus on the *advantages* of losing the struggle. She wasn't *stuck* with the upstairs. Now, as she talked she seemed to preside over it as her dominion. She would do the housework, but the house would feel like "hers." The new living-room couch, the kitchen cabinet, she referred to as "mine." She took up "supermom-speak" and began referring to *my* kitchen, *my* living-room curtains, and, even in Evan's presence, to *my* son. She talked of machines that helped *her,* and of the work-family conflict itself as *hers.* Why shouldn't she? She felt she'd earned that right. The living room reflected Nancy's preference for beige. The upbringing of Joey reflected Nancy's ideas about fostering creativity by giving a child controlled choice. What remained of the house was Evan's domain. As she remarked: "I never touch the garage, not ever. Evan sweeps it and straightens it and arranges it and plays with tools and figures out where the equipment goes—in fact, that's one of his hobbies. In the evening, after Joey has settled down, he goes down there and putzes around; he has a TV down there, and he figures out his fishing equipment and he just plays around. The washer and dryer are down there, but that's the only part of the garage that's my domain."

Nancy could see herself as the "winner"—the one who got her way, the one whose kitchen, living room, house, and child these really were. She could see her arrangement with Evan as *more* than fair—from a certain point of view.

As a couple, Nancy and Evan together explained their division of the second shift in ways that disguised their struggle. Now they rationalized that it was a result of their two *personalities.* For Evan, especially, there was no problem of a leisure gap; there was only the continual, fascinating interaction of two personalities. "I'm lazy," he explained. "I like to do what I want to do in my own time. Nancy isn't as lazy as I am. She's compulsive and very well organized." The comparisons of his work to hers, his fatigue to hers, his leisure time to hers—comparisons that used to point to a problem—were melted into freestanding personal characteristics, his laziness, her compulsiveness.

Nancy now agreed with Evan's assessment of her, and described herself as "an energetic person" who was amazingly "well organized." When I asked her whether she felt any conflict between work and family life, she demurred: "I work real well overnight. I pulled overnights all through undergraduate and graduate school, so I'm not too terribly uncomfortable playing with my family all evening, then putting them to bed, making coffee, and staying up all night [to write up reports on her welfare cases] and then working the next day—though I only do that when I'm down to the wire. I go into overdrive. I don't feel any conflict between the job and the child that way at all."

Evan was well organized and energetic on his job. But as Nancy talked of Evan's life at home, he neither had these virtues nor lacked them; they were irrelevant. This double standard of virtue reinforced the idea that men and women cannot be compared, being "naturally" so different.

Evan's orientation to domestic tasks, as they both described it now, had been engraved in childhood, and how could one change a whole childhood? As Nancy often reminded me, "I was brought up to do the housework. Evan wasn't." Many other men, who had also done little housework when they were boys, did not talk so fatalistically about "upbringing," because they were doing a lot of it now. But the idea of a fate sealed so very early was oddly *useful* in Nancy's program of benign resignation. She needed it, because if the die had been cast in the dawn of life, it was inevitable that she should work the extra month a year.

This, then, was the set of mental tricks that helped Nancy resign herself to what had at one time seemed like a "bad deal." This was how she reconciled believing one thing and living with another.

HOW MANY HOLTS?

In one key way the Holts were typical of the vast majority of two-job couples: their family life had become the shock absorber for a stalled revolution whose origin lay far outside it—in economic and cultural trends that bear very differently on men and women. Nancy was reading books, newspaper articles, and watching TV programs on the changing role of women. Evan wasn't. Nancy felt benefited by these changes; Evan didn't. In her ideals and in reality, Nancy was more different from her mother than Evan was from his father, for the culture and economy were in general pressing change faster upon women like her than upon men like Evan. Nancy had gone to college; her mother hadn't. Nancy had a professional job; her mother never had. Nancy had the idea that she should be equal with her husband; her mother hadn't been much exposed to that idea in her day. Nancy felt she should share the job of earning money, and that Evan should share the work at home; her mother hadn't imagined that was possible. Evan went to college, his father (and the other boys in his family; though not the girls) had gone too. Work was important to Evan's identity as a man as it had been for his father before him. Indeed, Evan felt the same way about family roles as his father had felt in his day. The new job opportunities and the feminist movement of the 1960s and '70s had transformed Nancy but left Evan pretty much the same. And the friction created by this difference between them moved to the issue of second shift as metal to a magnet. By the end, Evan did less housework and childcare than most men married to working women—but not much less. Evan and Nancy were also typical of nearly 40 percent of the marriages I studied in their clash of gender ideologies and their corresponding difference in notion about what constituted a "sacrifice" and what did not. By far the most common form of mismatch was like that between Nancy, an egalitarian, and Evan, a transitional.

But for most couples, the tensions between strategies did not move so quickly and powerfully to issues of housework and childcare. Nancy pushed harder than most women to get her husband to share the work at home, and she also lost more overwhelmingly than the few other women who fought that hard. Evan pursued his strategy of passive resistance with more quiet tenacity than most men, and he allowed himself to become far more marginal to his son's life than most other fathers. The myth of the Holts' "equal" arrangement seemed slightly more odd than other family myths that encapsulated equally powerful conflicts.

Beyond their upstairs-downstairs myth, the Holts tell us a great deal about the subtle ways a couple can encapsulate the tension caused by a struggle over the second shift without resolving the problem or divorcing. Like Nancy Holt, many women struggle to avoid, suppress, obscure, or mystify a frightening conflict over the second shift. They do not struggle like this because they started off wanting to, or because such struggle is inevitable or because women inevitably lose, but because they are forced to choose between equality and marriage. And they choose marriage. When asked about "ideal" relations between men and women in general, about what they want for their daughters, about what "ideally" they'd like in their own marriage, most working mothers "wished" their men would share the work at home.

But many "wish" it instead of "want" it. Other goals—like keeping peace at home—

come first. Nancy Holt did some extraordinary behind-the-scenes emotion work to prevent her ideals from clashing with her marriage. In the end, she had confined and miniaturized her ideas of equality successfully enough to do two things she badly wanted to do: feel like a feminist, and live at peace with a man who was not. Her program had "worked." Evan won on the reality of the situation, because Nancy did the second shift. Nancy won on the cover story; they would talk about it as if they shared.

Nancy wore the upstairs-downstairs myth as an ideological cloak to protect her from the contradictions in her marriage and from the cultural and economic forces that press upon it. Nancy and Evan Holt were caught on opposite sides of the gender revolution occurring all around them. Through the 1960s, 1970s, and 1980s masses of women entered the public world of work—but went only so far up the occupational ladder. They tried for "equal" marriages, but got only so far in achieving it. They married men who liked them to work at the office but who wouldn't share the extra month a year at home. When confusion about the identity of the working woman created a cultural vacuum in the 1970s and 1980s, the image of the supermom quietly glided in. She made the "stall" seem normal and happy. But beneath the happy image of the woman with the flying hair are modern marriages like the Holts', reflecting intricate webs of tension, and the huge, hidden emotional cost to women, men, and children of having to "manage" inequality. Yet on the surface, all we might see would be Nancy Holt bounding confidently out the door at 8:30 A.M., briefcase in one hand, Joey in the other. All we might hear would be Nancy's and Evan's talk about their marriage as happy, normal, even "equal"—because equality was so important to Nancy.

CHAPTER 11

Domestic Violence

The problem of violence against women in families and in other intimate settings is not new. Yet only within the last decade or two has much attention been paid to it. The feminist movement deserves much of the credit for placing violence against women on the political agenda. Even so, government responses were modest. The U.S. Congress did not pass the Violence Against Women Act until the summer of 1994, when the murder of Nicole Simpson, O.J. Simpson's wife, focused the public's attention on battered women. It can be very difficult, and even life-threatening, for a woman to leave an abusive relationship with a husband or intimate partner. The following article by Kathleen Ferraro describes in detail the stages battered women tend to pass through before they attempt to leave a violent partner.

Child abuse is the other major form of domestic violence. In 1995, six-year-old Elisa Izquierdo of New York City was beaten to death by her mother. After her death, it came to light that her mother had been reported seven times to local child protective authorities for suspected child abuse. Yet no action had been taken. In response, outraged legislators in New York passed strict rules aimed at requiring social service agencies to take more at-risk children from their parents and place them in foster homes.

Just two decades earlier, however, public unhappiness with the quality and cost of foster care had led to a "family preservation" movement that urged social service agencies to make greater efforts to keep potentially abusive families together by helping them increase their parenting skills and solve their other problems. In truth, public sentiment about what to do about child abuse has seesawed between family preservation and removing children from their families because neither position has solved the problem of child abuse.

There is some evidence of a rise in child abuse recently, although it is very difficult to determine how much of the apparent increase merely reflects a rise in the number of existing cases that are now reported to authorities.[1] Douglas Besharov, the first director of the U.S. National Center on Child Abuse and Neglect, tries to disentangle reporting from reality in the following article. Besharov also argues that we

---

[1] See Cherlin, *Public and Private Families.*

shouldn't treat all forms of officially noted child abuse similarly. He argues that some of the problems that are officially labeled as child abuse are more appropriately viewed as problems of poverty instead. None of this is meant to question the seriousness of the child abuse problem; rather, it suggests that social policy could be more effective if we took a closer look at the different types of cases that are often lumped together as abusive.

Battered Women: Strategies for Survival

Kathleen J. Ferraro

Women in violent intimate relationships often continue to live with abusers for many years or until the death of one partner. Over the past decade, scholarship on the battering of women has been critical of analyses that focus on the reasons women remain in violent relationships (Jones, 1994; Loseke & Cahill, 1984; Tifft, 1993; Radford & Russell, 1992). The question, "Why do battered women stay?" is misinformed and misdirected. Most women not only eventually leave their abusive partners, but they are more likely to be battered in the process of leaving or after they leave than while living with an abusive partner (Schwartz, 1988; Harlow, 1991; Barnett & LaViolette, 1993). More fundamentally, the question of why women stay implies that the battered women's behavior is problematic, rather than that of their abusive partners. The more relevant questions are "why do men batter?" and "why do they stay when women tell them to go?" (see Marano, 1993).

Over the past five years, scholars have begun recasting the image of battered women from "victim" to "survivor" (Gondolf, 1990; Hoff, 1990; Kelly, 1988; Campbell et al., 1994). This shift emphasizes the competent decision making women perform to end intimate violence. The obstacles to escape are daunting, and some women may never lead lives free of male violence. Still, many women are able, over time, to eliminate violence either through divorce or

through other help-seeking efforts. Campbell and others (1994, p. 105) found that after two and a half years, 43 percent of battered women had left their abusers and two-thirds of the women were living in nonviolent situations. The researchers' interviews with women who had escaped do not suggest a simple solution to violence, but complex and persistent strategies for survival.

Although focusing on women's behavior may be a form of "victim blaming," most of our understanding of battering has come from listening to women. From women, we know that it is extremely difficult to escape from intimate violence. The contextual nature of woman battering differentiates it from other forms of interpersonal violence. One goal of this [reading] is to discuss some of the many dimensions of the context within which women who are battered develop strategies for survival. Both the context of the violence and the process women go through in their responses to battering are important issues for those concerned with women's well-being. By examining these issues, we hope to develop and implement policies that effectively respond to women's needs and desires. Battering is not a simple phenomenon, but a complex experience involving relational, institutional, and cultural contexts. Each of these contexts will be explored in this [reading] with an emphasis on the process by which women develop strategies for survival.

The analysis and examples are drawn from empirical work with women who have lived in battering relationships with husbands or lovers. Thus, the focus is on heterosexual battering, which . . . is not always identical in nature to same-sex battering. The cases are drawn from research in shelters, on police ride-alongs, with women who called the police, with battered women who killed their abusers, and with women who came to talk to me about their problems. While the interviews were conducted for separate purposes, they illuminate different aspects of the context and processes addressed here.

The [reading] outlines the stages of engagement and disengagement with the intimate relationship in which battered women participate, including ardor, accommodation, ambivalence, and terror. The factors that influence the engagement process (relational, situational, institutional, and cultural) will be examined as they support or discourage women's safety. Individual-, relational-, and institutional-level strategies will be presented for each stage, emphasizing the successful and detrimental aspects of strategies and institutional responses. The [reading] concludes with recommendations for understanding the contextual and process-oriented nature of women's responses to battering and their strategies for survival.

STAGES OF ENGAGEMENT

Ardor

Intimacy neither begins nor ends instantaneously, but follows an emotional career. Retrospective interpretations by women often identify clues that could have predicted their partners' future violence. However, the early stages of courtship are characterized by physical and emotional attractions that overshadow negative characteristics and forewarnings of danger. It is in this stage of *ardor* that individuals become bonded to the relationship and the positive feelings it generates. Most women report no experiences of physical violence during the first six months of their relationships. As described by Dobash and Dobash (1979), Walker (1979), and Kelly (1987), the first stage of a battering relationship often involves increasing isolation of the woman from her friends and family. In this stage of ardor, she usually enjoys the time alone with her partner and does not perceive his desire for social exclusivity as oppressive or abusive, but as an expression of their mutual affection. The isolation that begins to occur in this early phase, however, may establish conditions that facilitate the batterer's efforts to control his partner at a later time.

Observers, both official agents and the general public, often express surprise and sometimes disdain for women who say they love the men who have assaulted them. But this love is the dominant theme of contemporary culture, in children's films (e.g., *Beauty and the Beast*); adult literature, film, and theater; and all kinds of music and advertising. Because of the glorification of heterosexual romantic love, a high value is placed on intimate relationships; this value is socially reinforced through elaborate and expensive engagement and marital rituals. It should not be surprising that women "love" the men they live with.

At the relational level, the intense physical attraction and emotional involvement that usually are part of new intimate relationships builds ardor. Women who have been battered often discuss the deep feelings of kinship that they share with their partners; often women say that their partners are the only ones who really know and understand them. Women describe their partners as "charismatic" or "charming" and uniquely suited to meet their needs. As one woman said:

> He's all I've got. My dad's gone, and my mother disowned me when I married him. And he's really special. He understands me, and I understand him. Nobody could take his place (Ferraro & Johnson, 1983, p. 330).

Recently, Goldner and Walker have examined battered women's and their partners' perceptions that "the other knows them more profoundly and accepts them better than anyone before" (Marano, 1993, p. 49). These feelings contribute to a context in which initial violence is perceived as a profound violation of trust and intimacy, but rarely as a justification for the outright rejection of the violent man who, until then, represented her soul mate.

Accommodation

The first act of physical violence marks the beginning of the transition from ardor to the next stage of engagement—that is, *accommodation.* It is extremely unusual for a woman to leave an abusive man after the first incidence of violence. Physical violence is so inconsistent with expectations of an intimate partner that most women perceive the first instance as an exceptional aberration. A tremendous emotional commitment is threatened by recognition of battering, and most women protect that commitment through techniques of rationalization. These techniques draw on cultural scripts, excuses by abusers, and reactions of acquaintances and institutional actors to provide these women with accounts of the battering that preserve the image of intimacy between the partners (Ferraro & Johnson, 1983). Specific techniques include appeals to the salvation ethic; denials of injury; denials of victimization; denials of who the victimizer is; denials that there are options; and appeals to higher loyalties. At the relational level, the denials related to the injury, victimization, victimizer, and options represent an internalization by the women of some of the excuses and justifications offered by batterers (Ptacek, 1988). The denial of victimization, for example, reflects the batterer's attempt to reject responsibility for his violence by focusing on the woman's behavior, which he defines as provocative or deficient. As one woman told me, "I just can't learn to keep my mouth shut. I shouldn't have asked him. I don't know why I had to ask him." These statements describe her feelings of responsibility for an incident in which her partner shattered the door of their apartment and threw her against the wall because she had asked him if he wanted to take a piece of his birthday cake to work.

The strategies of denial become intertwined with the women's diminishing sense of self-worth, which results from physical and emotional battering. Men who continually denigrate their partners, particularly when the women are isolated from other sources of nurturance, establish a definition of the situation that encourages self-blame. Women usually express feelings of bewilderment (e.g., "What did I do wrong?"), but simultaneously they believe they must have done *something* to provoke the violence. For example, one woman commented on her feelings of responsibility for her husband's violence to others as well as to herself in the following manner:

> I blamed me, and I still feel sometimes like it was my fault that he did things to other people. What was it about me that made him want to hit me? I don't think I was the terrible person he said I was. Someone would call and get the wrong number, and just hang up, and I cannot tell you how many times I was thrown against walls for that.

This viewpoint exemplifies part of the confusion many women experience when they try to understand how they can control a batterer's violence with their own behavior, yet simultaneously see that accusations against them are not justified. It is particularly obvious to women that they are *not* having affairs with men walking down the street, at the grocery store, on the other end of a wrong telephone number, or anywhere else. When their partners beat them for these imagined infidelities, the women know they are not at fault. Still, many of these same women try to analyze why their abusers have such bizarre fantasies and what they could do to prevent future violence. They know at one level that they are not "that terrible person" their partner accuses them of being but, at the same time, believe there must be *something* wrong with them to evoke such rage.

Discussions with women who are trying to cope with battering reveal two forms of self-blame: behavioral and characterological (Manley, 1982; Barnett & LaViolette, 1993). Behavioral blame focuses on "specific controllable actions that led to the occurrence of the negative events," while characterological blame "is the identification of an enduring quality or trait that caused the hurtful events" (Barnett & LaViolette, 1993, p. 79). Behavioral blame encourages women to identify and eliminate behaviors, and it may contribute to a sense of control over their lives. While the women's behavior usually has nothing to do with their partner's violence, the perception that controlling behaviors will diminish his violence helps to maintain a sense of "internal locus of control"; that is, women maintain a sense of human dignity in which their actions matter. This may explain why Walker (1984) found that battered women were much more likely to have an internal locus of control than the general population of women. They may believe that by "walking on eggshells" they can maintain a safe environment.

Characterological blame, on the other hand, represents an internalization of the batterer's denigration of the woman's core sense of self. She begins to accept her partner's definitions, namely, that she is "a bad person," "a whore," "ugly," and undesirable to anyone but him. Characterological blame is debilitating, and it leads to depression, because there is nothing a woman can do to change. It is this form of self-blame that accompanies the feelings of "learned helplessness" described by Walker (1979). Through repeated experiences of noncontingency, a woman learns that there is nothing she can do to control the abusive context; thus, she begins to lose the ability to perceive alternatives to terror.

At the extreme end of the continuum of battering, abuse may be inflicted without any immediate prior interaction or even during a woman's sleep. The same woman quoted previously, who was beaten because of wrong telephone numbers, also said:

He very much believed that a home is a man's castle, and he can do anything he wants there. I just found it easier not to argue. I knew there was just so far I could go, and I couldn't cross that line. Sometimes it wouldn't even matter, I wouldn't

cross that line. He would wake me up in my sleep and start beatin' on me.

Batterings that occur "out of the blue" contradict the notion that men become violent when women resist their domination (see Wesson, 1994, p. 3). Once violence becomes an established pattern, there is not much a woman can do to prevent its occurrence. Nevertheless, most women try.

At the relational level, women try to control their own behavior based on their historical knowledge of their partners' violence. At the accommodation stage, women try to eliminate those conditions that have preceded violent incidents in the past, knowing that it is impossible to predict which specific behaviors will become an excuse for violence. Thus, large categories of behavior, such as talking to people or looking at strangers, are excluded from a woman's repertoire of actions. For example, one woman described how she learned not to speak or look at anyone while driving.

It just got to the point where I don't say anything, if you say anything, he just starts yellin' at you. So I just let it be, and I just let a lot of things go . . . And then you can't even look at somebody walkin' down the street or road, and he'll get mad at you, tell you "Get your————eyeballs back in your eyes," you know, stuff like that, so, wherever I used to go, I used to just go to sleep . . . or just pretend to sleep, half the time until we get to where we're going.

Another woman explained how she learned not to express her own opinions.

There's been times when we'd be sitting there having a conversation about anything, and maybe I didn't agree with him, and he'd haul off and smack me one. I got so I didn't express my opinion, I found out how he felt about it, and that's what I'd say. It was just easier.

In accommodating violence, or trying to do what is "easier" because it might diminish the violence, women relinquish both autonomy and support. Learning not to talk or express opinions may work as a temporary strategy, but it also lessens the women's sense of self-sufficiency, as well as any sense of intimacy. Similarly, eliminating contact with friends and family as a strategy for controlling the jealous partner also eliminates important sources of support and validation. In this respect, most women describe how their friends and relatives were scared away from them, and how the women themselves stopped trying to interact with others to avoid accusations of infidelity. One woman explained that her husband beat her after a visit to her family.

> When I used to go see my brothers and my family, and I used to come back and he used to accuse me.

He accused you of being with your brothers?

> And my father, and stuff like that. And he gave me certain time to go over there, and if I was so many minutes late, he would start beating up on me, hitting me around. And that was one of the reasons why I didn't go see my relatives or my family, because of the way he used to act. I just started ignoring my friends, my relatives, my family. He didn't do anything when they were there, but when we get home, he would just start hitting me, cussin' at me, and start beating me up.

Some women tell of their efforts to "do everything right," which suggests that all of their actions are oriented toward pleasing the batterer and preventing future violence. This strategy is all-consuming, and encourages women to abandon their own standards and judgments to meet those set by the batterer. In extreme cases, it is possible for the ethical perceptions of a woman to be deformed or distorted by attempts to adhere to a violent partner's criteria. One woman indicated how her efforts never really succeeded in improving the ways in which her husband treated her.

> He used to wake up in the mornings grouchy, and I used to have everything done before he gets up, so he won't start with me, start beating me and

cussing me, I always wanted everything to be clean and ready for him so that he would appreciate me at least that one day. But I never got that.

The relational strategies that women develop for controlling male violence are also accompanied by institutional and cultural components. At the institutional level, responses by law enforcement agencies, courts, social service agencies, and religious institutions all cooperate with or undermine techniques of rationalization. Denial of victimization, for example, is enhanced when police, under mandatory arrest policies, arrest women who have fought back, even verbally, against their batterer. In Phoenix, Arizona, in 1993, 18 percent of domestic violence arrests were of women. Norris (1994) in interviewing 10 of these women, found that all had been battered women. In terms of the effectiveness of mandatory arrest laws, one woman incarcerated for killing her abuser said:

> I've seen women in jail taken in because of defending themselves from their husbands. I wouldn't call the police, no, uh huh, who's gonna' protect me when he gets out? No one. And its gonna' be worse, I know, I been there. I think that law is crazy. They say, well, "Why didn't you call the police?" Well, what was I supposed to do, say, excuse me a minute while I go use the phone? In [country], he was so mad at me, he locked me in a trunk and left for the day. When he got back, I was so glad to get out of there, calling the police was the furthest thing from my mind.

Even when arrests of batterers do occur, unless the physical damage is severe, punishment will usually consist of a night in jail and probation. At the felony level of aggravated assault, Ferraro & Boychuk (1992) found that 16 percent of cases involving intimate partners were dismissed against the wishes of the victim. Furthermore, the vast majority of successfully prosecuted cases resulted in minor sanctions; only 11 percent of all defendants received prison sentences for violent offenses including homicide and rape. Among those cases involving violent assault by an intimate partner, severe sentences were even less common. Only in those instances involving separated couples in which severe physical injury was inflicted on the woman was a prison sentence likely to be imposed, and when administered, was usually less than two years in length (Ferraro & Boychuk, 1992). While the evidence that the incarceration of batterers is an effective deterrent of such behavior has not been convincingly demonstrated, the release of these offenders with little or no consequences is likely to send battered women the message that their abuse is not only unimportant, but that there are few options for achieving a safe haven.

Although the development of temporary restraining orders (TROs) and orders of protection was intended to provide potential victims with greater legal means for protection, the orders appear to be effective only in certain types of battering relationships. Those men who are in the early stages of battering and who are less likely to be influenced by alcohol or drugs are more likely to be deterred from harassment or stalking behavior by a court order. On the other hand, those men with long histories of dangerous and persistent violence are unlikely to be deterred from such behavior by a court order (Chaudhuri & Daly, 1992; Klein, 1996).

In addition, some women who do obtain court orders are often themselves held to be in violation of the intent of the court order by their own behavior. Thus, women who show a positive response to visits or contact by partners, when the court order required them to refrain from such behavior, are usually informed by police that they have violated the court order by allowing these individuals on their property, thereby precluding any further enforcement of the order (Ferraro, 1989). In these instances, women are given a message that it is *their* responsibility to control the violence of their partners, and *their* fault if their partners fail to do so.

Social service agencies, especially child welfare agencies, may also contribute to a woman's sense of self-blame. One woman had her children placed in foster care after she was hospitalized for three weeks because of a brutal beating; after nine months, she was unable to regain custody of her children, and may only visit them under supervised conditions. Furthermore, she has been categorized as "emotionally unstable," certainly an understandable reaction to a beating from her husband that resulted in a coma, but dubious grounds for removing children from her custody. Another woman was told by a shelter counselor during couple counseling that she had to promise not to do anything to make her partner hit her. Even when institutions intend to help, through mandatory arrest policies, laws, and the like, they often serve to reinforce the mechanisms that define the violence as appropriate and inevitable and the woman as responsible for controlling the men's behavior.

The best-trained criminal justice personnel and most sensitive legal policies depend on women who are convinced that invoking external parties is the best course of action for their families. The current cultural context is not, however, conducive to such a decision. During the administrations of Ronald Reagan and George Bush, "family values" became a focus for resolving the social problems that plagued the United States. The simplistic media portrayal of "broken families" suggested that poverty, drug abuse, teen pregnancy, HIV, and gangs were direct consequences of the breakdown in the patriarchal nuclear family. Women were bombarded with media images that inform them of the shortage of men, the perils of delayed childbearing, and the misery of choosing careers over marriage (Faludi, 1991). In *Mrs. Doubtfire,* one of the most successful 1993 films, a professional woman becomes the source of her family's downfall when she seeks divorce. Her husband, who is sympathetically portrayed as her victim, resorts to transvestism in order to be hired as his children's nanny. *Mrs. Doubtfire* reinforces the myth that divorce is disastrous to children and that women who divorce unsatisfactory men betray themselves and their children.

Battered women who are trying to survive in violent marriages at the accommodation stage must negotiate these cultural messages as they evaluate their own alternatives. Within the context of husbands' or boyfriends' accounts of victim provocation, isolation from supportive friends and family, and lack of effective intervention by criminal justice and social service agencies, these cultural scripts reinforce a woman's belief that it is her responsibility to control her partner's violence and to make the best of a bad situation.

Ambivalence

Despite the weight of forces colluding to support women's accommodation to violence, behaviors that challenge commitment may lead to the stage of *ambivalence*. The transitions in individual women's lives are impossible to predict, and some women may never move past the stage of accommodation to their partners' violence and abuse. For others, however, ambivalence about continued engagement in the relationship may be instigated by actions that are clearly at odds with intimacy and caring. These catalysts may be physical, such as a sudden increase in the severity of violence, or emotional, such as partners' flagrant affairs with other women. Sudden increases in the severity of violence may break through a woman's prior efforts at minimization and may shock a woman into realizing the potential lethality of her partner's actions. While slaps, kicks, and even beatings may be rationalized as confusing, regrettable aspects of a relationship, stabbings and threats with loaded guns are significantly more blatant violations of personal safety. As one woman said:

It was like a pendulum. He'd swing to the extremes both ways. He'd get drunk and beat me up, then he'd get sober and treat me like a queen. One day he put a gun to my head and pulled the

trigger. It wasn't loaded. But that's when I decided I'd had it. I sued for separation of property. I knew what was coming again, so I got out. I didn't want to. I still loved the guy, but I knew I had to for my own sanity (Ferraro & Johnson, 1983, p. 331).

At the emotional level, bonding to an abuser is sometimes facilitated when periods of love and contrition are interspersed with phases of tension building and battering (Walker, 1979). Dutton and Painter (1981) refer to the traumatic bonding that can occur as a consequence of intermittent violence followed by kindness. Living with "a pendulum" perpetuates hope for many women. When episodes of kindness and affection diminish or disappear, women may begin to question the nature of their relationships. The disappearance of any outward signs of emotional commitment from their partners, combined with an awareness of their partners' sexual infidelities, may lead women to reevaluate their strategies of accommodation. One woman who left her abuser to stay in a shelter said:

At first, you know, we used to have so much fun together. He has kind've, you know, a magnetic personality; he can be really charming. But it isn't fun anymore. Since the baby came, it's changed completely. He just wants me to stay at home, while he goes out with his friends. He doesn't even talk to me, most of the time . . . No, I don't really love him anymore, not like I did.

In the stage of ambivalence, prior efforts to control behavior may give way to strategies of controlling the violence that focus less on self-blame and more on protection. One such strategy is selective fighting back. Women's violence against men has been a controversial topic in the literature, with a small group of researchers claiming parity or even greater violence by women against men (Straus & Gelles, 1990). The few detailed examinations of violence by women that do exist demonstrate that women usually use physical violence as an episodic defensive tactic, rather than a habitual offensive strategy of domination (Berke et al., 1983; Saunders, 1988; Norris, 1994; Dobash et al., 1992; Campbell et al., 1994). Selective fighting back may be used to demonstrate resistance and lack of acceptance of abuse. It is not usually effective in stopping male violence, and it may even escalate abuse.

Occasionally, however, fighting back is an effective strategy in deterring violence by male partners. One woman, in describing her perception of the police response to her call, recounted her successful use of defensive violence as follows:

> He had his arms around me and . . . and I didn't want him to get the loaded gun. So I shot him to get him to let me go and leave me alone . . . I just looked at them [the police] and I said, "I was tired of being hit. I wasn't going to be hit anymore" . . . I told him that I wasn't going to be hit again because I had been married to two other abusive husbands and I'm just, I'm tired of it.

And how is your relationship now?

> It's very, very good: quite stable. We have plans you know, going on ahead and staying married and being together . . . You couldn't ask for a happier, more content couple.

The use of defensive violence in this instance is unusual both in terms of its effectiveness and in terms of the absence of any punitive response by the criminal justice system. Both the woman and her husband received alcohol counseling and stopped drinking after the shooting incident, which had occurred after two years of wife abuse and heavy drinking by both partners.

The vast majority of women who employ defensive violence are less fortunate, however. When their response to abuse involves minor property damage or assault without injury, they are usually arrested for misdemeanor violence. When the women's response becomes lethal, they are almost always charged with homicide and later sentenced to prison.

Another strategy in the ambivalence stage is to leave the relationship. In contrast to popular views of battering, more women are battered *after*

they leave a relationship than during it. According to National Crime Survey data, most victims of battering are divorced or separated from their assailants (Lehnen & Skogan, 1981). Attempts to leave a violent man are dangerous; women are more likely to be killed while trying to leave a relationship than by trying to remain in it.

While most women in violent relationships eventually attempt to leave, the first attempts do not usually result in permanent separation. Shelters for battered women report that about half their residents return to the relationships they have fled (Pagelow, 1984). Women return for a variety of reasons, including fear, continuing emotional involvement, desire to keep the family together, and lack of viable alternatives. Generally, the process of leaving begins after accommodation strategies have begun to break down. Women usually make between five and seven attempts to leave before they leave for good.

A violent man's pleas and promises are commonly cited by women as reasons for returning. Such promises are almost always never kept, however. As one woman explained:

> Every time I tried to take my kids home with me, get away from him, either he would drink and be there with my parents, he would come with his mother, and they would say, "come home" he would cry, and say he would never do it again, and I'd go home, and two days later, my other black eye would be goin' away, and he would say, "why did you tell them? why did you go to your mom, why did you have to tell them, they have nothing to do with our problems," and it just continued.

Other women try to get their abusers to leave but find that the abusers keep returning and that they beg to come back and threaten those women who refuse to take them back.

> Sometimes, you know, [it] gets so bad sometimes, I just take him to [town], and tell him to go home, and go, you know, and he won't get out until you leave him. And he'll come back, you know, bother you, call us, or he'll threaten that he's gonna' burn the house down, or lay there and

shoot everybody that comes in the house, and stuff like that.

A significant factor in determining a woman's ability to leave is her economic independence. Battering crosses all classes, races, occupations, and nationalities. While celebrity status and seven-digit incomes do not protect women from battering, economic independence is an essential factor in the ability to terminate a violent relationship. In Johnson's (1992) study of 426 battered women, income and employment were found to be more important to decisions to leave violent men than psychological characteristics, such as self-esteem. Of the 85 women in her sample who were unemployed, severely abused, and whose husbands earned over $10,000, 88 percent returned to their abusers after leaving a shelter (Johnson, 1992, p. 173). As Johnson notes:

> A battered woman with few or no marketable skills or access to employment may perceive her alternatives inside the marriage as being more rewarding than alternatives outside the relationship, even though she is subjected to severe abuse. No abuser is violent 24 hours a day, and the victim may evaluate her costs and benefits and decide that it would be less costly to stay with an abuser who is financially capable of supporting her and her dependents. In such cases, the woman's economic needs may take precedence over her physical and emotional need to be free from abuse (1992, p. 175).

Women's decision making reflects relational as well as individual needs (Ferraro & Pope, 1994). When a woman's abuser is unemployed, leaving the relationship will probably not decrease her children's economic well-being. An abuser who provides a high level of income to a woman who does not work outside the home, however, poses the threat of deprivation if she tries to leave. Such men also have the means to challenge maternal custody and, according to Chesler's research (1986), usually succeed. Women who have been most obedient to traditional sex-role ideology, devoting their lives to mothering and homemaking, thus face the most difficult obstacles in achieving economic independence and freedom from abusive partners.

Many women discover that although *they* reach a point at which they no longer desire to go on with the relationship, their partners will not let them go. Beyond crying or threatening, some men employ severe violence or psychological torture when women try to leave. It is at this point that some women move beyond ambivalence to the stage of terror.

Terror

At the *terror* stage, women perceive their abusers as possessing superhuman power to control and destroy them. Constant surveillance, threats, and punishments convince these women that the men they live with pose an omnipotent and omnipresent danger. It is important to note that this terror is not mere fantasy on the women's part. It is based on experiences that would be categorized as terrorism if they involved military opponents. The perception that there is no escape from this terror is based on concrete encounters intended to demonstrate the woman's lack of alternatives. One woman who told her husband that she was going to leave him was given the following "lesson."

> He made me get in the car and drove me way out in the middle of nowhere, out in the desert, and made me get out of the car and kneel on the ground. He put the gun at the back of my head and cocked it and said, "if you ever try to leave me, I'll kill you."

Other women are exposed to the murder of pets and death threats against their children. One woman who recanted her courtroom testimony regarding her assault informed me that her partner had said that he would cut out her son's liver if she persisted with the prosecution. Prior to this threat, the husband had driven her to a remote location and bragged to her about committing a similar murder. Another woman was threatened as follows:

"If you try to leave me, first I'll take [their daughter] and make you watch me kill her, and then I'll kill you." I didn't know it at the time, but he was saying the same thing to her.

These terrorist tactics convince most women that leaving an abuser is more dangerous for them and their children than staying. It is at this point that women enter a period of despair, characterized by use of prescription and illegal drugs and alcohol and thoughts of suicide. Physicians and psychiatrists who are untrained in the phenomenon of battering often prescribe psychotropic medication to hide the symptoms of depression and posttraumatic stress syndrome (Kurz & Stark, 1988). Many women begin to view suicide as their only alternative.

There was one time I thought about shootin' myself, and in fact I had the gun in my mouth, and I was gonna' pull the trigger, and then I thought about [daughter] having to be raised by him, without me there, and it stopped me. Several times, I came close to doin' it, but every time, I thought about her. I thought about doin' a lot of different things. I thought about taking medication, but somethin' stopped me every time. One time in [country] I thought about driving off a mountain, but I think I just chickened out. I thought about it several times. To me, it was the only solution. But I think [daughter] would've really gotten it bad, because I wasn't there to protect her.

At this point of despair, women find that external, decisive intervention, such as police arrest, is most desired and most to be mistrusted. The distrust stems from the women's perception that such arrests will not only lead to more violence, but that the arrests will increase their vulnerability to such violence. As one woman said, "I don't think anything can help."

Homicide

Homicide is not a "strategy for survival," because it is not consciously planned. Women who resort to lethality in their struggle for survival are not strategically calculating the best method

to ensure their safety. It is relevant to discuss homicide, however, since it is increasingly the outcome when other survival strategies fail. Overwhelmingly, it is an outcome that does not benefit the battered woman, whether she is sentenced to prison or remains free. Homicide is not a solution that leads to peace and happiness.

. . . [M]ost homicides committed by battered women occur in the context of an immediate confrontation. These confrontations often do not meet the legal criteria for self-defense, but they exceed the battered woman's definition of "imminent danger" based on her past experiences. Over the course of a long-term battering relationship, women become adept at reading the cues that predict violent assaults. As one woman, who is currently in prison for killing her abuser, told me:

I *lived* it, that's how I knew, I'm not ESP, not psychic. I just didn't want him to hurt me anymore. How did I know he was gonna' hurt me? I had been through it so many times [italics added].

Some women when told by their partners that they are going to be severely beaten or killed react in defensive violence that leads to death. In one such case, a woman walked in her door to find her drunk husband lying on the couch pointing a gun at her and saying, "You're gonna' die bitch." He threw the gun at her, and she shot him. She later was charged with second-degree murder. The prosecutor said that since she had the gun, she should have walked back out the door. Another woman awoke in the middle of the night to find her estranged husband pointing a gun at her. She alleged that he turned the gun around, put her hand on the trigger, and shot himself. She also was charged with second-degree murder.

The same cultural context that encourages women to remain married and denies adequate protection from abuse reacts punitively when battered women kill. When death of the abuser is the final outcome of a battering relationship, most women are sent to prison. There are approximately 2,000 women serving prison time in the United States for defending themselves against a batterer (MCTFADA, 1994, p. 4). Since the late 1970s, efforts have been initiated to educate criminal justice personnel about the impact of battering. Now a few states have laws that require judges to admit testimony about battering when it is relevant to the defense of women who kill. The National Clearinghouse on Battered Women's Self-Defense keeps records and literature on efforts to provide alternatives to incarceration. Currently, there are efforts under way in many states to require review of such cases for consideration of clemency. Most of these women pose no threat to society, and they are often separated from their children who have already lost one parent.

Even women who are not sentenced to prison for homicide continue to suffer after the death of their abusers. If they blamed themselves for being battered, they torture themselves for killing their abuser. Both their love and their fear survive the physical death of the partner. Three women who killed their abusers described their feelings as follows.

> I was screaming for help, someone to call the ambulance. It took almost an hour. They pulled me away from him. It was just like a nightmare . . . I never did hurt him, I never did try to fight back or anything, I loved him so much. . . . and when I think about it, I think to myself, I didn't do that, I didn't do that. No, at times I still do love him, sometimes I think I'm crazy, after all the things that I went through, all the pain.
>
> Sometimes I don't even know if I'm comin' or goin'. I try not to cry in front of the kids, it's mostly at night that I have to go through all this. Sometimes, I just get to the point that—I miss him, I miss him a lot. No matter what he put me through, I miss him. There are days where I wonder, why am I alive, stuff like that.
>
> Even when he's dead, he got me . . . he still has this control over me, I still catch myself saying, "Oh, I can't do that, [husband] won't let me do that." I feel like he's watching me still, I catch myself looking.

For these women, the scars of being battered and the grief of losing a partner to whom they were bonded will last for many years. They escaped with their lives, but they remain lonely, fearful, and guilt-ridden. Their stories, however, may be helpful to women in the earlier stages of battering relationships who are looking for support.

SUCCESSFUL SURVIVAL STRATEGIES

Given the overwhelming barriers to escape, it is amazing that women do survive battering relationships. Factors that facilitate survival depend on the available resources, the current context of the relationship, and the women's stage of engagement. The most important aspect of the context is the batterer's level of dependency. Men who are extremely dependent emotionally on their partners are difficult to change or to leave. They will not accept a woman's decision to end the relationship, often responding with "If I can't have you, no one else will." They stalk, harass, threaten, and often assault or kill the women for whom they proclaim undying love. This drastic response requires drastic survival strategies, which disrupt women's lives. It is, of course, true that battered women should not be the ones to leave their homes, friends, and jobs. However, they cannot depend on their partner's fear of arrest for protection. When it is clear that men will continue to prey on their partners, regardless of the expressed wishes and efforts by women to separate, the most realistic strategy, under current law, is for women to leave and begin new lives. In fact, during the course of my research, several women with children left their communities and assumed new identities in new locations. The shelter network operates like a modern version of the Underground Railroad acting as a referral and support system for women who need to take radical steps to escape from abusers who are determined to own and control them, and who need to protect themselves and their children (Ferraro & Johnson, 1985).

In terms of social policy, a more desirable approach would be to require repetitive batterers and stalkers to leave the state in which their partner resides. Such men could be banished from the state, logged onto FBI data files, similar to those kept on federal fugitives, and arrested if they set foot in the prohibited state. Violation of banishment orders could result in lengthy prison terms. The danger of this approach is that women in other states would be unaware of the violent pasts of these men. Banishment is also inconsistent with current criminal justice policies, which prohibit punishments that infringe on an individual's right to serve a specified sentence length and then continue life as a free person. Because banishment is an unlikely prospect, women will continue to bear the burden of escape from persistently violent men.

For women involved with violent men who are not intent on keeping or killing their abusive partners, strategies that focus on the development of emotional and practical resources seem to offer the best hope of escape. Several studies, for example, have found that the major reason cited by women who leave shelters to return to abusive partners is the lack of alternative housing and income (Roy, 1977; Schechter, 1982; Johnson, 1992). Furthermore, because many women need legal assistance in obtaining child support and spousal maintenance and because attorneys usually request retainers of between $1,500 and $3,000 for contested divorce cases, many women are effectively prohibited from obtaining the legal help needed to permanently escape from an abusive relationship. Legal aid services not only are limited and involve lengthy waiting periods, but qualification for such aid is often based on family income. One result is that battered women who are married to men with above-poverty-level incomes are disqualified from receiving such assistance. Battered women who are not legally married to their abusers are usually not able to obtain any court-ordered financial assistance when they leave.

The amount of low-income housing, especially for women with children, is far from adequate. One source estimates that 50 percent of homeless women are escaping violent relationships (Schneider, 1994). Because shelters provide only temporary refuge, they cannot accommodate the large numbers of women seeking assistance. To establish a societal commitment to battered women would necessitate increasing the availability of low-income housing.

The list of resources required for survival outside of a battering relationship is lengthy. Women need day care, health care, transportation, housing, clothing, food, utility assistance, and employment. Many women need job training after having devoted themselves to bearing and rearing children and maintaining the household. In the current economic environment, women, especially older women, who have nontechnical or entry-level job skills will be noncompetitive in the job market. A basic level of income maintenance will be required for many women who are unable to obtain steady employment (Albelda et al., 1988).

While the idea that battered women need therapy has been rejected by most advocates and analysts (Dobash & Dobash, 1992; Martin, 1976), women do need advocacy, information, and support. Because of the obtuse character of the legal processes involved in filing criminal charges, obtaining orders of protection, and maintaining child custody, it is difficult to obtain the necessary information that women need for effective advocacy. Women need advocates familiar with the legal system to help make phone calls and fill out appropriate forms. While individual therapy focusing on the women's psychological issues may not be appropriate, it is important to recognize that women who have been battered have experienced both trauma and loss. These experiences create depression, confusion, and grief, so the women need emotional support in order to successfully return to a violence-free life. For some of these women therapy may be entirely appropriate.

SUMMARY

Realistically, with all the practical and emotional resources provided, some women will continue to live with violent men. For an outsider to the relationship, it is difficult to know how to be most helpful in these situations. It is important to recognize that every woman has her own complex understanding of her situation and needs that is not accessible to outsiders. The most beneficial form of assistance will depend on the woman's level of engagement with the relationship. If she is still in the stages of ardor or accommodation, any demands that she recognize and act on the danger of her situation will only increase her sense of alienation. It is especially important that agency representatives, such as law enforcement officers and social workers, respect the ability of women to interpret their situation and make choices that are best for them.

The best survival strategies for women in violent relationships cannot be divorced from the social and cultural context that supports intimate violence and the subordination of women. In this respect, it is essential that any discussion of women's experiences not overshadow the macrolevel forces that encourage male violence against women and limit the practical and emotional options available to them.

REFERENCES

Albelda, Randy, McCrate, Elaine, Melendez, Edwin, Lapidus, June, & the Center for Popular Economics. (1988). *Mink coats don't trickle down.* Boston: South End.

Barnett, Ola W., & LaViolette, Alyce D. (1993). *It could happen to anyone: Why battered women stay.* Newbury Park, CA: Sage.

Berk, R. A., Berk, S. F., Loseke, D. R., & Rauma, D. (1983). Mutual combat and other family violence myths. In D. Finkelhor, R. J. Gelles, G. T. Hotaling, & M. A. Straus (Eds.), *The dark side of families: Current family violence research.* Beverly Hills, CA: Sage.

Campbell, Jacquelyn C., Miller, Paul, & Cardwell, Mary M. (1994). Relationship status of battered women over time. *Journal of Family Violence, 9*(2): 99–111.

Chaudhuri, M., & Daly, K. (1992). Do restraining orders help? Battered women's experience with male violence and legal process. In E. S. Buzawa & C. G. Buzawa (Eds.), *Domestic violence: The changing criminal response* (pp. 227–252). Westport, CT: Auburn House.

Chesler, Phyllis. (1986). *Mothers on trial.* New York: McGraw-Hill.

Dobash, R. E., & Dobash, R. P. (1979). *Violence against wives: A case against the patriarchy.* New York: Free Press.

Dobash, R. E., & Dobash, R. P. (1992). *Women, violence, and social change.* London: Routledge.

Dobash, Russell P., Dobash, R. Emerson, Wilson, Margo, & Daly, Martin. (1992). The myth of the symmetrical nature of domestic violence. *Social Problems, 39:* 71–91.

Dutton, Donald, & Painter, Susan. (1981). Traumatic bonding: The development of emotional attachments in battered women and other relationships of intermittent abuse. *Victimology 6*(1–4): 139–155.

Faludi, Susan. (1991). *Backlash: The undeclared war against American women.* New York: Doubleday.

Ferraro, K. J. (1989a). The legal response to woman battering in the United States. In J. Hanmer, J. Radford, & E. Stanko (Eds.), *Women, policing and male violence* (pp. 155–184). London: Routledge.

———. (1989b). Policing woman battering. *Social Problems, 6*(1): 6174.

Ferraro, Kathleen, & Boychuk, Tascha. (1992). The court's response to interpersonal violence: A comparison of intimate and nonintimate assault. In E. S. Buzawa & C. G. Buzawa (Eds.). *Domestic violence: The changing criminal justice response* (pp. 209–226). Westport, CT: Auburn House.

Ferraro, Kathleen, & Johnson, John M. (1983). How women experience battering: The process of victimization, *Social Problems 30*(3): 325–339.

———(1985). The new underground railroad. *Studies in Symbolic Interaction, 6:* 377–386.

Ferraro, Kathleen, & Pope, Lucille. (1993). Irreconcilable differences: Battered women, police, and the law. In N. Z. Hilton (Ed.). *Legal responses to wife assault* (pp. 96–123). Newbury Park, CA: Sage.

Gondolf, E. W. (1990). Battered women as survivors. Holmes Beach, FL: Learning Publications.

Harlow, C. W. (1991). *Female victims of violent crime.* Rockville, MD: U.S. Department of Justice.

Hoff, Lee A. (1990). *Battered women as survivors.* London: Routledge.

Johnson, Ida M. (1992). Economic, situational, and psychological correlates of the decision-making process of battered women. *Families in Society, 73*(3): 168–176.

———. (1994). *Next time she'll be dead: Battering and how to stop it.* Boston: Beacon Press.

Kelly, Liz. (1987). The continuum of sexual violence. In J. Hanmer & M. Maynard (Eds.), *Women, violence and social control* (pp. 46–60). Atlantic Highlands, NJ: Humanities Press.

———. (1968a). How women define their experiences of violence. In K. Yllö & M. Bograd (Eds.), *Feminist perspectives on wife abuse* (pp. 114–132). Newbury Park, CA: Sage.

Klein, A. (1994). *Recidivism in a population of court-restrained batterers after two years.* Unpublished dissertation, Northeastern University.

Kurz, Demie, & Stark, Evan. (1988). Not so benign neglect: The medical response to battering. In K. Yllö & M. Bograd (Eds.) *Feminist perspectives on wife abuse* (pp. 249–268). Newbury Park, CA: Sage.

Lehnen, R. G., & Skogan, W. G. (1981). The national crime survey. In R. G. Lehnen & W. G. Skogan (Eds.), *Working papers: Vol. 1. Current and historical perspectives.*

Loseke, Donileen R., & Spencer E. Cahill. (1984). The social construction of deviance: experts on battered women. *Social Problems, 31:* 296–310.

Manley, N. J. (1982). Battered women: The victim's perceptions. Unpublished master's thesis, California State University, Sacramento.

Marano, Hara Estroff. (1993). Inside the heart of marital violence. *Psychology Today, 26*(6): 48, 89–91.

Martin, D. (1976). *Battered wives.* San Francisco, CA: Glide Publications.

———. (1981). *Battered wives.* San Francisco, CA: Volcano Press, Inc.

MCTFADA (Maricopa County Task Force Against Domestic Abuse) (1994). Why don't batterers leave? MCTFADA Newsletter, p. 5.

Norris, Lynn. (1994). Dangerously equal or equally dangerous? An analysis of women's violence against male intimate partners. Unpublished master's thesis, Arizona State University, Tempe.

Pagelow, M. D. (1984). *Family violence.* New York: Praeger.

Ptacek, James. (1988). Why do men batter their wives? In Kersti Yllö & Michele Bograd (Eds.). *Feminist Perspectives on Wife Abuse* (Ch. 6, pp. 133–157). Newbury Park, CA: Sage.

Radford, Jill, & Russell, Diana E. H. (1992). *Femicide.* New York: Twayne.

Roy, Maria. (1977). *Battered women.* New York: Van Nostrand Reinhold.

Saunders, D. G. (1988a). Other 'truths' about domestic violence: A reply to McNeely and Robinson-Simpson. *Social Work.* March–April, 179.

———. (1988b). Wife abuse, husband abuse or mutual combat? In K. Yllö & M. Bograd (Eds), *Feminist perspectives on wife abuse* (pp. 90–113). Newbury Park, CA: Sage.

Schechter, Susan. (1982). *Women and male violence.* New York: Macmillan.

Schneider, Elizabeth. (1994). Legal reform efforts for battered women. Cited in MCTFADA Newsletter, p. 5.

Schwartz, M. D. (1988a). Ain't got no class: Universal risk theories of battering. *Contemporary Crises, 12:* 373–392.

Schwartz, M. D. (1988b). Marital status and woman abuse theory. *Journal of Family Violence, 3:* 239–259.

Straus, M. A., & Gelles, R. (1990). How violent are American families? Estimates from the National Family Violence Resurvey and other studies. In M. A. Straus & R. J. Gelles (Eds.), *Physical violence in American families* (pp. 95–132). New Brunswick, NJ: Transaction Publishers.

Tifft, L. L. (1993). *Battering of women: The failure of intervention and the case for prevention.* Boulder, CO: Westview Press.

Walker, L. E. (1979). *The battered woman.* New York: Harper and Row.

Wesson, Mimi. (1994). Digging up the roots of violence. *Women's Review of Books, 11*(6): 1, 3.

Don't Call It Child Abuse If It's Really Poverty

Douglas J. Besharov with Lisa A. Laumann

In 1997, about 3 million reports of suspected child abuse or child neglect were made to the police and child protective agencies. This reading argues that a large proportion of these reports—between a quarter to a half—is more properly considered a symptom of poverty, and is more appropriately handled outside the nation's child protection system. Helping these families does not require mandatory reporting laws, involuntary investigations, central registers of reports, and psychologically oriented treatment interventions.

For me, this is not an abstract issue. I prosecuted my first child abuse case 30 years ago, when the issue was far from public and professional attention. I have seen my share of brutally battered children, with open wounds and broken bones; of sexually abused children, who trembled at the touch of an adult; and of filthy, melancholy children, who received less care than a child provides to a hamster. I have spent a large part of my professional life trying to protect these children, first as a prosecutor, then as director of a state legislative committee, and, later, as the first director of the U.S. National Center on Child Abuse and Neglect.

But throughout this period, I have also seen families weakened, if not torn apart, by a system that fails to recognize the overlap between what we now label as child maltreatment and the conditions of poverty—especially among families headed by single mothers. In this [reading], I argue that society should cease treating these disadvantaged families as if they suffer from some form of psychological deviancy and, instead, should develop intervention strategies that better address their broader problems.

This [reading] is divided into four sections: The first section summarizes what is known about the nature and extent of child abuse and neglect. The second section describes the available evidence showing the overlap between poverty and child maltreatment. The third section presents a framework for understanding different levels of government intervention and proposes an alternative to child protective intervention in poverty-related cases. The last section proposes a plan for implementation and assesses its political feasibility.

I. NATURE AND EXTENT

The first step in policy making in this area, one hopes, is understanding the nature and scope of child abuse and child neglect. But this is not such a simple matter, considering that maltreatment usually occurs in the privacy of the home. Hence, to understand the size of this problem, one must make distinctions among:

1. *Annual prevalence*—the total number of children who have been abused or neglected at least once in a particular year (whether or not reported to the authorities).[1]
2. *Reported cases*—the total number of families or children[2] reported under formal procedures to child protective agencies (usually a social service agency but sometimes a law enforcement one).
3. *Substantiated (or "indicated") reports*—the total number of reports (counted either as

Douglas J. Besharov with Lisa Laumann, "Don't Call It Child Abuse If It's Really Poverty." Paper prepared for the conference "Social Policies for Children," Woodrow Wilson School of Public and International Affairs, Princeton University (Washington, D.C.: The American Enterprise Institute for Public Policy Research, 1996), pp. 1–30. Updated with the assistance of Carra M. Cote. Reprinted with the permission of Douglas J. Besharov.

children or families) that were determined, after an investigation, to be supported by specific evidence. (The legal test is often "some credible evidence.")

As will be shown, each category results in a vastly different estimate of the amount of child maltreatment—but taken together, they provide a useful portrait of the situation.

Prevalence

Three major efforts have been made to estimate the total number of abused and neglected children (whether or not reported to the authorities): "The National Study of the Incidence and Severity of Child Abuse and Neglect" (1980),[3] the "Study of National Incidence and Prevalence of Child Abuse and Neglect" (1986),[4] and "The Third National Incidence Study of Child Abuse and Neglect" (1996).[5] All were funded by the federal government's National Center on Child Abuse and Neglect and were conducted by Westat, Inc.

All three studies use essentially the same methodology: In a stratified sample of counties, a broadly representative sample of professionals who serve children was asked whether, during the study period, the children they had seen in their professional capacities appeared to have been abused or neglected.[6] This methodology does not allow Westat to estimate the number of children seen by nonprofessionals, such as friends, neighbors, and relatives. Thus, even if these studies had no other problems, the methodology inherently underestimates the prevalence of maltreatment because it does not count those children whose condition was either not seen or not recognized by a professional. (Complicated issues of sample frame and weighting also limit the ability of these studies to make more precise estimates of prevalence.)

Nevertheless, these three federally sponsored studies are the best source of information about unreported child abuse and neglect. Unfortu-

nately, design and definitional differences make the findings from the third incidence study not comparable with the first two, so they are not presented here in the same detail.[7] However, there is substantial internal consistency between the findings of the first two studies, conducted six years apart, as well as between them and data about officially reported cases. Thus, it seems reasonable to use them to provide a general picture of the nature, extent, and distribution of the various types of child maltreatment. What do they tell us?

About 1 million children are victims of child abuse or neglect each year. The first two Westat studies had a rigorous definition of countable cases that required that the child suffer demonstrable harm that lasted at least 48 hours (e.g., bruises, emotional distress, or depression).[8] However, since child protective agencies accept cases of "threatened harm" to children, the 1986 study also employed an additional (or optional) definition which included cases where the child's "health or safety was endangered through abusive or neglectful treatment." This broader definition resulted in about 500,000 additional countable cases.

The third national incidence study (NIS-3) had broader definitions of abuse and neglect or perhaps an inability to control for expanding professional interpretations of its original definitions. The result was a 60 percent increase in estimated prevalence of actual abuse and neglect under the so-called "Harm Standard," from 931,000 to 1,622,000 children.[9] However, NIS-3 also applied an "Endangerment Standard," which counted children who were not actually harmed by maltreatment, but were "*in danger of being harmed* according to the views of community professionals or child-protective agencies."[10] Under this much broader definition, the estimates rose from 1,424,000 to 2,845,000.[11] These higher estimates may be significant for what they say about changing professional attitudes, but they almost certainly do not reflect an actual increase in abuse and neglect.[12]

In the second incidence study, Westat examined the distribution of child maltreatment by sex, age, race, and family size. Except for sexual abuse, rates did not differ greatly between males and females. Females were, however, about three times more likely to be sexually abused than males (2.9 per 1,000 female children versus .9 per 1,000 male children).

The study found that the risk of maltreatment increased with age (2.4 per 1,000 children ages 0 to 2 versus 21.8 per 1,000 children ages 12 to 14). However, this may be an artifact of the study methodology, which relied on what professionals saw, and, since they tend to see older children who are in day care, schools, and so forth, there is a natural bias against finding maltreatment among infants and toddlers. Also, the large proportion of educational neglect cases (described in a moment), which, by definition, only involve older children, also raises the average age.

Rates of maltreatment did not differ by race, a surprising result given the relationship between reported maltreatment and poverty, discussed below. It may be that Westat's definitions are so broad that they pick up many cases of problematic child rearing among the middle class. The only difference found was that blacks were marginally more likely than whites to die as a result of abuse or neglect (.01 per 1,000 white children versus .05 per 1,000 black children). But because there were so few fatalities, this difference was not found to be statistically significant.

Family size likewise did not seem to be associated with differing rates of child maltreatment.

A relatively small proportion of maltreated children suffered battering, sexual abuse, or serious neglect. The Westat studies establish six categories of child maltreatment. The largest proportion of maltreated children experienced educational neglect (31 percent), followed by physical abuse (29 percent), physical neglect (18 percent), emotional abuse (17 percent), sexual abuse (13 percent), and emotional neglect (5 percent).[13] The majority of the maltreated children found by the study suffered from educational neglect (31 percent) and emotional maltreatment (both abuse and neglect) (22 percent)—situations of concern, certainly, but probably not what comes to mind when the public thinks of "child abuse" and "child neglect."

The vast majority of maltreated children suffered from nonserious conditions. The Westat studies establish four categories of severity: fatal, serious, moderate, or inferred.

Fatal: death as a result of child maltreatment during the study period.

Serious: a life-threatening condition, requiring treatment to prevent long-term impairment.

Moderate: injuries or impairments for which observable symptoms persisted for at least 48 hours (e.g., bruises, depression, or emotional distress).

Inferred: the nature of the maltreatment itself gives reasonable cause to assume that injuries or impairment have occurred.

By far, the greatest proportion of children suffered moderate injuries (73 percent). Only about .1 percent of maltreated children died as a result of child abuse or neglect. Fifteen percent of the children experienced serious injuries and 11 percent had injuries that were inferred.[14]

Although rating the cases by their severity is extremely helpful, some questionable classifications were made. For example, the definition of "serious" sexual abuse excluded penile penetration if the child was not considered to have suffered serious emotional trauma. As a result, only 6 percent of all sexual abuse cases were considered serious, even though over one third of them included penile penetration.[15]

Conversely, the definition of "serious" emotional neglect included the delaying or refusal of psychiatric care and the permitting of maladaptive behavior. While these conditions might be a cause for child protective concern, they are hardly the equivalent of child battering. Yet, the study labels them both "serious."

Public and professional definitions of child maltreatment seem to have expanded to include more cases of "moderate" harm to children. Although Westat counted a 49 percent increase in the prevalence of child maltreatment between its first and second studies, most of this increase was among cases of "moderate" physical abuse and neglect and educational neglect (with no corresponding increase among "fatal" or "serious" cases).[16] Hence, it seems reasonable to conclude that the level of child maltreatment did not grow nearly as much as suggested by the findings of the second incidence study. As Westat is careful to note, the increase "probably reflected an increase in the likelihood that professionals will recognize maltreatment rather than an increase in the actual occurrence of maltreatment."[17]

Awareness of possible child sexual abuse seems to have increased. Between 1980 and 1986, for example, the rate of *observed* sexual abuse cases nearly tripled, increasing from .7 per 1,000 children to 1.9 per 1,000 children (or from 44,700 to 119,000 victims).[18] It seems highly improbable that the underlying prevalence of sexual abuse could increase almost threefold in only six years. Hence, much of this increase is probably due to greater professional awareness of this heretofore hidden problem. Professionals who become more sensitive to possible abuse, or more adept at noticing it, would make more reports to Westat—even if the actual incidence has not risen at such a rapid rate.[19]

NIS-3 reported a further increase in cases of sexual abuse—to 217,000 victims (3.2 per 1,000 children). However, it was operating on a broader definition that included nonparental situations that are not considered included within the *child welfare definition* of child sexual abuse, that is, "adult caretakers other than parent(s)/substitute(s) permitted sexual abuse and situations where nonparental teenagers perpetrated or permitted sexual abuse." The "Endangerment Standard" increased this figure to 300,000.[20]

The Westat statistics are for all cases of child maltreatment seen by the surveyed professionals—whether reported or not. How many of these cases are reported?

Reported Cases

Since the early 1960s, all states have passed laws that mandate designated professionals to report specified types of child maltreatment. Over the years, both the range of designated professionals and the scope of reportable conditions have been steadily expanded.

Initially, mandatory reporting laws applied only to physicians—who were only required to report "serious physical injuries" and "nonaccidental injuries." In the ensuing years, however, increased public and professional attention, sparked in part by the number of abused children revealed by these initial reporting laws, led many states to expand their reporting requirements. Now, almost all states have laws which require the reporting of all forms of suspected child maltreatment, including physical abuse, physical neglect, emotional maltreatment, and, of course, sexual abuse and exploitation.[21]

Under threat of civil and criminal penalties, these laws require most professionals who serve children to report suspected child abuse and neglect. About 20 states require all citizens to report, but in all states, any citizen is permitted to report. In addition, there have been extensive public awareness campaigns and professional education programs.

It is surprisingly difficult to get nationwide information about official reports of child maltreatment. Federal efforts to collect state data have been uneven, and actually, were suspended a number of times.[22] Filling the gap have been a number of private organizations, primarily the National Committee to Prevent Child Abuse (NCPCA), now called Prevent Child Abuse of America (PCA), and the American Public Welfare Association (APWA), now called the American Public Human Services Association (APHSA).

In essence, each of these efforts uses the same methodology: a survey of state child protective agencies to determine how many reports were made in a particular year. This is not as easy as it sounds. Definitions and procedures vary sharply. For example, some states use family-based reports, while others use child-based reports. Some states collect their data on a calendar-year basis, while others use a fiscal year.[23] Compiling a national total requires a fair amount of interpretation and, thus, presents opportunity for error. Nevertheless, like the two incidence studies, there is a sufficient amount of consistency across the various studies to tell a reasonably reliable story.

In 1997, nearly 3 million reports of children suspected of being abused or neglected were made.[24] This is a 20-fold increase since 1963, when about 150,000 children were reported to the authorities. As we will see, however, this figure is bloated by reports that later turn out to be unfounded and by substantial double counting.

A relatively small percentage of reported cases involve serious harms to children. AHA found that, in 1986, about 10 percent of physical abuse cases (less than 3 percent of all substantiated reports) involved serious injury to the child, which is consistent with Westat's prevalence findings.[25]

Professionals still fail to report many of the children they see who have observable signs of child abuse and neglect. According to Westat, in 1986, 56 percent of apparently abused and neglected children, about 500,000 children, were not reported to the authorities. This is a decline in nonreporting from 1980, when professionals failed to report nearly two-thirds of the maltreated children they saw.[26] (The study methodology, which involved asking professionals about children they had seen in their professional capacities, did not allow Westat to estimate the number of children seen by nonprofessionals, let alone their nonreporting rate.)

Professionals seem to report most of the children they see who are suffering from serious *forms of abuse and neglect.* Basically, the more serious the maltreatment, the more likely a report. The surveyed professionals failed to report only 15 percent of the fatal or serious physical

abuse cases they saw. They also failed to report about 28 percent of the sexually abused children they saw, and 40 percent of the moderate physical abuse cases they saw.

Nonreporting was concentrated in five types of cases: educational neglect (85 percent not reported); emotional neglect (76 percent); moderate physical neglect cases (75 percent); serious physical neglect cases (67 percent); and emotional abuse (56 percent).[27]

This means that, in 1986, about 2,000 children with observable physical injuries severe enough to require hospitalization were not reported, over 100,000 children with moderate physical injuries were also not reported, as were over 30,000 apparently sexually abused children.

These results are difficult to interpret, however, in part because of the problems with Westat's classifications of severity described above. The most recent incidence study found that investigations of child abuse and neglect dropped 36 percent, but this number deserves closer scrutiny as well.[28] In producing the number of uninvestigated cases, the study compared the number of cases identified by professionals with those known to local agencies. Emotional abuse and neglect cases, 30 percent of cases not investigated, are usually avoided by child protective agencies because they tend to involve subjective judgments, and there is little that a quasi-law-enforcement agency can do about them. Another 33 percent of cases not reported involve educational neglect—but most communities do not consider them to be within the jurisdiction of child protective agencies.

Many people ask whether this vast increase in reporting signals a rise in the incidence of child maltreatment. Although some observers believe that deteriorating economic and social conditions have contributed to a rise in the level of abuse and neglect, it is impossible to tell for sure. So many maltreated children previously went unreported that earlier reporting statistics do not provide a reliable baseline against which to make comparisons. One thing is clear, however; the great bulk of reports now received by child protective agencies would not be made but for the passage of mandatory reporting laws and the media campaigns that accompanied them.

Although child protective programs still have major problems, some of which are discussed in this paper, the results of this 20-year effort to upgrade them have been unquestionably impressive. All states now have specialized child protective agencies to receive and investigate reports, and treatment services for maltreated children and their parents have been expanded substantially. Federal and state expenditures for child protective programs and associated foster care services are almost $7 billion a year.[29]

As a result, many thousands of children have been saved from death and serious injury. The best estimate is that over the past 20 years, child abuse and neglect deaths have fallen from over 3,000 a year—and perhaps as many as 5,000—to about 1,100 a year.[30] In New York state, for example, within five years of the passage of a comprehensive reporting law which also created specialized investigative staffs, there was a 50 percent reduction in child fatalities, from about 200 a year to under 100.[31]

This is not meant to minimize the remaining problem. Even at this level, maltreatment is the fourth largest cause of death for children under 14 years of age.[32]

Substantiated Reports

After a report is made, a child protective agency is supposed to investigate it to determine whether there is reason to be concerned about the child and, if so, what action should be taken. All states make this a formal process which concludes with a determination that the report was "substantiated," "founded," or "indicated" (terminology differs) or, conversely, that the report was "unsubstantiated," "unfounded," or "not indicated."

Collecting data on state substantiation rates is even more difficult than collecting data about raw reports, partly because states do not always keep the information and partly because there can be a long delay between the making of the report and a final decision about its validity. Nevertheless, all the efforts to collect nationwide data on the subject point toward a decline in the substantiation rate in the past 20 years.

More recently, HHS reported that, in 1997, only about 34 percent of the reports received by child protective agencies were substantiated or indicated.[33] This is a sharp contrast to 1975, when about 65 percent of all reports were substantiated (American Humane Association 1976, 11). Thus, of the approximately 3 million reports to child protective agencies in 1997, only about 1 million were substantiated or indicated.

But even this is an overestimation. Most states are unable to tell how many reports are repeat reports on the same child. Hence, these national estimates are based on duplicated counts—meaning that repeat reports on the same child are added to the total. In its analysis of the Illinois State Central Registry, the Chapin Hall Center for Children found that within one year about 20 percent of the founded reports were repeat reports.[34] So have other studies.[35]

Subtracting unsubstantiated cases and duplicated cases from the total number of reports reveals a vastly different picture of child abuse and neglect: The three million reports made in 1997 melt down to about 800,000 children involved in substantiated cases of child maltreatment.

But this is children—not families. If we want to see how many families are involved in substantiated cases, a better way to gauge caseloads, we need to divide the number of substantiated reports of children by the average number of children in a family. The National Center on Child Abuse and Neglect estimated that, in 1993, there were about 1.7 children per reported family.[36] This means that, if a case is a family, child protective agencies handled about 470,000 cases of substantiated child maltreatment.

As mentioned above, most experts attribute the increase in reports to greater public and professional awareness. But recent increases in social problems such as out-of-wedlock births, inner-city poverty, and drug abuse, may have raised the underlying rates of child maltreatment. On the other hand, a substantial portion of what we call child maltreatment is more properly considered a symptom of poverty and is more appropriately handled outside the nation's quasi-criminal child protection system. The expansion of child protective programs to cover such poverty-related cases could also explain the increase in reports.

II. THE POVERTY CONNECTION

A visit to any child welfare office would suggest a strong relationship between child maltreatment and poverty. And yet, data on income, poverty status, and welfare recipiency is rarely collected in the studies described above. What is available, however, reveals an unambiguous association between maltreatment and poverty.

Income

Across all types of maltreatment, prevalence rates are highest among low-income families. Comparing families with incomes above and below $15,000, the second national incidence study found that the rate of maltreatment was over five times higher in low-income families than high-income families (29.3 versus 5.5 per 1,000 children).[37] Two-thirds (66 percent) of all cases of maltreatment identified by the study involved families with incomes below $15,000. (No further divisions by income were made.)

These low-income families were more concentrated among particular types of maltreatment. They were nine times more likely than high-income families to be involved in cases of educational neglect and physical neglect, but only three to five times more likely across the remaining types of maltreatment.

Poor families also make up the majority of families reported to the authorities. The Virginia Department of Social Services, for example, found that 45 percent of the families reported to the child protective agencies in 1991 had incomes of less than $12,000.[38] (In 1991, the poverty rate for a family of four was $13,924.) Similarly, in 1976, AHA found (based on incomplete data) that the median family income for reported families was only about one-third of the national median income ($5,051 versus $13,900). Almost 30 percent had incomes below $3,000.[39]

The association is even greater for AFDC (cash welfare) families. In Illinois, for example, 48 percent of the children with founded reports of child abuse or neglect also received AFDC.[40] Likewise, welfare families made up about half of all reported families. Nationwide, AHA found that 49 percent of the families reported for any type of child maltreatment received public assistance, while almost 62 percent of the families reported for neglect received assistance.[41]

Further, Pelton found that AFDC parents who maltreated their children were palpably poorer than AFDC parents who did not. They were, for example, more likely to live in crowded housing and to have to share their child's sleeping spot, and they were less likely to have a shower or a telephone in their home.[42]

Poor children also predominate in foster care. National data on the income of the families of foster children do not exist. To fill this gap, researchers look at the proportion of foster care children who are Title IV–E eligible,[43] that is, whose families received or would have been eligible for AFDC prior to the child's removal from the home. Data from HHS show that, in 1998–1999, 56 percent of the national foster care caseloads were Title IV–E eligible.[44] In some states, however, the proportions of AFDC children in foster care are considerably higher. For example, in 1998–1999, the percentages were 67 percent in California, 77 percent in New York, and 71 percent in Illinois. (Together, these three states account for 50 percent of all Title IV–E foster care children.)

A study in Illinois found that children who received AFDC within the first five years of their life were twice as likely as children who did not to be placed in foster care during this period (2 percent versus .8 percent). Title IV–E eligible children made up over 58 percent of the state's foster care population.[45]

The level of poverty-related child protective intervention could grow even higher. Westat's second incidence study found that professionals did not report over 85 percent of the children who had been educationally neglected and 75 percent of the children with moderate cases of physical neglect. As noted earlier, poor children were particularly concentrated in these two types of maltreatment. If greater proportions of these types of "child maltreatment" were reported, an even higher proportion of child protective cases would involve the problems of poverty.

Family Demographics

This sharp connection between poverty and child maltreatment is further concentrated among families headed by single mothers, especially those who had their first babies as unwed teens.

Reported child maltreatment is many times more prevalent among single-parent families than among two-parent families. In Minnesota, for example, families headed by single parents were almost seven times more likely than two-parent families to have founded reports of maltreatment (28.7 per 1,000 children living in single-parent families versus 4.3 per 1,000 children living in two-parent families). About 57 percent of all substantiated victims lived in single-parent homes.[46] In New Jersey, this proportion was even higher (69 percent).[47]

The second Westat showed this relationship by maltreatment type. While less than 24 percent of the nation's children lived in single-parent families in 1986, 36 percent of those with substantiated reports of educational neglect lived in such homes. The proportions of single-parent families among the other maltreatment types

were: physical neglect (33 percent); sexual abuse (32 percent); and physical abuse (31 percent).[48]

Reported child maltreatment is more prevalent among families headed by teen mothers than families headed by nonteen mothers. For instance, in Illinois, 7 percent of teen-headed families had founded reports of maltreatment, as compared to only 3 percent of families headed by mothers who delayed their birth until their 20s.[49]

Among mothers on welfare in Illinois, families headed by mothers under 16 years at the time of their first birth were almost twice as likely as those headed by mothers who delayed childbirth until their 20s to have founded reports of maltreatment (16 percent versus 9 percent for a four-year period). The likelihood of maltreatment decreased as the age of the mother increased. Thirteen percent of the welfare families headed by mothers who were 16 to 17 at first birth, 11 percent of those with mothers 18 to 19 at first birth, and 9 percent of those with mothers 20 or over at the time of first birth had founded reports of maltreatment.[50] (A study of foster care children in Oregon found that 83 percent of their biological mothers and 85 percent of their fathers were high school dropouts.)[51]

A strong association exists between race and reported maltreatment. Although the Westat studies found no association between the two, this was probably due to the broad definition of maltreatment that they used. HHS found that, in 1997, black children were greatly overrepresented in reported cases—making up 29.5 percent of substantiated reports. (In 1997, blacks comprised about 15 percent of the national population of children under 18, whites about 66 percent, and Hispanics about 15 percent).[52] And, according to APHSA, black children were even more prevalent among the foster care population: In FY 1995, 45.1 percent of the children who entered foster care were black, 36.5 percent were white, and 11.3 percent were Hispanic.[53]

A study in Illinois found that black children were almost three times as likely as white and

Hispanic children to have a substantiated report of child maltreatment in their first five years of life. (The rates were 85 per 1,000 black children, 29 per 1,000 white children, and 23 per 1,000 Hispanic children).[54]

Endangering Abused Children

Ironically, this overreaction to poverty-related "child maltreatment" can endanger children who are in real jeopardy. Inconsistent as it may seem, given the overuse of child protective programs, workers and judges are deeply conscious of the hazards of foster care. Hence, they hesitate to remove children from their parents' custody except in the most extreme cases. Unfortunately, after dealing with so many cases of social deprivation, caseworkers become desensitized to the obvious warning signals of immediate and serious physical danger. Many children are left in the custody of parents who have repeatedly abused them. One study of child abuse fatalities, for example, described how: "In two of the cases, siblings of the victims had died previously . . . In one family, two siblings of the victim had died mysterious deaths that were undiagnosed. In another family, a twin had died previously of abuse."[55]

The result, all too often, is the child's tragic death. Studies in several states have shown that about 35 to 55 percent of all child fatalities attributed to abuse or neglect involve children previously reported to a child protective agency.[56] In 1996, the NCPCA reported that, of the estimated 1,046 child maltreatment fatalities, 41 percent had prior or current contact with CPS.[57] Tens of thousands of other children receive serious injuries short of death while under child protective supervision.

Part of the problem is the misuse of the child protective system. Social agencies fail to protect children who need help the most—the victims of physical brutality—by not removing them from their abusive parents. At the same time, they overreact to cases of social deprivation in poor families. In fact, poor, socially deprived children are more likely to be placed in foster care than are abused children. Poor children, in no real danger of physical injury, languish for years in foster care. Living in emotionally traumatic conditions, hundreds of thousands of poor children suffer more harm than if they were simply left at home. When it comes to the plight of these children, we should remember the ancient medical maxim: *Primum, non nocere*—first, do no harm.

Given these realities, many commentators blame poverty for the parents' abusive or neglectful behavior. Certainly, "poverty exposes parents to the increased likelihood of additional stresses that may have deleterious effects upon their capacities to care adequately for their children."[58] However, lest all families be stigmatized, it is important to remember that most poor families do not abuse or neglect their children. In any one year, fewer than 15 percent of welfare families are reported for suspected abuse or neglect.[59]

III. AN ALTERNATIVE INTERVENTION

Past Good Intentions

The harmful use of child protective programs for what is, in essence, a problem of poverty is another example of good intentions gone awry. Socially deprived children living in poor families have been known to public welfare agencies for decades. Until the mid 1970s, though, these children were the responsibility of the welfare caseworkers assigned to *each* AFDC recipient family. But then the provision of cash assistance was separated from the delivery of social services.

Besides providing a more efficient means of distributing AFDC funds, the separation of income maintenance from social services was supposed to upgrade the quality of social services for poor families. The planners had dreams of a greatly expanded network of specialized family service agencies to replace the all-purpose welfare caseworker. Unfortunately, this network of services never appeared. But the need for it remained, so cases of poverty-related maltreatment were transferred to the rapidly growing child protective system. (At the time, state child abuse reporting laws were being amended to require the reporting of child neglect, including emotional neglect.) Thus, responsibility for AFDC children whose needs were not being met by their parents was assumed by the newly expanded child protection system.

There was a major difference, however, between how the child protection system and the welfare system handle these cases. The welfare caseworker saw the family as the client, and was inclined to view poor child-rearing as a correlate of poverty, requiring aid to the family as a unit. The child protective worker, on the other hand, rightly sees the child as the client, with poor child-rearing as a reason for coercive state intervention. And, most significantly, the two types of caseworkers had entirely different orientations to foster care and court ordered removal. Welfare caseworkers were rarely in court; they were not trained—nor deployed—toward easy access to court and court ordered removal of children from the home. Child protective workers are.

In the context of heightened concern for the "abused" child, giving child protective agencies responsibility for these poverty-related cases of social deprivation inexorably led to more poor children being placed in foster care. (In addition, federal funding for foster care, rather than for in-home services, created an added incentive to resort to foster care.)

In a paper for the U.S. Advisory Board on Child Abuse and Neglect, Leroy Pelton wrote that, ". . . the most effective way to reduce child abuse and neglect would be to raise family income."[60] If only it were that simple.

Normal A. Polansky, Regent's Professor of Social Work at the University of Georgia, is the nation's foremost expert on the relationship between poverty and child maltreatment. Through 15 years of research, he and his colleagues have concluded that the poverty/child maltreatment connection is a complex interaction: "parental personality plays a major role in determining how much income is available [to a family], as well as how it is handled."[61] Polansky's research depicts maltreating parents as

> a group of people with a modal personality: less able to love, less capable of working productively, less open about their feelings, more prone to living planlessly and impulsively, but also susceptible to psychological symptoms and to phases of passive inactivity and numb fatalism. The image is one of men and women who do not cope well with life.[62]

These parents are extremely difficult to reach, let alone successfully treat. As Polansky concludes, programs "aimed simply at increasing income will not solve the problem of child neglect."[63]

Thinking Long Term

If these families are to be helped, they will need long-term assistance. Unfortunately, child protective agencies can rarely provide intensive services over the long haul, even if that is merely defined as over 90 days. Propelled by a combination of budgetary constraints, misplaced faith in our ability to help deeply troubled clients, and single-minded prescriptions, child welfare agencies are focusing more and more on short-term services and treatment interventions.

In fact, it has even come into vogue to support short-term services like Homebuilders, the first family preservation program. There are times in people's lives when an immediate and decisive intervention can redirect their life course. Such crisis-oriented interventions can often accomplish beneficial change in family functioning more effectively—and more economically—than can long-term, intensive services. This is the essential, theoretical core of programs such as Homebuilders, and it is valid. We have a name for the process: "crisis intervention."

Many other families known to child welfare agencies, however, cannot be helped so easily and so quickly. They have more deep-seated problems, with roots in a host of social, economic, and familial troubles—and often going back many generations. For these families, to think that sustainable change can occur in 30 days, in 60 days, or in 90 days is wishful thinking. Worse, it undermines support for the kinds of on-going efforts that must be made on behalf of these deeply troubled families.

There is an analogy here. It is unpleasant to talk about it this way, but if you accept that some of these clients have severe emotional handicaps as real as the physical disabilities that other people face, then picture a world in which we give someone a wheelchair, for 30 days or 60 days or 90 days—and then take it away. In child welfare work, this is what happens all too often.

When I was first appointed director of the National Center on Child Abuse and Neglect, I visited an inner-city multiservice treatment center. The center had a wonderful therapeutic day-care nursery and a counseling program for some relatively dysfunctional families. After the program had been set up, the staff realized that the three-room apartment over the day-care center could be used as a residential facility for severely dysfunctional families. Their plan was to place a family in the apartment and to nurture the family with services until it no longer needed their help—and then to move in another family, and then another family, and so on.

I visited this center about three years after it had opened. The same family that had moved in three years earlier was still living there. The parents were coping well, I should add, and were taking proper care of their children. But, speaking metaphorically, they were still in the wheelchair. They could have been moved out of the apartment but, and this is the point, they still would have needed sustained support and supervision.

To help families like this one—and there are more of them than any of us would like to acknowledge—we must develop an infrastructure of long-term services. There is no magic about how to do this. The answer comes from the past, from the types of services that we have let atrophy in recent years.

In most communities, for example, the public child welfare agency used to maintain a "family service" or "preventive service" unit for long-term family supervision. Never well funded, these units have shrunk considerably as agencies have responded to the often crushing burden of investigating an ever-increasing number of reports of suspected child abuse and neglect.

In-home services have likewise suffered. Homemakers, for example, were always in short supply, and many questioned how they were used. Nevertheless, most public child welfare agencies once could place homemakers with troubled families for extended periods of time. Now, budgets for homemaker services have all but withered away.

In thinking about long-term services, however, it is a mistake to think solely about what child welfare agencies can provide. At some point, child welfare agencies need to be able to turn families over to less intensive, more voluntary, community-based service programs.

As mentioned above, caseworkers used to be assigned to every AFDC family, and these caseworkers used to visit the families at home on a regular basis. There were, of course, abuses of the process: Many of us remember the notorious bed checks. Some of these workers thought their only job was to enforce the man-in-the-house rule, but many more saw themselves as helpers, as facilitators, and as encouragers of improvements in their clients' lives. Many assessed the functioning of the families on their caseloads to determine which needed on-going supervision and support. For these families, caseworkers made sure that the children got to school, even if that meant signing them up themselves; made sure that children were immunized, even if that meant going with the family to the clinic; and made sure that a host of other needs were also met.

With the separation of income maintenance and social services in the mid 1970s, this capability to provide on-going and noncategorical social services was lost. It is time to build a new and improved version of this lapsed infrastructure. Such preventive and supportive services would help families across the spectrum of social welfare programs, including AFDC, Medicaid, Food Stamps, and WIC. This is the only way to provide coherent and coordinated long-term services to disadvantaged and at-risk families.

The challenge would be to build a program that is capable of both sustaining the long-term participation of the mothers and achieving some constructive change in their behavior. Developing plans for such a program would be a major objective for the project and, although much work still needs to be done, the program's essential elements would probably include: *educational services,* including classes in cooking and housekeeping, literacy, and child development and parenting; *child care* for the mothers while they are in classes, work, or other activities; *health services* for the mothers and the children; some form of *home visitation* for families at risk of other social problems; sadly, for a large group, *drug and alcohol abuse treatment services; antismoking services;* and finally, *contraceptive services,* especially for the younger mothers. (These latter services should be voluntary in every sense of the word, but they should be provided with a clear message that, just as doing drugs is stupid, so is having another child out of wedlock.)

One important element of this service would be a modified version of a home-visitor service, an idea that C. Henry Kempe personally nurtured for many years and that was recently endorsed by the Federal Advisory Board on Child Abuse and Neglect. I say modified because I think that the home visitors should be an adjunct to the standard package of child welfare/child protective services. In addition, an attempt should be made to recruit entry-level staff who have more in common with the families they are seeking to help, that is, who share similar social and economic backgrounds as their clients.

The base for such a program could be the expanded Head Start program, which every-one seems to support. There is even a name for the revised approach, "two-generation programs," and it has three interrelated elements: (1) reaching disadvantaged children much earlier with more intensive developmental services, (2) helping low-income parents to nurture and teach their own children, and (3) encouraging unemployed parents to work or continue their education.

Finally, humility and caution should infuse any new effort to create such a service structure. The problems faced by poor families make action along the lines described in this [reading] necessary, but too many questions remain unanswered to rush headlong into radically new programs. The history of social engineering is strewn with examples of perverse and unintended consequences from even the most promising of programs.

Planning should be based on properly controlled, multiyear experiments to determine the effects of new policies. Tentative as it may seem, we should adopt a step-by-step approach, securing sound successes and avoiding over-promising and over-reaching. After all, we are tinkering with the lives of some of the most deprived and the least powerful among us.

ENDNOTES

1. As contrasted to annual "incidence," which would count the total number of "incidents." An incidence study would add five incidents to its count if a child was abused five times during a year, while a prevalence study would add just one child to its count. The difference, obviously, could result in widely different counts, which, as we will see, seems to be distorting official reporting statistics.
2. This is a substantial and confusing difference, since some states include all children in the family automatically, whether or not they have actually been abused or neglected.
3. Westat, Inc., "The National Study of the Incidence and Severity of Child Abuse and Neglect," (Washington, D.C.: National Center on Child Abuse and Neglect, 1981).

4. The original report for this study contained inaccurate information because of weighting errors by Westat. The revised report is: Andrea Sedlak, "National Incidence and Prevalence of Child Abuse and Neglect: 1988, Revised Report" (Rockville, MD: Westat, September 1991).

5. The U.S. Department of Health and Human Services, National Center on Child Abuse and Neglect, *The Third National Incidence Study of Child Abuse and Neglect: Final Report (NIS-3)* (Washington, D.C.: General Printing Office, 1996).

6. Actually, the professionals were not asked the ultimate question of whether the children appeared to be "abused" or "neglected." Instead, they were asked to identify children with certain, specified harms or conditions which were then decoded into a count of various types of child abuse and neglect.

7. For a further discussion of the findings of the third incidence study, see Douglas J. Besharov and Jacob W. Dembosky, "Child Abuse: Threat or Menace?" *Slate,* October 4, 1996.

8. See Appendix for more detailed description of the national incidence studies' definitions of maltreatment by types and levels of severity.

9. The U.S. Department of Health and Human Services, National Center on Child Abuse and Neglect, *The Third National Incidence Study of Child Abuse and Neglect: Final Report (NIS-3)* (Washington, D.C.: General Printing Office, 1996), pp. 3–5.

10. The U.S. Department of Health and Human Services, National Center on Child Abuse and Neglect, *The Third National Incidence Study of Child Abuse and Neglect: Final Report (NIS-3)* (Washington, D.C.: General Printing Office, 1996), pp. 2–9 (emphasis added).

11. The U.S. Department of Health and Human Services, National Center on Child Abuse and Neglect, *The Third National Incidence Study of Child Abuse and Neglect: Final Report (NIS-3)* (Washington, D.C.: General Printing Office, 1996), pp. 3–19.

12. For a further discussion of the implications of findings in the third incidence study, see Douglas J. Besharov and Jacob W. Dembosky, "Child Abuse: Threat or Menace?" *Slate,* October 4, 1996.

13. Andrea Sedlak, "Supplementary Analyses of Data on the National Incidence of Child Abuse and Neglect, Revised Report" (Rockville, MD: Westat, 1991), pp. 2–15. The percentages add to over 100, because one calculation was made for children falling within each applicable category of maltreatment and a separate one was made for the total number of maltreated children.

14. Ibid., pp. 2–15.

15. Ibid., pp. 2–7, 2–15.

16. The estimated number of maltreated children increased from 625,100 children in 1980 to 931,000 in 1986. Over 90 percent of this increase was among moderate cases. A proportion of these moderate cases, however, were cases of sexual abuse, which, for the reasons described above, might more properly be classified as "serious." Unfortunately, Westat's published report does not provide sufficient information to enable us to exclude sexual abuse cases from the increase in moderate cases. Andrea Sedlak, "National Incidence and Prevalence of Child Abuse and Neglect," pp. 3–11.

17. Ibid., pp. 3–12.

18. Andrea Sedlak, *National Incidence and Prevalence of Child Abuse and Neglect: 1988 Revised Report* (Rockville, MD: Westat, 1991), pp. 3–6.

19. For a further discussion of questions raised by the NIS-3, see Douglas J. Besharov and Jacob W. Dembosky, "Child Abuse: Threat or Menace?" *Slate,* October 4, 1996.

20. The U.S. Department of Health and Human Services, National Center on Child Abuse and Neglect, *The Third National Incidence Study of Child Abuse and Neglect: Final Report (NIS-3)* (Washington, D.C.: General Printing Office, 1996), pp. 2–9; and U.S. Department of Health and Human Services, National Center on Child Abuse and Neglect, *Executive Summary of the Third National Incidence Study of Child Abuse and Neglect (NIS-3)* (Washington, D.C.: General Printing Office, 1996), p. 5.

21. *See generally,* Douglas Besharov, *Recognizing Child Abuse: A Guide for the Concerned* (New York: Free Press, 1990).

22. The two major efforts were conducted for the federal government's National Center on Child Abuse and Neglect by the American Humane Association (1974 to 1987) and Walter R. McDonald & Associates, in conjunction with Bowers & Associates and the American Humane Association (1990 to present).

23. Walter R. McDonald & Associates, et al., "National Child Abuse and Neglect Reporting Data

System: Working paper 2" (Washington, D.C.: National Center on Child Abuse and Neglect, May 1993), pp. 4–7.

24. Estimates based on Ching-Tung Wang and Deborah Daro, "Current Trends in Child Abuse Reporting and Fatalities: The Results of the 1996 Annual Fifty State Survey" (Chicago: National Committee to Prevent Child Abuse, April 1997), Table 1 (3,126,000 reports of abuse and neglect); and U.S. Department of Health and Human Services, Administration on Children, Youth, and Families, *Child Maltreatment 1997: Reports from the States to the National Child Abuse and Neglect Data System* (Washington, D.C.: U.S. Government Printing Office, 1999), p. 3–2 ("nearly three million children were reported to CPS agencies as alleged victims of maltreament").

25. American Association for Protecting Children, "Highlights of Official Neglect and Abuse Reporting: 1986" (Denver, CO: American Humane Association, 1988), p. 22.

26. Andrea Sedlak, "National Incidence and Prevalence of Child Abuse and Neglect," p. 6–23.

27. Andrea Sedlak, "Supplementary Analyses of Data on the National Incidence of Child Abuse and Neglect," pp. 3–19.

28. For a further discussion of the findings of the third incidence study, see Douglas J. Besharov and Jacob W. Dembosky, "Child Abuse: Threat or Menace?" *Slate,* October 4, 1996.

29. Federal expenditures for foster care, child welfare, and related services, which make up less than 50 percent of total expenditures (federal plus state) for these services: In 1998, they were: $292 million for Title IV–B child welfare services; $1.66 billion for Title IV–E foster care maintenance; $1.7 billion for foster care administration and training; $70 million for Title IV–E independent living program; and $495 million for Title IV–E adoption assistance, totaling $4,217 million. House Committee on Ways and Means *1998 Green Book* (Washington, D.C.: U.S. Government Printing Office, 1998), Table 11–2. In addition, states may use a portion of the $2.2 billion federal Social Services Block Grant for such services, though detailed data on these expenditures are not available. Additional federal appropriations will fund family preservation and support services (an estimated $239 million in 1998). *Budget of the United States Government: Appendix, Fiscal Year 2000* (Washington, D.C.: U.S. Government Printing Office, 1999), pp. 456, 458. In addition, $68 million was appropriated in FY 1999 for the Child Abuse and Neglect Prevention and Treatment Act (CAPTA) to carry out Title I (General Program) and Title II (Community-Based Family Resource and Support Grants). The Child Abuse and Neglect Prevention and Treatment Act, *Amendments of 1996 (P.L. 104-235, 10/3/96),* U.S. Code Citation: 42 USC 5101 *et seq;* 42 USC 5116 *et seq.*

30. Estimates based on U.S. Department of Health and Human Services, Administration on Children, Youth, and Families, *Child Maltreatment 1997: Reports from the States to the National Child Abuse and Neglect Data System* (Washington, D.C.: U.S. Government, Printing Office, 1999) p. 6–1 (1,196 fatalities); Ching-Tung Wang and Deborah Daro, "Current Trends in Child Abuse Reporting and Fatalities: The Results of the 1996 Annual Fifty State Survey" (Chicago: National Committee to Prevent Child Abuse, April 1997), Table 2 (1,046 fatalities); and Andrea Sedlak, *National Incidence of Child Abuse and Neglect: 1988 Revised Report,* pp. 3–10 (1,000 fatalities).

31. N.Y.S. Department of Social Services, "Child Protective Services in New York State: 1979 Annual Report" (New York, 1980), Table 8.

32. Based on comparison data from "Vital Statistics of the United States for 1980: Advanced Report of Final Mortality Statistics" (Washington, D.C.: Government Printing Office, 1980).

Based on comparison calculations from National Center for Health Statistics, *National Vital Statistics Reports,* Vol. 47, No. 19 (Hyattsville, MD: National Center for Health Statistics, 1999), Table 8. The six leading causes of death for children were: (1) accidents (10,752); (2) neoplasms (1,629); (3) congenital anomalies and perinatal conditions (1,111); (4) child maltreatment fatalities (1,046); (5) diseases (788); and (6) homicide (656). [Note that homicide would be the fifth leading cause of death if it included the 176 homicide deaths listed as Child Abuse Fatality on the death certificate. We removed this from the figure to avoid duplication and based the number of child-maltreatment fatalities on the data from NCPCA (1997).]

33. U.S. Department of Health and Human Services, Administration on Children, Youth, and Families, *Child Maltreatment 1997: Reports from the States to the National Child Abuse and Neglect Data System* (Washington D.C.: U.S. Government Printing Office, 1999), pp. 3–4, 6–1, reporting that, of 1,485,658 investigations in 46 states, only 33.8 percent were "substantiated" or "indicated," 56.2 percent were "unsubstantiated" 8.1 percent were "other," and 1.9 percent were "closed without a finding." *See also* Ching-Tung Wang and Deborah Daro, "Current Trends in Child Abuse Reporting and Fatalities: The Results of the 1996 Annual Fifty State Survey" (Chicago: National Committee to Prevent Child Abuse, April 1997), Table 2, based on data from 37 states, 31 percent of the reports of maltreatment were "substantiated" or "indicated."

34. A rough estimate calculated using 1990 data from the Illinois State Registry by Bong Joo Lee, Research Associate, Chapin Hall Center for Children, phone conversation with Lisa Laumann, 26 April 1994.

35. In its study, AHA found that about 25 percent of all reports to child protective agencies were repeat reports. AHA also cites a 20 percent duplication rate for official reports analyzed in Westat's second incidence study. American Association for Protecting Children, "Highlights of Official Aggregate Neglect and Abuse Reporting: 1986" (Denver, CO: American Humane Association, 1988), p. 9.

36. Walter R. McDonald & Associates, et al., "National Child Abuse and Neglect Data System: Working Paper 2," p. 21.

37. Andrea Sedlak, "National Incidence and Prevalence of Child Abuse and Neglect," pp. 5–27.

38. Virginia Child Protective Services, "Virginia Cares About its Children: 1991–1992 Annual Report" (Richmond, VA, 1992), p. 10.

39. American Humane Association, "National Analysis of Official Child Neglect and Abuse Reporting" (Boulder, CO: American Humane Association, 1976), pp. 13–14.

40. This figure refers to first-born children born in 1988. Of the children who had a founded report of maltreatment at some point in their first five years of life, 48 percent also received AFDC at some point during this time. Robert Goerge, et al., "A Longitudinal Analysis of Public Aid and Child Welfare Experiences of Illinois Families with Children" (Report prepared for the American Enterprise Institute, November 1993), p. 14.

41. American Association for Protecting Children, "Highlights of Official Child Neglect and Abuse Reporting: 1984" (Denver, CO: American Humane Association, 1986), p. 28.

42. Leroy Pelton, *For Reasons of Poverty* (New York: Praeger Press, 1989), p. 39.

43. Title IV–E funding supports the placement and maintenance of AFDC children in foster care.

44. Although the data used to determine these figures were from different years and were not calculated in the same manner, these differences do not appear to bias the findings. The data on the number of Title IV–E eligible children were from FY 1998 and were given as an average monthly number. The foster care data were from October 1, 1998 to March 31, 1999 (period #99A) and were given as a snapshot of all the foster care children served on March 31, 1999. The calculated percentages were determined by dividing the number of Title IV–E eligible children by the total number of children in foster care. This method was used to calculate the national percentage of Title IV–E eligible children as well as the state percentages of Title IV–E eligible children. Source: For data on the number of children in foster care, see U.S. Department of Health and Human Services, Administration on Children, Youth, and Families, Children's Bureau, Adoption and Foster Care Analysis and Reporting System (AFCARS), #99A; and for data on the number of Title IV–E eligible children, see U.S. Department of Health and Human Services, Administration on Children, Youth, and Families, Children's Bureau, Adoption and Foster Care Analysis and Reporting System (AFCARS), *Title IV–E Financial Report.*

45. This study looked at first-born children born in 1988. Robert Goerge, et al., "A Longitudinal Analysis of Public Aid and Child Welfare Experiences of Illinois Families with Children," p. 15.

46. Minnesota Department of Human Services, "Child Maltreatment Report: 1982–1991" (St. Paul, MN, 1993), pp. 48–49.

47. N.J. Department of Human Services, "Child Abuse and Neglect in New Jersey: 1992 Annual Report" (Trenton, NJ, July 1993), p. 23.

48. Andrea Sedlak, "Supplementary Analyses of Data on the National Incidence of Child Abuse and Neglect," pp. 5–2.

49. These figures represent the proportion of families that had their first child in 1988 that had founded reports of child abuse or neglect within five years of the birth of the child. Robert Goerge, et al., "A Longitudinal Analysis of Public Aid and Child Welfare Experiences of Illinois Families with Children," Table 49.

50. These figures represent the proportion of welfare families who had founded reports of child maltreatment at any time in the four-year period, 1986 to 1990. Robert Goerge, et al., "The Point-in-Time Multiple Service Use of Illinois Families with Children" (Report prepared for the American Enterprise Institute, Washington, D.C., August 1993), Table 19.

51. Leroy Pelton, *for Reasons of Poverty,* p. 63.

52. Not included are the percentages of American Indian, Eskimo, Aleut, Asian, and Pacific Islander children under age 18. Together, these comprise the remaining 5 percent. U.S. Bureau of the Census, *Statistical Abstract of the United States: 1998* (118th edition.) Washington, D.C., 1998, Table No. 22.

53. Toshio Tatara. "U.S. Child Substitute Care Flow Data and the Race/Ethnicity of Children in Care for FY 95, Along with Recent Trends in the U.S. Child Substitute Care Populations," p. 2.

54. Robert Goerge, et al., "A Longitudinal Analysis of Public Aid and Child Welfare Experiences of Illinois Families with Children," Table 48.

55. Confidential report held by author.

56. See, e.g., Region VI Resource Center on Child Abuse, "Child Deaths in Texas," (1981), p. 26; Mayberry, "Child Protective Services in New York City: An Analysis of Case Management" (Albany, NY: Welfare Research Inc., 1979), p. 109.

57. Ching-Tung Wang and Deborah Daro, "Current Trends in Child Abuse Reporting and Fatalities: The Results of the 1996 Annual Fifty State Survey" (Chicago: National Committee to Prevent Child Abuse, April 1997), Table 2.

58. Giovannoni & Billingsley, "Child Neglect Among the Poor: A Study of Parental Adequacy in Families of Three Ethnic Groups," *Child Welfare* 49 (1970): 196, 204.

59. The 15 percent figure is the upper bound, calculated by dividing the number of substantiated cases in 1997 (597,470) by the average monthly AFDC caseload in FY 1997 (3,945,000). This almost certainly exaggerates the number of welfare families reported for abuse or neglect because (1) it assumes that *all* of the 597,470 cases were from families on welfare; and (2) it underestimates the number of families that received AFDC for FY 1997 because the average monthly number of families is a point-in-time figure and does not reflect the total number of families that received AFDC throughout the year.

60. Leroy Pelton, "The Role of Material Factors in Child Abuse and Neglect," in the U.S. Advisory Board on Child Abuse and Neglect Report, "Neighbors Helping Neighbors: A New National Strategy for the Protection of Children" (Washington, D.C., 1993).

61. Norman Polansky, et al., *Damaged Parents: An Anatomy of Child Neglect* (Chicago: University of Chicago Press, 1981), p. 25.

62. Ibid., p. 109.

63. Ibid., p. 25.

CHAPTER 12

Divorce

[handwritten note: emotional, legal, coparental and economic divorce]

The process of adjustment to divorce has many facets. In my sociology of the family textbook, I wrote about the emotional divorce, the legal divorce, the coparental divorce, and the economic divorce. Others have written about the "community divorce," involving the loss of friends and neighbors, and the "psychic divorce," involving regaining autonomy.[1] The readings in this section focus on two of these aspects.

The first is the coparental divorce. One of the important postdivorce tasks is for the ex-spouses to work out arrangements for raising the children. Central to this task, obviously, is the physical location of the children: are they to live with the mother, the father, or split their time between both? By far the most common arrangement is for the children to live most of the time with their mothers and visit their fathers occasionally—perhaps every other weekend and during vacations. This arrangement is called maternal physical custody. Less common is pa-

ternal physical custody, in which fathers are the primary caretakers for their children. It is still rare enough that it often signals a mother's serious problem, such as depression or alcoholism. The third arrangement is joint physical custody, in which the children spend substantial amounts of time at each parent's home. It only occurs in a minority of families in large part because it requires substantial communication and cooperation between the ex-spouses.

In *Dividing the Child: Social and Legal Dilemmas of Custody,* a northern California study of over 1,000 families that initiated divorces in 1984 and 1985, 66 percent agreed that the children would live with the mother, 8 percent agreed that the children would live with the father, and 20 percent agreed on joint physical custody. (The remaining families had other arrangements or did not specify the arrangement.) The California families were interviewed three times over a three-year period. The authors, Eleanor E. Maccoby, a developmental psychologist, and Robert H. Mnookin, a lawyer, studied a broad range of postdivorce issues. In the following excerpt, they discuss the process by which parents must adjust their childrearing activity from the jointly

---

[1] Paul Bohannan, "The Six Stations of Divorce," in Paul Bohannan, ed., *Divorce and After* (New York: Anchor Books, 1971), pp. 33–62.

supportive style of most married couples to the individualized styles that divorced parents adopt.

The second aspect for which a reading is presented is the economic divorce. Probably no other consequence of divorce for adults has received as much attention as the sharp economic slide experienced by many women. The reasons are simple: husbands tend to earn more than their wives, and after divorce many ex-husbands pay little or no child support to their ex-wives. Some divorced wives may have done little or no work for pay while raising the couple's children. So after the breakup of their marriages, women frequently find that their standard of living plummets. Terry Arendell interviewed 60 divorced women in the San Francisco area in 1983 for her book, *Mothers and Divorce: Legal, Economic, and Social Dilemmas.* All had been divorced for at least two years (the median was four years), had custody of at least one child, and had considered themselves middle-class during their marriages. Nearly all of the women reported sharp economic declines. Their stories are told in the excerpt reprinted here.

Keep in mind that Arendell's subjects aren't representative of all divorced mothers. For one thing, she excluded women who had remarried, and remarriage is the main route out of economic decline for divorced women. So, almost by definition, her sample overrepresents divorced women with long-lasting financial problems. Also, women who shared physical custody of their children with their ex-husbands—an arrangement that typically eases the financial burdens on mothers—were underrepresented. (Only three women shared custody.) In addition, some of the women responded to advertisements, bulletin board notices, and even a newspaper article asking divorced mothers to participate in the project. It is possible that the women who replied overrepresented those with poignant stories to tell. Nevertheless, there are many divorced mothers in America with situations as moving as the ones captured by Arendell in her book.

The Parental Divorce: Coparenting Before and After Separation

Eleanor E. Maccoby and Robert H. Mnookin

While parents are dealing with the distress of the spousal divorce and the relentless pressures of the economic divorce, they must also redefine their parental roles and responsibilities. We now turn to the parental divorce, and examine in some detail the ways in which divorcing parents characteristically must modify their old patterns . . . In focusing on this central concern of our study, how divorce changes parental roles and responsibilities, we begin by considering in some detail what coparenting involves in predivorce families. Then we examine the changes in the coparental relationship that occur when parents move into separate households while each continues to see the children. From the perspective of family systems theory, we consider the implications of these changes for postseparation family organization and therapeutic approaches.

COPARENTING IN PREDIVORCE FAMILIES: THE PARENTAL ALLIANCE

In the past, most research on how parents socialize a child focused on the mother–child pair. More recently, the role of fathers in child rearing has been given more attention, and two aspects of the paternal role in the family have been emphasized: the father's role in giving support (both emotional and material) to the

Eleanor E. Maccoby and Robert H. Mnookin, "The Parental Divorce: Co-parenting Before and After Separation" from *Dividing the Child: Social and Legal Dilemmas of Custody,* pp. 24–39. Copyright © 1992 by the President and Fellows of Harvard College. Reprinted with the permission of Harvard University Press.

mother as major child rearer, and his direct interactions with the children. The interest in fathers' role in child rearing emerged partly in response to pressure for gender equality. Feminists asked why women should be the ones primarily responsible for child-care duties. Because women have traditionally occupied the primary child-rearing role in all human societies—particularly for young children—one question posed for child development researchers was whether this had to be so. In a sense, the question many studies addressed was: can men "mother" as well as women? Work by Parke and O'Leary (1976) illustrates this approach.[1] They observed fathers and mothers interacting one-on-one with infants, and found fathers to be as skillful in bottle-feeding, and as gentle and responsive, as were mothers.

Although it appears that fathers, like mothers, can successfully nurture even very young children, in most American families the two parents do not have the same functions in child rearing. When fathers are asked what it means to be a father, they are likely to mention first their role as breadwinner. Studies show that most two-parent families with young children—even those where both parents are working—adopt a division of labor such that the mother assumes more responsibility for child care and household management while the father brings in a higher portion of the family income. If either parent is to reduce the time spent in outside employment in order to care for children, many families find that it makes more economic sense for the family as a whole for the mother to be the one who does so.

Lamb and colleagues (1987), summarizing a considerable body of research, report that although there is great variation among families in the extent of the father's involvement in child rearing, fathers on the average are considerably less involved even when mothers are working. On average, fathers are "available" (that is, present and accessible) to their children for about half as much time as are mothers; mothers spend about three times as much time in face-to-face interaction with children as do fathers. And mothers are overwhelmingly more likely to be the person *responsible* for the children—the only person at home with them, the one who stays home from work with them if they are ill, the person who arranges the child care, makes medical appointments, takes the children to lessons and doctor's appointments, decides about their clothing, and so forth. In terms of the time spent as the responsible parent, mothers outweigh fathers nine to one.

When one considers the "role overload" that many women experience when they are both working outside the home and carrying the major responsibility for child care, it may come as a surprise to learn that many are not enthusiastic about their husbands' taking on a larger role with the children. Yet this is the case (Pleck, 1983), and there is evidence that when economic circumstances force a reversal of roles—with the mother as the major wage earner and the father staying home with the children—mothers express considerable dissatisfaction with the way their husbands are managing the household. It would seem that many if not most women wish to retain their dominant role in the management of household and children.

While the division of child-care labor has been extensively studied, the nature of parental cooperation in dealing with children has not been examined in as much detail. However, family systems theorists have contributed to our understanding of some of the elements of coparenting relations. They tell us, first of all, that families are indeed systems, having their own dynamic properties, boundaries, and subsystems. In well-functioning two-parent families, the strongest and most cohesive dyad is the one between the mother (wife) and father (husband) (Feldman & Gehring, 1988). Children perceive the parental pair as jointly exercising authority, and as being affectively close.

Patricia Minuchin (1985), in discussing the family, points out that much interaction between parents and children goes on when both parents are present, and the mother-father-child triad has its own dynamics in the socialization of the child. Minuchin gives an example of an interaction that was observed while the parents of a young child were being interviewed:

> The two-year-old knocks over a box of chalks and they spill out onto the carpet.
>
> Mother [soft voice]: "Brian, pick them up, please." (She turns back to adult conversation.)
>
> Father [voice raised slightly]: "Brian, put the chalks in the box." [Pause; voice stronger]: "Brian, put the chalks in the box!"
>
> Mother: "Yeah come on. Don't muck up the carpet." [Adult conversation resumes. Child is examining the chalk.]
>
> Father: "Brian, listen! You're not supposed to have the chalk on the carpet. Now pick them up. Come on."
>
> Child: "I'm doing it."
>
> Father: "You're not. You're playing. Come, pick them up first. Quickly. If I get up, you know you will. Now come on!"
>
> Adult discussion resumes. Mother glances at child, stands up and goes to him, kneeling and talking softly. As he dallies over the chalk, she says, "Don't throw them. Put away all of them." Father, seated, says "Come on," and watches as the mother tells the child he will have to sit on her lap and not play if he doesn't pick them all up. The child says, "I want to play," and gathers the chalk up more quickly. Father relaxes and mother returns to the adults. (Minuchin, 1985, p. 296)

The dynamics of this interaction are complex. Possibly, the mother sees a confrontation brewing between the father and child, and moves to forestall it. But the major feature of the interaction is that the two parents are working together in the exercise of joint authority.

A similar dynamic may be seen in the following incident, recently observed by Maccoby:

> Six-year-old girl exuberantly runs out the back door of her home, bumping into the sliding screen

door and knocking it off its track. Father gets up to reset the screen, saying irritably:

"Janie, that's the *third* time you've knocked that door off."

Janie: "I didn't do it."

Father: "Yes you did!"

Janie: "No I didn't!"

Father leaves door, goes to girl, holds her shoulders firmly, looks directly into her face, and says loudly: "Don't tell me you didn't do it. I *saw* you. You didn't mean to, but you *did* do it."

Child wails and goes to mother. Father returns to door. Mother puts arm around daughter, rubs her back, says: "It's all right, honey. You didn't mean to. But you have to be more careful. So daddy won't always have to be fixing the screen door."

Here the roles of the two parents were different—mother as comfort-giver, father as disciplinarian. Also, their momentary socialization goals were somewhat different: the father was focusing on truth telling, the mother on being considerate of another family member. Yet they were mutually supportive. In many families, instances of joint parenting such as these may be fairly rare—most of the time, only one parent at a time directly interacts with a child, although in family dinner-table conversations, three-way exchanges do occur. The point is, however, that it may not take many instances of jointly exercised parental authority for the children to form a picture of their parents as a mutually reinforcing team.

Most parental couples not only adopt a division of labor in terms of child-rearing roles and responsibilities; the father and mother may also have different characteristic styles of interaction with children. In both the vignettes, the mothers were to some extent mediating between the father and the child. That is, they softened the impact of the fathers' power-assertive style, while supporting him in his attempts to teach relevant lessons to the child. There is evidence that in most families mothers do more of the work of sustaining positive moods among family members than fathers do; fathers are observed gener-

ally to be more power-assertive in the way they speak to children (Gleason, 1987).

But fathers do much more than merely play the "heavy" role of authority figure. From the earliest period of the child's life, fathers typically spend a higher proportion of their interactive time in play than mothers do (Parke & Tinsley, 1981; Russell & Russell, 1987), and they do more joking. While father-child play involves more roughhousing, mother-child play involves more reciprocal role-taking in fantasy scripts (Maccoby & Jacklin, 1983). In addition, mothers are the primary comfort-givers for children at times of distress. Moreover, they chat more with them, and spend more time listening to what they have to say. Indeed, mothers appear to be better able to understand what a very young child is saying at a time when the child's speech can be quite unclear (Gleason, 1987). Russell and Russell (1987) report that although mothers issue more directions than fathers to school-age children (second-graders)—for example, telling the child to take a bath, come to the table, put away toys—mothers also consult the child's viewpoint more, and respond more positively than fathers do when the child makes an independent decision. Perhaps as a consequence, the children in their study expressed their feelings more freely to their mothers.

Our interpretation of the existing research is that while the affectional bonds are normally very strong between the children and each of the parents, typically there is more reciprocal give-and-take between mothers and children in the course of daily life, even though fathers may be the favorite playmates. One corollary of the maternal style is that mothers usually know more about the child's interests, friends, preferences, and goals. Adolescents report that their mothers know them better than their fathers do, even though they regard their two parents as equally important as standard-setters (Youniss & Smollar, 1985). In many households, then, the two parents play complementary roles in the lives of their children.

How a parent interacts with a child may depend, according to some research, on whether the parent is alone with the child. Per Gjerde (1986) has observed mothers and fathers interacting with their teenage children, either one-on-one or in the mother-father-child trio. He found that a parent's mode of interaction with the children does change somewhat, depending on whether the other parent is present. Fathers appeared to be somewhat inhibited in the presence of the child's mother, and when alone with the child, interacted more freely and became more relaxed and humorous. When both parents are present many fathers regard the management of the children as more in their wives' domain than their own, and they are careful about invading her territory. Mothers, on the other hand, interacted with teenage sons more comfortably and more assertively when their husbands were present. Thus, fathers may serve as "backup" authority, helping to keep children—especially sons—in line. Many a boy has heard his father say: "Young man, I don't want to hear you talking to your mother like that." Lytton (1979), in observing parents with much younger children, found that mothers were more effective in controlling their 2-year-old sons when the father was present than when he was not.

We do not have comparable information on the effect of a mother's presence on children's compliance to their fathers' demands, but suspect that her presence would not make as much difference, considering that there is evidence that fathers are usually more successful in exacting compliance even when the mother is not there. For example, in observations of mothers and fathers interacting separately with a preschool child, Hetherington and colleagues (1982) found that children complied more readily to a father's than a mother's demands, in both intact and divorced families. Furthermore, it has been reported that school-age children treat fathers as though they were more powerful than their mothers (Cowan, Drinkard, & MacGavin, 1984). Thus, mothers on the average may derive more benefit from their spouse's authority backup than do fathers.

During marriage, successful parents forge a parental alliance. When parents are closely allied, they make most decisions concerning the children jointly; or at least, they have an understanding concerning which decisions need to be discussed and which can be left to either parent acting singly. Allied parents also relieve each other of child-care duties when one parent is ill, overstressed, or subject to special demands outside the home. At such times, the other parent will step in to manage or entertain the children. When the children simply need someone to stay with them at times when no formal child care has been arranged, one parent will usually "sit" with the children so that the other can do necessary errands, or participate in out-of-home functions or recreational activities to which the children cannot be taken.

The parental alliance also involves agreeing on rules for the children, backing up the other parent's authority, and conveying an atmosphere of mutual respect and affection. Even in well-functioning families, of course, parents do not always manage to present a united front, and children become expert at finding weaknesses in the parental alliance. As they grow older, children learn which parent is more likely to soften a particular rule under particular circumstances. They try out "divide and conquer" tactics: for example, saying, "But Mom, Daddy said I could." They quickly learn whether their parents are communicating well enough so that each knows what the other has demanded or decided. Parents with a strong alliance learn, for their part, to respond to a child's demands with "We'll see" or "I'll talk to your mother (father)," so as to allow themselves time for working out a joint strategy.

In two-parent households, each parent may at times protect children from potentially damaging behavior by the other parent. Hetherington and colleagues (1982) have called this parental "buffering." Their research suggests that in intact families, one well-functioning parent can shield children from the risks entailed in exposure to a depressed, abusive, or neglectful parent. Parents know each other's behavior patterns well enough so that one parent can often anticipate a blowup on the part of the other parent, and may be able to forestall it. If one parent does become enraged or drunk or potentially abusive, the more stable parent may be able to get the children out of reach of the endangering one. In less extreme situations, if a parent has misgivings about something the other parent is doing vis-à-vis the children—for example, doing things that frighten them, or allowing too much or too little autonomy—there are opportunities for the parents to discuss the issue and perhaps influence each other's parental style.

COPARENTING AS THE PARENTAL ALLIANCE BREAKS UP

New Family Structures

In some divorcing families, the parental alliance has already begun to crumble before the couple actually separates. One parent may form an alliance with the child to exclude the other parent, thus forming what family therapists consider an unhealthy subsystem (Minuchin, 1985). Parents may also compete for the children's loyalty, and differences in their values and standards may have become evident to all family members. Recent evidence indicates that parents in conflict do not hold their children to as high standards as do parents who have a harmonious relationship (Goldberg, 1990). This research suggests that as the parental alliance weakens, the behavior standards for the children decline. If parents quarrel openly in front of the children, and show contempt for each other, the atmosphere of mutual respect that underlies their joint authority and effective coparenting is seriously weakened. In some families, however, the decision to separate is rather sudden (perhaps triggered by one parent's discovery of the other's extramarital af-

fair), and the parental alliance may have been well maintained up to the point of separation.

When the parents do actually separate, the parental alliance must obviously be profoundly affected. For children and adults alike, the separation of spousal roles from parental roles is difficult. The mere fact of spousal divorce means that one parent (or both) no longer considers the other lovable as a spouse. Even when a mother says to a child: "I don't love your father any more, but *you* should (may) love him," the message is a mixed one. The kind of teamwork that was illustrated in the vignettes presented earlier can hardly occur when each parent is operating from a different household.

Divorce requires that the division of child-rearing responsibilities must be renegotiated. In order to understand the degree and kind of coparenting that can occur following divorce, we now consider the nature of the postdivorce family structure or structures that take the place of the predivorce structure. When therapists or mediators deal with couples who have passed the point of attempting reconciliation, a major goal is to help the couple dampen or at least manage their interpersonal conflict so that they can complete their spousal detachment from each other while still being able to do necessary business together concerning the children. Still, there are some differences among therapists concerning the kind of family structure that should be the outcome. One set of theorists suggests that so long as a child is continuing to spend time with both parents, the child is a member of a single family structure that includes both parents. The predivorce family structure continues (or can, or should continue) as a structural entity, and is merely reorganized so that the nonresident parent becomes an extended family member in the same sense that grandparents are: living in a different household, but nevertheless linked to the resident family by family ties and obligations. A contrasting viewpoint suggests that the prior nuclear family structure no longer exists, and is replaced by *two* new structures, organized within each of the two parental households. In the case of a child who spends time in both households, the child is a member of two families.

These differences in viewpoint are more than merely semantic. They affect the way mediators and family therapists define the goals of intervention. Working from the first point of view, for example, Isaacs and colleagues (1986) say:

> We place special emphasis on problem solving—parent with parent, and parent with child—that allows family members to struggle face to face with each other during the process of reorganizing the unit. We view the immediate family (mother, father and their children) as the unit of direct intervention. (Isaacs, Montalvo, & Abelsohn, 1986, p. 5)
>
> The unit has to maintain some subsystems, shed others, and develop new ones. In working with subsystems, we follow two elementary principles: we support those that will help the family fulfill its functions, and we attempt to limit the influence of antagonistic groupings. (p. 6)
>
> Separation and divorce need not herald the death of the family. For some, separation can be a transition and not an end. The well-being of parents and children can be enhanced as the family—albeit considerably changed—attempts to remain a viable, self-propelled and interprotective unit. (p. 219)

These therapists make it clear that a guiding principle of their therapeutic efforts is to prevent either parent from "abdicating"—to keep both parents involved and functioning together as coparents.

In contrast, Preston and Madison (1984), two therapists working in the Family Court of Australia, see the postdivorce family as made up of the custodial parent and children. For a child living with the mother, the mother's household is "home" for the child, even if the child visits the father. The boundary around the old system is gone, and a new boundary is formed around the mother and children. The father does not have a place within this new boundary. His visits may be experienced as intrusions, particularly if visitation is imposed against the wishes of the pri-

mary parent. Preston and Madison argue that visitation arrangements should have rules that give the new family (that is, the mother-child dyad) control over the conditions of the father's presence in their household. They say:

> Following separation, the family boundary becomes disturbed. The departure of one spouse from the family makes this boundary diffuse; it becomes more permeable and less able to provide a sense of security and containment for the members of the family. This is because of disturbance in the spousal sub-system which is responsible for maintaining the family boundary. The important task in the initial period after separation is to reestablish the boundary around the family. Disputes over access (visitation) can serve to prevent the formation of a clear family boundary. (Preston & Madison, 1984, p. 39)

In short, Preston and Madison believe that access by the father should be limited and/or clearly regulated in the interest of strengthening the boundary around a new family structure that does not include him.[2]

We are not completely satisfied with either view about the changes in family structure. Let us consider first the most common residential situation, that in which the children are living with the mother and maintaining some degree of contact with a nonresidential father. Certainly if the father is continuing to pay child support, he is joining with the mother in the enormously important function of providing food and shelter for the family. In this sense, he continues as part of the original nuclear family. Yet in other equally important respects, he is not part of this family because of the spousal divorce. He no longer has a key to the house; he cannot arrive at the house and expect to join the family for dinner; he does not share in the plans the mother and children have for their joint activities, nor in their confidences with one another. The child's family household is not the father's "home," and normally he no longer shares in the household upkeep and chores. It has been said that home is the place where "they always have to take you in." A divorced nonresident father does not have the right to be "taken in," nor to have his needs considered by other family members, and he no longer functions as a coparent in the day-to-day rearing of the children. Indeed, it may be said that a couple's decision to divorce is in effect a decision no longer to be members of the same family.

A nonresident father is not a member of an extended family, in the same sense that grandparents are. In sociological writings, the term "extended family" usually refers to a network of kin (people related by blood, marriage, or adoption) who exchange goods and services. Thus members of the extended family might baby-sit for the nuclear family, help in finding jobs for the parents or the young people as they grow into adulthood, help to provide the down payment for a house, and so on. In addition, members of an extended family usually share important symbolic occasions: birthdays, holidays, weddings, funerals. Usually, loyalty, a common identity, and pride mark an extended family. Clearly the children's father and his parents are not part of the mother's extended family as so defined. They are kin to the *child* (related by blood ties), but not kin to the extended *family* of which the child and mother are the central system.

As we see it, divorce necessarily involves the formation of at least one new family structure, having its own boundaries. When one parent simply disappears from the children's lives at the time of divorce, the family is "reconstituted" as a single-parent family. It may later be transformed in structure once more with the addition of a stepparent. When the children continue to spend time with both parents, this need not imply that mother, father, and children are now a "reconstituted" version of the original family. True, from the *child's* standpoint, both parents (and both sets of grandparents) may still be seen as members of the child's family (Funder, 1991). But when both parents remain involved

in the children's lives following divorce, we believe that from a structural standpoint it is more accurate to say that a single family (both nuclear and extended) has been replaced by two family structures, and that the child may be a member of both.

Do any vestiges of the old boundary around the original family as a unit remain? This, we think, is a matter of degree, and varies from family to family. Clearly, it depends on whether, and in what way, the parental alliance is maintained. There may be no residual vestiges in circumstances where the divorced parents no longer communicate with one another concerning the children. On the other hand, there are situations in which divorced parents cooperate actively, attempting to coordinate rules for the children in the two households and jointly making decisions about the children's lives. Here, one aspect of the old family unit continues to exist, but the structure is qualitatively very different from its predecessor. The old family unit was one whose members lived together, shared many plans and activities with one another, and had unlimited access to one another. The new version of the original mother-father-child "unit" involves only a limited sharing of information and plans about the child (which can be seen as a limited overlap between the two family structures). Other aspects of the family life are separate, even in this "ideal" case of high parental cooperation. Even for those parents who succeed in the important task of developing a cooperative coparenting relationship, we see their parental unit not as a simple continuation of their old coparenting processes but as something that must be constructed anew to fit their greatly changed circumstances.

Single Parenting in Separate Households

We have seen that in intact families, mothers and fathers frequently have somewhat different roles and interactive styles where parenting is concerned. These differences, we believe, have implications for the way the two parents will function as single parents. In view of the division of labor that typically prevails in preseparation households, with mothers having the predominant role in child rearing, we may expect that there would be considerable continuity in the way mothers carry out parenting functions during the times when the children are with them following the separation. And indeed, Hetherington and colleagues (1982) have reported that the quality of a mother's parenting after divorce can be fairly well predicted from her preseparation parenting activities. The way divorced fathers interacted with their children when the children were with them was not so predictable, however. Fathers, as single parents, or even as visiting parents, typically have more to learn than single mothers do.

Nevertheless, for mothers there are important changes. Although the mother has the advantage of greater experience in household management and day-to-day child care, she must continue to do these things when there are increasing demands on her time for other activities (for example, increased working hours outside the home). The spousal backup for her authority is largely absent. Furthermore, children tend to believe that parenting is primarily the responsibility of mothers rather than fathers. Consequently, they do not experience (or at least, do not express) any particular indebtedness to custodial mothers for their caretaking, whereas they do express such appreciation to custodial fathers, who are seen by the children as doing something beyond what might be expected (Ambert, 1982). In short, in the eyes of children, being cared for by one's mother is a right; being cared for by one's father is more a privilege. Hence, children may feel they "owe" more respect and obedience to a custodial father, and may be less responsive to a custodial mother's attempts at control. There is reason to expect, then, that custodial mothers may encounter more difficulty in maintaining discipline. Furthermore, the additional financial pressures and the lack of a

partner to share household chores and child-care duties can produce sufficient stress to make the mother more irritable toward the children, less responsive, and less patient.[3] For some mothers, on the other hand, the father's departure from the household may relieve stress and simplify parenting.

Single fathers, we predict, will have a different set of problems during the times when they have responsibility for the children. Discipline should not pose any special difficulties for them. For nonresidential fathers who see the child only on brief weekend visits—particularly if the children do not stay overnight—the father may become mainly a "pal," playmate, or friend and not so much an important authority figure. But for fathers who have their children with them for any substantial portion of residential time, the "playmate" relationship must be transformed into a managerial one. As noted above, fathers may have an advantage in terms of the children's readiness to comply to parental directives. Hetherington and colleagues (Hetherington, Cox, & Cox, 1982) report that the young children in their study obeyed their divorced fathers more readily than their divorced mothers. However, all these fathers were noncustodial, and we have no information concerning how these influence patterns would work out with custodial fathers.

There is probably great variability among custodial fathers in what and how much they have to learn. A small group of fathers may have assumed primary parental management duties before the divorce, sometimes because their wives were unwilling or unable to assume them. For many fathers, however, assuming the primary parental role will be new. When the children are young, fathers who have not been especially vigilant before must learn to pay attention to small noises (or silences) that signal impending dangers or otherwise call for parental action. They must plan agendas for the children, and modify their own schedules to fit in with the children's schedules. They must monitor the whereabouts, friendships, activities, and moods of the children if they are to provide effective guidance, control, and support.

Fathers, like mothers, may experience some parental gains as well. Now they can interact directly with their children without the mother's mediation. Fathers who have taken on a major role in child rearing report that they get to know their children much better than they did in a traditional father's role, and feel closer to them (Russell, 1982). But, at least initially, their lack of familiarity with the details of the children's lives may make it more difficult to monitor the children's whereabouts and supervise their activities.

Coparenting After Separation

In some families, divorce means that one parent essentially drops out of the parental role—that is, he or she seldom sees the children, and does not participate in child care or child rearing. For such families, the question of parental cooperation hardly arises. In other families, both parents continue to be involved, and for these families important new issues emerge: What kind of agreement can the parents come to concerning the amount of time the children will spend with each parent? How will they divide responsibilities for getting the children back and forth? Should they operate independently, or should they try to achieve some form of coordination between the two households with respect to standards of behavior set for the children, discipline, chores, allowances, privileges, and so forth? When important decisions need to be made concerning the child's life (for example, what school the child should attend, medical care, religious training), should the parents plan to discuss each issue and decide jointly? What decisions should be left to the independent decision making of whichever parent has the child with him/her at the time?

It is possible for parents who are both seeing the children to carry out their parental functions almost entirely separately from each other—that is, to practice "parallel" parenting. Alternatively,

parents can maintain contact with each other in connection with their joint responsibilities for the children—and this contact can be either cooperative or conflicted. Although we have argued that the parental alliance can no longer function as before, it is certainly possible for divorced parents to create a new coparental relationship that permits them to do business together concerning the children in a cooperative and mutually supportive way. Indeed, this is the goal of many mediators and family therapists who work with divorced parents. Yet clearly, many parents are so caught up in the emotional turmoil of their spousal divorce that they cannot construct a coparental relationship.

The parental divorce is especially complex in cases of joint custody. A joint custody decree implies that parents will share responsibility for the children after divorce. Joint legal custody gives both parents the right and responsibility to be involved in decisions about the children's education, medical care, and religious training. When the decree is for joint physical custody, this suggests that the two will share in day-to-day responsibility for the upbringing of the children. Such arrangements presumably call for a considerable degree of cooperative coparenting. However, little is known about how joint-custodial parents manage their coparental functions: the extent to which they are able to cooperate, the degree of conflict, the amount of joint decision making, and the way they carry on their parental business together. In fact, we do not know how coparental functions are managed between divorced parents in *any* of the three custodial arrangements . . . Clearly, joint decision making and other forms of cooperation should be possible when both parents are eager to sustain each other's involvement with the children. But what about cases in which joint custody is ordered over the objections of one of the parents? Or cases where the parents agree to it because they can find no other solution to a serious conflict over custody? The nature of coparenting under conditions in which parents have initially been in conflict about custody has seldom been examined . . .

A final word should be said about "buffering." Hetherington and colleagues (1982) have noted that as time goes on following parental separation, the quality of children's functioning becomes more and more dependent on the quality of the residential parent's functioning, and less and less related to characteristics of the nonresidential parent. This can have either positive or negative implications—sometimes both—as far as the children are concerned. A competent residential parent can raise the children without having to worry about interference from a spouse or—in more extreme cases—about protecting the children from the other parent's endangering behavior. On the other hand, the children are left more vulnerable to the residential parent in terms of that parent's mood states, lack of parenting skills, or life style.

Parents functioning in two different households can hardly serve as effective buffers or mediators between the children and the other parent when the children are at the other parent's house. For a parent who is deeply committed to the children's welfare, this can be one of the most frustrating situations a divorced parent faces. Some parents are in the fortunate position of feeling that the former spouse is entirely reliable as a parent. But others are not; they remember all too well the former spouse's flash points and weaknesses. Indeed, they are probably more aware of these weaknesses than of the other parent's strengths. Some of their concerns will surely be unrealistic, but others will be accurate appraisals of kinds of situations that can arise between a given parent and child in the course of ordinary life situations.

ENDNOTES

1. See also Parke & Sawin (1976).
2. One sees some kinship here with the position advocated by Goldstein, Freud, & Solnit (1973).

3. See Maccoby & Martin (1983) for a review of research on the effects of stress on parent-child interaction.

REFERENCES

Ambert, A. 1982. Differences in children's behavior toward custodial mothers and custodial fathers. *Journal of Marriage and the Family 44,* 73–86.

Cowan, G., J. Drinkard, & L. MacGavin. 1984. The effects of target, age and gender on use of power strategies. *Journal of Personality and Social Psychology 47,* 1391–1398.

Feldman, S.S., & T. Gehring. 1988. Changing perceptions of family cohesion and power across adolescence. *Child Development 59,* 1034–1045.

Funder, K. 1991. Children's constructions of their post-divorce families: A family sculpture approach. In *Images of Australian families,* ed. K. Funder. Australian Institute of Family Studies. Melbourne: Longman-Cheshire.

Gjerde, P.F. 1986. The interpersonal structure of family interaction settings: Parent-adolescent relations in dyads and triads. *Developmental Psychology 22,* 297–304.

Gleason, J.B. 1987. Sex differences in parent-child interaction. In *Language, gender and sex in comparative perspective,* ed. S.U. Philips, S. Steele, and C. Tanz. Cambridge: Cambridge University Press.

Goldberg, W.A. 1990. Marital quality, parental personality, and spousal agreement about perceptions and expectations for children. *Merrill-Palmer Quarterly 36,* 531–556.

Goldstein, J., A. Freud, and A. J. Solnit. 1973. *Beyond the best interests of the child.* New York: Free Press.

Hetherington, E.M., M. Cox, & R. Cox. 1982. Effects of divorce on parents and children. In *Nontraditional families,* ed. M.E. Lamb. Hillside, N.J.: Lawrence Erlbaum Associates.

Isaacs, M.B., B. Montalvo, & D. Abelsohn. 1986. *The difficult divorce: Therapy for children and families.* New York: Basic Books.

Lamb, M.E., J.H. Pleck, E.L. Chernov, & J.A. Levine. 1987. A biosocial perspective on paternal behavior and involvement. In *Parenting across the lifespan: A biosocial perspective,* ed. J.B. Lancaster, A. Rossi, J. Altman, and L. Sherrod. New York: Aldine de Gruyter.

Lytton, H. 1979. Disciplinary encounters between young boys and their mothers: Is there a contingency system? *Developmental Psychology 15,* 256–268.

Maccoby, E.E., & C.N. Jacklin. 1983. The "person" characteristics of children and the family as environment. In *Human development: An interactional perspective,* ed. D. Magnusson and V. Allen. New York: Academic Press.

Maccoby, E. E., and J. Martin. 1983. Parent-child interaction. In *Charmichael's manual of child psychology,* vol. 4, ed. P. Mussen. New York: Wiley.

Minuchin, P. 1985. Families and individual development: Provocations from the field of family therapy. *Child Development 56,* 289–302.

Parke, R.D., & S. O'Leary. 1976. Father-mother-infant interaction in the newborn period: Some findings, some observations and some unresolved issues. In *The developing individual in a changing world,* vol. 2, *Social and environmental issues,* ed. K.A. Riegel and J. Meacham. The Hague: Mouton.

Parke, R. D., and D. B. Sawin. 1976. The father's role in infancy: A re-evaluation. *The Family Coordinator* 25:365–371.

Parke, R.D., & B.R. Tinsley. 1981. The father's role in infancy: Determinants of involvement in caregiving and play. In *The role of the father in child development,* ed. M.E. Lamb, 2d ed. New York: John Wiley and Sons.

Pleck, J. 1983. Husbands' paid work and family roles: Current research issues. In *Research in the interweave of social roles,* vol. 3, *Families and jobs.* ed. H. Lopata and J.H. Pleck. Greenwich, Conn.: JAI Press.

Preston, G., & M. Madison. 1984. Access disputes in the context of the family structure after marital separation. *Australian Journal of Sex, Marriage and Family 5(1),* 36–45.

Russell, G. 1982. Shared-caregiving families: An Australian study. In *Nontraditional families: Parenting and child development,* ed. M.E. Lamb. Hillsdale, N.J.: Lawrence Erlbaum Associates.

Russell, G., & A. Russell. 1987. Mother-child and father-child relationships in middle childhood. *Child Development 58,* 1573–1585.

Youniss, J., & J. Smollar. 1985. *Adolescent relations with mothers, fathers and friends.* Chicago: University of Chicago Press.

READING 12-2

Downward Mobility

Terry Arendell

These women had assumed that after divorce they would somehow be able to maintain a middle-class life-style for themselves and their children. Those in their 20s and 30s had been confident that they could establish themselves as capable employees and find positions that would provide sufficient incomes. Most of the older women, who had been out of the work force longer, had been less confident about their earning abilities, but they had assumed that the difference between the former family income and their own earnings would be adequately compensated for by court-ordered child support and spousal support payments. In fact, virtually all of the women had assumed that family management and parenting efforts, which had kept most of them from pursuing employment and career development while they were married, would be socially valued and legally recognized in their divorce settlements. What had worried them most was not economic difficulty but the possible psychological effects of divorce on themselves and their children. Still, they had believed that they would probably recover from the emotional trauma of divorcing in a matter of months and would then be able to reorganize their lives successfully.

DRASTICALLY REDUCED INCOMES

But even the women who had worried most about how they would manage financially without their husbands' incomes had not imagined

Terry Arendell, "Downward Mobility" from *Mothers and Divorce: Legal, Economic, and Social Dilemmas,* pp. 36–52. Copyright © 1986 by The Regents of the University of California. Reprinted with the permission of the University of California Press.

the kind of hardship they would face after divorce. All but 2 of the 60 women had to cope with a substantial loss of family income. Indeed, 90 percent of them (56 out of 60) found that divorce immediately pushed them below the poverty line, or close to it. As wives and mothers, they had been largely dependent on their husbands, who had supplied the family's primary income.* Without that source of income, they suffered a drastic reduction in standard of living—an experience not shared by their ex-husbands.[1] Like women generally, they were "declassed" by divorce.

The economic decline experienced by these 60 women, all of whom remained single parents, was not temporary.[2] With caution and careful spending, most could meet their essential monthly expenses. But few had any extra money for dealing with emergencies or unexpected demands, and some continued to fall further behind, unable even to pay their monthly bills. One of them, divorced for nearly eight years, described her experience this way:

> I've been living hand to mouth all these years, ever since the divorce. I have no savings account. The notion of having one is as foreign to me as insurance—there's no way I can afford insurance. I have an old pickup that I don't drive very often. In the summertime I don't wear nylons to work because I can cut costs there. Together the kids and I have had to struggle and struggle. Supposedly struggle builds character. Well, some things simply aren't character building. There have been times when we've scoured the shag rug to see if we could find a coin to come up with enough to buy milk so we could have cold cereal for dinner. That's not character building.

Although they had been living for a median period of over four years as divorced single parents, only 9 of these 60 women had managed to halt the economic fall prompted by divorce; four of these nine had even managed to reestablish a standard of living close to what they had had while married. Thus the remaining majority—51 women—had experienced no economic recovery. Few had any savings, and most lived from paycheck to paycheck in a state of constant uncertainty. One of them, a woman in her late 40s and divorced more than four years, told me:

> I can't go on like this. There's no way. I can manage for another year, maybe a year and a half, but no more. I don't have the stamina. It's not that I don't have a job. My problem is money, plain and simple. That's all that counts in this situation.

This group of recently divorced mothers was by no means unique. All female-headed households experience high rates of economic hardship, and the gap in median income between female-headed families and other types of families has actually widened between 1960 and 1983.* Part of the reason is obvious: certain fixed costs of maintaining a family—such as utility bills and home mortgages or rent—do not change when the family size declines by one, and many other expenses, such as food and clothing, do not change significantly. Additionally, in most cases when the mother obtained employment, it provided a low income that was substantially re-

---

*According to Lee Rainwater (1984) and the U.S. Bureau of the Census (1985), the earnings of working married wives contribute only 22 percent of the average family's total income. For this reason, poverty, which occurs in only 1 of 19 husband-wife families and in only 1 of 9 families maintained by a single father, afflicts almost one of every three families headed by a woman.

---

*Between 1960 and 1983, the median income of female-headed families with no husband present dropped by the following percentages: from 61 to 57 percent of the median income of male-headed families with no wife present, from 43 to 41 percent of the median income of married couples, and from 51 to 38 percent of the median income of married-couple families in which the wife was also employed. In 1983, the median income for female-headed families was $11,484; for male-headed families with no wife present, $20,140; for married-couple families, $26,019; and for married couples in which the wife was employed, $30,340 (U.S. Bureau of the Census, 1985).

duced by new expenses, such as the costs of transportation and child care.*

These women understood how their economic dependency in marriage had contributed to their present economic situation. One of them, who had been married nearly 20 years before divorcing, said:

> Money does wonders in any situation. I'm sure women with more education and better jobs don't have situations quite as desperate as mine. But I quit school when I married and stayed home to raise my children.

Unfortunately, they arrived at such understanding the hard way, through experience. Before divorcing, they had expected to receive "reasonable" child support and had thought they could probably find jobs that paid "reasonable" wages. They had only the vaguest understanding of other women's divorce experiences. Thus two of them said:

> Friends of mine had ended up divorced with children, and they would tell me some of these things. But I had no empathy at all. I might say, "Gee, that doesn't seem fair" or "Gee, that's too bad." But it never *really* hit me how serious it is until it happened to me. So I think there must be a lot of people out there who don't have the foggiest idea what it feels like.

> I had no idea how *much* money it takes. You don't have the [husband's] income, but you still have your family. There's the rub.

Their experiences led them to conclude that in America today, divorced women generally must accept a reduced standard of living. And as women with children, they were keenly aware that only remarriage could offer a quick escape from economic hardship.* A mother of three told me:

> I have this really close friend. She was a neighbor and often kept my daughter until I got home from school. She and her husband had two darling little kids. One day he just up and left. Surprised us all—he married his secretary eventually. My friend hadn't worked before, so I helped her get some typing skills. She worked for two weeks and said, "No more." She called me and said, "Well, I'm not going through what you did. I'm getting married." That was like a slap in the face. Gosh, did I look that bad? I started to doubt myself. Was I doing that bad a job? Should I have gone the marriage route? Gone out and gotten a job and then married somebody? I still wonder about that. Things would have been a lot easier financially. The kids would have had a father. And I would have done what society looks at favorably. I don't know. I still don't know what to do.

Economically these women lost their middle-class status, but socially their expectations of themselves and their children remained the same. They still identified with the middle class, but their low incomes prevented them from participating in middle-class activities. This contradiction created many dilemmas and conflicts:

> I went to a CETA workshop, and I started crying when all they talked about was how to get a job. A woman came after me in the hallway, and I just bawled. I'd been searching for a job for months. I had a degree and teaching credential, and here I was being told how to fill out a stupid job application. And I had three kids at home that I didn't know how I was going to feed that week and a lovely home I couldn't afford.

---

*From his Michigan study, David Chambers (1979) concludes that the custodial parent needs 80 percent of the predivorce income to maintain the family's standard of living. The total income of most family units of divorced women and children falls below 50 percent of their former family income. Sweden, in fact, has determined that single-parent families actually need more income than others and provides cash supports that give them incomes comparable to those of two-parent families (Cassetty, 1983a).

---

*Research supports the commonsense belief that the surest way to reverse the economic decline resulting from divorce is to remarry (Sawhill, 1976; Duncan & Morgan, 1974, 1979; Johnson & Minton, 1982). Do women remarry because they conclude, pragmatically, that being a single woman is too costly, for themselves and perhaps also for their children? Would fewer women remarry if they could successfully support themselves? The answers to such questions will have interesting political implications.

I moved here after the divorce because the school had a particularly good program for gifted children. Kids were classed by ability and not just by grade level. So my kid was in a really good spot for what he needed. I didn't realize at the time that I was the only single parent in that group. One reason those kids can achieve at that level is because they have a very stable home life, two parents to work with every child on the enrichment and the projects and the homework. I hate to say this, but it's all socioeconomic. Every kid in there belonged to a high socioeconomic group. Oh, they can rationalize that it's not really like that, but it's completely WASPish, all two-parent families where the mothers don't work. Mothers are available to take kids to music lessons, soccer lessons, gymnastic lessons, and all of that whenever it's needed. I had to take my son out of that class. I couldn't keep up the level of activity required of the kids and the parents. The gap was growing greater and greater. If I'd lived like this a long time, I might have known how to cope, but this was all new. And it all came down to money.

The women resented their precarious positions all the more because they knew that their former husbands had experienced no loss in class status or standard of living and could have eased their struggles to support the children.

Five hundred dollars here or there—or taking over the orthodontist's bills—anything like that would have meant a lot. I don't see why this kid should have to live with jaw and tooth problems because I got a divorce. His jaw had to be totally realigned, so it wasn't just cosmetic. His father could easily have paid that monthly [orthodontist] bill and deducted it. That would have made a tremendous difference. But he wouldn't. By making me suffer, he made his child suffer too.

When the children retained some access to middle-class activities through involvement with their fathers, their mothers had ambivalent feelings. They were grateful that their children were not neglected by their fathers and could enjoy some enriching and entertaining activities with them; but they found their former hus-

bands' greater financial resources a painful reminder of how little they themselves could provide. One woman, who had to let her child get free meals through the subsidized school lunch program, despite her many efforts to make more money, told me this:

His father seldom buys him anything. But his stepmother sometimes does. She can give him all these nice things. She's given him nice books, a stereo headset. I have no idea what her motivation is, but it's a very funny feeling to know that I can't go and buy my son something he would love to have, but this perfect stranger can. And how will that affect my son ultimately? He must know how difficult things are here, and that I'm not deliberately depriving him. But it's kind of ironic—I helped establish that standard of living, but I end up with none of it, and she has full access to it.

EXPENSES AND ECONOMIZING

Living with a reduced budget was a constant challenge to most of these women because they had no cushion to fall back on if expenses exceeded their incomes. Their savings were depleted soon after they divorced; only 12 of the 60 women I talked to had enough money in savings to cover a full month's expenses. Most said they had radically cut back their spending.[3] The major expenses after divorce were housing, food, and utilities. The women with young children also had substantial child-care expenses, and several had unusually high medical bills that were not covered by health insurance.

Within a short time after their divorces, more than one-third of the women—16 women living in homes they owned and 7 living in rented places—had to move to different housing with their children in order to reduce their expenses. Two of the women had moved more than four times in the first two years after their divorces, always for financial reasons.[4] During marriage, 49 of the 60 women had lived in homes owned with their husbands. After divorce, only nine of them retained ownership of the family home. Of these nine, six were able to acquire ownership by buying out their husbands as part of the community property settlement (five of them only because they were able to get financial assistance from their parents); two retained the home by exchanging other community assets for it; and one received the home according to the dictates of the religion she and her husband shared.

Home ownership brought with it many expenses besides mortgage payments. Several women neglected upkeep and repairs for lack of money. A woman who was in her 50s reported this common dilemma:

> I owe $16,000 on this house. I could get about $135,000 for it, so I have a large equity. But it would have taken all of that to get that condominium I looked at, and my payments would still have been about $400 a month. I don't know how I'll be able to keep up the house, financially or physically. The house needs painting, and I can't keep up the yard work. I'd like to move. I'd like a fresh start. But the kids don't want to move, and I can't imagine how I'll handle all of this once they're gone. When the alimony [spousal support] stops, there'll be no way I can manage a move. I'm stuck here now. The mortgage is really low and the interest is only 5 percent.

Two of the mothers reduced expenses by moving their children from private to public schools. Two others were able to keep their children in private schools only after administrators waived the tuition fees. Seven mothers received financial assistance for preschoolers' child care costs, five from private and two from public agencies. One of these women, who worked full-time, had this to say about her expenses:

> I'm buying this house. I pay $330 a month for it. Child care for my two kids runs to almost $500 a month. Since I bring home only a little more than $900, there's no way I could make it without the child care assistance. There'd be nothing left.

About half of these women had economic situations so dire that careful budgeting was not enough, and they continued to fall further behind economically. Those living close to the margin managed by paying some bills one month and others the next. Their indebtedness increased, and opportunities for reversing the situation did not appear:

> I'm so far in debt. Yes indeed. I keep thinking, why should I worry about the bills? I'll never get out of debt! All I can do is juggle. Without my charge cards, my kids would be bare-assed naked. And school is coming up again. What am I going to do for school clothes? And they've all grown fast this year . . . I probably owe $3,000 on charge cards, and I still owe rent—I haven't paid this month or last. The landlord I have has been very understanding. He's let us go along as best he can. We've been here four years, and he knows what I'm going through. Over the years, he's given me several eviction notices, but this last time he hired a lawyer and everything. I decided I'd just pitch my tent on the capitol mall in Sacramento and say, "Here I am." I've written my congressman again, because I qualify for subsidized housing. But it'll take forever to get any action on that.

For many, however, even the persistent realities of economic hardship could not extinguish middle-class hopes:

> My husband liked really good food and always bought lots and the best. So when he left, it was really hard to cut the kids back. They were used to all that good eating. Now there's often no food in the house, and everybody gets really grouchy when there's no food around . . . I think I've cut back mostly on activities. I don't go to movies anymore with friends. We've lost $150 a month now because my husband reduced the support. It gets cut from activities—we've stopped doing everything that costs, and there's nowhere else to cut. My phone is shut off. I pay all the bills first and then see what there is for food . . . I grew up playing the violin, and I'd wanted my kids to have music lessons—piano would be wonderful for them. And my older two kids are very artistic. But lessons are out of the question.

Obtaining credit had been a real problem for many, for the reasons given by this woman, who had worked during the marriage while her husband attended school:

> My kids and I were very poor those first years after the divorce. I had taken care of our finances during marriage. But I didn't have accounts in my own name, so I couldn't get credit. I got a job as soon as I could. I was getting $65 a month for child support and paying $175 a month for rent. Between the rent and the child care and the driving to work, I was absolutely broke. I really didn't have enough to live on. I had no benefits either, with my first job. I was living dangerously, and with children. I could barely pay the basic bills. There wasn't enough money for food lots of times. I cried many times because there wasn't enough money. I couldn't get any credit. [When I was married] my husband could get any credit he wanted, but it was on the basis of *my* job, which had the higher income. He couldn't even keep his checkbook balanced, but now I'm the one who can't get credit! It was a hard lesson to learn. Now whenever I get a chance, I tell women to start getting a credit rating.

The woman who told me this, incidentally, had managed to overcome initial impoverishment and gain a middle-class income from her job.

Some women regarded personal possessions such as jewelry, furniture, and cars as things they might sell to meet emergencies or rising indebtedness:

> I sold jewelry to have my surgery, to pay for the part that wasn't covered. I still have some silver, and I have some good furniture, which could probably bring something. That's probably what I'd do in an emergency, sell those things. What else do people do?

Teenage children helped by earning money through odd jobs and babysitting. Older teenagers changed their college plans, and several entered community colleges instead of universities. One woman's daughter was already in the Navy, pursuing her schooling in languages and working as a translator, and the daughter of another was considering military service as a way of saving money for a college education.

Most women compared their own hardship and forced economizing to the economic freedom enjoyed by their ex-husbands. For example:

> I know my ex-husband goes somewhere almost every weekend, and he usually takes a friend along. I wonder how he can do that. How can he go somewhere every weekend? The only way I could do that is find a rich man! I couldn't possibly work enough hours to pay for that much stuff. I'd be doing well to finance a [20-mile] trip to San Francisco!

There were some exceptions to the general pattern of economic decline. Nine of the 60 women had regained some latitude for discretionary spending, though only three of them had managed this economic reversal without help. These nine were a distinct subgroup; the others did not share their higher standards of living or their feelings and approaches to the future. Still, only two of these nine women had not experienced a major decline in income immediately upon divorcing (or separating). One had been living on welfare because her husband's excessive drinking and erratic behavior had prevented him from holding a job; she found employment immediately after separating from him. The other one had been the primary family wage earner during her marriage.* Four of the women whose incomes had dropped significantly had managed to stop and even reverse the economic decline very soon after divorce because they were granted temporary spousal support awards and acquired some money and assets from their community property settlement; two of them, who had been divorced after more than 20 years of

---

*A recent study by Lee Rainwater (1984, p. 84) shows how economic dependency in a previous marriage makes it difficult for a woman to recover economically from divorce: "By the fourth year that they headed their own families, women who had regular work experience before becoming female heads had family incomes equal to 80 percent of their average family income while a wife. Women who had not worked at all had incomes slightly less than half that of their last married years."

marriage, also received substantial amounts of money from their parents. Although these four did not experience the degree of hardship shared by the others, they did not fully recover their formerly high income levels and therefore also had to alter their life-styles. As one of them said:

> Essentially, I took an $80,000 drop in annual income. And I had to borrow again last year. This year I finally sold the house, and that was really the only way I've made it. My change in life-style has been *tremendous*. Just my heating and electricity bill for our home was $350 a month. We just barely got by on $2,000 a month. I stopped buying household things; I stopped buying clothes for myself. And I rented out a room in the house. It was a huge house, and that helped out. I let the cleaning woman and the gardener go. I didn't paint. I let the property taxes go until I sold the house and paid them then. I quit taking trips. This house I'm in now has much lower operating expenses. My son doesn't have the same things he'd had. His grandparents buy most of his shoes and clothes now. He used to have lots and lots, so it's been a change for him.

Of the other five women who succeeded in improving their economic situations after a few years, three did so entirely through their own work efforts, and the other two managed with help from their former husbands—one took in the child for more than a year while his ex-wife worked at several jobs, and the other accepted a shared parenting arrangement.

EMOTIONAL RESPONSES TO ECONOMIC LOSS

None of the nine women who had experienced substantial economic recovery reported suffering serious emotional changes. Forty-four of the others, however, spoke of frequent struggles with depression and despair. Every one of them attributed these intense feelings, which often seemed overwhelming, directly to the financial

hardships that followed divorce. This woman spoke for many others in describing the effects that economic loss had had on her:

> I think about money a great deal. It's amazing. I used to get so bored by people who could only talk about money. Now it's all I think about. It's a perpetual thought, how to get money—not to invest, or to save, but just to live. The interesting thing is that you develop a poverty mentality. That intrigues me. I would never have thought that could happen. But if I had had money, several times in the last year I would have fought what was happening to me in a way I no longer think of fighting. You tend to accept what's coming because there's so much you *have* to accept. You get so you accept everything that comes your way. For example, I accepted at first what I was told about treating this cancer on my face: that the only surgery possible would leave my face disfigured with one side paralyzed. I knew it would ruin any possibility of my teaching if they did that to my face, but I would have just accepted it if a friend hadn't told me to go to someone else for consultation. I wouldn't have done that on my own. That's not how I would have behaved at other times in my life. I think it must happen to a lot of divorced women. It was only this year that I realized how strange this has become. I'm educated, I've come through a wealthy phase of my life, and now here I am, being shuttled around and not even fighting. It continues to fascinate me. After a while, you develop a begging mentality in which you'd like to squeeze money out of anybody. I guess I'm somewhere in the realm of poverty. I know there are poorer people, but I'm pretty well down near the bottom. If I were to lose this job—which is always possible, there's no security to it—I'd be finished. Finished. I'd lose the house. I'd lose everything. There's no way I could survive.

The first year of divorce was traumatic for most, especially because legal uncertainties were mixed with other fears. A vicious circle was common: anxieties brought sleepless nights, and fatigue made the anxieties sharper. Although economic hardship remained, by the end of the first year most of the women had learned to control some of the anxiety surrounding it.*

Depression overtook a majority of these women at some time or other. Their feelings of despair over financial troubles were worsened by concerns for their children. One of them said:

> I thought about running away, but who would I have turned my kids over to? I also thought about suicide—especially when the youngest was still a baby and I had so much trouble with child care and it cost me so much. I kept thinking that if I were gone, it would take a major burden off of everybody.

In fact, such despair was a common experience: 26 of the 60 women volunteered that they had contemplated suicide at some time after divorce. They mentioned various contributing factors, such as emotional harassment from their husbands and uncertainty about their own abilities and identities, but all said that economic hardship was *the* primary stress that pushed them to the point of desperation.

One mother gave a very detailed account of her experience with suicidal depression, which occurred at a time when she had been barely managing for several months. She would drag herself to work and then collapse in bed when she got home. When she would get out of bed, she told me, the sight of her 10-year-old son sitting in front of the television set, alone in a cold room and eating cold cereal, would send her back to bed, where her exhaustion and despair would be exacerbated by hours of crying. She went on:

> I came home to an empty house that night—it was February. I had gotten my son's father to take him

that weekend so I could go to my class—the one about learning to live as a single person again. I'd hoped that by getting some encouragement, I'd be able to pull myself out of this and find a way to make a better living. About 11 o'clock, I just decided this was no way to live. I couldn't take care of this child. I'd gone to Big Brothers, and they wouldn't take him because he had a father. But his father wasn't seeing him. Family Services weren't any help. The woman there did try to help, I think. She cared. But she'd been married more than 25 years and just didn't understand. All I could do in the 50-minute appointment with her was cry. My attorney wasn't giving me any help or getting me any money. My mother was mad at me—she said it was my fault for leaving my husband.

> I just couldn't see it ever being any different, so I decided to kill myself. I'm sure that's not a unique thing. It was the most logical thing in the world. I knew exactly how I was going to do it. I was going to fill the bathtub with warm water and cut my wrists. It would be fine then—that thought was the only thing that made me feel any better. Nothing was as bad as the thought of getting up the next day. So I called my son's father—he was going to bring him back the next day—and I asked him if he thought he could take care of him. I didn't think I gave any evidence [of my feelings] or anything—it wasn't a desperate call for help, or a threatening call, or anything like that, because I'd already made up my mind. I just didn't want him to bring my son in here and find me like that. I wanted him to make some kind of arrangements to take care of him. He didn't say anything on the phone, but in about 20 minutes the doorbell rang. Two young men in blue uniforms were standing there. They wanted to take me to an emergency room. It was a crisis place, they said. They were young and scared themselves and acted like they didn't know what to do.

> I guess the shock of realizing how far I'd gone was enough to snap me out of it. I'd spent those 20 minutes [after the phone call] piddling around taking care of some last-minute things, tidying up and so on. It seems that once I made the decision, it gave me such inner peace, such a perfect reconciliation. It seemed the most logical, practical thing in the world. Then their coming stopped me from doing it. I didn't go with them, but they gave

---

*Various studies argue that the first year or so after divorce is the most stressful and traumatic (Hetherington, Cox, & Cox, 1976; Wallerstein & Kelly, 1979, 1980; Weiss 1979a, 1979b). Additionally, both Pett (1982) and Buehler and Hogan (1980) found that financial concerns were among the factors that limited divorced mothers' emotional recovery from divorce. None of these studies, however, attempts to distinguish the effects of economic uncertainty from more generalized separation emotions.

me a phone number and told me there were people there who would come and get me anytime.

I've only recently put into perspective what happened. It wasn't so much my inability to cope as it was the convergence of everything in my situation. That person at Family Services did help, actually, when she pointed out that some people who've never had trouble dealing with anything don't know what else to do when they feel like they can't cope. That fit. I'd never had a crisis I couldn't deal with in some way. I'd gotten myself into bad situations before, but I could always see cause-and-effect relationships, and I'd always felt like I could make some changes right away that would change things in my life. In this case, I couldn't figure anything out. I don't even know how to tell you what I thought.

This woman had been divorced before and had not suffered depression; but she had had no child then, no one else for whom she was responsible.

These women who were new to poverty had no ideas about how to cope in their new situations, and they found little help in the society at large. Some of the most desperate were unable to afford professional counseling. One of them said:

At one point during the eviction, I was getting hysterical. I needed help. So I called a program called Women's Stress. Good thing I wasn't really suicidal, because they kept me on hold a long time. They said, "Well, this program is just for women with an alcohol or drug problem. Does that fit you?" I said, "No, but if I don't get help, it will." They said they'd send me a pamphlet, which they did. It cost twenty-five dollars to join. I never did find any help.

The worst personal pain these women suffered came from observing the effects of sudden economic hardship on their children. Here is one woman's poignant account:

I had $950 a month, and the house payment was $760, so there was hardly anything left over. So there we were: my son qualified for free lunches at school. We'd been living on over $4,000 a month, and there we were. That's so humiliating. What that does to the self-esteem of even a child is absolutely unbelievable. And it isn't hidden:

everybody knows the situation. They knew at his school that he was the kid with the free lunch coupons . . . My son is real tall and growing. I really didn't have any money to buy him clothes, and attorneys don't think school clothes are essential. So he was wearing these sweatshirts that were too small for him. Then one day he didn't want to go to school because the kids had been calling him Frankenstein because his arms and legs were hanging out of his clothes—they were too short. That does terrible things to a kid, it really does. We just weren't equipped to cope with it.

But the need to cut costs—on food, clothing, and activities for the children—was not the only source of pain. Most of the mothers reported that their parenting approaches changed and that their emotions became more volatile, and even unstable, in periods of great financial stress. Mothers who went to work full-time resented the inevitable loss of involvement in their children's lives:

I wish I could get over the resentment. [In the first years after the divorce] I spent half the time blaming myself and the other half blaming their father. Because I was so preoccupied, I missed some really good years with them, doing things I'd looked forward to and wanted to do. Those years are gone now.

Some of the mothers also thought the experience of economic hardship after divorce might eventually affect the society at large, as more and more women and children come to share it.[5] For example:

It's not just the mother [who's affected]. It's a whole generation of kids who don't even know how to use a knife and a fork, who don't sit at a table to eat, who don't know how to make conversation with people of different ages. There are so many awful possibilities, and it's a whole society that's affected. I'm not talking about people who have lived for years in poverty. We planned and lived one way with no idea of the other reality. Then this harsh reality hits, and everything becomes a question of survival. I think it must be different if that's all you've experienced. At least then your plans fit your possibilities—that sort of thing. You can't spend your whole day trying to survive and then care anything about what's going on in the world around you. You really can't . . . Maybe it's going to take 50 percent of the population to be in this shape before we get change. But some of us have to be salvaged, just so we can fight. We can't all be so oppressed by trying to survive that we can't do anything at all.

Although their despair was worsened by concern for their children, it was the children who gave these women their strongest incentive to continue the struggle:

Sure, I think about suicide. And I'm a smart lady who's been creative and able to do things to change our situation. But I'm tired—*tired*. And it's real hard. What keeps me alive is my kid. I may be boxed in, but if I give up, what will happen to her? She doesn't deserve that.

Most of these women also admitted to having lost a sense of the future. A 50-year-old woman, who said she wondered if she would someday become a bag lady, told me:

That's what I started to say at the beginning—*I don't have a future.* I can sit around and cry about that for a while, but then I have to move on and ask, what am I going to do about it? And there's not much I can do. What career can I start at my age? How do I retrieve all those years spent managing a family?

And another somewhat younger woman said:

The worst poverty is the poverty of the spirit that sets in when you've been economically poor too long, and it gets to the point where you can't see things turning around.

To avoid this sense of hopelessness, a majority of the 60 women tried not to think about the future and made only short-term plans:

I learned very quickly that I couldn't think too far into the future or I'd drive myself crazy. The future became, "What will I do next month?" I learned I had to go day to day and just do the best I could. That's been my major technique for cop-

ing, and I learned it right away. I've built up some retirement and Social Security through work, thank heavens. But I have to live right now. I just can't think about the future. The worst that can happen is that the state will take care of me, and I'll end up in a crappy old folks' home. But I don't think about that.

Ten of the 60 women—a unique subgroup—said they had not experienced serious depression or despair after divorce. But the reasons they gave simply reemphasize the central importance of economic loss in the lives of divorced women. Four of these 10 had various sources of income that protected them from poverty and enabled them to work actively toward improving their situation. Two of them were using income from the divorce property settlement to attend graduate school, and they hoped to regain their former standard of living by pursuing professional careers. Two were receiving financial support from their parents while they sought employment and planned for the possible sale of their homes as part of the property settlement. The remaining six said they were generally optimistic *in spite of* their poor economic positions. Like the others, they found the financial hardships imposed by divorce surprising and difficult to handle; they simply found these hardships easier to cope with than the despair they had known in their marriages.

In summary, these women discovered that the most important change brought about by divorce was an immediate economic decline, which for most of them had not been reversible. Despite their economizing efforts and dramatically altered life-styles, many of them continued to lose ground financially. In addition, economic circumstances had a powerful effect on their emotional lives. Only a very few escaped feelings of despair and hopelessness. Most found that economic uncertainties fostered depression, discouragement, and despair, and nearly all said they had endured periods of intense anxiety over the inadequacy of their income and its effects on the well-being of their children. Most of them felt trapped in their present circumstances and said they had no sense of the future.

ENDNOTES

1. Glick (1983); data from U.S. Bureau of the Census (1980).
2. Duncan and Morgan (1974, 1976, 1978, 1979); M. Hill (1981).
3. U.S. Bureau of the Census (1985). There has been no significant change in the proportion of children living with a single parent father since 1960 (U.S. Bureau of the Census, 1983, 1985).
4. National Advisory Council of Economic Opportunity (1981:46).
5. U.S. Bureau of the Census (1985). In fact, more than half of all families in poverty are headed by women, even though female-headed households make up only about 20 percent of all households; and 55.4 percent of all children in female-headed households live in poverty; children in two-parent and male-headed families who live in poverty total 13.4 percent (U.S. Bureau of the Census, 1985).

REFERENCES

Buehler, C., & J. Hogan. 1980. "Managerial Behavior and Stress in Families Headed by Divorced Women: A Proposed Framework." *Family Relations 29(4),* 525–532.

Cassetty, J. 1983. "Emerging Issues in Child-Support Policy and Practice." In J. Cassetty (ed.), *The Parental Child-Support Obligation.* Lexington, Mass.: Lexington Books.

Chambers, D. 1979. Making Fathers Pay: The Enforcement of Child Support. Chicago: University of Chicago Press.

Duncan, G., & J. Morgan (eds.). 1974. *Five Thousand Families,* vol. 4. Ann Arbor: University of Michigan Press.

———. 1976. *Five Thousand Families,* vol. 5. Ann Arbor: University of Michigan Press.

———. 1978. *Five Thousand Families,* vol. 6. Ann Arbor: University of Michigan Press.

———. 1979. *Five Thousand Families,* vol. 7. Ann Arbor: University of Michigan Press.

Glick, P. 1977. "Updating the Life and Cycle of the Family." *Journal of Marriage and the Family* 39:3–15.

Hetherington, E., M. Cox, & R. Cox. 1976. "Divorced Fathers." *The Family Coordinator 25,* 417–428.

Hill, M. 1981. "Some Dynamic Aspects of Poverty." In G. Duncan and J. Morgan (eds.). *Five Thousand Families,* vol. 9. Ann Arbor: University of Michigan Press.

Johnson, W., & M. Minton. 1982. "The Economic Choice in Divorce: Extended or Blended Family?" *Journal of Divorce 5(1–2),* 101–113.

National Advisory Council on Economic Opportunity (NACEO). 1981. *The American Promise: Equal Justice and Economic Opportunity.* Washington, D.C.: NACEO.

Pett, M. 1982. "Predictors of Satisfactory Social Adjustment of Divorced Single Parents." *Journal of Divorce 5(3),* 1–17.

Rainwater, L. 1984. "Mothers' Contributions to the Family Money Economy in Europe and the United States." In P. Voydanoff (ed.), *Work and Family.* Palo Alto, Calif.: Mayfield.

Sawhill, I. 1976a. "Discrimination and Poverty Among Women Who Head Families." *Signs 1,* 201–221.

———. 1976b. "Women with Low Incomes." In M. Blaxall and B. Reagan (eds.), *Women and the Workplace.* Chicago: University of Chicago Press.

U.S. Bureau of the Census. 1980. "Child Support and Alimony: 1978." In *Current Population Reports,* series P-23, no 106. Washington, D.C.: U.S. Government Printing Office.

———. 1983. "Households, Families, Marital Status, and Living Arrangements." *Current Population Reports,* series P-20, no. 382. Washington, D.C.: U.S. Government Printing Office.

———. 1985. *Statistical Abstract of the United States, 1985. National Data Book and Guide to Sources.* Washington, D.C.: U.S. Government Printing Office.

Wallerstein, J., & J. Kelly. 1979. "Children and Divorce: A Review." *Social Work* (November): 469–475.

Weiss, R. 1979a. *Going It Alone: The Family Life and Social Situation of the Single Parent.* New York: Basic Books.

———. 1979b. "Growing Up a Little Faster: The Experience of Growing Up in a Single-Parent Household." *Journal of Social Issues 35(4),* 97–111.

CHAPTER 13

Remarriage

At current rates, about one-third of all adults can expect to marry, divorce, and remarry during their lifetimes—a far higher proportion than in previous generations. When neither spouse has children from their previous marriages, remarried life can be very similar to life in first marriages. To be sure, the spouses tend to be older, more established in their careers, and more set in their preferences about personal life, but the basic day-to-day interaction isn't all that different. When one or both partners, however, have children from previous marriages, then the remarriage creates a stepfamily. In past times, most stepfamilies formed after the death of a parent; today the overwhelming number form after the parents' divorces. In both types of stepfamilies, the new stepparent must adjust to the immediate presence of the children of the other spouse. This adjustment can be difficult, not just for the stepparent but for the biological parent and the stepchildren as well.

When the remarriage follows a divorce, the stepfamily often faces additional complications. The stepchildren often create links with other households as they go back and forth between their mothers' and their fathers' homes. Ex-spouses also play a larger role in the remarried parents' lives. In this situation, it can be difficult for the remarried couple to forge a strong, viable partnership because of the tugs and pulls of stepchildren, biological children, and former spouses. Most family therapists believe that the creation of a strong bond between the remarried partners is central to the long-term success of the stepfamily. Yet this is not an easy task. In the following excerpt from a chapter in the edited volume, *Relative Strangers: Studies of Stepfamily Processes,* Jamie K. Keshet, a family therapist, shares the stories of several couples whom she has counseled. They illustrate the diverse ways in which married couples shape their sense of themselves as a couple. She illustrates some common reasons for conflict in stepfamilies. The difficulties, Keshet argues, arise not from personality defects of the couples but rather from the complex structure and history of their family lives.

Many remarried couples, nevertheless, build successful partnerships. Keshet also analyzes the development of successful coping styles among the couples she counseled. The key, she asserts, is "building a boundary that separates them from the rest of the family and by becoming a team in solving stepfamily problems." Building a barrier may mean deferring some of the demands of children for time and attention, but by creating a strong alliance the couple may make the family system work better for the children as well as for themselves.

Looking to the future, one might ask what will happen when the current generation of stepchildren grows up. Young adults rely on their parents for support when they need funds for college, babysitting help for a newborn, or a security deposit for an apartment. Adults in old age rely on their adult children for help carting groceries, assistance cleaning the house, and transportation when they no longer can drive. But will adult stepchildren receive the same amount of support from their stepfather or stepmother as they would have from a biological parent? Will an elderly stepfather be able to call up his adult stepchild when he needs help? With the growth in the number of stepfamilies in the United States, these questions will become increasingly important in the decades ahead.

In the second reading in this chapter, Lynn White reviews four theories of stepfamily life and concludes that all four predict that stepparents and stepchildren, on average, will not provide as much support for each other as biological parents and children usually do. Later in the article, in a section not included here, she examines data from a national survey of families that show, as predicted, that stepparents and their adult stepchildren report fewer exchanges of support and less emotional closeness than do parents and their biological adult children. At the end of the article, she concludes (using the anthropological term *affines,* which means people who are related to each other through marriage, such as a mother-in-law and a daughter-in-law):

> Stepfamilies are weaker support networks than intact families. The effects are not simply statistically significant; they are of substantive magnitude. Thus, I think we can set aside the view that stepfamilies mean more relatives, broader networks, and more support. This potential is generally not realized.
>
> Overall, I think stepfamily members are best viewed as affines, much like parents-in-law or children-in-law. The relationship is created and sustained by a marriage; although affectionate relationships may develop, the primary impetus for exchange with the affine is to benefit or please the biological relative. When the marriage ends, the relationship falters or dies (p. 130).

White is speaking in general terms; she does not mean to suggest that stepparents and stepchildren never support each other in adulthood. She would agree that there are many stepparents who form strong bonds with stepchildren that lead to mutual support later in life, even in some cases in which the stepfamily has been broken by divorce. But on average, she suggests, the ties between steprelatives may not lead to the same levels of support later in life as do the ties to biological parents.

The Remarried Couple: Stresses and Successes

Jamie K. Keshet

In every marriage there is a tension between the need for stability in the couple relationship and the desire of each member to maintain and develop an individual identity. Each relationship has different parameters of how much closeness is too much and how much separateness can be tolerated. These limits change as the couple relationship matures and in response to pressures on the couple from other family members, work, and community. In this space between ultimate oneness or union and extreme separateness and uniqueness, the drama of marriage takes place. The tension between these poles leads to creative solutions and to growth in the individual members. Along the way it can cause arguments, disappointment, and frustration. (See Askham [1984] for a description of the relationship between identity and stability in first marriages.)

A remarried family differs from a family formed by a first marriage because one or both partners have been married before and have children from that first marriage. The partners' past and present ties to their former families create special opportunities and constraints for the second marriage. This [reading] describes some of these opportunities and constraints. The emphasis is on remarriage following divorce, which is more common than remarriage follow-

ing death of a spouse, and which is more likely to involve children young enough to live in the couple's home (Cherlin, 1981).

The material in this [reading] is based primarily on the author's experience working as a family therapist and family educator with remarried couples and stepfamilies. In this capacity I have made the acquaintance of a wide variety of families—from those experiencing mild difficulties in making the transition to a stepfamily, to those with major crises in family life. I work with a family systems perspective that influences the way in which I perceive others. A fuller description of the theoretical basis of my work can be found in Keshet (1980, 1981, 1985, and 1987). (References to available research or theories about remarriage are included in this [reading].) Even so, not nearly enough research has been done in this area to guide us.

Remarriage becomes a fact of life for a half-million couples each year (Prosen & Farmer, 1982). When people enter a second marriage they find themselves in a new and unusual situation. The remarried couple is the foundation of a stepfamily. They have brought together diverse stepfamily members and are responsible for keeping them together. Their couple relationship, however, is likely to have a shorter history and less power than the relationship between either parent and child. Nonetheless, the couple has the tremendous task of building a lasting relationship with each other at the same time that they are completing divorces from former partners, raising their children, and pursuing their careers . . .

CONCEPTS OF FAMILY

As the couple define and create their marital relationship, they are also creating a family for themselves and their children. Each brings with him concepts of what a family is and should be. These concepts are likely to need adjusting to fit the new family that is formed. Not many people envision a honeymoon with five teenagers or a home with three different last names on the mailbox.

Each person's family concept is unique and contains elements from his or her family history. In addition, the concept of family is likely to contain two important cultural beliefs: the overriding importance of blood ties among family members (Schneider, 1980), and the superiority of the nuclear family for child rearing (Burgoyne & Clark, 1984; Duberman, 1975; Perkins, 1977). Both beliefs are challenged by the stepfamily, in which blood ties link some members and not others.

Stepfathers often have concepts of the family ideal that differ from their perceptions of their current families (Perkins, 1977; Woodruff, 1982). This difference between real and ideal families is greater for stepfathers than for fathers in nuclear families. In one study the greater the difference between real and ideal family concepts, the more dissatisfaction was expressed by stepfamily members (Woodruff, 1982). Similar studies of stepmothers have not been undertaken (Keshet, 1986). Biological parents in first families may also have ideas about family that do not fit their actual families. In a study of parents, Galinsky (1981) identified the first stage of parenthood, which takes place before the birth of the first child, as image making, becoming aware of memories and fantasies of what it means to be a parent. Part of the parent's growth process in the family is the adjustment of these old images to fit new realities.

In a stepfamily, each partner can be at a different stage of adjusting these images. A stepparent who has never had children of his own may be functioning with the kind of images of parenthood he would have if he were expecting his first child. His stepchild, however, is already a teenager. His wife has already adjusted her images and her expectations many times as she has reared her son.

One of the tasks of the remarried couple is to create a family concept, similar to the marital definition, that can help them to provide leadership for their new family. If the couple hold similar family concepts, the areas of disagreement between them are fewer and stability in their marriage is increased. Moreover, the decisions they make and the ways they behave in the family will make sense to each other, because they will be founded on the same beliefs about family.

For example, a stepfather-father comes home at the end of the day. His wife is already home and has started cooking dinner. He finds the family room, dining room, and kitchen littered with the children's coats, lunchboxes, and toys. He starts to straighten up and asks his eight-year-old stepson, who is sitting nearby reading, to help him.

If this stepfather and his wife both share a family concept in which everyone pitches in to do what needs to be done, his wife will appreciate his beginning a task she has not had time to do. She will approve of his involving her son, as he, too, is a family member. If, on the other hand, she has a concept of family in which everyone has fixed roles and responsibilities, she may see her husband's action as a criticism of her housekeeping: he would not be doing her work if he thought she did it well. She may be angry that he asked her son to help, because cleaning up is not his responsibility, either.

If the stepfather had the first concept of family and the mother the second, they could become embroiled in a large conflict. His effort to help is interpreted by his wife as a criticism of her and an exploitation of her child.

Working out a mutually acceptable concept of family may be more difficult than working out a definition of marriage. The family involves many more people, who are related differently to each member of the couple; the marital relationship involves only two.

In the formation of the stepfamily, it is likely that one's former concept of family will have to be adjusted to cope with the ways in which stepfamilies differ from nuclear families. Family membership and living in the same house are not synonymous. The couple members have different commitments and different relationships with the family children. Decisions about the children may involve adults living outside the household. Children are likely to call one adult "Mom" or "Dad" and the other by a first name.

Burgoyne and Clark, who studied stepfamilies in Sheffield, England, (1984), developed a typology to describe five different ways that remarried couples reconcile their desires to be like ordinary families with the realities of their stepfamily lives.

Type 1. *Not really a stepfamily.* These couples did not have to change their concept of the nuclear family and the stepparent was able to function as a parent. Either the children were quite young when the remarriage took place, or they had no contact with their parents outside the stepfamily home. Many couples had children in the stepfamily fairly soon after remarriage, and these mutual children increased their similarity to nuclear families.

Type 2. *Looking forward to the empty nest.* These couples could not resolve the discrepancy between their ideal families and the ways in which the stepparent functioned within the current stepfamily. They avoided this dilemma by focusing on their ideal of a couple relationship that they hoped to achieve in the future. Looking forward to a time when the stepfamily would be less difficult sustained them in the present.

Type 3. *The progressive stepfamily.* These couples changed their family ideals so they were no longer modeled after the nuclear family. They recognized that they had a different kind of family and saw themselves as part of a historical trend. In this way, they functioned according to a new family concept that fit their daily life.

Type 4. *The conscious pursuit of ordinary family life.* These couples attempted to live by the nuclear family imagery. The stepparent performed the functions of parents without having blood ties to the children. In this way they reconciled their family concept and function. In doing so, however, they reduced their allegiances to biological children who were living outside the home.

Type 5. *Conscious pursuit of ordinary family life frustrated.* These couples attempted to become Type 4 families but were unable to do so, largely due to the interventions of former spouses or to unresolved problems dating back to the divorce. The stepparent was unable to function as a parent, and the family did not fit the couple's concept. These couples were the most uncomfortable with their new families.

The authors point out that they had trouble placing some couples in their typology because the husband and wife did not seem to belong in the same type. These differences between husbands and wives are likely to reflect differences in family concept as well as different perceptions of the family's daily life together.

This typology illustrates how couples combine their ideas about family with such factors as the ages of the children and the amount of contact they have with former spouses to create a way of describing their families to themselves and others. Most of the couples preferred to approximate the nuclear family ideal even if that meant living in the future or breaking ties with children in other homes. Only a few were willing to restructure their view of family to suit the situation in which they found themselves.

CONFLICTS THAT RESULT FROM DIFFERENCES

In my clinical and educational work with stepfamilies I meet many couples who are in the midst of difficult struggles to resolve differences about their identity as a couple or their handling of the children. Sometimes these differences are compounded by the fact that one member of the couple is a stepparent and the other is not.

Different Definitions of the Family

When one partner in a remarriage is in a first marriage, the couple members may have particular problems in working out a definition of their marriage that works for both of them. The following incident illustrates this difficulty.

Mr. and Mrs. Abraham were attending a holiday cookout in their suburban community. Mr. Abraham, a remarried father, had joint custody of two boys, aged four and seven, who spent every other week with him. Mrs. Abraham had never been married. Most of the couples at the cookout were first-married parents of babies or young children.

When a new neighbor asked the Abrahams if they had any children, Mr. Abraham indicated his two boys. The neighbor, a new mother herself, asked Mrs. Abraham whether she had breastfed the boys. Mrs. Abraham gave her husband a dirty look for opening her up to this awkward question and replied that she was the boys' stepmother and had never breastfed anyone.

As a result, each of the Abrahams felt betrayed by the other. Mrs. Abraham was angry that Mr. Abraham did not make her role clear and opened her up to embarrassing questions. Mr. Abraham wished his wife could have kept up the illusion that these were their children.

In this example, the members of the couple, due to their different biological relationships to the children and their different marital histories, experienced the dialogue differently. They also had different ways of handling public and private realities. Mr. Abraham had chosen his new wife, in part, because she was a pediatric nurse and knew how to handle children. He wished her to be the "real mother" of his children instead of the mother they had. He took every opportunity to include the children in his new family. He would not have minded public misrepresentation that they were a fine, suburban family consisting of Mom, Dad, and two kids, and did not understand why his wife became upset by the details.

Mrs. Abraham, slightly overwhelmed by the responsibilities of caring for the two children, missed the excitement she had expected from her first marriage. When her birthday celebration, during the first year of marriage, was not a candlelit dinner in an elegant restaurant but a visit from two muddy little boys to share cake and ice cream, she spent the late-night hours crying. At the cookout, she wished she was one of the new mothers, that she knew the history of every tooth and every fever as the new mothers did. Not only had she no desire to perpetuate the illusion that she was the mother of her stepsons, she felt she would set a trap for herself if she did. How strange it would seem to the others if they called her by her first name instead of Mom.

In their private life, Mr. and Mrs. Abraham also had different ways of understanding their reality. Mr. Abraham criticized his wife for being too strict about chores, planned outings with the children without informing her, and allowed the boys to greet him with big hugs and ignore their stepmother. In other words, Mr. Abraham maintained his role as the biological parent of the children, the one they favored and the parent who had the final say in their upbringing. He already resented the amount of control he had to relinquish to the children's biological mother, and did not want to lose more control to his new wife.

In private Mrs. Abraham wanted to be treated more like a mother. She longed for the boys to give her hello hugs, good-night kisses, and homemade cards. She wanted to be part of the planning for the family and to refer to the boys as "our kids" rather than "your kids." She wanted Mr. Abraham to support her authority and let her have the control over the household, which she felt commensurate with the amount of housework she did to create a home for him and his children.

This example illustrates the difficulty this type of remarried couple (a remarried father with a wife who has not been previously married or has been married but has not had children) has in establishing a common concept of their family reality. If we ask a childless couple in a first marriage whether they have children, we will assuredly receive the same reply from both of them. If they are expecting a child, or have a child, they will also answer in the same way. Their reality around the issue of having children is the same. They may differ in their goals for having children, but they have some time and space in which to resolve those differences.

The Abraham couple actually experienced their reality around children differently. From the difference in their identities as a parent and a stepparent came many other differences in their day-to-day experiences. Within their step-family, Mr. Abraham received affection from his wife and his two sons; Mrs. Abraham received affection primarily from her husband. Mr. Abraham was living with a woman he chose as a partner and two children he chose to father; Mrs. Abraham was living with a man she chose as a mate and two children about whose presence she had no choice. Mr. Abraham's history with his sons dated back seven years. Mrs. Abraham had known them for two years, the same amount of time she has known Mr. Abraham. The children respected Mr. Abraham and followed his commands; they tested the authority of Mrs. Abraham. To Mr. Abraham they were "fine kids" who became rambunctious (boys will be boys). To Mrs. Abraham they often seemed disrespectful and sloppy (she demanded order and neatness, and they listened to her less often).

Every married couple has to make decisions about how to spend their money and how much they should each work as they raise children. Financial decisions created immediate differences for the Abrahams. Mr. Abraham was proud that his income supported his boys in his home and

helped support them in their mother's home (the amount of child support had been worked out by Mr. Abraham, his first wife, and their lawyers, before his marriage to his second wife). Mrs. Abraham resented the money that the former Mrs. Abraham received for the boys, which improved her lifestyle as well. Mrs. Abraham also resented that she and her husband had to use her savings to have a special vacation or a new car.

These differences in family definition created communication problems. When they discussed a vacation, Mrs. Abraham pictured two adults on a deserted beach; Mr. Abraham envisioned the four of them in a camper. The same weekend with the children could be a great success for Mr. Abraham and a large disappointment for his wife.

Couples like the Abrahams are more common in counseling than in the population at large. These couples seem to have a particularly hard time when the wife takes the major responsibility for the nurturance and support of the couple relationship itself. She may feel that she looks after the couple and her husband looks after his children. She plans an evening out with him, and he has expended so much energy with his children during the day that he's too tired to enjoy their time out. She wants new furniture in the living room, and he wants to buy a climbing structure. She can easily feel abandoned if this split is too great. In a couple in which the wife is the remarried parent and the stepfather has no children, often the wife takes on the responsibility for the couple relationship as well as for the parenting. Stepfathers rarely feel they are taking prime responsibility for the couple relationship.

Different Orientations to Child-Rearing

The next example illustrates the differences that can occur between parent and stepparent about discipline.

Mr. Russell, the stepfather of a 13-year-old daughter, criticized his wife for the way she handled her daughter for coming in late the night before. "Listen, last night she came in an hour late. In my family, when I broke a rule, I got punished. Right then and there. You sweettalk her, you ask her if everything's all right, and tuck her in with a good night kiss. Why didn't you lay out a punishment last night? I think we should ground her for a month."

"Look," Mrs. Russell answered, "she's the kind of kid who will apologize and listen tomorrow. Last night we just would have had a huge argument, she would have been stubborn, I would have lost my temper, and we would all have been up for another hour fighting. This way I'll remind her how important it is for her to be in on time—she was very foolish not even to call us—and I'll cut back on her phone time for the next week."

"There you go again, being so namby-pamby. What kind of kid are you raising anyway? If she's gonna be a daughter of mine, even a stepdaughter of mine, she's got to learn to obey."

The Russells illustrate another common difference in remarried couples, a difference that frequently arises in this form when a divorced or widowed mother marries a man who has never been married or has never had children of his own, but has very strong ideas about how children should be reared.

Two ways of looking at morality, a rules orientation and a response orientation, have been described by Gilligan (1982) and Lyons (1983). In the rules orientation, the priority is to fulfill one's responsibility according to an explicit code of behavior. In the response orientation, the priority is the maintenance of relationship even when that means diverging from the formal code. Most people are able to use both these orientations and use them in different settings.

Mrs. Russell expressed the response orientation and Mr. Russell the rules orientation in coping with Jennifer's misbehavior. This difference in outlook between parent and stepparent is typical for remarried couples. Mrs. Russell, as the parent, had a relationship with her child to maintain. In the context of this relationship, she could make exceptions to the rules. Mrs. Russell knew that her daughter would be apologetic and cooperative the following morning but stubborn and defiant the night of the offense. She had learned this way of handling Jennifer by trial and error over their years together. Moreover, she had a stake in handling Jennifer in a way that did not increase the emotional distance between them.

Mr. Russell, lacking this kind of intimate relationship, needed to rely on the rules to bring some order and predictability into his life. He was evaluating the child's behavior from a distance. He was also more aware and more upset by the ways in which transgressions of the rules disrupted his adult life and intruded into the private space for him and his wife. Mrs. Russell expected worry about a daughter to be part of her life; she had had 13 years to become accustomed to the strains of parenthood. Mr. Russell wanted a quiet evening, to relax, and to go to bed on time. He wanted Mrs. Russell to be attentive to him, not to listening to every footstep on the sidewalk or to look at the phone to make it ring.

This difference was also apparent in Mr. Russell's wish to return to a neat home, to walk inside without tripping over skate boards, being accosted by the blare of rock and roll, or finding books and coats piled on the dining room table. Mr. Russell interpreted these acts as a deliberate lack of consideration. To Mrs. Russell, they were minor infringements that she considered part of life with a teenager. She knew her daughter loved her; she did not interpret her messiness as disrespect or lack of caring. Mr. Russell was not sure his stepdaughter even liked him; he looked for signs of acceptance or rejection in all her behavior.

What happened in the Russells' argument is common. The conflict is likely to escalate as each one becomes more entrenched in his or her position. The more critical Mr. Russell became, the more Mrs. Russell felt she had to protect her daughter. The more Mrs. Russell defended her daughter, the more unsupported and rejected Mr. Russell felt and the angrier he became. His anger, evoked by his wife, was often displaced onto his stepdaughter so that he thought her punishment should be even greater than he did originally.

Mr. Russell is not atypical. Research on stepfather families indicates that stepfathers tend to be more authoritarian and traditional in their views about family and child-rearing than are natural fathers (Bohannon & Yahraes, 1979; Perkins, 1977; Woodruff, 1982). One reason that stepfathers express such authoritarian views may be that the family system needs more authority. Divorced mothers tend to be more permissive and less firm in disciplining their children than either mothers in intact families or mothers in stepfamilies (Hetherington, Cox & Cox, 1982; Santrock et al., 1982). When the stepfather joins the family there is a good chance that the children are behaving in ways that many adults would not accept. The mother had tolerated this behavior because she felt guilty about the divorce or because she did not have the strength to take control. Unless the stepfather is an extremely tolerant person, he is likely to be pulled into the role of bringing some order to the family. Someone needs to present the rules orientation.

A similar phenomenon does occur with stepmothers if the remarried father has been very permissive with his children. The stepmother then feels she has to establish order in the household. Her emphasis is often getting chores done, doing homework, and keeping things neat. The stepfather's concern is more often obedience to adults and showing respect. Each stepparent may enforce limits in those areas that the natural parent has let slide since the divorce. Stepmothers, however, tend to resent it when they fall into the role of "heavy" in the family. They complain that their husbands should make these demands on the children and they should

not have to (an old-fashioned nuclear family model). In contrast, although stepfathers become angry at their partners for allowing the children to misbehave, they are willing to take the children on directly. They may be fulfilling what they have been taught is the masculine role—to be the authority.

These differences in orientation and the fact that the parent has gone through years of the intense experience of parenting sometimes make it hard for the couple to see eye-to-eye on these issues. Mr. Russell felt he was helping out by laying down the law and having his stepdaughter follow the rules. Mrs. Russell appreciated his strictness but at times felt he was being too harsh or did not know her daughter well enough.

Disagreement about the Former Spouse

The former spouse of one member of the remarried couple can also continue to exert an influence on that partner, which makes it more difficult for the couple to establish stability between them. The Jordan couple illustrate this problem.

Mrs. Jordan's parents had just arrived for their first visit to the new couple since the wedding. Mrs. Jordan had planned five days of sightseeing and visiting. Mr. Jordan received a phone call from his former wife, who had sprained her ankle and would not be able to drive his children to summer camp. Nor had she finished shopping for them. Mr. Jordan agreed to take the children shopping the next day and to drive them to camp the day after.

Mrs. Jordan remonstrated: "She always does this. That woman runs my life. I want to have a nice weekend with my parents and my kids and you and now this."

Mr. Jordan replied, "She didn't sprain her ankle on purpose. The kids need me to help them. I can't refuse to help my kids."

Mrs. Jordan answered, "Helping your kids hurts mine. They want their grandparents to share their new family. You're important to them, too. There's always something. Why couldn't she find a friend to drive them up? Why can't they go on a bus? Why do you always say yes to her right away?"

The continuing relationship with a former spouse can interfere with the autonomy of the remarried couple. Many decisions cannot be made without checking with the former spouse. Events in the former spouse's life, such as this sprained ankle, affect the new couple. Sometimes both members of the new couple have the same reaction—whether anger or acceptance. When they have different reactions, additional problems arise for the couple. Mrs. Jordan saw Mr. Jordan as being manipulated by his ex-wife. This limited her own power in the couple relationship and also lowered her respect for her husband. Mr. Jordan saw Mrs. Jordan as unsympathetic and unsupportive of his parenting of his children.

The ex-wife is frequently a character to be reckoned with. Problems seem to occur more frequently with former wives of remarried husbands than with former husbands. A former wife is more likely than a former husband to have custody of the children: she is more involved with her children's lives and may want to be in charge of the children-father relationship. Even when mothers do not have custody, they are more likely to remain involved with their children than fathers without custody (Furstenberg & Nord, 1985).

Mr. Jordan viewed his children and their mother as a unit as they were when he was married—his wife-n-kids. He helped his ex-wife pay her rent so the children would have a roof over their heads. Since he was somewhat removed from the daily care of the children, he wanted the person providing that care, his ex-wife, to do it well.

Mrs. Jordan was more likely to separate the ex-wife and the children in her thinking. She saw the children when they spent time in her home; she rarely saw the former wife. She also had a tremendous respect for the bond created

between a man and a woman when they have a child together. She knew that a marriage can be ended through a divorce, but that the children, and the bonds they create, remain forever. She was jealous that the former Mrs. Jordan had this bond with her husband and she did not. Even though she knew rationally that Mr. Jordan had no desire to return to his former wife, the new Mrs. Jordan was readily jealous of the kinds of attention, assistance, and cooperation that Mr. Jordan gave his ex-wife.

Feelings about the former spouse came between the couple members when Mr. Jordan had some direct contact with his former wife and Mrs. Jordan did not. In a long phone conversation or even in a face-to-face meeting, Mr. Jordan could express his anger and frustration at some of their dealings. At these times he could find her responsive and reasonable, and might end the conversation with an improved opinion of his former wife. Mrs. Jordan, without this outlet for her feelings and without the direct exchange with her husband's ex-wife, had no way to release her anger. She often felt abandoned by her husband when he told her that his ex-wife was trying to be reasonable.

LIVING IN THE STEPFAMILY STRUCTURE

The Abraham, Russell, and Jordan couples illustrate some characteristic conflicts in remarried couples. These problems are not caused by personality defects in the partners; they are a result of the stepfamily's complex structure and history. A look at this structure is helpful in understanding the couples' dilemmas.

The remarried couple is embedded within the larger and more complex family constellation of a stepfamily. Through their children they are tied to former spouses who may also be in stepfamilies of their own. The couple, their children, and their children's parents are all functioning within a larger system that Ahrons (1984) calls the binuclear family and Bohannon (1970) refers to as a kinship chain.

Being part of a stepfamily has a very specific influence on the couple. On the positive side, the other adults in the binuclear family may be resources for the couple when they need time without children or when the children are having difficulties. On the negative side, the couple may find their autonomy, intimacy, and power limited by the larger system. An example will illustrate:

Marge was a single parent with two children. Her mother, who lived in another state, needed surgery, and Marge wanted to spend two weeks with her after the operation. She called her former husband, Peter, to see if he could take the children for that time (Peter is a resource for her). Peter talked to his second wife, Jessica, and they agreed. (Marge's request can be seen as a disruption of their lives. They are not autonomous in planning their time.) Jessica had two children from her first marriage. She called her ex-husband, Ron, to see if he could switch his visitation weekend so it would come after Peter's kids had gone, rather than in the middle of their stay. (Ron is a potential resource for Jessica and Peter in helping them have time alone together). Ron agreed but found himself thinking, "I am expected to change my plans because my ex-wife's second husband's ex-wife's mother is ill." (His autonomy is now limited and his concept of family is being stretched). So that he could care for his children, he called the new woman in his life to reschedule a ski weekend they had planned.

This story demonstrates how the various adults can be resources for each other and how their doing so puts restraints on their own autonomy and on the intimacy of the new couples. This particular family demonstrated flexibility and cooperation. Marge, Peter, Jessica, and Ron seem to have accepted living in a kinship chain. Peter's new woman friend, Liz, is not yet a member of this system and is less likely to un-

derstand why Peter chose to agree to this change. As the newest adult in the kinship chain, she could easily feel resentful and powerless. Jessica, earlier in her marriage to Peter, might have felt the same way about Marge's request, but she has become used to changing arrangements and recognizes that an occasion may arise when she and Peter will ask Marge for a similar favor.

Peter and Jessica, because they are settled in their stepfamily and have learned to put each other first when communicating about stepfamily events, are not likely to argue about this new childcare plan. Liz and Ron, on the other hand, may have some conflict about it. Ron said yes to his ex-wife even before he consulted Liz. The Russell couple above were still experiencing conflict about similar behavior on the part of the husband toward his ex-wife.

Limits on Intimacy

Couples in remarriages usually want intimacy and closeness. Many of them have had first marriages in which they never became as intimate as they would have liked. Individuals going through the divorce process often begin to share with other people in new ways. They think about their lives, their choices, and their relationships more seriously. Some men, who care for their children after a marital separation, learn to be more attentive to feelings, more nurturant, and more responsive to others than they have been before. Couples also enter new relationships with a fear of the vulnerability they know accompanies closeness. A determination to make the relationship work despite the risks often keeps the remarried couple together as they face the hurdles of stepchildren and former spouses.

Children themselves interfere with intimacy (it is hard to hug a man who has two children on his lap). Love is not supposed to be a quantifiable entity with only so much to go around. Yet time, energy, front seats in the car, and hands to hold are finite. The romance quickly goes out of a day in the woods when two children are along. A pizza shop is not as conducive to intimacy as a candlelit café. Children often make a point of disregarding hints from the couple that they want to be alone.

Old concepts of the family often get in the way of ensuring the couple's privacy. Parents feel guilty saying no to requests their children make for help or time together. They often dislike closing or locking their bedroom doors. Stepparents feel ashamed to admit they feel jealous when their partners are loving and intimate with their children.

A parent can feel close to the new partner and the child at the same time; a stepparent rarely can. The stepfather of a six-year-old girl expressed his embarrassment when his wife would allow her daughter to come into their room while they dressed in the morning. When the stepparent experiences the child as a hindrance to couple intimacy and requests time alone, the parent often feels that the child is being rejected. When the parent can understand the motivation for the stepparent's request, the chances of resolving differences are increased.

The daily tasks of childcare can be tedious and frustrating. Preparing meals, washing dishes, doing laundry, driving the children to their lessons and appointments are not intrinsically pleasant but give parents the satisfaction of being good parents and watching their children develop. An afternoon pushing kids on swings in the park can be a meaningful, great Sunday for the visiting father and a bore for his wife. Watching a school play can be a thrill for the proud mother and a chore for her new husband. This difference in their experience, if not acknowledged, can lead to a sense of resentment and neglect on the part of the stepparent.

The former spouse can also interfere with intimacy. A phone call from an ex-husband or ex-wife interrupts an evening together far more than a call from a family member or friend. Conflicts that arise between former spouses spill over into the new marriage. The new couple may disagree about how to handle the "ex." Even when they agree, they may feel emotionally burned out from discussing the problems with a former mate. It is hard to switch gears from this kind of problem solving to intimate relations.

Reminders of the past, if they upset one member of the couple, can cause friction. The children themselves often look or behave like their other parent. A cute story about a child when he was little may include a reference to the child's mother, which sets off jealousy in the stepmother. Some stepparents hate hearing about family history that occurred before they were on the scene.

The Russell couple's dilemma is a good illustration of how the former spouse can interfere with the couple's time together and sense of shared purpose and create disagreements between them. Although difficulties between former spouses seem to be the worst in the first years of courtship and remarriage, they may occur as long as the children are in touch with both parents. For many divorced parents, major milestones in the child's life, such as graduation or marriage, include some kind of contact with the former spouse. This contact itself may create conflict for the stepparent or differences of opinion between parent and stepparent.

Limits on Autonomy and Power of the Couple

Being a couple in a stepfamily limits the couple's power in several ways. Within their household they have to work hard for each parent's authority to be respected by all the children. The children's needs and requests often interfere with couple goals and priorities. Unless the couple take charge of the family and act as its executive team, they are not likely to feel any sense of stability and order in their marriage. When they attempt to manage the family and establish standards in their household about the kind of food served, the hours at which children are allowed to wake or sleep, or the participation of the children in family activities, they often meet resistance from children who were accustomed to another way of doing things before the marriage.

As a unit within the larger system, the remarried couple is not as autonomous as a first-married couple would be. They cannot even choose when to have their first child—the children are there already. A remarried couple often need to talk with former spouses in order to make vacation plans to go away with their own children. Many couples cannot decide to send a child to a private school, seek a therapist for a child, or move out of state without complex negotiations. Often the couple are not independent financially; a wife may be receiving child support from her former husband, while a husband is making support payments to his former wife. Changes in the financial status of the former spouses can suddenly affect the new family's economic stability as well.

Both parents and stepparents express pain and frustration at having their hands tied in dealing with the ways the former spouses treat the children. The couple members can work together to minimize these effects, but they rarely experience the satisfaction of solving this kind of problem together. The remarried couple simple do not have the power to change the behavior of the child's other parent. They cannot, for example, make a visiting parent be responsible, be punctual, or plan appropriate activities. Sometimes when one parent remarries, the parent who is still living as a single parent puts pressure on the children to miss their visitation time and stay with her because she is alone. Although parents can go as far as the courts to enforce divorce agreements, they cannot effectively stop a parent's guilt-inducing tactics on the children.

Gender Differences

It is almost impossible to write about couple relationships without considering the effects of male and female roles and socialization. In a remarriage the gender of the stepparent (especially if he or she is not a parent already) affects the kind of differences that the couple are likely to have to work out. A stepmother's experience and a stepfather's experience are not interchangeable, primarily because being the partner of a divorced mother is different from being the partner of a divorced father.

The ways in which custody is usually awarded following divorce contributes to the ways in which the roles of stepfather and stepmother differ. These differences, in turn, create particular patterns of couple interaction.

Because most mothers are awarded custody or have joint custody following divorce (Cherlin, 1981), most stepfathers see their stepchildren regularly and share their primary household. But stepfathers vary considerably in how directly involved they are with the children. In many households the provider role is considered sufficient involvement for a stepfather or a father. The children are used to living in their mother's household. Although they have to adjust to a stepfather, he is not defined as their primary caretaker. The stepfather, by living in the custodial home of the children, shares their daily routines, sees them when they are relaxed, and has some leisure time alone with his wife if the children visit their father.

Most stepmothers, who live with fathers who do not have custody of their children, see the children only at those times designated for visitation. When the children spend time with them, they seem to be a cross between family members and guests and may be particularly anxious or rebellious. Some divorced fathers feel they do not have enough time with their children and are reluctant to allow the stepmothers to become close to them. Others expect the stepmothers, as females, to take the primary responsibility for the children during their visits, especially if the stepmother is caring for children of her own or is in charge of running the household. Some stepmothers find themselves in this role because their paychecks are smaller and are more easily sacrificed when their stepchildren move in.

When fathers do have custody of their children, it is often because the mother is considered unfit or because the children have moved from the mother's home to the father's. In these cases, the children are more likely to be confused, to feel rejected, or to be lacking in basic security and social skills because of the family history. Caring for these children may be more difficult than dealing with children who are in their mother's custody. Moreover, visiting mothers are in touch with their children more frequently than visiting fathers, so the child in father custody may feel conflicted in loyalty to the two parents.

Differences in the socialization of men and women also influence the expectations they bring to the stepparent role. Both fathers and stepfathers are expected to be more distant from children than mothers. Both are expected to be out of the house a good deal of the time and to concern themselves with providing for the material needs of the family. A stepfather who is ignored by a crying child running to her mother does not often feel rejected (many biological fathers are also ignored in the dash to get comfort from Mommy). A stepfather who helps out financially, does some activities with his stepchildren on the weekend, and gives his wife comfort and support in her role can feel that he is doing a pretty good job.

A stepmother's job, on the other hand, is often closer to the role of a father than that of a mother. A father is sometimes treated as the secondary parent in the family. A stepmother is also a secondary parent, second to the father. But her ideal of a parent is usually that of a mother. She may feel like a failure when the crying child pushes past her to find Daddy's arms for comfort.

As a woman, a stepmother is also more likely to use her relationships as a measure of how her life is going. If her relationships are in good shape, other areas of her life may seem less important. Because of the structure of the visiting stepfamily and because of her unrealistic expectations of her role, it is often hard for the stepmother to feel that her steprelationships are going well. This may be true even if she has already proven to be a good mother to her biological children.

The implications of these differences between stepmothers and stepfathers are twofold. First, within each marriage they create a role and a set of role expectations for the stepmother or the stepfather. The stepparent's adjustment to this role may cause discomfort or grievances, which the couple need to resolve. Different roles for stepfathers and stepmothers also create important differences among those remarried couples that contain a stepmother and father, a stepfather and mother, or a stepmother and stepfather (the Abraham, Jordan, and Russell couples above). Disagreements between the couple members are likely to be expressed differently in each type of couple, and the particular conflicts that arise are likely to be different.

Successful Coping Patterns

Being part of a larger system puts a particular and somewhat predictable set of limits on the couple's opportunities to be intimate, powerful, and autonomous. Within these structural and historical constraints, the remarried partners work out a balance between togetherness and individuality.

The couple's sense of connection is enhanced by building a boundary that separates them from the rest of the family and by becoming a team in solving stepfamily problems. Many couples set aside time to be alone together. Planning to have a discussion about how things are going every Tuesday after dinner might seem absurd to partners in a first marriage, but it may be a necessity in a remarriage. Having time alone together increases the sense of stability, because each partner is not pulled in a different direction by his or her ties to a set of children.

The couple also learn to say no to children and former spouses on issues that interfere with their needs as a couple. Sometimes a couple with two sets of stepchildren make time for themselves by having all the children at their home some weekends and none of the children on other weekends. Although this arrangement may be less satisfactory for the children who always have to share their parents with stepsiblings, the parents find it helpful. Other activities such as entertaining friends, playing sports, and do-it-yourself projects may also be limited so the couple can be together.

The identity of each couple member is respected and encouraged by the recognition of each one's different connections to other family members. Some remarried parents find it fulfilling to spend time alone with their biological children. Honoring this desire gives the other partner a chance to be with his or her children or to pursue other interests. Some childless stepmothers find that leaving the house while the children are visiting and doing things they like by themselves or with other adults is a good antidote to feeling exploited or excluded. When they feel gratified by their own activities they are likely to be better partners in the marriage.

Remarried partners are often able to express their individual needs and interests more easily than partners in first marriages because they are more mature, have insights about themselves gained from a divorce, or have a vision of marriage that allows them to express their uniqueness. Giving up the concept of marriage as a total unity and merger of two people provides freedom for individual differences.

Remarried couples can handle their finances by pooling their resources into a common pot (Fishman, 1983) or by pooling some resources for household needs and keeping some separate for one's biological children and oneself. Fishman found that pooled resources increased family integration. Keeping some money separate can give partners a sense of independence and the freedom to spend some money without

consulting the other. Each approach has some benefits.

The improved communication that happily remarried couples describe can enhance both couple stability and individual identity. Talking things over enables couples to come to agreement and to form common goals, thereby increasing the stability in the relationship. Good communication also includes listening to the other person and respecting the differences that arise. By continuing to talk together, a remarried couple can learn that differences are not always a threat to their marriage.

Stresses and Successes

Second marriages end in divorce as frequently or more frequently than first marriages (Cherlin, 1981). When one thinks about why so many remarriages are shortlived, it is important to consider both the particular stresses felt by the remarried couple and their strengths in coping with these stresses.

The stresses of the stepfamily seem to take their toll. Having stepchildren in the remarriage increases the likelihood of divorce, and having two sets of stepchildren increases it even more (White & Booth, 1985). This implies that the pressures of being a couple in the midst of a stepfamily may make some remarriages less viable. Yet the Pennsylvania couples described by Furstenberg and Spanier (1984) are living with these stresses and feel their marriages are better the second time around. They seem to represent a category of remarried couples who are well equipped to survive the difficulties of stepfamily life.

When couples in remarriages do divorce, it is likely that the difficulties of living in a stepfamily are not the only reason. Couples who divorce after a second marriage probably break up for the same reasons that their first marriages did. Many second marriages for one partner are first marriages for the other. The desire for individual gratification that is not found in the marriage may lead to divorce. Both the strengths and weaknesses of the couple relationship itself and the nature and extent of the pressures upon it are likely to influence the marriage's success or failure.

One factor that may help a remarried couple to survive is their ability to reformulate their concepts of marriage and family to fit the remarried couple and stepfamily. If they cannot do this, the frustration of trying to live up to nuclear family and first-marriage ideals may increase the tension between the partners. Not all successful remarried couples, however, give up the model of the nuclear family. Some prefer to sever ties with children in other households and treat their stepfamily as a nuclear family (Burgoyne & Clark, 1984).

Despite the similar dilemmas faced by remarried couples, there are many differences among them. There is no right way or best way for a remarried couple to achieve the balance of stability and identity that works for them. Successful stepfamilies have developed their own strategies to cope with the differences between the spouses and the differences between the parts of their stepfamily. The stepfamily can be a place for learning that differences can generate excitement and energy and that people who have different histories and different opinions can remain married and care for each other and all their children.

REFERENCES

Ahrons, C. 1984. "The Binuclear Family: Parenting Roles and Relationships." In *Parent-Child Relationships, Post-Divorce: A Seminar Report.* Copenhagen: Danish National Institute of Social Research.

Askham, J. 1984. *Identity and Stability in Marriage.* Cambridge: Cambridge University Press.

Bohannon, P. 1970. "Divorce Chains, Households of Remarriage and Multiple Chains." In Bohannon, ed., *Divorce and After: An Analysis of the Emotional and Social Problems of Divorce.* New York: Doubleday.

Bohannon, P., & H. Yahraes. 1979. "Stepfathers as Parents." In *Families Today: A Research Sampler on Families and Children,* ed. E. Corfman.

Burgoyne, J., & D. Clark. 1984. *Making a Go of It: A Study of Stepfamilies in Sheffield.* London: Routledge and Kegan Paul.

Cherlin, A. 1981. *Marriage, Divorce, Remarriage: Changing Patterns in the Post-war United States.* Cambridge: Harvard University Press.

Duberman, L. 1975. *The Reconstituted Family: A Study of Remarried Couples and Their Children.* Chicago: Nelson-Hall.

Fishman, B. 1983. "The Economic Behavior of Stepfamilies." *Family Relations 32,* pp. 359–66.

Furstenberg, F., and C. Nord. 1985. "Parenting Apart: Patterns of Childrearing after Marital Disruption." *Journal of Marriage and the Family 47,* pp. 893–904.

Furstenberg, F., and G. Spanier. 1984. *Recycling the Family: Remarriage After Divorce.* Beverly Hills, Calif.: Sage.

Galinsky, E. 1981. *Between Generations: The Six Stages of Parenthood.* New York: Times Books.

Gilligan, C. 1982. *In a Different Voice.* Cambridge: Harvard University Press.

Glick, P. 1980. "Remarriage: Some Recent Changes and Variations." *Journal of Family Issues* 1: 455–77.

Hetherington, E., M. Cox, & R. Cox. 1982. "Effects of Divorce on Parents and Children." In *Nontraditional Families: Parenting and Child Development,* ed. M. Lamb. Hillsdale, N.J.: Lawrence Erlbaum Associates.

Keshet, J. 1980. "From Separation to Stepfamily: A Subsystem Analysis." *Journal of Family Issues 1,* pp. 517–32.

———. 1981. "The Minifamily in the Stepfamily." In *Parenting After Divorce,* ed. C. Baden. Boston: Wheelock Center for Parenting Studies.

———. 1986. "The Stepparent Role: A Review of the Literature." Unpublished paper. Harvard University Graduate School of Education.

———. 1987. *Love and Power in the Stepfamily: A Practical Guide.* New York: McGraw-Hill.

Lyons, N. 1983. "Two Perspectives: On Self, Relationships, and Morality." *Harvard Educational Review 53,* pp. 125–46.

Perkins, T. 1977. *Natural-Parent Family Systems vs. Stepparent Family Systems.* Ph.D. dissertation, University of Southern California.

Prosen, S., & J. Farmer. 1982. "Understanding Stepfamilies: Issues and Implications for

Counselors." *Personnel and Guidance Journal 60,* pp. 393–97.

Santrock, J., R. Warshak, C. Lindbergh, and L. Meadows. 1982. "Children's and Parents' Observed Social Behavior in Stepfather Families." *Child Development 53,* pp. 472–80.

Schneider, D. 1980. American Kinship: A Cultural Account. Chicago: University of Chicago Press.

White, L., & A. Booth. 1985. "The Quality and Stability of Remarriages: The Role of Children." *American Sociological Review 50,* pp. 689–98.

Woodruff, L. 1982. "Traditionalism in Family Ideology: Effects on Adjustment and Satisfaction Comparing Biological and Stepfather Families." Ph.D. dissertation, University of Alabama.

READING 13-2

Stepfamilies over the Life Course: Social Support

Lynn White

Most of the research on stepfamilies rightly focuses on the stepfamily with young children. Childrearing and social replacement are clearly the most important functions of families in any society, and knowing how well stepfamilies perform these functions is crucial to understanding how children and society will fare under this increasingly common family form.

Families are much more than childrearing organizations, however. Relationships between parents and children remain important long after co-residence ends and the children are

Lynn White, "Stepfamilies Over the Life Course: Social Support" from Alan Booth and Judy Dunn (eds.), *Stepfamilies: Who Benefits? Who Does Not?* Copyright © 1994 by Lawrence Erlbaum Associates, Inc. Reprinted with the permission of Lawrence Erlbaum Associates.

grown. Although the actual quantity of goods and services exchanged between generations may be rather small under routine conditions, family members remain important sources of identity and perceived social support. In the National Survey of Families and Households (NSFH), for example, 80% of adults listed a family member as their first source of assistance in at least one of three emergencies. This perceived supportiveness has been found to be more important than actual exchange of mental health outcomes (House, Umberson, & Landis, 1988).

Thus, one question we need to ask about stepfamilies is whether they will provide these sorts of services to their members. Do people feel confident about relying upon their stepmothers or stepfathers in emergencies? Do stepchildren provide the same kinds of social integration and assistance as biological children?

There has been much speculation on these questions, but few definitive answers. Some scholars have taken a positive stance, arguing that remarriage and stepfamilies enrich the kinship network and provide us with an enlarged pool of potential kin (Furstenberg & Spanier, 1984; Wald, 1981). Others suggest that stepfamily bonds will be weaker than those in biological families, with a resulting shortfall in social support (Bartlema, 1988). In 1979, Troll, Miller, and Atchley (1979) wrote that "we know so little about kinship relations among reconstituted families that we cannot even speculate about them" (p. 69). In the ensuing 15 years, modest steps were taken to fill this gap . . .

THEORETICAL FRAMEWORKS

I briefly review sociobiological, social psychological, social network, and institutionalization perspectives on stepfamilies as support networks. Each leads to the prediction that stepfamilies will be less supportive than biological families.

Sociobiology: They're Not Carrying My Genes

The sociobiological argument (taken from Daly & Wilson, 1978) suggest that animals are reproductive strategists who maximize the survival of their genes into the next generation, in part by focusing nurturance on their own offspring. Not only is there no genetic predisposition to nurture another's children, such children may be seen as rivals who endanger one's own children's survival. In many species (including some primates), males will kill a mate's young from former unions, increasing the chances that her attention and resources will be devoted to bearing and nurturing his offspring. This argument was noted by some scholars as an explanation for the higher likelihood that stepchildren will be abused or killed (Dobash, Dobash, Wilson, & Daly, 1992; Finkelhor, 1979).

From a sociobiological perspective, not all conflict in stepfamilies will be between stepparent and stepchild. Van den Berghe hypothesized (personal communication, March 5, 1986) that as stepchildren reach puberty, they will become sexual competitors to their parents. In the usual structure of stepfamilies—biological mother/stepfather—his model implies that postpubertal stepdaughters will be the most troublesome element in stepfamilies and that this family configuration will be most unstable.

Although sociobiology is controversial, I do not introduce it as a straw man. To paraphrase Alice Rossi (1984), failure to recognize the extent to which biology shapes our lives cripples our efforts to understand the role that social structures play. It may be that, given biological predispositions, human stepfamilies are amazingly successful.

Social Psychological Perspectives

Taking a very different approach, scholars who approach the family from a social–psychological orientation argue that what sets parent–child relationships apart from others is the long-term, cumulative nature of the affective bond (Atkinson, 1989). The issue is not whether you like or love your parents/children, but the extent to which your relationship to these persons is a defining characteristic of your identity.

Turner (1970) introduced the concept of *crescive bonds* to describe incrementally built bonds that "link irreplaceable individuals . . . into a continuing relationship" (p. 89). According to Turner, the development of such bonds requires that the relationship: (a) have a long history and an open-ended future orientation, (b) be a label others use to identify you (e.g., "you are John's father"), (c) be a label you use to identify yourself, and (d) provide rewards, particularly enhanced self-esteem. When all criteria are met, the relationship becomes an integral part of identity, and it is maintained even if it ceases to be rewarding.

Empirical evidence about family identities tends to focus on parents rather than children. Research suggests that "parent" is a defining role, a role that sits at or near the top of men's and women's identity salience hierarchies. Parenthood is, after all, an incredibly time-consuming role that, for many years, shapes and constrains lifestyle choices. It would be surprising, indeed, if parenthood was not nearly as important as age and gender in determining our sense of "Who am I?" Stepparenting, however, should be substantially less important to our identities: Stepparenting takes fewer years of our lives, we can walk away, identification is incomplete and tentative ("No, I'm not John's father; I'm his stepfather"), and social recognition is weak and inconsistent. As a result, we would anticipate weaker role performance.

In recent research, Thoits (1992) documented the difference in role salience for parenting and stepparenting. Although her results must be tentative because of the small number of stepparent respondents, differences in role salience are more dramatic than those found in behavioral domains. Thoits asked her respondents to rank each of 17 roles (if occupied) on a scale of 0 (respondent held the role but did not list it as one of his or her nine top role identities) to 3 (most important identity). Although parenthood received ratings of 2.7–2.9 (the highest ratings of any role), the stepparent role ranged in salience from only 0.2–0.6. Nearly a dozen roles—including neighbor, churchgoer, in-law, relative, friend—intervened between parenthood and stepparenthood, and in general, being a stepparent was about as important as belonging to voluntary associations or having a hobby.

Thus, social psychological theory and evidence suggest that stepfamily roles are less salient to parents than are biological family roles. We might expect that this salience would be significantly greater when the stepfamily relationship had lasted longer and been formed earlier in the child's life. It is startling in Thoits' data, however, to note that stepparent roles were only marginally more salient for married than for divorced respondents.

The consequences of low role salience remain to be established. It seems likely that social support to stepchildren will be far higher than these salience rankings suggest—at least as long as the marriage creating the stepfamily lasts. Stepparents may aid stepchildren in order to please their spouse, rather than because of their own relationship to the stepchildren; likewise, stepchildren may maintain cordial relationships with the stepparent in order to please their parent. In the face of such very low role salience, the enactment of role obligations must depend on external forces—in this case, the biological parent.

Social Network Perspectives

In the last decade, a body of work has developed around the notion of social network—an interacting group whose exchanges are regulated by the density and duration of social relationships. Although the family is distinct from voluntary groups in many ways, the structural factors that operate to make other groups cohesive also apply to the family. Briefly, social network characteristics may partly explain why the family is more cohesive than other social groups: The family has high levels of density (everyone knows one another) and so has higher social control capacity (Fischer, 1982); long and open-ended interaction, and so greater likelihood of cooperation and diffuse reciprocity (Axelrod, 1984; Carley, 1991, Ekeh, 1974); and strong similarity, which reduces the cost of exchange (Carley 1991; Knoke, 1990). In every case, the stepfamily is structurally weaker than the biological family. The uniformly dense network of the biological family breaks into cliques where stepchildren and stepparent may have nonoverlapping sets of ties (to noncustodial fathers, noncustodial children, former affines), ties are of shorter duration and not so open-ended (stepparents can walk away), and genetic and, perhaps, even social similarity is less.

The structural weakness of the stepfamily implies that stepfamilies will be less able to maintain and enforce obligations to one another. They may be more apt to operate as a voluntary group, characterized by demands for immediate as opposed to diffuse reciprocity, and more dependent on affect. This line of reasoning leads to the direct hypothesis that stepfamilies will be weaker support mechanisms than biological families. It also leads to subsidiary hypotheses that exchange within stepfamilies will be greater when the stepfamily has lasted longer and when there are fewer competing ties (stepparent has no own children, noncustodial parent is dead or absent); it also implies that affect will have a greater effect on exchange within stepfamilies than biological families.

Institutionalization Perspectives

Many family scholars argue that what sets the family apart from other collections of individuals is not genetics, crescive bonds, or density of networks, but institutionalized norms of obligation—

norms that hold us responsible for our children or parents even if we don't like them (Finch, 1989).

Norms of family obligation are weakening in contemporary society for blood relatives. Certainly, many fathers have found ways to walk away from their children without being, apparently, overwhelmed with guilt or ostracized by polite society. As Cherlin (1978) noted, these norms are even weaker for stepfamilies, and it is not at all clear how much obligation stepparents and stepchildren owe one another. How much guilt do stepparents/children impose on themselves if they fail to meet a need in the other? How much censure will others impose on the individual? Two kinds of evidence can be brought to bear on these questions: evolving legal obligation among stepfamily members and survey evidence about perceived normative obligation.

Legal Obligations Laws about family obligation reflect, sustain, and create behavior. Thus, laws about stepfamilies are informative about how our society views these obligations. Two issues are of particular relevance: child support and inheritance. Fine and Fine (1992) provided important insight into stepparent/stepchild relationships by reporting on legal rights and responsibilities in these areas.

In 45 states, stepparents have no obligation to support minor stepchildren even while they live with the child's parent; in no state are they required to continue providing support if their marriage to the child's parent ends or they cease to live with the child.

In regard to inheritance, stepparents *may* choose to specify that their stepchildren receive a share of their estate, but in cases where they die without a will, the courts will assume that they intended to omit their stepchildren. If a will directs that the estate is to be divided among "my children," the courts will interpret that phrase as excluding stepchildren. No evidence exists to support or refute the assumption of such an intention on the part of stepparents.

California has recently permitted stepchildren to inherit if "the relationship of parent and child [began] during the person's minority and continued throughout the parties' joint lifetimes [and if] it is established by clear convincing evidence that the foster parent or stepparent would have adopted the person but for a legal barrier" (Waggoner, Wellman, Alexander, & Fellows, 1991, p. 131). The problem with this doctrine is that very few stepparents formally adopt their stepchildren, even though (in the many cases where the noncustodial parent disappears from the child's life and provides no support) such adoptions could probably be achieved even over the noncustodial parent's objections (Waggoner et al., 1991). Failure to adopt signals to the courts an absence of commitment. Does it carry the same signal to the child or the child's parent? Social science research could make a useful contribution, here.

From their review of statutes and judicial findings, the Fines deduce a judicial assumption that "stepfamily status entails no rights or obligations" (Fine & Fine, 1992, p. 335). If this assumption accurately reflects the feelings of stepfamily members—and little evidence exists one way or the other—then it is an inescapable conclusion that stepfamilies are seriously weak organizations whose roles lack substance.

Normative Obligations to Stepfamily Members Bartlema (1988) argued that as serial monogamy replaces monogamy, we will find kinship networks filled with "all kinds of affinal kin of varying degree of relationships" (p. 218). In many cases, we may not even be sure that these people are, in fact, relatives or what we should call them (Day, 1988). Such confusion "leaves the individual free to fill in the nature and degree of affinity of such relationships according to his or her own needs and preferences" (Bartlema, 1988, p. 218). The result is less normative pressure and more dependence on individual characteristics, such as affection, affluence, and proximity.

Rossi and Rossi's (1990) study of three-generational family relationships in the Boston area provided unique information about norms of stepfamily obligations. Rossi and Rossi gave each of their respondents a set of 32 vignettes that randomized hundreds of combinations of situation, relationship, and gender. For each vignette, respondents were asked how obligated they would feel to provide the assistance specified to the kin member named. Stepparents and adult stepchildren were among the relationships examined.

The vignettes represented hypothetical situations, and the vast majority of respondents reporting on kinship obligations to adult stepchildren and stepparents had no such relatives in their own families. Evidence that those with stepfamily experience are less likely to carry negative stereotypes about stepchildren/parents than others (Fine, 1986; Fluitt & Paradise, 1991) suggests that these hypothetical reports may underestimate actual feelings of obligation among stepfamily members. On the other hand, Thoits' data showing extraordinarily low salience of stepparent roles suggests that stepparents may distance themselves from their stepchildren even more than the public anticipates. Because generalized norms affect the degree to which stepfamily members will be sanctioned for failing to meet obligations, however, they are important.

Rossi and Rossi (1990) showed that normative obligations to stepchildren fall very materially below those to own children, but they are nevertheless substantial.[1] Obligation was rated

on an 11-point scale, where 0 represented *no obligation at all* and 10, *a very strong obligation.* Averaging obligation ratings across the four crisis situations for which the Rossis provide tabular data (p. 173), the average obligation rating was 8.3 for own children and 6.4 for stepchildren. These figures suggests a public perception that stepparents ought to feel a moderate obligation to assist adult stepchildren, and that, although the obligation to assist stepchildren falls materially below the obligation to help own children, obligations to stepchildren are rated higher than those to nieces/nephews, aunts/uncles, cousins, friends, and neighbors. Stepparents fared somewhat less well than stepchildren, and the gap between biological and stepparents was greater than that between biological children and stepchildren. Stepparents rated below friends, but ahead of neighbors, nieces/nephews, aunts/uncles, and cousins. Average obligation to stepparents was 5.8, compared to 8.3 for own parents.

The Rossi and Rossi data suggest that public opinion (presumably reflected in internalized normative pressure) would support giving less to stepparents and stepchildren than to biological parents and children. Public opinion would condemn those who failed to provide comfort or support in times of crisis, or who failed to keep up normal intercourse with stepfamily members.

A question unanswered by the Rossis' hypothetical data is whether obligations to the two types of kin might be more or less determined by circumstances. It seems likely that the normative obligations between stepchildren and stepparent like the very modest legal obligations discussed earlier, depend on an intact marriage between parent and stepparent. Normative obligations probably also depend on such factors as duration of the stepfamily relationships, the age of the child when the stepfamily was formed, length of co-residence with the stepparent, and whether one has relatives in the higher ranked categories (e.g., whether one has own children).

---

[1]The same general finding is reported in Schwebel, Fine, and Renner's (1991) small study of college students' perceptions of stepparent obligations to school-age children. Averaging across several vignettes in which the child needed some sort of assistance or support, 80% of the students thought stepparents ought to provide assistance, compared to 83% of biological parents—a significant, but quite small difference. These authors note that standard deviations differ more across categories than do the means, suggesting less consensus on norms about stepfamily obligations.

Whether normative and legal obligations extend beyond the marriage between stepparent and parent brings up an even more basic question: Does the relationship itself extend beyond the marriage? Is John still your stepson if you divorce his parent? Day (1988) noted that we have no readily agreed-upon terms to refer to such people, and that the vagueness of the role relationship is likely to be paralleled by the vagueness and ambiguity of the role expectations. In this regard, however, it is interesting that Thoits' research on role identities found that 11% of divorced men and 3% of divorced women (compared to 19% of married women and men) reported being a stepparent—and that the majority of these divorced stepparents claimed the role by saying they thought of themselves as stepparents. These data imply that role relationships, and perhaps, role obligations between stepparents and stepchildren may have a lasting quality not entirely embedded in the marriage between parent and stepparent.

The extent and determinant of normative obligations in stepfamilies are empirical questions worth further study. Both theory and the limited existing evidence, however, suggest that members of stepfamilies will feel less normative obligation (internal and external) to provide social support.

Conclusion

From each of the theoretical perspectives reviewed here, we come to the hypothesis that stepfamilies will not be as effective as biological families in providing social support to members. The extent of supportiveness in stepfamilies is likely to be enhanced by longer duration of childhood co-residence, weakness of competing ties, and especially by the continued marriage of the stepparent to the biological parent. In the absence of this last critical link and the absence of strong institutionalized support, exchange among stepparents and stepchildren is likely to be fragile . . .

REFERENCES

Aquilino, W. S. (1990). The likelihood of parent–adult child coresidence. Effects of family structure and parental characteristics. *Journal of Marriage and the Family, 52,* 405–419.

Aquilino, W. S. (1991a). Family structure and home-leaving: A further specification of the relationship. *Journal of Marriage and the Family, 53,* 999–1010.

Aquilino, W. S. (1991b). Predicting parents' experiences with coresident adult children. *Journal of Family Issues, 12,* 323–342.

Astin, A., Korn, W., & Berg, E. (1989). *The American freshman: National norms for Fall 1989.* Los Angeles: University of California, Los Angeles, American Council on Education.

Atkinson, M. (1989). Conceptualizations of the parent–child relationship: Solidarity, attachment, crescive bonds, and identity salience. In J. Mancini (Ed.), *Aging parents and adult children* (pp. 81–97). Lexington, MA: Lexington.

Axelrod, R. (1984). *The evolution of cooperation.* New York: Basic Books.

Bartlema, J. (1988). Modeling step-families: Exploratory findings. *European Journal of Population, 4,* 197–221.

Brody, E. M. (1990). *Women in the middle: Their parent-care years.* New York: Springer.

Carley, K. (1991). A theory of group stability. *American Sociological Review, 56,* 331–354.

Cherlin, A. (1978). Remarriage as an incomplete institution. *American Journal of Sociology, 84,* 634–649.

Collins, S. (1991). British stepfamily relationships, 1500–1800. *Journal of Family History, 16,* 331–344.

Daly, M., & Wilson, M. (1978). *Sex, evolution, and behavior.* North Scituate, MA: Duxbury.

Day, A. T. (1998). Kinship networks and informal support in the later years. In E. Grebenik. C. Hohn, & R. Mackensen (Eds.), *Later phases of the family cycle: Demographic aspects* (pp. 184–207). Oxford, England: Clarendon.

Dobash, R. P., Dobash, R. E., Wilson, M., & Daly, M. (1992). The myth of sexual symmetry in marital violence. *Social Problems, 39,* 71–91.

Eggebeen, D. J. (1992). Family structure and intergenerational exchanges. *Research on Aging, 14,* 427–447.

Ekch, P. (1974). *Social exchange theory: The two traditions.* Cambridge, MA: Harvard University Press.

Finch, J. (1989). *Family obligations and social change.* Oxford, England: Polity Press.

Fine, M. A. (1986). Perceptions of stepparents: Variation in stereotypes as a function of current family structure. *Journal of Marriage and the Family, 48,* 537–543.

Fine, M. A., & Fine, D. R. (1992). Recent changes in laws affecting stepfamilies: Suggestions for legal reform. *Family Relations, 44,* 334–340.

Finkelhor, D. (1979). *Sexually victimized children.* New York: The Free Press.

Fischer, C. (1982). *To dwell among friends: Personal networks in town and city.* Chicago: University of Chicago Press.

Fluitt, M. S., & Paradise, L. V. (1991). The relationship of current family structure to young adults' perceptions of stepparents. *Journal of Divorce and Remarriage, 15,* 159–173.

Furstenberg, F. F., Jr., & Spanier, G. (1984). *Recycling the family: Remarriage after divorce.* Beverly Hills, CA: Sage.

Glick, P. C. (1989). Remarried families, stepfamilies, and stepchildren: A brief demographic profile. *Family Relations, 38,* 24–27.

Glick, P. C. (1990). American families: As they are and were. *Sociology and Social Research, 74,* 139–145.

Goldscheider, F. K., & Goldscheider, C. (1991). The intergenerational flow of income: Family structure and the status of black Americans. *Journal of Marriage and the Family, 53,* 499–508.

Goldscheider, F. K., & Goldscheider, C. (1993). *Leaving home before marriage: Ethnicity, familism, and generational relationships.* Madison: University of Wisconsin Press.

Granovetter, M. (1973). The strength of weak ties. *American Journal of Sociology, 78,* 1360–1380.

House, J. S., Umberson, D., & Landis, K. R. (1988). Structures and processes of social support. *Annual Review of Sociology, 14,* 293–318.

Kiernan, K. (1992). The impact of family disruption in childhood on transitions made in young adult life. *Population Studies, 46,* 218–234.

Knoke, D. (1990). Networks of political action: Toward theory construction. *Social Forces, 68,* 1041–1063.

Kulis, S. S. (1992). Social class and the locus of reciprocity in relationships with adult children. *Journal of Family Issues, 13,* 482–504.

McLanahan, S., & Bumpass, L. (1988). Intergenerational consequences of family disruption. *American Journal of Sociology, 94,* 130–152.

Mitchell, B. A., Wister, A. V., & Burch, T. K. (1989). The family environment and leaving the parental home. *Journal of Marriage and the Family, 52,* 605–613.

Rossi, A. S. (1984). Gender and parenthood. *American Sociological Review, 49,* 1–18.

Rossi, A. S., & Rossi, P. H. (1990). *Of human bonding: Parent–child relations across the life course.* Hawthorne, NY: Aldine de Gruyter.

Schwebel, A. I., Fine, M. A., & Renner, M. A. (1991). A study of perceptions of the stepparent role. *Journal of Family Issues, 12,* 43–57.

Speare, A. Jr., & Avery, R. (1993). Who helps whom in older parent–child families? *Journal of Gerontology, 48*(2), S64–73.

Sussman, M. B. (1985). The family life of old people. In R. S. Binstock & E. Shanas (Eds.) *Handbook of aging and the social sciences* (2nd ed., pp. 415–443). New York: Van Nostrand.

Sweet, J., Bumpass, L., & Call, V. (1988). *The design and content of the National Survey of Families and Households* (Working Paper No. NSFH-1). Madison: University of Wisconsin Center for Demography and Ecology.

Thoits, P. A. (1992). Identity structures and psychological well-being: Gender and marital status comparisons. *Social Psychology Quarterly, 55,* 236–256.

Troll, L., Miller, S. J., & Atchley, R. C. (1979). *Families in later life.* Belmont, CA: Wadsworth.

Turner, R. H. (1970). *Family interaction.* New York: Wiley.

Waggoner, L. W., Wellman, R. V., Alexander, G. S., & Fellows, M. L. (1991). *Family property laws: Cases and materials on wills, trusts, and future interests.* Westbury, NY: Foundation Press.

Wald, E. (1981). *The remarried family: Challenge and promise.* New York: Family Service Association of America.

White, L. K. (1992). The effect of parental divorce and remarriage on parental support for adult children. *Journal of Family Issues, 13,* 234–250.

White, L. K., & Booth, A. (1985). The quality and stability of remarriages: The role of stepchildren. *American Sociological Review, 50,* 689–698.

White, L. K., & Riedmann, A. C. (1992a). When the Brady Bunch grows up: Relations between fullsiblings and stepsiblings in adulthood. *Journal of Marriage and the Family, 54,* 197–208.

White, L. K., & Riedmann, A. C. (1992b). Ties among adult siblings. *Social Forces, 71,* 85–102.

LINKS ACROSS THE GENERATIONS

CHAPTER 14

Children and Parents

How are children faring in America? This is a question that more and more observers of our society have been asking, and the answers are disquieting. Nearly one in four American children lives in a family whose income is below the federal poverty line. Some of these poor children are growing up in neighborhoods where few adults work full time, the streets are infested with drugs and gangs, and killings are common occurrences. The proportion of children living in poverty declined sharply during the prosperous 1950s and 1960s but has increased since the 1970s.

Many commentators have associated this increase in poverty with the changing family structure of the poor. More than one-half of all poor families were headed by single mothers in the 1990s, compared to about one-fourth in the 1960s. It is alleged that children growing up in these households are not only economically disadvantaged but also receive less supervision and guidance. Defenders of these families counter that they could do just as good a job if they had more economic and child-care support.

In the political debates over welfare reform in the mid-1990s, critics of welfare maintained that open-ended economic support of poor families had created a dependent population that had lost its initiative and independence. They argued that if welfare recipients were forced to work, their self-esteem would rise, they would be better parents, and their children would have better role models. Their opponents said that welfare was the result of being poor, not the cause of it, and that cutting families off from cash assistance would hurt many more poor children than it would help.

Among children who are not poor, another large group seem to be just getting by. Their parents—like Kenny and Bonita Merten, whom you read about in Chapter 4—earn just enough to keep them above poverty but too little to support them in comfort. Some of these children will not graduate from high school and many will not graduate from college. Consequently, their job prospects will be limited.

Still, some children are faring well. A large group of children from middle-class homes, most of whom live with two parents, are comfortable, healthy, dressed in the latest styles, and headed for college. Using census data, Donald Hernandez showed that the proportion of

341

children living in relatively prosperous families increased during the 1970s and 1980s, even as the proportion in poor families also increased.[1] In contrast, the proportion of children who were neither prosperous nor poor decreased. So for children, as for adults, inequality increased as the numbers at both extremes rose.

Pharoah and Lafeyette Rivers are two children from the poorest group. The brothers were profiled in a book, *There Are No Children Here: The Story of Two Boys Growing Up in the Other America,* by journalist Alex Kotlowitz. Pharoah, who is nine when the book begins, is an especially poignant example of the kind of child that developmental psychologists call "resilient." For reasons that experts cannot fully determine, some children who grow up in deprived circumstances have the internal resources to successfully battle, and often triumph over, the daily trials they face. These resilient children show ingenuity and creativity in developing survival strategies. In the following excerpts, note the ways in which Pharoah is able to isolate himself from the worst of his world, gain the attention

and protection of adults, and satisfy his need to learn. But note also that even a child as resourceful as Pharoah cannot avoid developing a stammer in reaction to the tension of living in his dangerous neighborhood.

The first part of this excerpt introduces Pharoah's family. The second part, which takes place a year later, describes Pharoah's hiding place. In the third part, two years later, Pharoah celebrates his birthday and recites a poem at a school assembly—always against the constant backdrop of drugs, alcohol, and violence.

The second reading addresses a very different kind of parenting experience: adopting a child. Elizabeth Bartholet, in her early 40s, decided to adopt a child after several years of unsuccessful fertility treatments. In that regard, she was not unlike many women who have postponed childbearing into their 30s or early 40s, only to find it difficult to become pregnant. But Bartholet was also a law professor, and she was able to observe the complex world of adoption through her professional lens. She found it to be governed by rules and principles that, in many ways, seemed to be just the opposite of the principles applied to biological childbearing. She argues, in this article, for encouraging adoption through a less restrictive and less regulated approach.

---

[1]Donald J. Hernandez, *America's Children: Resources from Family, Government, and Economy* (New York: Russell Sage Foundation, 1993).

READING 14-1

There Are No Children Here

Alex Kotlowitz

The children called home "Hornets," or, more frequently, "the projects" or, simply, the "jects" (pronounced *jets*). Pharoah called it "the graveyard." But they never referred to it by its full name: the Governor Henry Horner Homes.

Nothing here, the children would tell you, was as it should be. Lafeyette and Pharoah lived at 1920 West Washington Boulevard, even though their high-rise sat on Lake Street. Their building had no enclosed lobby; a dark tunnel cut through the middle of the building, and the wind and strangers passed freely along it. Those tenants who received public aid had their checks sent to the local currency exchange, since the building's first-floor mailboxes had all been broken into. And since darkness engulfed the building's corridors, even in the daytime, the residents always carried flashlights, some of which had been handed out by a local politician during her campaign.

Summer, too, was never as it should be. It had become a season of duplicity.

On June 13, a couple of weeks after their peaceful afternoon on the railroad tracks, Lafeyette celebrated his 12th birthday. Under the gentle afternoon sun, yellow daisies poked through the cracks in the sidewalk as children's bright faces peered out from behind their windows. Green leaves clothed the cottonwoods, and pastel cotton shirts and shorts, which sat for months in layaway, clothed the children.

And like the fresh buds on the crabapple trees, the children's spirits blossomed with the onset of summer.

Lafeyette and his nine-year-old cousin Dede danced across the worn lawn outside their building, singing the lyrics of an L.L. Cool J rap, their small hips and spindly legs moving in rhythm. The boy and girl were on their way to a nearby shopping strip, where Lafeyette planned to buy radio headphones with $8.00 he had received as a birthday gift.

Suddenly, gunfire erupted. The frightened children fell to the ground. "Hold your head down!" Lafeyette snapped, as he covered Dede's head with her pink nylon jacket. If he hadn't physically restrained her, she might have sprinted for home, a dangerous action when the gangs started warring. "Stay down," he ordered the trembling girl.

The two lay pressed to the beaten grass for half a minute, until the shooting subsided. Lafeyette held Dede's hand as they cautiously crawled through the dirt toward home. When they finally made it inside, all but 50 cents of Lafeyette's birthday money had trickled from his pockets.

Lafeyette's summer opened the way it would close, with gunshots. For Lafeyette and Pharoah, these few months were to be a rickety bridge to adolescence.

If the brothers had one guidepost in their young lives these few months, though, it was their mother LaJoe. They depended on her; she depended on them. The boys would do anything for their mother.

A shy, soft-spoken woman, LaJoe was known for her warmth and generosity, not only to her own children but to her children's friends. Though she received Aid to Families with Dependent Children, neighbors frequently knocked on her door to borrow a can of soup or a cup of flour. She always obliged. LaJoe had often mothered children who needed advice or comforting. Many young men and women still

Alex Kotlowitz, "There Are No Children Here" from *There Are No Children Here: The Story of Two Boys Growing Up in the Other America*, pp. 8–18, 142–145, and 249–256. Copyright © 1991 by Alex Kotlowitz. Reprinted with the permission of Doubleday, a division of Random House, Inc.

called her "Mom." She let so many people through her apartment, sometimes just to use the bathroom, that she hid the toilet paper in the kitchen because it had often been stolen.

But the neighborhood, which hungrily devoured its children, had taken its toll on LaJoe as well. In recent years, she had become more tired as she questioned her ability to raise her children here. She no longer fixed her kids' breakfasts every day—and there were times when the children had to wash their own clothes in the bathtub. Many of the adults had aged with the neighborhood, looking as worn and empty as the abandoned stores that lined the once-thriving Madison Street. By their mid-30s many women had become grandmothers; by their mid-40s, great-grandmothers. They nurtured and cared for their boyfriends and former boyfriends and sons and grandsons and great-grandsons.

LaJoe, in her youth, had been stunning, her smooth, light brown complexion highlighted by an open smile. When she pulled her hair back in a ponytail, she appeared almost Asian, her almond-shaped eyes gazing out from a heart-shaped face. She had been so pretty in her mid-20s that she briefly tried a modeling career. Now she was 35, and men still whistled and smiled at her on the street. Unlike many other women her age, she hadn't put on much weight, and her high-cheekboned face still had a sculptured look. But the confidence of her youth had left her. Her shoulders were often hunched. She occasionally awoke with dark circles under her eyes. And her smile was less frequent now.

LaJoe had watched and held on as the neighborhood slowly decayed, as had many urban communities like Horner over the past two decades. First, the middle-class whites fled to the suburbs. Then the middle-class blacks left for safer neighborhoods. Then businesses moved, some to the suburbs, others to the South. Over the past 10 years, the city had lost a third of its manufacturing jobs, and there were few jobs left for those who lived in Henry Horner. Unemployment was officially estimated at 19 percent; unofficially, it was probably much higher. There were neighborhoods in Chicago worse off than Horner, but the demise of this particular community was often noted because it had once been among the city's wealthiest areas.

Ashland Avenue, a six-lane boulevard just east of Henry Horner, was named for the Kentucky estate of Henry Clay. By the mid-19th century, it had become one of the city's smartest thoroughfares, lined with dwellings constructed of elegant Attic marble, fashionable churches, and exclusive clubs. "People would parade along the sidewalk to ogle at the notables and to be seen themselves; to watch the fine carriages spin along the macadam boulevard, to see the latest manifestation of changing fashion," read one newspaper account. But the neighborhood slowly changed. As immigrants, primarily German, Irish, and Eastern European Jews, settled on the west side, the city's glitter moved eastward to the lake, just north of the Loop, a strip now known as the Magnificent Mile and the Gold Coast.

The Ashland Avenue area quickly lost its luster. Jane Addams's founding of the renowned Hull House in 1889 signaled the west side's growing decline. It was one of the nation's first settlement houses, delivering various services to the poor of the area and acting as their advocate in housing, health care, and children's rights. Soon, the mansions on Ashland were transformed into headquarters for local unions or rooming houses for the transients of Skid Row. By 1906, the neighborhood had deteriorated still further, and tuberculosis claimed 5 percent of the west side's population. The Chicago Lung Association, then called the Chicago Tuberculosis Institute, opened its office on the west side, where it is still located.

The blight has continued and is particularly evident today west of Horner, a section of the city that, along with the south side, during the 1930s, 1940s, and 1950s became home to over a half-million blacks who migrated from the South, displacing the earlier immigrants. Western Avenue, now a strip of fast-food outlets, car washes, and family-run stores, borders Henry Horner to the west, though it is not a boundary of much significance, since on the other side the rubble continues. The two- and three-family tenements sag and lean like drunkards. Many of the buildings are vacant, their contents lying on the sidewalk.

To LaJoe, the neighborhood had become a black hole. She could more easily recite what wasn't there than what was. There were no banks, only currency exchanges, which charged customers up to $8.00 for every welfare check cashed. There were no public libraries, movie theaters, skating rinks, or bowling alleys to entertain the neighborhood's children. For the infirm, there were two neighborhood clinics, the Mary Thompson Hospital and the Miles Square Health Center, both of which teetered on the edge of bankruptcy and would close by the end of 1989. Yet the death rate of newborn babies exceeded infant mortality rates in a number of Third World countries, including Chile, Costa Rica, Cuba, and Turkey. And there was no rehabilitation center, though drug abuse was rampant.

According to a 1980 profile of the 27th ward—a political configuration drawn, ironically, in the shape of a gun and including Henry Horner and Rockwell Gardens, a smaller but no less forbidding public housing complex— 60,110 people lived here, 88 percent of them black, 46 percent of them below the poverty level. It was an area so impoverished that when Mother Teresa visited it in 1982, she assigned nuns from her Missionaries of Charity to work at Henry Horner. They had set up a soup kitchen, a shelter for women and children, and an afterschool program. Where there used to be 13 social service agencies there were now only three: the Missionaries of Charity, the Boys Club, and the Chicago Commons Association. The latter two provided recreational activities as well as tutoring, counseling, and day care, but they had limited funds. A Chicago Commons' program called Better Days for Youth targeted children under 13 who were having problems in school or with the police, but there was money to serve only 28 children at a time.

LaJoe sometimes believed that the city had all but given up here. A local billboard warned NEEDLES KILL. There was a time when such a message read DRUGS KILL.

And despite Horner's proximity—one mile— to the city's booming downtown, LaJoe and her neighbors felt abandoned. Horner sat so close to the city's business district that from the Sears Tower observation deck tourists could have watched Lafeyette duck gunfire on his birthday. But city residents never had reason to pass the housing complex unless they attended a basketball or hockey game at the Chicago Stadium, just a block away.

Exacerbating the isolation was the fact that nearly half of the families in Henry Horner, including the Riverses, had no telephone. Residents also felt disconnected from one another; there was little sense of community at Horner, and there was even less trust. Some residents who didn't have a phone, for instance, didn't know any others in their building who would let them use theirs. Some neighbors wouldn't allow their children to go outside to play. One mother moved aside her living room furniture to make an open and safe place where her children could frolic.

But though the isolation and the physical ruin of the area's stores and homes had discouraged LaJoe, it was her family that had most let her down. Not that she could separate the two. Sometimes she blamed her children's problems on the neighborhood; at other times, she attributed the neighborhood's decline to the change in people, to the influx of drugs and violence.

Her three oldest children, to whom she felt she'd given everything she could, had all disappointed her. All had dropped out of school. All had been in jail at least once. All had been involved with drugs. The oldest, LaShawn, a slender 20-year-old, was so delicately featured some called her "China Doll." She worked as a prostitute from time to time to support her drug habit. The next oldest, 19-year-old Paul, named after his father, had served time in an Indiana prison for burglary. Terence, now 17, had been the most troublesome problem for LaJoe and, because of their extraordinary closeness, her biggest disappointment. He began selling drugs at the age of 11 and had been in and out, usually in, trouble with the law ever since.

LaJoe also had a set of four-year-old triplets: Timothy, Tiffany, and Tammie. The two girls so resembled each other that not even their father could tell them apart.

All eight children had the same father, Paul, to whom LaJoe had been married for 17 years. But the two had long ago fallen out of love. He lived at home only sporadically.

LaJoe wanted it to be different for Lafeyette and Pharoah, different from the way it had been for her three oldest children and different from the way it had been for her.

In her husband's absence, Lafeyette had become LaJoe's confidant. She relied on him. So did the younger children. Lafeyette watched after Pharoah and the triplets. He wouldn't let anything happen to them. He had been a carefree child, a bit of a ham, in fact. For a photograph taken when he was about four, he shoved a big cigar in his mouth and plopped a blue floppy hat on his small head. It was Christmastime, and Lafeyette's cousins, who in the photo were all crowded behind him, seemed amused by his antics. When he got older, around eight or nine, he'd hop on the Madison Street bus by himself to visit his grandmother, who lived in an apartment farther west. And he loved to draw, mostly pictures of superheroes. He boasted that his name appeared on all seven floors of his building. He was a boy bubbling with energy and verve.

But over the past year Lafeyette had begun to change, LaJoe thought. The past spring, he'd been caught stealing candy from a Walgreen's downtown. It was the first time he'd gotten into any kind of trouble. He had been hanging out with a youngster, Keith, who was known among the neighborhood kids for his ability to swipe expensive bottles of cologne from the display cases at downtown department stores. Lafeyette was placed in the Chicago Commons' Better Days for Youth. One of the first children in the new six-month program, Lafeyette received help with his school work as well as counseling. Keith moved out of town, and Lafeyette made friends with Chicago Commons' staff members, whom he'd periodically visit after his completion of the program.

Lafeyette still laughed and played with Pharoah and friends, but he could be bossy, ordering around his younger brother and the triplets with cockiness and the fury of a temperamental adult. He had inherited his mother's temper and could turn on the younger ones in an instant. It wasn't that Lafeyette and they didn't get along; it was that he worried about them, like a father worrying about his children. He admonished them for hanging out with the wrong people or straying too far from his sight. He cared almost too much about everything and everybody. Sometimes the strain of responsibility showed in his thin, handsome face; it would tighten, like a fist, and it seemed as if he would never smile again. He'd purse his lips and clench his jaw; his deep-set, heavy-lidded eyes would stare straight ahead. His face revealed so little, his mother thought, and yet so much.

Pharoah was different, not only from Lafeyette but from the other children, too. He didn't have many friends, except for Porkchop, who was always by his side. LaJoe had given him his name but, like his brother's name, spelled it in an unusual way. At the time, LaJoe hadn't known the story of Moses and the Pharoah, but in later years when she found out she laughed. Pharoah was anything but a king.

Pharoah clutched his childhood with the vigor of a tiger gripping his meat. He wouldn't let go. Nobody, nothing would take it away from him. When he was two, Pharoah would run around the apartment naked; sometimes he'd be wearing just small white shoes. When he was four or five, he told LaJoe that he wanted to live on a lake so that he could always feel the wind on his back. At the age of five, he had an imaginary friend, Buddy, whom he'd talk to and play with in his bedroom. Frequently, Pharoah got so lost in his daydreams that LaJoe had to shake him to bring him back from his flights of fancy. Those forays into distant lands and with other people seemed to help Pharoah fend off the ugliness around him.

Now, at the age of nine, he giggled at the slightest joke; he cried at the smallest of tragedies. He had recently developed a slight stutter, which made him seem even more vulnerable. And he listened to classical music on the radio because, he said, it relaxed him. He sensed that his playfulness delighted the adults, so he would tease them and they him. He wanted to be recognized, to know that he was wanted. At the age of eight he wrote a short letter to his Aunt LaVerne, one of LaJoe's sisters.

Jan. 1986
Pharoah Rivers
I love you do you love me. You are my best aunt verny. I love you very much. The people I love.

> Verny
> Grandmother
> Linda
> Randy
> Moma
> Dad
> Brothers
> Sisters
> Cousins
> Aunt

"Oh, that Pharoah," family and neighbors would say to LaJoe, recounting some enchanting incident involving the nine-year-old. They adored him.

Pharoah liked to tell people he was big-boned "like my mama," though she was, in fact, a small woman. He had LaJoe's open and generous smile, and, like his mother, who was only five feet two, he was short, so that LaJoe could, until he was nine or ten, pass him off as a five-year-old to get him on the bus without paying fare.

Where the adults found Lafeyette handsome, they found Pharoah cute. The women would josh both of them, saying that someday they'd be lady killers. The local Boys Club used a photograph of Pharoah in one of its fund-raising brochures. In the picture, Pharoah, along with four other young boys, was dressed in marching cap and cape with a drum set, almost as large as Pharoah himself, slung around his neck. As he often did, he had cocked his head to one side for the camera and grinned cheerfully, a pose he must have known made him look even cuter.

The boys got along, and for that LaJoe was grateful. The two shared a room and, on most mornings, walked to school together. Occasionally, Lafeyette played rough with Pharoah or told him off, but LaJoe knew that if Pharoah ever needed his older brother, he'd be there. Older and bigger, he offered Pharoah some protection from the tougher kids in the neighborhood.

LaJoe knew that Lafeyette and Pharoah were like millions of other children living in the nation's inner cities. She knew that she was not alone in her struggles, that other women in other cities were watching their children grow old quickly, too. She had heard of some mothers who moved their families to Milwaukee or to the suburbs, some of which were poorer than Henry Horner, in an effort to escape the neighborhood's brutality. In the end, LaJoe would almost always learn, these families were up against the same ruthless forces they had faced in Chicago.

It wouldn't happen to Lafeyette and Pharoah, she had vowed to herself. It just wouldn't happen. They would have a childhood. They would have a chance to enjoy the innocence and playfulness of youth and to appreciate the rewards of school and family. They would bring home high school diplomas. They would move out of the neighborhood. They would get jobs and raise families. She had made mistakes with the older children that she was determined not to repeat with her younger ones.

But during the summer of 1987, when drugs and the accompanying violence swept through the neighborhood, she lived in daily fear that something might happen to her young ones. Though she would never say as much, she worried that they might not make it to their 18th birthday. Too many hadn't. Already that year, 57 children had been killed in the city. Five had died in the Horner area, including two, aged eight and six, who died from smoke inhalation when firefighters had to climb the 14 stories to their apartment. Both of the building's elevators were broken. Lafeyette and Pharoah knew of more funerals than weddings.

So that summer LaJoe wanted to be prepared for the worst. She started paying $80 a month for burial insurance for Lafeyette, Pharoah, and the four-year-old triplets.

Lafeyette had promised his mother he wouldn't let anything happen to Pharoah. But for a brief moment, he thought he had lost him.

Three days after Lafeyette's birthday, gunfire once again filled the air. It was 2:30 in the afternoon; school had just let out. As Lafeyette and his mother hustled the triplets onto the floor of the apartment's narrow hallway, a drill they now followed almost instinctually, they caught glimpses through the windows of young gunmen waving their pistols about. One youth toted a submachine gun.

The dispute had started when two rival drug gangs fired at each other from one high-rise to another.

From his first-floor apartment, Lafeyette, who had left his fifth-grade class early that day, watched hopefully for Pharoah as the children poured out of the Henry Suder Elementary School, just a block away. Panicking, many of the youngsters ran directly toward the gunfire. Lafeyette and his mother screamed at the children to turn back. But they kept coming, clamoring for the shelter of their homes.

Lafeyette finally spotted his brother, first running, then walking, taking cover behind trees and fences. But then he lost sight of him. "Mama, lemme go get him. Lemme go," Lafeyette begged. He was afraid that Pharoah

would run straight through the gunfire. Pharoah would later say he had learned to look both ways and that's why he'd started walking. "My mama told me when you hear the shooting, first to walk because you don't know where the bullets are coming," he explained. LaJoe refused Lafeyette's request to let him go after his brother. She couldn't even go herself. The guns kept crackling.

Lafeyette's friend James, who was cowering behind a nearby tree, sprinted for the Riverses' apartment. Pharoah saw him and ran, too. The two frantically pounded with their fists on the metal door. "Let us in!" James wailed. "Let us in! It's James and Pharoah!" James's heart was beating so hard that he could hear it above the commotion. But with all the noise, no one heard their frenzied pleas, and the two ran to a friend's apartment upstairs.

Meanwhile, the police, who at first thought they were the targets of the shooting, had taken cover in their cars and in the building's breezeway. Passersby lay motionless on the ground, protected by parked vehicles and a snow-cone vending stand. Then, as suddenly as it began, the battle ended. No one, amazingly, had been hurt. Lafeyette learned later that one errant bullet pierced a friend's third-floor window with such force that it cut through a closet door and lodged in the cinder-block wall.

The police made no arrests. And when a reporter called the police department's central headquarters the next day, he was told that there was no record of the shoot-out.

But Lafeyette knew. So did Pharoah.

* * * * *

Three blocks south of Horner sits a condominium complex called Damen Courts. Its manicured lawns and graffiti-free walls seem immaculate next to the rubble of Horner. The three-story red brick buildings look elegant and proper beside Horner's grim and worn high-rises.

Pharoah can't recall when he first discovered this small paradise, but when he did, he retreated regularly to the comfort of the lush lawns that circled the buildings. He was there when his mother returned from shopping.

The grass carpet offered a quiet resting place; it was like going to the beach. Pharoah found a shady place on the lawn and shot marbles or read a *Captain America* or *Superman* comic. Or, if the mood fit him, he just sat and daydreamed. He thought about school and next year's spelling bee. He urged on the Chicago Cubs and imagined himself a professional wrestler. It was at Damen Courts that he came up with the name for a scraggly gray cat that was now staying with the family: Useless. "He hardly don't catch no mice. He just want to freeload off our heat," he explained.

Pharoah had long sought such a refuge. For a few months last spring, he'd attended Bible classes at the First Congregational Baptist Church. Washington Boulevard was lined with churches, but most of them now served people who had since moved from the neighborhood. Churches had lost their authority in areas like Horner. Pharoah grew bored with the classes and began to question whether there was indeed a God. He often prayed to him, asking that he let them move from the projects. But, Pharoah would say, "I be praying but he don't do nothing. Maybe there ain't no God." It was as much a question as it was a statement.

At Damen Courts, Pharoah found some respite. No one knew of his discovery, not his mother, his cousin Porkchop, his friend Rickey, or Lafeyette. He wanted it that way. He wanted a place that he could escape to by himself, where nothing would interrupt his daydreaming, where no one would try to fight him, where he didn't have to worry about gunshots or fire-bombings. When his mother asked where he was going, he said to the corner store to play video games. He didn't want anybody to know about his hideaway.

In the weeks immediately following Jimmie Lee's conviction, an unusual calm descended over Horner. Several other gang leaders had been jailed. The drug dealing and beatings didn't stop, but they certainly slowed down in comparison with the relentless battles of the previous summer.

With fewer shootings and a reprieve from some of the family's troubles, Pharoah's stutter became less noticeable. In later months, it would recur, but never would it get so bad that it would immobilize or silence him as it had during the past year. LaJoe had taken Pharoah to the Miles Square Health Center, where a counselor urged Pharoah to slow down when he spoke. Think about what you want to say before speaking, he told Pharoah. The stuttering is partly due to nerves, he explained. Pharoah was bewildered. "What's it got to do with nerves?" he later asked his mother, who did her best to explain that when people started fighting and shooting, he got nervous and scared and would begin to stutter. It acted as a kind of warning mechanism to himself to be vigilant and cautious. Pharoah understood. He always seemed to understand—when he wanted to.

With the uneasy calm, Pharoah found other distractions in addition to Damen Courts. He and Lafeyette frequented the outdoor swimming pool in Union Park, four blocks to the east, and in this large pool filled with flailing bodies, both boys learned to swim. They also regularly visited the Boys Club to play basketball or shoot pool or to get free sandwiches, which had become endearingly known among the children as a "chokes." Or they might just hang about their building, playing basketball on the jungle gym or wading in the permanent pool created by the fire hydrant. Sometimes Red, a small man in his 50s who lived in their building, would ride around the highrise on his adult-size tricycle with presents for the neighborhood children stuffed in his basket. He found the used gifts in trash bins or behind stores. He'd give the little girls plastic necklaces and metal pendants; the little boys got tennis balls. To LaJoe and the other mothers, he presented gladioli and daisies which, in their late bloom, florists had thrown away. Over the years, Red had become like a year-round Santa to the building's kids. The triplets in particular adored him, and on his arrival on his tricycle could be heard screaming, "Red, oh, Red! What it is, Red?" as they ran up and surrounded him and gave him hugs in exchange for the presents.

Pharoah continued to badger Lafeyette and Rickey and any other older friend he could corner to take him back to the railroad tracks, which he remembered for the quiet and solace he'd found there. But no one would take him. The stories from last year of lost legs were still fresh in their minds. And now there were exaggerated children's tales of "raper mans" and other loonies hiding in the buildings by the viaduct. So, with the older boys' refusal and his own fear of what he might meet at the tracks, Pharoah spent more time at his private sanctuary.

He stayed on the lawn at Damen Courts until a security guard or janitor shooed him away, but he always left happy and satisfied. Being there for even an hour gave him a chance to catch his breath, to find the tranquillity he treasured.

On this particular afternoon, after his mother had finished putting away the groceries, Pharoah wandered through the front door, his head cocked slightly to one side. "Where you been, Pharoah?" his mother asked.

"Nowheres," he said, turning away. It was hard for him to lie, especially to his mother.

"Pharoah?"

Pharoah thought about telling her but didn't. "I been playing video games with Porkchop," he said and walked back to his room.

In later weeks, he finally confided in his mother abut his discovery. "My mind be cleared of everything there," he told her.

* * * * *

On Friday, May 19, LaJoe and Rochelle taped the last of the streamers to the walls; the narrow strips of crepe paper crisscrossed the living room like tangled vines. Balloons hung from the ceiling and bounced unfettered on the floor. Party hats and party favors lay on the table, which was covered with a paper cloth adorned with Disney cartoon characters. A gold crown, also made of paper, sat to the side for the birthday boy. Eleven candles circled the strawberry shortcake, which read: I LOVE YOU. FROM MAMA AND ROCHELLE.

"LaJoe, here, put it up here," Rochelle urged. LaJoe pulled the last of the banners from the package. They read, "It's a Boy." LaJoe and Rochelle laughed. They hoped Pharoah wouldn't notice.

A few weeks earlier, after Pharoah had attended a birthday celebration for a friend, he mentioned to his mother that he'd never had a party. So she decided to throw him one—and to keep it a surprise. Rochelle had helped her buy the decorations and the cake. She seemed nearly as excited as LaJoe.

Since the incident the month before in which she lost control of herself, LaJoe had slowed down and tried to pull herself and her family together. With summer fast approaching, she wanted to be prepared. She did what she could to lift her spirits and her children's. She had finally made the last of the down payments on the five bunk beds, so Lafeyette, Pharoah, and the triplets now each had one. The wooden bunks were used but in good condition. LaJoe had paid $479 for them. Lafeyette and Pharoah kept the plastic covering on their mattresses. "It keeps them clean," Pharoah explained. They dreamed about what they would do now to decorate their room. Lafeyette wanted to paint it black "'cause then it won't get dirty 'so easy." He had taken a steel door off a vacant apartment to replace their broken wooden one, and he had installed a new lock so that only he and Pharoah could enter. They had hung a torn venetian blind over the windows, which kept the room dark but private.

LaJoe also bought a handsome wooden table and chairs from the same used-furniture dealer who had sold her the beds. The storekeeper liked LaJoe and gave her a good buy—$80 for the table and chairs—and even delivered the goods, though he refused to carry the items into the building, because he feared for his safety. Neighbors helped haul the furniture from the truck into the apartment. Pharoah particularly loved the new wooden table; he told his mother that it was the kind they had in mansions.

The triplets and Lafeyette traipsed home from school, wet from the spring downpour. Other youngsters soon arrived, mostly children the triplets' age. They awaited the birthday boy. Someone knocked on the door. The children, giggling, put their fingers to their lips. "Shh. Shh. Shh." The knocking got louder and more forceful. Lafeyette moved to the side of the door and undid its lock.

"SURPRISE!" Lafeyette slapped the back of Pharoah's head with his open palm. In all the excitement, he didn't quite know how to greet his brother. Pharoah shuffled into the living room, surprised and embarrassed by the attention. Just as he had done during the first spelling bee, he balled his hands up under the fold of his shimmery green raincoat, where he nervously played with the plastic. The children, about 10 in all, quickly scattered, many running into the kitchen for hot dogs. Pharoah stood by the door, his toothy smile lighting his face. He didn't say anything. Instead, he walked back to his room and sat on the plastic-covered mattress, trying to take it all in. Lafeyette sat with him.

"I thought you forgot it," he told his mother, who poked her head through the door. She rubbed the back of his head and gave him his present, a green shorts set. Pharoah put it on. With the suspenders and knee-length shorts, he looked quite handsome. He silently readied himself for the party: he found a new pair of white socks, and scrubbed his face and hands; he ran jell through his long, curly hair and then secured the gold paper crown on his head. And as he did almost everything, he did it all slowly and with great deliberation. The dressing and preening took him half an hour—and when he was done he wasn't fully satisfied. "I should have greased my legs," he told his brother.

"You look proper," Lafeyette told his brother. Rickey, who had been invited to the party by Lafeyette, wandered into the bedroom. With his hands in his pocket, he looked uncomfortable. He often did. "You look straight, Pharoah," he assured him. "Happy birthday."

"Thanks," Pharoah said. He didn't say much that afternoon. He mostly grinned and giggled. In Polaroid photos of the day, his smile seems to cover his face; his big grin forces his cheeks into plump balls and squeezes his eyes neatly shut. In one photo, he stands behind his seated grandmother, who has come over for the party, with his arm affectionately around her neck. In another, he sits behind the cake in one of the new chairs, his paper crown sliding off his head, looking pleased with the festivities. In yet another, LaJoe steadies Pharoah's small hands as he cuts the cake with a big kitchen knife.

Once Pharoah was dressed and had made his entrance into the party amid the screaming gaggle of kids, Lafeyette and Rickey sneaked out the door. Lafeyette told his mother he didn't want to hang around "no children's party." It was LaJoe's one disappointment. All the guests were much younger than Pharoah; no one Pharoah's age came. He didn't have many good friends, except for his cousin Porkchop. But even he wasn't there. Throughout the festivities, Pharoah asked, "Where's Porkchop?" or could be heard muttering, "I hope Porkchop comes." Porkchop showed up two hours after the party began; he'd forgotten all about it. The two, as usual, embraced. "Happy Birthday," Porkchop mumbled through his soft giggles.

The children, with half-eaten hot dogs squirting out of their hands, danced to the rap music of L. L. Cool J. Pharoah, who sat with his mother and grandmother and his Aunt LaVerne as they admired his new outfit, mouthed the words to one of his favorite songs.

> When I'm alone in my room sometimes I
> stare at the walls
> And in the back of my mind I hear my
> conscience call
> Telling me I need a girl that's as sweet as
> a dove
> For the first time in my life—I see I need
> love
> I need love.

"Keep the kids inside," a panicky voice hollered to LaJoe, distracting Pharoah from the rap music. "Keep them here. Someone's figuring to get killed at four trey." Dawn had come by with her four kids. Four trey was how everyone referred to the building next door, whose address was 1943 West Lake. LaJoe locked the door.

"Y'll stay inside, you hear," she told the children, who had momentarily stopped their dancing, knowing that something was wrong. Apparently there had been an altercation between drug dealers in the building, and Dawn was worried it might erupt into something more. Nothing, though, happened. The children resumed dancing. Dawn gave Pharoah a hug.

Just as Pharoah blew out the candles—after an off-key, half-shouted rendition of "Happy Birthday"—something heavy fell in the living room. The crash startled everyone. A relative of LaJoe's, who had passed out on the couch and had been there throughout the noisy party, had tried to get up to go to the bathroom. He didn't make it. He lay face down, urine seeping through his blue jeans onto the linoleum door.

Pharoah took Porkchop's hand and the two went outside to get away from their drunken relative and the screaming kids. As they walked out the building's back door, they stopped. A teenage girl stood there vomiting. The two boys quietly walked around her. Pharoah hadn't stopped smiling.

It was a good few weeks for Pharoah. Not only did he celebrate his birthday, but he had been picked to recite a short poem at Suder's year-end assembly. Pharoah had gotten his stammer under control. It wasn't gone entirely, but he managed it better, having learned, when necessary, to slow down before he spoke. And so this was a big honor for him; it was as if his teachers were recognizing Pharoah for conquering his stutter.

As soon as Pharoah got a copy of the rhyme he was to recite, he set it to memory. He felt so confident that he eventually threw away the crumpled piece of paper he'd been carrying around in his back pocket for weeks. He wouldn't forget it.

He wanted to look tidy for the assembly, so he had his hair shorn. He also cleaned and ironed a black-striped sport coat that his mother had bought for him two Easters ago. He didn't have many occasions to wear it. With his neatly pressed white pants and olive-green shirt buttoned at the collar, LaJoe thought, he looked very handsome.

LaJoe got to the school's gymnasium early. She was as excited as Pharoah. When she saw her son on stage, she couldn't help thinking, There's the one. There's the one. I'm going to get it back.

Lafeyette sat with his class. He too was "happy for my little brother." Ms. Barone was so proud of her former student that she took a snapshot of him in his new clothes and haircut.

Pharoah had been on this platform before for the spelling bees, so he knew what to expect. He knew that he had to speak loud and clear, and that he needed to speak deliberately so as not to stumble. But in his excitement, as he stretched to reach the microphone, he realized that he had to go to the bathroom something awful. His bladder felt ready to burst. Not here, he told himself. He locked his knees together, tensing his bladder muscles. He wasn't going to pee on himself, not in front of all these people. He tried to look relaxed.

He spotted his mother in the crowd, with her full and open grin. But he tried to avoid her eyes and fixed his stare at the back of the auditorium. That way, he'd been told, it would look as if he were talking to everyone.

"Uh-uh-uh . . . uh," Pharoah paused. He wasn't going to stutter. Not here. Not now. Slow down, he told himself. Take your time.

"Try, try, try, try, that's what special effort means." His soft, amplified voice rang through the auditorium; once he got through the first line, his confidence returned. His heart was in it. He indeed believed hard work could overcome all.

And when you put your best foot forward, it
    really isn't hard as it seems.
Success comes to those who when given
    a chance

Do their very best and work hard to advance.
The special effort award is what they've
   earned.
Though it can't begin to match the things
   they've learned.

The applause rang in Pharoah's ears. He looked over to his mother. She winked. Lafeyette clapped so hard and long that his teacher had to ask him to stop. "Nice job," Ms. Daigre, the principal, whispered to Pharoah. He thanked her, stepped off the stage, and then sprinted for the bathroom.

That morning Pharoah received two certificates: one for placing second in the school's spelling bee, the other for special effort in math and reading. His brother Timothy got three, including the much coveted principal's list as well as one for scholastic achievement and another for excellent conduct. Tammie received one for outstanding student, another for excellent conduct. Tiffany got one for special effort in handwriting. "The only person who didn't get a ribbon was Lafie," Pharoah said later. "That made me feel bad." Along with the certificates came ribbons. LaJoe was so proud of her children's accomplishments that she pinned all eight of them to her white sweatshirt. She paraded around the neighborhood all day with a rainbow of green, purple, white, and red ribbons hanging from her chest; she looked like a decorated war hero.

After the assembly, Pharoah and his mother attended a meeting at which it was announced that Pharoah was one of 25 Suder students chosen for Project Upward Bound, a summer school designed to assist minority students in bringing up their math and reading scores. Primarily a program for high school students, this Upward Bound, which operated at the University of Illinois, had in recent years begun to focus some of its efforts on sixth-, seventh-, and eighth-graders with the hope of following them through their four years of high school, working with them on Saturdays and during the summers.

The Upward Bound staff described the Summer Scholars program and then asked the as

sembled children what they wanted to be when they grew up. Pharoah knew. A congressman.

"I want to change a lot of rules," he told the others. "I want to change them and everybody move out of the projects. I'll pay people to build housing. Let the people who live in the projects live in other houses. Any gang member who has their hat turned, they'd go directly to jail. Stop stealing and stuff. A little kid got to come into a store with their parent or guardian or they can't come in. They'd probably steal."

He paused, then added, "If you be a congressman, there be people guarding me so you won't get hurt. I like that."

LaJoe and the children got caught up in the warmth and beauty of those first few days of summer. The children shot baskets on the jungle gym. At night, they wandered over to the stadium to watch cars and make a few dollars. Pharoah's and the triplets' awards at school had brightened the family's outlook. LaJoe displayed them on the wobbly shelves in the living room. They offered some promise of a better tomorrow. And everyone was thrilled with Pharoah for being picked to participate in the summer program. Pharoah would come back with tales of the University of Illinois campus that delighted LaJoe. He talked of the footbridges and the big glass buildings and of the students who seemed to be everywhere, always carrying books. Pharoah would tell LaJoe that he planned to attend college there. But it wasn't long before LaJoe was rudely reminded of summer's true character at Horner.

One afternoon, she and Rochelle were walking down Washington Boulevard to a corner store. She waved to two teenage boys she knew who were walking on the other side of the street; both wore red, the Vice Lords' color, in Disciples' territory. LaJoe noticed that two children, one no bigger than Pharoah, and a young man were tailing the two teens. They'd duck into alleys and behind the porches of the two-family homes on Washington. LaJoe yelled to the two teens that they were being followed.

Then she watched in horror as the man handed a pistol to the little boy who reminded LaJoe of Pharoah in his small size and bobbing gait.

"Go kill the motherfucker," LaJoe overheard him say. The boy aimed the pistol, his entire body straining just to hold it straight, and opened fire on the two teens. POW. POW. LaJoe and Rochelle ducked into the corner store for cover. The two teens ran. They escaped unharmed.

The incident angered and frightened LaJoe. How did that little boy even know whom he was shooting at? All he saw was a couple of people wearing red and their hats turned to the left. From the back, they could have been girls. Later that day, LaJoe ripped the red Louisville cap off Lafeyette's head and told him he couldn't wear any hats. No earrings, either, she told him. That was that. She was putting her foot down. That could have been Lafeyette the boy was shooting at.

READING 14-2

Blood Knots: Adoption, Reproduction, and the Politics of Family

Elizabeth Bartholet

In the fall of 1985, I flew from Boston to Lima, Peru, to adopt a four-month-old child. Some 18 years earlier I had given birth to my first child. During the last 10 of those years, I had strug-

gled to give birth again, combating an infertility problem that had resulted, as is often the case, from use of a contraceptive device during the intervening years. I had been married when I produced my first child, but my husband and I divorced when my son was just a few years old. Years later I decided I wanted more children, regardless of whether I was married. But I found that I was unable to conceive.

I subjected myself to every form of medical treatment that offered any possibility of success. I had operations to diagnose my problem, I took fertility drugs and charted my menstrual cycles and my temperature, and I had sexual intercourse according to the prescribed schedule. I had surgery to remove scar tissue from my fallopian tubes. And I went through in vitro fertilization (IVF) repeatedly in programs in three different states. As a single person in my early forties, I was officially excluded from every IVF program in the country that I learned about. Almost all had a maximum age of 40, and all limited their services to married couples. But I was determined. I begged my way into programs that were willing to consider bending their age rules, and I presented myself as married, with the help of a loyal and loving friend who was willing to play the part of husband. Unaccustomed to a life of fraud, I spent much of my IVF existence terrified that I would be discovered.

Then I got lucky. I ran out of money. IVF treatment was excluded from health insurance coverage during this period, and I had cursed my fate and timing, as it seemed likely that the exclusion would eventually be eliminated. I had been paying the going price, $5,000 for a full treatment cycle, and had about run through what savings I had.

I woke one morning in March 1985—I learned later that it was the month, and for all I know the very day, my son-to-be was born—and lay in bed thinking that I didn't want to spend all my remaining money on IVF. I would need it if I was to adopt. And I didn't want to spend any more time and energy or any more of my life on the fertility pursuit. I wanted a child, and I wanted to move on. I called my IVF program that day and said I would not go forward with another treatment cycle.

I was one of the fortunate infertility patients, because I did move on to adoption and to parenting. Treatment enables only a limited number of the infertile to conceive and bear children, and it prevents many from ever considering adoption as a form of parenting. I now look back in amazement at the person I was, traversing the country from one IVF program to another in search of an infertility fix. I am bemused at my shifting notions of "natural" and of "choice." It had seemed natural to pursue biologic parenting, even when the pursuit led me into the high-tech world of IVF where the doctors and lab technicians took over the business of conception, "harvesting" the eggs they had cultivated in the patient's body and inseminating them in glass dishes. It also had seemed that I was making choices when I decided to move on to new stages of treatment. Indeed, I had felt thrilled with the sense that I was pushing against the social and biologic constraints that prevented a single woman with damaged fallopian tubes from giving birth. Now I look back and see a woman driven by the forces that had told her since birth that she should go forth and multiply, that her ability to bear a child was central to her meaning as a human being, and that "real" parenting involved raising that biologically linked child.

The adoption experience changed me profoundly. It changed my life and my thinking about life. It changed my understanding of parenting and my view of the law, even though I had been a parent and lawyer all my adult life.

It was, of course, predictable that adoption would change my day-to-day life. I went back to Peru in 1988 and adopted another infant, so I am now the mother of two young children. My days start with small warm bodies crawling into my bed, my floors are covered with miniature cars and trucks and Lego pieces, my calendar is scrawled with the kids' doctor appointments and play dates. All this is familiar from 20 years ago, as are the middle-of-the-night coughing fits, the trips to the emergency room to stitch a bloody cut, the sense that there is not enough time to fit it all in.

But I could not have predicted these two particular magical children. I could not have imagined the ways in which they would crawl inside my heart and wrap themselves around my soul. I could not have known that I would be so entirely smitten, as a friend described me, so utterly possessed. And I could not have anticipated that these children thrown together with me and with each other, with no blood ties linking us to each other or to a common history, would seem so clearly the children meant for me.

The process I went through to form this family affected my understanding of many legal issues. As a lawyer, I had thought of the law largely in terms of its potential for advancing justice and social reform. In the adoption world, I experienced the law as something that operated primarily to prevent good things from happening. You need only to step through the door of this world and look around to realize that there are vast numbers of children in desperate need of homes and vast numbers of adults anxious to become parents. It seems overwhelmingly clear that efforts to put these groups of children and adults together would create much human happiness. But the legal systems in this and other countries have erected barriers that prevent people who want to parent from connecting with children who need homes.

Adoption also affected my understanding of discrimination. Because of my background, first as a civil rights lawyer and then as a law professor, my initial reaction to the adoption world was one of shock. I was familiar with a social realm increasingly governed by the principle that such human characteristics as race, religion, sex, age, and handicap should not matter. In the adoption world, just such factors are central in deciding who gets to parent and which kids get homes.

The adoption process also forced me to think on a personal level about discrimination. When you fill out a form for the adoption agency that asks what disabilities you could accept in a child—mental retardation, blindness, a missing limb, Down syndrome—you think about the meaning of disability in a new way. If you check the box that says "none of the above disabilities," you are pushed to think about how your act of discrimination compares with the act that excludes a disabled person from employment or housing. If your goal is to adopt children who fall in the "healthy infant" category, as my goal was, you may spend many guilty hours questioning whether you measure up as a loving human being and fit prospective parent.

Adoption transformed my feelings about infertility and my understanding of parental love. For years I had felt that there was only one less-than-tragic outcome of my infertility battle, and that was to reverse the damage that had been done to my body. I had felt that there was only one really satisfactory route to parenthood, and that was for me to conceive and to give birth. I had assumed that the love I felt for my first child had significantly to do with biologic connection. The experience of loving him was wrapped up in a package that included pregnancy, childbirth, nursing, and the genetic link that meant I recognized his eyes and face and personality as familial.

I discovered that parental love grows out of the experience of nurturing and that adoptive parenting is in fundamental ways identical to biologic parenting. Pregnancy and childbirth were for me enormously satisfying but now seem of limited relevance to the parenting relationship. I do not see biologic links as entirely irrelevant to parenting, but neither do I see an obvious hierarchical system for ranking biologic and adoptive parenting.

I can, of course, be seen as privileged by virtue of having experienced both kinds of parenting. It may therefore be hard for those who have never borne a child to identify with me. If,

for example, there is some primal need to project oneself into future generations by reproduction, I have had the luxury of satisfying that need. But it seems that not much is gained by leaving a genetic legacy. You do not live on just because your egg or sperm has contributed to another life. The sense of immortality that many seek in parenting has more to do with the kind of identification that comes from the parent-child relationship and the way it helps shape the child's being.

This is not to say that *becoming* a parent through adoption is comparable to *becoming* a parent through giving birth. Adoption involves choice on a scale most of us don't generally experience. You can't fall accidentally into adoption as you can into pregnancy. You exercise choice down to the wire. And the choice to go forward with an adoption means a lifelong commitment, which simply isn't true of most other choices that we make. If you make a mistake in choosing a house, a job, or even a spouse, you can get out of it. Few of those who consciously enter an adoptive parenting relationship would feel comfortable opting out of their commitment.

While choice is difficult and uncomfortable for most of us, there are obvious advantages for children and parents in parenting that results from conscious choice. In the world of biologic parenting, too many children are raised by parents who neither planned for nor wanted them, and the evidence shows that this is problematic for both the parents and the children.

MAKING ADOPTION THE LAST RESORT

As a society, we define personhood and parenthood in terms of procreation. We push the infertile toward ever more elaborate forms of high-tech treatment. We are moving rapidly in the direction of a new child production market, in which sperm, eggs, embryos, and pregnancy services are for sale so that those who want to parent can produce a child to order. At the same time, we drive prospective parents away from children who already exist and need homes. The claim is that no children are available for adoption, but the fact is that millions of children the world over are in desperate need of nurturing homes. The politics of adoption in today's world prevents these children from being placed in adoptive homes. Our policies make no sense for people interested in parenting, for children in need of homes, or for a world struggling to take care of its population.

The medical profession has a near-monopoly on the information given out as people discover their infertility and explore and exercise their options. When people who have been trying to have a baby realize that something may be wrong, they usually consult their family doctor or their gynecologist, and then, if they can afford it, a fertility specialist. The specialist educates them about the range of treatment possibilities and, if they are willing and financially able, begins to lead them down the same treatment path I traveled: from scheduled sex to fallopian tube surgery to IVF.

The adoption world does essentially nothing to reach out to the infertile. Indeed, adoption agency rules push them away and prevent them from obtaining the information they need to consider adoption at an early stage. The accepted ethic among adoption workers is that prospective parents must resolve feelings about infertility before they pursue adoption. The idea behind this makes some sense: they should not enter into adoption thinking of their adopted child as a second-best substitute for the biologic child they still ache to produce. But it may be impossible to know whether the desire to parent will be satisfied by adoption without knowing what adoption is about.

Other factors contribute to the bias toward the medical process. Infertile people are bombarded with messages that reinforce the idea that adoption is an inferior form of parenting and *should* be thought of as a last resort. They are lured into IVF by aggressive advertising.

If infertile people do manage to get accurate information about their parenting options, they find that our society gives vastly preferential treatment to people seeking to produce children. First and foremost, those seeking to reproduce operate in a free market world in which they are able to make their own decisions subject only to financial and physical constraints. Those seeking to adopt operate in a highly regulated world in which the government asserts the right to determine who will be allowed to parent.

The parental screening requirement deters many who might otherwise consider adoption. People don't like to become helpless supplicants, utterly dependent on the grace of social workers, with respect to something as basic as parenting. Screening turns the process of becoming a parent into a bureaucratic nightmare of documents endlessly accumulated and stamped and submitted and copied.

Regulation also sends a powerful message. By subjecting adoptive but not biologic parents to regulation, society suggests that it trusts what goes on when people raise a birth child but profoundly distrusts what goes on when a child is transferred from a birth to an adoptive parent.

Society also discriminates in financial terms. People covered by health insurance are reimbursed for many of the costs involved in infertility treatment, pregnancy, and childbirth. Although insurance plans typically do not cover IVF treatment, the trend is toward expanding coverage to include it. Treatment and childbirth expenses that are not covered by insurance are tax deductible if they exceed a certain percentage of income. By contrast, those who adopt are generally on their own in paying for the adoption, and only limited subsidies are available for those who adopt children with special needs. There is no equivalent of insurance coverage for the expenses involved in adoption, nor are those expenses generally tax deductible. The expenses typically range from $5,000 to $12,000, and they often amount to as much as $35,000. Of course, expenses are as high as they are *because* we regulate adoption so extensively.

SCREENING PROSPECTIVE PARENTS

The parental screening system constitutes one of the major barriers to adoption. Both public and private agencies conduct home studies designed to assess eligibility for adoptive parenthood and to rank prospective parents for child assignments. The children waiting for homes are ranked and categorized as well.

The system operates on the basis of what looks roughly like a market system, one in which financial ranking produces buying power. The most "desirable" parents are matched with the most "desirable" children, and the less desirable with the less desirable, on down the list. The "marginally fit" parents are matched with the hardest-to-place children, which often means the children with the most extreme parenting needs and demands. Black parents are given black children, and Catholic parents are given the children surrendered by Catholic birth parents.

Discrimination is the name of the game. Those who procreate live in a world of near-absolute rights with respect to parenting. Those who would adopt have no rights. They must beg for the privilege of parenting and do so in a state-administered realm that denies them both the right to privacy and the "civil rights" that we have come to think of as fundamental in the rest of our communal life. Only the adoption system proudly proclaims not just the right to discriminate but the importance of doing so.

Moreover, because agencies simultaneously counsel and screen prospective parents, there is little incentive for parents to be honest about any anxieties or issues they might have about adoptive parenting. Most applicants want to score well in the process to improve their chances of adopting the kind of child they want. Those with any game-playing abilities will know that to score well, they should not bring up any issues that might concern a social worker. Thus they avoid frank discussion about legitimate issues that *should* be explored— what kinds of children they would find difficult to raise or how they would deal with their adopted child's birth family and ethnic or racial heritage. The eager applicant strives to come up with the best possible version of a life story and a series of "right" answers to difficult questions.

Money, however, enables prospective adopters to bypass the parental screening system. The more money they have, the greater their ability to shop around and escape the strictures of the system.

With money, you can venture into the world of the private adoption agency, which uses a variety of screening systems and offers a much larger proportion of healthy infants and young children. Some private agencies screen and match according to the classic home study criteria, but others are much more sympathetic to nontraditional parents. Still others are willing to place children with virtually all applicants who satisfy minimal criteria. Prospective adopters can shop among the private agencies and select the one most sympathetic to their personal profile and most likely to provide the kind of child they want. Fees vary significantly, with the agencies that are most open to nontraditional parents tending to charge higher fees.

Money also gives access to the world of "independent" adoption, which accounts for roughly one-third of all nonrelative adoption in the United States. Here home studies are not required at all. Some intermediaries and some birth parents apply their own screening criteria, and nontraditional parents have a harder time adopting than young married couples do. But many of those who place children in the independent process do little or no screening, and those who are more selective differ widely on what qualities they seek. Many parents who surrender infants at birth are attracted to independent adoption, so prospective adopters with enough money to explore the possibilities are able to avoid classic screening and to find their way to a healthy newborn. The state subjects these parents to only minimal scrunity in the court process that formalizes the adoption.

Judged in terms of the very values it purports to serve, the screening system fails. Together with the rule against baby-buying, parental screening is supposed to ensure that children are assigned not to the highest bidder but to those deemed most fit to parent. The fact that money enables those deemed least fit to buy their way to the children who are most in demand makes a farce of the entire system.

FOR THE CHILDREN'S SAKE

We now place an extremely high value on the right to procreate and the related right to hold on to our biologic product. We place no real value on the aspect of parenting that has to do solely with relationship. There is essentially an absolute right to produce a child, but there is no right to enter into a parenting relationship with a child who is not linked by blood—no right to adopt. Foster parents, stepparents, and others who develop nurturing relationships with children are deemed by the law to have no right to maintain such relationships. They and the children who may have come to depend on them are subject to the whim of the blood-linked parent. Such parents, in contrast, have enormous proprietary power over their children. Even in situations of serious abuse and neglect, the government is reluctant to interfere with parental rights. Everyone knows that children require nurturing homes and parenting relationships, but it is painfully obvious that they have no enforceable rights to these things.

We need to flip this rights picture, upend this value system. We need to give priority to children and their interest in growing up in nurturing relationships. We need to recognize a right to provide the nurturing piece of parenting and give it equal status with the right to procreate. Any such revision of parenting rights and responsibilities would lead to a very different view of the role that adoption agencies should play. It would seem obvious that their primary function should be to create parent-child relationships—to find

homes for children in need of nurturing parents and to find children for adults who want to nurture. In this new world, agencies would become adoption advocates. They might devote some resources to screening out those who are demonstrably unfit to parent, but they would be conscious of the importance of not creating barriers that would discourage people from providing homes to existing children in need. Their respect for adult interests in enjoying parenting relationships would make them reluctant to impose any screening requirements that do not seem necessary to protect children.

Parental screening in adoption has always been justified as necessary for the protection of children. But children have much to gain—homes and parents—and little to lose from scrapping the system.

Many traditionalists claim that children will lose appropriate parenting if we abandon the screening and matching process. The argument for parental screening rests largely on the assumption that children are subject to special risks when there is no biologic link between parent and child. But the fact that adoptive parents have consciously chosen parenthood would seem more than enough to compensate for any difficulties that might be inherent in adoptive parenting.

Nor is there any *evidence* that the absence of a biologic link affects the successful establishment of a parent-child relationship. Studies indicate that adoptive families function very well compared with biologic families and that adoptive parents are successful in helping their children overcome unfortunate pre-adoptive histories. There is no evidence that adoptive parents are more likely than biologic parents to abuse their children. The adoption literature makes many *claims* that adoptive relationships are inherently problematic. But only recently have empirical studies compared nonclinical groups of children adopted in infancy with control groups of children raised in their birth families. These studies reveal no significant disadvantages to adoptive parenting. Indeed, some studies indicate there may be *advantages* to adoptive parenting—that adoptive parents may, for example, be more caring and responsive to their children's needs.

Screening is said by some to be an appropriate way of allocating a scarce resource. If there is a limited supply of children available for adoption, why not select those parents who will do the best job? But the supply is *not* limited. There are many more children in need of adoptive homes than there are homes available for them. While it is true that limited numbers of healthy infants born in this country are available for adoption, more than 400,000 children were in foster care at the end of 1990, and the numbers are going up at a frightening rate, with experts predicting that this figure will double by 1995. Tens of thousands of these children are free for adoption and waiting for homes. Many of them will wait for years before being placed with adoptive families, and many will grow up in foster or institutional homes. In other countries untold millions of children need homes. Many of them are free for adoption, and many more could be free if adoptive homes were available.

It is very likely that we do not know what we think we know about what makes for good parenting or happy families. Our views are necessarily shaped by a model of parenting sanctioned by biology and tradition. But single people and older people who ask for the chance to parent usually don't look much like their counterparts in the general population. Moreover, many of the married couples preferred by adoption agencies will be divorced within a few years, and their children will be subject to the traumatic change that divorce represents. Generally, those children will be left with just one parent, who often will be less prepared to function as a single parent than the person who deliberately adopts on his or her own.

People who choose to become parents in their late thirties and forties often testify that this is a good stage of life in which to parent because they feel less torn by the conflict between work and family and more capable of giving of themselves to a child than they did when they were younger. Some gays and lesbians maintain that for children with a same-sex or bisexual orientation, growing up with determinedly heterosexual parents can be oppressive.

The studies that exist provide no indication that the objective factors relied on by the current screening system are useful predictors of good parenting. There is no evidence that these factors are correlated with success as an adoptive parent, and there is no evidence that those who become adoptive parents by virtue of the agency screening process are more successful than those who avoid such screening by using the independent adoption system. Studies do, however, reveal that children raised by parents rated by the agency system as "marginal," such as straight singles and gay and lesbian couples, suffer no significant disadvantages compared with children raised in traditional households.

Parental screening has enormous costs from the perspective of those screened and categorized by the system. A declaration that a person is unfit, or marginally fit, to parent another human being is a serious condemnation. A denial of the opportunity to parent constitutes for many people a denial of what is most meaningful in life. The government should have to demonstrate a powerful interest in screening in order to justify such costs.

The government has traditionally asserted an interest in promoting heterosexual marriage and parenting in the context of such a marriage. But adoptive screening does little to promote this vision of the family. Instead it drives some gays and lesbians underground to pose as straight adoptive parents, and others, together with older applicants and singles, into the private and the independent adoption worlds, where they can avoid the strictures of the traditional screening system. Furthermore, it drives many of those who are fertile but would nonetheless be interested in adoption into the world of biologic parenting. Straight singles and gay singles and couples meet with no real restrictions if they seek to form families by reproduction, either naturally or with the help of reproductive technology. Even assuming that the government has a valid interest in promoting a traditional model of the family, this interest is not served by driving the socially unorthodox away from adoptive and into biologic parenting.

It is hard to identify any way in which the current system furthers the goal of ensuring children the best homes. What is clear is that it deprives many children altogether of the homes they need.

THE ADOPTION ALTERNATIVE

Adoptive family relationships are often built on a foundation of human misery. Birth parents generally surrender children for adoption or abandon them because they feel forced to do so by poverty, discrimination or the chaos that results from war or some other disaster. Many of those interested in adoption feel forced into it by infertility. In an ideal world, we would eliminate the social ills that force some to give up the children they bear and that deprive others of their fertility. But in the world in which we live today and will live tomorrow, these social ills do and will exist. Adoption should be understood as an institution that works well for birth parents, for the infertile, and for children.

But adoption should not be seen simply as a partial solution for some of the world's social ills. It should be understood as a positive alternative to the blood-based family. Adoption creates a family that in important ways is *not* "nuclear." It creates a family that is *connected* to another family, the birth family, and often to different cultures and different racial, ethnic, and national groups. Adoptive families have much to teach us about the meaning of parenting and about the value for families of connection with the larger community.

The politics of adoption is complex. Traditionalists often portray themselves as pro-adoption but tend to promote adoption simply as a preferred alternative to abortion. They do little to support adoption as a legitimate choice, either for the infertile who want to parent or for women who give birth but do not want to parent.

Progressives often voice concern with adoption's potential for exploitation of the poor and single birth mother by the well-off adoptive couple, exploitation of racial and ethnic minority groups by the dominant white cultures, and exploitation of the Third World by the industrialized West. But while adoption holds the potential for exploitation, it is not *inherently* exploitative. Adoption expands reproductive choice for women, and it gives children increased opportunities to grow up in nurturing homes.

Adoption adds to the choices enjoyed by the fertile, enabling those who become pregnant but do not abort and do not want to parent to give their children to others for parenting. We could add to the sense of choice by constructing adoption so that a woman could make the decision to relinquish her child without undue guilt. It would be liberating for women and for their children if we were to enable birth parents to think more positively about giving their children to those who are in a better position to provide the nurturing piece of parenting. Adoption, of course, also adds to the choices enjoyed by the infertile. A more positive construction of adoption would help free the infertile from the obsession to restore their sense of personhood by obtaining a medical fix.

We need to expand the concept of reproductive rights to include adoption rights: the birth mother's right to give up her child, the infertile woman's right to parent the child who has no parent, and the child's right to a home. The twin stigmas that surround adoption and infertility shape and constrain choice in ways that promote a traditional understanding of women's roles. Anti-abortion forces have pushed adoption as the *only* appropriate route for the woman who does not want or feel able to raise the child she is carrying. They have helped create the impression that to be pro-adoption is to be anti-abortion. But there is no necessary inconsistency between abortion rights and adoption rights, and we should not let abortion opponents hoodwink us so easily. Women should be free to choose whether to carry a child to term or to abort and free to choose whether to raise a child or give it up for others to raise. True reproductive freedom includes all these choices.

Progressives should recognize that adoption is not the cause of socioeconomic disadvantages that result in some people and some groups and some countries producing children that they are unable to care for. And they should recognize that while children are often termed "precious resources," it does not make sense to think of them that way. Giving up children, like deciding to abort, may be the best choice among the options available at a particular time. Also, children deserve to be treated as human beings with their own entitlements, rather than as resources in which adult individuals and communities have a property interest. From the child's perspective, being given up means being given a chance at a permanent nurturing home.

It makes no sense for a society that thinks of itself as sane and humane to drive people in the direction of child production rather than adoption. It makes no sense for children—those who have already been born and who will grow up without homes unless they are adopted. A sane and humane society should encourage people to provide for these existing children rather than bring more children into the world.

It makes no sense for adults either. Of course infertile people are begging for treatment, and of course those who manage to produce a child will say it has all been worth it. But they have been conditioned to feel that pregnancy and childbirth are the only solutions to their problem. Those who give birth cannot know what they would have done with the years spent in doctors' offices or what the experience of parenting an adopted child would have been. Moreover, most people who go down the treatment road will not succeed in producing a child. A 1988 Office of Technology Assessment report, "Infertility: Medical and Social Choices," estimates that only

about half of those who pursue an extensive series of treatment programs, including tubal surgery and two IVF cycles, will produce children. Of those who do not, some will move on to adoption. They will often ask themselves later why they wasted all those years on the treatment treadmill. But most unsuccessful infertility patients will never become adoptive parents. Many will find that after years of struggling to conquer infertility, they are too old, too tired, too poor, or too broken in spirit to begin another uphill battle. And that is what adoption is.

We need to correct the biologic bias to give children a better chance and to give adults more genuine choices. We need to restructure our understanding of infertility and parenting. We need to make counseling available on a widespread basis to those suffering from infertility so that early in their struggles they can begin to deal with feelings of loss and inadequacy, can try to unravel what part of their pain, if any, relates to a desire to parent, and can begin to puzzle out what parenting is and should be about. We need to make meaningful information about various parenting options available early. Counseling and information should come from groups that are not tied to or part of any medical establishment. We need to create new support organizations for the infertile. Adoption agencies and organizations should become adoption advocates active in outreach efforts.

We also need radically to reform the regulatory system that structures adoption. Adoption should not look like an uphill struggle. We need to change our laws and policies so they facilitate rather than impede the process of matching people who want to parent with children who need homes. And we need simultaneously to question current practices that push the infertile to pursue treatment.

Adoption generally works to expand life opportunities for birth mothers, for the infertile, and for children in need of nurturing homes. It would work even better if we eliminated the stigma and reformed the restrictive regulation that shapes adoption as we know it today.

The Elderly
and Their Families

Many observers of the changing lives of children have concluded that the family is in crisis. The litany is familiar: more divorce, more stepfamilies, more childbearing outside of marriage, more day care, more sex and violence in the media, and so forth. Even commentators who disagree with this position feel compelled to explain why divorce, day care, and so on, don't have the negative effects that one might expect. In other words, when you look at the family from the vantage point of its youngest members, the changes that occurred during the last half of the 20th century seem problematic.

But when you look at families from the vantage point of their oldest members, the picture is quite different. The changes that occurred in the lives of the elderly in the last half of the 20th century were generally positive: longer life expectancy, higher incomes, and greater independence. In a 1986 book on grandparents, Frank F. Furstenberg, Jr., and I argued that, on balance, the elderly and their adult children were satisfied with their family lives.[1] The better health and greater affluence of the elderly had allowed them to lead independent lives while still retaining frequent contact with their children and grandchildren—a style of life both the elders and their children, for the most part, preferred.

In 1988 and 1989, John R. Logan and Glenna D. Spitze conducted a survey of 1,200 persons aged 40 and over in the Albany-Schenectady-Troy, New York, metropolitan area. The survey included detailed questions about the family lives and well-being of these middle-aged and elderly adults. The authors published their analyses of the survey in several journal articles and a 1996 book, *Family Ties: Enduring Relations between Parents and Their Grown Children* (Philadelphia, Temple University Press). The excerpt reprinted here consists of a few pages from their introductory chapter and several

---

[1]Andrew J. Cherlin and Frank F. Furstenberg, Jr., *The New American Grandparent: A Place in the Family, A Life Apart* (New York: Basic Books, 1986. [Reprinted by Harvard University Press, 1992.])

pages from the concluding chapter of their book. The authors found little support for the view that family life is in crisis. They argue that a look at the later years of the family life course could alter our sense of the consequences of recent changes.

Demographer Samuel Preston, in a 1984 article, first noted the paradox that the well-being of the elderly was improving even as their numbers in the population were increasing (in part due to longer life expectancy). One would think, Preston observed, that the well-being of the elderly would be worsening because of the difficulty of caring for their vast numbers. Moreover, the well-being of children seemed to be decreasing, even though their numbers were diminishing (due to a lower birth rate). One might have expected children's lot to improve because there were fewer of them to care for.

Why was this occurring? Preston's answer was that the political power of the elderly was growing as a result of their greater numbers, compelling state and federal governments to expand Social Security, institute Medicare (the government health insurance program for the elderly), and take other measures designed to benefit them. Moreover, Preston argued, since every nonelderly person hopes that she or he will one day be elderly, the political demands of the elderly struck a responsive chord in the general population. In contrast, children do not vote and had few effective groups advocating on their behalf. And no one anticipates being a child again.

Although more than a decade has passed since the article was published and although the number of children is increasing (because the baby boomers of the 1950s and early 1960s are in their prime childbearing ages), Preston's point is still relevant. Public policy has rewarded the elderly with increased benefits, but little has been done for children. The 1996 welfare reforms actually cut spending for cash welfare and food stamps for families with children and subsidies to the families of disabled children.

When the baby boomers begin to retire after about 2010, it is questionable whether the nation will be able to pay for all the benefits they will be entitled to. But few politicians have the courage to confront that difficult issue now for fear of incurring the wrath of elderly voters. Still, critics of Preston's article have stated that there is no reason why benefits for children must fall just because their numbers are falling relative to the elderly. Our country could continue to increase benefits to both groups, the critics say. Strictly speaking, they are correct; but in practice, it is the elderly who have been accruing most of the new government benefits.

Extending the Family

John R. Logan and Glenna D. Spitze

THE EFFECTS OF FAMILY CHANGE ON THE OLDER FAMILY

Family Ties is a study of how Americans deal with family in adulthood. We look closely at people who are now middle-aged and older (the respondents in our research were all aged forty and above). We explore their social networks: with whom do they live, what kinds of people are they in touch with, whom do they support, and from whom do they receive help? What is the role of family, and what part is played by contacts outside of the family—by neighbors, for example, or particularly for the elderly, by public programs? We also consider how people interpret and respond to their situations. How do people experience the transition from thinking of themselves as young, to middle-aged, to old? Are there generational conflicts in expectations of support, within the family or in the public arena? For the "middle generation," what are the effects of multiplication of roles?

Our conclusions are decidedly upbeat in the following senses. First, we find that families continue to be at the center of people's lives and that people link their family roles smoothly with other commitments. Second, we find that growing older is not generally associated with loss of autonomy, and that the dependency sometimes attributed to older people should better be understood as interdependence between the generations. Our results do not confirm worries about the continuing viability of

families in people's daily lives, and they reject images of aging (from middle age to elderly) as self-centered dependency.

To be more precise, we believe that families have retained their role as the central core of social support through midlife and old age, despite speculation to the contrary. This has been possible for the following reasons, which it is our purpose to establish in this book.

First, although it is true that the frail elderly often rely on their spouse and adult children for help, such dependence makes up only a small part of the aging experience. Most people of retirement age, for most of their senior years, are quite capable of managing daily routines on their own. Therefore it would be misleading to base our image of this generation on the reality of health problems that typically appear near the end of life. The older generation on the whole is autonomous, and in fact provides more assistance to adult children than vice versa.

Second, we find evidence that the bonds between generations are strong, founded on mutual caring rather than on generational self-interest. It was popular in the days of the Gray Panthers to anticipate a time when the older generation would develop a highly politicized age consciousness and mobilize in its own interest, and it is clear that the aging lobby today has become very effective in government. Nevertheless, the value system to which the majority of older Americans subscribe is more indelibly marked by concern for the younger generation. The values of mutual caring are the key to understanding how ties between parents and adult children can remain stronger than most other social ties throughout the life course.

Third, parents do not rely exclusively on daughters for contact and help. Intergenerational bonds are sustained by the activities of both men and women in their roles as mothers and fathers, as daughters and sons. There are to be sure differences in the kinds of activities that men and women carry out, and our research bears only tangentially on the special emotional investment in families that is commonly attributed to women or intensive caregiving near the end of life. But time and again throughout this book we will examine the evidence regarding gender differences in various aspects of relationships between parents and adult children, and repeatedly we will show that differences are small, mixed, or in an unexpected direction. The participation of both men and women in maintaining family ties is another key to their durability.

We also consider several ways in which demographic trends may disrupt or limit intergenerational relations. The literature has focused particularly on negative effects of employment or divorce on adult children's, especially daughters', relations with parents. We find no such effects. And turning to the broader question of how adult children combine their various work and nuclear family roles with dealing with their own parents, we detect no cause for concern. Typical relations with aging parents are well within the range of children's ability to manage them without suffering stress. Even in the extreme cases of caregiving for dependent elderly parents (just as may be true in other forms of caregiving, as to a handicapped spouse, child, or sibling) we believe that the full picture includes both anxiety and fulfillment. In this respect perhaps the research literature has put forward an unrealistic image of caregivers as victims, when the reality is more diverse.

Finally, we will show that family ties remain at the core of other sorts of social relations. Much intergenerational support is based on the neighborhood—indeed, families are at the center of neighboring as a social form—belying theories of the withering away of the traditional community/kinship nexus. And public services for the noninstitutionalized older population, despite their expansion over the last several decades, are used by relatively few seniors, and even then principally only in the absence of intimate family members . . .

CENTRALITY OF FAMILY TIES

Our analyses are remarkable for the apparent resilience of parent-child ties in later life. Even more noteworthy is the importance of these ties compared to other parts of people's social networks. Whether measured as contact, visiting, help given, or help received, these family ties are at the very core of people's networks outside the home. And the most traditional of them—family neighbors, that is, parents or children living within the same neighborhood—retain a special weight in social relationships. Rather than being displaced by secondary associations, by friends or coworkers living at a distance or by paid helpers or public services, we find that family ties—when they are present—are people's preferred source of routine assistance. Others play distinctly subordinate roles. These conclusions are parallel to those of Rossi and Rossi regarding normative obligations. They describe a pattern of normative social relations as a set of concentric circles, with parent and child in the center.

No doubt the family is being stretched today, as could only be expected under conditions of growing social inequality and poverty, weakening job security, and reduced public assistance. Even the most affluent households bear the emotional scars of divorce, the strains of remarriage, and the pressures of long working hours. Family patterns including high incidence of female-headed households, resulting from divorce and out-of-wedlock childbirth, have extended well beyond the confines of the inner city and the minority community. Yet there are reasons to believe that the family is also being regenerated, and the task of sociologists is not only to identify the failures of the old family but also to perceive the emergence of the new one. Vital institutions don't just cease to function; they may be battered and punished by change, but people must and do find ways to adapt to their conditions. It is not a Pollyana but a realist who, like Stacey (1991, p. 16), looks for the ways in which people "have been creatively remaking American family life." Stacey describes the current period as one where little is taken for granted about family form and people struggle to adapt existing institutions to new needs. No single family structure has emerged to replace the modern family: this is "a transitional and contested period of family history, a period after the modern family order, but before what we cannot foretell" (1991, p. 18).

Our own view is that less is changing than meets the eye. Any interpretation reflects the particular blinders of the theorist. Our interpretation may reflect the emphases of the gerontological literature in which we have worked together for nearly ten years. Let us be clear about what we mean. Sociologists are now more inclined than ever before to study family issues in the context of people's whole life histories, from childhood to retirement and widowhood (Elder 1985). Yet the core of family studies has been, and perhaps still is, that phase of family life that runs from marriage to nest leaving: the family, the nuclear family or the modern family, is a childbearing and childraising institution. Social gerontologists, grounded in a medical and social work tradition and specializing in the problems of older people, have been separated from this theoretical core. The linkage between aging and family studies was established by the recognition that adult children were often the primary caregivers for the frail elderly. But the framing of the issues at that time—the concern about whether these caregivers would continue to be available because of divorce, women's employment, etc.—simply reflected the questions that family theorists were already asking about the younger family. The crisis of the younger family became a crisis in support for older family members.

EXTENDING THE FAMILY

Thus our tendency has been to study the younger family only insofar as it is mirrored in intergenerational relations in the older family. The corresponding bias of most family researchers has been to assume that the extended family died out long ago, and that only the

younger nuclear family has survived. For example, a single-minded focus on the young family is found in the recent essay on the decline of the family by David Popenoe (1993) cited in our Preface. Though he recognizes that family change is not necessarily family decline, he regards recent changes as "both unique and alarming." This is because, in his view, "it is not the extended family that is breaking up but the nuclear family. The nuclear family can be thought of as the last vestige of the traditional family unit; all other adult members have been stripped away, leaving but two—the husband and the wife. The nuclear unit—man, woman, and child—is called that for good reason: It is the fundamental and most basic unit of the family. Breaking up the nucleus of anything is a serious matter. . . . Adults for their own good purposes, most recently self-fulfillment, have stripped the family down to its nucleus. But any further reduction—either in functions or in number of its members—will likely have adverse consequences for children, and thus for generations to come" (Popenoe 1993, pp. 539–40).

We do not dispute the importance of this younger nuclear family. The family of parents and minor children is the site of many key activities. It is first of all the setting where most child-raising issues arise. It is where divorce has its greatest incidence and perhaps its greatest impact. And it is arguably where the greatest gender-related tensions are found, particularly because the tasks of economic support, homemaking, and child-rearing are typically most stressful for young parents. Perhaps for these same reasons it is the least secure component of the American family.

But it is not the whole family. On the contrary, as others have argued persuasively (Rossi and Rossi 1990), the nuclear family is a lifelong and multigenerational event. It is a network of two sorts of relationships of central importance in people's lives: with their parents, lasting until their parents' death (when, in many cases, they themselves are well into middle age), and with their own children, usually extending through their own lifetime. We all acknowledge this point, when confronted by it, but family sociologists have focused particularly on the childhood years.

The research literature on young families and on grandparenting demonstrates the relevance for children of relationships with older kin. The well-known ethnographic accounts of resilient kin and neighbor networks of poor single mothers by Stack (1974) offer at least the possibility that there are workable alternatives to the two-parent family, even in the worst conditions. There is evidence that intergenerational ties do play a strong role in coping with difficult family situations. Only a small minority of the grandparents studied by Cherlin and Furstenberg (1986) were "involved" in a parent-like relationship with grandchildren, but others were viewed by the authors as "sources of support in reserve. This latent support may never be activated; but, like a good insurance policy, it is important nevertheless" (p. 206). They predict that demographic trends including the increase in divorce will work to make this support more salient in the future.

The great majority of teenage mothers live in a larger family environment (Voydanoff and Donnelly 1990), typically in the grandmother's home, and this may occur even when the mother is married. This is particularly true for black teen mothers (married or unmarried), who are twice as likely to live with other adult kin than are white teen mothers (Hogan et al. 1990; see also Taylor et al. 1993). White mothers, though less likely to coreside with kin, are more likely to receive other forms of assistance (Hofferth 1984).

Coresidence may create problems for grandparents, who may feel burdened by and conflicted with the contradictory norms of noninterference and obligation to help if needed, but grandchildren and their mothers may benefit from these arrangements (Aldous 1995). Generally, mothers who live with kin benefit from higher levels of assistance in child care, psychological support, and help in returning to school

or work (Hogan et al. 1990). And the payoff of this intergenerational presence is evident in the performance of the children: the negative effects of having been born to a teenage mother are partly offset by the presence of other adults in the household (Voydanoff and Donnelly 1990, p. 90). McLanahan and Sandefur (1994) note that studies of younger families have found that "being raised by a mother and grandmother is just as good as being raised by two parents, at least in terms of children's psychological well-being" (p. 74; see also Cherlin and Furstenberg 1986). Their own study of teenage grandchildren found no positive effect.

Adopting a multigenerational view of the family leads in a different direction than the reports of its decline. A recent essay by Matilda White Riley and John Riley (1993) offers an alternate perspective. Riley and Riley argue that the "simple kinship structure" of a young nuclear family that only sometimes included a surviving older generation has already been supplanted by an "expanded" structure. Because people live longer, the number of generations surviving jointly has increased. As a result, "linkages among family members have been prolonged. Thus parents and their offspring now survive jointly for so many years that a mother and her daughter are only briefly in the traditional relationship of parent and little children; during the several remaining decades of their lives they have become status equals" (1993, p. 163).

This expanded family, extended in generations and in duration, points the way toward an even more flexible type of kinship structure, a "latent matrix" of kin connections. Riley and Riley (1993, p. 169) point to four features of this new family:

"First, numerous social and cultural changes—especially cohort increases in longevity—are yielding a large and complex network of kin relationships. Second, these many relationships are flexible . . . increasingly matters of choice rather than obligation. A plethora of options is potentially at hand. Third, these relationships are not constrained by age or generation; people of any age, within or across generations, may opt to support, love, or confide in one another. Fourth, many of these kinship bonds remain latent until called upon. They form a safety net of significant connections to choose from in case of need."

The "latent matrix" loses "the sharp boundaries set by generation or age or geographical proximity . . . the boundaries of the family network have been widened to encompass many diverse relationships, including several degrees of stepkin and in-laws, single-parent families, adopted and other 'relatives' chosen from outside the family" (1993, p. 174). Further, it adds the element of greater choice rather than obligation to family relationships—even for motherhood itself.

THE FUTURE OF THE FAMILY

So we can't equate the future of the family with the future of the nuclear family, or the "modern" nuclear family, as Stacey calls it. It is the family as a latent matrix or multigenerational network that has to be evaluated, the family that endures throughout adulthood and that only sometimes is characterized by living together. This is a family structure in which people are relatively independent and self-sufficient, but nonetheless they maintain core relationships.

In this family form (the "extended" family, by which we mean the nuclear family extended through time and generations), we certainly find consequences of the changing nuclear family, though in most respects we do not share a sense of crisis. Perhaps the most often discussed set of family issues is associated with divorce and single-parent families. The harshest impacts here are probably on children in their younger years, most commonly including poverty and weakened or absent ties to their fathers. Our own research bears only on intergenerational relations at a later stage in the life cycle. Goldscheider (1990; see also Bumpass 1990) argues that there are special risks for people, especially men, who will become old in the next century, due to their weak ties to chil-

dren (already visible in their relationships to these children today). But it is hard to predict the future impact of the single-parent or blended families of today.

We cannot be sure of the degree to which the multigenerational family network can substitute for the two-parent nuclear family that became our cultural model in the 1950s. Commentators have often pointed out that divorce and remarriage simultaneously undermine a child's links to one parent while expanding the universe of potential kin in the form of stepparents, stepsiblings, and stepgrandparents. But as Furstenberg and Cherlin (1991, pp. 91–95) point out, little is known about the long-term consequences of exchanging one very close tie for a wider network of weaker ties (see also Bumpass 1990). This is largely uncharted territory. The evidence so far, however, is that intergenerational ties in adulthood remain strong in spite of the social currents that have been expected to disrupt them. These ties are a firm foundation for the family of the future.

REFERENCES

Aldous, Joan. 1995. "New Views of Grandparents in Intergenerational Context." *Journal of Family Issues* 16: 104–22.

Bumpass, Larry L. 1990. "What's Happening to the Family? Interactions between Demographic and Institutional Change." *Demography* 27: 483–98.

Cherlin, Andrew J., and Frank F. Furstenberg, Jr. 1986. *The New American Grandparent*. New York: Basic Books.

Furstenberg, Frank, Jr. and Andrew Cherlin. 1991. *Divided Families*. Cambridge, MA: Harvard University Press.

Goldscheider, Frances K. 1990. "The Aging of the Gender Revolution: What Do We Know and What Do We Need to Know?" *Research on Aging* 12 (December): 531–45.

Hofferth, Sandra. 1984. "Kin Networks, Race, and Family Structure." *Journal of Marriage and the Family* 46: 791–806.

Hogan, Dennis P., Ling-Xin Hao, and William Paris. 1990. "Race, Kin Networks, and Assistance to

Mother-Headed Families." *Social Forces* 68: 797–812.

McLanahan, Sara, and Gary Sandefur. 1994. *Growing Up with a Single Parent: What Hurts, What Helps.* Cambridge, MA: Harvard University Press.

Popenoe, David. 1993. "American Family Decline, 1960–1990: A Review and Appraisal." *Journal of Marriage and the Family* 55: 527–55.

Riley, Matilda White, and John W. Riley Jr. 1993. "Connections: Kin and Cohort." Pp. 169–89 in *The Changing Contract across Generations,* eds. Vern Bengston and W. Andrew Achenbaum. New York: Aldine de Gruyter.

Rossi, Alice S., and Peter H. Rossi. 1990. *Of Human Bonding: Parent-Child Relations Across the Life Course.* New York: Aldine de Gruyter.

Stacey, Judith. 1991. *Brave New Families: Stories of Domestic Upheaval in Late Twentieth Century America.* New York: Basic Books.

Stack, Carol. 1974. *All Our Kin: Strategies for Survival in a Black Community.* New York: Harper and Row.

Taylor, Robert Joseph, Linda M. Chatters, and James S. Jackson. 1993. "A Profile of Familial Relations among Three-Generation Black Families." *Family Relations* 42: 332–41.

Voydanoff, Patricia, and Brenda Donnelly. 1990. *Adolescent Sexuality and Pregnancy.* Newbury Park, CA: Sage.

READING 15-2

Children and the Elderly in the United States

Samuel H. Preston

In the 1960s and 1970s two developments that had not been expected by demographers changed the age structure of the U.S. population in a dra-

matic way. The first was a decrease in the number of children. From 1960 to 1982 the number of children younger than 15 fell by 7 percent. The decline was mainly due to the drop in the birth rate that followed the "baby boom."

The second development was a rapid increase in the number of elderly people. Between 1960 and 1980 the number of people 65 or older grew by 54 percent. The increase was caused mainly by a sharp reduction in the death rate among older people, acting on a population that already was large because of the large number of babies born between 1890 and 1915. As a result, during the 1970s the elderly population of the United States increased at a higher rate than the total population of India.

One might expect such a change in age structure to help the young and hurt the old. Fewer children should mean less competition for resources in the home and greater per capita availability of social services such as public schools. More old people, on the other hand, should put great pressure on resources such as hospitals, nursing homes, and Social Security funds. I believe, however, that exactly the opposite has happened. Since the early 1960s the well-being of the elderly has improved greatly whereas that of the young has deteriorated. Demographic trends underlie these changes: in the family, in politics and in industry the growing number of older people and the declining number of children have worked to the advantage of the group that is increasing in size.

In order to account for what has happened to children and older people in the United States it is first necessary to document the changes in living conditions among the two groups. The measures that are commonly used by social scientists to measure the well-being of large groups include levels of income, health, educational achievement, and reports of satisfaction with life.

One of the most straightforward ways to compare children with the elderly is to measure the fraction of the two groups that live in poverty. Since children generally do not have independent incomes, one cannot directly compare personal income. One can, however, measure the incomes of the families in which the children live and compare the incomes to a minimum standard of need. The Bureau of the Census uses an Economy Food Plan drawn up by the Department of Agriculture as the basis of such a standard. Families that have an income equal to an amount less than three times the cost of the food plan are said to be living in poverty.

By this standard there have been remarkable changes in the proportion of children who live in poverty compared with the corresponding proportion of the elderly. In 1970, 16 percent of those under 14 lived in poverty compared with 24 percent of those older than 65. By 1982 the situation had been reversed: 23 percent of children lived in poverty compared with 15 percent of the elderly.

Monetary income is not the only measure of material well-being. Noncash transfer payments such as food stamps and Medicare have a strong influence on the condition of society's dependents. The Census Bureau estimated that in 1982 the market value of noncash transfers was $98 billion, much of it in medical payments to the elderly. If this sum is taken into account, the disparity in poverty status between children and the elderly is increased further. The fraction of the elderly living in poverty in 1982 falls from 15 to 4 percent. The corresponding reduction for children is only from 24 to 17 percent.

An examination of public outlays as a whole reinforces the idea that the elderly have done better than children at society's hands in recent years. Mary Jo Bane of Harvard University concluded that in 1960 the average government expenditure (including federal, state and local funds) on each elderly person was about three times the expenditure on each child. Both types of spending increased rapidly in the succeeding decades; hence the ratio remained about the same through 1979. Because the expenditure on the elderly started from a higher level, however,

the absolute gain for each elderly person was much larger than the gain for each child.

Since 1979 there has been a sharp break in the pattern of government expenditure that kept the ratio of per-capita outlays for the two groups roughly constant. Many public programs for children have been cut back while those for older people have been expanded. For example, the Aid to Families with Dependent Children (AFDC) program has been substantially reduced. In 1979, out of every 100 children in poverty 72 were enrolled in AFDC. By 1982 only 52 out of 100 were in the program. In comparison, Medicare outlays rose from $3.4 billion in 1967 to $57.4 billion in 1983, and it has been estimated that they will rise to $112 billion by 1988.

The Federal Office of Management and Budget has recently begun estimating the fraction of all federal benefits that are directed to those who are 65 or older. Older people got $44 billion in federal funds in 1971 and $217 billion in 1983. The 1983 figure is equivalent to about $7,700 per person who is about than 65 and is a sum larger than the total spent on national defense in that year.

Federal expenditures on children are harder to calculate, but I have attempted to do so from budget documents. The total federal outlay on the major child-oriented programs (AFDC, Head Start, food stamps, child health, child nutrition and aid to education) is about $36 billion for 1984; this is about a sixth of the total spending on the elderly. Because there are more children than old people, the expenditure per child through these programs is less than a 10th the expenditure per older person. These figures are not strictly comparable to the data collected by Bane, but they do give a sense of the increasing disparity between public outlays on the young and those on the old.

The gulf in well-being that separates the old and the young has been widened still further by the fact that public spending on the young has become less effective. The largest portion of public money spent on the young goes to public schools. Many indicators suggest the quality of public schooling has declined drastically in the past two decades.

The sum of the scores on the verbal and mathematics sections of the Scholastic Aptitude Test (S.A.T.) declined by 90 points from 1963 through 1980. The Wirtz Commission, which was the most authoritative group to investigate this trend, concluded that about half of the decline was due to the fact that a wider range of students now take the test than took it in the 1960s. About half of the decline, however, represents an actual decline among students with qualifications similar to those taking the test earlier. Most of the real decline took place in the early 1970s. In addition there has been a decrease in the proportion of U.S. teen-agers who finish high school. In 1965 the fraction was 76.3 percent; by 1980 it had fallen to 73.6 percent.

Education is the principal public service for the young; health care is the principal service for the old. Some 69 percent of the medical bills of people 65 or older are paid for with public funds. The Congressional Budget Office estimates that in 1984 the Federal Government will spend an average of $2,948 on health care for each person 65 or older.

A good index of the effectiveness of public spending on health care is the mortality rate. Between 1968 and 1980 mortality rates improved in all age groups in the United States. The improvements, however, were not equally distributed between the young and the old. Demographers employ statistical standards called *model life tables* to compare the relations of death rates in different age groups with the relations that would be expected from international and historical experience. If model life tables are used to analyze the recent changes in mortality in the United States, it can be shown that the greatest improvements in the death rate have occurred in the older age groups. By normal standards of progress, children and young adults gained the least . . .

Thus according to several measures, including health, educational achievement and poverty status, the elderly appear to be doing better than the young. The elderly are not oblivious to the improvement in their welfare. A Gallup poll made in 1982 found that 71 percent of those 65 or older reported they were highly satisfied with their standard of living, by far the greatest level of satisfaction in any age group. The proportion of the elderly who scored "Very high" on a psychological scale of anxiety fell from 22 to 15 percent between 1957 and 1976, while the corresponding proportion of younger adults rose sharply. Furthermore, since 1960 there have been reductions in the suicide rate among the elderly, which also seems to suggest increased well-being.

Although suicide is rare among children, the trend appears to be upward. Other indicators also suggest that a deterioration has occurred in the mental health of children. The U.S. Health Examination Survey asked parents whether "anything had ever happened to seriously upset or disturb your child?" The fraction of parents who answered in the affirmative rose from 27 percent in 1963–65 to 37 percent in 1976.

The major reason for the increased emotional disturbance among children, as reported by parents, seems to be the intensification of marital discord. Indeed, changes in the structure of the family appear to be closely connected to what has happened to both children and the elderly in recent years.

One reason that changes in family structure can have such a strong effect on the status of dependent groups is that the family is an important vehicle for the transfer of society's resources. James N. Morgan of the University of Michigan estimated that roughly a third of the U.S. gross national product takes the form of transfers from income earners to nonearners within family groups that live together.

As a result, any change in the family's capacity to care for its dependents has powerful consequences for those who are being taken care of. These consequences are more significant for children than they are for the elderly because the family has relinquished to the state an increasing share of responsibility for elderly dependents. Hence older people are to some extent protected against changes in family structure.

The situation is very different for children. The government assumes a much smaller share of support for the young than it does for the elderly. The conjugal family is the chief source of support for children. In recent years it has begun to divest itself of its responsibility for the young, just as earlier it abandoned much of its responsibility for the elderly. Absent fathers are the main factor in this divestiture. In 1960 only 5.3 percent of births were out of wedlock. By 1980 the figure had risen to 18.4 percent. The rate of illegitimacy has a strong influence on resources available for children because in most out-of-wedlock births the father takes no lasting responsibility for his child.

Even for children born in wedlock, the situation has deteriorated. According to Larry Bumpass of the University of Wisconsin at Madison, persistence of the divorce rates that prevailed at the end of the 1970s will mean that 43 percent of the children born in wedlock will experience parental separation before they are 16. If the rate of increase in divorce of the past decade continues, the proportion could reach two-thirds. Furthermore, fathers contribute little on the average to the support of children from previous marriages. A recent study by the Census Bureau found that fewer than half of all children living with their mother after a divorce were supported by payments from their father. The immediate consequence is that the economic condition of mothers and children deteriorates after a divorce. Morgan and his colleague Greg J. Duncan conclude that in divorces occurring from 1972 through 1978, 72 percent of the affected children experienced a reduction in their family's income in relation to the minimum standard of need.

It is obvious that the economic consequences of marital disruption have much to do with the increase in the number of children who live in poverty. Census Bureau data show that 69 percent of the increase in the number of children living in poverty from 1970 through 1982 occurred in households headed by women. Evidence suggests that the instability of the nuclear family is also responsible for some of the decline in educational achievement.

The main vehicle other than the family for transferring resources to dependents is the state. In a pluralistic democracy such as that of the United States the formation of public policy is strongly influenced by the relative power of interest groups. In recent decades the old have become a far more powerful interest group, while the constituency for children has declined in power.

In exerting their political influence the elderly draw on support from three overlapping but substantial groups. The first group consists of the elderly themselves. The second consists of members of the under-65 population acting on behalf of elderly family members who are currently or potentially in need of financial assistance. The third consists of the entire under-65 population acting on behalf of themselves in their own (future) old age. The elderly, unlike some other special interests, make up a group we all expect, or at least hope, to join eventually. Most government programs for those more than 65 years old are to some extent perceived as a social contract enabling middle-aged adults to transfer resources to themselves later in life.

Children have only one of these three sources of political influence. Young people cannot vote. Furthermore, adults cannot agitate to improve conditions in their own childhood, since that is the past. Children's only remaining source of political influence is parents acting on behalf of their progeny.

Because of the imbalance between the sources of political support available to older people and the sources available to children, the change in age structure can have a "multiplier" effect on public policy. The sharp mortality decline in the older age groups has led not only to an increase in the number of voters older than 65 but also to an increase in the number of middle-aged adults who have living parents and an increase in the number of years beyond 65 that the average adult can expect to live.

The most significant of these changes is probably the increase in the number of elderly. In the past decade the increase has been combined with a high level of political participation. In the 1982 congressional elections 65 percent of those age 65 through 74 voted. This was the highest percentage of any age group and more than twice the rate among people aged 20 through 29. Once again the trend reverses earlier patterns: in the congressional elections of 1966 the voting rate for those older than 65 was lower than it was for any age group between 35 and 64.

The elderly probably have also come to exercise a stronger claim on the political allegiance of those younger than 65. I estimate that in 1980 the average 40-year-old couple had 2.59 living parents and 2.72 living children. If present fertility and mortality rates persist, however, the average 40-year-old couple would eventually have 2.88 living parents and 1.78 living children. It would not be until age 52 that the average couple would have as many living children as they would have living parents.

When parents are 52, of course, most children have left home. It turns out that under current fertility and mortality rates there is no stage in the life cycle when the average married couple will have more children under the age of 20 than they will have surviving parents. The dependency concerns of the middle-aged are thus shifting toward the elderly, at least in numerical terms.

None of this would matter if people of different ages and in different domestic circumstances saw public issues in the same light. But they do not. For example, the 1983 Gallup Poll of public

attitudes toward the public schools asked whether people would vote to raise taxes for schools if asked to do so by the local school board. Those younger than 50 were evenly split; those older than 50 were opposed by 62 to 28 percent.

The foregoing discussion of politics deals only with the part of political behavior that is motivated by self-interest. What about altruism? Altruism is not a negligible motive in human affairs, particularly altruism directed toward people with whom an individual shares some corporate identity. I suspect, however, that W. Norton Grubb and Marvin Lazerson, then at the University of California at Berkeley, were at least partially correct in proposing that we have drifted toward a form of society and government based mainly on self-interest and adversarial relations between groups. Grubb and Lazerson argue that in U.S. society there has never been a strong sense of collective responsibility for other people's children. Furthermore, the wide availability of effective contraception could well have exaggerated this split between private and collective concerns. Reliable contraceptives give a married couple a high degree of control over whether they have children. Since children are now the result of a private decision rather than of chance, many people today think the parents should bear the cost of child rearing. On the other hand, we do not choose to have parents and so there is no equivalent motive for insisting that parents be privately supported.

A second factor that probably helps to suppress altruism toward other people's children is the fact that these children are increasingly from minority groups with whom the majority have trouble identifying: 24 percent of those younger than 15 are black or Hispanic, compared with only 11 percent of those older than 65 . . .

Some readers may be disturbed by the fact that in demonstrating the existence of the demographic mechanisms affecting the elderly and the young, age has been emphasized to the exclusion of other traditional demographic variables, including race. In discussing the changing status of children and the elderly in the United States, however, I see no reason to analyze the races separately. For those who think the current problems of children are confined to racial minorities it should be pointed out that there is not one trend described above that does not apply to both blacks and whites. On the contrary, in the case of some of the most significant trends, including rising illegitimacy rates and declining school achievement, the changes have been much greater among whites than they have among blacks.

In summarizing the lessons to be learned from recent demographic trends I do not want to paint the elderly as the villains of the piece. I am primarily concerned about the fate of children and in that context the elderly serve largely for comparison. Nevertheless, it is unrealistic simply to wish away the possibility that there is direct competition between the young and the old for society's resources.

Even if the young and the old are to some extent competitors, however, the elderly alone do not decide where society's resources are to be expended. That is a collective, political decision that society makes. It is certainly reasonable to ask whether such decisions in recent decades have taken us along a useful course. There is surely something to be said for a system in which conditions improve as we pass through life.

On the other hand, the failure to devote resources to children cannot be defended so easily. Whereas expenditure on the elderly can be thought of mainly as consumption, expenditure on the young is a combination of consumption and investment. The quality of education and the psychological well-being of children are crucial to the future productive capacity of the United States.

If we care about our collective future rather than simply about our futures as individuals, we are faced with the question of how best to safeguard the human and material resources represented by children. These resources have not been carefully guarded in the past two decades. Rather than assuming collective responsibility, as has been done in the case of the elderly, U.S. society has chosen to place almost exclusive responsibility for the care of children on the nuclear family. Marital instability, however, has much reduced the capacity of the family to care for its own children. Hence insisting that families alone care for the young would seem to be an evasion of collective responsibility rather than a conscious decision about the best way to provide for the future.

CHAPTER 16

Social Change and Families

Having studied the sociology of the family, you should be in a better position to evaluate the debates over its current and future state. That's not to say that you should necessarily choose a side: the issues are complex and the institution itself is always changing. It's not always clear what is the "conservative" or "liberal" or "feminist" position. If the course you are completing increases your power to critically evaluate the arguments that you will hear in the future, whether or not you sympathize with the people who are doing the arguing, then it will have been a success.

The issue on which the debates have been centered over the past few decades is how well families are caring for children. Critics ask whether the decline of life-long marriage between a father who earns the family's income and a mother who stays home and raises the children has lowered the quality of parenting that children receive today. They cite statistics that purport to show a drop in the well-being of children and link this drop to the changes in family life. Conservatives often blame the trends on a cultural drift toward greater individualism—a focus on individual growth and self-fulfillment—

which is said to have eroded the strength of social ties, including marriage.

In contrast, the defenders of contemporary families often argue that the drop in children's well-being is exaggerated and that, in any case, forces outside of the family's control are responsible for both the lowered well-being and the changes in family life. Liberals maintain that an important force is a deterioration in the job prospects for people—and especially young men—without college degrees. The worsening job market is said to have discouraged young adults from marrying and made marriages that do occur more fragile. Feminists defend the movement of married women into the work force for broadening women's lives; if, as a result, working parents are stressed and children sometimes don't receive optimal care, the solution they suggest is to provide more social support for working parents.

In the following selection, Janet Z. Giele outlines the essentials of what she sees as three different political positions in the debate about the family: conservative, liberal, and feminist. The descriptions of the conservative and liberal positions are standard ones, and the author does a good job of summarizing them. Giele's feminist position is more original—she claims that there is a coherent feminist viewpoint that is neither liberal nor conservative. Not every contributor to the debate, not even every feminist contributor, would agree with her. Giele obviously favors this third way, and you should evaluate her position as critically and thoughtfully as you would evaluate the other two.

Whether or not the family has declined, it is hard to argue against the proposition that marriage plays a lesser role in family life than it did a few decades ago, when cohabitation was rare outside of the lower classes, divorce was much less common, and the vast majority of children were born to married couples. In the second reading, Steven Nock attempts to construct an argument for restoring marriage to a privileged status. This position is strongly opposed by many liberal and feminist writers who believe that all family forms should be regarded as equally deserving and privileged. The critics also charge that marriage has privileged men more than women because men have received more benefits from it than women have. What makes Nock's argument interesting is that he acknowledges from the start that marriage has traditionally been organized in ways that benefit men, and he urges a restructing of marriage in such as way that women and men benefit equally. Nock further recognizes that marriages need to be held together by more than love, and he suggests some radical policy prescriptions to support gender-neutral marriage. His essay is a response to an article by Jean Bethke Elshtain, "A Call to Civil Society,"[1] that argues, in part, for stronger family bonds but, in Nock's view, ignores the crucial problem of gender inequalities in family life.

---

[1]Jean Bethke Elshtain, "A Call to Civil Society." *Society* (July/August 1999): 11–19.

READING 16-1

Decline of the Family: Conservative, Liberal, and Feminist Views

Janet Z. Giele

In the 1990s the state of American families and children became a new and urgent topic. Everyone recognized that families had changed. Divorce rates had risen dramatically. More women were in the labor force. Evidence on rising teenage suicides, high rates of teen births, and disturbing levels of addiction and violence had put children at risk.

Conservatives have held that these problems can be traced to a culture of toleration and an expanding welfare state that undercut self-reliance and community standards. They focus on the family as a caregiving institution and try to restore its strengths by changing the culture of marriage and parenthood. Liberals center on the disappearance of manual jobs that throws less educated men out of work and undercuts their status in the family as well as rising hours of work among the middle class that makes stable two-parent families more difficult to maintain. Liberals argue that structural changes are needed outside the family in the public world of employment and schools.

The feminist vision combines both the reality of human interdependence in the family and individualism of the workplace. Feminists want to protect diverse family forms that allow realization of freedom and equality while at the same time nurturing the children of the next generation.

Janet Z. Giele, "Decline of the Family: Conservative, Liberal, and Feminist Views" from David Popenoe, et al., eds., *Promise to Keep: Decline and Renewal of Marriage in America,* pp. 89–115. Copyright © 1996 by Rowman & Littlefield Publishers, Inc. Reprinted with the permission of the publishers.

THE CONSERVATIVE EXPLANATION: SELFISHNESS AND MORAL DECLINE

The new family advocates turn their spotlight on the breakdown in the two-parent family, saying that rising divorce, illegitimacy, and father absence have put children at greater risk of school failure, unemployment, and antisocial behavior. The remedy is to restore religious faith and family commitment as well as to cut welfare payments to unwed mothers and mother-headed families.

CONSERVATIVE MODEL

Cultural and moral weakening $\rightarrow$ Family breakdown, divorce, family decline $\rightarrow$ Father absence, school failure, poverty, crime, drug use

Cultural and Moral Weakening

To many conservatives, the modern secularization of religious practice and the decline of religious affiliation have undermined the norms of sexual abstinence before marriage and the prohibitions of adultery or divorce thereafter. Sanctions against illegitimacy or divorce have been made to seem narrow-minded and prejudiced. In addition, daytime television and the infamous example of Murphy Brown, a single mother having a child out of wedlock, helped to obscure simple notions of right and wrong. Barbara Dafoe Whitehead's controversial article in the *Atlantic* entitled "Dan Quayle Was Right" is an example of this argument.[1]

Gradual changes in marriage laws have also diminished the hold of tradition. Restrictions against waiting periods, race dissimilarity, and varying degrees of consanguinity were gradually disappearing all over the United States and Europe.[2] While Mary Ann Glendon viewed the change cautiously but relativistically—as a process that waxed and waned across the centuries—others have interpreted these changes as a movement from status to contract (i.e., from attention to the particular individual's characteristics to reliance on the impersonal considerations of the marketplace). The resulting transformation lessened the family's distinctive capacity to serve as a bastion of private freedom against the leveling effect and impersonality of public bureaucracy.

Erosion of the Two-Parent Family

To conservatives, one of the most visible causes of family erosion was government welfare payments, which made fatherless families a viable option. In *Losing Ground,* Charles Murray used the rise in teenage illegitimate births as proof that government-sponsored welfare programs had actually contributed to the breakdown of marriage.[3] Statistics on rising divorce and mother-headed families appeared to provide ample proof that the two-parent family was under siege. The proportion of all households headed by married couples fell from 77 percent in 1950 to 61 percent in 1980 and 55 percent in 1993.[4] Rising cohabitation, divorce rates, and births out of wedlock all contributed to the trend. The rise in single-person households was also significant, from only 12 percent of all households in 1950 to 27 percent in 1980, a trend fed by rising affluence and the undoubling of living arrangements that occurred with the expansion of the housing supply after World War II.[5]

The growth of single-parent households, however, was the most worrisome to policymakers because of their strong links to child poverty. . . . Of all poor children in 1959, 73 percent had two parents present and 20 percent had a mother only. By 1988, only 35 percent of children in poverty lived with two parents and 57 percent lived with a mother only. These developments were fed by rising rates of divorce and out-of-wedlock births. Between 1940 and 1990, the divorce rate rose from 8.8 to 21 per thousand married women. Out-of-wedlock births exploded from 5 percent in 1960 to 26 percent in 1990.[6]

To explain these changes, conservatives emphasize the breakdown of individual and cultural commitment to marriage and the loss of stigma for divorce and illegitimacy. They understand both trends to be the result of greater emphasis on short-term gratification and on adults' personal desires rather than on what is good for children. A young woman brings a child into the world without thinking about who will support it. A husband divorces his wife and forms another household, possibly with other children, and leaves children of the earlier family behind without necessarily feeling obliged to be present in their upbringing or to provide them with financial support.

Negative Consequences for Children

To cultural conservatives there appears to be a strong connection between erosion of the two-parent family and the rise of health and social problems in children. Parental investment in children has declined—especially in the time available for supervision and companionship. Parents had roughly 10 fewer hours per week for their children in 1986 than in 1960, largely because more married women were employed (up from 24 percent in 1940 to 52 percent in 1983) and more mothers of young children (under age 6) were working (up from 12 percent in 1940 to 50 percent in 1983). By the late 1980s just over half of mothers of children under a year old were in the labor force for at least part of the year.[7] At the same time fathers were increasingly absent from the family because of desertion, divorce, or failure to marry. In 1980, 15 percent of white children, 50 percent of black children, and 27 percent of children of Hispanic origin had no father present. Today 36 percent of children are living apart from their biological fathers compared with only 17 percent in 1960.[8]

Without a parent to supervise children after school, keep them from watching television all day, or prevent them from playing in dangerous neighborhoods, many more children appear to be falling by the wayside, victims of drugs, obesity, violence, suicide, or failure in school. During the 1960s and 1970s the suicide rate for persons aged 15 to 19 more than doubled. The proportion of obese children between the ages of 6 and 11 rose from 18 to 27 percent. Average

SAT scores fell, and 25 percent of all high school students failed to graduate.[9] In 1995 the Council on Families in America reported, "Recent surveys have found that children from broken homes, when they become teenagers have 2 to 3 times more behavioral and psychological problems than do children from intact homes."[10] Father absence is blamed by the fatherhood movement for the rise in violence among young males. David Blankenhorn and others reason that the lack of a positive and productive male role model has contributed to an uncertain masculine identity which then uses violence and aggression to prove itself. Every child deserves a father and "in a good society, men prove their masculinity not by killing other people, impregnating lots of women, or amassing large fortunes, but rather by being committed fathers and loving husbands.[11]

Psychologist David Elkind, in *The Hurried Child,* suggests that parents' work and time constraints have pushed down the developmental timetable to younger ages so that small children are being expected to take care of themselves and perform at levels that are robbing them of their childhood. The consequences are depression, discouragement, and a loss of joy at learning and growing into maturity.[12]

Reinvention of Marriage

According to the conservative analysis, the solution to a breakdown in family values is to revitalize and reinstitutionalize marriage. The culture should change to give higher priority to marriage and parenting. The legal code should favor marriage and encourage parental responsibility on the part of fathers as well as mothers. Government should cut back welfare programs which have supported alternative family forms.

The cultural approach to revitalizing marriage is to raise the overall priority given to family activities relative to work, material consumption, or leisure. Marriage is seen as the basic building block of civil society, which helps to hold together the fabric of volunteer activity and mutual support that underpins any democratic society.[13] Some advocates are unapologetically judgmental toward families who fall outside the two-parent mold. According to a 1995 *Newsweek* article on "The Return of Shame," David Blankenhorn believes "a stronger sense of shame about illegitimacy and divorce would do more than any tax cut or any new governmental program to maximize the life circumstances of children." But he also adds that the ultimate goal is "to move beyond stigmatizing only teenage mothers toward an understanding of the terrible message sent by all of us when we minimize the importance of fathers or contribute to the breakup of families."[14]

Another means to marriage and family revitalization is some form of taking a "pledge." Prevention programs for teenage pregnancy affirm the ideal of chastity before marriage. Athletes for Abstinence, an organization founded by a professional basketball player, preaches that young people should "save sex for marriage." A Baptist-led national program called True Love Waits has gathered an abstinence pledge from hundreds of thousands of teenagers since it was begun in the spring of 1993. More than 2,000 school districts now offer an abstinence-based sex education curriculum entitled "Sex Respect." Parents who are desperate about their children's sexual behavior are at last seeing ways that society can resist the continued sexualization of childhood.[15]

The new fatherhood movement encourages fathers to promise that they will spend more time with their children. The National Fatherhood Initiative argues that men's roles as fathers should not simply duplicate women's roles as mothers but should teach those essential qualities which are perhaps uniquely conveyed by fathers—the ability to take risks, contain emotions, and be decisive. In addition, fathers fulfill a time-honored role of providing for children as well as teaching them.[16]

Full-time mothers have likewise formed support groups to reassure themselves that not having a job and being at home full-time for their children is an honorable choice, although it is typically undervalued and perhaps even scorned by dual-earner couples and women with careers. A 1994 *Barron's* article claimed that young people in their 20s ("generation X") were turning away from the two-paycheck family and scaling down their consumption so that young mothers could stay at home. Although Labor Department statistics show no such trend but only a flattening of the upward rise of women's employment, a variety of poll data does suggest that Americans would rather spend less time at work and more time with their families.[17] Such groups as Mothers at Home (with 15,000 members) and Mothers' Home Business Network (with 6,000 members) are trying to create a sea change that reverses the priority given to paid work outside the home relative to unpaid caregiving work inside the family.[18]

Conservatives see government cutbacks as one of the major strategies for strengthening marriage and restoring family values. In the words of Lawrence Mead, we have "taxed Peter to pay Paula."[19] According to a *Wall Street Journal* editorial, the "relinquishment of personal responsibility" among people who bring children into the world without any visible means of support is at the root of educational, health, and emotional problems of children from one-parent families, their higher accident and mortality rates, and rising crime.[20]

The new congressional solution is to cut back on the benefits to young men and women who "violate social convention by having children they cannot support."[21] Sociologist Brigitte Berger notes that the increase in children and women on welfare coincided with the explosion of federal child welfare programs—family planning, prenatal and postnatal care, child nutrition, child abuse prevention and treatment, child health and guidance, day care, Head Start, and Aid to Families with Dependent Children (AFDC), Medicaid, and Food Stamps. The solution is to turn back the debilitating culture of welfare dependency by decentralizing the power of the federal government and restoring the role

of intermediary community institutions such as the neighborhood and the church. The mechanism for change would be block grants to the states which would change the welfare culture from the ground up.[22] Robert Rector of the American Heritage Foundation explains that the states would use these funds for a wide variety of alternative programs to discourage illegitimate births and to care for children born out of wedlock, such as promoting adoption, closely supervised group homes for unmarried mothers and their children, and pregnancy prevention programs (except abortion).[23]

Government programs, however, are only one way to bring about cultural change. The Council on Families in America puts its hope in grassroots social movements to change the hearts and minds of religious and civil leaders, employers, human service professionals, courts, and the media and entertainment industry. The Council enunciates four ideals: marital permanence, childbearing confined to marriage, every child's right to have a father, and limitation of parents' total work time (60 hours per week) to permit adequate time with their families.[24] To restore the cultural ideal of the two-parent family, they would make all other types of family life less attractive and more difficult.

ECONOMIC RESTRUCTURING: LIBERAL ANALYSIS OF FAMILY CHANGE

Liberals agree that there are serious problems in America's social health and the condition of its children. But they pinpoint economic and structural changes that have placed new demands on the family without providing countervailing social supports. The economy has become ever more specialized with rapid technological change undercutting established occupations. More women have entered the labor force as their child-free years have increased due to a shorter childbearing period and longer lifespan. The family has lost economic functions to the urban workplace and socialization functions to the school. What is left is the intimate relationship between the marital couple, which, unbuffered by the traditional economic division of labor between men and women, is subject to even higher demands for emotional fulfillment and is thus more vulnerable to breakdown when it falls short of those demands.

LIBERAL MODEL

Changing economic structure	→	Changing family and gender roles	→	Diverse effects: poor v. productive children

The current family crisis thus stems from structural more than cultural change—changes in the economy, a pared-down nuclear family, and less parental time at home. Market forces have led to a new ethic of individual flexibility and autonomy. More dual-earner couples and single-parent families have broadened the variety of family forms. More single-parent families and more working mothers have decreased the time available for parenting. Loss of the father's income through separation and divorce has forced many women and children into poverty with inadequate health care, poor education, and inability to save for future economic needs. The solution that most liberals espouse is a government-sponsored safety net which will facilitate women's employment, mute the effects of poverty, and help women and children to become economically secure.

Recent Changes in the Labor Market

Liberals attribute the dramatic changes in the family to the intrusion of the money economy rather than cultural and moral decline. In a capitalist society individual behavior follows the market. Adam Smith's "invisible hand" brings together buyers and sellers who maximize their satisfaction through an exchange of resources in the marketplace. Jobs are now with an employer, not with the family business or family farm as in preindustrial times. The cash economy has, in the words of Robert Bellah, "invaded" the diffuse personal relationships of trust between family and community members and transformed them into specific impersonal transactions. In an agricultural economy husbands and wives and parents and children were bound together in relationships of exchange that served each others' mutual interests. But modern society erodes this social capital of organization, trust among individuals, and mutual obligations that enhances both productivity and parenting.[25]

The market has also eroded community by encouraging maximum mobility of goods and services. Cheaper labor in the South, lower fuel prices, and deeper tax breaks attracted first textile factories, then the shoe industry, and later automobile assembly plants which had begun in the North. Eventually, many of these jobs left the country. Loss of manufacturing jobs has had dramatic consequences for employment of young men without a college education and their capacity to support a family. In the 1970s, 68 percent of male high school graduates had a full-time, year-round job compared with only 51 percent in the 1980s. Many new jobs are located in clerical work, sales, or other service occupations traditionally associated with women. The upshot is a deteriorating employment picture for less well educated male workers at the same time that there are rising opportunities for women. Not surprisingly, ever more middle-income men and women combine forces to construct a two-paycheck family wage.[26]

Changing Family Forms

Whereas the farm economy dictated a two-parent family and several children as the most efficient work group, the market economy gives rise to a much wider variety of family forms. A woman on the frontier in the 1800s had few other options even if she were married to a drunken, violent, or improvident husband. In today's economy this woman may have enough education to get a clerical job that will support her and her children in a small apartment where the family will be able to use public schools and other public amenities.[27]

Despite its corrosive effect on family relations, the modern economy has also been a liberating force. Women could escape patriarchal domination; the young could seek their fortune without waiting for an inheritance from their elders—all a process that a century ago was aligned with a cultural shift that Fred Weinstein and Gerald Platt termed "the wish to be free."[28] Dramatic improvements took place in the status of women as they gained the right to higher education, entry into the professions, and the elective franchise.[29] Similarly, children were released from sometimes cruel and exploitive labor and became the object of deliberate parental investment and consumption.[30] Elders gained pensions for maintenance and care that made them economically independent of their adult children. All these developments could be understood as part of what William J. Goode has referred to as the "world revolution in family patterns" which resulted in liberation and equality of formerly oppressed groups.[31]

The current assessment of change in family forms is, however, mostly negative because of the consequences for children. More parental investment in work outside the family has meant less time for children. According to liberals, parents separate or divorce or have children outside of marriage because of the economic structure, not because they have become less moral or more selfish. Young women have children out of wedlock when the young men whom they might marry have few economic prospects and when the women themselves have little hope for their own education or employment.[32] Change in the family thus begins with jobs. Advocates of current government programs therefore challenge the conservatives' assertion that welfare caused the breakup of two-parent families by supporting mothers with dependent children. According to William Julius Wilson, it is partly the lack of manual labor jobs for the would-be male breadwinner in inner-city Chicago—the scarcity of "marriageable males"—which drives up the illegitimacy rate.[33]

Among educated women, it is well known that the opportunity costs of forgone income from staying home became so high during the 1950s and 1960s that ever increasing numbers of women deserted full-time homemaking to take paid employment.[34] In the 1990s several social scientists have further noted that Richard Easterlin's prediction that women would return to the home during the 1980s never happened. Instead women continued in the labor force because of irreversible normative changes surrounding women's equality and the need for women's income to finance children's expensive college education.[35] Moreover, in light of globalization of the economy and increasing job insecurity in the face of corporate downsizing, economists and sociologists are questioning Gary Becker's thesis that the lower waged worker in a household (typically the woman) will tend to become a full-time homemaker while the higher waged partner becomes the primary breadwinner. Data from Germany and the United States on the trend toward women's multiple roles suggests that uncertainty about the future has made women invest more strongly than ever in their own careers. They know that if they drop out for very long they will have difficulty re-entering if they have to tide over the family when the main breadwinner loses his job.[36]

Consequences for Children

The ideal family in the liberal economic model, according to political philosopher Iris Young, is one which has sufficient income to support the parents and the children and "to foster in those children the emotional and intellectual capacities to acquire such well-paid, secure jobs themselves, and also sufficient to finance a retirement,"[37] Dependent families do not have self-sufficient income but must rely on friends, relatives, charity, or the state to carry out their contribution to bringing up children and being good citizens.

Among liberals there is an emerging consensus that the current economic structure leads to two kinds of underinvestment in children that are implicated in their later dependency—material poverty, characteristic of the poor, and "time" poverty, characteristic of the middle class.

Thirty years ago Daniel Patrick Moynihan perceived that material poverty and job loss for a man put strain on the marriage, sometimes to the point that he would leave. His children also did less well in school.[38] Rand Conger, in his studies of Iowa families who lost their farms during the 1980s, found that economic hardship not only puts strain on the marriage but leads to harsh parenting practices and poorer outcomes for children.[39] Thus it appears possible that poverty may not just be the result of family separation, divorce, and ineffective childrearing practices; it may also be the *cause* of the irritability, quarrels, and violence which lead to marital breakdown. Material underinvestment in children is visible not just with the poor but in the changing ratio of per capita income of children and adults in U.S. society as a whole. As the proportion of households without children has doubled over the last century (from 30 to 65 percent), per capita income of children has fallen from 71 percent of adult income in 1870 to 63 percent in 1930 and 51 percent in 1983.[40]

The problem of "time" poverty used to be almost exclusively associated with mothers' employment. Numerous studies explored whether younger children did better if their mother was a full-time homemaker rather than employed outside the home but found no clear results.[41] Lately the lack of parental time for children has become much more acute because parents are working a total of 21 hours more per week than in 1970 and because there are more single-parent families. In 1965 the average child spent about 30 hours a week interacting with a parent, compared with seventeen hours in the 1980s.[42] Moreover, parents are less dependent on their children to provide support for them during old age, and children feel less obligated to do so. As skilled craftsmanship, the trades, and the family farms

have disappeared, children's upbringing can no longer be easily or cheaply combined with what parents are already doing. So adults are no longer so invested in children's futures. The result is that where the social capital of group affiliations and mutual obligations is the lowest (in the form of continuity of neighborhoods, a two-parent family, or a parent's interest in higher education for her children), children are 20 percent more likely to drop out of high school.[43]

It is not that parents prefer their current feelings of being rushed, working too many hours, and having too little time with their families. Economist Juliet Schor reports that at least two-thirds of persons she surveyed about their desires for more family time versus more salary would take a cut in salary if it could mean more time with their families. Since this option is not realistically open to many, what parents appear to do is spend more money on their children as a substitute for spending more time with them.[44]

Fixing the Safety Net

Since liberals believe in a market economy with sufficient government regulation to assure justice and equality of opportunity, they support those measures which will eradicate the worst poverty and assure the healthy reproduction of the next generation.[45] What particularly worries them, however, is Charles Murray's observation that since 1970 the growth of government welfare programs has been associated with a *rise* in poverty among children. Payments to poor families with children, while not generous, have nevertheless enabled adults to be supported by attachment to their children.[46] Society is faced with a dilemma between addressing material poverty through further government subsidy and time poverty through policies on parental leave and working hours. It turns out that the United States is trying to do both.

Measures for addressing material poverty would stimulate various kinds of training and job opportunities. The Family Support Act of 1988 would move AFDC mothers off the welfare rolls by giving them job training and requiring them to join the labor force. Such action would bring their economic responsibility for supporting their children into line with their parental authority. A whole program of integrated supports for health insurance, job training, earned income tax credits for the working poor, child support by the noncustodial parent, and supported work is put forward by economist David Ellwood in *Poor Support*.[47] An opposite strategy is to consolidate authority over children with the state's economic responsibility for their care by encouraging group homes and adoption for children whose parents cannot support them economically.[48]

Means for addressing time poverty are evident in such legislative initiatives as the Family and Medical Leave Act of 1993. By encouraging employers to grant parental leave or other forms of flexible work time, government policy is recognizing the value of parents having more time with their children, but the beneficiaries of such change are largely middle-class families who can afford an unpaid parental leave.[49] Another tactic is to reform the tax law to discourage marital splitting. In a couple with two children in which the father earns $16,000 annually and the mother $9,000, joint tax filing gives them no special consideration. But if they file separately, each taking one child as a dependent, the woman will receive about $5,000 in Earned Income Tax Credit and an extra $2,000 in food stamps.[50] Changing the tax law to remove the incentives for splitting, establishing paternity of children born out of wedlock, and intensifying child support enforcement to recover economic support from fathers are all examples of state efforts to strengthen the kinship unit.

INTERDEPENDENCE: THE FEMINIST VISION OF WORK AND CAREGIVING

A feminist perspective has elements in common with both conservatives and liberals, a respect for the family as an institution (shared with the conservatives) and an appreciation of modernity (valued by the liberals). In addition, a feminist perspective grapples with the problem of women's traditionally subordinate status and how to improve it through both a "relational" and an "individualist" strategy while also sustaining family life and the healthy rearing of children.[51] At the same time feminists are skeptical of both conservative and liberal solutions. Traditionalists have so often relied on women as the exploited and underpaid caregivers in the family to enable men's activities in the public realm. Liberals are sometimes guilty of a "male" bias in focusing on the independent individual actor in the marketplace who does not realize that his so-called "independence" is possible only because he is actually *dependent* on all kinds of relationships that made possible his education and life in a stable social order.[52]

By articulating the value of caregiving along with the ideal of women's autonomy, feminists are in a position to examine modern capitalism critically for its effects on families and to offer alternative policies that place greater value on the quality of life and human relationships. They judge family strength not by their *form* (whether they have two parents) but by their functioning (whether they promote human satisfaction and development) and whether both women and men are able to be family caregivers as well as productive workers. They attribute difficulties of children less to the absence of the two-parent family than to low-wage work of single mothers, inadequate child care, and inhospitable housing and neighborhoods.

FEMINIST MODEL

Lack of cooperation among community, family, and work	→	Families where adults are stressed and overburdened	→	Children lack sufficient care and attention from parents

Accordingly, feminists would work for reforms that build and maintain the social capital of volunteer groups, neighborhoods, and communities because a healthy civil society promotes the well-being of families and individuals as well as economic prosperity and a democratic state. They would also recognize greater role flexibility across the life cycle so that both men and women could engage in caregiving, and they would encourage education and employment among women as well as among men.

Disappearance of Community

From a feminist perspective, family values have become an issue because individualism has driven out the sense of collective responsibility in our national culture. American institutions and social policies have not properly implemented a concern for all citizens. Comparative research on family structure, teenage pregnancy, poverty, and child outcomes in other countries demonstrates that where support is generous to help *all* families and children, there are higher levels of health and general education and lower levels of violence and child deviance than in the United States.[53]

Liberal thinking and the focus on the free market have made it seem that citizens make their greatest contribution when they are self-sufficient, thereby keeping themselves off the public dole. But feminist theorist Iris Young argues that many of the activities that are basic to a healthy democratic society (such as cultural production, caretaking, political organizing, and charitable activities) will never be profitable in a private market. Yet many of the recipients of welfare and Social Security such as homemakers, single mothers, and retirees are doing important volunteer work caring for children and helping others in their communities. Thus the social worth of a person's contribution is not just in earning a paycheck that shows economic independence but also in making a social contribution. Such caretaking of other dependent citizens and of the body politic should be regarded as honorable, not inferior, and worthy of society's support and subsidy.[54]

In fact it appears that married women's rising labor force participation from 41 percent in 1970 to 58 percent in 1990 may have been associated with their withdrawal from unpaid work in the home and community.[55] Volunteer membership in everything from the PTA to bowling leagues declined by over 25 percent between 1969 and 1993. There is now considerable concern that the very basis that Alexis de Tocqueville thought necessary to democracy is under siege.[56] To reverse this trend, social observers suggest that it will be necessary to guard time for families and leisure that is currently being sucked into the maw of paid employment. What is needed is a reorientation of priorities to give greater value to unpaid family and community work by both men and women.

National policies should also be reoriented to give universal support to children at every economic level of society, but especially to poor children. In a comparison of countries in the Organization for Economic Cooperation and Development, the United States ranks at the top in average male wages but near the bottom in its provision for disposable income for children. In comparison with the $700 per month available to children in Norway, France, or the Netherlands in 1992, U.S. children of a single nonemployed mother received only slightly under $200.[57] The discrepancy is explained by very unequal distribution of U.S. income, with the top quintile, the "fortunate fifth," gaining 47 percent of the national income while the bottom fifth receives only 3.6 percent.[58] This sharp inequality is, in turn, explained by an ideology of individualism that justifies the disproportionate gains of the few for their innovation and productivity and the meager income of the poor for their low initiative or competence. Lack of access to jobs and the low pay accruing to many contingent service occupations simply worsen the picture.

Feminists are skeptical of explanations that ascribe higher productivity to the higher paid and more successful leading actors while ignoring the efforts and contribution of the supporting cast. They know that being an invisible helper is the situation of many women. This insight is congruent with new ideas about the importance of "social capital" to the health of a society that have been put forward recently by a number of social scientists.[59] Corporations cannot be solely responsible for maintaining the web of community, although they are already being asked to serve as extended family, neighborhood support group, and national health service.

Diversity of Family Forms

Those who are concerned for strengthening the civil society immediately turn to the changing nature of the family as being a key building block. Feminists worry that seemingly sensible efforts to reverse the trend of rising divorce and single parenthood will privilege the two-parent family to the detriment of women; they propose instead that family values be understood in a broader sense as valuing the family's unique capacity for giving emotional and material support rather than implying simply a two-parent form.

The debate between conservatives, liberals, and feminists on the issue of the two-parent family has been most starkly stated by sociologist Judith Stacey and political philosopher Iris Young.[60] They regard the requirement that all women stay in a marriage as an invitation to coercion and subordination and an assault on the principles of freedom and self-determination that are at the foundation of democracy. Moreover, as Christopher Jencks and Kathryn Edin conclude from their study of several hundred welfare families, the current welfare reform rhetoric that no couple should have a child unless they can support it, does not take into account the uncertainty of life in which people who start out married or with adequate income may not always remain so. In the face of the world-wide dethronement of the two-parent family (approximately one-quarter to one-third of all families around the globe are headed by women), marriage should not be seen as the cure for child poverty. Mothers should not be seen as less than full citizens if they are not married or not employed (in 1989 there were only 16 million males between the ages of 25 and 34 who made over $12,000 compared with 20 million females of the same age who either had a child or wanted one).[61] National family policy should instead begin with a value on women's autonomy and self-determination that includes the right to bear children. Mother-citizens are helping to reproduce the next generation for the whole society, and in that responsibility they deserve at least partial support.

From a feminist perspective the goal of the family is not only to bring up a healthy and productive new generation; families also provide the intimate and supportive group of kin or fictive kin that foster the health and well-being of every person—young or old, male or female, heterosexual, homosexual, or celibate. Recognition as "family" should therefore not be confined to the traditional two-parent unit connected by blood, marriage, or adoption, but should be extended to include kin of a divorced spouse (as Stacey documented in her study of Silicon Valley families), same-sex partnerships, congregate households of retired persons, group living arrangements, and so on.[62] Twenty years ago economist Nancy Barrett noted that such diversity in family and household form was already present. Among all U.S. households in 1976, no one of the six major types constituted more than 15–20 percent: couples with and without children under 18 with the wife in the labor force (15.4 and 13.3 percent respectively); couples with or without children under 18 with the wife not in the labor force (19.1 and 17.1 percent); female- or male-headed households (14.4 percent); and single persons living alone (20.6 percent).[63]

Such diversity both describes and informs contemporary "family values" in the United States. Each family type is numerous enough to have a legitimacy of its own, yet no single form is the dominant one. As a result the larger value system has evolved to encompass beliefs and rules that legitimate each type on the spectrum. The regressive alternative is "fundamentalism" that treats the two-parent family with children as the only legitimate form, single-parent families as unworthy of support, and the nontraditional forms as illegitimate. In 1995 the general population appears to have accepted diversity of family forms as normal. A Harris poll of 1,502 women and 460 men found that only two percent of women and one percent of men defined family as "being about the traditional nuclear family." One out of 10 women defined family values as loving, taking care of, and supporting each other, knowing right from wrong or having good values, and 9 out of 10 said society should value all types of families.[64] It appears most Americans believe that an Aunt Polly single-parent type of family for a Huck Finn that provides economic support, shelter, meals, a place to sleep and to withdraw is better than no family at all.

Amidst gradual acceptance of greater diversity in family form, the gender-role revolution is also loosening the sex-role expectations traditionally associated with breadwinning and homemaking. Feminists believe that men and women can each do both.[65] In addition, women in advanced industrial nations have by and large converged upon a new life pattern of multiple roles by which they combine work and family life. The negative outcome is an almost universal "double burden" for working women in which they spend 84 hours per week on paid and family work, married men spend 72 hours, and single persons without children spend 50 hours.[66] The positive consequence, however, appears to be improved physical and mental health for those women who, though stressed, combine work and family roles.[67] In addition, where a woman's husband helps her more with the housework, she is less likely to think of getting a divorce.[68]

The Precarious Situation of Children

The principal remedy that conservatives and liberals would apply to the problems of children is to restore the two-parent family by reducing out-of-wedlock births, increasing the presence of fathers, and encouraging couples who are having marital difficulties to avoid divorce for the sake of their children. Feminists, on the other hand, are skeptical that illegitimacy, father absence, or divorce are the principal culprits they are made out to be. . . . Arlene Skolnick and Stacey Rosencrantz cite longitudinal studies showing that most children recover from the immediate negative effects of divorce.[69]

How then, while supporting the principle that some fraction of women should be able to head families as single parents, do feminists analyze the problem of ill health, antisocial behavior, and poverty among children? Their answer focuses on the *lack of institutional supports* for the new type of dual-earner and single-parent families that are more prevalent today. Rather than attempt to force families back into the traditional mold, feminists note that divorce, lone-mother families, and women's employment are on the rise in every industrialized nation. But other countries have not seen the same devastating decline in child well-being, teen pregnancy, suicides and violent death, school failure, and a rising population of children in poverty. These other countries have four key elements of social and family policy which protect all children and their mothers: (1) work guarantees and other economic supports; (2) child care; (3) health care; and (4) housing subsidies. In the United States these benefits are scattered and uneven; those who can pay their way do so; only those who are poor or disabled receive AFDC for economic support, some help with child care, Medicaid for health care, and government-subsidized housing.

A first line of defense is to raise women's wages through raising the minimum wage, then provide them greater access to male-dominated occupations with higher wages. One-half of working women do not earn a wage adequate to support a family of four above the poverty line. Moreover, women in low-wage occupations are subject to frequent lay-offs and lack of benefits.

Training to improve their human capital, provision of child care, and broadening of benefits would help raise women's capacity to support a family. Eisenberg reports that the Human Development Index of the United Nations (HDI), which ranks countries by such indicators as life expectancy, educational levels, and per capita income, places the United States fifth and Sweden sixth in the world. But when the HDI is recalculated to take into account equity of treatment of women, Sweden rises to first place and the United States falls to ninth. Therefore, one of the obvious places to begin raising children's status is to raise the economic status and earning power of their mothers.[70]

A second major benefit which is not assured to working mothers is child care. Among school-age children up to 13 years of age, one-eighth lack any kind of after-school child care. Children come to the factories where their mothers work and wait on the lawn or in the lobby until their mothers are finished working. If a child is sick, some mothers risk losing a job if they stay home. Others are latchkey kids or in unknown circumstances, such as sleeping in their parents' cars or loitering on the streets. Although 60 percent of mothers of the 22 million preschool children are working, there are only 10 million child care places available, a shortfall of one to three million slots.[71] Lack of good quality care for her children not only distracts a mother, adds to her absences from work, and makes her less productive, it also exposes the child to a lack of attention and care that leads to violent and antisocial behavior and poor performance in school.

Lack of medical benefits is a third gaping hole for poor children and lone-parent families. Jencks and Edin analyze what happens to a Chicago-area working woman's income if she goes off welfare. Her total income in 1993 dollars on AFDC (with food stamps, unreported earnings, help from family and friends) adds up to $12,355, in addition to which she receives Medicaid and child care. At a $6 per hour full-time job, however, without AFDC, with less than half as much from food stamps, with an Earned Income Tax Credit, and help from relatives, her total income would add to $20,853. But she would have to pay for her own medical care, bringing her effective income down to $14,745 if she found free child care, and $9,801 if she had to pay for child care herself.[72]

Some housing subsidies or low-income housing are available to low-income families. But the neighborhoods and schools are frequently of poor quality and plagued by violence. To bring up children in a setting where they cannot safely play with others introduces important risk factors that cannot simply be attributed to divorce and single parenthood. Rather than being protected and being allowed to be innocent, children must learn to be competent at a very early age. The family, rather than being child-centered, must be adult-centered, not because parents are selfish or self-centered but because the institutions of the society have changed the context of family life.[73] These demands may be too much for children, and depression, violence, teen suicide, teen pregnancy, and school failure may result. But it would be myopic to think that simply restoring the two-parent family would be enough to solve all these problems. . . .

CONCLUSION

A review of the conservative, liberal, and feminist perspectives on the changing nature of the American family suggests that future policy should combine the distinctive contributions of all three. From the conservatives comes a critique of modernity that recognizes the important role of the family in maintaining child health and preventing child failure. Although their understanding of "family values" is too narrow, they deserve credit for raising the issue of family function and form to public debate. Liberals see clearly the overwhelming power of the economy to deny employment, make demands on parents as workers, and drive a wedge between employers' needs for competitiveness and families' needs for connection and community.

Surprising though it may seem, since feminists are often imagined to be "way out," the most comprehensive plan for restoring family to its rightful place is put forward by feminists who appreciate both the inherently premodern nature of the family and at the same time its inevitable interdependence with a fast-changing world economy. Feminists will not turn back to the past because they know that the traditional family was often a straightjacket for women. But they also know that family cannot be turned into a formal organization or have its functions performed by government or other public institutions that are incapable of giving needed succor to children, adults, and old people which only the family can give.

The feminist synthesis accepts both the inherent particularism and emotional nature of the family and the inevitable specialization and impersonality of the modern economy. Feminists are different from conservatives in accepting diversity of the family to respond to the needs of the modern economy. They are different from the liberals in recognizing that intimate nurturing relationships such as parenting cannot all be turned into a safety net of formal care. The most promising social policies for families and children take their direction from inclusive values that confirm the good life and the well-being of every individual as the ultimate goal of the nation. The policy challenge is to adjust the partnership between the family and its surrounding institutions so that together they combine the best of private initiative with public concern.

ENDNOTES

1. Barbara Dafoe Whitehead, "Dan Quayle Was Right," *Atlantic Monthly* (April 1993), p. 47. Her chapter in this volume on the "Story of Marriage" continues the theme of an erosion of values under the guise of tolerance for cultural diversity.

2. Mary Ann Glendon, "Marriage and the State: The Withering Away of Marriage," *Virginia Law Review 62* (May 1976), pp. 663–729.

3. Charles A. Murray, *Losing Ground: American Social Policy, 1950–1980* (New York: Basic Books, 1984). Critics point out that the rise in out-of-wedlock births continues, even though welfare payments have declined in size over the last several decades, thereby casting doubt on the perverse incentive theory of rising illegitimacy.

4. U.S. Bureau of the Census, *Statistical Abstract of the United States: 1994,* 114th ed. (Washington, DC: 1994), p. 59.

5. Suzanne M. Bianchi and Daphne Spain, *American Women in Transition* (New York: Russell Sage Foundation, 1986), p. 88.

6. Donald J. Hernandez, *America's Children: Resources from Family, Government, and the Economy* (New York: Russell Sage Foundation, 1993), pp. 284, 70; Janet Zollinger Giele, "Woman's Role Change and Adaptation, 1920–1990," in *Women's Lives through Time: Educated American Women of the Twentieth Century,* ed. K. Hulbert and D. Schuster (San Francisco: Jossey-Bass, 1993), p. 40.

7. Victor Fuchs, "Are Americans Underinvesting in Children?" in *Rebuilding the Nest,* ed. David Blankenhorn, Stephen Bayme, and Jean Bethke Elshtain (Milwaukee: Family Service America, 1990), p. 66. Bianchi and Spain, *American Women in Transition,* pp. 141, 201, 226. Janet Zollinger Giele, "Gender and Sex Roles," in *Handbook of Sociology,* ed. N. J. Smelser (Beverly Hills, CA: Sage Publications, 1988), p. 300.

8. Hernandez, *America's Children,* p. 130. Council on Families in America, *Marriage in America* (New York: Institute for American Values, 1995), p. 7.

9. Fuchs, "Are Americans Underinvesting in Children?" p. 61. Some would say, however, that the decline was due in part to a larger and more heterogeneous group taking the tests.

10. Council on Families in America, *Marriage in America,* 6. The report cites research by Nicholas Zill and Charlotte A. Schoenborn, "Developmental, Learning and Emotional Problems: Health of Our Nation's Children, United States, 1988." *Ad-*

vance Data, National Center for Health Statistics, Publication # 120, November 1990. See also, Sara McLanahan and Gary Sandefur, *Growing Up with a Single Parent* (Cambridge, MA: Harvard University Press, 1994).

11. Edward Gilbreath, "Manhood's Great Awakening," *Christianity Today* (February 6, 1995), p. 27.

12. David Elkind, *The Hurried Child: Growing Up Too Fast Too Soon* (Reading, MA: Addison-Wesley, 1981).

13. Jean Bethke Elshtain, *Democracy on Trial* (New York: Basic Books, 1995).

14. Jonathan Alter and Pat Wingert, "The Return of Shame," *Newsweek* (February 6, 1995), p. 25.

15. Tom McNichol, "The New Sex Vow: 'I won't' until 'I do'." *USA Weekend,* March 25–27, 1994, p. 4 ff. Lee Smith, "The New Wave of Illegitimacy," *Fortune* (April 18, 1994), p. 81 ff.

16. Susan Chira, "War over Role of American Fathers," *New York Times,* June 19, 1994, p. 22.

17. Juliet Schor, "Consumerism and the Decline of Family and Community: Preliminary Statistics from a Survey on Time, Money and Values," Harvard Divinity School, Seminar on Families and Family Policy, April 4, 1995.

18. Karen S. Peterson, "In Balancing Act, Scale Tips toward Family," *USA Today,* January 25, 1995.

19. Lawrence Mead, "Taxing Peter to Pay Paula," *The Wall Street Journal,* November 2, 1994.

20. Tom G. Palmer, "English Lessons: Britain Rethinks the Welfare State," *The Wall Street Journal,* November 2, 1994.

21. Robert Pear, "G.O.P. Affirms Plan to Stop Money for Unwed Mothers," *New York Times,* January 21, 1995, p. 9.

22. Brigitte Berger, "Block Grants: Changing the Welfare Culture from the Ground Up," *Dialogue* (Boston: Pioneer Institute for Public Policy Research), no. 3, March 1995.

23. Robert Rector, "Welfare," *Issues '94: The Candidate's Briefing Book* (Washington, DC: American Heritage Foundation, 1994), chap. 13.

24. Council on Families in America, *Marriage in America,* pp. 13–16.

25. Robert Bellah, "Invasion of the Money World," in *Rebuilding the Nest,* ed. David Blankenhorn, Steven Bayme, and Jean Bethke Elshtain (Milwaukee: Family Service America, 1990), pp. 227–36.

James Coleman, *Foundations of Social Theory* (Cambridge, MA: Harvard University Press, 1990).

26. Sylvia Nasar, "More Men in Prime of Life Spend Less Time Working," *New York Times,* December 1, 1994, p. A1.

27. John Scanzoni, *Power Politics in the American Marriage* (Englewood Cliffs, NJ: Prentice-Hall, 1972). Ruth A. Wallace and Alison Wolf, *Contemporary Sociological Theory* (Englewood Cliffs, NJ: Prentice-Hall, 1991), p. 176.

28. Fred Weinstein and Gerald M. Platt, *The Wish to Be Free: Society, Psyche, and Value Change* (Berkeley, CA: University of California Press, 1969).

29. Kingsley Davis, "Wives and Work: A Theory of the Sex-Role Revolution and Its Consequences," in *Feminism, Children, and the New Families,* ed. S. M. Dornbusch and M. H. Strober (New York: Guilford Press, 1988), pp. 67–86. Janet Zollinger Giele, *Two Paths to Women's Equality: Temperance, Suffrage, and the Origins of American Feminism* (New York: Twayne Publishers, Macmillan, 1995).

30. Vivianna A. Zelizer, *Pricing the Priceless Child: The Changing Social Value of Children* (New York: Basic Books, 1985).

31. William J. Goode, *World Revolution in Family Patterns* (New York: The Free Press, 1963).

32. Constance Willard Williams, *Black Teenage Mothers: Pregnancy and Child Rearing from Their Perspective* (Lexington, MA: Lexington Books, 1990).

33. William Julius Wilson, *The Truly Disadvantaged: The Inner City, the Underclass, and Public Policy* (Chicago: University of Chicago Press, 1987).

34. Jacob Mincer, "Labor-force Participation of Married Women: A Study of Labor Supply," in *Aspects of Labor Economics,* Report of the National Bureau of Economic Research (Princeton, NJ: Universities-National Bureau Committee of Economic Research, 1962). Glen G. Cain, *Married Women in the Labor Force: An Economic Analysis* (Chicago: University of Chicago Press, 1966).

35. Richard A. Easterlin, *Birth and Fortune: The Impact of Numbers on Personal Welfare* (New York: Basic Books, 1980). Valerie K. Oppenheimer, "Structural Sources of Economic Pressure for Wives to Work—Analytic Framework" *Journal of Family History 4,* no. 2 (1979), pp. 177–97; and Valerie K. Oppenheimer, *Work*

and the Family: A Study in Social Demography (New York: Academic Press, 1982).

36. Janet Z. Giele and Rainer Pischner, "The Emergence of Multiple Role Patterns Among Women: A Comparison of Germany and the United States," *Vierteljahrshefte zur Wirtschaftsforschung* (Applied Economics Quarterly) (Heft 1–2, 1994). Alice S. Rossi, "The Future in the Making," *American Journal of Orthopsychiatry 63,* no. 2 (1993), pp. 166–76. Notburga Ott, *Intrafamily Bargaining and Household Decisions* (Berlin: Springer-Verlag, 1992).

37. Iris Young, "Mothers, Citizenship and Independence: A Critique of Pure Family Values," *Ethics 105,* no. 3 (1995), pp. 535–56. Young critiques the liberal stance of William Galston, *Liberal Purposes* (New York: Cambridge University Press, 1991).

38. Lee Rainwater and William L. Yancey, *The Moynihan Report and the Politics of Controversy* (Cambridge, MA: MIT Press, 1967).

39. Glen H. Elder, Jr., *Children of the Great Depression* (Chicago: University of Chicago Press, 1974). Rand D. Conger, Xiao-Jia Ge, and Frederick O. Lorenz, "Economic Stress and Marital Relations," in *Families in Troubled Times: Adapting to Change in Rural America,* ed. R. D. Conger and G. H. Elder, Jr. (New York: Aldine de Gruyter, 1994), pp. 187–203.

40. Coleman, *Foundations of Social Theory,* p. 590.

41. Elizabeth G. Menaghan and Toby L. Parcel, "Employed Mothers and Children's Home Environments," *Journal of Marriage and the Family 53,* no. 2 (1991), pp. 417–31. Lois Hoffman, "The Effects on Children of Maternal and Paternal Employment," in *Families and Work,* ed. Naomi Gerstel and Harriet Engel Gross (Philadelphia: Temple University Press, 1987), pp. 362–95.

42. Juliet Schor, *The Overworked American: The Unexpected Decline of Leisure* (New York: Basic Books, 1991). Robert Haveman and Barbara Wolfe, *Succeeding Generations: On the Effects of Investments in Children* (New York: Russell Sage Foundation, 1994), p. 239.

43. Coleman, *Foundations of Social Theory,* pp. 596–97.

44. Schor, "Consumerism and Decline of Family."

45. Iris Young, "Mothers, Citizenship and Independence," puts Elshtain, Etzioni, Galston, and Whitehead in this category.

46. Coleman, *Foundations of Social Theory,* pp. 597–609.

47. Sherry Wexler, "To Work and to Mother: A Comparison of the Family Support Act and the Family and Medical Leave Act" (Ph.D. diss. draft, Brandeis University, 1995). David T. Ellwood, *Poor Support: Poverty in the American Family* (New York: Basic Books, 1988).

48. Coleman, *Foundations of Social Theory,* pp. 300–321. Coleman, known for rational choice theory in sociology, put forward these theoretical possibilities in 1990, fully four years ahead of what in 1994 was voiced in the Republican Contract with America.

49. Wexler, "To Work and to Mother."

50. Robert Lerman, "Marketplace," National Public Radio, April 18, 1995.

51. Karen Offen, "Defining Feminism: A Comparative Historical Approach," *Signs 14,* no. 1 (1988), pp. 119–51.

52. Young, "Mothers, Citizenship and Independence."

53. Robert N. Bellah et al., *Habits of the Heart* (Berkeley, CA: University of California Press, 1985), pp. 250–71. Gosta Esping-Andersen, *The Three Worlds of Welfare Capitalism* (Princeton, NJ: Princeton University Press, 1990). Susan Pedersen, *Family, Dependence, and the Origins of the Welfare State: Britain and France, 1914–1945* (New York: Cambridge University Press, 1993).

54. Young, "Mothers, Citizenship and Independence."

55. Giele, "Woman's Role Change and Adaptation" presents these historical statistics.

56. Elshtain, *Democracy on Trial;* Robert N. Bellah et al., *The Good Society* (New York: Knopf, 1991), p. 210; Robert D. Putnam, "Bowling Alone: America's Declining Social Capital," *Journal of Democracy 4,* no. 1 (1995), pp. 65–78.

57. Heather McCallum, "Mind the Gap" (paper presented to the Family and Children's Policy Center colloquium, Waltham, MA, Brandeis University, March 23, 1995). The sum was markedly better for children of employed single mothers, around $700 per mother in the United States. But this figure corresponded with over $1,000 in 11 other countries, with only Greece and Portugal lower than the U.S. Concerning the high U.S. rates of teen pregnancy, see Planned Parenthood advertisement, "Let's Get Serious About Ending Teen Childbearing," *New York Times,* April 4, 1995, p. A25.

58. Ruth Walker, "Secretary Reich and the Disintegrating Middle Class," *Christian Science Monitor,* November 2, 1994, p. 19.

59. For reference to "social capital," see Coleman, *Foundations of Social Theory;* Elshtain, *Democracy on Trial;* and Putnam, "Bowling Alone." For "emotional capital," see Arlie Russell Hochschild, *The Managed Heart: The Commercialization of Human Feeling* (Berkeley, CA: University of California Press, 1983). For "cultural capital," see work by Pierre Bourdieu and Jurgen Habermas.

60. Judith Stacey, "Dan Quayle's Revenge: The New Family Values Crusaders," *The Nation,* July 25/August 1, 1994, pp. 119–22. Iris Marion Young, "Making Single Motherhood Normal," *Dissent* (winter 1994), pp. 88–93.

61. Christopher Jencks and Kathryn Edin, "Do Poor Women Have a Right to Bear Children," *The American Prospect* (winter 1995), pp. 43–52.

62. Stacey, "Dan Quayle's Revenge"; Arlene Skolnick and Stacey Rosencrantz, "The New Crusade for the Old Family," *The American Prospect* (summer 1994), pp. 59–65.

63. Nancy Smith Barrett, "Data Needs for Evaluating the Labor Market Status of Women," in *Census Bureau Conference on Federal Statistical Needs Relating to Women,* ed. Barbara B. Reagan (U.S. Bureau of the Census, 1979) Current Population Reports, Special Studies, Series P-23, no. 83, pp. 10–19. These figures belie the familiar but misleading statement that "only 7 percent" of all American families are of the traditional nuclear type because "traditional" is defined so narrowly—as husband and wife with two children under 18 where the wife is not employed outside the home. For more recent figures and a similar argument for a more universal family ethic, see Christine Winquist Nord and Nicholas Zill, "American Households in Demographic Perspective," working paper no. 5. Institute for American Values, New York, 1991.

64. Tamar Levin, "Women Are Becoming Equal Providers," *New York Times,* May 11, 1995, p. A27.

65. Marianne A. Ferber and Julie A. Nelson, *Beyond Economic Man: Feminist Theory and Economics* (Chicago: University of Chicago Press, 1993).

66. Fran Sussner Rodgers and Charles Rodgers, "Business and the Facts of Family Life," *Harvard Business Review,* no. 6 (1989), pp. 199–213, especially 206.

67. Ravenna Helson and S. Picano, "Is the Traditional Role Bad for Women?" *Journal of Personality and Social Psychology* 59 (1990), pp. 311–20. Rosalind C. Barnett, "Home-to-Work Spillover Revisited: A Study of Full-Time Employed Women in Dual-Earner Couples," *Journal of Marriage and the Family 56* (August 1994), pp. 647–56.

68. Arlie Hochschild, "The Fractured Family," *The American Prospect* (summer 1991), pp. 106–15.

69. Leon Eisenberg, "Is the Family Obsolete?" *The Key Reporter 60,* no. 3 (1995), pp. 1–5. Arlene Skolnick and Stacey Rosencrantz, "The New Crusade for the Old Family," *The American Prospect* (summer 1994), pp. 59–65.

70. Roberta M. Spalter-Roth, Heidi I. Hartmann, and Linda M. Andrews, "Mothers, Children, and Low-Wage Work: The Ability to Earn a Family Wage," in *Sociology and the Public Agenda,* ed. W. J. Wilson (Newbury Park, CA: Sage Publications, 1993), pp. 316–38.

71. Louis Uchitelle, "Lacking Child Care, Parents Take Their Children to Work," *New York Times,* December 23, 1994, p. 1.

72. Jencks and Edin, "Do Poor Women Have a Right," p. 50.

73. David Elkind, *Ties That Stress: The New Family in Balance* (Boston: Harvard University Press, 1994).

READING 16-2

The Problem with Marriage

Steven L. Nock

A Call to Civil Society[1] warns that the institutions most critical to democratic society are in decline. "What ails our democracy is not simply

---

Steven L. Nock, "The Problem with Marriage" from *Society* (July/August 1999). Copyright © 1999 by Transaction, Inc. Reprinted with the permission of Transaction Publishers. All rights reserved.
[1]Jean Bethke Elshtain, "A Call to Civil Society." *Society* (July/August 1999): 11–19.

the loss of certain organizational forms, but also the loss of certain organizing ideals—moral ideals that authorize our civic creed, but do not derive from it. At the end of this century, our most important challenge is to strengthen the moral habits and ways of living that make democracy possible." I suggest that American institutions have traditionally been organized around gender and that the loss of this organizing principle explains many of the trends discussed in the report. Specifically, the continued centrality of gender in marriage—and its growing irrelevance everywhere else—helps explain many contemporary family problems. The solution is to restore marriage to a privileged status from which both spouses gain regardless of gender.

The family trends we are now seeing reflect a conflict between the ideals central to marriage and those that define almost all other institutions. Growing numbers of Americans reject the idea that adults should be treated differently based on their gender. But it is difficult to create a new model of marriage based on such a premise. For many people, assumptions about gender equality conflict with the reality of their marriages. It may hardly matter if one is male or female in college, on the job, at church, in the voting booth, or almost anywhere else in public. But it surely matters in marriage. The family, in short, is still organized around gender while virtually nothing else is. Alternatively, marriage has not been redefined to accommodate the changes in male-female relations that have occurred elsewhere. This, I believe, is the driving force behind many of the problematic trends identified in *A Call to Civil Society*.

Stable marriages are forged of extensive dependencies. Yet trends toward gender equality and independence have made the traditional basis of economic dependency in marriage increasingly problematic. The challenge is to reinvent marriage as an institution based on dependency that is not automatically related to gender. Both partners, that is, must gain significantly

from their union, and both must face high exit costs for ending it.

Despite dramatic changes in law and public policy that have erased (or minimized) distinctions between men and women, married life has changed more slowly and subtly. In the last four decades, the percentage of married women in the paid labor force increased from 32 percent to 59 percent, and the number of hours that wives commit to paid labor increased apace. While men do not appear to be doing much more housework today than they did two decades ago, women are doing less in response to their commitments to paid labor. Women did 2.5 times as much household labor as their husbands in 1975. By 1987, the ratio was 1.9. Wives' share of total (reported) household income increased marginally, from 35 percent in 1975–1980 to 38 percent in 1986–1991. In such small ways, husbands and wives are increasingly similar. Still, marriages are hardly genderless arrangements. My research for *Marriage in Men's Lives* showed that most marriages in America resemble a traditional model, with husbands as heads of households, and wives who do most housework and child care. Given the pace at which gender distinctions have been, or are being, eliminated from laws, work, school, religion, politics, and other institutions, the family appears to be curiously out of step.

One reason gender is still a central motif in marriage is because masculinity (and possibly, femininity) are defined by, and displayed in marriage. As the title of Sara Berk's book proclaimed, the family is *The Gender Factory*. Consider the consequences of unemployment for husbands. If spouses were economically rational, then the unemployed (or lower-paid) partner would assume responsibility for housework. Sociologist Julie Brines found just the opposite. After a few months of unemployment, husbands actually *reduced* their housework efforts. The reason is that housework is much more than an economic matter. It is also symbolic. "Men's" work means providing for the family and being a "breadwinner," whereas "women's" work means caring for the home and children. Such assumptions are part of our cultural beliefs. Doing housework, earning a living, providing for the family, and caring for children are ways of demonstrating masculinity or femininity. When wives are economically dependent on their husbands, doing housework is consistent with traditional assumptions about marriage. Such women conform to cultural understanding about what it means to be a wife, or a woman. However, a dependent husband departs from customary assumptions about marriage and men. Were he to respond by doing more housework, his deviance would be even greater. Marriage is still the venue in which masculinity and femininity are displayed.

The husband and wife who construct a new model of marriage that doesn't include gender as a primary organizing principle will face challenges. The husband who decides to be the primary child-care provider or the wife who elects to be the sole wage earner will find these unusual marital roles difficult but not impossible to sustain. Relationships with parents may be awkward. Friends may struggle to understand the arrangement if it differs from their own. Employers may also find such an arrangement difficult to understand and accept. Yet as difficult as it may be to forge a new model of marriage, it seems certain that some change is necessary if marriage is to endure.

The title of Goldscheider and Waite's recent book asks a stark question: *New Families, or No Families?* In "new" families, husbands and wives will share family economic responsibilities *and* domestic tasks equitably. The alternative, according to these authors, is "no" families. Quite simply, marriage must be redefined to reflect the greater gender equality found everywhere else, or women will not marry. Or those who do will face increasing difficulties reconciling their public and private lives. Indeed, young women today value marriage less than young men do. Three in four (75 percent)

never-married men under age 30 described getting married as important for their lives in 1993. A smaller percentage (66 percent) of comparable women replied that way (1993 General Social Survey).

Research confirms that most women who marry today desire marriages that differ importantly from those of their grandmothers because women's lives have changed in so many other ways in recent decades. However, though the options available to women have expanded in other respects, the basic pattern of marriage is pretty much the same as it has been for decades. The revolution in gender has not yet touched women's marriages. Part of the reason is that men have been excluded from the gender revolution. While almost any young woman today will notice enormous differences between her life options and those of her great-grandmother, the differences between men and their great-grandfathers are minimal, at most. The script for men in America has not changed. In short, despite enormous changes in what it means to be a woman, marriage does not yet incorporate those changes. Neither men nor women have yet figured out how to fashion "new" families.

Many of our problems are better seen as the result of institutional change than of individual moral decline. The *personal problems* that lead to family decline are also legitimate *public issues*. Institutions like the family are bigger than any individual. So when large numbers of people create new patterns of family life, we should consider the collective forces behind such novel arrangements. And if some of those innovations are harmful to adults or children, fixing them will require more than a call for stronger moral habits (though there is certainly nothing wrong with such advice). Fixing them will require restructuring some basic social arrangements.

Since *A Call to Civil Society* focuses on *institutional* decline, I want to consider the meaning of an institution. A society is a cluster of social institutions, and institutions are clusters of *shared* ideals. Only when people agree about how some core dimension of life should be organized is there a social institution. The family is a good example.

Although individual families differ in detail, collectively they share common features as a result of common problems and tested solutions. In resolving and coping with the routine challenges of family life such as child care, the division of household labor, or relations with relatives, individuals draw on conventional (i.e., shared) ideals. As disparate individuals rely on shared answers to questions about family life, typical patterns emerge that are understood and recognized—mother, father, son, daughter, husband, and wife. To the extent that such ideals are widely shared, the family is a social institution. Were individuals left completely on their own to resolve the recurring problems of domestic life, there would be much less similarity among families. Alternatively, were there no conventional values and beliefs to rely on, the family would not be an institution. The family, as an institution, differs in *form* from one culture to another. Yet everywhere, it consists of patterned (i.e., shared and accepted) solutions to the problems of dependency (of partners, children, and the elderly).

The problem today is that an assumption that was once central to all social institutions is no longer so compelling. Beliefs about gender have long been an organizing template that guided behaviors in both public and private. Yet while gender has become increasingly unimportant in public, neither women nor men have fully adjusted to these changes in their private married lives. If men and women are supposed to be indistinguishable at work or school, does the same standard apply in marriage? Americans have not yet agreed about the answer. As a result, the institution of the family (the assumptions about how married life should be organized) no longer complements other social arrangements. Increasingly, the family is viewed as a problem for people because the assumptions about domestic life no longer agree with those in other settings.

When husbands and wives return home from work, school, church, or synagogue, they often struggle with traditional ideals about marriage that do not apply in these other areas. No matter what her responsibilities at work, the married mother will probably be responsible for almost all child care at home, for instance. Responsibilities at work are unlikely to be dictated by whether the person is male or female. But responsibilities at home are. This contradiction helps explain the trends identified in *A Call to Civil Society.*

High rates of divorce, cohabitation, and unmarried childbearing are documented facts, and all have clearly increased this century. Do such trends suggest that the family is losing its institutional anchor? In fact, the traditional arrangements that constitute the family are less compelling today than in the past. In this respect, the institution of the family is weaker. To understand why, I now consider the traditional basis of the family, legal marriage.

LEGAL MARRIAGE AND THE INSTITUTION OF THE FAMILY

The extent to which the family *based on legal marriage* is an institution becomes obvious when one considers an alternative way that adult couples arrange their intimate lives. Certainly there is no reason to believe that two people cannot enjoy a harmonious and happy life without the benefit of legal marriage. In fact, growing numbers of Americans appear to believe that unmarried *cohabitation* offers something that marriage does not. One thing that cohabitation offers is freedom from the rules of marriage because there are no widely accepted and approved boundaries around cohabitation. Unmarried partners have tremendous freedom to decide how they will arrange their legal and other relationships. Each partner must decide how to deal with the other's parents, for example. Parents, in turn, may define a cohabiting child's relationship as different from a married child's. Couples must decide whether vacations will be taken together or separately. Money may be pooled or held in separate accounts. If children are born, cohabiting parents must decide about the appropriate (non-legal) obligations each incurred as a result. In such small ways, cohabiting couples and their associates must *create* a relationship. Married couples may also face decisions about some of these matters. However, married spouses have a pattern to follow. For most matters of domestic life, marriage supplies a template. This is what cohabiting couples lack. They are exempt from the vast range of marriage norms and laws in our society.

A man can say to his wife: "I am your husband. You are my wife. I am expected to do certain things for you, and you likewise. We have pledged our faithfulness. We have promised to care for one another in times of sickness. We have sworn to forego others. We have made a commitment to our children. We have a responsibility and obligation to our close relatives, as they have to us." These statements are not simply personal pledges. They are also enforceable. Others will expect these things of the couple. Laws, religion, and customs bolster this contract. When this man says to someone, "I would like you to meet my wife," this simple declaration says a great deal.

Compare this to an unmarried couple living happily together. What, if any, are the conventional assumptions that can be made? What are the limits to behavior? To whom is each obligated? Who can this couple count on for help in times of need? And how do you complete this introduction of one's cohabiting partner: "I would like you to meet my . . ."? The lack of a word for such a partner is a clear indication of how little such relationships are governed by convention. Alternatively, we may say that such a relationship is *not* an institution, marriage is. I believe this helps explain why cohabiting couples are less happy, and less satisfied with their relationships than married couples.

Almost all worrisome social trends in regard to the *family* are actually problems related to *marriage:* declining rates of marriage, non-marital fertility, unmarried cohabitation, and divorce. Any understanding of the family must begin with a consideration of marriage. I now offer a *normative definition of marriage;* a statement of what Americans agree it *should* be, the assumptions and taken-for-granted notions involved. In so doing, I will lay the foundation for an explanation of family decline.

In *Marriage in Men's Lives,*[2] I developed the details of normative marriage by consulting three diverse sources. First, I examined large national surveys conducted repeatedly over the past two decades. Second, I read domestic relations law, including state and federal appellate decisions. Finally, I consulted sources of religious doctrine, especially the Bible. Throughout, my goal was to identify all aspects of marriage that are widely shared, accepted as legitimate, and broadly viewed as compelling.

A normative definition of marriage draws attention to the central idea that marriage is more than the sum of two spouses. As an institution, marriage includes rules that originate outside the particular union that establish boundaries around the relationship. Those boundaries are the understood limits of behavior that distinguish marriage from all other relationships. Married couples have something that all other couples lack; they are heirs to a system of shared principles that help organize their lives. If we want to assess changes in the family, the starting point is an examination of the institutional foundation of marriage. Six ideals define legal marriage in America.

1. Individual Free Choice Mate selection is based on romantic love. In the course of a century, parents have come to play a smaller and

---

[2]Steven L. Nock, *Marriage in Men's Lives* (New York: Oxford University Press, 1998).

smaller role in the choice of married partners. Dating supplanted courtship as compatibility, attractiveness, and love replaced other bases for matrimony. National surveys show that "falling in love" is the most frequently cited reason for marrying one's spouse, and that the most important traits in successful marriages are thought to be "satisfying one another's needs" and "being deeply in love." Western religious ceremonies admonish partners to love one another until death, and every state permits a legal divorce when love fails ('incompatibility', 'irreconcilable differences' or similar justifications). Love is associated with feelings of security, comfort, companionship, erotic attraction, overlooking faults, and persistence. Since love and marriage are so closely related, people expect all such feelings from their marriages.

2. *Maturity*   Domestic relations law defines an age at which persons may marry. Throughout the U.S., the minimum is 18, though marriage may be permitted with approval by parents or the court at earlier ages. Parental responsibilities for children end with legal *emancipation* at age 18. Thus, marriage may occur once parents are released from their legal obligations to children, when children are legally assumed to be mature enough to enter binding contracts, and once children are assumed able to become self-sufficient and able to provide for offspring. Traditional religious wedding ceremonies celebrate a new form of maturity as Genesis states: "A man leaves his father and mother and cleaves to his wife and they become one flesh."

3. *Heterosexuality*   Traditionally, and legally, the only acceptable form of sex has been with one's spouse. Sex outside of marriage (fornication or adultery) is still illegal in half of U.S. states. And sexual expression within marriage has traditionally been legally restricted to vaginal intercourse (sodomy laws). Though such laws are rarely enforced even where they exist, they remind us of the very close association of marriage and conventional forms of heterosexual sexuality. Recent efforts to legalize homosexual marriage have been strenuously resisted. Since the full-faith-and-credit clause of the Constitution requires that marriages conducted legally in one state be recognized as legal in others, the possibility of legal homosexual marriage in Hawaii prompted an unprecedented federal "Defense of Marriage Act" in September 1996. This law will allow states to declare homosexual Hawaiian marriages void in their jurisdiction. Despite growing acceptance of homosexuality, there is very little support for homosexual marriages. The 1990 General Social Survey showed that only 12 percent of Americans believe homosexuals should be allowed to marry.

4. *Husband as Head*   Though Americans generally endorse equality between the sexes, men and women still occupy different roles in their marriages. Even if more and more couples are interested in egalitarian marriages, large numbers of people aren't. The 1994 General Social Survey shows that adults are almost evenly divided about whether both spouses should contribute to family income (57 percent approve of wives working, and in fact, 61 percent of wives are employed). Four in ten adults endorse a very traditional division of roles, where the wife takes care of the home and family, and the husband earns all the income. Traditional religious wedding ceremonies ask women to "honor and obey" their husbands. In reality, most husbands have more authority than their wives do. The spouse who is primarily responsible for income enjoys more authority, and in the overwhelming majority of American marriages, that is the husband. Demands made of husbands at work are translated into legitimate demands made on the family. So most husbands have more authority than their wives do, regardless of professed beliefs.

5. Fidelity and Monogamy   In law, sexual exclusivity is the symbolic core of marriage, defining it in more obvious ways than any other. Husbands and wives have a legal right to engage in (consensual) sex with one another. Other people may not have a legal right to engage in sex with either married partner. Adultery is viewed as sufficiently threatening to marriages that homicides provoked by the discovery of it may be treated as manslaughter. Extramarital sex is viewed as more reprehensible than any other form, including sex between young teenagers, premarital sex, and homosexual sex. Eight in ten adults in the 1994 General Social Survey described extramarital sex as "always wrong." Adultery, in fact, is rare. Recent research reported by Laumann and his colleagues in *The Social Organization of Sexuality* revealed that only 15 percent of married men and 5 percent of married women have ever had extramarital sex. Among divorced people these percentages are only slightly higher, 25 percent for men and 10 percent for women. Monogamy is closely related to fidelity because it restricts all sexual expression to one married partner. With the exception of Utah where some Mormons practice polygamy (against the canons of the Mormons Church), monogamy has gone largely unchallenged in the United States since 1878 when the U.S. Supreme Court upheld the conviction of a Mormon who practiced polygamy.

6. Parenthood   With rare exceptions, married people become parents. Despite high rates of unmarried fertility, there is little to suggest that married couples are less likely to have, or desire to have children today than they were several decades ago. Only 13 percent of ever-married women aged 34 to 45 are childless today. Two decades ago, the comparable figure was 7 percent. The six-point difference, however, is due to delayed fertility, rather than higher childlessness. Overall completed cohort fertility (i.e., the total number of children born to women in their lifetime) has remained stable since the end of the Baby Boom. And while the legal disabilities once suffered by illegitimate children have been declared unconstitutional, marital and nonmarital fertility differ in important respects. Unmarried fathers may, through legal means, obtain the custody of their children, although few do. Indeed, a vast legal apparatus exists to enforce the parental obligations of men who do not voluntarily assume them. On the other hand, married men are automatically presumed to be the legal father of their wife's children, and nothing (except the absence of "unfitness") is required of them to establish custody.

CHALLENGES TO NORMATIVE MARRIAGE

This ensemble of behaviors and beliefs describes how most Americans understand marriage. Even if particular marriages depart in some ways from this model, this should be the starting point when attempting to assess family change. If "the family" has declined, then such change will be obvious in one or more of the foregoing dimensions. Widespread attempts to change normative marriage, or wholesale departures from it, are evidence that Americans do not agree about the institution. I now briefly review three obvious challenges to the normative model of marriage just outlined. High divorce rates, late ages at marriage, and declining rates of remarriage are a reflection of an underlying theme in such challenges. That theme is the importance of gender in marriage.

The increasingly common practice of unmarried *cohabitation* is an example of a challenge to normative marriage. In 1997, 4.1 million opposite-sex cohabiting couples were counted by the U.S. Bureau of Census, the majority of whom (53 percent) have never married, and one in five of whom (22 percent) is under 25 years old. Research on cohabiting partners has identified a central theme in such relationships. Cohabiting individuals are more focused on gender equality in economic and other matters than married spouses. They are also less likely to have a gender-based division of tasks in most forms of household labor except the care of infants.

Yet another challenge to normative marriage is unmarried childbearing. One in three children in America is born to an unmarried woman; six in ten of those children were conceived outside of marriage (the balance were conceived prior to a divorce or separation). The historical connection between sexual intercourse and marriage weakened once effective contraception and abortion became available. Without contraception, married women became pregnant if fecund. There was no reason to ask a married woman why, or when she would have a child. Parenthood in an era of universal contraception, however, is a choice. It is now possible to ask *why* someone had a child. Since childbearing is thought to be a choice, it is viewed as a decision made chiefly by women. And the type of woman who chooses to have children differs from the childless woman because motherhood now competes with many other legitimate roles in a woman's life. Research has shown that women who choose motherhood give occupational and income considerations lower priority than childless women.

By the late 1960s, feminists who argued that wives should not be completely dependent on husbands joined this critique of the exclusive breadwinner role of husbands. Just as the exclusive breadwinner role for men was criticized, the exclusive homemaker-mother role for married women was identified as oppressive. And, of course, such women are the statistical exception today. Maternity must be balanced with many other adult roles in women's lives, and traditional marriage is faulted as creating a "second shift" for women who return home from work only to assume responsibility for their households with little help from their husbands.

All significant challenges to marriage focus on various aspects of gender. The traditional assignment of marital roles based on sex (i.e., hus-

band as head of household) is the core problem in marriage. Other dimensions of normative marriage are less troublesome. There is little evidence of widespread disagreement about the ideas of free choice of spouses, fidelity, monogamy, heterosexual marriage, maturity, or parenthood.

Whether Americans are now less committed to common moral beliefs than in the past is an empirical question. Values (i.e., moral beliefs) are researchable issues, and it would be possible to investigate their role in matters of family life. Increases in divorce, cohabitation, illegitimacy, or premarital sex are certainly evidence that some beliefs are changing. However, social scientists have yet to identify all the various causes of these family trends. Undoubtedly there are many, including demographic (e.g., longer life, lower fertility), technological (e.g., contraception, public health) and cultural (e.g., shifting patterns of immigration). Changing values about gender are but one cause of family change. Still, I suspect they are the most important. When something as basic and fundamental as what it means to be a man or woman changes, virtually everything else must change accordingly. Now we must incorporate such new ideas into the institution of marriage.

NEW FAMILIES

It is easy to imagine how a new model of marriage would look. None of the basic elements of normative marriage are likely to change except the gender assumptions about who heads the family. Husbands and wives are already familiar with this new model of marriage, even if we have yet to acknowledge it. In 1995, virtually all (95 percent) of married men with children in the household were employed. Two-thirds (65 percent) of wives in such families were employed. Husbands are still breadwinners, but so are wives. While employment does not typically eliminate a wife's dependency on her husband, it does mean that husbands are also dependent on wives. Most American marriages now involve a pooling of incomes. The resulting lifestyle, therefore, is produced jointly by wives and husbands. Income pooling has increasingly replaced the breadwinner/homemaker pattern.

These new economic realities of married life have not been fully incorporated into the institution of normative marriage—the way we think about marriage. Husbands and wives have yet to reconcile their joint economic dependency with the routine of married life. Even if most married couples today depend on one another's earnings, traditional patterns of domestic responsibilities persist. Such gendered marriages are a problem because they do not fit with the assumptions about men and women in all other spheres of their lives.

The trends in the family that worry us might better be viewed as a consequence of redefining the institution. We are now struggling to resolve ideas about what is proper in our marriages with ideas about what is proper outside of them. Repeated studies have shown that conflicts over gender (Should the wife work? Who should do what?) are leading causes of divorce. Growing numbers of women find it difficult to live in marriages that appear to devalue their roles as breadwinners. On the other hand, full-time housewives feel that housework is devalued. Growing numbers of couples opt for "informal" marriage, or cohabitation, as a way to live without strict gender assumptions. Large numbers of women decide to pursue parenthood without the limitations and restrictions that would be imposed by marriage. It is easy to see why people make these choices. But though understandable, they are costly. Adults and children thrive in stable, nuclear families, even if they are not always happy. No feasible alternative comes close in its economic or emotional benefits for children or adults.

But the solution is not complete independence in marriage. Cohabitation has taught us that two soloists do not make a very good duet. Such equal partnerships do not last very long, and cohabiting couples report low levels of happiness and satisfaction. That is probably because nothing binds cohabiting couples together except love and affection. As desirable as those emotions are, they are a flimsy basis for an enduring relationship without alternative bonds. Stable, enduring marriages must be forged of extensive dependencies. Each person must depend on the other for many things. But such dependencies need not be inequitable or unfair.

What is the problem with marriage? The problem is the role of gender in the institution. More accurately, the problem is how to deal with widespread social change in matters of gender. But there is good reason to believe that we will come to terms with such challenges. Few boys today will grow up with mothers who are not employed. Young men are unlikely to inherit their fathers' or grandfathers' traditional views about marriage or women. Fewer men work with colleagues who openly view women and wives in traditional restricted roles. More and more of the youthful life course is spent in nontraditional families or outside of families altogether. Children, especially boys, who experience such childhoods (employed mothers, divorce, non-family living) are more accepting of women's new roles and options and are willing to perform more housework. It is not, therefore, a dramatic change in the basic institution of normative marriage that we need. Rather, it is a recognition and accommodation to the changes in women's lives and patience for intergenerational (cohort) change to catch up with current expectations. And men must become a part of the gender revolution. Even if this is not a fundamental redefinition of marriage, it will have profound consequences for how marriage is experienced because the tension between public and private lives will be reduced.

MARRIAGE AND PUBLIC POLICY

Social institutions can be changed intentionally, but not easily, not quickly, and not without widespread discussion and debate. I have been studying covenant marriage in Louisiana for the past year. In that state (and in Arizona) couples may elect one of two marriage regimes: the traditional one based on no-fault divorce rules, and covenant marriage which requires premarital counseling, and is governed by traditional fault-grounds for divorce. Covenant marriage laws are the first in over 200 years in America designed explicitly to make *marriage more permanent and divorce more restrictive.* Not surprisingly therefore, they are extremely controversial. It is much too early to know if this legal innovation will affect divorce rates. But one thing is clear. The passage of more restrictive divorce laws, even if optional, has provoked intense debate and discussion about the meaning of marriage and the role of the state in family affairs. Covenant marriage is discussed and debated almost weekly in the Louisiana media. A public discussion about marriage has begun in that state. Only through such *megalogues,* as Etzioni calls them, will institutions change. Social change is not being legislated. It is simply being encouraged, debated, and discussed.

Proposals that marriage be recognized, promoted, and protected by revisions in federal tax codes, increased use of pre-marital counseling, and revisions in divorce laws are a good start. I believe we must go further, however, to create and reinforce dependencies in marriage. Dependency based automatically on gender will eventually be purged from marriage, as it is now being purged from work, school, and other public realms. The transition is clearly difficult and painful as we now can see. But what will bind couples to such new families? The answer is that bases of dependency other than gender must be created. Significant benefits must flow from the marriage, and significant exit costs must exist for both partners.

The most sensible, though controversial way to achieve these goals is for states to establish a preference for married couples in the distribution of discretionary benefits. My research on covenant marriage has convinced me that any attempt to privilege marriage over other statuses will be controversial and resisted, especially by those who see traditional marriage as unfair to women. Since the inequities in marriage are being resolved, I would focus on ways to privilege marriage by granting significant economic benefits to couples willing to commit to a restrictive regime. The purpose would be to create a new distinction between married and unmarried persons, though not one automatically based on gender. If marriage is to thrive, significant benefits *other than emotional ones* must flow from the status. And men and women alike must benefit from the status of marriage.

Marriage has traditionally been founded on dependencies of many types. But unequal (i.e., women's) economic dependencies are the most obvious (and often the source of inequity). In a world where men and women may each be economically independent, the benefits of pooled incomes may not suffice to sustain couples during those inevitable times when love fades. What the authors of *A Call to Civil Society* refer to as "the philosophy of expressive individualism—a belief in the "sovereignty of the self" is fostered by gender equality and individual economic independence. In the absence of unequal economic dependencies, marriage must become a privileged status again, or else divorce rates will remain high, and marriage rates will continue to fall. To make it a privileged status, we should establish significant economic incentives. To the extent that people benefit economically in obvious and large ways by virtue of their marriages, (and to the extent that such benefits are not available to unmarried people) each spouse is dependent on *the union, per se* (dependency is typically measured by the costs of exiting a relationship).

The state has an enormous economic interest in promoting stable marriages. Strangely, the *macroeconomic* costs of divorce are rarely discussed in deliberations about public policy. Yet the *microeconomic* consequences are well known. Divorce and single-parenthood take a toll on earnings, educational attainment, labor-force attachment, subsequent marital stability, and the likelihood of poverty for the adults and the children involved. The aggregate consequences of all such individual losses are vast, even if unknown. Promoting marriage makes very good economic sense, beyond any other benefits to children or adults.

There are many ways we might promote marriage. Here I offer one example. We should consider significant tax credits for some married couples to create an economic interest in the marital union and significant exit costs for both partners. Americans will not tolerate mandatory family policy, so states should follow the lead of Louisiana in offering couples the option of two marriage regimes. Any couple could elect to be married under the customary no-fault divorce system without requirements for pre-marital and marital counseling. The more restrictive marriage regime would require pre-marital and marital counseling (as a prerequisite for a divorce), and would apply prevailing "best interests of the child" custody standards in granting a divorce. Divorce would be denied if the court determined that it was not in the best interest of the child (or children) involved. ("Best interests of the child" divorce proposals have been considered in several states, though never enacted.)

Couples who marry under the more restrictive marriage regime would qualify for very significant tax credits. Such credits must be quite large—$2,500 or $3,500 a year—sufficient to offset the costs of a college education for the children of married parents, or to underwrite the costs of a home, for example. Such tax credits would create a financial interest in the marriage *per se,* a benefit that flows to married couples by virtue of their marital status and nothing else. It also creates a significant exit cost at divorce. Both partners benefit so long as they remain married, both lose at divorce. How will we pay for such generous benefits? In fact, it is not certain that there would be net costs. A more appropriate question is how we will continue to pay for single parenthood and divorce.

Such a proposal seeks to restore marriage to a privileged status. It also addresses the need for a new basis of dependency in modern marriages where both spouses are likely to be breadwinners. It is intended to foster higher rates of marriage, lower rates of unmarried childbearing, and delays in divorce. Were any policy to be partially successful in having these consequences, the long-term economic ledgers (i.e., costs and benefits) may balance. Even if they didn't, such proposals would surely provoke discussion and debate about the importance of marriage in America. *A Call to Civil Society* asks us to begin such a debate about the loss of organizing ideals. Let's start with a consideration of the centrality of gender to the problem with marriage.